HTML

THIRD EDITION – ILLUSTRATED

COMPLETE

Vicki L. Cox
Lynn Wermers
Elizabeth Eisner Reding

THOMSON ™
COURSE TECHNOLOGY

Australia • Canada • Mexico • Singapore • Spain • United Kingdom • United States

THOMSON
™
COURSE TECHNOLOGY

HTML, Third Edition - Illustrated Complete
Vicki L. Cox, Lynn Wermers, Elizabeth Eisner Reding

Executive Editor:
Rachel Goldberg

Senior Acquisitions Editor:
Marjorie Hunt

Product Manager:
Jennifer Muroff

Associate Product Manager:
Shana Rosenthal

Editorial Assistant:
Janine Tangney

Senior Production Editor:
Catherine G. DiMassa

Developmental Editor:
Barbara Clemens

Marketing Manager:
Joy Stark

Marketing Coordinator:
Melissa Marcoux

QA Manuscript Reviewers:
John Freitas, Susan Whalen, Ashlee Welz

Text Designer:
Joseph Lee, Black Fish Design

Composition House:
GEX Publishing Services

The Illustrated Series Vision

Teaching and writing about computer applications can be extremely rewarding and challenging. How do we engage students and keep their interest? How do we teach them skills that they can easily apply on the job? As we set out to write this book, our goals were to develop a textbook that

- works for a beginning student
- provides varied, flexible, and meaningful exercises and projects to reinforce skills
- serves as a reference tool
- makes your job as an educator easier, by providing resources above and beyond the textbook to help you teach your course

Our popular, streamlined format is based on advice from instructional designers and customers. This flexible design presents each lesson on a two-page spread, with step-by-step instructions on the left, and screen illustrations on the right. This signature style, coupled with high-caliber content, provides a comprehensive yet manageable introduction to HTML—it is a teaching package for the instructor and a learning experience for the student.

Acknowledgments

I want to thank all the people at Course Technology who helped bring this project together. Many thanks to managing editor Marjorie Hunt for giving me the opportunity to write this book. My gratitude also goes to product managers Christina Kling-Garrett and Jennifer Muroff, who skillfully guided this project from concept to completion; and production editor Catherine DiMassa, who put it all together. Quality assurance tester John Freitas helped us immeasurably. My special thanks go to my developmental editor, Barbara Clemens, who worked so hard to guide me through the painful process of learning to author textbooks. I also want to thank my loving husband and best friend, Rick, whose gentle patience kept me going, and my children, who love me enough to nag, "Mom, get some sleep!"

Vicki L. Cox

I would like to thank Barbara Clemens for her insightful contributions, great humor, and patience.

Lynn Wermers

Preface

Welcome to *HTML, Third Edition–Illustrated Complete*. Each lesson in this book contains elements pictured to the right.

How is the book organized?

This book is organized into 15 units covering essential HTML skills, including creating, linking, and formatting HTML documents, as well as adding images and multimedia components. A glossary and appendix provide supplemental reference information.

What kinds of assignments are included in the book? At what level of difficulty?

The lessons use Paradise Mountain Family Resort, a fictional resort in the Rocky Mountains, as a case study. The assignments on the light purple pages at the end of each unit increase in difficulty. Data files and case studies, with international examples, provide a variety of engaging and relevant Web development possibilities. Continuing cases at the end of each unit include site development for: a local water district promoting water conservation, a startup company in the timeshare vacation rental business, and an established computer sales and service business. Students also have the chance to research Web accessibility and usage issues. Assignments include:

- **Concepts Reviews** include screen identification, matching, and multiple-choice questions.

- **Skills Reviews** provide additional hands-on, step-by-step reinforcement.

- **Independent Challenges** feature case projects requiring critical thinking and application of the unit skills. The Independent Challenges increase in difficulty, with the first one in each unit being the easiest (most step-by-step with detailed instructions). Subsequent Independent Challenges become

---

Each 2-page spread focuses on a single skill.

Concise text introduces the basic principles in the lesson and integrates a real-world case study.

UNIT A
HTML

Importing Web Content

You have learned that content added to the body section appears in the browser window. However, it is not necessary for you to type in all the page content. You will often discover that the content you need is already saved in digital format, such as a word-processed document, for another purpose. You can easily **import**, or bring in, that content instead of retyping it. To avoid retyping company information, you decide to use a rich text file (.rtf) you obtained from the Public Relations Department as the main content on your new page.

STEPS

> **TROUBLE**
> Do not select the closing body (</body>) or closing HTML (</html>) tags, or the "Page modified by" paragraph.

1. **Click before the first opening paragraph tag (<p>), drag to select all of the content through and including the second closing paragraph tag (</p>), then press [Delete] to remove the page content**

2. **Start Microsoft Word or another word-processing program, then open the document htm_a-1.rtf from the location where you store your Data Files**

3. **Click before the word Located in the first paragraph below the page heading in the htm_a-1.rtf document, then drag to select all the remaining text**

4. **Click Edit on the menu bar, click Copy, then click the text editor program button on the taskbar**
   You copied the text and returned to the index.htm file that is open in your text editor.

> **TROUBLE**
> If you accidentally copied and pasted the page heading from the RTF file, delete it now.

5. **Click in the line below the level-one heading, click Edit on the menu bar, then click Paste**
   You pasted the copied text into the content area of the index.htm file. Your file should now resemble Figure A-9.

6. **Close the rtf file, then save your work**
   Although you are not finished, it is time to preview your new page in a browser. Saving your work ensures that your recent changes will appear in your browser.

7. **Start your browser, then cancel any dial-up operations**
   The procedure for opening the page may vary, depending on your browser.

> **TROUBLE**
> If you are warned that Windows security settings will not allow you to open a local file from the browser, find the file in My Computer, then double-click it to open it in a browser.

8. **Click File on the menu bar, click Open or Open Page, click Browse or Choose File**

9. **Navigate to and then click the file index.htm in your paradise site folder, click Open, then click Open or OK**
   Compare your page with Figure A-10. The level-one page heading appears in boldface type and is larger than the rest of the text. See Table A-3 for a list of heading levels you can use with text. The paragraph text runs together because it is not marked with paragraph tags; the browser does not read blank lines and other white space typed into the HTML code of a document.

Clues to Use

Viewing Web page source code

An excellent way of learning what other designers are doing is to view the source code of other pages on the World Wide Web. To view a page's source code in Internet Explorer, click View on the menu bar, then click Source. The page opens in Notepad. In Navigator, click View on the menu bar, then click Page Source. The code is not editable, but you can copy and paste it into a Notepad document. It is acceptable to copy the HTML code itself, but it is not acceptable to copy and use someone else's content, including text, graphics, or logos. All Web content is considered copyrighted and using someone else's content without permission is a violation of copyright laws.

HTML A-10 CREATING AN HTML DOCUMENT

Hints, as well as troubleshooting advice, are located right where you need them–next to the step itself.

Clues to Use boxes provide concise information that either expands on the major lesson skill or describes an independent task that in some way relates to the major lesson skill.

Every lesson features large, full-color representations of what the screen should look like as students complete the numbered steps.

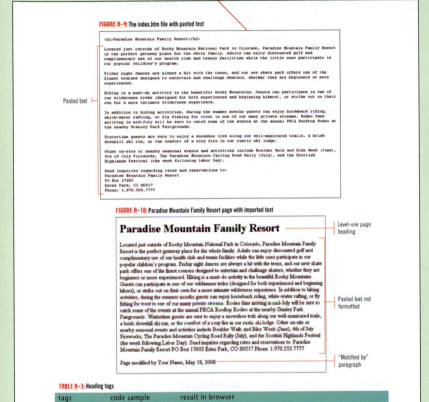

FIGURE A-9: The index.htm file with pasted text

FIGURE A-10: Paradise Mountain Family Resort page with imported text

TABLE A-3: Heading tags

tags	code sample	result in browser
<h1>...</h1>	<h1>Heading 1</h1>	# Heading 1
<h2>...</h2>	<h2>Heading 2</h2>	## Heading 2
<h3>...</h3>	<h3>Heading 3</h3>	### Heading 3
<h4>...</h4>	<h4>Heading 4</h4>	Heading 4
<h5>...</h5>	<h5>Heading 5</h5>	Heading 5
<h6>...</h6>	<h6>Heading 6</h6>	Heading 6

HTML

CREATING AN HTML DOCUMENT HTML A-11

Tables provide quickly accessible summaries of key terms, toolbar buttons, or keyboard alternatives connected with the lesson material. Students can refer easily to this information when working on their own projects at a later time.

increasingly open-ended, requiring more independent problem solving.

- **E-Quest Independent Challenges** are case projects with a Web focus. E-Quests require the use of the World Wide Web to conduct research to complete the project. The E-Quests in this text focus on real-world Web accessibility issues associated with the subject matter of each unit.

- **Your Site Independent Challenges** give students the greatest degree of flexibility as they develop their own Web sites. Students who complete these challenges will develop a business or personal site of their choice, which they complete as they work through the text.

- **Advanced Challenge Exercises** set within the Independent Challenges provide optional steps for more advanced students.

- **Visual Workshops** are practical projects that require independent problem solving and critical thinking skills. Students are shown layout sketches or completed Web pages and, based on the skills they gained in the unit, are asked to create the pages.

Instructor Resources

The Instructor Resources CD is Course Technology's way of putting the resources and information needed to teach and learn effectively into your hands. We believe that with an integrated array of teaching and learning tools that offers you and your students a broad range of technology-based instructional options, this CD represents the highest quality and most cutting edge resources available to instructors today. Many of these resources are available at www.course.com. The resources available with this book are:

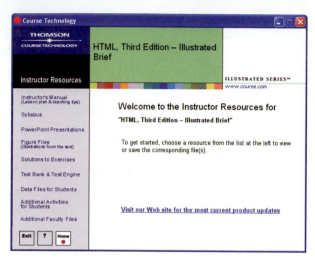

• **Data Files for Students**—To complete most of the units in this book, your students will need Data Files. Put them on a file server for students to copy. The Data Files are available on the Instructor Resources CD-ROM and the Review Pack, and can also be downloaded from www.course.com.

Instruct students to use the **Data Files List** located at the back of this book, on the Review Pack and the Instructor Resources CD. This list gives instructions on copying and organizing files.

• **Solutions to Exercises**—Solutions to Exercises contains every file students are asked to create or modify in the lessons and End-of-Unit material. A Help file on the Instructor Resource CD includes information for using the Solution Files. There is also a document outlining the solutions for the End-of-Unit Concepts Review, Skills Review, and Independent Challenges.

• **PowerPoint Presentations**—Each unit has a corresponding PowerPoint presentation that you can use in lecture, distribute to your students, or customize to suit your course.

• **Instructor's Manual**—Available as an electronic file, the Instructor's Manual is quality-assurance tested and includes unit overviews and detailed lecture topics with teaching tips for each unit.

• **Sample Syllabus**—Prepare and customize your course easily using this sample course outline.

• **Figure Files**—The figures in the text are provided on the Instructor Resources CD to help you illustrate key topics or concepts. You can create traditional overhead transparencies by printing the figure files. Or you can create electronic slide shows by using the figures in a presentation program such as PowerPoint.

• **ExamView**—ExamView is a powerful testing software package that allows you to create and administer printed, computer (LAN-based), and Internet exams. ExamView includes hundreds of questions that correspond to the topics covered in this text, enabling students to generate detailed study guides that include page references for further review. The computer-based and Internet testing components allow students to take exams at their computers, and also save you time by grading each exam automatically.

Brief Contents

Contents

HTML

Using Forms to Control Input   G-1

HTML

Controlling Page Layout with Frames and Tables   H-1

HTML

Designing Web Pages   I-1

HTML

Scripting for HTML J-1

HTML

Working with Dynamic HTML (DHTML) K-1

Read This Before You Begin

Software Information and Required Installation
In order to use this book, you will need:

Hardware and Software

- **An IBM or compatible** computer with at least a Pentium processor, 16 MB of RAM and a Windows 98 or higher operating system or **a Macintosh computer** with similar memory, color, graphics, and video capabilities.
- **A text editor program** such as Notepad or the Macintosh equivalent.
- **A Web browser:** This book was written to be non-browser specific, and was tested using several browsers including Netscape Navigator, Microsoft Internet Explorer, Opera, and Mozilla Firefox. While you need only one browser installed to use this book, establish the good practice of testing Web pages in different browsers to ensure that your pages appear as you intended.
- **Access to the Internet**.
- **E-mail software** that will support attachments such as Microsoft Outlook, or one of the free e-mail services available through providers such as Hotmail or Yahoo, or your online course e-mail interface.
- **An FTP client software program** (if using FTP to transfer files to a remote directory).
- **An external media storage device** such as a Zip disk, a "thumb" (USB) drive, or other external storage device. If you use floppy disks for data storage, be aware that even though Web documents are small, Web support files such as images and multimedia can be very large in file size and might not fit on a floppy disk.
- **Some type of graphics-editing software** is helpful, but not required for this text. Students without graphics-editing capabilities can use graphics provided in the student Data Files or can download them from links provided on the Student Online Companion for this text or can surf the Web to find suitable graphics download sites.

FTP Configuration: This text provides instructions on transferring files to a server using FTP Commander by InternetSoft, which can be downloaded free of charge by clicking the FTP Commander link in the Student Online Companion for this text. Links to download sites and instructions for using other FTP Client programs are also available through the Student Online Companion. Students who are not transferring files as part of their course/project assignments can complete the course by following guidelines set by their individual instructor.

Data Files: To complete the units in this book, you need to use Data Files. A Data File contains a partially completed document that allows you to focus on the core lesson material without losing valuable time setting up the framework for each lesson by typing all the information in the document yourself. Your instructor will either provide you with copies of the Data Files or ask you to make your own copies. Your instructor can give you instructions on how to organize your files, as well as a complete file listing. You can also find the list and the instructions for organizing your files in the Review Pack.

Saving your files

The author assumes no specific location for the Data Files you are provided or site files you create. Whatever location you or your instructor chooses, carefully organize your files by case project. If you are using floppy disks for site file storage, it is recommended that you have at least one floppy disk per site. Be aware that some case studies can become quite large and will require more than one floppy disk.

Why is my screen different from the book?

Your desktop components and some dialog box options might be different if you are using an operating system other than Windows XP. Depending on your computer hardware and the Display settings on your computer, you may notice the following differences:

- Your screen may look larger or smaller because of your screen resolution (the height and width of your screen).
- Your title bars and dialog boxes may not display file extensions. To display file extensions, right-click the Start button on the taskbar, click Explore, click Folder Options on the View menu, click the View tab in the Folder Options dialog box, click Hide extensions for known file types to deselect it, then click OK. Your dialog boxes and title bars should then display file extensions
- Your browser may display different menu and toolbar choices than those shown.

Creating an HTML Document

OBJECTIVES

Understand Web concepts
Plan an HTML document
Write an HTML document
Understand W3C coding standards
Import Web content
Mark up Web page content
Print an HTML document
Understand file transfer methods
Transfer files with FTP Commander

The **World Wide Web** (also referred to as simply the **Web**) is information contained on the vast **network** of interconnected computers known as the **Internet**. **Web sites** are related collections of files stored on those computers. Web files can be documents called Web pages; they can also be images or other files that are accessible through a Web browser program. Although navigating the World Wide Web with a browser is a useful skill, mastering just a few more basic concepts enables you to create and publish your own Web pages. You can create Web pages by learning Hypertext Markup Language (HTML), the language upon which all Web pages are based. Before you begin, you must plan your Web site and write its contents so that it conforms to specific standards. You can then publish those pages on the Web so others can view them. You work in the Information Technology (IT) Department at Paradise Mountain Family Resort, a family vacation destination specializing in "something for everyone." The resort owners have decided they need a Web site to publicize their goods and services, and you have been given the job of creating the Web site.

Understanding Web Concepts

HTML, which stands for **Hypertext Markup Language**, is the authoring language used to create pages for the World Wide Web (WWW). HTML allows various computer systems to interpret Web information in the same way. Web pages, also called **HTML documents** or **HTML files**, are text files made up of text and HTML instructions. Each of these instructions is called a **tag**. Together these tags and text make up the document's **source code**, often called the **source** or the **code**. You need to design and create a Web site that is easy to use, so vacation-bound families can easily find information about Paradise Mountain Family Resort. Before you begin, however, you review some basic Web terms and concepts.

Some basic Web terms and concepts are:

- **Web page**

  Also known as a Web document, a **Web page** is a single text file that has been **marked up** (annotated) with HTML tags so it is viewable on any operating system using any browser.

- **Tags**

  HTML includes many tags that allow you to describe how you want each of your Web page elements to appear in browsers. Although most HTML tags are part of a **tag set** that contains an opening and a closing tag, it is proper, and easier, to refer to the set as simply a tag. For example, you can refer to <p>...</p> as a **paragraph tag set** or as a **paragraph tag**. Sometimes tags with no closing counterparts are referred to as **open tags**.

- **Web browser**

  A **Web browser** is a software program installed on your computer that allows you to view Web pages. Some popular browsers are Microsoft Internet Explorer, Netscape Navigator, Mozilla Firefox, and Opera, which was created by a European consortium research project. Figure A-1 shows a Web page displayed in Microsoft Internet Explorer.

- **Web site**

  A **Web site** is a collection of related Web pages and other files housed in the same directory on a Web server. Pages in a Web site are connected by hyperlinks that visitors can click to navigate from one page to another.

- **Hyperlinks**

  Commonly called links, **hyperlinks** are specially-formatted text or graphics users click to move from one file to another on the World Wide Web. Hyperlinks give users an easy way to pursue information they find useful or interesting.

- **Web server**

  A **Web server**, or **server**, is a computer that is connected to the Internet and accessible to anyone with an Internet connection and a Web browser. Each server has its own four-part numeric address, called an **Internet Protocol (IP) address**, such as 1.160.10.40, that makes it possible for Web users to find site information.

- **URL**

  A **uniform resource locator (URL)** is the exact Internet address of a Web file. Figure A-2 shows the parts of a URL.

- **Search engine**

  A **search engine** is a Web-based program that helps you locate information on the Web. To use a search engine, type a word or phrase into a blank area called a **search box**, then click a **search button**. Some popular search engines are Google and Yahoo.

- **World Wide Web Consortium (W3C)**

  The **World Wide Web Consortium (W3C)** is an independent industry consortium that develops common protocols and sets new Web standards to promote WWW evolution and ensure interoperability among products and platforms.

FIGURE A-1: Web page with hyperlinks

Hyperlinks

URL

FIGURE A-2: Parts of a URL

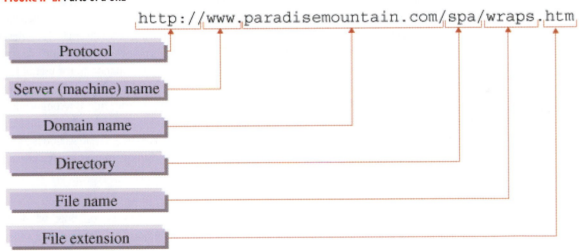

Protocol

Server (machine) name

Domain name

Directory

File name

File extension

Clues to Use

Understanding URLs

Each URL consists of several parts including the **protocol**—a standardized format for sending and receiving data, the machine or server name, the domain name, and the file name. The protocol for delivering Web documents is `http://`—**Hypertext Transfer Protocol**— or `https://`—**Hypertext Transfer Protocol Secure**. The **Web server name** or **machine name** is assigned by the server administrator and can be almost any combination of characters but is often "`www,`" for World Wide Web. A **domain name** is a unique name chosen by the site's owner. It represents a group of computers at the same Internet address. Each domain name contains a suffix, such as .com, representing a top-level domain, the highest category in the Internet naming system. A top-level domain can indicate the site's function or its country of origin. Common top-level domains include: commercial (.com), educational (.edu), governmental (.gov), nonprofit organizational (.org), network (.net), United States (.us), Canada (.ca), or Thailand (.ta). The last part of a URL is the file path, which consists of the directory, file name, and extension. Figure A-2 shows the parts of a URL.

Planning an HTML Document

Before writing an HTML document, you should have a preliminary idea of how you want your final Web page to look. Although you'll inevitably modify your initial page format as you go along, a master plan helps keep you focused on the information you want to convey. You decide to use the Web to research the process of creating an HTML document and to find a list of suggested steps for planning and creating a Web page.

Follow these steps to plan and create a Web page:

- ### Sketch your Web page

    Create a rough sketch showing the desired appearance of your final Web page. The goal of this process—which is called **storyboarding**—is to show the elements you want to include and how you want them arranged on the Web page. You then can make sure you know how to use the necessary tags for each element, and you can research those that you haven't used before. Figure A-3 presents a **storyboard layout sketch**, or **storyboard**, showing the first few elements you want to add to the Paradise Mountain Family Resort home page.

- ### Enter structuring tags for the file

    Every Web page begins with an opening HTML tag and ends with a closing HTML tag. These beginning and ending HTML tags identify the file as an HTML document and provide basic information about it to the browser. A Web page also contains tags that divide it into two main structural sections, the head and body sections, which hold section-specific content. See Figure A-4 for examples of these tags.

- ### Enter the head section elements

    The **head section** contains identifying and descriptive information. It can contain **meta tags**, which add information that helps search engines identify and describe your page content. The most commonly-used metatags are the **keywords** meta tag, which allows you to list words users might type into a search engine, and **description**, which lets you give more detail about your page content. Other head section elements can include **scripts**, lists of commands that run automatically on the Web page to provide extra information to the user or to track user movements. The head section also often contains some page formatting information. Although many different head section elements *can* be included in a Web page, only one element, the page title, is recommended for every Web page. **Page title** information does not appear in the browser window; instead, it appears in the title bar at the top of the browser window, as shown in Figure A-5. All content of a Web page's head section is coded between the opening and closing head tags (`<head>...</head>`). Your Paradise Mountain page will include a title and a keyword meta tag. (For more information on meta tags, see the appendix.)

- ### Enter each Web page body element

    Web page content, the information that appears in the browser window, is contained within the **body section** of the Web page and falls between the opening and closing body tags (`<body>` and `</body>`). The most common Web page elements are heading and paragraph elements and tags containing source references used to display graphics and multimedia elements on a Web page. You can enter tags to add special formatting to text, to create tables, or to add links to other Web pages. It is generally best to add one new element at a time, and then preview the Web page. If the page doesn't appear as you expect, you then have a good idea of which HTML tag or tag set is likely to contain the error. Figure A-4 shows the source code for a basic Web page.

- ### Preview the Web page

    As you create your page, you should preview it often in a Web browser. Figure A-5 shows the output from the code shown in Figure A-4. Such previews allow you to notice any elements that don't appear as you intended. Correcting errors often can be as simple as adding or editing an HTML tag. Because different Web browsers, such as Microsoft Internet Explorer or Netscape Navigator, sometimes display the same code differently, it is best to preview your work in multiple browsers to ensure that it appears as you planned for all users.

- ### Test links

    If your document contains links to other Web pages, preview your page in a Web browser and test each link by clicking it. If clicking a link does not open the Web page you intended as the target, you can edit the code.

FIGURE A-3: Storyboard for Paradise Mountain Web page

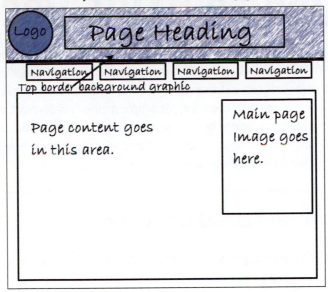

FIGURE A-4: Web page source code

HTML tag set

Head tag set

Body tag set

Opening and closing title tags (title tag set)

Content in body section with level-one heading and paragraph tags

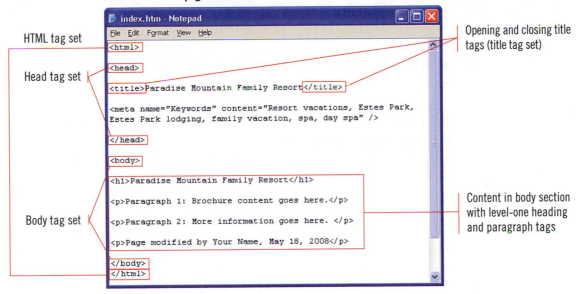

FIGURE A-5: Web page preview in browser

Page title

Level-one heading

Paragraph output

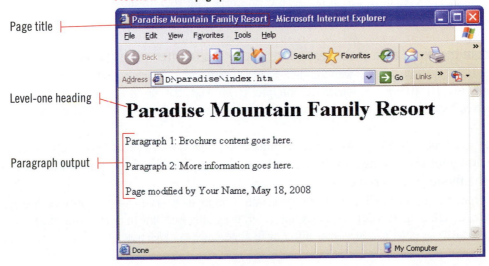

HTML

Writing an HTML Document

Once you've planned how you want your document to look, you can start creating its structure and adding page elements. You can create an HTML document in any application that allows you to enter and save text. Notepad, a text editor program installed with Windows, and the Macintosh Text Editor, are popular tools for writing HTML code. These applications include simple methods of saving a document in text format without the additional formatting added by some word processors. You decide to create your first HTML document using Notepad and begin coding the Paradise Mountain home page by entering the structuring tags and adding some basic page elements.

STEPS

QUICK TIP

Use a plain text editor instead of a word processor to ensure results like those found in these lessons.

1. **Click the Start button**  **start** **on the taskbar**

2. **Point to All Programs, point to Accessories, click Notepad, then maximize the Notepad window, if necessary**
   A blank Notepad document opens.

QUICK TIP

Be sure you do *not* use the Save As HTML command if you are creating your HTML document in a word processor.

3. **Click File on the menu bar, then click Save**
   The Save As dialog box opens.

4. **Click the Save in list arrow, then navigate to the location where you want to store your site files**

5. **Click the Create New Folder icon , type paradise as the new folder name, then double-click the paradise folder to open it**
   It is important to organize your Web files as you create them. The paradise folder will serve as the home or **root folder,** which is the top-level folder for your Web site.

6. **Click the Save as type arrow, then click All Files**
   Choosing All Files when you save your HTML file prevents your file from being saved with the .txt extension appended to the filename such as index.htm.txt.

TROUBLE

Make sure to type a period followed by htm after the file name. Otherwise, your text editor will automatically add the .txt extension to your filename when you save it. Double-check your filename to make sure it ends with .htm.

7. **Click in the File name text box, type index.htm, compare your dialog box with Figure A-6, then click Save**
   On most servers, the default file name for a home page or the main page in a Web folder is index.htm or index.html. However, other default filenames exist. Check with your instructor or webmaster to determine the default name for your server and name your page accordingly.

8. **Click in the blank area of the text editor, type <html>, then press [Enter]**
   Every HTML document begins with the <html> tag and ends with a closing </html> tag. Table A-1 lists commonly used HTML tags. A browser can interpret HTML tags that are in either uppercase or lowercase. However, because of new W3C Web standards, it is best to consistently use all lowercase characters.

9. **Type the remaining tags, as shown in Figure A-7, using extra return characters after each tag and your own name and the current date in the "Modified by" paragraph, click File on the menu bar, then click Save**
   You typed a level-one heading and three paragraphs. Because browsers do not recognize extra spaces, hard returns, or tabs in most HTML code, pressing [Enter] twice after each line to create extra white space makes your HTML code easier to read without affecting its appearance as a Web page.

FIGURE A-6: Notepad Save As dialog box

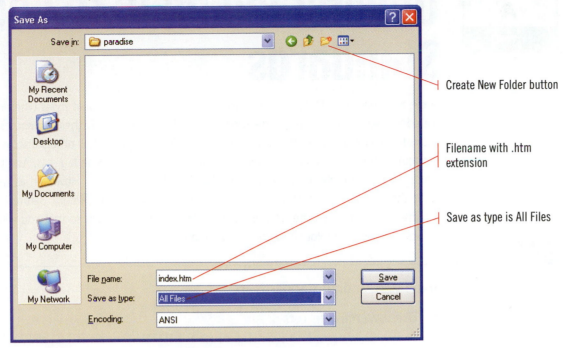

Create New Folder button

Filename with .htm extension

Save as type is All Files

FIGURE A-7: Paradise Mountain Family Resort HTML code

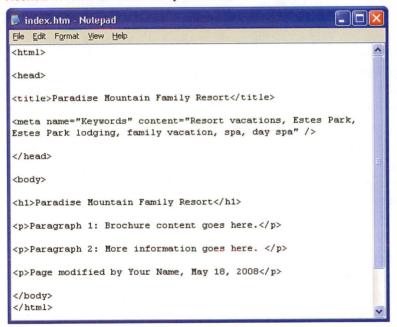

TABLE A-1: HTML tag sets

tag set	purpose
`<html>...</html>`	Identifies the file as an HTML document to the program opening it
`<head>...</head>`	Identifies the document's head area, where you can code information about your document, including its title
`<title>...</title>`	Formats the document title, which appears in the browser's title bar; search engines use information found in the title to help identify page content and rank pages for search queries
`<body>...</body>`	Identifies the document's body area, which contains the Web page contents that appear in the browser window
`<p>...</p>`	Defines a paragraph, the basic content unit for Web text

Understanding W3C Coding Standards

In the early days of HTML, designers used a hodgepodge of personal styles when coding or marking up a Web document. For example, some used all capital letters to specify their tag names. Others used all capital letters for opening tags and lowercase type for their closing tags. Still others discovered that they could use shortcut methods of coding by leaving out the closing tags of some tag sets. As a result, many Web documents were extremely untidy with code that was difficult to read. However, as newer Web technologies make their presence felt, Web coding standards are tightening. Before coding any more of the Paradise Mountain Web site, you review the W3C coding standards so that you will be in a better position to tackle newer technologies as your Web site grows and matures.

DETAILS

Some W3C coding standards are:

QUICK TIP

Be aware that UNIX servers are case sensitive, meaning that they distinguish between upper- and lowercase letters. So if you use fileName.htm, use that same capitalization throughout your site so that UNIX machines will be able to find your file.

- **Use lowercase letters**

  Because many newer Web technologies such as **DHTML** (dynamic HTML) and **XML** (extensible markup language)—often used for creating database connections—are case sensitive, the W3C recommends using all lowercase letters for HTML documents.

- **If you open it, close it**

  Most HTML tags are part of a tag set, except for open tags which, as you learned earlier, have no closing counterpart. Tags representing line breaks, images, and horizontal rules are open tags. These open elements are now closed by inserting a single space followed by the closing slash (/) after the tag name (if no **attributes**—additional instructions inside the opening tag that change the appearance or behavior of the affected element—are applied). You will further explore the proper method of closing tags in Unit D. A list of old and new tag elements is shown in Table A-2.

- **No spaces in folders or file names**

  From the time that Microsoft introduced the first Windows 9*x* system with support for long file names, computer users began to learn that they could place spaces in folders or file names to make their file names easier to understand. This practice is not accepted on the Web. In fact, giving HTML documents and other Web files names with spaces can cause linking, display, and scripting problems down the road. If you must use more than one word to identify a file, combine words with an underscore character (file_name.htm) or run both words together, but capitalize the second word of the file name (fileName.htm).

- **Keep it neat**

  When a browser reads the code of a Web document, it starts at the beginning and reads the document straight through to the end, paying no heed, in most cases, to line breaks, tabs, and extra spaces that occur within the code. However, code that does not include extra carriage returns, spaces and/or tabs is extremely difficult to read for humans. Sloppily coded pages are much more likely to contain coding errors than are pages to which "code-beautification tactics" such as extra carriage returns, spaces, and/or tabs have been applied.

- **Put everything in its place**

  Stacked tags are tags that are closed before the next tag begins or are opened after the previous tag has ended. **Nested tags** are tags that are fully contained within another tag. There is a proper tag nesting and stacking standard for HTML documents and, with XML standards in mind, it is important to adhere to the standard. According to the standard, when stacking tags, the opening tag of a subsequent HTML element must not be inserted into a document until the closing tag of the previous tag element has been inserted. With nested tags the rule is that the first element opened is the last element closed. Figure A-8 shows an example of a Web page with stacked and nested HTML elements.

FIGURE A-8: Stacked and nested tags

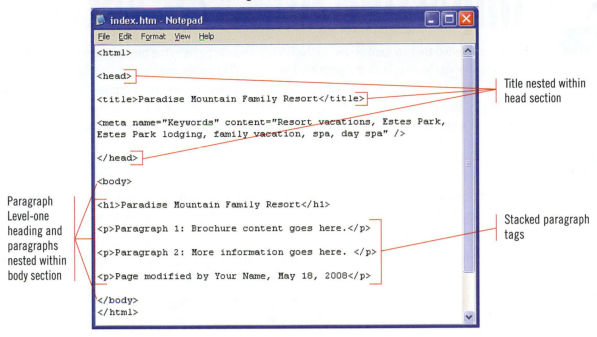

Title nested within head section

Paragraph Level-one heading and paragraphs nested within body section

Stacked paragraph tags

TABLE A-2: Coding to W3C standards

tag	old style	new style
Paragraph	`<P>...</P>` or `<p>`	`<p>...</p>`
META	`<META Description="...">`	`<meta description="..." />`
Line break	` ` or ` `	` `
Horizontal rule	`<hr>` or `<HR>`	`<hr />`
Image	`<img src="filename.jpg">`	`<img src="filename.jpg" />`
List item	`<li>List item`	`<li>List item</li>`

Clues to Use

Using a text editor versus a word processor or other program

Many word processors and desktop publishing programs, such as Microsoft Word or Microsoft Publisher, offer a Save as HTML command on the File menu. This feature allows you to create and format a document using word-processing features with which you are familiar, and then automatically create a Web page that contains the same information and layout. Such a feature makes Web page authoring possible even for people who don't know anything about HTML. However, this automated method has its drawbacks. In some cases, page elements do not appear in a Web browser exactly as they did in the word processor. Also, the generated code is usually full of extra formatting information and making any change to the Web page requires regenerating the HTML code from the word processor. Creating pages by entering the HTML tags yourself— known as **hand coding**—gives you more precise control over the exact appearance of your Web pages. You can fine-tune a page's appearance by making direct and specific changes to the HTML code. Because you are studying HTML, you should use a plain text editor such as Notepad (for Windows) or SimpleText (for MAC systems) to complete these lessons. If you choose to use a word processor instead, be sure to save each file in text format with an .htm extension. Do not use the word processor's **native format** (.doc or .wpd) or its HTML document type.

HTML

Importing Web Content

You have learned that content added to the body section appears in the browser window. However, it is not necessary for you to type in all the page content. You will often discover that the content you need is already saved in digital format, such as a word-processed document, for another purpose. You can easily **import**, or bring in, that content instead of retyping it. To avoid retyping company information, you decide to use a rich text file (.rtf) you obtained from the Public Relations Department as the main content on your new page.

STEPS

TROUBLE

Do not select the closing body (`</body>`) or closing HTML (`</html>`) tags, or the "Page modified by" paragraph.

1. **Click before the first opening paragraph tag (`<p>`), drag to select all of the content through and including the second closing paragraph tag (`</p>`), then press [Delete] to remove the page content**

2. **Start Microsoft Word or another word-processing program, then open the document htm_a-1.rtf from the location where you store your Data Files**

3. **Click before the word Located in the first paragraph below the page heading in the htm_a-1.rtf document, then drag to select all the remaining text**

4. **Click Edit on the menu bar, click Copy, then click the text editor program button on the taskbar**

   You copied the text and returned to the index.htm file that is open in your text editor.

TROUBLE

If you accidentally copied and pasted the page heading from the RTF file, delete it now.

5. **Click in the line below the level-one heading, click Edit on the menu bar, then click Paste**

   You pasted the copied text into the content area of the index.htm file. Your file should now resemble Figure A-9.

6. **Close the rtf file, then save your work**

   Although you are not finished, it is time to preview your new page in a browser. Saving your work ensures that your recent changes will appear in your browser.

7. **Start your browser, then cancel any dial-up operations**

   The procedure for opening the page may vary, depending on your browser.

8. **Click File on the menu bar, click Open or Open Page, then click Browse or Choose File**

TROUBLE

If you are warned that Windows security settings will not allow you to open a local file from the browser, find the file in My Computer, then double-click it to open it in a browser.

9. **Navigate to and then click the file index.htm in your paradise site folder, click Open, then click Open or OK**

   Compare your page with Figure A-10. The level-one page heading appears in boldface type and is larger than the rest of the text. See Table A-3 for a list of heading levels you can use with text. The paragraph text runs together because it is not marked with paragraph tags; the browser does not read blank lines and other white space typed into the HTML code of a document.

Clues to Use

Viewing Web page source code

An excellent way of learning what other designers are doing is to view the source code of other pages on the World Wide Web. To view a page's source code in Internet Explorer, click View on the menu bar, then click Source. The page opens in Notepad. In Navigator, click View on the menu bar, then click Page Source. The code is not editable, but you can copy and paste it into a Notepad document. It is acceptable to copy the HTML code itself, but it is not acceptable to copy and use someone else's content, including text, graphics, or logos. All Web content is considered copyrighted and using someone else's content without permission is a violation of copyright laws.

FIGURE A-9: The index.htm file with pasted text

```
<h1>Paradise Mountain Family Resort</h1>

Located just outside of Rocky Mountain National Park in Colorado, Paradise Mountain Family Resort
is the perfect getaway place for the whole family. Adults can enjoy discounted golf and
complimentary use of our health club and tennis facilities while the little ones participate in
our popular children's program.

Friday night dances are always a hit with the teens, and our new skate park offers one of the
finest courses designed to entertain and challenge skaters, whether they are beginners or more
experienced.

Hiking is a must-do activity in the beautiful Rocky Mountains. Guests can participate in one of
our wilderness treks (designed for both experienced and beginning hikers), or strike out on their
own for a more intimate wilderness experience.

In addition to hiking activities, during the summer months guests can enjoy horseback riding,
white-water rafting, or fly fishing for trout in one of our many private streams. Rodeo fans
arriving in mid-July will be sure to catch some of the events at the annual PRCA Rooftop Rodeo at
the nearby Stanley Park Fairgrounds.

Wintertime guests are sure to enjoy a snowshoe trek along our well-manicured trails, a brisk
downhill ski run, or the comfort of a cozy fire in our rustic ski lodge.

Other on-site or nearby seasonal events and activities include Boulder Walk and Bike Week (June),
4th of July Fireworks, The Paradise Mountain Cycling Road Rally (July), and the Scottish
Highlands Festival (the week following Labor Day).

Send inquiries regarding rates and reservations to:
Paradise Mountain Family Resort
PO Box 17603
Estes Park, CO 80517
Phone: 1.970.555.7777
```

Pasted text

FIGURE A-10: Paradise Mountain Family Resort page with imported text

Paradise Mountain Family Resort

Located just outside of Rocky Mountain National Park in Colorado, Paradise Mountain Family Resort is the perfect getaway place for the whole family. Adults can enjoy discounted golf and complimentary use of our health club and tennis facilities while the little ones participate in our popular children's program. Friday night dances are always a hit with the teens, and our new skate park offers one of the finest courses designed to entertain and challenge skaters, whether they are beginners or more experienced. Hiking is a must-do activity in the beautiful Rocky Mountains. Guests can participate in one of our wilderness treks (designed for both experienced and beginning hikers), or strike out on their own for a more intimate wilderness experience. In addition to hiking activities, during the summer months guests can enjoy horseback riding, white-water rafting, or fly fishing for trout in one of our many private streams. Rodeo fans arriving in mid-July will be sure to catch some of the events at the annual PRCA Rooftop Rodeo at the nearby Stanley Park Fairgrounds. Wintertime guests are sure to enjoy a snowshoe trek along our well-manicured trails, a brisk downhill ski run, or the comfort of a cozy fire in our rustic ski lodge. Other on-site or nearby seasonal events and activities include Boulder Walk and Bike Week (June), 4th of July Fireworks, The Paradise Mountain Cycling Road Rally (July), and the Scottish Highlands Festival (the week following Labor Day). Send inquiries regarding rates and reservations to: Paradise Mountain Family Resort PO Box 17603 Estes Park, CO 80517 Phone: 1.970.555.7777

Page modified by Your Name, May 18, 2008

Level-one page heading

Pasted text not formatted

"Modified by" paragraph

TABLE A-3: Heading tags

tags	code sample	result in browser
<h1>...</h1>	<h1>Heading 1</h1>	# Heading 1
<h2>...</h2>	<h2>Heading 2</h2>	## Heading 2
<h3>...</h3>	<h3>Heading 3</h3>	### Heading 3
<h4>...</h4>	<h4>Heading 4</h4>	#### Heading 4
<h5>...</h5>	<h5>Heading 5</h5>	##### Heading 5
<h6>...</h6>	<h6>Heading 6</h6>	###### Heading 6

Marking up Web Page Content

Two basic tags, the line break <br /> and the paragraph tag <p>...</p>, allow you to control the space between lines of text and to determine where those lines break on the screen. Other tags allow you to apply special formatting styles to Web content. For example, heading tags, which come in a range from h1 (the largest) to h6 (the smallest) act like paragraph tags in that they cause extra white space to appear above the tag; however, unlike paragraph tags, heading tags also cause their content to appear as boldface type in the browser window. Table A-4 shows the descriptions and samples of paragraph and line break tags. It is important to note that text formatted with heading tags appears with slight differences in different Web browsers. The best way to make sure your Web page appears as you intended is to preview it in all of the most common Web browsers. To make your page appear as expected, you want to format it as a Web page by using HTML markup tags.

STEPS

1. **Click the text editor program button on the taskbar, click before the word Located, type <p>, click in the white space after "program." at the end of the paragraph, then type </p>**

2. **Add opening and closing paragraph tags at the beginning and end of each paragraph, like the tags shown in Figure A-11, then save your work**

> **QUICK TIP**
> In Internet Explorer, you can press F5 as a keyboard shortcut for the Refresh button.

3. **Click the browser program button** `Paradise Moun...` **on the taskbar, then click your browser's Reload or Refresh button**

   The browser displays the new version of your Web page, in which the paragraphs are displayed as separate blocks of text. However, because the browser recognizes only *coded* line breaks—those that are forced by using the HTML line break tag—the contact information at the bottom of the page runs together, as shown in Figure A-12.

> **QUICK TIP**
> Be sure to type a space between the "br" and the slash.

4. **Click the text editor program button on the taskbar, click after the line that reads, Send inquiries regarding rates and reservations to:, then type <br />.**

5. **Type a line break at the end of the next three lines, as shown in Figure A-13, then save your work**

6. **Return to the browser window, then click the browser's Reload or Refresh button**

   The browser opens the most recently saved version of the Web page showing that the line break tags you entered produced a hard line return at the end of each line, but, unlike the paragraph tag, did not produce any extra white space, as shown in Figure A-13.

TABLE A-4: Basic HTML text tags

tag	description	sample	result in browser
 	Adds a line break; this open tag has no closing counterpart and so the closing slash is placed within the opening following a single space after the tag name (br)	line 1 line 2	line 1 line 2
<p>...</p>	Adds a blank line before and after the current paragraph; does require a closing tag	<p>paragraph 1</p> <p>paragraph 2</p>	paragraph 1 paragraph 2

FIGURE A-11: Text marked up with paragraph tags

Opening and closing paragragh tags surround paragraph sections

Add opening and closing paragraph tags to the next four paragraphs

```
<h1>Paradise Mountain Family Resort</h1>

<p>Located just outside of Rocky Mountain National Park in Colorado,
Paradise Mountain Family Resort is the perfect getaway place for the whole
family. Adults can enjoy discounted golf and complimentary use of our health
club and tennis facilities while the little ones participate in our popular
children's program.</p>

<p>Friday night dances are always a hit with the teens, and our new skate
park offers one of the finest courses designed to entertain and challenge
skaters, whether they are beginners or more experienced.</p>

<p>Hiking is a must-do activity in the beautiful Rocky Mountains. Guests can
participate in one of our wilderness treks (designed for both experienced
and beginning hikers), or strike out on their own for a more intimate
wilderness experience.</p>

<p>In addition to hiking activities, during the summer months guests can
enjoy horseback riding, white-water rafting, or fly fishing for trout in one
of our many private streams. Rodeo fans arriving in mid-July will be sure to
catch some of the events at the annual PRCA Rooftop Rodeo at the nearby
Stanley Park Fairgrounds.</p>

<p>Wintertime guests are sure to enjoy a snowshoe trek along our
well-manicured trails, a brisk downhill ski run, or the comfort of a cozy
fire in our rustic ski lodge. </p>

<p>Other on-site or nearby seasonal events and activities include Boulder
Walk and Bike Week (June), 4th of July Fireworks, The Paradise Mountain
```

FIGURE A-12: Reloaded page after paragraph markup

Friday night dances are always a hit with the teens, and our new skate park offers one of the finest courses designed to entertain and challenge skaters, whether they are beginners or more experienced.

Hiking is a must-do activity in the beautiful Rocky Mountains. Guests can participate in one of our wilderness treks (designed for both experienced and beginning hikers), or strike out on their own for a more intimate wilderness experience.

In addition to hiking activities, during the summer months guests can enjoy horseback riding, white-water rafting, or fly fishing for trout in one of our many private streams. Rodeo fans arriving in mid-July will be sure to catch some of the events at the annual PRCA Rooftop Rodeo at the nearby Stanley Park Fairgrounds.

Wintertime guests are sure to enjoy a snowshoe trek along our well-manicured trails, a brisk downhill ski run, or the comfort of a cozy fire in our rustic ski lodge.

Other on-site or nearby seasonal events and activities include Boulder Walk and Bike Week (June), 4th of July Fireworks, The Paradise Mountain Cycling Road Rally (July), and the Scottish Highlands Festival (the week following Labor Day).

Send inquiries regarding rates and reservations to: Paradise Mountain Family Resort PO Box 17603 Estes Park, CO 80517 Phone: 1.970.555.7777

Page modified by Your Name, May 18, 2008

Added paragraph tags create white space between paragraphs

Address elements on same line because there are only paragraph marks between them in source code

FIGURE A-13: Coded line breaks and output

Hiking is a
our wildern
their own f

In addition
white-wate
arriving in
Rodeo at t

```
<p>Send inquiries regarding rates and reservations to:<br />
Paradise Mountain Family Resort<br />
PO Box 17603 <br />
Estes Park, CO 80517<br />
Phone: 1.970.555.7777 </p>

<p>Page modified by Your Name, May 18, 2008</p>

</body>
</html>
```

`<br />` tags added to force line breaks in output

Wintertime guests are sure to enjoy a snowshoe trek along our well-manicured trails, a brisk downhill ski run, or the comfort of a cozy fire in our rustic ski lodge.

Other on-site or nearby seasonal events and activities include Boulder Bike Week (June), 4th of July Fireworks, The Paradise Mountain Cycling Road Rally (July), and the Scottish Highlands Festival (the week following Labor Day).

Contact paragraph output with coded line breaks

Send inquiries regarding rates and reservations to:
Paradise Mountain Family Resort
PO Box 17603
Estes Park, CO 80517
Phone: 1.970.555.7777

Page modified by Your Name, May 18, 2008

Printing an HTML Document

Even though HTML documents are designed to facilitate information exchange over the Internet, sometimes you need to print hard copies. You can print the HTML source code for your pages using the same text editor you used to create them. For a fully developed Web page, the source code can span many printed pages, so you might want to print only selected pages if you are checking specific lines of code. Web browsers also allow you to print your Web pages as they appear in the browser window. You want to present your preliminary work on the Paradise Mountain Family Resort Web page at your design team meeting later today. You will print both the HTML source code and the Web browser display.

STEPS

1. **Click the text editor button on the taskbar, click File on the menu bar, then click Print**
   The Print dialog box opens, allowing you to select your printer. Your dialog box should resemble the one shown in Figure A-14, although your printer may display different options.

2. **Verify that your preferred printer is selected, then click Print**
   The text editor prints a single copy of the source code, as shown in Figure A-15. By default, the filename prints at the top of each page, and the page number at the bottom.

3. **Click the browser program button on the taskbar**

4. **Click the Print button 🖨 on the browser toolbar, then, if necessary, click OK**
   Figure A-15 displays the page printed from the browser window. Notice that the page title appears at the top of the page and the file path or URL appears at the bottom of the page.

5. **Click the browser window Close button**

6. **If necessary, click the text editor program button on the taskbar, then click the text editor window Close button**

Clues to Use

Changing browser headers and footers

When you print a Web page from a browser, the output includes information about the Web page, such as its location and the page title, as shown in Figure A-15. Both Netscape Navigator and Microsoft Internet Explorer Web browsers allow you to customize the information that prints, whether you created the Web page or not. In both browsers, you click File, then click Page Setup to change header and footer information. In Navigator, the Header and Footer sections include list arrows that allow you to select or deselect header and footer items. The default selections print the Title and URL at the top of the page, and the Page number, date, and time at the bottom. Instead of list arrows, Internet Explorer uses codes consisting of an ampersand (&) and a letter, such as &u for the URL and &p for the page number as shown in Figure A-16. Although using codes takes a bit more work, Internet Explorer offers more choices of what you can show in the header and the footer, and also allows you to choose the order of the elements. You can also enter text before or after the codes. To display an index of the Internet Explorer codes and their meanings, click in the Header or Footer text box, then press F1.

FIGURE A-16: Internet Explorer Page Setup options

FIGURE A-14: Notepad print dialog box

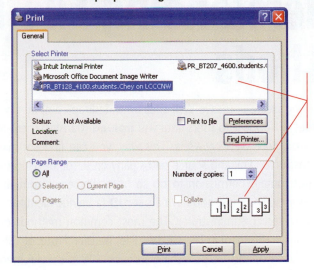

Depending on your printer and printer choices, your options may differ

FIGURE A-15: Paradise Mountian home page printouts from Notepad and from Internet Explorer

File name

Page title

Page number

File path or URL

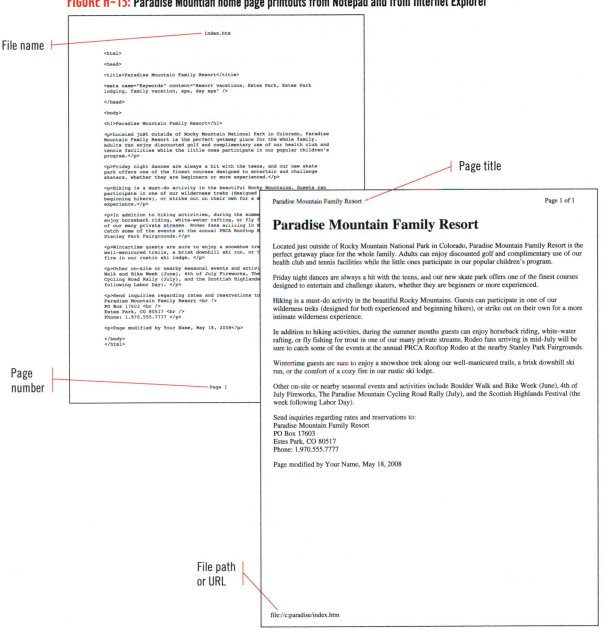

HTML

Understanding File Transfer Methods

While you usually create and save Web sites on a desktop computer, you can never really be sure exactly how your pages will appear to users until you **upload** (transfer) them to a Web server and view the "live" site using one or more Web browsers. This way, you can find and fix display problems stemming from improperly constructed link and source paths early on in the development cycle. Before you post files to a server, you must obtain permission to do so from the server administrator; this is called having **write access** to the server. You must also have a **user ID** (a unique identifying name) and a valid password, also assigned by your server administrator. The most common methods of transferring files to a Web server include File Transfer Protocol (FTP), Secure File Transfer Protocol (SFTP), direct file transfer through a mapped network drive, and file publishing through a Web development software application's publishing interface. You are eager to begin transferring Paradise Mountain's Web pages to the Web server so you can see how they look in a live setting. You set up a meeting with your network manager to review the various methods of transferring files and determine which one is best for you.

DETAILS

- ### File Transfer Protocol (FTP)
  File Transfer Protocol (FTP) is one of the most common methods of transferring files to a server. You can use DOS command-line FTP instructions to transfer files, but most people find it easier to use a special program called an FTP client. **FTP client** programs, such as InternetSoft FTP Commander, Ipswitch WS_FTP, and Fetch Softworks Fetch (for Macintosh users), let you transfer files without having to remember a list of command-line FTP instructions. Instead, most FTP client programs use a graphical user interface, which uses windows, icons, pointers, and the like, to navigate among folders and subfolders in much the same way that you do with your computer's file system. Figure A-16 shows the FTP Commander interface.

- ### Secure File Transfer Protocol (SFTP)
  Secure File Transfer Protocol (SFTP) works like FTP, except that files transferred with SFTP are encrypted for additional security. If your file transfers must be secure, it is important that you choose an FTP client application that supports SFTP.

- ### Mapped Network Drive
  Direct transfer through a mapped drive is as easy as copying or moving files on your own computer. You simply drag files from your local disk to the desired server location. However, this method is also the most dangerous because it can alter file path integrity. For example, files transferred in this manner often end up with drive letters and file designators such as file:///C:/mydirectory/myfile.htm in their file paths. If you test your remote files from your development station after transferring them in this manner, file-path problems will not be evident because your local files and "live" files have access to the same mapped and local drives. To prevent this type of error, examine your source code before transferring files to ensure that there are no drive-letter references in your file paths.

- ### Web Site Development Program Publishing Interface
  Web development software packages, such as Macromedia Dreamweaver (now owned by Adobe Systems), and Microsoft FrontPage utilize their own publishing interfaces to transfer files. In fact, some sites developed with these applications are **extension specific**, meaning that they do not perform properly unless specific files, called extensions, are stored on the Web server and unless the sites are published and updated using the application's publishing interface. Hand coded sites are not extension dependent and so have no need of a program-specific publishing interface.

FIGURE A-16: FTP Commander interface

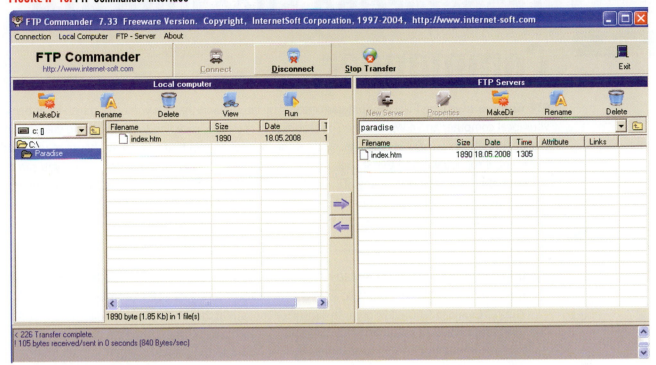

Clues to Use

Downloading FTP Commander

Although you can use any FTP client program to transfer your files, the freeware program, FTP Commander, is easy to install and to use. Complete the steps below to download and install FTP Commander. (These steps describe the download process from Internet Explorer; your browser steps may differ.)

1. Open your browser, then go to the InternetSoft Web site: Go to the Student Online Companion for this book and find the links for Unit A.

2. Click the DOWNLOAD link in the navigation bar near the top of the page.

3. On the Download page, click the Download link next to FTP Commander. (Notice that there is no charge for this program.)

4. If the Windows File Download - Security Warning dialog box displays the message, "Do you want to run or save this file?" click Run. (If you are on a very slow connection, you might want to save the file first and run it later.)

Wait a few moments while the small FTP Commander Install file downloads to your Temporary folder.

5. Click Run when the Internet Explorer - Security Warning dialog box displays the message: "The publisher could not be verified. Are you sure you want to run this software?"

6. After reading the FTP Commander License Agreement, click to select the check box indicating that you agree with the license terms.

7. Click Next.

8. When the FTP Commander Destination Directory dialog box appears, click Browse to select a different storage location or

click Start to accept the default destination. FTP Commander unpacks and installs the necessary files.

9. When the files are installed, make sure that the Run Installed Application box is checked, then click OK. You are now ready to begin using FTP Commander. The first time you run the application, a Windows Security Alert dialog box may warn you that Windows Firewall has blocked some features of this program. If this happens, click Unblock, as shown in Figure A-17.

For information on using WS_FTP Home for Windows or Fetch for MAC operating systems, see Using Other FTP Programs in the appendix of this text or in the FTP Resources section of the Student Online Companion.

FIGURE A-17: Windows Security Alert dialog box

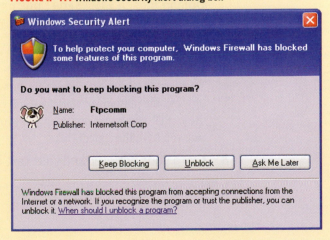

HTML

Transferring Files with FTP Commander

FTP Commander is an FTP client program created by InternetSoft that lets you easily transfer files between your local computer and a Web server. The program is **freeware**, meaning that you can download it at no charge from the Internet; it is readily available at the Internet-Soft Web site. You may choose to use another FTP client; if so, you will find that it operates in a similar manner to FTP Commander. In fact, you can apply the same basic steps to almost any FTP client. Now that you have a basic understanding of file transfer methods, you are eager to see how your site will appear on a "live" server and decide to use FTP Commander to transfer them there.

STEPS

TROUBLE

If FTP Commander is not installed on your computer, you need to download and install it. To do so, complete the steps in the Clues to Use in the previous lesson. You will also need access to a server directory with an assigned user-name and password that grants your permission to control files in that directory.

1. **If FTP Commander is not already running, click the Start button** ![start] **on the taskbar, point to All Programs, point to FTP Commander, then click FTP Commander**
The FTP Commander window opens to display the contents of the FTP Commander folder in the local directory (left pane) and a list of servers on the remote site in the right pane. These servers are public access FTP sites where you can go to download information. Before transferring files to and from a server, you must first define your local and remote directories.

2. **Click the Browse local drives list arrow shown in Figure A-18, then navigate to the location where you store your site files**
Any available folders in your selected drive are displayed in the Folders pane. When a folder is selected, the folder content, which could include other folders as well as files, is displayed in the Folder content pane. You need to define the path to your remote server.

3. **Click New Server under FTP- servers**
The FTP Server Properties box appears.

QUICK TIP

If you need to change your Server Definition Properties again later, select the server name in the SERVER LIST pane, and then click the Modify FTP server properties ![Properties] button.

4. **Type your information as described in Table A-5, then click Save**
FTP Commander Server Properties settings may change over time. If necessary, go to the Student Online Companion for this text and unit, then click the FTP Resources link to see an updated table.

5. **In the SERVER LIST pane, double-click the name of the server you just defined to open an FTP connection to your server**
Your remote site content appears in the server pane. If you have not yet transferred any files to your remote site, your files list contains no items.

6. **Click index.htm in the Folder content pane of the Local computer window, then click the Upload files to FTP - server button** ![arrow] **to start the file transfer to the server**
The paradise home page file is copied to the FTP server, as shown in Figure A-18.

7. **Start your Internet browser, type your remote URL in the browser's Address box, then click Go or press [Enter]**
Your remote page is displayed in the browser window. Your remote URL is usually a combination of your FTP server name plus any subdirectory and filename (with extension). However, on occasion, some FTP servers use an FTP alias that is not the same as your URL. Check with your instructor or server administrator to make sure you have the correct URL.

8. **Close your browser and your text editor**

FIGURE A-18: Transferring a file using FTP Commander

Browse local drives button

Click to select local file

Folders pane

Folder content pane

File appears in server file listing

Click Upload Files to FTP Server button

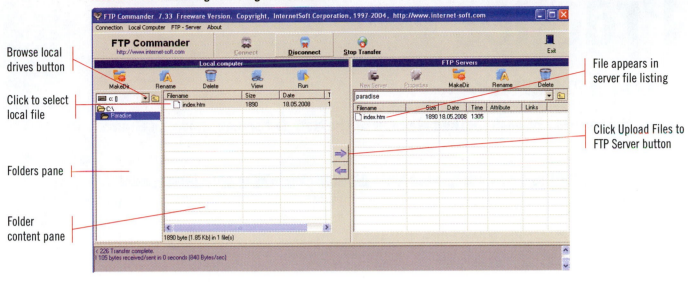

TABLE A-5: FTP Commander Server Properties settings

section	property	value
Server	Name	An identifying name for your site
Server	FTP Server	Use the FTP server name, including any subdirectory paths, as assigned by your instructor or server administrator. Do not include any protocol designation such as ftp:// or http://.
Server	FTP Port	21 (unless otherwise instructed)
User	User ID	Obtain from your instructor or server administrator
User	Password	Obtain from your instructor or server administrator
User	Save Password	If computer is your own, leave checked; if computer is shared, do not check this box
User	Mask Password	Checked
User	Passive Mode	Unchecked unless otherwise instructed
User	Anonymous Login	Unchecked unless otherwise instructed
User	E-Mail	Leave blank unless otherwise instructed
Additional Options	Use "/" as initial directory on FTP server	Unchecked unless otherwise instructed
Additional Options	Shared virtual host	Unchecked unless otherwise instructed
Additional Options	Use relative pathname	Unchecked unless otherwise instructed
FTP Server response type	Drop-down menu	Obtain from your instructor or server administrator. For Microsoft servers, choose the current Windows server version; for UNIX servers, choose Default.

HTML

Practice

▼ CONCEPTS REVIEW

Name the function of each marked element of the Notepad screen shown in Figure A-19.

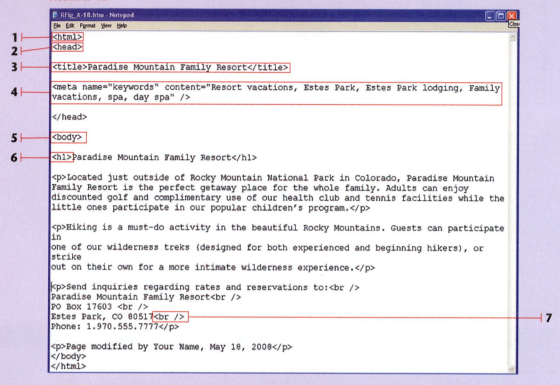

FIGURE A-19

Match each term with the statement that best describes it.

8. **Tag**

9. **<title>...</title>**

10. **Web site**

11. **Search engine**

12. **<body>...</body>**

13. **Source code**

a. A Web-based program that helps you find information you are seeking

b. An instruction in HTML

c. Tag set surrounding Web page contents that appear in the browser window

d. Tag set for text to appear in the browser's title bar

e. A collection of related Web pages

f. The HTML code used to create a Web page

Select the best answer from the list of choices.

14. **If you wanted to reduce the text size of a level four heading, which tag set would you use?**

    a. <head>...</head>

    b. <h3>...</h3>

    c. <h5>...</h5>

    d.
...</br>

15. **In the URL http://www.paradisemountain.com/spa/wraps.htm, paradisemountain.com is the:**

    a. Machine name.

    b. Domain name.

    c. Directory name.

    d. Protocol.

16. **Which is the proper method of coding a line break?**

    a.

    b. <break>

    c.

    d. <lb>

▼ SKILLS REVIEW

1. **Plan an HTML document.**
   a. Consider a Web page you might create for Paradise Mountain's spa. Assume it will have a page title, a level-one heading, a subheading, and two text paragraphs.
   b. Create a sketch of how the page will eventually look.
   c. On your sketch, identify each heading and/or subheading.
   d. On your sketch, identify your page content area.
   e. On your sketch, use boxes to identify areas that will eventually contain images.

2. **Write an HTML document.**
   a. Locate and open the paradise folder in the directory where you store your site files.
   b. Create a subfolder in your paradise folder called **spa**.
   c. Start your text editor with a blank document.
   d. Save your new file as **index.htm** inside your spa folder. (*Note*: Be careful *not* to save the new file in your paradise folder. Be sure to type the .htm extension and use the All Files file type.)
   e. Enter the HTML code shown in Figure A-20.
   f. Format the text "Paradise Garden Day Spa" in the body section as a level-one heading.
   g. Format the text "Your Eden in the Rockies" in the body section as a level-two heading, then save your document.

3. **Import Web content.**
   a. Open the file **htm_a-2.rtf** in your word processor and copy all of the text.
   b. In the index.htm document, click to place the insertion point after the closing tag for the subheading, "Your Eden in the Rockies" and press [Enter] to add a new line.
   c. Paste the copied text into the document, then save the file.
   d. Close the RTF file, then preview the index.htm file in your browser.

FIGURE A-20

```
<html>
<head>

<title>Paradise Garden Day Spa</title>

<meta name="keywords" content="Paradise Mountain Resort, spa, day spa,
massages, hair care, nail care, spa treatments" />

</head>
<body>

Paradise Garden Day Spa
Your Eden in the Rockies

</body>
</html>
```

4. **Mark up Web page content.**
   a. Return to the source code and surround each of the paragraph sections with opening and closing paragraph tags.
   b. Click after phone: in the second to the last paragraph, then add a line break.
   c. Update the "modified by" paragraph with your name and the current date.
   d. Save your work.
   e. Reload the page in your browser to display the latest version of the document.

5. **Print an HTML document.**
   a. In your text editor, print the source code for the spa/index.htm file.
   b. In your browser program, print the Web page.
   c. Close the browser window.
   d. If necessary, close the text editor program.

6. **Transfer an HTML document.**
   a. Start FTP Commander (or whichever FTP program you are using).
   b. Find the server definition you created during your FTP lesson and double-click it to establish a connection to your remote directory.
   c. Double-click your remote paradise folder to open it on the server.
   d. Use the Browse local drives list arrow to browse to the directory where you save your site files.
   e. Single-click the spa folder to select it, then click the Upload files to FTP server button to transfer the folder and its contents to your server.
   f. Open a browser window and type the URL to your remote file in the browser Address bar. (*Hint*: Don't forget to add the folder and file name to the remote path.)
   g. In the browser program, print the spa/index.htm file from its remote location.

▼ INDEPENDENT CHALLENGE 1

You have recently started a vacation resort rental agency called Star Vacations that brokers rentals of time-share properties in the United States, Canada, and the Bahamas. It is a priority for you to provide a Web site so potential clients can research your available services. Using the skills you learned in this unit, plan and create a Web page for your agency. Use a text editor to write your HTML tags, then use your browser to view the finished page. Your page should include at least two headings, as well as some placeholder text and contact information for your company.

a. Create a sketch of your Web page, including a page title, a heading, and at least one paragraph of descriptive text.

b. On your sketch, define which HTML tags you will use for each page element.

c. Start your text editor and enter the structuring tags for the page, along with the title and heading elements; be sure to add a "Modified by" paragraph at the bottom of the page with your name and current date.

d. Create a new folder called **vacations** in the location where you store your site files. (*Hint*: Do not create the new folder inside your paradise folder.)

e. Save your work inside your vacations folder as **index.htm**.

f. Preview your page in your Web browser, then edit the source code, if necessary, to format the page as you want it to appear.

g. Print the document in your text editor and in your browser.

h. Transfer your new folder and its contents to your remote server directory, then view the remote file in your browser.

i. Print your remote vacations/index.htm file from the browser.

▼ INDEPENDENT CHALLENGE 2

You are the Water Resources Manager at Metro Water, the local water department, and have volunteered to help create a Web site for your employer. Your priority is to create an information source about your community's water resources and to encourage water conservation. Because you are familiar with the topic of water resources in your area, you will also gather additional information to include in the site.

a. Create a sketch that includes the items you want to include on your Web page.

b. Add notations about the HTML elements and the code needed to create each element.

c. Create a new folder called **water** in the directory where you save your site files.

d. Start your text editor and enter the structuring tags for the page, along with the title and the heading elements, add some general page heading and paragraph placeholder content, then save your file as **index.htm** in your water folder.

e. Preview your page in your browser, edit the source, if necessary, to format the page as you want it to appear, then save your page.

f. Edit the page by adding the following contact information paragraph, making sure to insert a line break after each colon (:):
For more information, contact: Your Name, Water Resources Manager at: (303) 555-4H2O (555-4426).

g. Save your work and preview it; print the document in your text editor and in your browser, then close your source code file.

h. Transfer your new folder and its contents to your remote server directory, then view the remote file in your browser.

i. Print the remote file from your browser window.

Advanced Challenge Exercises

- You want to start creating a page with links to online resources. Open your text editor, start a new document, and add basic page formatting elements with a page title.
- Connect to the Internet and use your favorite search engine to find at least 5 sites that contain information on water resources and water conservation that you can include in a list of linked resources.
- Copy the complete URLs of each of your resources, then paste each URL into your document, pressing [Enter] once after each one, and adding a short description of the site below it.
- Press [Enter] twice after each description, then paste the next URL into the document.
- Save your file as **resources.htm** in your water folder.
- Add a level-two or level-three heading with the text **Water Conservation Resources** above your list of URLs.
- Separate each item from the others by enclosing each URL and its description in an opening and closing paragraph tag.
- Add line breaks to the end of each URL to force its description to the next line.
- Save and preview your page and then transfer your water directory to the server.
- View your new page in your browser from the remote location, then print the page and close all programs.

▼ INDEPENDENT CHALLENGE 3

In this unit you have practiced using basic HTML tags to create some of the fundamental elements of a Web page. As you learn more tags and their functions, you will be able to add different elements and formats to your Web pages. The Web itself can be one of the most useful tools for learning more about HTML. Try it out by seeing what you can find on the Web about a tag or a tag set that you haven't used yet.

a. Use your favorite search engine to locate one of the following online HTML references: W3C, Webmonkey, or WebReference, or go to the Student Online Companion for this book and see the Unit A links.

b. Click the link for HTML if you see one, then use the site's search utility to find information about one of the following tag sets:

<em>...</em>, <i>...</i>, <ol>...</ol>, or <ul>...</ul>

c. If you're using Internet Explorer, enter your name in the header section of the Page Setup dialog box, after any codes you see there.

d. Print at least two pages that discuss what the selected tag does and how you use it in Web page code. (If you are using a browser that doesn't allow you to add text to the header, write your name on the printout.)

e. Write a paragraph about your selected tag. Include the following information:

- Its name (what the letters in the tag stand for)
- What feature(s) it adds to a Web page
- An example of where in Web page design you think the selected tag would be useful

▼ INDEPENDENT CHALLENGE 4

You have decided to create your own Web site. Because it is your site, you can use your imagination in determining a site theme and topic. Your site can be a business site, an informational site, a fan site, or a personal site. One of the most basic sources of design ideas is published Web pages. After determining your site subject, use a search engine to find good examples of similar sites. Analyze the sites to determine what makes them effective. Then create a basic Web page as the initial home page for your Web site.

a. Use your favorite search engine such as Google, Alta Vista, or Yahoo to find Web pages similar to the site you want to create. If you have trouble locating a search engine, go to the Student Online Companion for this book, and use the links for Unit A as a starting point.

b. Add your name to the footer, then print the home page from the site you like the best.

c. On your printout, indicate familiar elements (such as titles, headings, empty lines, and paragraphs of text) and indicate the tag you think was used to create each element.

d. List at least two design aspects that you think make the page functional, such as placement of elements, colors, and text phrasing. List at least one aspect that could be improved. Write a paragraph describing how you would improve the design of each Web page.

e. Sketch your own page design using boxes to indicate the items you want to include, such as images, page navigation elements, headings, and paragraph content, then add your name at the top.

f. Create a basic home page for your site with at least a page title, a page heading, and placeholder paragraphs describing what you will eventually include on your site, as well as a paragraph containing your contact information.

g. Save your page as **index.htm** in a folder you create and designate as your site folder, then transfer the folder to your remote site.

Advanced Challenge Exercises

- View and print the page source for the site you critiqued.
- Compare your speculations with the actual code used to create the page you viewed. Then consider the following: How close did you come to guessing the code tags? List up to three tags that you do not recognize.
- Search the Web for information on one of the tags that is new to you.
- Write one or two paragraphs about that tag and its purpose.

HTML

▼ VISUAL WORKSHOP

You work for a local computer store called Bits and PCs, which is celebrating its 20th year in business. Your employer has asked you to design a Web site to promote the store's anniversary celebration and to highlight its advertised specials. You sketched a storyboard of page ideas and want to use it for reference as you add the basic elements for your home page. Create a folder in the place where you store your site files, called **bitspcs**. Then, using the skills you have learned, create a page based on the layout sketch shown in Figure A-21. Save it as index.htm in your bitspcs folder, then transfer the folder to your remote directory.

FIGURE A-21

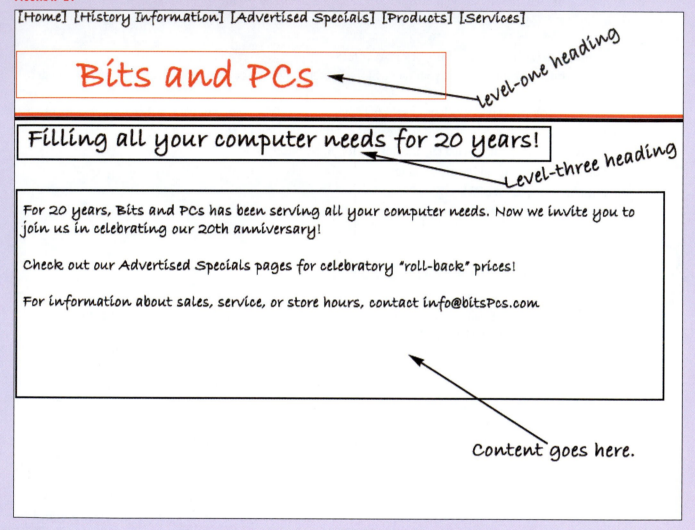

Creating Links to Web Pages and Other Files

OBJECTIVES

Plan a Web Site

Create internal links

Create links to other directories

Create external links

Create e-mail links

Create jump links

Open links in new windows

Add link titles

What makes the Web so useful is its ability to present **non-linear content**—content that need not be read in any particular order—through hyperlinking. **Hyperlinking** is the ability to jump from one content point to another by clicking on **hypertext links**—text or graphics that, when clicked, direct site visitors to other information. The ability to link one page to another allows you, the site designer, to make it easier for site visitors to find the information they are seeking. Using hyperlinks, Web site visitors can jump from place to place within a page, from file to file within a site, or across cyberspace to a file in another site. You can also create links that launch external e-mail programs for sending messages or that cause linked files to open in a new window. You have a lot of information to present and want to organize it into sections that you can link to your home page. You also want to create links to external information you think will interest your site visitors.

Planning a Web Site

Before you start creating your Web site, you need to plan it. Decide what type of site you want to create, identify your target audience, determine your content sources, and define your site's purpose and goals. In addition, you should organize your content into logical divisions and create a site structure chart. You decide to meet with the Paradise Mountain Family Resort owners and their Public Relations Director to plan the site structure and content and to identify its target audience.

DETAILS

Steps to planning a Web site include:

QUICK TIP

Business sites often start out as brochure sites, then later add interactive features such as shopping carts, payment processing, and order-tracking pages.

- **Determine your site type**

Before you start creating your site pages, you need to determine your site type and define the content for each page. Three common Web site categories are business, support, and personal. **Business sites** are divided into two main categories: **brochure sites**, which display information similar to that found in a printed brochure; and **e-commerce sites**, which contain catalog information and order-processing elements such as shopping carts and order-tracking pages. Brochure sites are not designed to sell a product, but may contain links to e-commerce sites where products and services are sold. **Support sites** often contain downloadable user manuals, forms, and software drivers. **Personal sites** offer the greatest degree of flexibility in design; they can be used to communicate with friends, post professional résumés or portfolios, or honor a favorite public figure. You determine that the Paradise Mountain site will be a brochure site.

QUICK TIP

When available, always list your business address including your city and state, and your contact information, including your area code and phone number.

- **Define the site's purpose**

Is the purpose of your site to sell goods, provide general information, or showcase your own talents? Answering this question helps determine the type of content to include on your pages. Paradise Mountain's site will deliver information about the resort and provide a listing of resort and area activities.

- **Identify the target audience**

Your **target audience** is the group or groups of people you are trying to attract. Are they young or middle-aged? Are they male or female? What is their income level? What technology do they have available? Knowing your target audience enables you to design pages that include content, features, and colors attractive to them. Paradise Mountain Family Resort caters to families who are attracted to "the Great Outdoors," so you decide to use primarily blues and greens to represent clear skies and trees.

QUICK TIP

All information posted on the Internet is copyrighted. Taking information from one Web site and using it on your own without written permission is a violation of federal copyright law.

- **Identify content sources**

If you are starting a new business or developing a personal site, you will probably create your own original content. However, for an existing business or organization, you will probably find that you can repurpose existing information such as company brochures, mission statements, and catalogs, for use on the Web. Remember that you must have permission to use any information you collect. Paradise Mountain's Marketing Department already has many documents that you can repurpose for use on the company's Web site.

- **Organize your site content**

To make your content accessible to site visitors, organize it by subject matter into sections and pages, then create navigation elements to help your site visitors find the information they need. You decide to include pages with general information about the resort, as well as two content sections—one for the resort's spa and one for resort and area activities.

- **Create a site storyboard**

Once you have determined your site categories, you can further organize your site structure by creating a diagram called a **site storyboard** or **site map**, which can help you design your site navigation elements. Figures B-1 and B-2 show common site structures, a **net structure** (also called a Web structure), where all pages are linked to one another, and a **hierarchical** structure, in which information is organized in content sections, moving from general to more specific. Net structure is effective for organizing very small sites; hierarchical structure is perfect for organizing large sites or sites with potential for fast growth. Figure B-2 shows the hierarchical structure you will use for the Paradise resort site.

FIGURE B-1: Net site structure

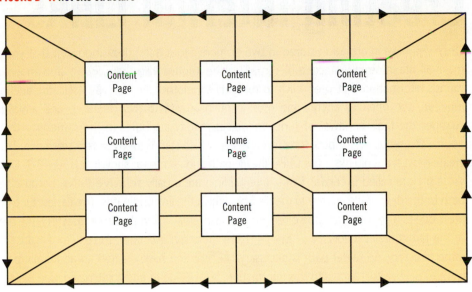

FIGURE B-2: Hierarchical site structure for Paradise Mountain

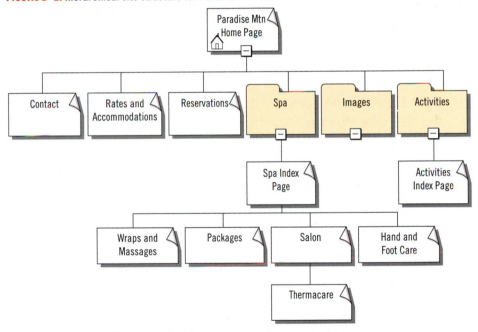

Clues to Use

Designing for company intranet sites

Intranet sites are private Web sites available only to authorized users who log in with special credentials. These sites often contain links to company support materials and allow employees to upload and download company documents nd to access shared databases.

Intranet sites offer a greater flexibility in design because you can develop pages based on technology known to be available to company employees.

Creating Internal Links

Once you have information stored in two or more pages (files), it is important that you link those pages to make all site information accessible. In a link, the **anchor tag** (<a>...</a>), also known as a **link tag**, surrounds information that users click to navigate to another location. By itself, the anchor tag is useless. To function, the opening anchor tag must contain an **attribute**, (feature), and a **value** that specifies or changes the tag's behavior or function. Values modify attributes in the same way that adjectives modify nouns. The required attribute for a link is **href**—which stands for hypertext reference. The href value used to create most types of links is the URL—the file path and name—as shown in Figure B-3. Links to files within the same site are called **internal links**. Internal links are usually **relative links**, because the link URL traces a path to the desired file *relative to* the file from which the link originates. The easiest type of relative link to create is one to a page in the same directory. For an internal link in the same directory, the href value is the name of the target file as follows: `<a href="file.htm">View the file</a>` Because both files are in the same directory, no folder path is necessary. ▨ You have created an additional page for your site and want to give visitors access to this information. You decide to add a site navigation bar to link your pages.

STEPS

1. **Using your file management system, locate and open the folder where you store your Unit B Data Files, click to select contact.htm, click Edit on the menu bar, then click Copy**
   The contact.htm file is copied to the clipboard

TROUBLE
If you did not complete the Skills Review in Unit A, the spa folder will not be part of your directory structure. If it is not, you may copy the spa folder from your Data Files into the paradise folder at this time.

2. **Locate and click to select the paradise folder in the directory where you save your site files, click Edit on the menu bar, then click Paste**
   The contact.htm file is copied to your folder as shown in Figure B-4. In the following step, and in all HTML code you type, make sure that your text editor or word processor does not have the smart quote feature turned on; you must use straight quotation marks or the links will not work correctly.

3. **Open the paradise\index.htm file in your text editor from the place where you save your site files, click after the </h1> tag, then press [Enter] twice**

4. **Type `<p>|<a href="index.htm">Home</a>|`, press [Spacebar], type `|<a href="contact.htm">Contact Us</a>|</p>`, then save your work**
   You have created links to your home and contact pages. These links are the first part of your site navigation bar.

5. **Drag to select the navigation bar code (including opening and closing paragraph tags), then copy it**

6. **Open the paradise\contact.htm file in your text editor, click after </h1>, press [Enter] twice, paste the code, update the "modified by" paragraph, then save the file**

7. **Start your browser program, click File on the menu bar, click Open, click Browse, navigate to the index.htm file in your paradise folder, double-click index.htm, then click OK to open it in the browser**

8. **Move the mouse pointer over the links**
   As you rest the mouse pointer over each link, the linked file's URL appears in the browser status bar and the mouse pointer turns into a hand pointer ⍟, indicating that the link is active.

9. **Click the Contact Us link, then from the contact.htm file, click the Home link**
   When you click the Contact Us link, the target page appears in the browser window. Clicking the Home link from the contact.htm page returns you to the index.htm file. Figure B-5 shows a completed navigation bar. Notice the single space between the links.

Opening anchor tag

`<a href="http://www.course.com/contact.cfm">Course Technology contact page</a>`

Closing anchor tag

Tag name   href attribute   URL   Linked text

FIGURE B-4: Files copied to paradise folder

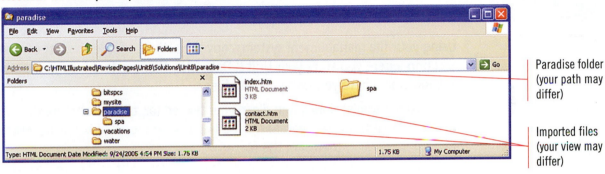

Paradise folder (your path may differ)

Imported files (your view may differ)

FIGURE B-5: Site navigation with target URL displayed in navigation bar

Linked text

Single space between links

Target URL (your path may differ)

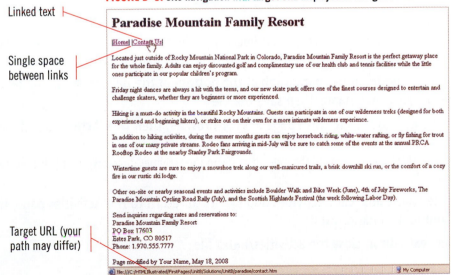

HTML

Creating Links to Other Directories

As your site grows and matures, you will likely need to organize some of your content into subdirectories. Creating relative links to files in other directories is easy once you understand relative file paths. As shown in Figure B-6, to direct the browser to move from one directory to another, use **dot-slash notation**, a combination of dots and forward slashes that serve as path designators from one folder to another up and down the directory tree. A pair of dots followed by a slash direct the browser to move one level up the directory tree before seeking the linked file. A folder name followed by a slash tells the browser that the file is one directory-level down in the designated folder. The owners of Paradise Mountain Family Resort have asked you to develop a set of pages to promote the resort's activities center and to link it to the Paradise Mountain home page.

STEPS

1. **Using your file management system, copy the activities folder and its contents from the location where you store your Unit B Data Files, then paste it into your paradise folder in the location where you save your site files**

QUICK TIP

Although system folder paths are designated using backslashes (\), Web paths are always specified with forward slashes (/). You might see backslashes in file paths when a local file is displayed in the browser, but *do not* use backslashes in your file paths.

2. **Open your paradise\index.htm file in your text editor, click just before the `</p>` in the navigation bar code, press [Spacebar], type `|<a href="activities/index.htm">Activities and Events</a>|`, then save the file**
   The Activities link directs the browser down from the root folder to the activities folder and finds the activities/index.htm file.

3. **Drag to select the modified navigation bar, click Edit on the menu bar, then click Copy**

4. **Open your paradise\activities\index.htm file in your text editor, click after `</h1>`, press [Enter] twice, click Edit on the menu bar, then click Paste**
   The navigation bar code you just pasted from your site home page must be modified so that the links will work from the activities directory.

5. **Locate the Home link, click between the first quotation mark and the file name index.htm, then type `../`**

6. **Click between the first quotation mark and the file or folder name in each of the other URLs and the two other links, type `../`, then save the file**
   By adding ../ to the beginning of each root-level page link and to the sub-folder link, as shown in Figure B-7, you instruct the browser to move to the parent directory before searching for the root- or sub-level file, creating a universal navigation bar that will work from any page in a first-level sub directory. Because the structure of this site has only one sublevel, the root directory is the parent directory for your subfolders.

7. **Locate the "modified by" paragraph at the bottom of the page, change the text "Your Name" to your own name, then save the file**

TROUBLE

If the linked files do not display as expected, check your code to ensure that ../ precedes each link path and that each href value is enclosed in straight quotes.

8. **Open the activities/index.htm page in your browser, then click Activities and Events to test the link**
   Because the HREF value points to the index.htm file in the activities directory, the file is reloaded when you click the link.

9. **Click the Home link, click Activities and Events to return to the Activities page, then click the Contact Us link to test it**

10. **In your text editor, close the activities/index file**

FIGURE B-6: Relative file paths

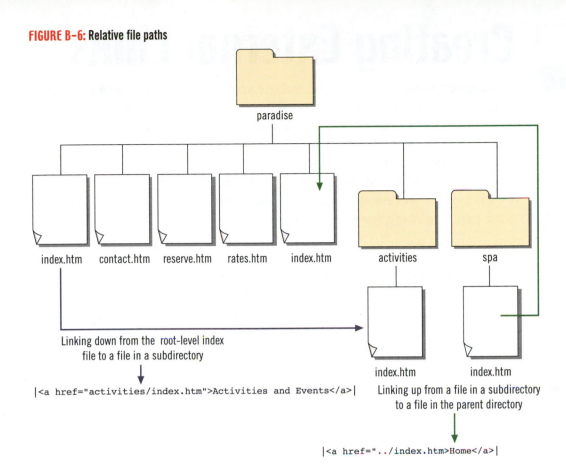

Linking down from the root-level index
file to a file in a subdirectory

```
|<a href="activities/index.htm">Activities and Events</a>|
```

Linking up from a file in a subdirectory
to a file in the parent directory

```
|<a href="../index.htm>Home</a>|
```

FIGURE B-7: Linking from a first-level subdirectory

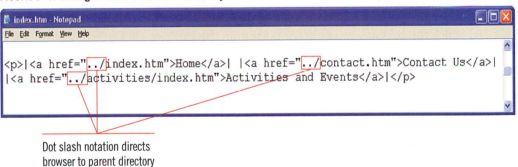

Dot slash notation directs
browser to parent directory

Design Matters

Creating a Text-Based Navigation Bar

Including a text-based navigation bar is an easy method of enhancing your site's accessibility and usability. Properly formatted text-based navigation bars are easy to read, understand, and click. The following tips will help you create effective text-based navigation bars. 1) Never include spaces between the opening link tag and the start of the linked text, or between the end of the linked text and the closing link tag; doing so causes spaces on either side of the linked text to be formatted as underlined spaces. 2) Set off links by surrounding each one with characters such as pipes, |linked text|, or square brackets, [linked text] to make them easier to click. 3) To prevent your linked text item from "wrapping" between the text and the pipe or bracket, make sure that no spaces occur between the pipe or bracket and the start of the opening link tag or the end of the closing link tag. 4) Insert a single space between the linked item to make them easier to select. 5) Avoid the use of decorative fonts in your text-navigation bars. Decorative fonts are difficult to read and can negate the effectiveness of your text navigation bar.

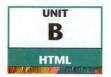

Creating External Links

An excellent method of providing additional resources and information for your site visitors is to create links to **external Web files**—files that are hosted on another server or Web site. External links are easy to create. In an external link, use an absolute URL as the href property value. An **absolute URL** is the complete URL including the protocol (http://), server name, domain name, path, and filename of the file you want to open. To create a link to an external file, type its absolute URL between the opening and closing quote marks that follow the href attribute. The Paradise Mountain Family Resort home page contains references to several area events of interest to Paradise Mountain's visitors. You want to create links from your home page to existing online information about those events.

STEPS

1. If necessary, open your paradise\index.htm file in your text editor, from the paradise folder in the directory where you save your site files

2. Click in front of the word annual in the phrase annual PRCA Rooftop Rodeo in the fourth paragraph, then type `<a href="http://www.estesnet.com/events/rooftoprodeo.htm">`

> **QUICK TIP**
> To save a file using the keyboard, press [Ctrl][S].

3. Click just after Rodeo, type `</a>`, click File on the menu bar, then save your work
   Your text should look similar to Figure B-8.

4. Open paradise\index.htm in your browser, move the mouse pointer over the linked text
   The text that you typed between the link anchor tags appears underlined. When you point to the link, the pointer changes to the hand icon and the target URL appears in the status bar.

> **QUICK TIP**
> If the target page does not appear, check your code to make sure that you typed the URL correctly, that you have included (http://), and that you have enclosed the entire href attribute value in straight quotation marks. If the page still does not appear, use your favorite search engine to search for the appropriate URL.

5. Click the link to display the PRCA Rooftop Rodeo page, scroll down the page to view its content, shown in Figure B-9, then click your browser's Back button to return to the index.htm page
   While the target page is displayed, the external URL is shown in the browser address location box.

6. Click the text editor program button on the taskbar, click in front of Boulder in the first sentence of the last paragraph, type `<a href="http://www.ci.boulder.co.us/goboulder/WBW/">`, click after "Week" in "Boulder Walk and Bike Week", then type `</a>`

7. Click before Scottish in the last paragraph, type `<a href="http://www.scottishgames.org/">`, click after Festival, then type `</a>`

8. Save the document, click the browser program button on the taskbar, then click your browser's Reload or Refresh button
   The updated version of your page appears in the browser window.

> **QUICK TIP**
> If the appropriate target URLs do not display, refer to QuickTip next to step 5.

9. Click each link to verify that it works properly, then click the text editor program button on the taskbar

FIGURE B-8: External link code

External link

```
<p>In addition to hiking activities, during the summer months guests can enjoy
horseback riding, white-water rafting, or fly fishing for trout in one of our many
private streams. Rodeo fans arriving in mid-July will be sure to catch some of the
events at the <a href="http://www.estesnet.com/events/rooftoprodeo.htm">annual
PRCA Rooftop Rodeo</a> at the nearby Stanley Park Fairgrounds.</p>
```

FIGURE B-9: External link displayed in browser

External URL

Content may
have changed

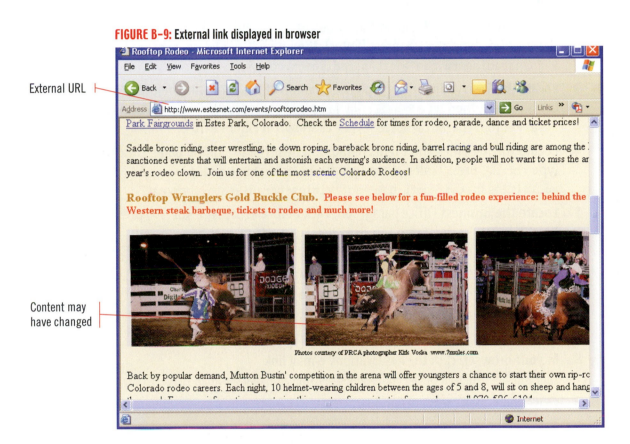

Design Matters

Linking to high-quality external files

You can help boost your site's search engine ratings by creating **content-specific links**—links from keywords in your page content area. You may create links to any publicly accessible Web site. A **publicly accessible site** is one that is hosted on an Internet server and does not require log-in permission for file viewing. Use a search engine to find quality link material by typing a keyword or phrase in the search box before initiating the search. Disregarding **sponsored links**—those that site owners have paid search engines to place at the top of the list—and reading the page description under the linked text can help you narrow your choices. If a page appears to be a likely candidate as a quality linked resource, click the link and view the page to ensure that the information is what you are seeking.

HTML

Creating E-Mail Links

E-mail links are simple code instructions that give your site visitors an additional way to contact you for information. E-mail links use the mailto protocol with an e-mail address as the href attribute value, as shown in Figure B-10. When a site visitor clicks the e-mail link, an e-mail message window appears, similar to the one shown in Figure B-11. The new message is addressed using the mailto value you entered. 🎨 You decide to update your "Contact Us" page to include clickable e-mail links with each person's contact information.

STEPS

1. In your text editor, open the paradise/contact.htm page from the location where you store your paradise site files

2. Locate the Paradise Mountain Family Resort paragraph at the bottom of the page, click before `</p>`, type `<br />`, press [Enter], then type `E-mail: <a href=mailto: info@paradisemtn.com">info@paradisemtn.com</a>`

QUICK TIP

Because not all users are surfing the Web using a browser on which e-mail has been enabled, it is a good idea to include the full e-mail address as the linked text when you create an e-mail link. This allows the user to copy or print the e-mail address for later use.

3. Locate the Reservations paragraph near the top of the page, click before `</p>`, type `<br />`, press [Enter], then type `E-mail: <a href=mailto:reservations@paradisemtn.com"> reservations@paradisemtn.com</a>` as shown in Figure B-10

4. Locate the Activities and Events paragraph near the top of the page, click before `</p>`, type `<br />`, press [Enter], then type `E-mail: <a href=mailto: activities@paradisemtn.com">activities@paradisemtn.com</a>`

5. Locate the Business Office paragraph, click before `</p>`, type `<br />`, press [Enter], then type `E-mail: <a href=mailto:business@paradisemtn.com"> business@paradisemtn.com</a>`

6. Click before `</p>` in the "modified by" paragraph at the bottom of the page, type `<p>For questions or comments about this site, contact: <br /> <a href="mailto:web-master@paradisemtn.com">webmaster@paradisemtn.com</a> </p>`, then press [Enter]

7. Save the contact.htm file, then open it in your browser

QUICK TIP

If no e-mail account has been set up on your browser, the default e-mail program setup box will display when you click an e-mail link. If this happens, click the Cancel button on the e-mail program setup dialog box.

8. In your browser, click the Reservations e-mail link
   Your e-mail program creates an untitled message, similar to that shown in Figure B-11.

9. Close the e-mail message window

FIGURE B-10: Mailto link source code

Protocol

```
<h3>Reservations</h3>

<p>Reservations Desk<br />
Office Hours: 7 a.m. - 10 p.m. MST *<br />
Phone: 1.970.555.7780<br />
* After-hours callers, please leave a message and one of our helpful reservations
specialists will return your call. <br />
E-mail: <a href="mailto:reservations@paradisemtn.com">reservations@paradisemtn.com</a>
</p>
```

href attribute

Code for e-mail link

FIGURE B-11: A mailto link and e-mail message window

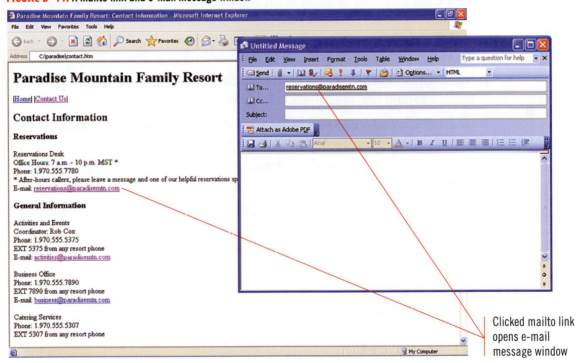

Clicked mailto link opens e-mail message window

Creating Jump Links

When you must create an exceptionally long page, it is handy to create **jump links**, also known as **menu links**, that allow users to jump from a link on a page to a specific point on that page or a specific point on another page. Jump links are unlike other links in that they target HTML element IDs rather than an entire file. An **ID** is an identifier for any HTML element that can serve as an anchor point for jump links. The URL for a jump link on the same page is a pound sign (#) followed by the target element's ID. The URL for a jump link to another page is the file URL with the # and ID appended to the end of the file name.  You decide to create jump links at the top of the page to specific locations on the same page. You also want to create links back to the top of the page.

STEPS

1. Click the **text editor program button** to return to your **contact.htm** source code

> **QUICK TIP**
> Make sure that no two elements on the page use the same ID.

2. Locate the level-one heading at the top of the page, click between h1 and > in the opening tag, press [Spacebar], then type `id="top"`
   You just set the ID value of "top" for the navigation bar paragraph, which you will use as an anchor point for creating links that allow visitors to navigate back to the top of the page.

3. Locate the level-three heading, **Reservations**, near the top of the page, click just after h3 in the opening tag, press [Spacebar], then type `id="reservations"`

4. Locate the level-three heading, **General Information**, click just after h3 in the opening tag, press [Spacebar], then type `id="geninfo"`

5. Locate the level-three heading, **Paradise Garden Day Spa and Fitness Center**, click just after h3 in the opening tag, press [Spacebar], then type `id="spa"`

6. Locate the level-three heading, **Front Desk**, click just after h3 in the opening tag, press [Spacebar], then type `id="fdesk"`

> **QUICK TIP**
> Don't forget to type square brackets ([....]) around each jump link.

7. Locate the level-two heading near the top of the page, click after </h2>, press [Enter] twice, then type the following, pressing [Spacebar][Enter] after each item:
   ```
   <p>[<a href="#reservations">Reservations</a>]
   [<a href="#General Information">General Information</a>]
   [<a href="#spa">Day Spa and Fitness Center</a>]
   [<a href="#fdesk">Front Desk</a>]</p>]
   ```
   You created jump links to each of the id points you set on the page.

8. Locate the paragraph containing the Reservations contact information near the top of the page, click before </p>, press [Enter], then type `<br /><a href="#top">Return to top</a>`

9. Drag to select the **Return to** top link you just created, including the opening and closing anchor tags, copy it to your clipboard, then paste it before </p> in the Human Resources Office and the Paradise Mountain Family Resort paragraphs
   Your page code appears similar to that shown in Figure B-12.

10. Save the file, then reload it in the browser to test your links
    Your completed page should resemble Figure B-13.

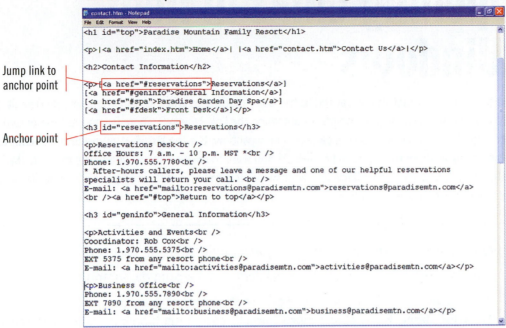

Jump link to anchor point

Anchor point

FIGURE B-13: Completed menu bar

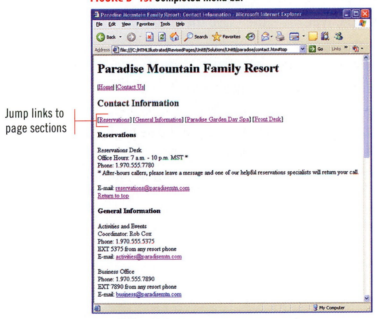

Jump links to page sections

Clues to Use

Creating jump links with anchor name points

For years jump links were set using named anchor points rather than element IDs. Jump links created in this manner require two parts: the link and the named anchor point. Named anchor points have been deprecated by the W3C, but they are still in use today; consequently you might be called upon to modify pages with jump links to named anchor points, so it is good to know how they are created.

Links to named anchors are created in exactly the same manner as those to element IDs (<a href="URL#">Linked text</a>). To set the anchor point, click in front of the desired target element and type the anchor name code as follows: <a name="name"></a>. Set the name value as appropriate, as you would for an ID.

Opening Links in New Windows

Earlier you learned that the target URL is the page that opens when users click a link. By default, that URL opens in the same window as the page containing the link. However, there is another type of target associated with links; this target opens a page in a new window. Use the target attribute of the anchor tag with a value _blank as shown in Figure B-14.  You want to create a link to one of the many Rocky Mountain National Park sites. The site is large and your site visitors might lose their way back to your site, so you want the link to open in a new window.

1. **Open the index.htm page from your paradise site folder in your text editor**

2. **Click before Rocky Mountain National Park in the second paragraph**

3. **Type `<a href="http://www.nps.gov/romo" target="_blank">`**
   The value, _blank, is one of four **magic targets**, each of which begins with an underscore character. Although magic targets are generally reserved for use in sites that use **frames** (sites that display parts of the page in several windows simultaneously), the _blank target is useful for opening linked files in a new window from any page. Using the _blank target ensures that a new window will open every time and no content will be hidden behind already opened windows.

4. **Click after Park, type `</a>`, then save the document**

5. **Open paradise/index.htm in your browser**
   The page opens in your browser and the words "Rocky Mountain National Park" appear blue and underlined.

6. **Click the Rocky Mountain National Park link**
   The target URL opens in a new window as shown in Figure B-15.

7. **Close the target window to return to your home page**
   When the new window closes, the original page appears.

8. **Click the text editor program button to return to your source code**

Clues to Use

Targeting windows

When coding a link to open in a new window, some designers like to use "new" or "new_window". Declaring a value other than "_blank" causes the browser to assign an internal name to the generated window. Whenever a target attribute value is declared in a link tag, the linked file will open in another window provided that no other window of the same name is already open. However, one cannot always count on users closing the pop-up window after viewing its contents. This can cause content to open in hidden windows. Your option, then, is to give each target a unique name or to use the _blank name, which opens a file in a new window every time.

FIGURE B-14: Code for opening a file in a new window

```
<a href="http://www.nps.gov/romo/" target="_blank">Rocky Mountain National Park</a>
```

Target value

FIGURE B-15: Linked URL opened in new window

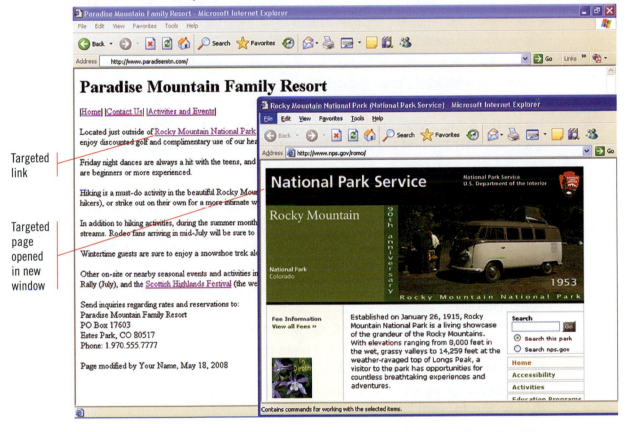

Targeted
link

Targeted
page
opened
in new
window

Adding Link Titles

Link titles produce ScreenTips (pop-up text balloons) that appear when site visitors rest the mouse pointer over a link in which a link title has been specified. Link titles are useful **accessibility tools**—objects that make a site more usable to disabled users. They also give visitors extra information about the link. Visitors using a standard browser see a ScreenTip as shown in Figure B-16 when they rest the mouse pointer over the link. When visitors using a text reader come to a titled link, they hear the contents of the link title. This description can be much more valuable to site visitors than hearing only the link's URL. Link titles can be used to describe the content at the other end of the link, display file size, or supply download time information. Link titles can also be used to add additional, searchable information to a page. You want to warn site visitors that your external Rocky Mountain Park link opens a page in a new window. You also want to make your site more accessible to all visitors, so you decide to add link titles to your page links.

STEPS

1. Locate the opening Rocky Mountain National Park anchor tag, click after the the href attribute value "_blank", press [Spacebar], then type `title="Rocky Mountain National Park home page - opens in new window."`
   Your code should resemble Figure B-16.

2. Locate the "PRCA Rooftoop Rodeo" opening anchor tag, click just after "...rooftoprodeo.htm", press [Spacebar], then type `title="PRCA Rooftop Rodeo Web site. Click here for event schedules and dates."`

> **QUICK TIP**
> Because link titles are descriptions, you can use punctuation (except quotation marks) and spacing within a link title.

3. Locate the Boulder Walk and Bike Week opening anchor tag, click after the closing quotation mark after the href attribute value, press [Spacebar], then type `title="Experience the fun and excitement of Boulder Walk and Bike Week. Visit Boulder Walk and Bike Week's Web site."`

4. Locate the Scottish Highlands Festival opening anchor tag, click after the closing quotation mark after the href attribute value, press [Spacebar], then type `title="Visit the official Estes Park/Scottish Highlands Festival Web site for more information."`, then save the document

5. Click the browser program button on the taskbar, then click your browser's Reload or Refresh Button

6. Move the mouse pointer over the Rocky Mountain National Park link; observe that a ScreenTip displays the sentence, Rocky Mountain National Park home page - opens in new window., as shown in Figure B-17

7. Move the mouse pointer over the other three links; observe that the ScreenTip displays the title text for each link

8. Click the text editor program button on the taskbar to return to your code, print and close all files, then transfer your updated files to your remote server directory

```
<p>Located just outside of
<a href="http://www.nps.gov/romo/" target="_blank" title="Rocky Mountain National
Park home page - opens in new window.">Rocky Mountain National Park</a> in Colorado,
Paradise Mountain Family Resort is the perfect getaway place for the whole family.
Adults can enjoy discounted golf and complimentary use of our health club and tennis
facilities while the little ones participate in our popular children's program.</p>
```

Link title code

FIGURE B-17: Linked text with title in ScreenTip

Link title screen tip

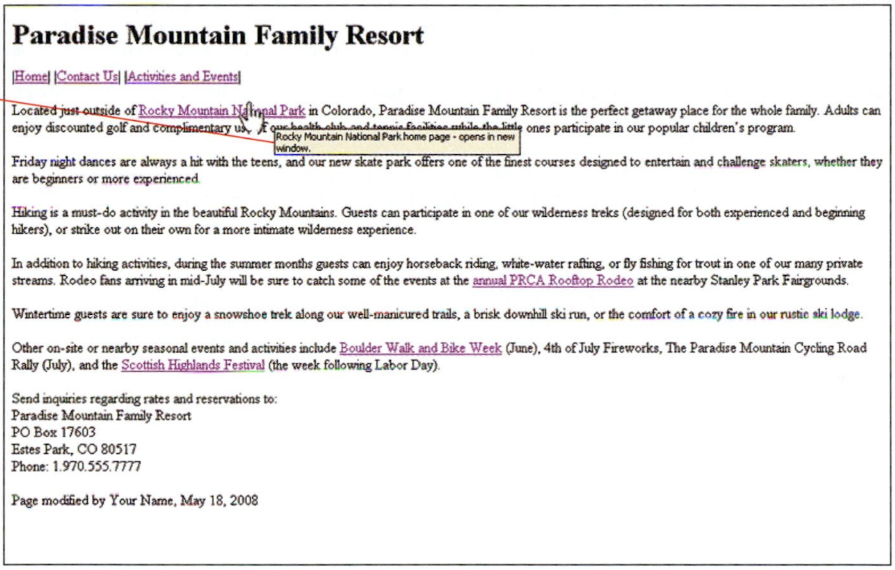

Paradise Mountain Family Resort

|Home| |Contact Us| |Activities and Events|

Located just outside of Rocky Mountain National Park in Colorado, Paradise Mountain Family Resort is the perfect getaway place for the whole family. Adults can enjoy discounted golf and complimentary use of our health club and tennis facilities while the little ones participate in our popular children's program.
Rocky Mountain National Park home page - opens in new window.

Friday night dances are always a hit with the teens, and our new skate park offers one of the finest courses designed to entertain and challenge skaters, whether they are beginners or more experienced.

Hiking is a must-do activity in the beautiful Rocky Mountains. Guests can participate in one of our wilderness treks (designed for both experienced and beginning hikers), or strike out on their own for a more intimate wilderness experience.

In addition to hiking activities, during the summer months guests can enjoy horseback riding, white-water rafting, or fly fishing for trout in one of our many private streams. Rodeo fans arriving in mid-July will be sure to catch some of the events at the annual PRCA Rooftop Rodeo at the nearby Stanley Park Fairgrounds.

Wintertime guests are sure to enjoy a snowshoe trek along our well-manicured trails, a brisk downhill ski run, or the comfort of a cozy fire in our rustic ski lodge.

Other on-site or nearby seasonal events and activities include Boulder Walk and Bike Week (June), 4th of July Fireworks, The Paradise Mountain Cycling Road Rally (July), and the Scottish Highlands Festival (the week following Labor Day).

Send inquiries regarding rates and reservations to:
Paradise Mountain Family Resort
PO Box 17603
Estes Park, CO 80517
Phone: 1.970.555.7777

Page modified by Your Name, May 18, 2008

Design Matters

Creating effective link titles

Link titles help users predict where they are going and what they can expect from the linked page or site when they arrive. However, titles are not a substitute for good visual clues—descriptive icons and detailed text in and around the link that give site visitors navigation information. Visitors should be able to navigate your site even without link titles. If the link leads the visitor out of the current site, the link title can include the name of the linked site; the predicted page download time—especially if the linked page is graphic heavy; whether the link will open a page in a new window; whether any specific scripting has been applied to the linked page that might require users to change their browser settings; and if the site requires user registration. Although you can write link titles in sentence format, try to limit them to between 60 and 80 characters.

HTML

Practice

▼ CONCEPTS REVIEW

Identify the function of each numbered item in Figure B-18.

FIGURE B-18

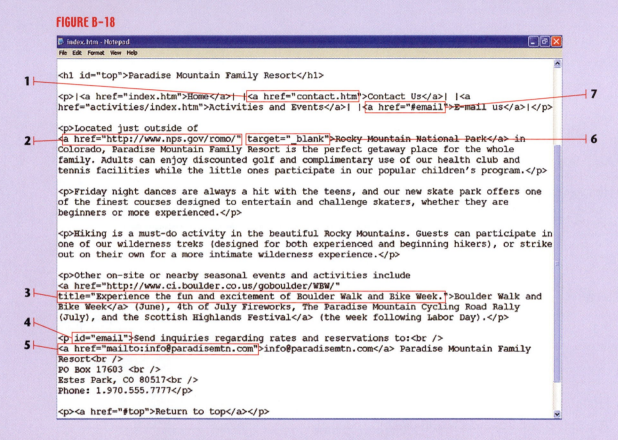

Match each directory path with its correct browser interpretation.

8. http://	a. The object a user clicks to navigate to another file or location
9. href	b. An attribute that can be set in almost any HTML element and can be used as an anchor point for jump links
10. Link	c. Hypertext transfer protocol designation—must be part of the link path when the file is on another server
11. id	d. Directs the browser to move up one level to the parent directory
12. ../	e. Most often-used anchor tag attribute—when paired with a file URL, creates a hyperlink

Select the best answer from the list of choices.

13. **Which of the following statements about brochure sites are true? (Choose all that apply.)**
    a. Brochure sites contain information similar to what one would find in a printed brochure.
    b. Brochure sites often serve as start-up sites for businesses that later develop more comprehensive sites.
    c. Brochure sites offer the greatest degree of flexibility in design.
    d. Brochure sites utilize shopping carts and order-tracking pages.

14. **Which Web structure is best for organizing sites with a potential for fast growth?**
    a. Cluster
    b. Net
    c. Linear
    d. Hierarchical

15. **In the URL, `http://www.paradisemountain.com/spa/wraps.htm`, "spa" is a _____.**
    a. Root directory
    b. Top-level page
    c. Subdirectory
    d. File name

▼ SKILLS REVIEW

1. **Plan a site**
   a. Although a part of Paradise Mountain Family Resort, the Garden of Eden Day Spa offers its services to community members and resort visitors. The spa and salon do offer a few items for sale, but the key focus is spa services. Which type of site is best?
   b. List three main objectives you think the site should satisfy.
   c. Identify and describe your site's target audience.
   d. What are some potential content sources for the new site?
   e. What type of structure do you think it best suited for the site?

2. **Create internal links**
   a. Locate and open the **UnitB** folder in the location where you store your Data Files, then copy the hands.htm, packages.htm, salon.htm, services.htm, and thermacore.htm files.
   b. Paste the files you just copied into the paradise/spa directory in the location where you save your site files.
   c. Open the **salon.htm** page in your text editor and link the text in the top-level navigation bar as follows: Spa Services/services.htm; Spa Packages/packages.htm; Aphrodite's Salon/salon.htm; and Hand and Foot Care/hands.htm. (*Hint*: Place an href tag inside the opening square bracket of each navigation bar item, remembering to include closing tags after the linked items.)
   d. Save your work.

3. **Create links to other directories.**
   a. Click before "Paradise Mountain Resort" in the top-level navigation bar, then type `<a href="../index.htm">` to start a link to the resort home page.
   b. Click after the Paradise Mountain Resort text and type `</a>` to close the link.
   c. Click in front of Day Spa in the same navigation bar, then type the code to create a link to the index.htm file in the spa directory, then save your work.
   d. Open the **paradise/index.htm** page in the parent directory. (*Hint*: A parent directory is one that contains the current directory.)
   e. Click after Events</a>|, insert a space, then type the code to create a link to the spa index.htm page that is one level down in the directory structure using Day Spa as the linked text.
   f. Save your work, then open your **spa/salon.htm** page in your browser and click the links to move between pages to test your links, clicking the Back button as necessary to return to your salon.htm page.

4. **Create external links.**
   a. Open your **salon.htm** file in your text editor.
   b. Locate the line of text that begins "Aphrodite's Salon uses only ...," then create external links to the Web sites for the hair-care products listed in that line using the information shown in Table B-1.
   c. Save your work, then open your **salon.htm** file in your browser to test your links.
   d. Return to your text editor.

TABLE B-1: External links for salon.htm page

Product	Link URL
Redken	http://www.redken.com
Nioxin	http://www.nioxin.com
Tigi	http://www.tigihaircare.com
Paul Mitchell	http://www.paulmitchell.com

HTML

5. Create e-mail links.

   a. In your salon.htm file, locate the questions and comments paragraph at the bottom of the page, click before spainfo@paradisemtn.com.

   b. Using the e-mail address listed in the line, type the code to create an e-mail link. (*Hint*: E-mail links use the mailto protocol. Be sure to display the e-mail address on the page.)

   c. Replace Your name with your own name, then save your work.

   d. Open your **salon.htm** page in your browser to test the link, then return to your text editor program.

6. Create jump links.

   a. On the salon.htm page, click inside the opening level-one heading tag between the h1 and the >, press [Spacebar], then type `id="top"` to set the heading id.

   b. Locate the level-three heading in front of Hair Care, click between the h3 and the >, press [Spacebar], then type `id="haircare"`.

   c. Set the remaining IDs as indicated in Table B-2.

   d. In the second menu bar at the top of the page, click in front of the text "Hair Care" and type `<a href="#haircare">`

   e. Click between "Care" and "|" in the menu bar and type `</a>`.

   f. Create the rest of the menu bar links as indicated in Table B-3, then save the document

   g. Click in front of `</p>` in the hair care list, type `<br /> <a href="#top">Return to menu</a>`

   h. Copy the line break and link you just typed and paste it before the `</p>` tag in the Facials, Depilatory Services, Makeup, and Limited-time specials lists. (*Hint*: The facials list is long. Be sure to set your "Return to menu" link before the closing paragraph tag of the "Super-Lifting" item.)

   i. Save the salon.htm file then test the links in your browser.

7. Open a link in a new window.

   a. Click the text editor program button to return to your salon.htm page code.

   b. Click in front of Thermacore in the list of hair care services.

   c. Type the code to create a link to the thermacore page. (*Hint*: You copied the thermacore.htm file into your spa directory at the beginning of this Skills Review.)

   d. Click inside the link you just created and type the code `target="_blank"` to cause the link to open in a new window.

   e. Click after Thermacore and type the code to close the link.

   f. Cause the Paul Mitchell link that you created earlier to open in a new window, then save your work.

8. Add link titles.

   a. Verify that your **salon.htm** file is still open.

   b. Click after the closing quotation mark of the Redken URL inside the opening anchor tag for the redken link, then press [Spacebar].

   c. Type `title="Redken introduces Color Extend for color-treated hair"`, then save the page.

   d. Create the rest of the link titles on the salon page as shown in Table B-4.

   e. If necessary, replace Your Name at the bottom of any open code files with your own name and today's date.

   e. Save all source code files, test them in your browser, then print and close the files.

   f. Transfer your spa folder and it contents to your remote site.

TABLE B-2: Name anchor points

ID location	ID value
Inside of <h3> next to Facials	facials
Inside of <h3> next to Depilatory	depil
Inside of <h3> next to Makeup	makeup
Inside of <h3>, next to Limited-time specials	specials

TABLE B-3: Menu bar links

Linked text	URL
Facials	#facials
Depilatory	#depil
Makeup	#makeup
Specials	#specials

TABLE B-4: Link titles for salon external

Product	Link Title
Nioxin	Skincare for the scalp - keep healthy-looking hair longer
Tigi	The fastest-growing professional hair care company in the industry
Paul Mitchell	Site opens in new window. Site is graphic-heavy and uses Flash animation - visitors may experience download delays

▼ INDEPENDENT CHALLENGE 1

You are developing a Web site for your new resort rental business, Star Vacations. You know that supplying listing and rental information as well as Frequently Asked Questions (FAQs) and featured resorts pages on your site will make your business more successful. You want to use the skills you have learned to link the pages you are developing. You also want to create links to some of your featured resorts. Your featured resorts page should contain at least three links to off-site resorts.

a. Determine your organizational structure and sketch a site storyboard.

b. Copy the files faq.htm, features.htm, and rentals.htm, and the listings folder from the location where you store your Data Files and paste them into your vacations directory in the location where you store your site files.

c. In your text editor, open the features.htm page from the place where you save your site files.

d. Click after `<p>|` in the navigation bar that is positioned below the comment that reads, `<!-- Add links to the navigation bar below -->`

e. Type the code `<a href="index.htm">` to link the text "Home" to the site home page, then click after Home and type the closing anchor tag to complete the link.

FIGURE B-19: Tomahawk resort link target opens in new window

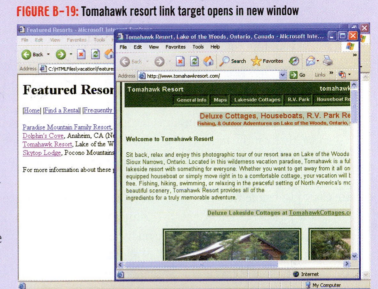

f. Link the rest of the navigation bar text as follows: Featured Resorts (features.htm), Find a Rental (rentals.htm) and Frequently Asked Questions (faq.htm).

g. Click after the pipe following the Frequently Asked Questions link, insert a space, add a link to the listings/index.htm page, using the text "List a Rental," then save your work.

h. Create external links to the featured resorts using the link information indicated in Table B-5, then type the code to cause each link to open in a new window as shown in Figure B-19. (*Hint*: If a target page fails to appear, go to the Student Online Companion for this book and click the appropriate link.)

l. Use the contact text at the bottom of the page to create an e-mail link, then replace "Your Name" with your own name.

m. Save your work, then preview your vacations/features page in the browser, click each link to check it, then return to your source code.

n. Make any necessary corrections to your page code, then save your work, print the page code, and transfer your updated files to your remote vacations directory on the server.

TABLE B-5: Features page links

Resort	Link
Paradise Mountain Family Resort	Use the absolute URL to your paradise site on your remote server. If you are not transferring the paradise site to a server, create a relative path to the site.
Dolphin's Cove Resort	`http://www.resortime.com/resorts/profile.asp?resortid=18`
Tomahawk Resort	`http://www.tomahawkresort.com/`
Skytop Lodge	`http://www.skytop.com/`

Advanced Challenge Exercises

- Copy the navigation bar from your features.htm page, then paste it after the closing level-one heading tag on your vacations/index.htm page.
- Surf the Web to find and read the privacy statements of several Web sites.
- Create a new page with your own privacy statement, then save it as privacy.htm in your vacations directory.
- At the bottom of your privacy.htm page, create a paragraph that contains the text, "Close the window to return to the previous page," then save your work.
- Return to the source code for your vacations/index.htm page, place the insertion point below the "Page modified by" paragraph at the bottom of the page and create a new paragraph containing a link to your privacy statement.
- Supply an appropriate link title, then add the code to cause the target URL to open in a new window.
- Replace Your Name with your own name, save and preview the file, then print and close all files.

▼ INDEPENDENT CHALLENGE 2

You have been researching water-conservation issues for your employer, Metro Water, and are ready to begin creating and linking your pages in order to present your findings to the people of Denver, Colorado and surrounding areas. Your site will contain a home page, a resources page, tips on water conservation and a landscaping and irrigation section. (*Hint*: You created the index.htm page for this site in Unit A. If you did not complete Independent Challenge 2 in Unit A, follow the instructions in Unit A to create this file or obtain a copy from your instructor.)

a. Copy the outside.htm, inside.htm, and saver.htm files, as well as the irrigation folder with all its files, from the place where you store your Data Files, and paste them into the water directory you created in Unit A.

b. Open the **inside.htm** page in your text editor and scroll through the code to observe that three level-three page headings have been given IDs and that the phrase "Return to menu" which appears in several locations on the page, has been linked to #menu.

c. Locate the level-three subheading tag for the "What about water?" subheading near the bottom of the page, insert a space, then set the heading id as "wells."

d. Locate the paragraph near the top of the page that begins, <p>[General Tips, and assign an id of "menu" to the opening paragraph tag.

e. Click just before General Tips in the same line and type the code `<a href="#tips">` to start a link to the tips heading on the page, click after General Tips and type the code, </a>, to finish the link.

f. Link the rest of the text in the menu bar as follows: "Conserving in the Kitchen," #kitchen, "Conserving in the Bathroom," #bathroom, and "What about Wells," #wells.

g. Locate the line of text at the bottom of the page that reads, "For more information about saving water, contact:
Your Name at: yourname@metrowater.net" and create an e-mail link substituting your own name for the text "yourname", edit the "Page modified by" paragraph at the bottom of the page using your own name and today's date, then save your work.

h. Locate the site navigation bar at the top of the page and link the navigation bar text to the files as indicated: "Home," index.htm; "Conserving Inside," inside.htm; "Conserving Outside,"outside.htm; "Resources," resources.htm, "Super Saver," saver.htm; "Landscaping and Irrigation," irrigation/index.htm," then save the page and test it in your browser. (*Hint*: Click the browser Back button to return to the inside.htm page. If you did not complete the ACE steps in the Unit A Independent Challenge 2, open htm_b-1.txt then save it as resources.htm in your water site folder.)

i. Copy the site navigation bar from inside.htm, open water/irrigation/index.htm in your text editor and paste the navigation bar above the level-two page heading. Then modify the link paths by using dot-slash notation (../) to direct the browser to the parent directory before searching for the pages.

j. Save your work, then preview the page in your browser to test the links. (*Hint*: Click the Back button when you access pages without a link bar.)

k. Preview your page in your browser and click to test each link, then print the page and close the browser.

l. Close all files, then transfer your new and updated pages to your remote directory.

Advanced Challenge Exercises

- Use your favorite search engine to find sites about agricultural irrigation and water conservation.
- Using the information you found, write some content describing best agricultural irrigation practices.
- Create a Web page with appropriate page headings and title information, to display your information and add links to the cited sources, then create appropriate link titles.
- Add a "Page modified by" paragraph using your own name and today's date, then save the page as **agri_irrigation.htm** in your irrigation subdirectory, then print your page source code.
- Open your **irrigation/index.htm** page, then create a link from the text "agricultural irrigation" to your new page, then save the irrigation/index.htm page
- Edit the "Page modified by" paragraph to the bottom of the page using your own name and today's date, then save your work and transfer your updated pages to your remote directory.

▼ INDEPENDENT CHALLENGE 3

You have been using link titles because you know that they are part of the accessibility initiative. You are interested in learning more about the use of link titles and their part in making Web sites more accessible. You also want to find out what else you can do to make your site more user-friendly.

a. Go to the W3C Web Accessibility page and review the information regarding HTML links in section 6.1. Go to the Student Online Companion for this text, then locate the Unit B links. Write one or two paragraphs answering the following questions:

1. How can the use of link titles make your site more user-friendly?
2. What other steps can you take to enhance the effectiveness of your site's navigation interface to make it more accessible?
3. Add your name and today's date to the top of your paper, then print it.

▼ INDEPENDENT CHALLENGE 4

Now that you've studied site structure and linking principles, you are ready to add and link additional pages to your Web site.

a. Determine what additional pages your proposed site requires and whether it would benefit from the use of sub-directories, then make a sketch of your proposed site structure, labeling each of your intended pages.

b. In addition to your home page, create at least four placeholder pages with appropriate page titles, headings and placeholder text. (You may add actual content if you wish.)

- Make sure to name your home page file, and the main file in each directory, index.htm or use the default file name given to you by your instructor or server administrator.
- Make sure each page contains page headings and titles. (*Hint*: Page titles belong in the head section of your document.)
- Name one file about_me.htm and add some information about yourself. (*Hint*: If you are creating a business, name the file about_us.htm and add information about the business.)
- Create at least one page in a subdirectory of your site.
- Create at least one page with a list of links to sites related to your site content. (*Hint*: If you are creating a personal site, off-site links could be a list of your favorite Web sites, vacation places, work-related sites, or sites belonging to your family and friends.)

c. Add appropriate content to your home page. (*Hint*: Content can be changed as necessary as your site develops.)

d. Add a navigation bar to the top of each page to link all the pages.

e. On your site home page or your about_me.htm page, create at least one e-mail link.

f. On at least one page, create a jump-link menu to take the site visitor to specific points on that page.

g. Make sure to create a link that will take the site visitor back to the jump-link menu.

h. Add appropriate link titles to all your external links.

i. Cause at least one external link to open in a new window.

j. Save all your pages and transfer them to your remote server.

▼ VISUAL WORKSHOP

You are excited as you continue to build your Bits and PCs Web site and you decide to organize the entire site into logical folders and files. Create a directory structure and some placeholder pages with page heads and titles based on the site design shown in Figure B-20, then create navigation bars for each file based upon its relative placement in the file structure.

FIGURE B-20

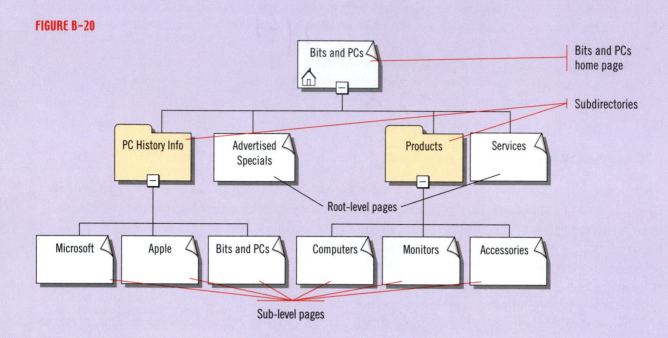

Formatting Page Elements with HTML

OBJECTIVES

Understand HTML formatting methods
Align text
Format characters
Define an address block
Control font selection
Customize fonts
Create ordered lists
Create unordered lists

Just as HTML allows you to include different kinds of text elements on your Web pages, it also enables you to determine the way text appears in the browser window. You can use HTML formatting and style tags to alter text appearance. You can apply attributes to block-level tags—tags that define an entire section of content—to modify the alignment of page content in the browser window. You can also use tag attributes to add color to your page or to change text appearance by altering fonts. Formatting text in your Web pages can improve the organization of information and make it easier for users to find what interests them.  You are excited to start enhancing the pages you are developing for the Paradise Mountain Family Resort Web site using text formatting.

Understanding HTML Formatting Methods

HTML provides some effective methods of organizing page content by allowing you to format text at the tag level, making it easier for users to identify valuable content and navigate your site. Because HTML was not designed to format text in complex ways, you cannot use traditional HTML formatting alone to format a Web page in the same manner you would if you created the page in a word processor. However, HTML does include several tags that allow you to add basic formatting to your Web pages, and there are literally millions of pages on the World Wide Web to which formatting of this type has been applied. Figure C-1 shows a sample page that uses several of these formats. The HTML code that produced it is shown in Figure C-2. You begin to review the formatting methods that you want to use for the Paradise Mountain Web site.

DETAILS

HTML pages can be formatted using the following methods:

- **Alignment**

  By default, Web page text is aligned along the left edge of the browser window. HTML's alignment options allow you to quickly and easily customize your Web page's appearance. **Alignment attribute options**—left, right, center, and, justify—can be applied to paragraphs, headings, and text blocks.

- **Character Formatting**

  HTML character formatting can affect text **weight** (such as boldfaced), **posture** (such as italicized), and **decoration** (such as underlined). Character formatting is useful for emphasizing words or short sections of text.

- **Font Formatting**

  HTML includes a tag set for changing the font formatting in small sections of text as well as a tag for specifying font formatting at the page level. When used appropriately, both of these tags let you customize your Web page appearance by changing the typeface, color, and size of text. Font formatting is useful for creating pages that appeal to specific target audiences and for adding personality to your pages.

- **Block-Level Formatting**

  Block-level tags—tags in which other elements, such as paragraphs and headings can be nested—allow you to control entire sections of content. Some block-level tags require the use of attributes and values. Others are predefined to produce changes and are often used without additional attributes. Block-level tags include **division** (`<div>...</div>`), which uses attributes to effect changes in text, **blockquote** (`<blockquote>...</blockquote>`), which alters the amount of white space on either side of the effected text, and **address** (`<address>...</address>`), which both alters the physical appearance and marks content to make it recognizable to text readers as well as to indexing and cataloging software.

- **Lists**

  The most commonly used lists are **ordered lists**, in which list items appear with sequential numbers or letters, and **unordered lists**, which have bullets instead of numbers or letters. To format an ordered list, you designate a series of text lines as list items and then enclose them in the appropriate **parent element**—a tag set in which another tag set is nested. You use the same method to create an unordered list. The parent list element for an ordered list is `<ol>...</ol>`, and the parent list element for an unordered list is `<ul>...</ul>`. Both ordered and unordered lists use the **child element** (an element within a parent tag) list item, `<li>...</li>`, to define each item in the list.

FIGURE C-1: Web page with applied formatting

Centered text

Colored text

Unordered list

Ordered list

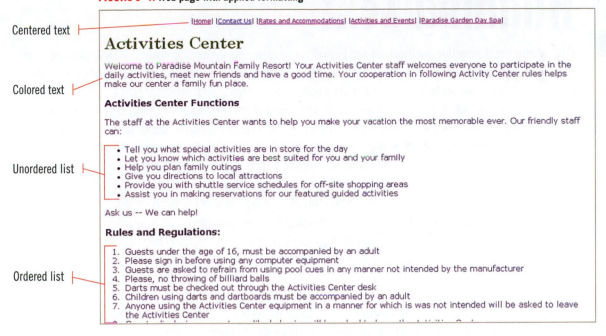

FIGURE C-2: Code for formatted text

Centers
navigation
bar

Sets font color

Creates
unordered list

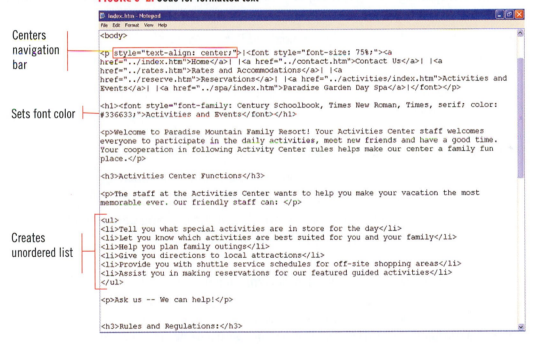

Design Matters

Guidelines for Web page formatting

Using element formatting in moderation can make your Web pages easier to use. However, the overuse of formatting can make pages more difficult to understand and navigate. Web users tend to scan text rather than read it, so presentation is critical in the Web environment. Properly formatted items such as page headings and navigation elements help users to quickly determine the most important content on a page; however, applying the same formatting technique to all page elements makes none of them stand out. Adhering to the "rules of three" can help make your pages more inviting to users: Increase the amount of white space on your page by limiting text blocks (paragraphs) to three average sentences. When possible, constrain your page length to scroll no more than three screens. Select no more than two or three font faces, usually one for the body type, one for headings, and a third, if necessary, for captions and/or non-text navigation elements. Use no more than three main colors consistently throughout your site.

HTML

Aligning Text

One of the most effective methods of setting off page elements is text alignment. HTML provides some basic control over where text appears on the page. Attribute values such as "text-align: center;" can be applied to block elements such as the paragraph (`<p>...</p>`) and heading (`<h1>...</h1>` through `<h6>...</h6>`) tag sets. The default text-align style value is left, meaning that if no style alignment value is applied, each line of text is flush with the left edge of the browser window. Other text-align style settings are right, which sets each line of text even with the right edge of the window, center, which centers each line between the two edges of the window, and justify, which stretches each line of text so it is flush with both the left and right edges of the browser window. Using justified text can cause text spacing problems. This is especially problematic when text wraps around an image or when a window is resized. Therefore, it is best to leave justified text in the hands of textbook publishers and keep it off your Web pages. Table C-1 summarizes the text-align attribute.  You think your page navigation bars would look better centered on the page. You also want to experiment with other alignment options.

STEPS

1. **Open the htm_C-1.txt file in your text editor from the location where you store your data files, then save it as rates.htm in your paradise site folder**

2. **Locate the opening paragraph tag of your site navigation bar at the top of the page, then click between p and >**

3. **Press [Spacebar], then type `style="text-align: center;"`**
   You may have seen earlier versions of HTML documents in which alignment was specified using the `align="value"` method as follows: `<p align="center">`. Although this is easier to type, formatting text in this manner has been deprecated by the W3C. Therefore, it is best to learn to format to newer standards so that you are prepared to apply newer formatting techniques at a later date.

4. **Locate the paragraph that begins with "Call the resort office," click just before > in the opening paragraph tag, press [Spacebar], then type `style="text-align: justify;"`**

5. **Locate the next paragraph, which begins "For questions or comments," click in the opening paragraph tag just before >, press [Spacebar], then type `style="text-align: center;"`**

6. **Locate the "Page modified by" paragraph, click in the opening paragraph tag just before >, press [Spacebar], then type `style="text-align: right;"`**
   Your code should appear similar to that shown in Figure C-3.

7. **Save your work, start your browser program, then view the rates.htm file in your browser**
   As shown in Figure C-4, the site navigation bar and contact paragraph are aligned in the center of the page. However, the "Page modified by" paragraph is right aligned and the "Call the resort office" paragraph displays some odd spacing due to justified alignment. You are not pleased with the results produced by the right and justify align styles.

8. **Click the text editor program button on the taskbar, locate the "Call the resort office" paragraph, click and drag to select the style attribute and value in the opening paragraph tag, press [Delete], then press [Backspace], if necessary, to remove the extra space**
   The justified formatting has been removed from the paragraph.

9. **In the opening paragraph tag of the "Page modified by" paragraph, drag to select "right" after "text-align:", press [Delete], type `center`, then save the page and reload it in your browser**
   The right alignment formatting has been removed from the paragraph and center alignment has been applied.

FIGURE C-3: Style text-align attribute values

Center alignment

Right alignment

Justified alignment

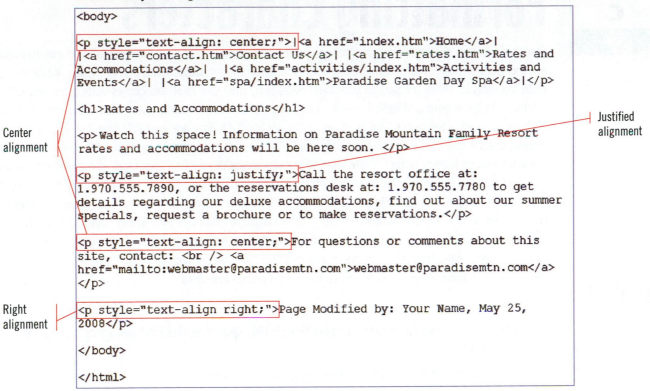

```
<body>

<p style="text-align: center;">|<a href="index.htm">Home</a>|
|<a href="contact.htm">Contact Us</a>| |<a href="rates.htm">Rates and
Accommodations</a>|  |<a href="activities/index.htm">Activities and
Events</a>| |<a href="spa/index.htm">Paradise Garden Day Spa</a>|</p>

<h1>Rates and Accommodations</h1>

<p>Watch this space! Information on Paradise Mountain Family Resort
rates and accommodations will be here soon. </p>

<p style="text-align: justify;">Call the resort office at:
1.970.555.7890, or the reservations desk at: 1.970.555.7780 to get
details regarding our deluxe accommodations, find out about our summer
specials, request a brochure or to make reservations.</p>

<p style="text-align: center;">For questions or comments about this
site, contact: <br /> <a
href="mailto:webmaster@paradisemtn.com">webmaster@paradisemtn.com</a>
</p>

<p style="text-align right;">Page Modified by: Your Name, May 25,
2008</p>

</body>

</html>
```

FIGURE C-4: Web page with applied text-align style attribute values

Justified text with irregular spacing

Center-aligned text

Right-aligned text

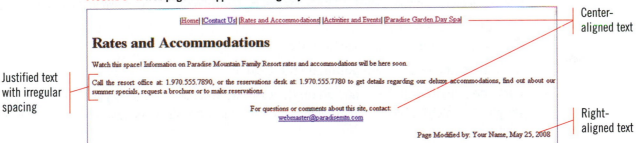

TABLE C-1: HTML text-align attribute values

value	examples	results
text-align: left	`<p style="text-align: left;"> This text has been aligned to the left. </p>`	This text has been aligned to the left.
text-align: right	`<p style="text-align: right;"> This text has been aligned to the right. </p>`	This text has been aligned to the right.
text-align: center	`<p style="text-align: center;"> This text is centered. </p>`	This text is centered.
text-align: justify	`<p style="text-align: justify;"> This text is justified. Justified text can cause display problems like this. </p>`	This text is justified. Justified text can cause display problems like this.

HTML

Formatting Characters

Sometimes words or phrases on your Web pages need to stand out. In documents created in a word processor, this is most often accomplished using three standard formats: **bold**, *italic*, and <u>underline</u>. While you can easily add any of these formats to your Web page text, their use in HTML comes with some restrictions. Additionally, both bold and italic formatting can each be created by using two different tag sets. The most obvious choices—`<b>...</b>` for bold and `<i>...</i>` for italic—are available only to devices that can visually display text. Because of this restriction, these formats are known as **physical formats**. However, some Web users require different interfaces—for example, audio devices that read Web content to visually impaired people. To render character formatting in such a manner that it can be heard as well as seen, one must use the **logical formatting** tags `<strong>...</strong>`, for boldfaced text, and `<em>...</em>` for emphasized text. Table C-2 summarizes the tags available for character formatting. You have identified a small section on two pages where extra formatting would provide a needed contrast. You decide to apply bold and italic formatting using logical character formatting tags to ensure that Paradise Mountain Family Resort page content is accessible to the widest possible audience.

STEPS

1. **In the rates.htm file, locate the text Watch this space! in the first paragraph under the page heading**

2. **Click before the word Watch, then type `<strong><em>`**
   The `<strong>` tag marks the beginning of the section you want to appear as boldfaced; `<em>` marks the beginning of the section of text you want to italicize.

3. **Click after space! then type `</em></strong>`**
   The `</em>` tag ends the emphasized formatting; `</strong>` ends the boldfaced formatting. Following the rules of tag order that you learned in Unit A, the first tag opened is the last tag closed in these nested tags.

4. **Save the rates.htm file**
   Compare your code to that shown in Figure C-5.

5. **Click the browser program button on the taskbar**

6. **Click the Reload or Refresh button on the browser toolbar to update your rates.htm page**
   The phrase "Watch this space!" stands out from the rest of the text as shown in Figure C-6, because it is bold-faced and italicized.

Design Matters

Using text emphasis

As you have learned, linked text is underlined by default. Therefore, to avoid confusing users, it is best not to underline unlinked text on a Web page. If you need to emphasize text, use bold, italic, a font color, or a combination of these three methods instead.

FIGURE C-5: Logical formatting tags

```
<p><strong><em>Watch this space!</em></strong> Information on Paradise
Mountain Family Resort rates and accommodations will be here soon. </p>
```

Opening and closing
emphasized tags

FIGURE C-6: Logical formatting elements displayed in browser

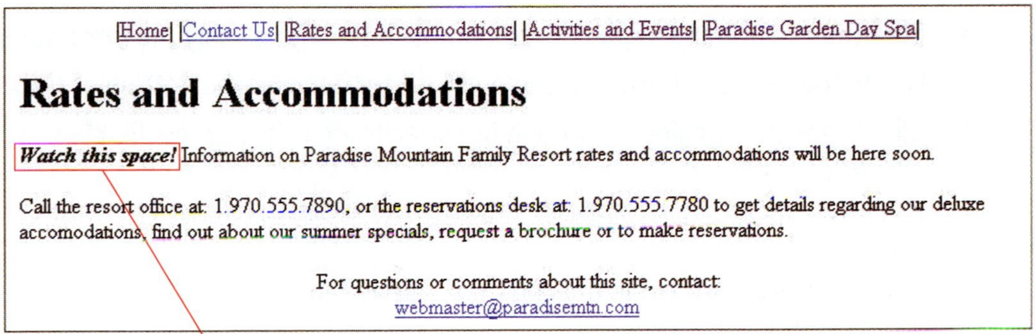

|Home| |Contact Us| |Rates and Accommodations| |Activities and Events| |Paradise Garden Day Spa|

Rates and Accommodations

Watch this space! Information on Paradise Mountain Family Resort rates and accommodations will be here soon.

Call the resort office at: 1.970.555.7890, or the reservations desk at: 1.970.555.7780 to get details regarding our deluxe accomodations, find out about our summer specials, request a brochure or to make reservations.

For questions or comments about this site, contact:
webmaster@paradisemtn.com

`<strong> ... </strong>` and `<em> ... </em>`
formatting displayed in browser

TABLE C-2: HTML text formatting tags

name	tag(s)	function	notes
Underlined text	`<u>...</u>`	Adds underline format to text	Avoid using; may be confused with linked text
Boldface text	`<b>...</b>`	Adds bold format to text	Applies to visual format only; use `<strong>...</strong>` instead to allow widest accessibility
Italicized text	`<i>...</i>`	Adds italic format to text	Applies to visual format only; use `<em>...</em>` instead to allow widest accessibility
Strong text	`<strong>...</strong>`	Marks text as strong; interpreted by browsers as bold	Interpretable by different Web interfaces; use instead of `<b>...</b>`
Emphasized text	`<em>...</em>`	Marks text as emphasized; interpreted by browsers as italic	Interpretable by different Web interfaces; use instead of `<i>...</i>`

HTML

Defining an Address Block

Just as character formatting allows you to change the appearance of text and to add logical formatting at the character level by enclosing small sections of text in character formatting tags, HTML also offers a method of applying logical formatting at the block level. One such tag set, **blockquote** (`<blockquote>...</blockquote>`), allows you to control white space on the page by indenting the affected text approximately 40 pixels on each side. Although there are other methods of controlling white space on the page, the block quote is still useful when a "quick-fix" is necessary. Another block-level tag set that appeared to be "on the way out" is making a comeback: The **address tag** (`<address>...</address>`) was originally designed to be recognized as address content by indexing and cataloging software, but it is also recognized by most accessibility devices, such as text readers and is, therefore, an accessibility tool recommended by the Web Accessibility Initiative (WAI). In most browsers, address text is rendered using an italic typeface. You decide to format your contact and "modified by" content using the address tag set.

STEPS

1. Click the text editor program button on the taskbar to display the rates.htm page code

2. Locate the "For questions or comments" paragraph near the bottom of the page

TROUBLE

If you deleted the space between the tag name, "address," and the tag style attribute, click after "address" and press the space-bar once.

3. Click inside the opening paragraph tag directly after the p, press [Backspace], then type address

   You changed the opening paragraph tag into an opening address tag, but left the formatting that you applied earlier.

4. Click directly after the p in the closing paragraph tag, press [Backspace], type address, then save your work

   Your page code appears similar to that shown in Figure C-7.

5. Click the browser program button on the taskbar, then reload your page in the browser window

   The "For questions or comments" address block appears in italic type as shown in Figure C-8.

6. Click the text editor button on the taskbar to display the rates.htm page code

   You want the navigation bar on your home page to match the one on your rates page, so you decide to copy it.

7. Locate the navigation bar code near the top of the body selection, drag to select from the opening paragraph tag through the closing paragraph tag, then copy the selected code to your clipboard

8. Open the paradise/index.htm file, drag to select the navigation bar code, press [Delete], then paste the copied code and save your work

Design Matters

Using address blocks for inline display

Many designers like to use address blocks in the middle of a line to emphasize inline e-mail links. However, some browsers display address blocks with extra white space above and/or below them. If you use inline address blocks, be sure to test your page in several browsers.

FIGURE C-7: Address block code

Opening tag

Closing tag

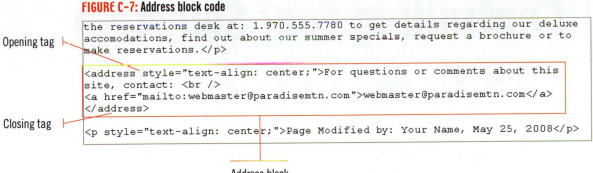

```
the reservations desk at: 1.970.555.7780 to get details regarding our deluxe
accomodations, find out about our summer specials, request a brochure or to
make reservations.</p>

<address style="text-align: center;">For questions or comments about this
site, contact: <br />
<a href="mailto:webmaster@paradisemtn.com">webmaster@paradisemtn.com</a>
</address>

<p style="text-align: center;">Page Modified by: Your Name, May 25, 2008</p>
```

Address block

FIGURE C-8: Address block text displayed in browser window

|Home| |Contact Us| |Rates and Accommodations| |Activities and Events| |Paradise Garden Day Spa|

Rates and Accommodations

Watch this space! Information on Paradise Mountain Family Resort rates and accommodations will be here soon.

Call the resort office at: 1.970.555.7890, or the reservations desk at: 1.970.555.7780 to get details regarding our deluxe accomodations, find out about our summer specials, request a brochure or to make reservations.

Address block

For questions or comments about this site, contact:
webmaster@paradisemtn.com

Controlling Font Selection

You have used character- and block-formatting features to change the weight, posture, and alignment of text. You can also alter text appearance by changing its typeface. You can do this by using the `<font>...</font>` tag in the body of the document. You can also apply changes to text at the page level by adding formatting instructions in the head section of your document using the `<basefont />` tag. The style value `font-family` changes the typeface in which text appears. In recent years, basefont and font tags have been deprecated by the W3C in favor of newer formatting methods; however, there are literally millions of pages on the Web that still use font tags to format pages, so it is a good idea to learn how to use these tags. ▦ You are accustomed to working with different fonts in a word processor, and now you want to see how the Paradise Mountain Resort pages look in another font.

STEPS

1. **Open paradise/index.htm in your browser program and view the formatting**

   As shown in Figure C-9, the page heading is heavier than the rest of the text, but the heading and body text all use the same typeface.

2. **Return to the paradise/index.htm page in your text editor**

QUICK TIP

The semicolon (;) at the end of the style value signifies the end of that style element. While some browsers apply the style correctly when the semicolon is missing, not all do, so it is important to include the semicolon at the end of the value string and before the closing quotation mark.

3. **Click between `<h1>` and the page heading text, type `<font style="font-family: Century Schoolbook, Times New Roman, Times, serif;">`**

   You used an **inline style**—a style applied as an attribute—to change the page heading text to the serif typeface, Century Schoolbook, which is available on most systems. To make sure your page appears as close to your design as possible, you decide to list similar-looking font families used in three operating systems in case your chosen font is not available. You did this by creating a **font stack**—a list of acceptable fonts—in which you specified Times New Roman—the default serif font on Windows systems, Times (Macintosh), and serif (UNIX).

4. **Click after Resort and before `</h1>`, then type `</font>`**

   The opening and closing font tags surround the page heading text. You want to add basefont formatting to format the rest of the text on the page in a sans serif font. For information on modifying fonts without using style attributes, see the appendix.

5. **Click before the closing head tag in the head section, type `<basefont style="font-family: Verdana, Arial, sans serif;" />`, then press [Enter] twice**

   The basefont tag is now inserted in the head section of your code as shown in Figure C-10.

TROUBLE

Based on your monitor size and display settings, your output may appear differently.

6. **Save your file, click the browser program button on the taskbar, then reload your paradise/index.htm page in the browser window**

   The page heading is now set in the Century Schoolbook (or the default serif font on your computer), and the rest of the document is set in Verdana or a sans serif font as shown in Figure C-11. You like the new look, but notice that the navigation bar now wraps to a second line.

Design Matters

Understanding fonts and typefaces

A **font** is a complete set of characters, including letters, numbers, and special characters, in a particular size and style of type. A **typeface** contains a series of fonts such as Times Bold, Times Italic, and Times New Roman, which are different fonts in the same family. In Web design, the terms "font," "typeface," "font family," and "font face" are used interchangeably. Typefaces are divided into families. The majority of fonts fall into one of two categories: serif or sans serif. **Serif** fonts take their name from the decorative "tails," called serifs, at the ends of the lines that make up each letter. The most common serif fonts are Times New Roman, the default serif font on most Windows computers, and Times, the default serif font on most Macintosh computers. **Sans serif** literally means "without serifs"; fonts in this group do not have decorative "tails." In traditional print media, large blocks of normal-sized text usually appear in a serif font so they are easier to read. Page headings traditionally appear in sans serif. On a computer screen, however, light emissions from the monitor make serif fonts more difficult to read. Therefore, the roles of serif and sans serif fonts are often reversed on the Web.

FIGURE C-9: Paradise Mountain home page before formatting

Paradise Mountain Family Resort

|Home| |Contact Us| |Rates and Accommodations| |Activities and Events| |Paradise Garden Day Spa|

Located just outside of Rocky Mountain National Park in Colorado, Paradise Mountain Family Resort is the perfect getaway place for the whole family. Adults can enjoy discounted golf and complimentary use of our health club and tennis facilities while the little ones participate in our popular children's program.

Friday night dances are always a hit with the teens, and our new skate park offers one of the finest courses designed to entertain and challenge skaters, whether they are beginners or more experienced.

Heading and body are all the same typeface

FIGURE C-10: Home page code with applied formatting

Basefont formatting in head section

Opening font tag with style formatting

Closing font tag

```
<title>Paradise Mountain Family Resort</title>

<meta name="Keywords" content="Resort vacations, Estes Park, Estes Park lodging,
family vacation, spa, day spa" />

<basefont style="font-family: Verdana, Arial, san serif;" />

</head>

<body>

<h1><font style="font-family: Century Schoolbook, Times New Roman, Times,
serif;">Paradise Mountain Family Resort</font></h1>

<p style="text-align: center;">|<a href="index.htm">Home</a>| |<a
href="contact.htm">Contact Us</a>| |<a href="rates.htm">Rates and Accommodations</a>|
|<a href="activities/index.htm">Activities and Events</a>| |<a
href="spa/index.htm">Paradise Garden Day Spa</a>|</p>
```

FIGURE C-11: Paradise Mountain home page with text formatting

Serif font in level-one heading

Sans serif font applied with <basefont /> tag

Paradise Mountain Family Resort

|Home| |Contact Us| |Rates and Accommodations| |Activities and Events| |Paradise Garden Day Spa|

Located just outside of Rocky Mountain National Park in Colorado, Paradise Mountain Family Resort is the perfect getaway place for the whole family. Adults can enjoy discounted golf and complimentary use of our health club and tennis facilities while the little ones participate in our popular children's program.

Friday night dances are always a hit with the teens, and our new skate park offers one of the finest courses designed to entertain and challenge skaters, whether they are beginners or more experienced.

Hiking is a must-do activity in the beautiful Rocky Mountains. Guests can participate in one of our wilderness treks (designed for both experienced and beginning hikers), or strike out on their own for a more intimate wilderness experience.

In addition to hiking activities, during the summer months guests can enjoy horseback riding, white-water rafting, or fly fishing for trout in one of our many private streams. Rodeo fans arriving in mid-July will be sure to catch some of the events at the annual PRCA Rooftop Rodeo at the nearby Stanley Park Fairgrounds.

Clues to Use

Selecting and specifying page fonts

Rules governing typeface selection apply to both print and screen media: If you are going to use more than one font face, use one family (serif or sans serif) for headings and select a font from the other family for body text. Do not mix several different font faces from the same family. A sans serif font such as Verdana, which was designed for Web display, Arial, or Helvetica are all excellent choices for Web page text. Although you can specify any font family for a document or marked section of text, only the fonts that are installed on the user's system are available for display in the user's browser. If the font you specified is not installed, the user's computer displays the system's default font. Consequently, the best practice is to use fonts that are commonly available. When in doubt, you can "stack" multiple font families. When multiple font families are listed, the browser checks each family until it finds one that is available or, finding none, displays the system font.

HTML

Customizing Fonts

In addition to specifying a font family, the `<font>...</font>` and `<basefont />` tags also allow you to change the color and size of text on a page. By applying the color style and specifying a color code value such as the following, `<font style="color: #339999;">affected text</font>`, you can change text to a color other than black. (The color shown in the example is teal, but you can use any color code.) You also can customize font appearance by changing font size with the font style size value as follows `<font style="font-size: 80%;">`. Size can be specified in percentages or in point sizes. An older method of customizing fonts is to use the attributes **face**, **color**, and **size** as follows: `<font face="Century Schoolbook" size="5" color="#339999">Affected text</font>`. While this method of specifying fonts has been deprecated by the W3C, it is still widely in use today. The appendix summarizes the attributes and values for working with fonts in traditional HTML. You think adding color to the text on the Paradise Mountain Family Resort page will make the page more interesting to your site visitors. You also want to resize the navigation bar so that it does not wrap in the browser window.

STEPS

QUICK TIP

You can use descriptive words such as "green" or "navy" to specify your color choices; however, not all browsers interpret color words in the same manner.

1. **Return to the paradise\index.htm page in your text editor, locate the opening font tag in the level-one page heading, click between the semicolon (;) and the closing quotation mark, press [Spacebar], type `color: #336633;` (including the semicolon), then save the page**
   The number #336633 is a hexadecimal color code for a medium-green color. When setting text colors, be sure to select colors that are different from your link colors.

2. **Locate the basefont tag in the head section, click between ";" and the closing quotation mark, press [Spacebar], then type `color: #333366;` (including the semicolon)**
   The hexadecimal code you just typed sets the document text to a steel blue color, which you think is a good match for the company's image. By adding the color value to the style attribute, you are creating a series of attributes called an **attribute string**. Attribute strings allow you to assign more than one attribute to the same tag. This is useful when you want to display all of the marked content in the same manner. Using attribute strings rather than several individual tags of the same type enable you to keep your code neater and reduce the possibility of code errors.

3. **Locate the navigation bar at the top of the page, click after the opening paragraph tag and just before the first pipe, then type `<font style="font-size: 75%;">`**
   The font-size style you set causes the affected text to appear at 75 percent of (25 percent smaller than) the surrounding text. When no font size is specified, the page appears in the default font size. Font sizes can also be specified in traditional HTML as `<font size="4">affected text</font>`.

4. **In the site navigation bar, click between the final pipe and the `</p>`, type `</font>`, then save the page**
   Your page code should resemble the code shown in Figure C-12.

5. **Click the browser program button on the taskbar, then reload your page**
   The site navigation bar appears smaller than the rest of the page text, and the text colors change, as shown in Figure C-13.

FIGURE C-12: HTML code for typeface formatting

Basefont tag with font style and color values

Font tag nested inside level-one heading tag

Font size attribute

```
<basefont style="font-family: Verdana, Arial, san serif; color: #333366;" />

</head>

<body>

<h1><font style="font-family: Century Schoolbook, Times New Roman, Times, serif;
color: #336633;">Paradise Mountain Family Resort</font></h1>

<p style="text-align: center;"><font style="font-size: 75%;">|<a
href="index.htm">Home</a>|  |<a href="contact.htm">Contact Us</a>|  |<a
href="rates.htm">Rates and Accommodations</a>|  |<a
href="activities/index.htm">Activities and Events</a>|  |<a
href="spa/index.htm">Paradise Garden Day Spa</a>|</font></p>
```

FIGURE C-13: Page with font family, color, and size formatting

Navigation bar is 75% of surrounding text size

Heading is green

Body text is blue

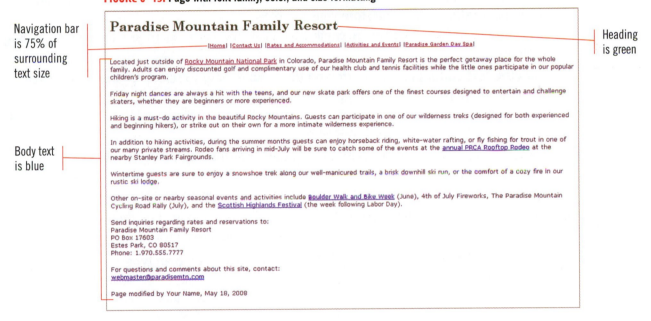

Design Matters

Working with hexadecimal colors

Hexadecimal is a base 16 numbering system that uses numerical and character values from 0 (zero) through 9 and "A" through "F." A color code is composed of three pairs of numbers. The code "#FF6666," produces a rose pink color. Although you can use descriptive words for colors, such as "green" or "navy," to specify your color choices, using the hexadecimal equivalent is a good habit to develop. Hexadecimal code tells the browser mathematically how to create the color you want and is interpretable by a wider range of browsers than are color names. There are literally millions of hexadecimal colors. However, there are only 216 colors that are considered "browser-safe." A table of browser-safe hexadecimal color codes is included in the appendix and in the Online Companion for this text.

HTML

Creating Ordered Lists

One of the keys to an effective online layout is to divide text into small pieces that users can easily comprehend. HTML list formats provide an easy avenue for keeping your pages Web friendly. An ordered list is an ideal format for steps, rankings, and other sets of information for which order is important. 🖌️ The Paradise Mountain Family Resort Activities Center staff prints a list of rules and regulations for guests using the Activities Center facilities and equipment. They have asked you to publish this list in the activities directory of the Paradise Mountain Family Resort Web site.

STEPS

QUICK TIP

If you are using a Microsoft browser, you can open your page source code from the browser menu bar. Simply click View on the menu bar and then click Source.

1. In your text editor, open the file htm_C-2.txt from the location where you store your Data Files, click File on the menu bar, then click Save As

2. Navigate to the location where you store your paradise site files, double-click activities, click the Save as type list arrow, click All Files, type the filename index.htm, click Save, then click Yes to replace the existing index file

3. Click the browser program button on the taskbar, then open the activities/index.htm file from the location where you store your site files

   The file includes a list of Activity Center rules. You think this content would look better formatted as a numbered list.

QUICK TIP

Most HTML tags are abbreviations; "ol" is short for "ordered list."

4. Click the text editor program button on the taskbar, drag to select <p> below the level-three heading, press [Delete], type <ol>, then press [Enter]

   The <ol> tag marks the start of an ordered list. By pressing [Enter] after the ordered list tag, you move the list text down one row and make it easier to identify.

5. Locate the end of the the rules list after "...the following day", drag to select the </p>, press [Delete], type </ol>, then press [Enter] twice

   You have just specified the beginning and end of the ordered list. You still need to format the list items.

6. Click before "Guests" in the line below the opening ordered list tag, then type <li>

   The <li> tag marks the text that follows it and identifies it to the browser as a list item.

7. Select the "<br />" tag at the end of the line, press [Delete], then type </li>

   The </li> marks the end of a list item. Some designers choose not to include the closing list tag. However, according to newer coding standards, list item tags, like all other tags, must be closed. On the other hand, <br /> tags aren't necessary in lists because each list item automatically starts on a new line.

TROUBLE

Be sure that you do not replace the line break in the contact paragraph with a closing list item tag.

8. Type <li> tags before the remaining list items, as shown in Figure C-14

9. Replace the remaining line break tags with closing list item tags, click just before the </ol>, type </li> to mark the end of the last list item as shown in Figure C-14, save the file, then view it in your browser

   Your completed file should resemble Figure C-15.

FIGURE C-14: Marked ordered list

```
<ol>

<li>Guests under the age of 16, must be accompanied by an adult</li>

<li>Please sign in before using any computer equipment</li>

<li>Guests are asked to refrain from using pool cues in any manner not
intended by the manufacturer</li>

<li>Please, no throwing of billiard balls</li>

<li>Darts must be checked out through the Activities Center desk</li>

<li>Children using darts and dartboards must be accompanied by an adult</li>

<li>Anyone using the Activities Center equipment in a manner for which is was
not intended will be asked to leave the Activities Center</li>

<li>Guests displaying unsportsmanlike behavior will be asked to leave the
Activities Center</li>

<li>Internet access is reserved for adult guests; however, a selection of
video games are available for youngsters</li>

<li>Video games may be checked out for up to three days at a time</li>

<li>Guests checking out videos and DVDs are reminded that all movies are due
for return by noon the following day.</li>

</ol>
```

FIGURE C-15: Completed page with ordered list

|Home| |Contact Us| |Rates and Accommodations| |Activities and Events| |Paradise Garden Day Spa|

Activities Center

Welcome to Paradise Mountain Family Resort! Your Activities Center staff welcomes everyone to participate in the daily activities, meet new friends and have a good time. Your cooperation in following Activity Center rules helps make our center a family fun place.

Rules and Regulations:

1. Guests under the age of 16, must be accompanied by an adult
2. Please sign in before using any computer equipment
3. Guests are asked to refrain from using pool cues in any manner not intended by the manufacturer
4. Please, no throwing of billiard balls
5. Darts must be checked out through the Activities Center desk
6. Children using darts and dartboards must be accompanied by an adult
7. Anyone using the Activities Center equipment in a manner for which is was not intended will be asked to leave the Activities Center
8. Guests displaying unsportsmanlike behavior will be asked to leave the Activities Center
9. Internet access is reserved for adult guests; however, a selection of video games are available for youngsters
10. Video games may be checked out for up to three days at a time
11. Guests checking out videos and DVDs are reminded that all movies are due for return by noon the following day.

For questions or comments about this site, contact:
webmaster@paradisemtn.com

Page Modified by: Your Name, May 25, 2008

Clues to Use

Nesting lists

Sometimes information is more easily organized when you break your lists down even further. For example, it might be necessary to include a list of subitems within a parent list. This process is known as **nesting** a list. You can nest lists of any type. You can nest an ordered list inside an unordered list, an unordered list inside of an ordered list, or you can nest lists of the same type. When nesting lists, make sure that you nest the sublist completely. In other words, make sure that you include an opening as well as a closing list tag and the opening and closing tags for all list items. Also remember to close the parent list. Figure C-16 shows the code used to produce a nested list as well as the browser output the code produces.

FIGURE C-16: Nested list code and browser output

```
<p>You can nest lists of any sort. Following are examples of nested lists:
</p>

<ol>
<li>This is the first list item in an ordered list</li>
<li>This is the second list item. What are some reasons that you might want
to nest a list?</li>
    <ol type="a">
    <li>To organize your content (we set the list type attribute for this
    nested list to "a".)</li>
    <li>To demonstrate your superb cod
    <li>Because it's so cool </li>
    </ol>
<li>This is list item three in the p
unordered list.</li>
    <ul>
    <li>This is unordered list item 1<
    <li>This is unordered list item 2.
        <ul>
        <li>This is unordered list ite
        <li>This is unordered list ite
        <li>This is unordered list ite
        </ul>
    <li>This is unordered list item 3
    </ul>
<li>This is the last list item in th
</ol>

<p>Indentions in your code help you
ends.</p>
```

You can nest lists of any sort. Following are examples of nested lists:

1. This is the first list item in an ordered list
2. This is the second list item. What are some reasons that you might want to nest a list?
   a. To organize your content (we set the list type attribute for this nested list to "a".)
   b. To demonstrate your superb coding abilities
   c. Because it's so cool
3. This is list item three in the parent list. It precedes a nested unordered list.
   ○ This is unordered list item 1
   ○ This is unordered list item 2. We'll add another nested list here:
      ■ This is unordered list item 1 in the nested list.
      ■ This is unordered list item 2 in the nested list.
      ■ This is unordered list item 3 in the nested list.
   ○ This is unordered list item 3 in the first ordered list
4. This is the last list item in the master list

Indentions in your code help you to keep track of when and where each list ends.

Creating Unordered Lists

Like an ordered list, an unordered list is a simple way to divide Web page text into smaller, easier-to-read portions. While the items in an ordered list are numbered in order, unordered list items appear with bullets before each item. This format works well for organizing a list of links or listing sets of ideas when each item is equally important and order doesn't matter. Table C-3 explains the HTML tags used to create an unordered list. The Activities Center director has asked you to post some additional information on the Center's main page.

STEPS

1. In your text editor, open the file htm_C-3.txt from the location where you store your Data Files, drag to select all the text on the page, click Edit on the menu bar, click Copy, then close the file

2. If necessary, open your activities/index.htm page in your text editor, locate the paragraph that ends with "… our center a family fun place," click after </p>, press [Enter] twice, click Edit on the menu bar, then click Paste

   The text and markup from htm_C-3.txt has been pasted into the activities/index.htm file between the welcome paragraph and the list of rules. This information would look better as bulleted text.

3. Drag to select <p> in the line that begins "Tell you what," press [Delete], type <ul>, then press [Enter]

   The <ul> marks the start of an unordered list. As with the ordered list, the paragraph tag is not necessary. Pressing [Enter] causes the first sentence of the pasted text to move to the next line.

4. Verify that the insertion point is before the word "Tell" in the first sentence of the list, then type <li>

5. Drag to select <br /> at the end of the line, press [Delete], then type </li>

   Just as in an ordered list, <li> marks the text that follows as a list item, and </li> closes that item. Line breaks are not required because each list item starts a new line.

QUICK TIP

You can use the Copy and Paste commands on the Edit menu to speed your work.

6. Repeat Steps 4 and 5 to set an opening and closing list item tag before and after each line, replacing the <br /> tags with </li> tags, then save the file

7. Drag to select the </p> after the list item that ends with "guided activities," press [Delete], type </ul>, then compare your screen to Figure C-17

8. Save your work, click the browser program button in the taskbar, reload the activities/index.htm page, then print the page

   The Activity Center functions appear next to bullet characters, while the Rules and Regulations list items are numbered, as shown in Figure C-18.

9. Close all files, then transfer your updated files to your remote directory on the server

---

Clues to Use

Customizing lists

Be default, ordered lists are displayed in the browser with items numbered sequentially beginning with 1. However, you can use attributes to customize the <ol> tag to display lists with letters or Roman numerals. Set the "type" attribute to "a" for lowercase letters, "A" for uppercase letters, "i" for lowercase Roman numerals, or "I" for uppercase Roman numerals. You can also change the starting point of a list by setting a start value. For example, to format a numbered list to begin with the number 4, add start="4", to the <ol> tag. You can also customize bulleted lists using type="value" to specify the appearance of the bullet as follows: <ul type="circle"> <li>Item 1</li></ul>. The bullet produced by the preceding code is an open circle rather than the usual filled disc. Possible values for unordered list types are: circle, square, and disc.

FIGURE C-17: Code for unordered list

```
<p>The staff at the Activities Center wants to help you make your vacation the most
memorable ever. Our friendly staff can: </p>

<ul>
<li>Tell you what special activities are in store for the day</li>
<li>Let you know which activities are best suited for you and your family</li>
<li>Help you plan family outings</li>
<li>Give you directions to local attractions</li>
<li>Provide you with shuttle service schedules for off-site shopping areas</li>
<li>Assist you in making reservations for our featured guided activities</li>
</ul>

<p>Ask us -- We can help!</p>
```

FIGURE C-18: Unordered and ordered lists displayed in Web page

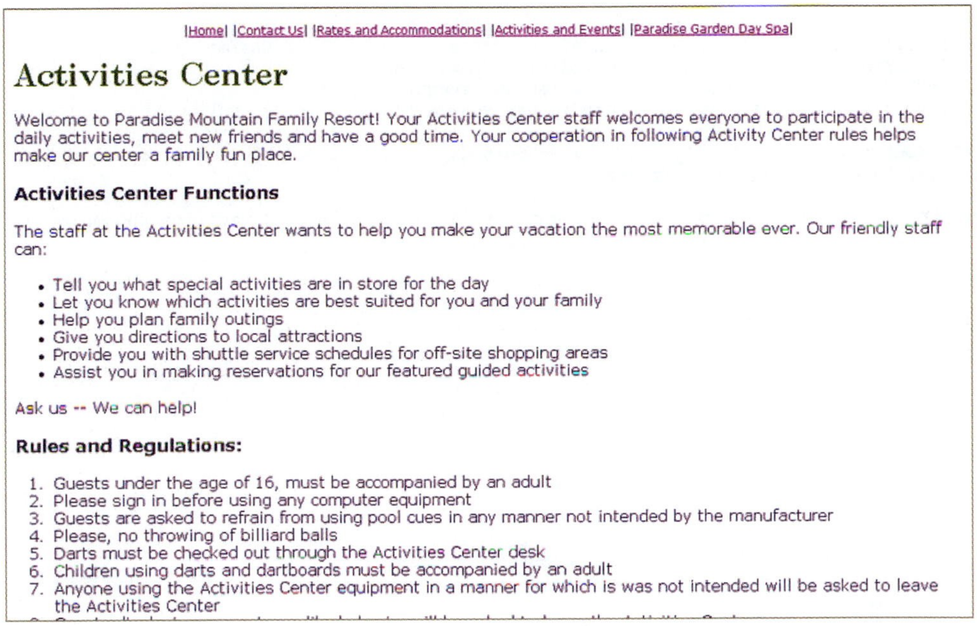

|Home| |Contact Us| |Rates and Accommodations| |Activities and Events| |Paradise Garden Day Spa|

Activities Center

Welcome to Paradise Mountain Family Resort! Your Activities Center staff welcomes everyone to participate in the daily activities, meet new friends and have a good time. Your cooperation in following Activity Center rules helps make our center a family fun place.

Activities Center Functions

The staff at the Activities Center wants to help you make your vacation the most memorable ever. Our friendly staff can:

- Tell you what special activities are in store for the day
- Let you know which activities are best suited for you and your family
- Help you plan family outings
- Give you directions to local attractions
- Provide you with shuttle service schedules for off-site shopping areas
- Assist you in making reservations for our featured guided activities

Ask us -- We can help!

Rules and Regulations:

1. Guests under the age of 16, must be accompanied by an adult
2. Please sign in before using any computer equipment
3. Guests are asked to refrain from using pool cues in any manner not intended by the manufacturer
4. Please, no throwing of billiard balls
5. Darts must be checked out through the Activities Center desk
6. Children using darts and dartboards must be accompanied by an adult
7. Anyone using the Activities Center equipment in a manner for which is was not intended will be asked to leave the Activities Center

TABLE C-3: HTML tags for creating ordered and unordered lists

tag	description	example

`<ol>...</ol>`	Marks beginning and end of an ordered list	`<ol>`
		`<li>Item 1</li>`
		`<li>Item 2</li>`
		`</ol>`

`<ul>...</ul>`	Marks beginning and end of an unordered list	`<ul>`
		`<li>Item 1</li>`
		`<li>Item 2</li>`
		`</ul>`

`<li>...</li>`	Marks the beginning and end of each item in an ordered or unordered list; as with most other tags, the closing tag is required	`<li>Item 1</li>` `<li>Item 2</li>`

Practice

▼ CONCEPTS REVIEW

Identify the function of each item labeled in Figure C-19.

FIGURE C-19

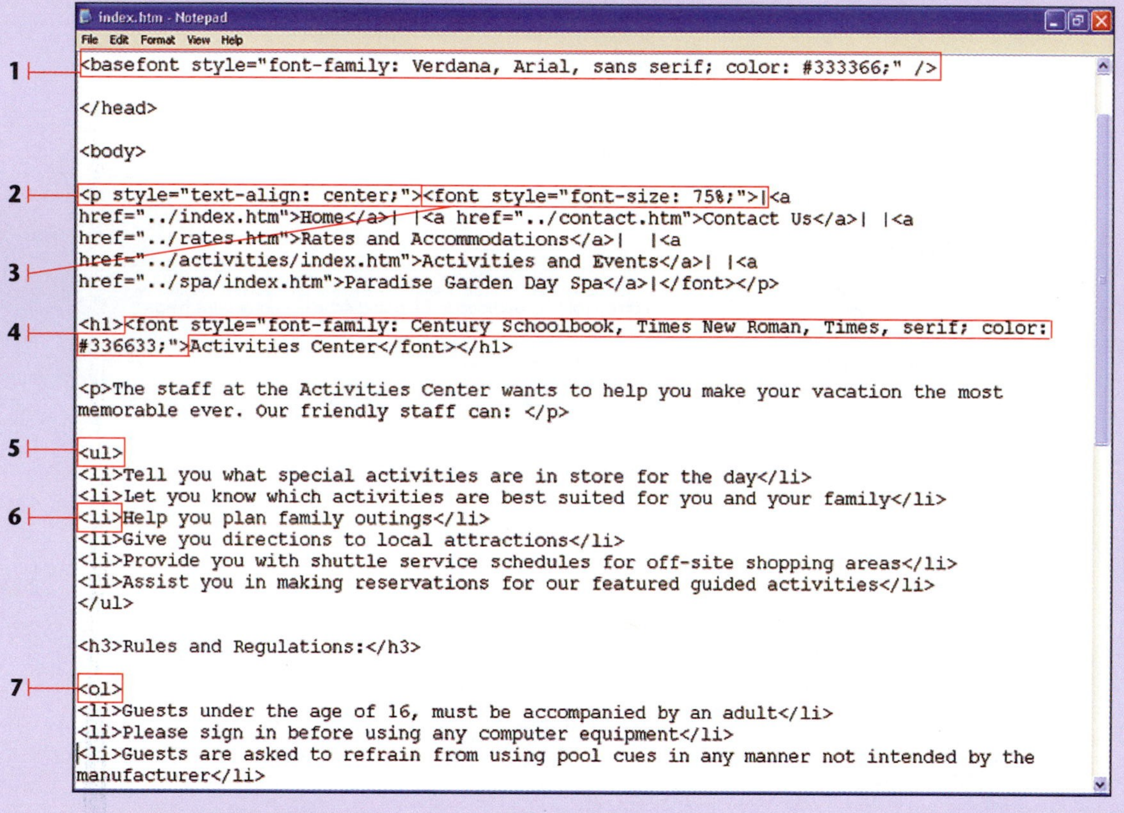

```
index.htm - Notepad
File  Edit  Format  View  Help

1 →  <basefont style="font-family: Verdana, Arial, sans serif; color: #333366;" />

     </head>

     <body>

2 →  <p style="text-align: center;"><font style="font-size: 75%;"><a
     href="../index.htm">Home</a>|  |<a href="../contact.htm">Contact Us</a>|  |<a
     href="../rates.htm">Rates and Accommodations</a>|  |<a
3 →  href="../activities/index.htm">Activities and Events</a>|  |<a
     href="../spa/index.htm">Paradise Garden Day Spa</a>|</font></p>

4 →  <h1><font style="font-family: Century Schoolbook, Times New Roman, Times, serif; color:
     #336633;">Activities Center</font></h1>

     <p>The staff at the Activities Center wants to help you make your vacation the most
     memorable ever. Our friendly staff can: </p>

5 →  <ul>
     <li>Tell you what special activities are in store for the day</li>
     <li>Let you know which activities are best suited for you and your family</li>
6 →  <li>Help you plan family outings</li>
     <li>Give you directions to local attractions</li>
     <li>Provide you with shuttle service schedules for off-site shopping areas</li>
     <li>Assist you in making reservations for our featured guided activities</li>
     </ul>

     <h3>Rules and Regulations:</h3>

7 →  <ol>
     <li>Guests under the age of 16, must be accompanied by an adult</li>
     <li>Please sign in before using any computer equipment</li>
     <li>Guests are asked to refrain from using pool cues in any manner not intended by the
     manufacturer</li>
```

Match each tag with its function.

8. `<ol>`

9. `<ul>`

10. `<font>`

11. `<address>`

12. `<blockquote>`

a. Alters the default white space on either side of the affected text

b. Useful for creating pages that appeal to specific target audiences and for adding personality to your pages

c. Produces a series of list items where a bullet character, instead of a number or letter, designates each list item

d. Produces a series of list items in which the items appear with sequential numbers or letters

e. Alters the physical appearance of a block of content and is recognized by some indexing and cataloging software

Select the best answer from the list of choices.

13. **Which of the following HTML codes could you use to change a character style to bold? (Choose all that apply)**
    a. `<p property="bold">`
    b. `<strong>...</strong>`
    c. `<b>...</b>`
    d. `<font color="#FFCC33">...</font>`

14. **Which one of the following HTML codes does not center-align a paragraph?**
    a. `<p style="text-align: center;">`
    b. `<p align="center">`
    c. `<ol>...</ol>`
    d. `<address style="text-align: center;">`

▼ SKILLS REVIEW

1. **Align text.**
   a. Start your text editor, then open the **salon.htm** file from your paradise/spa directory in the place where you save your site files. (If you did not complete the Skills Review in Unit B, see your instructor for a copy of the files you need.)
   b. In your text editor, locate the level-one heading that begins with "<h1 id="top" >Aphrodite's..." at the top of the page content section, then click directly before the > in the <h1> tag.
   c. Insert a space, then type the code `style="text-align: center;"` to center the page heading on the page.
   d. Apply the centered style you used on the page heading to both navigation bars and the "questions or comments" paragraph near the bottom of the page.
   e. Save the page, then open it in your browser to verify that the page heading, both navigation bars, and the questions and comments paragraph are centered.

2. **Format characters.**
   a. In your text editor, locate the line near the top of the page that starts with, "<p>Aphrodite's Salon full-service hair and nail salon", click directly before the phrase "full-service", then enter an `<em>` tag.
   b. Click directly after "full-service," then enter the closing tag `</em>`.
   c. Locate the "Limited-time specials" section heading near the bottom of the page.
   d. Apply the emphasized formatting to the "Limited-time specials" text using the same method you applied in Steps a and b above.
   e. Locate the line that begins "* Summer Special:".
   f. Click just before the *, then enter `<strong>`.
   g. Click just after the colon following the word "Special," enter a closing `</strong>` tag, then save your work.
   h. Reload the **salon.htm** page in your browser to verify that your formatting appears.

3. **Define an address block.**
   a. Return to your code, locate the questions or comments paragraph that you centered earlier, then click directly after the p in the opening paragraph tag.
   b. Press **[Backspace]**, then type `address`.
   c. If necessary, modify the content so that you are listed as the contact source.
   d. Locate the closing paragraph tag after </a> and change the closing paragraph tag into a closing address tag, then save your work.
   e. Reload the **salon.htm** file in your browser to verify that the contact paragraph is now an address block with italicized text.

4. **Control font selection.**
   a. In your text editor, locate the head section of the salon.htm page, click after </title>, then press **[Enter]** twice.
   b. Enter the code `<basefont style="font-family: Franklin Gothic Book, Arial, Helvetica, sans serif;" />`.
   c. Locate the level-one page heading at the top of the body section, click directly before the word "Aphrodite's," then enter the code `<font style="font-family: Pristina, Viner Hand ITC, Script MT Bold, serif;">`.

    d. Click between the word "Salon" and the </h1>, then type `</font>`.

    e. Save your work.

    f. Reload the page in your browser to verify that all the text on the page appears in a sans serif font and that the page heading appears in a decorative or serif font.

5. Customize fonts.

    a. In your text editor, locate the level-one page heading at the top of the page, click after the semicolon and before the closing quotation mark inside the opening font tag, then press **[Spacebar]**.

    b. Enter the code `color: #336633;`

    c. In the "Summer special" paragraph near the bottom of the document, click before the asterisk (*), then add a font tag that includes a color style set to `#FF3333;`

    d. Click directly after the colon (:) in the same line, then insert the `</font>` tag.

    e. Click directly before the first square bracket in the top-level navigation bar, then enter an opening font tag with a code that sets the font-size at 80% of the default font.

    f. Move to the end of the navigation bar and set a closing font tag directly before </p>, then save your work.

    g. Reload the **salon.htm** page in your browser to verify that the text color is changed in the heading and in the "Summer special" paragraph, and that the navigation bar appears smaller than the rest of the text on the page.

6. Create ordered lists.

    a. In your text editor, locate the line beginning with "<p>Apollo's haircut" under the level-three heading "Hair Care" near the top of the file, click after the <p>, then type `Aphrodite's has a number of hair-care services to make you feel like a god or goddess. View our list below:</p>`.

    b. Press **[Enter]** twice, enter the code `<ol>`, then press **[Enter]**.

    c. Enter the opening list item tag `<li>` before "Apollo's", then replace the line-break tag at the end of the line with the closing list item tag, `</li>`.

    d. Repeat Step c on the following lines through the line that begins "Chemical straightening." Replace the </p> with a closing ordered list tag. (*Hint*: The link tag and the Thermacore text are part of the same line.)

    e. Click before the Return to Menu link at the bottom of the list and enter the code `<p>`. (*Hint*: Recall that you deleted the original opening paragraph tag at the start of the parent list.)

    f. Save your file, then reload the page in your Web browser to verify that the ordered list appears as shown in Figure C-20.

7. Create unordered lists.

    a. In your text editor, locate the line <p>Eyebrow shaping - $18.00
, under the level-three heading tag near the bottom of the page, replace the opening paragraph tag with an opening unordered list tag, then press **[Enter]**.

    b. If necessary, click before "Eyebrow," and type the code to start a list item, then at the end of the line, replace the line break tag with a closing list item tag.

    c. Repeat Step b in the next five lines, adding opening list item tags and replacing the line break tags with closing list item tags.

FIGURE C-20

Aphrodite's Salon

|Paradise Mountain Resort| |Day Spa| |Spa Services| |Spa Packages| |Aphrodite's Salon| |Resort Activities|

Aphrodite's Salon *full-service* hair and nail salon - services include:

|Hair Care| |Facials| |Depilatory Services| |Makeup| |Specials|

Hair Care

Aphrodite's has a number of hair-care services to make you feel like a god or goddess. View our list below:

1. Apollo's haircut - $18.00
2. Aphrodite's haircut - $40.00
3. Shampoo and styling - $35.00
4. Single process color - $65.00
5. Highlighting/foil work - Partial - $55.00
6. Highlighting/foil work - Full - $85.00
7. Permanent - Short hair - $65.00
8. Permanent - Long hair - $95.00
9. Thermacore Therapy - $45.00
10. Chemical straightening - $65.00

    d. Press **[Enter]** after the final </li> tag, type the code to end the unordered list, press **[Enter]**, then type the code `<p>` to restore the opening paragraph tag that was removed from the beginning of the list section.

▼ SKILLS REVIEW (CONTINUED)

e. Use the steps above to format the content under the level-three heading "Makeup" as an unordered list, then save your work.

f. Reload the page in your browser to verify that the unordered lists appears correctly, then print the page.

g. Save and close **salon.htm**, then transfer your updated file to your remote directory.

▼ INDEPENDENT CHALLENGE 1

You are developing a Web site for your new resort rental business, Star Vacations. You want to use the skills you have learned to enhance your site and to highlight one of your new featured resorts. You've decided to use two primary fonts, Arial—a sans serif font—for the page content, and Lucida Calligraphy—a more modern, serif font—for the page headings. As alternate fonts, you have chosen Magneto and serif. You also want to apply special formatting and organize some of your content in lists to emphasize some of the new resort's amenities.

a. Open the **htm_C-4.txt** file from the place where you store your Data Files, then save it as **IslandSeas.htm** in your vacations folder in the place where you save your site files.

b. Use the basefont tag to set the page font family to Arial and specify an alternate font choice of sans serif, then set the page text color as `#000066`.

c. Apply a style to center the level-two heading at the top of the page as well as the level-three heading that follows it.

d. Add `<font>...</font>` tags to all the page headings and specify a style that changes the font to Lucida Calligraphy with alternate fonts Magneto, and serif, then include a style that changes the color of the affected text to the aqua color, `#009999`. (*Hint*: If your system does not have Magneto or Lucida Calligraphy, use another readable calligraphic font or choose a serif font that you think most users will have on their systems.)

e. Format the contact paragraph at the bottom of the page as an address block.

f. Locate the paragraph that begins with "`<p>`Nestled serenely," then format the words "you've DISCOVERED PARADISE" at the end of the paragraph by applying strong and em formatting to the text.

g. Locate the section of text that begins with "Rollaway Bed," and use the `<ol>...</ol>` and `<li>...</li>` tags to format the text starting with "Rollaway Bed" through "Hot Tub/Whirlpool," as a numbered list.

h. Use the `<ul>...</ul>` and `<li>...</li>` tags to format the paragraphs under Snorkeling Excursions and Tours into bulleted lists.

i. Update the "Page Modified by" paragraph, using your name and today's date. Save the file and preview it in your browser, then print the page.

j. Close the file, then transfer it to your remote vacations directory.

Advanced Challenge Exercises

- Open **htm_C-5.txt** from your Data Files folder, then save it as **faq.htm**, replacing the existing file.
- Locate the comment tag, `<!-- Format the paragraphs below this comment as a bulleted list. -->`, then format the paragraphs below it as a bulleted list.
- Locate the comment that reads `<!-- Format the items below this comment as a nested list using lowercase letters. -->`, then format the next three lines as directed in the comment tag. (*Hint*: Do not format any Return to top links.)
- Add your name and the date to the "Page Modified by" paragraph at the bottom of the page, save and print your work, close all programs, then transfer your updated page to your remote directory on the server.

▼ INDEPENDENT CHALLENGE 2

The water-conservation Web site you have been developing for your employer, Metro Water, is coming along nicely. Now that you have created several informational pages and linked them to your home page, you are ready to start enhancing those pages by formatting text, adding lists, and aligning page elements. You also want to use colors that will make your site visitors think about water and nature.

a. In your text editor, open **inside.htm** from your Data File location, then save it as **inside.htm** in the water folder in the place where you save your site files, replacing the file if prompted.

b. Format the top-level navigation bar to align in the center of the page, then use a font tag to make the navigation bar display at 85 percent of the size of the rest of the text on the page.

c. Copy the alignment and font formatting from the navigation bar paragraph to the jump menu in the middle of the page and to the "For more information" paragraph at the bottom of the page.

d. Use a basefont tag to change the default page font to Verdana and specify Arial, Helvetica, and sans serif as alternate fonts, then specify the default page text color as #333333.

e. Change the color of the level-two page heading to #000066 and change the page heading font to Georgia, specifying alternate fonts Times New Roman, Times, and serif.

f. Locate the sentence that ends with "substantially reduce your water usage." At the end of the line, type `Every drop helps . . . You CAN make a difference!`

g. Use logical formatting styles to italicize "You CAN make a difference!" and to cause the word "CAN" to be displayed in boldfaced type, then emphasize the word "CAN" even more by making it red. (*Hint*: Refer to the browser-safe color chart in the appendix of this text for a list of color codes.)

h. Format the questions in the second paragraph on the page as an ordered list.

i. Add your name and update the date at the bottom of the page, then save your file and preview it in your browser.

j. Transfer your updated page to your remote directory.

Advanced Challenge Exercises

- Format the paragraphs under the page headings, "General Tips," "In the Kitchen," "Conserving Water in the Bathroom," and "What About Well Water" as bulleted items, creating a new list for each section. (Hint: Do not make the page headings part of the lists.)
- Use the type attribute on each of your bulleted lists to make the bullets in each list appear as square.
- Save your page, then view it in your browser.
- Transfer your updated page to your remote directory.

▼ INDEPENDENT CHALLENGE 3

You are concerned about text colors and lists because you know that they are part of the accessibility initiative. You are interested in learning more about the use of text colors and their part in making Web sites more accessible. You want to use the latest and most elegant methods of creating lists, but you are concerned about accessibility. You also want to find out what else you can do to make your site more pleasing to customers.

a. Go to the Online Companion for this book and locate the links for this unit. Click the W3C Web Accessibility page link and review the information regarding HTML color contrast in section 9.1, then write one or two paragraphs answering the following questions:

1. How can the use of text color make your site more user friendly?
2. How would you test your site to see whether color contrast is sufficient to be read by people with color deficiencies?

b. From the color section on the W3C Web Accessibility pages, click to follow the Lighthouse links until you arrive at the Lighthouse site.

▼ INDEPENDENT CHALLENGE 3 (CONTINUED)

c. Type "Color" in the search box to find information about effective color contrast, then find what three things a designer can do to make effective color choices.

d. Write your name at the top of your report and print the page.

▼ INDEPENDENT CHALLENGE 4

Now that you've studied formatting and creating lists, you are ready to add these features to the pages on your Web site.

a. Based on your site content and purpose, determine what formatting your site requires, then make a list describing your choice of colors and font families.

- Tell why you have chosen each of your font and color style elements.
- Plan what your page background color will eventually be and make sure it contrasts with your font color. (*Hint*: If you are going to use a dark background and light text, you may have to choose a temporary font color until you learn how to set page backgrounds.)

b. Format your home page using at least two font families in appropriate sizes, with at least one color change from the default font color.

c. Add at least one list to one of your pages.

d. Add appropriate content to your home page. (*Hint*: Content can be changed as necessary as your site develops.)

e. Apply formatting to your site navigation bar, then apply it to all pages.

f. Add a centered address block to your home page or your about_me.htm page, then apply other alignment formatting to the rest of your site elements to achieve the look you want.

g. Preview the modified pages in your browser, then print them and mark on the printouts the areas you modified.

▼ VISUAL WORKSHOP

As you develop the PC history Web site for Bits and PCs, you have obtained quite a bit of information on the history of Apple Computers. Because Apple played such a large role in making personal computing accessible to a wider audience, you want to present this chronology right away. Open the file **htm_C-6.txt** from the place where you store your Data Files, then save it as **apple_hist.htm** in the History folder in your bitspcs site file location. Add a page heading and apply color, alignment, font, and list formatting to resemble the Web page shown in Figure C-22. When you finish, link the file to your apple page in your BitsPCs history folder and cause the page to open in a new window. Save and print the apple.htm page code, then preview it in your browser. Click the new link and print the page from the browser window. (*Hint:* The basefont is Arial.)

FIGURE C-22

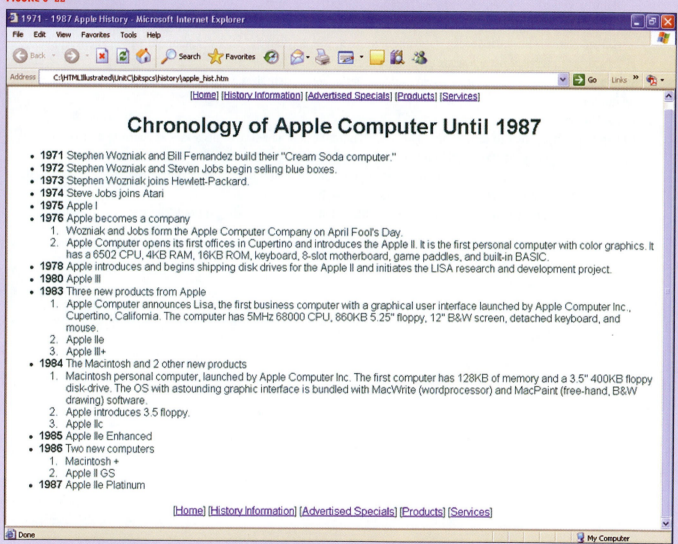

UNIT
D
HTML

Adding Graphics and Multimedia

OBJECTIVES

Plan graphics use

Insert images

Optimize images

Specify image size

Add a background image

Link images

Insert an image map

Explore multimedia options

Use multimedia

While text is often the most significant element of a Web page, graphics are also an important part of Web design. In addition to sometimes conveying information better than text, graphics can make a page easier to read and can give a page a unique style and mood. When resized and optimized for quick download, images can effectively serve as graphic content, page backgrounds, and navigation elements. Pages usually contain static graphics, but many also supplement content with multimedia, including animated graphics, sound, and video. You are leading the team of designers who are working to create the new Web site for Paradise Mountain Family Resort. Because so many of the resort's special features are better described in pictures, you want to use images to enhance the Web site and to better convey the information you are presenting. You also want to look into the possibility of using multimedia to further enhance the site.

Planning Graphics Use

The use of graphics is a popular and practical way to enrich Web pages. However, as with other design tools, moderation is the key to effective graphics use. A Web page filled with text but devoid of graphics can be uninviting and difficult for users to read. On the other hand, devoting too much space to graphics can overwhelm and distract users from the focus of the page. To use graphics most effectively, first clarify the goal of your Web page or Web site. Then plan and incorporate a graphics style that supports your layout without overwhelming it. Figure D-1 shows a Web page that balances text and graphics. You plan to incorporate the Paradise Mountain Family Resort logo into the Web site you are creating. You also want to add some graphics that depict some of the resort's many activities.

DETAILS

While planning the use of graphics, it's important to keep these few guidelines in mind:

QUICK TIP

To avoid potential problems with image display, make sure that all of your image files use lowercase extensions. If you are using a Windows system and cannot see your file extensions, click Folder Options on the Windows Explorer Tools menu, click the View tab, then uncheck Hide extensions for known file types, as shown in Figure D-2.

- ### Use supported file formats

  Unlike Web page text, which is actually a part of the HTML document that creates a Web page, Web page graphics are separate files that are referenced in a page's HTML code. Images that are displayed as content on the page are called **inline images** because the code used to **call** (pull in) the images is written "inline" with the other code on the page. Many graphic file formats exist, but only three are widely supported by Web browsers: GIF, JPG, and PNG. You can tell the format of a file by checking the filename's extension. For example, the name of a JPG file ends with .jpg or .jpeg. As you create or acquire graphics for your Web site, make sure they are GIF, JPG, or PNG files. When you request graphic files from others, you must either specify that they be in one of the three Web-compatible formats or you must have the ability to convert them into a Web-compatible format. Table D-1 gives more information about each of these three formats.

- ### Add alternate text

  Although images are widely supported by most of today's browsers, not all users are able to benefit from image-based content. Some users still surf the Web on computers without access to high-speed connections and choose not to view images in order to speed up Web page download time. What is more important to consider, however, is the fact that there are many individuals who are unable to view Web page images because of a visual impairment. To accommodate these users, it's important that Web pages convey the same information with or without the images. The HTML tag for adding an image to a Web page also supports an attribute that allows you to specify a text alternative that appears when your image does not. As you plan how you will incorporate graphics into your layout, you must also determine a text alternative that is appropriate for each graphic.

- ### Keep file size small

  Web page download time is an important usability factor in which the size of graphics plays a large role. Download time is the amount of time it takes for the page and its associated files to transfer from their location on a Web server to a user's computer. HTML files alone are relatively small, and, without their graphics, most download within a few seconds—even over the slowest Internet connection. Graphic files, however, can be much larger and can take much longer to download. High-speed technologies such as **DSL** (digital subscriber line), **ISDN** (Integrated Services Digital Network), **cable modem**, **T-1**, and **T-3** connections that allow faster downloads are becoming more widespread. Universities and many large corporations also have Web connections that enable near-instantaneous downloads. However, many parts of the world still use slower dial-up connections; this means that your design should ensure that your pages are easily viewable over all types of Internet connections.

- ### Use graphics wisely

  Some novice designers believe that if a few images are good, a lot of images are better. This is usually not the case. Placing too many images on a page can make the page difficult to understand and can distract the user from your intended message. The most reliable way to effectively use images on your Web pages is to restrict their use to those that support your page's structure and function. It is important that there be a purpose for every element, including images, on your page.

FIGURE D-1: Web page with text and graphics

Logo image

Top-border background image

Inline image

FIGURE D-2: Displaying file extensions in Windows Explorer

Hide extensions for known file types unchecked

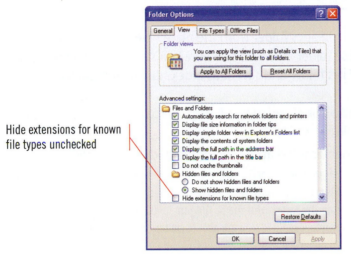

TABLE D-1: Web-compatible graphic formats

format	best for	notes
GIF	Line art and animations; also supports 1-bit transparency, which sets a single color as the transparent color	A proprietary format by CompuServ/Unisys: No licensing or fees required for using, viewing, or selling GIF images; companies producing software programs that *create* GIF images must pay licensing fees to CompuServ/Unisys
JPG (or JPEG)	Photographs and other images with gradient color	Variable compression allows a trade-off between better image quality and smaller file size
PNG	Line art and photographs, also supports 32-bit (gradient) transparency	Recently developed format; browser support not as widespread; in many browsers 32-bit transparency does not appear as expected; file size might be significantly larger or smaller depending upon image content—test image in more than one format

Clues to Use

Changing image file formats

While you can use your system's file management utility, such as Windows Explorer or Desktop Manager, to edit the name of an image file, you cannot use it to *convert* an image file from one type to another. In other words, you can use the utility to rename the file to use a lowercase extension, to remove spaces from folders or file names, to give the file a new name, or to change a JPG file extension from .jpeg to .jpg because .jpeg and .jpg, like .txt and .htm, are the same file type. But you cannot change a file type by renaming a file, such as changing logo.bmp to logo.gif, because BMP (bit mapped) files and GIF (Graphic Interchange Format) files are different file types. To convert a file from one type to another, you must open that file in an image-editing program and *convert* it to another file type.

Inserting Images

HTML uses the `<img />` tag to display images on a Web page. Because the `<img />` tag is not part of a tag set, you must close it by typing a closing slash at the end of the tag, just as you do for line break tags. Like the opening tag for a link, the `<img />` tag always requires an attribute. This required attribute for all image tags is the source attribute, src, which indicates the name and location of the graphic file. Another important image attribute is the alt attribute. Also known as alt statements, **alt attributes** are part of the Web Accessibility Initiative (WAI) because they supply alternative text that appears in the browser if for any reason the image does not appear. Alternative text is also used by screen readers to describe your graphics or your graphic links when you use graphics to create navigation bars. It is, therefore, critically important that you use good alt statements—simply stating the image's file name or size is not a good use of alt statements. The `<img />` tag supports many other attributes—several of which are explained in Table D-2. You want to add a logo graphic to the Paradise Mountain Family Resort's home page.

STEPS

TROUBLE

If you have already created an images folder in your paradise site, open the paradise\images folder from your Data Files directory and copy all of the images, then paste them into your existing images folder.

1. **Copy the paradise\images folder from the place where you store your Data Files and paste it into the paradise folder in the place where you store your site files; open htm_D-1.txt from your Data Files folder and save it as index.htm in your paradise folder, replacing the existing file**

   You want to try out the look of your page with a sans serif font, so you have removed the font reference from the basefont formatting.

2. **Locate the level-one heading at the top of the body section, click directly after `<h1>`, then type `<img src="images/pm_logo1.jpg" alt="Paradise Mountain Family Resort" />`**

   The code you typed adds the new company logo inline with the level-one page heading. The src attribute value maps a relative path from the index.htm file to the pm_logo1.jpg file in the images directory. By storing all of your image files in your images folder, you are able to better organize your site. Now you want to add a second image to the page.

QUICK TIP

Be sure to insert a single space between the closing quotation mark and the closing slash (/) in the image code.

3. **Locate the line that starts with `<p>` Located just outside of, click directly before `<p>`, type `<img src="images/trail_ride1.jpg" alt="The end of the trail -- A Paradise Mountain guide and guests return from a long day's ride exploring the resort wilderness." />`, press [Enter] twice, then save your work**

4. **Start your Web browser, then open index.htm from your paradise site folder**

   The resort logo and the photograph both appear on the left side of the page, and the page text has been pushed below the photo, leaving large amounts of white space, as shown in Figure D-3. Setting image alignment properties can help correct these problems.

QUICK TIP

The `<img />` align values set image alignment in relation to page text, not the page margins

5. **Click the text editor program button on the taskbar, click directly before `/>` inside the trail_ride1.jpg image tag, type `align="right"`, press [Spacebar], then save your file and reload it in your browser**

   Setting the `align="right"` property instructs the photograph to align on the right side of the text.

6. **Click the text editor program button on the taskbar, click directly before `/>` in the logo image tag, type `align="middle"`, press [Spacebar], then save your work**

   Your code should resemble Figure D-4.

7. **Reload the index.htm page in your browser, then rest the pointer over the photo**

   The heading text fills the white space to the right of the logo, and the alternate text appears, as shown in Figure D-5.

FIGURE D-3: Images with large amounts of white space

Logo and image
left-aligned on page

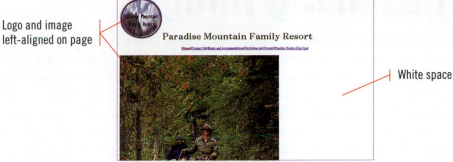

White space

FIGURE D-4: `<img />` tag code with attributes

Logo image inside
heading block

Image alt attribute

Image tag for
photo image

Image align
attribute

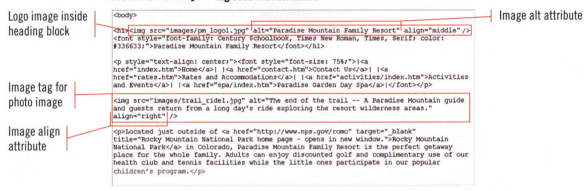

FIGURE D-5: Paradise Mountain home page with aligned images and alt statement

Logo image with
middle alignment

Right-aligned image

Hovering mouse pointer
displays alt text

TABLE D-2: Commonly used `</img>` tag attributes

attribute	specifies	possible values	examples
src	Name and location of image file	Name, including extension and path of image file	`src="filename.jpg"` or `src="filepath/filename.jpg"`
alt	Alternate text for users who don't use graphics	Almost any text, including spacing and punctuation—but not double quotation marks	`alt="Guests enjoy resort activities"`
align	Image's alignment in relation to page text, not in relation to page margins	Left, right, top, texttop, middle, absmiddle, baseline, bottom, absbottom, and center	`align="right"`
height	Image's display height in pixels	Whole number representing image height—do not use to resize image	`height="200"`
width	Image's display width in pixels	Whole number representing image width—not for use in resizing image	`width="275"`
border	Image border size	Whole number representing border width in pixels	`border="2"`

Optimizing Images

A picture may be worth a thousand words, but on the Web, that picture could also take up a thousand times more disk space. Images that are excessively large in file size cause problems for end users because large file sizes translate into long download times. Even one large image file can cause your page to download slowly. If you want your pages to download quickly, you must learn to optimize your images for display on the Web. To **optimize** an image is to make sure that it is properly sized and formatted for Web display. The four main factors affecting image file size are resolution, dimension, file type, and color depth. **Resolution** is specified in pixels per inch (ppi). **Pixels** (short for "picture elements"—abbreviated "px") are the points of light that make up the display on a computer screen. **Dimension** is the physical size of your image in terms of width and height. You can control dimension by changing file resolution, cropping out unnecessary elements, or by resizing the file in a graphics-editing program. **File type** is the format in which your file is saved, and **color depth** is the number of colors an image uses. You want your pages to download quickly, so you investigate methods of optimizing Web images for faster download time.

DETAILS

You can optimize your Web images by doing the following:

QUICK TIP

While many image-editing tasks, such as adjusting color, sharpness, and contrast, are better accomplished at higher resolutions, always be sure to set your file resolution to 72 ppi before cropping or resizing your Web image.

- #### Use the proper Web image resolution

  Print media uses dpi (dots per inch) to specify image resolution. A higher resolution for print media is advantageous because high-resolution images produce a better printed output. On the Web, however, high-resolution images take up too much file space and browser "real estate." The optimum resolution for Web images is 72 ppi. This might not seem like much, but as shown in Figure D-6, it is perfect for screen display. Sometimes, setting the resolution to 72 ppi is all that is required to optimize your Web image.

- #### Crop out unnecessary elements

  The next step in optimizing your images is to crop out any unnecessary image elements. Web designers often use photos or other images that contain unnecessary information. By cropping the image, you can trim unnecessary elements and cut the file size dramatically. Cropping an image can also make it more interesting by focusing on on the image subject.

- #### Resize the image

  After you have changed your file's resolution and cropped out unnecessary information, your image may still be too large for effective display. When selecting an output size for your Web images, it is important to consider browser dimensions and size your page elements accordingly. Most users have monitor resolution settings of 800 × 600 or 1024 × 768. Therefore graphic banners and headings should not exceed 700 pixels in width, and page content images should not exceed more than 300 pixels in width or height.

- #### Use the proper file format

  The format you choose for saving your Web images can greatly affect the image's file size. Save flat-color, clipart-type graphics as GIF or PNG files and save full-color images, such as photographs and images with gradient fills, in JPG format. Improperly saved images could be more than 10 times larger in file size than one that is saved in the proper format.

QUICK TIP

You can use image-editing programs such as Adobe Photoshop or ImageReady to change file resolution or reduce the number of available colors. If you do not own a full-scale image-editing program, you can search the Web for free programs.

- #### Control the color depth

  Color depth is defined by the number of bits per pixel that can be displayed on a computer screen. In a computer system, data is stored in bits. Each color bit represents two colors because it has a value of 0 or 1 (on or off). The more bits per pixel an image has, the more colors can be displayed. Since each bit represents two colors, it is easy to work out the number of colors for the various color depths. The number of possible colors is two to the power of the number of bits per pixel. Table D-3 demonstrates the relationship between color bits and the number of available colors. Some flat-color images use only four or five colors, but are saved with an 8-bit color depth (256 available colors—the maximum color depth for GIF or PNG-8 images). When this is the case, reducing the number of available colors can substantially reduce the file size of your image.

  Figure D-6 shows examples of a Web page before and after image optimization.

Optimized image fits in one screen (file size: less than 28KB)

Page after optimization

Oversized image scrolls off page (file size: nearly 569 KB)

Page before optimization

TABLE D-3: Color depth (bits) and available colors

color bit number	mathematic formula	number of available colors
1-bit	2^1 (2)	2
2-bit	2^2 (2 × 2)	4
3-bit	2^3 (2 × 2 × 2)	8
4-bit	2^4 (2 × 2 × 2 × 2)	16
5-bit	2^5 (2 × 2 × 2 × 2 × 2)	32
6-bit	2^6 (2 × 2 × 2 × 2 × 2 × 2)	64
7-bit	2^7 (2 × 2 × 2 × 2 × 2 × 2 × 2)	128
8-bit (the greatest number of colors available for a GIF or PNG-8 image)	2^8 (2 × 2 × 2 × 2 × 2 × 2 × 2 × 2)	256
24-bit (the greatest number of colors available for a JPG or PNG-24 image)	2^{24} (2 × 2 × 2 × 2 × 2 × 2 × 2 × 2 × 2 × 2 × 2 × 2 × 2 × 2 × 2 × 2 × 2 × 2 × 2 × 2 × 2 × 2 × 2 × 2)	16,777,216 (also called "millions of colors" in some monitor settings)
32-bit (generally refers to monitor color quality—not used for Web images)	2^{32} (2 × 2 × 2 × 2 × 2 × 2 × 2 × 2 × 2 × 2 × 2 × 2 × 2 × 2 × 2 × 2 × 2 × 2 × 2 × 2 × 2 × 2 × 2 × 2 × 2 × 2 × 2 × 2 × 2 × 2 × 2 × 2)	4,294,267,296 (also called "billions of colors" in some monitor settings)

Specifying Image Size

As you learned earlier, the <img /> tag supports many attributes, which are applied collectively as an attribute string. Among the attributes that should be added to your image attribute string are **width** and **height**, which specify a graphic's display dimensions in terms of pixels. An important use of width and height attributes is to reserve space on the page for the graphic as the page loads. This practice eliminates an event known as **text jumping**, an annoying condition in which text on a page begins to load and then must "jump" out of the way to make room for an image that appears later in the page-load process. Eliminating text jumping allows your pages to load more smoothly and gives the illusion that they load more quickly. Two other attributes that are usually part of an image attribute string are hspace and vspace. The **hspace** attribute controls the amount of horizontal white space and **vspace** controls the amount of vertical white space around an image. You want to add the height and width attributes to your page images to make the page load more smoothly. You also want to use an optimized image in the body of your document and add some additional white space around it.

STEPS

TROUBLE

If you are using Internet Explorer and the Internet Explorer information bar appears telling you that Internet Explorer has "restricted the file from showing active content," right-click the information bar, choose Allow Blocked Content from the shortcut menu, then click Yes.

1. **In your browser, right-click the Paradise Mountain Family Resort logo in the upper-left corner of the page, then click Properties on the shortcut menu**

   As shown in Figure D-7, the Properties dialog box appears. You can see that the image is 159 pixels wide by 156 pixels high and that the image file size is 5342 bytes or slightly more than 5 KB — there are 1024 bytes in a kilobyte.

2. **Click OK to close the dialog box**

3. **Click the text editor program button on the taskbar, locate the image tag that references pm_logo1.jpg, click just before the closing /, type `width="159" height="156"`, then press [Spacebar]**

4. **Locate the <img /> tag that references the graphic trail_ride1.jpg, click just after the "1" in the file name, press [Backspace], then type 2**

   You changed the source file to trail_ride2.jpg, a file that has been optimized for display on the Web. To prevent text jumping, you decide to reserve space for the graphic as the page loads.

5. **Click directly before the closing / in the same tag, then type `hspace="15" vspace="5"`**

   The hspace attribute adds horizontal space between the image and the page elements to the left and right of the image. The vspace attribute adds vertical space above and below the image. Although these attributes have been deprecated by the W3C in favor of CSS formatting, you see them in older pages and find that they still effectively control the amount of space around an image and are valuable tools for use until you are able to learn and apply style sheet formatting.

6. **Press [Spacebar], type `width="261" height="400"`, press [Spacebar], then save your work**

   See Figure D-8.

7. **Click the browser program button in the taskbar, then reload index.htm**

   Your completed page resembles the page shown in Figure D-9, with extra white space around the smaller, optimized image.

Clues to Use

Resizing Images

Although it is possible to use image width and height properties to cause an image to display on a Web page smaller than the image's actual dimensions, it is important that you not use these attributes for such a purpose. A large image with a large file size is still a big image—even if you have managed to make it appear smaller. If you need to use an image that is too large for your page design, use an image-editing program to reduce the file dimensions as well as the file size.

FIGURE D-7: Properties dialog box in browser window

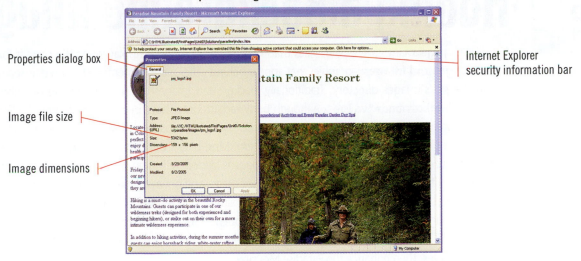

Properties dialog box

Image file size

Image dimensions

Internet Explorer security information bar

FIGURE D-8: Web page code for sized image

Image tag appears in code before other main page content

Align="right" attribute causes image to align to right of content

```
href="index.htm">Home</a>|  |<a href="contact.htm">Contact Us</a>|  |<a
href="rates.htm">Rates and Accommodations</a>|  |<a
href="reserve.htm">Reservations</a>|  |<a href="activities/index.htm">Activities
and Events</a>|  |<a href="spa/index.htm">Paradise Garden Day Spa</a>|</font></p>

<img src="images/trail_ride2.jpg" alt="The end of the trail -- A Paradise Mountain
guide and guests return from a long day's ride exploring the resort wilderness areas."
align="right" hspace="15" vspace="5" width="261" height="400"  />

<p>Located just outside of
<a href="http://www.rmnp.com" target="_blank" title="Rocky Mountain National Park
home page - opens in new window.">Rocky Mountain National Park </a> in Colorado,
Paradise Mountain Family Resort is the perfect getaway place for the whole family.
```

FIGURE D-9: Paradise Mountain Family Resort home page with optimized image

Extra white space between image and text

Smaller, optimized image

Adding a Background Image

Just as Web page images are separate files that the browser calls up for display when the page is loaded, Web page **background images**—graphics that appear behind other page elements—are stored as separate image files in the site's images directory. Traditionally, background images are specified in the opening body tag `<body>` as `background="value"`. Although body tag attributes have been deprecated by the W3C in favor of more advanced formatting techniques such as CSS, you will most likely have to edit or update pages with body tag attributes, so it is good to know about them. Most background images are very small in both dimension and file size so they display quickly when the page is loaded. Although small, a background image can fill a page because it is **tiled**, meaning that it repeats itself across and down the page until the entire page is filled. A well-designed background tile is **seamless**, making it almost impossible for the viewer to tell where one repetition of the image ends and the next begins. See the appendix for more information on applying body attributes and values. ▦▦ One of your design team members has created a background sampler page. You want to view the samples, then enhance the Paradise Mountain home page by adding a background graphic.

STEPS

1. **In a separate instance of your browser, open the file** bkg_samples.htm **from the samples folder in your paradise\images folder**

2. **Click each of the background samples to view the actual file, clicking the** Back to samples link **after viewing each file, then close the** bkg_samples.htm **browser window**

   You notice that each background image is quite small. You decide that the file pm_bkgnd.gif is the best choice for the Paradise Mountain home page.

3. **Click the** text editor program button **on the taskbar to return to your page code, click inside the** `<body>` **tag, directly before the closing** `>`**, press** [Spacebar]**, then type** `background="images/pm_bkgnd.gif"`

   The body's background attribute is similar to the src attribute of the image tag in that it directs the browser to find and display an image.

4. **Save your work, click the** browser program button **on the taskbar, then reload** index.htm

   As Figure D-10 shows, the small background image repeats, creating a border across the top of the page. However, a white square appears around the logo image. Because JPG images do not support transparency, the white matte—solid-colored, non-image area of a graphic that "frames" the graphic content—is displayed against the blue background image.

5. **Click the** text editor program button **on the taskbar, locate the logo image code, click directly before the closing quotation mark in the image file name, press** [Backspace] **five times, then type** 2.png

   You removed the .jpg file extension, the dot, and the number "1" from the file name. Then you replaced the image with one that supports transparency. You want to move the page content so it is somewhat higher on the page.

QUICK TIP

You can also use the leftmargin and rightmargin attributes in the body tag to control horizontal white space on your page. Some browsers support only the margin attribute, which sets equal left and right margins.

6. **Click directly before the** `>` **in the opening body tag, press** [Spacebar]**, type** `topmargin="5"`**, then save your work**

   Your code should be similar to that shown in Figure D-11. By default, most browsers have a top-border margin of approximately 10 pixels. By setting the topmargin attribute value in the opening body tag to "5," you reduced the size of the top margin and allowed the page content to move up five pixels on the page.

7. **Click the** browser program button **on the taskbar, then reload** index.htm

   As shown in Figure D-12, the logo and heading text have moved up slightly on the page, and the logo graphic no longer appears with a white background.

FIGURE D-10: Home page with background image and logo in JPG format

Logo image appears
in white box

Page background
image

FIGURE D-11: Web page code to adjust graphic elements

Background
image inserted in
opening body tag

```
<body background="images/pm_bkgnd.gif" topmargin="5">

<h1><img src="images/pm_logo2.png" alt="Paradise Mountain Family Resort"
align="middle" width="159" height="156" /><font style="font-family: Century
Schoolbook, Times New Roman, Times, Serif; color: #336633;">Paradise Mountain Family
Resort</font></h1>
```

Call to image file
changed

FIGURE D-12: Web page with transparent PNG-formatted logo and alignment adjustments

Transparent PNG
image replaces
opaque JPG image

Top margin reduced
and image and text
moved

Body content
moved up slightly
on page

Creating effective backgrounds

When you use backgrounds, make sure that there is enough contrast between the text and the background by using body attributes that determine text colors: **text**, for page text; **link**, for unclicked links; **vlink**, for visited links; and **alink**, for active links. In addition to using an image, you also can specify a background color for your Web page. A **background color** is the color that appears behind page text when no background image is supplied, if the background image is specified incorrectly, or when part of the page background image is transparent. You indicate a color in the <body> tag by setting the **bgcolor attribute** equal to the color's hexadecimal equivalent. As with a background image, it is important to select a background color that contrasts well with a page's text.

Linking Images

Just as you can link text, you can also add link formatting to Web page images. To do so, surround the `<img/>` tag with the `<a>...</a>` tag set, and add the appropriate href attribute. When using linked images as site navigation elements, it is good practice to place the images in the same location on every page for a consistent look. Most pages with linked images are more attractive when image borders are set to zero (0) using the `border="0"` attribute and value. Table D-4 lists additional image attributes. You have placed the Paradise Mountain logo in the upper-left corner of the home page and want to add it to your other pages as well. You think the logo would make an excellent link point to help keep users oriented as they view the site.

STEPS

1. Click the text editor program button on the taskbar, drag to select all of the code from the basefont tag through the navigation bar, as shown in Figure D-13, then copy the code

2. Open the contact.htm page in your text editor from the paradise folder in your site file location, click directly before `</head>`, drag to select all of the page code through `</p>` at the end of the site navigation bar, then paste the copied code

   The contact page is updated. You want to add an image link back to your home page.

QUICK TIP

Link titles may not appear on linked images with alt statements, but they still provide information for users with disabilities.

3. Click between the `<h1>` and the `<img` in the heading and logo section at the top of the page content code area, then type `<a href="index.htm" title="Return to Paradise Mountain Family Resort Home page">`

TROUBLE

If your image border is blue, you either have never displayed your home page in the browser, or your file path is incorrect.

4. Click directly after the `/>` at the end of the image tag, type `</a>`, save your work, click the browser program button on the taskbar, open contact.htm in your browser, then move the mouse pointer over the Paradise Mountain graphic logo

   The mouse pointer changes to a pointing hand, letting the site visitors know that the image is linked. Browsers handle alt statements and link titles differently. As shown in Figure D-14, the image alt statement rather than the link title appears in Internet Explorer. (Other browsers may display the link title rather than the alt statement.) In Internet Explorer, the image is bounded by a purple box, which spoils your page design.

5. Click the Paradise Mountain logo

   The Paradise Mountain home page opens.

6. Click the text editor program button on the taskbar to return to your contact.htm page code, click directly after the closing quotation mark following the align attribute "middle," press [Spacebar], type `border="0"`, then save your work

7. Click the browser program button on the taskbar, then click the Contact Us link to reload the contact page

   The linked logo now appears without the border, as shown in Figure D-15.

8. Return to your contact.htm source code, drag to select all the code from the basefont tag through the `</p>` of the top navigation bar, then copy the code

   You want to work with your rates.htm page next, so you begin by updating the logo and navigation bar with your most recent changes.

9. Open the rates.htm page in your text editor, drag to select from `</head>` through the closing `</p>` of the navigation bar paragraph, paste the copied code, then save your work

FIGURE D-13: Selected code for copying

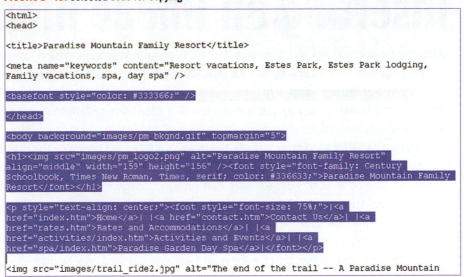

```html
<html>
<head>

<title>Paradise Mountain Family Resort</title>

<meta name="keywords" content="Resort vacations, Estes Park, Estes Park lodging,
Family vacations, spa, day spa" />

<basefont style="color: #333366;" />

</head>

<body background="images/pm_bkgnd.gif" topmargin="5">

<h1><img src="images/pm_logo2.png" alt="Paradise Mountain Family Resort"
align="middle" width="159" height="156" /><font style="font-family: Century
Schoolbook, Times New Roman, Times, serif; color: #336633;">Paradise Mountain Family
Resort</font></h1>

<p style="text-align: center;"><font style="font-size: 75%;">|<a
href="index.htm">Home</a>| |<a href="contact.htm">Contact Us</a>| |<a
href="rates.htm">Rates and Accommodations</a>| |<a
href="activities/index.htm">Activities and Events</a>| |<a
href="spa/index.htm">Paradise Garden Day Spa</a>|</font></p>

<img src="images/trail_ride2.jpg" alt="The end of the trail -- A Paradise Mountain
```

FIGURE D-14: Web page containing linked graphic in Internet Explorer

Linked logo image
displays border

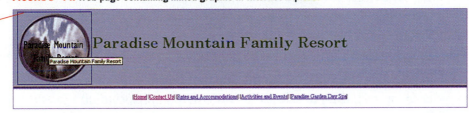

FIGURE D-15: Logo without border

Border="0" attribute
removes border from
linked image

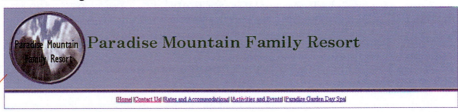

TABLE D-4: Additional `<img />` attributes

attribute	specifies	possible values	example
border	The width of an optional border placed around the image; by default, a blue border appears around a linked graphic	A number representing this width, in pixels; to remove default border from linked images, set value to 0	border="0"
vspace	The size of the space between the top and bottom of the graphic and the surrounding page elements; short for "vertical space"	A number representing this space, in pixels	vspace="5"
hspace	The size of the space between the left and right edges of the graphic, and the surrounding page elements; short for "horizontal space"	A number representing this space, in pixels	hspace="5"

Inserting an Image Map

Although the ability to link an image to a Web file is useful in Web page design, sometimes a single graphic conveys information that's appropriate for more than one link. You can take advantage of such an image by making it into an **image map**, a graphic that has different areas that are linked to different Web files. Each of these areas, known as **hot spots**, is defined with a coordinate system that uses the `<map>` and `<area>` tags. The image map information associated with a graphic can be located anywhere in a Web document; you specify a name for each map, and use the `usemap` attribute to reference the map name in the `<img />` tag that uses it. Because it is a challenging task to specify the exact pixel coordinates of areas within a graphic, most Web designers use software that simplifies image map creation by allowing you to draw the hot spots over the graphic. Table D-5 shows the available attributes for an image map.  You designed a graphic that shows a floor plan of a two-bedroom suite at Paradise Mountain Family Resort. You also created an image map for the graphic; the image map splits the image into seven hot spots. You want to insert the image map code into the Rates and Accommodations page you are designing for the resort.

STEPS

1. **Start another instance of your text editor program, then open the file imagemapParadise.txt from the paradise folder in the location where you store your Data Files**

   This file contains your image map information. Along with inserting the correct values in the `<map>` and `<area>` tags, the graphics software you used to create it also generated the `<img />` tag for the associated graphic.

2. **Drag to select all the text in the file, copy it to the clipboard, then close the file**

3. **In your rates.htm file, locate the line that begins with `<p><strong><em>Watch this space!`, drag to select the entire paragraph including `<p>` and `</p>`, then press [Delete] twice**

   You deleted the placeholder information and the blank line after it.

4. **Find the paragraph that ends with `or to make reservations.</p>`, click after `</p>`, press [Enter] twice, type `<p>Click a spot in the map below to view the rooms in one of our 2-bedroom units.</p>`, press [Enter] twice, paste the image map code from the clipboard, then press [Enter]**

   Figure D-16 shows the image map code in the Web page.

5. **Save your work, click the browser program button on the taskbar, then open the rates.htm page**

   The image map showing the floor plan of one of the units appears, as shown in Figure D-17.

6. **Move the mouse pointer over the graphic showing the two-bedroom floor plan**

   The text specified for each `<area>` tag's alt attribute appears in a box when the mouse pointer is over the matching hot spot. In addition to the pointing hand icon, the appearance of this text is another cue for the user that this image contains links.

7. **Click the master bath hot spot on the image map**

   An image of the master bath opens in a new window.

8. **Close the new window and return to the image map**

9. **Repeat Steps 7 and 8 for each of the other hot spots in the image map**

   All the hot spots work as you intended.

FIGURE D-16: Code for image map in Web page

```
<p>Click a spot in the map below to view the rooms in one of our 2-bedroom
units.</p>

<p><map name="resortMap">
<area target="_blank" href="images/masterbedroom.jpg" shape="rect" coords="12,
6, 123, 108" alt="view the master bedroom" />
<area target="_blank" href="images/masterbath.jpg" shape="rect" coords="5, 118,
101, 193" alt="The master bathroom features a Whirlpool hot tub"/>
<area target="_blank" href="images/bed2.jpg" shape="rect" coords="30, 252, 149,
342" alt="Two queen-sized beds and a sitting area provide ample comfort for
your family in the second bedroom." />
<area target="_blank" href="images/frontroom.jpg" shape="rect" coords="160, 48,
259, 183" alt="The DVD, 32-inch TV, and stereo system make this room ideal for
entertaining. The pull out queen-sized sleeper sofa is a delightful extra."  />
<area target="_blank" href="images/dine2.jpg" shape="rect" coords="112, 112,
156, 182" alt="U-shaped booth seating with additional chairs, gives plenty of
room for seating your entire family." />
<area target="_blank" href="images/bath2.jpg" shape="rect" coords="5, 203, 148,
242" />
<area target="_blank" href="images/kitchen.jpg" shape="polygon" coords="161,
302, 162, 187, 257, 188, 259, 253, 198, 303" alt="In the kitchen, built-in
Whirlpool appliances make cooking and cleanup a breeze." />
</map>
<img border="0" src="images/floorplan2bedroom.gif" width="266" height="351"
usemap="#resortMap"align="left" ></p>

<br clear="all" /><br /><br />

<address style="text-align: center;">For questions or comments about this site,
contact: <br /> <a
```

Pasted image map code

FIGURE D-17: Floor plan image map displayed in rates.htm page

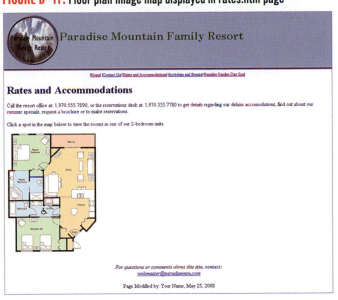

TABLE D-5: Image map tags

tag or tag set	function	attribute	specifies	example
`<map>...</map>`	Marks a section of HTML code as a named image map	name	Name of image map (for reference by `<img />` tag)	`<map name="2bedroom">`
`<area />`	Describes the shape and function of a hot spot	href	Target link address	`<area href="images/masterbedroom.jpg"`
		shape	Geometric shape of area; can be "circle," "rect" (rectangle), "poly" (polygon) or "default"	`shape="rect"`
		coords	pixel coordinates that describe the boundaries of the hot spot	`coords="12, 6, 123, 108"`
		alt	alternate text to display or speak	`alt="Click to view the master bedroom" />`

HTML

Exploring Multimedia Options

Advances in Web page design bring dynamic interactive pages to users instead of the static pages of yester-day. In addition to adding features to HTML, today's cutting-edge technology moves toward integrating sound and video with a page's basic text and graphics. The product of this integration is known as **multimedia**. In the past, **bandwidth**—the data transfer capacity of a Web user's Internet connection—was an obstacle to designers who wanted to incorporate multimedia in their sites. Because video and audio files are much larger than HTML and image files, the download time for a Web page that included video or audio blocked its smooth integration into Web pages. Recent trends in multimedia technology have enabled designers to provide a multitude of mul-timedia options knowing that most users will be able to experience all that the sites have to offer. These trends include **high-bandwidth Internet connections** (DSL and cable modems), **improved compression** that shrinks the size of video and audio files, and **streaming multimedia technology** (the ability to configure multimedia files to begin playing before they are fully downloaded). Table D-6 summarizes the requirements for creating and playing back the main multimedia technologies. You think multimedia would enhance your site and so you decide to explore your multimedia options to learn more about them.

DETAILS

Multimedia implementations on the Web include:

- ### Animated GIF

  The oldest of all multimedia options, and the easiest to use, the GIF file format allows you to combine two or more images into a single file and to include instructions on how the images are presented. Creating such a file, known as an **animated GIF**, was for years the only widely viewable multimedia effect on the Web. It costs very little and is often free, and online software is readily available for creating such effects. Animated GIFs are most often used in Web page banner advertisements, as they allow advertisers to display one or more images to attract a reader's interest before displaying the company logo or other target information. However, this type of advertising has been known to drive users away from a site, so be careful how often you use such a feature.

- ### Macromedia Flash animation

  A Macromedia innovation, Flash animation is rapidly becoming the most widely used Web animation. Flash ani-mation requires a proprietary player. However, the **object tag set** <object>...</object> used to implement Flash multimedia embeds a call to the Flash player download site, making it easy for users to obtain and install the program. Therefore a great majority of Web users have the Flash player installed on their machines. As early as March 2005, nearly 98 percent of Web users worldwide had the ability to view and listen to Flash video and sound, as shown in Figure D-18. Moreover, the Macromedia Flash program is no longer necessary to create Flash anima-tion; other licensed software allows designers to create complex and highly compressed multimedia animations.

- ### Streaming media

  Recent higher-bandwidth connections and more compressed formats have facilitated the wider incorpora-tion of traditional audio and video media into Web sites as streaming media. Many news organizations, such as printed newspapers and television stations, include relevant video clips alongside articles on their Web sites; musicians and record companies also use the Web to promote music and videos. Although clips are often embedded as links for downloading, today's faster Internet connections allow Web users to experience the audio or video without leaving the site. In addition, many radio and television stations have added **Webcasting** to their Web sites, meaning that they make their stations' normal programming available live on their Web sites. This technology also has allowed people and organizations to disseminate video and audio media programming without the financial costs of using traditional media channels.

- ### Embedded audio and video

  One of the easiest methods of making sound and video files available to site visitors is by delivering **embedded media**—simple sound and video files that are inserted through the use of the embed (<embed />) tag. Embedded media options are supported by most of the traditional audio and video types such as WAV, AVI, MPG, and MP3. When properly formatted, embedded media options allow site visitors to control the player and to stop or start a file as they see fit. Embedded media options are available for both sound and video files.

FIGURE D-18: Macromedia Flash statistics page

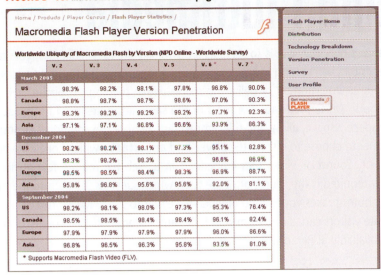

Clues to Use

Finding free graphics and animation

Numerous Web sites allow you to create your own background graphics, text images, and animations. In your favorite search engine, enter search terms such as "graphic generator" + "free" or "free animations," then initiate your search. Using your search results, you can create and download effective Web animations and graphics for your Web pages. For links to some of these sites, go to the Student Online Companion.

TABLE D-6: Comparison of multimedia options

technology	creation tool(s)	how used	playback tool
Animated GIF	Software commonly available for free or at low cost, or professional graphic editing tools such as Adobe ImageReady	`<img />` tag; implemented exactly like standard images; requires src attribute	Web browser
Flash animation	Macromedia Flash software and other tools such as Adobe ImageReady, Techsmith Camtasia, or free Web-based tools	`<object >...</object>` tag with specified param elements, required object attributes: classid with Flash class value, codebase, width, height, and name or id; required param names, movie with value	Web browser with Flash Player plug-in
Traditional audio and video	Audio and/or video computer translation hardware with associated software	`<embed />` tag, requires src attribute	Web browser with player plug-ins, such as Windows Media Player, Apple QuickTime Player, or one of the Real media players
RealOne Streaming audio and video	Audio and/or video computer translation hardware with associated software and streaming server	`<object >...</object>` with specified param elements, requires object attributes—classid with RealOne class value, width, height, and id; required param names, src with .rpm value; additional files—rpm file, which tells browser how to stream video or audio file	Web browser and add-on such as RealOne Player, QuickTime, or Windows Media player

HTML

UNIT D
HTML

Using Multimedia

If your page's only purpose is to serve as a download site for media files, you can make them available to your site visitors by creating links. However, in most cases, you want media files to enhance, not supplant, page content. One method of delivering media within the context of the Web page is to use the **embed tag** <embed />. Embed tags use most of the same attributes used by image tags including src, width, height, hspace, vspace, align, and title. Embed tags also use the additional attributes **hidden**—which allows the designer to choose to display the player, and **autostart**—which controls whether the file plays on page load or not. Sound or video files embedded in a Web file require few attributes. The only one that is absolutely required is the source attribute (src), which specifies the path to the media file. However, adding other attributes makes your sound or video file easier to use. You decide to provide a simple video file that site visitors can access from your Rates and Accommodations page to show site visitors some of the activities available at Paradise Mountain Family Resort.

STEPS

1. **Copy the media folder from the paradise folder in the place where you store your Data Files to the paradise folder in the place where you save your site files**

2. **Click the text editor program button on the taskbar to return to your rates.htm source code, click directly before `<br clear="all" /><br /><br />` near the bottom of the page, type `<p><embed src="media/paradise.wmv" width="300" height="400" /></p>`, press [Enter] twice, then save the file**

   The paradise.wmv file is a video clip. Most video clips display well at 300 × 400 pixels.

TROUBLE

If you open your file in Internet Explorer and the Information bar displays, right-click it and choose "Allow blocked content." Then click Yes to the prompt, "Are you sure you want to let this file run active content."

3. **Click the browser program button on the taskbar, then reload your rates.htm file**

   Depending upon your browser version, the file could start to play almost immediately. You realize that this is not necessarily in the best interests of the user, so you decide to add some attributes to allow the user to control the playback. You also notice that the object is too close to the floor plan image.

4. **Click the text editor program button on the taskbar to return to your rates.htm source code, locate the height attribute for the media file, click directly after the closing quotation mark following it, press [Spacebar], type `autostart="false" align="right" vspace="10" hspace="10"`, then save your work**

   The autostart="false" attribute prevents the player from starting automatically, thus enabling the users to decide whether they want to play the video. The align attribute moves the file to the right side of the page, and the vspace and hspace attributes add extra white space so the video is not crowded by other content on the page. The embedded file needs a title.

5. **Click after the closing quotation mark following the "hspace" attribute value, press [Spacebar], type `title="Click to play resort features video, or visit the site home page to learn more about the resort."`, make sure that your name and today's date appear in the "Page modified by" paragraph at the bottom of the page, then save your work**

   See Figure D-19. Although alt is not a supported attribute for the embed tag, you can use the title attribute to supply additional information for people whose disabilities prevent them from seeing the video display.

QUICK TIP

The multimedia file format can play a significant role in its initial appearance. Some files, like the WMV file you are using, are smaller in file size, but display no image until activated. Others are larger in file size but initially more attractive.

6. **Click the browser program button on the taskbar, reload the page, then print it**

   The page appears with a media player for the embedded media file, but the video does not start automatically.

7. **Click the Play button ⊙ on the media player to activate the video clip**

   The video plays in the media player, as shown in Figure D-20.

8. **Close any open files, then transfer your updated files to your remote directory on the server**

FIGURE D-19: Code for embedding a media file

```
<p><map name="resortMap">
<area target="_blank" href="images/masterbedroom.jpg" shape="rect" coords="12,
6, 123, 108" alt="View the master bedroom" />
<area target="_blank" href="images/masterbath.jpg" shape="rect" coords="5, 118,
101, 193" alt="The master bathroom features a Whirlpool hot tub"/>
<area target="_blank" href="images/bed2.jpg" shape="rect" coords="30, 252, 149,
342" alt="Two queen-sized beds and a sitting area provide ample comfort for your
family in the second bedroom." />
<area target="_blank" href="images/frontroom.jpg" shape="rect" coords="160, 48,
259, 183" alt="The DVD, 32-inch TV, and stereo system make this room ideal for
entertaining. The pull out queen-sized sleeper sofa is a delightful extra."  />
<area target="_blank" href="images/dine2.jpg" shape="rect" coords="112, 112,
156, 182" alt="U-shaped booth seating with additional chairs, gives plenty of
room for seating your entire family." />
<area target="_blank" href="images/bath2.jpg" shape="rect" coords="5, 203, 148,
242" />
<area target="_blank" href="images/kitchen.jpg" shape="polygon" coords="161,
302, 162, 187, 257, 188, 259, 253, 198, 303" alt="In the kitchen, built-in
Whirlpool appliances make cooking and cleanup a breeze." />
</map>
<img border="0" src="images/floorplan2bedroom.gif" width="266" height="351"
usemap="#resortMap"align="left" ></p>

<p><embed src="media/paradise.wmv" width="300" height="400" autostart="false"
align="right" vspace="10" hspace="10" title="Click to play resort features
video, or visit the site home page to learn more about the resort." /></p>

<br clear="all" /><br /><br />
```

Embed code ⟶

FIGURE D-20: Embedded media plays on Web page

HTML

Practice

▼ CONCEPTS REVIEW

Name the function of each section of code indicated in Figure D-21.

FIGURE D-21

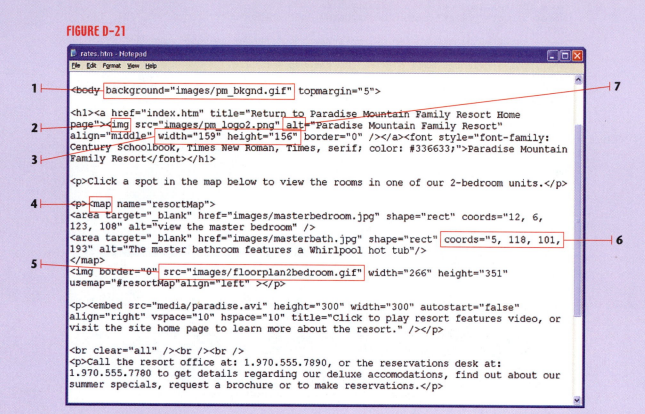

Match each statement with the term that best describes it.

8. A graphic that links different areas to Web pages
9. A linked area of a graphic
10. A graphic that allows any user to see text in a font selected by the designer
11. A group of technologies that allows faster downloads
12. One of the points of light that makes up the display on a computer screen

a. Broadband
b. Hot spot
c. Pixel
d. Image map
e. Text image

Select the best answer from the list of choices.

13. Which of the following is a graphics file format commonly used on the Internet? (Choose all that apply.)
    a. GIF
    b. JPG
    c. TIFF
    d. BMP
14. Which one of the following attributes for the <img /> tag adds space to the left and right of the image?
    a. align
    b. vspace
    c. src
    d. hspace

▼ SKILLS REVIEW

1. **Insert images.**
   a. In your text editor, open the file **htm_D-2.txt** from the place where you store your Data Files, then save it as **index.htm** in your paradise/spa folder in the place where you save your site files, replacing the existing file.
   b. Locate the level-two heading tag with the id "slogan", drag to select Paradise Garden Day Spa, press [Delete], then type the code `<img src="../images/spa_logo.gif" />`. (*Hint*: Because the spa site is in a subdirectory of the paradise site, the images folder is in the parent directory. Make sure that your src attribute correctly identifies the file path.)
   c. Add an alt statement to the image that indicates to the user that the image represents Paradise Gardens Day Spa, then save the file. (*Hint*: Use the code `alt="Paradise Garden Day Spa"`)
   d. In your text editor, open the **htm_D-3.txt** file from your Data Files location and save it as **hands.htm** in the spa folder in your site files location, replacing the existing file. Repeat Steps b and c to set the logo graphic at the top of the page, replacing Paradise Garden Day Spa, then add an appropriate alt statement.
   e. Click directly before the level-three heading tag for Hand Care, and insert the code to display the image pedi.jpg from your paradise images folder. (*Hint*: Use the code `<img src="../images/pedi.jpg" />`)
   f. Click inside the pedi.jpg image tag and insert the code to cause the image to align to the right, then type the code to insert an alt statement using the text, **Indulge yourself with a professional pedicure**, then save your work.

2. **Specify image size.**
   a. Open your **spa/hands.htm** file in your browser, locate and right-click the logo image and open the Image Properties dialog box, then record the width and height of the image. (*Hint*: In the Image Properties window, the width is always listed first.)
   b. Repeat Step a with the photograph, then click the text editor program button to return to your page code.
   c. Add the correct width and height attributes and set the hspace value for each image to 10 pixels, update the "Page modified by" paragraph with your name and the current date, then save your work.
   d. Open your **spa/index.htm** file in your text editor and use the information you recorded in Step a above to specify the proper image width and height for the page logo.
   e. Save your work, reload your **spa/hands.htm** file to view your changes, then click the Paradise Garden Day Spa link in the navigation bar to view changes to the spa/index.htm file.

3. **Add a background image.**
   a. Make sure that your **spa/index.htm** page is open in your text editor.
   b. Click directly after "body" in the opening body tag, insert a space, then type the code that causes the image bkg_spa.gif from the paradise/images folder to appear as the background image for your page. (*Hint*: Use the code `background="../images/bkg_spa.gif"`)
   c. Add a leftmargin attribute and value to the body tag that moves the page content 150 pixels from the left page margin and 50 pixels from the right margin. (*Hint*: Use the code `leftmargin="150" rightmargin="50"`)
   d. Save your work.
   e. Repeat Steps b through d to add the same background image and margins to your hands.htm page.
   f. Save and load each page in your browser to test your images.

4. **Link images.**
   a. Click the text editor program button to return to your hands.htm page code.
   b. Locate the `<img />` tag that references the spa logo graphic, click directly before `<img` and enter an opening anchor tag with the code to create a link to the spa/index.htm page, then click at the end of the image tag and type the closing anchor tag. (*Hint*: For the opening anchor tag, type `<a href="../spa/index.htm">`.)
   c. Click inside the opening link tag and directly after the href value, then insert the link title, **Link to Paradise Garden Day Spa home page**.
   d. Click inside the image tag and insert the code `border="0"` to prevent a border from being displayed on your linked image.
   e. Save your work, view the file spa/hands.htm in your browser, then click the logo graphic to make sure it links to the spa/index.htm page.

5. **Insert an image map.**
   a. In your text editor, open the file **imagemap.txt** from the UnitD spa folder in the location where you store your Data Files, select and copy all the text in the file, then return to your spa/index.htm file.

b. In the spa/index.htm file, locate, then delete the second-level navigation bar that starts with `<p id="spaNav"` `style="text-align: center;">`, and paste the image map code from the Clipboard.

c. Save your work, then reload the file **spa/index.htm** in your browser.

d. Copy the wraps.htm file from your Data Files spa folder and paste it into your paradise/spa folder.

e. Return to **index.htm** in your browser, then click the image map hot spots to test the image map.

6. Use multimedia.

a. Copy the media folder and its contents from the UnitD spa folder in the place where you store your Data Files to your paradise/spa folder in the place where you save your site files.

FIGURE D-22

b. Make sure that your **spa/index.htm** file is open in your text editor, click directly after the second line break following the image map, then press [Enter] twice.

c. Insert an embed tag with the source attribute and value `src="media/spa.wmv"` and the title `Tour our facilities`.

d. Right-align the embedded file, insert additional attributes to set the width and height to 300, then add an additional 10 pixels of horizontal white space around the player.

e. Type the code `hidden="false"` to make sure the player is visible in all browsers, then insert the code that prevents the file from playing when the page is loaded. (*Hint:* Set the autostart attribute to "false.")

f. Ensure that the "Page modified by" paragraph contains your name and the date is today's date, then print the code.

g. Save your work, then reload the file **spa/index.htm** in your browser.

h. Test your embedded multimedia file by clicking the Play button on the media player. Your page should resemble Figure D-22.

i. Close all files and transfer your updated files to your remote directory.

▼ INDEPENDENT CHALLENGE 1

As you continue developing the Web site for your resort rental business, Star Vacations, you want to use the skills you have learned to add graphics and multimedia to enhance the site.

a. Locate and copy the **images** directory with all of its contents, as well as the files, **eu.htm**, **ak.htm**, and **hi.htm**, from the UnitD vacations folder in the place where you store your Data Files.

b. Paste the copied folder and files inside your vacations site folder in the place where you store your site files.

c. In your text editor, open your **IslandSeas.htm** file from your vacations folder in the place where you save your site files (or obtain a copy of the file from your instructor).

d. Click just after "body" in the <body> tag and type the code to display the graphic **bkg_vaca.gif** as a background image. (*Hint:* The image is saved in your images folder.)

e. Click after the </h3> tag following the resort address at the top of the page, then enter two line breaks to move the rest of the content down on the page.

f. Locate the paragraph that begins with "<p>Nestled serenely", click before <p>, and enter the code `<img src="images/` `resort.jpg" hspace="10" vspace="10" align="right" />`, then insert an alt statement **Find fun in the sun at Island Seas**, update the "Page modified by" section with your name and today's date, then save your work.

g. Open **htm_D-4.txt** from the UnitD Data Files, save it as **index.htm** in your vacations folder, then repeat Step d to place the background graphic, bkg_vaca.gif, on the page and save your work.

h. Open a separate text editor window, open the **map.txt** file from the UnitD vacations Data Files folder, replacing the existing file, then copy all of the text to the Clipboard and close the map.txt file.

▼ INDEPENDENT CHALLENGE 1 (CONTINUED)

i. In the index.htm file, locate and select the comment tag, `<!-- Insert image map here -->`, then paste the copied code.

j. Update the "Page Modified by" section with your name and today's date, save your work and display the index.htm file in the browser, check your image map links, close all files, then transfer your completed pages to your remote directory.

Advanced Challenge Exercises

- Copy the media folder from your vacations_ace Data Files into your vacations folder, then edit the index.htm file to embed the audio file islandseas.wav in a separate centered paragraph just above the address block.
- Set the width and height attributes of the embed tag to 150 wide by 40 pixels high to cause only the media player control buttons to appear, then add code to prevent the file from playing automatically.
- Locate the text "Come to the Land of the Midnight Sun," currently linked to features.htm, and change its link to the Alaska Resort page, ak.htm.
- Locate the text "A tropical paradise awaits!", then change its link to the Hawaii Resorts page, hi.htm; if necessary, add your name and today's date to the "Page Modified by" section.
- Edit the Island Seas image map area to cause the page to open in a new window.
- Save your work, then reload the **vacations/index** file in your browser, and check all links; close all files, then transfer them to the remote site.

▼ INDEPENDENT CHALLENGE 2

The water conservation Web site you have been developing for your employer, Metro Water, is coming along nicely. You are ready to start enhancing your pages with graphics and sound.

a. Copy the images and media folders, as well as the saver.htm file from the water folder in the place where you store your Data Files and paste them into your water folder in the place where you save your site files. (*Hint:* If prompted to replace files, click Yes.)

b. In your text editor, **open htm_D-5.txt** from your Data File location, then save it as **index.htm** in your water folder, replacing the existing file.

c. Click after the closing paragraph tag in the "Page modified by" paragraph at the bottom of the page, then insert a return and enter the code to place and center the mw.gif file (located in the images folder) below the "Page modified by" text. (*Hint:* To center an image, place it in a paragraph or division and set alignment attributes in the parent element.)

d. Set the width and height of the graphic to 50 × 50, and add the alt attribute, "Metro Water reminds you that every drop counts" and link the graphic to saver.htm. (*Hint*: Be sure to remove the border from the linked graphic.)

e. Click just after `</a>` following the linked image at the bottom of the page, insert a line break, and embed the conserve.wav file. Set the media player to appear at 200 pixels by 20 pixels, update the "Page modified by" paragraph as necessary, then save, preview, and close your page and transfer your file to your remote directory.

Advanced Challenge Exercises

- Open **water/index.htm** and add the background image water_bg1.jpg or water_bg2.jpg.
- Replace the level-one heading text with the graphic waterHead2.gif, then add an alt statement for the graphic, then save your work.
- If necessary, open the page in your browser and view it to determine the best text and link color choices for the background, then use the color chart in the appendix of this text to help determine an appropriate text, link, and background color palette for this page.
- Use the text attribute of the body tag to set your page text color.
- Use the link, vlink, and alink body tag attributes to set the link, visited link, and active link colors.
- Use the bgcolor attribute to set a page background color that closely matches the background graphic.
- Save, preview, print, and close your file and transfer it to the remote site.

▼ INDEPENDENT CHALLENGE 3

Graphics and multimedia are a necessary part of presenting content on the Web today. You want to use the latest and most elegant methods of displaying graphics, but you are concerned about accessibility.

a. Go to the Student Online Companion, then click the link to open the W3C Web Accessibility page and review the information regarding graphics and multimedia, then answer the following:
   1. How can the use of graphics make your site more user friendly?
   2. How would you test your site to see whether the graphics you included can be read by people with sight deficiencies?
   3. What steps should you take when using graphics and multimedia to ensure accessibility?
   4. What are the issues of accessibility when using sound on your pages?
   5. Add your name and today's date to the top of your paper, then print it.

▼ INDEPENDENT CHALLENGE 4

Now that you've studied graphics and multimedia, you are ready to add these features to the pages on your Web site.

a. Locate or create graphics, multimedia, and background images that are appropriate for your site.
b. Make sure each page contains a background image and at least one inline graphic; include at least one multimedia file in your site. Then add appropriate content to your pages. You may include image maps, but they are optional.

VISUAL WORKSHOP

Work progresses on your Bits and PCs Web site and you decide to add images to the apple_hist.htm file. You received permission from photographer A. Luckow to use pictures he took of Steve Jobs and Steve Wozniak. Using the files provided, revise your apple_hist.htm page to resemble the page shown in Figure D-23. Copy the images and media folders from the UnitD bitspcs folder in the place where you store your Data Files into the bitspcs folder in the place where you save your site files. The images folder contains the files apple.gif, applebg.gif, and woz-jobsbyLuckow.jpg and the media folder contains the apple.wav file. (*Hint:* The base font in Figure D-23 is Arial.)

FIGURE D-23

[Home] [History Information] [Advertised Specials] [Products] [Services]

Chronology of the Apple Computer until 1987

Apple History

Click to hear some Apple history

- **1971** Stephen Wozniak and Bill Fernandez build their "Cream Soda computer."
- **1972** Stephen Wozniak and Steven Jobs begin selling blue boxes.
- **1973** Stephen Wozniak joins Hewlett-Packard.
- **1974** Steve Jobs joins Atari
- **1975** Apple I
- **1976** Apple becomes a company
  1. Wozniak and Jobs form the Apple Computer Company on April Fool's Day.
  2. Apple Computer opens its first offices in Cupertino and introduces the Apple II. It is the first personal computer with color graphics. It has a 6502 CPU, 4KB RAM,16KB ROM, keyboard, 8-slot motherboard, game paddles, and built-in BASIC.
- **1978** Apple introduces and begins shipping disk drives for the Apple II and initiates the LISA research and development project.
- **1980** Apple III
- **1983** Three new products from Apple
  1. Apple Computer announces Lisa, the first business computer with a graphical user interface launched by Apple Computer Inc., Cupertino, California. The computer has 5MHz 68000 CPU, 860KB 5.25 *floppy*, B&W screen, detached keyboard, and mouse.
  2. Apple IIe
  3. Apple III+

Formatting with Cascading Style Sheets

OBJECTIVES

Explore CSS formatting
Control text formatting
Set background colors and images
Set link properties
Apply margins
Apply text alignment and format lists
Use CSS class rules
Use linked style sheets

Cascading Style Sheets (CSS) are a powerful method of formatting Web pages according to a series of rules you create and apply to your Web pages. A fundamental feature of CSS formatting is its ability to **cascade**—apply multiple styles to the same document. CSS rules allow you to control page elements in ways that traditional HTML formatting cannot. You can use CSS to control the appearance of text, set background colors, apply page margins, set link properties, and align text. Moreover, you can create style sheets that can be linked to multiple pages to instantly control formatting throughout an entire site. As the Paradise Mountain Family Resort Web site grows and matures, you begin to realize how difficult it is to implement formatting changes across all pages, so you decide to investigate the possibility of using CSS.

Exploring CSS Formatting

In the first four units of this book, you used inline styles, which you entered within formatting tags. Although useful for formatting pages, inline styles require that you format each element individually. **Cascading Style Sheets (CSS)** allow you to format your Web files efficiently without adding HTML formatting tags and attributes to the document body. You apply CSS styles by creating and using **CSS style rules**—special instructions that describe the formatting you want to apply to each element. When HTML was introduced, it was not intended as a formatting language, but rather as a method of making documents available to users on a variety of operating systems. Over the years, formatting elements, such as `<font>...</font>` were introduced to make HTML documents more appealing to the general public. With new elements being introduced yearly, the need to standardize HTML led to **Extensible Hypertext Markup Language (XHTML)**. Well-formed XHTML documents use CSS to format page output. In addition to making pages more attractive, CSS formatting also enables designers to create pages that are accessible to a wider range of display devices, such as computer screens, personal digital assistants (PDAs), and digital phone displays. You want to learn how you can use CSS to enhance your pages, so you begin to study CSS formatting options.

DETAILS

You can accomplish the following tasks using CSS:

- ### Control text formatting
  As with HTML formatting, CSS enables you to control font color and size. However, CSS moves beyond the limitations of **standard HTML** (HTML prior to version 4.0) because it allows you to control font size in fixed values, such as points and pixels, as well as in relative values such as **em** (the height of the lowercase letter "m" of your chosen font family) and in percentages. Figure E-1 shows a Web page formatted with CSS.

- ### Set background properties
  Using CSS formatting you can apply background color and images to the entire page, to page block elements such as block quotes, divisions, and address tags and to specific page elements such as paragraphs and headings. In addition, CSS allows you to control the way page backgrounds appear by controlling the background's position and its repetition behavior.

- ### Control page margins and spacing
  With CSS formatting, you have more margin control than ever before. You can specify page margins in terms of pixels, points, or percentages. You can also control white space around specific page elements by applying **padding**—added space within an element—and **margins**—added space around an element. In addition, CSS lets you also control white space by adding CSS rules to control **line spacing**—the space between lines, **character kerning**—the space between letters within a word, and **word spacing**—the amount of space between words.

- ### Control element alignment and decoration
  You can use CSS to align block-level page elements such as `<div>...</div>`, `<blockquote>...</blockquote>`, and `<address>...</address>`. Using CSS you can also add decorative borders above, below, or around page block elements, paragraphs, and headings.

- ### Format multiple pages within the same site
  Once you have created your document styles, you can save them in a separate style sheet file with a .css extension and then apply that document to multiple pages throughout your site. Formatting your documents in this manner allows you to make global changes to your site by making those changes to a single file.

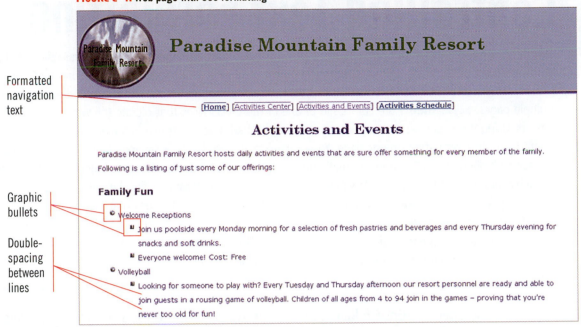

Formatted navigation text

Graphic bullets

Double-spacing between lines

Design Matters

Creating a "well-formed" document

According to W3C, a "well-formed" document follows certain syntax rules. This syntax is: All attributes must be enclosed in quotation marks and assigned values; the elements must be properly nested; all elements, even empty elements, must to be closed; element names must be in lowercase; and everything must be contained within the opening and closing html tags, which are together known as the **root element**. "Well-formed" usually describes XML documents. XHTML is HTML that is written to follow the XML syntax rules for a well-formed document.

Clues to Use

Understanding XHTML variations

XHTML language rules and structure, or **syntax**, is based on the stricter XML (Extensible Markup Language) standards. These standards declare that all tag elements must be closed and recommends that all documents contain a **document type definition (DTD)** tag written as the first line of code to tell the browser what type of XHTML you are using so it knows how to interpret the page code. According to the W3C, there are three "flavors" of XHTML: Strict, Transitional, and Frameset, each with its own DTD. Use **XHTML Strict** in documents that contain no layout or formatting markup and that use CSS to apply any formatting effects. Use **XHTML Transitional** for formatting pages that take advantage of CSS but that might contain small markup adjustments, such as bgcolor or text and link attributes in the body tag, to make page formatting visible in older browers. Use **XHTML Frameset** when you want to use frames to divide the browser window into two or more windows. (You will learn more about frames in Unit H.) The W3C also recommends that XHTML documents include a meta tag to describe the document's character set. A **character set** is a defined list of characters recognized by the computer hardware and software. Most Web documents use the ISO-8859-1 character set as defined by the International Organization for Standardization (ISO); the set includes standard ASCII characters plus additional characters for European languages. Figure E-2 shows a DTD that declares the document type to be transitional XHTML. It also shows a meta tag that defines the character set as ISO-8859-1.

FIGURE E-2: Transitional DTD and meta character type tag

Transitional DTD

```
<!DOCTYPE html PUBLIC "-//W3C//DTD XHTML 1.0 Transitional//EN"
    "http://www.w3.org/TR/xhtml1/DTD/xhtml1-transitional.dtd">

<html>
<head>

<title>Paradise Mountain Family Resort Weekly Activities List</title>

<meta name="description" content="Paradise Mountain Family Resort weekly
activities schedule for more information contact the activities center at:
1.970.555.7890">

<meta http-equiv="Content-Type" content="text/html; charset=iso-8859-1">

</head>
```

Meta character type tag

HTML

Controlling Text Formatting

Cascading Style Sheets provide document-formatting techniques that were previously available only for word-processed documents. You can apply styles to text as inline style attributes, as you did in Unit C. But it is much more effective to use style sheets because they can control the formatting for an entire page or for multiple pages. **Style sheets** are composed of one or more CSS rules that dictate the way page content appears. Using the `<style>...</style>` tags, you can embed style sheets within the head section of a document to control formatting on one page. You can also save style sheets as separate files to control formatting for multiple pages. **CSS rules** are made up of a selector and a declaration that together describe the characteristics of XHTML elements. As shown in Figure E-3, the **selector** specifies the element to which the style is applied. The **declaration** contains one or more properties and values that describe the style. A colon follows each declaration property and a semicolon (;) follows each declaration property value. The entire style declaration is enclosed in curly brackets ({}). 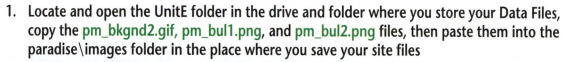 The activities center has asked you to post some information about their many activities, and you decide to use CSS to format the document.

STEPS

1. **Locate and open the UnitE folder in the drive and folder where you store your Data Files, copy the pm_bkgnd2.gif, pm_bul1.png, and pm_bul2.png files, then paste them into the paradise\images folder in the place where you save your site files**

2. **In your text editor, open htm_E-1.txt from the location where you store your Data Files, then inspect the code**

    The first tag in the file includes the XHTML doctype description (also called a **doctype declaration**), which tells the browser that this is a Transitional XHTML document. Above the `</head>` tag, the meta character set tag tells the browser to interpret the document using the ISO-8859-1 character set.

3. **Save the file as activities.htm in the paradise\activities folder in the location where you save your site files, replacing the existing activities.htm file if prompted**

4. **Click before </head>, then type the following code, pressing [Enter] after each line:**

    ```
    <style>
    <!--
    -->
    </style>
    ```

    You entered the opening and closing style tags as well as opening and closing comment tags. You place your style rules inside the comment tags to hide the style code from browsers that do not support CSS.

5. **Click after <!--, press [Enter], then type the following code, pressing [Enter] after each line:**

    ```
    body    {
            font-family: Verdana, Arial, Helvetica, sans-serif;
            font-size: 14px;
            color: #333366;
            line-height: 2em;
    }
    ```

    As shown in Figure E-4, an opening curly bracket starts the style rule declaration, which defines your font family, font size and color, and line spacing selections for the document.

6. **Save the activities.htm file, start your browser, then open activities.htm**

    Most of the formatting applied to your other pages, as well as your background graphic, are missing, as shown in Figure E-5. However, you like the readability of the double-spaced text.

FIGURE E-3: Parts of a CSS style rule

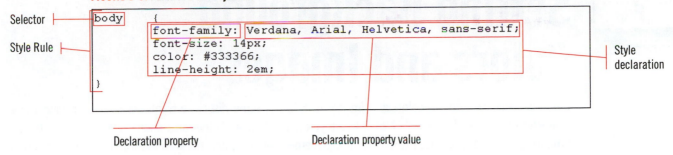

Selector — `body`

Style Rule —

```
body        {
            font-family: Verdana, Arial, Helvetica, sans-serif;
            font-size: 14px;
            color: #333366;
            line-height: 2em;

}
```

Style declaration

Declaration property

Declaration property value

FIGURE E-4: Embedded style sheet with body style rule

```
<head>

<title>Paradise Mountain Family Resort Weekly Activities List</title>

<meta name="description" content="Paradise Mountain Family Resort weekly
activities schedule for more information contact the activities center at:
1.970.555.7890">

<meta http-equiv="Content-Type" content="text/html; charset=iso-8859-1">

<style>
<!--
body        {
            font-family: Verdana, Arial, Helvetica, sans-serif;
            font-size: 14px;
            color: #333366;
            line-height: 2em;
}

-->
</style>
</head>
```

Opening style tag

Style rule

Closing style tag

Embedded style sheet in head section

FIGURE E-5: Activities page with CSS formatting

No background image

Your links may appear purple (visited)

Double-spaced text

HTML

Setting Background Colors and Images

Defining page background colors and images in CSS has some distinct advantages over specifying those characteristics in standard HTML. Not only can you use CSS to apply the same changes to all your Web documents; you can also use CSS to control the placement of inline and background images and the tiling of background images. (The appendix lists CSS background properties.) When you defined the style for your page in the first lesson of this unit, you used a type selector that specified the body element. **Type selectors**, also called **tag selectors**, specify elements by their names and apply the rule to all tags of the same name. The CSS rule to specify a page background also uses the body type selector. The declaration used to set the page background image is `background-image: url(imagepath);`. You decide to use CSS to apply background image and color properties. You also want to experiment with new color choices.

STEPS

1. **Click the text editor program button to return to your source code, click just before } in the body rule of your embedded style sheet, then press [Tab]**

   The insertion point is properly positioned for adding additional formatting commands to your CSS body style rule.

2. **Type the following code, pressing [Enter] after each line, save your work, then preview it in your browser:**

   ```
   background-image: url(../images/pm_bkgnd2.gif);
   margin-left: 0px;
   margin-top: 5px;
   margin-right: 0px;
   ```

   As shown in Figure E-6, you extended the CSS body rule to set a background image and margin properties for the page. Now you would like to experiment with background color.

3. **Select the color code in the color declaration, type `#FFFFFF;`, press [Enter], press [Tab], type `background-color: #336699;`, then save your file**

4. **Click the browser program button on the taskbar, then click the Reload/Refresh button to preview your updated file**

   As shown in Figure E-7, the white text is displayed against the blue background, but the link colors are almost invisible. The page is much easier to read with a white background and blue text.

5. **Click the text editor program button, change the color value to `#333366;`, change the background color to `#FFFFFF;`, then save your work and view the page in your browser**

   As shown in Figure E-7, the links are easier to read.

FIGURE E-6: Extended body rule sets background image and margin properties

Background image

Page margin zero px (pixels)

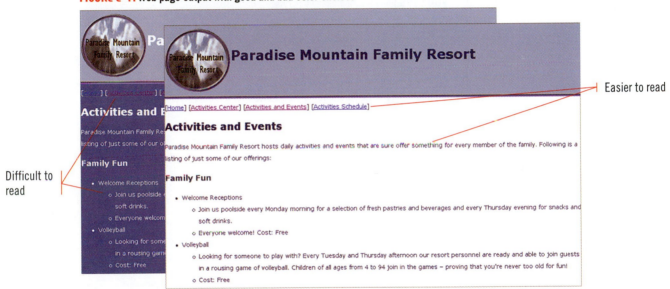

```
<style>
<!--
body     {
          font-family: Verdana, Arial, Helvetica, sans-serif;
          font-size: 14px;
          color: #333366;
          line-height: 2em;
          background-image: url(../images/pm_bkgnd2.gif);
          margin-left: 0px;
          margin-top: 5px;
          margin-right: 0px;

          }
         -->
</style>
</head>

<body>
```

Background image and margin declarations

FIGURE E-7: Web page output with good and bad color choices

Easier to read

Difficult to read

HTML

Design Matters

Working with page colors and backgrounds

When working with colors and images, always make sure that your background color or image contrasts adequately with your foreground text colors. Backgrounds that too closely match text colors in hue and intensity make text almost impossible to read (even when they are a different color). A good way to test the readability of your pages is to print them, with the Print background image command active, on a gray scale printer, or print them and then make gray scale photocopies to see if there are any readability problems. Too often, designers forget that the default background color in most browsers is white (the default background color in some older browsers is gray). This is not a problem unless you are using a dark background graphic that requires the use of white text. In this case if a background color is not set to match the content area of a background, the text is unreadable if for some reason the background images are not displayed. Additionally, never use high-contrast, patterned backgrounds on which to display text. The light areas of the background are too light to display light-colored text, and the dark areas are too dark to display dark text. For more information on working with color, go to the Student Online Companion for this book, which has links to several sites, such as the Color Schemer Online and Lighthouse International.

Setting Link Properties

As you learned in Unit D, you can change link colors using alink, vlink, and link attributes in standard HTML, but CSS allows you to do much more. With CSS formatting, you can not only change link colors from their default colors, but also cause links to be displayed in different colors on different sections of a page, and make linked text respond to **click events**—when the site visitor clicks a link—and **hover events**—when the site visitor rests the mouse pointer over the link. You format links separately for its three **states**: visited, hover, and active (those that are in the process of being clicked or that have just been clicked). You want the links on your page to stand out a little more, so you apply text decoration and other formatting to the links in their various states.

STEPS

1. Click the text editor program button on the taskbar, click just after the closing } at the end of the body CSS rule, then press [Enter] twice

2. Type the code shown below, pressing [Enter] after each line:

```
a:link    {
    font-weight: bold;
    color: #006699;
    text-decoration: underline overline;
}
a:visited{
    color: #666699;
    text-decoration: underline overline;
}
a:hover    {
    font-style: italic;
    font-weight: bold;
    color: #CC0000;
    text-decoration: underline overline;
}
a:active   {
    font-style: italic;
    font-weight: bold;
    color: #FF0000;
    text-decoration: underline overline;
}
```

> **TROUBLE**
> The Activities Schedule Link will not work because you haven't created that page yet.

3. Save your work, click the browser program button on the taskbar, then reload your activities.htm page

> **TROUBLE**
> If you have already clicked all your links, your unclicked formatting is not visible.

4. Move the mouse pointer over each link, then click to test each one

As shown in Figure E-8, the unclicked link appears in a steel blue as boldfaced type with over- and underlining. Hovered links—those over which you rest the mouse pointer—change to boldfaced, italicized, dark red. As you click each link to make it active, the red color intensifies. Clicking the back button to return to the page allows the link to remain active until another link or another part of the page is clicked. Visited links appear gray and lose their boldfaced qualities.

Hovered link

Active link

Visited link

Unclicked link

Design Matters

Specifying alternate link colors

Many Web sites are built with a dark-colored navigation area and a light-colored page content area. Prior to CSS formatting, this meant that either all links in the navigation area had to be graphic links to ensure they would appear against the dark background, or links in the content area were difficult to read because they were too light.

CSS formatting allows you to solve this problem by defining an alternate class of link color values that can work with your dark background. You then apply the class to the dark section of the page. You will learn more about style class selectors in a later lesson.

Applying Margins

White space is any empty area on a page and may not necessarily be white. Too much white space on a page gives the reader an unbalanced, uncomfortable feeling. Too little white space, a more common occurrence, makes page elements appear overcrowded and causes eye strain for the site visitor. Applied properly, white space can be a great enhancement to Web design. CSS formatting allows you to format page elements to include not only margins around the edges of a page, but also around elements within a page.  You have identified some elements of your page that need adjusting. As shown in Figure E-9, the page heading is too close to the logo and there is not enough white space on the edges of the page. You will also add some additional formatting to your headings.

STEPS

1. **Return to your page code, click just after the } that closes the active link rule, press [Enter] twice, then type the following code, pressing [Enter] after each line:**

```
h1      {
            font-family: Century Schoolbook, Times New Roman, Times, serif;
            color: #336633;
            font-size: 36px;
            margin: 0px;
}
```

Your new style rule makes the Paradise Mountain heading appear in 36-pixel green text, and sets the margins to zero. Because the logo is part of the heading, the zero-pixel margin setting ensures that the logo stays flush left with the page border. The rest of the page still needs adjusting.

QUICK TIP

In Unit D you learned that the hspace attribute applies horizontal space to both sides of an image; using CSS you can control the spacing on just one side of an image.

2. **Press [Enter] twice, then type the following code, pressing [Enter] after each line:**

```
img     {
            margin-right: 25px;
}
```

The image rule causes any image to be displayed on the page with a 25-pixel space to its right.

3. **Press [Enter] twice, then type the following code, pressing [Enter] after each line:**

```
div     {
            margin-left: 40px;
            margin-right: 40px;
}
```

Your new rule formats any page areas enclosed by <div>...</div> (division) tags with 40-pixel left and right margins. Usually used with an ID attribute, **divisions** are block-level elements often used to control several elements at once. On this page, you set a default div value to control the page-content borders. You still need to specify what block of text the div tag affects.

4. **Locate the line at the beginning of the navigation bar code that begins**
   <p>[<a href="../index.htm">, **click just before <p>, then type** <div>

5. **Move to the end of the source code, click just before the closing body tag, type** </div>,
   press [Enter], then save the file

6. **Preview the page in your browser**
   As shown in Figure E-10, the page content moves in 40 pixels on the left and right, leaving ample white space on the page margins.

FIGURE E-9: Activities and Events page with identified problems

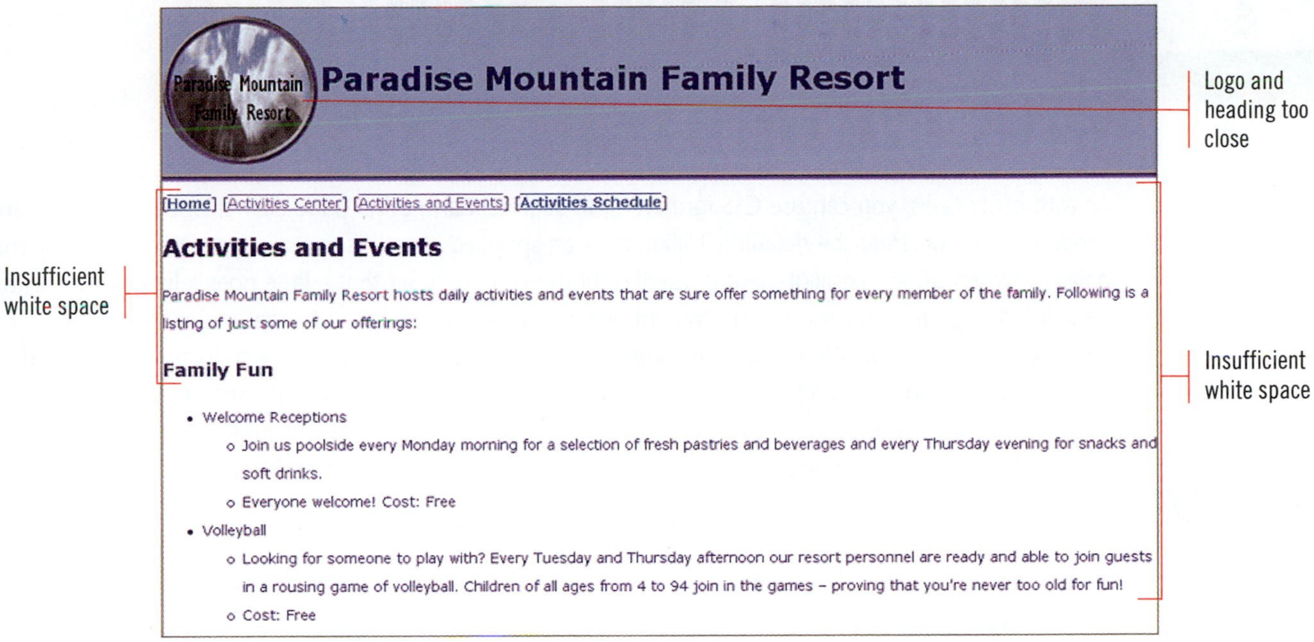

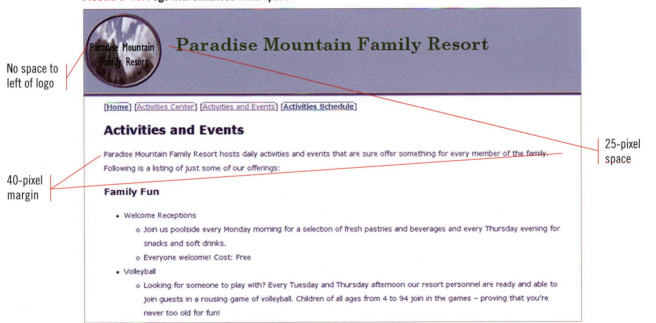

Logo and heading too close

Insufficient white space

Insufficient white space

FIGURE E-10: Page with enhanced white space

No space to left of logo

40-pixel margin

25-pixel space

Applying Text Alignment and Formatting Lists

As with other tasks, you can use CSS formatting to align text and other page elements. Setting alignment properties that override the default left alignment on specified elements can give your pages interest and balance. When using text alignment properties, however, remember that a little goes a long way. Use the default left alignment for most page content and apply special alignment formatting in moderation. The most accepted uses for other alignment options include right-aligning columns containing numeric data and center-aligning main page headings, some navigation bars, photo galleries, contact blocks, and copyright information. You want to add CSS formatting to some of your page elements in order to change their default alignment. You also want to add some specialized formatting.

STEPS

1. **Return to your text editor**

2. **Locate the h1 style rule you created earlier, click just after the } that closes the rule, press [Enter] twice, then type the following code, pressing [Enter] after each line:**

```
h2      {
        font-family: Century Schoolbook, Times New Roman, Times, serif;
        color: #000066;
        font-size: 28px;
        text-align: center;
}
```

You defined a style and set the alignment properties for level-two page headings.

3. **Click after } of the level-two heading rule, press [Enter] twice, then type the following code, pressing [Enter] after each line**

```
address     {
        text-align: center;
}
```

You center-aligned the address block.

TROUBLE

Be sure you type the number 1 after "pm_bul" instead of the letter L.

4. **Click after } of the division rule, press [Enter] twice, then type the following code, pressing [Enter] after each line:**

```
ul      {
        list-style-image: url(../images/pm_bul1.png);
}
```

You specified pm_bul1.png as the bullet image. Your code should resemble Figure E-11.

5. **Save your page, then view it in your browser**

Verify that the level-two page heading and the address block are centered on the page, and that the lists now use a graphic bullet, as shown in Figure E-12.

FIGURE E-11: Text formatting code

```
h1      {
        font-family: Century Schoolbook, Times New Roman,
        Times, serif;
        color: #336633;
        font-size: 36px;
        margin: 0px;
}

h2      {
        font-family: Century Schoolbook, Times New Roman, Times, serif;
        color: #000066;
        font-size: 28px;
        text-align: center;
}

address {
        text-align: center;
}



img     {
        margin-right: 25px;
}

div     {
        margin-left: 40px;
        margin-right: 40px;
}

ul      {
        list-style-image: url(../images/pm_bul1.png);
}
```

FIGURE E-12: Activities page with centered heading, address block, and graphic bullets

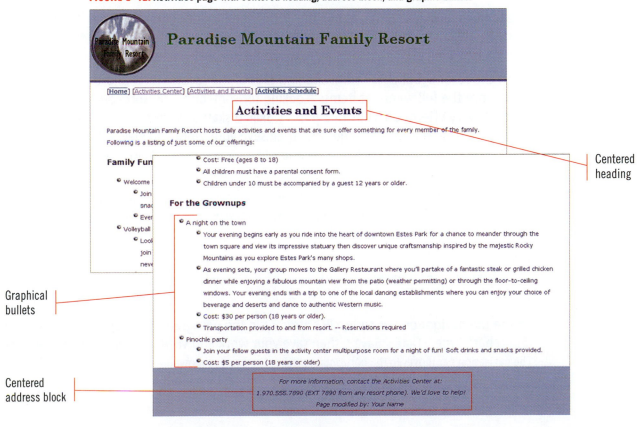

Centered heading

Graphical bullets

Centered address block

HTML

Using CSS Class Rules

Up until now, you have used type selector rules to apply CSS formatting to specific HTML elements. You have changed formatting while keeping your code relatively free of nonessential markup. However, there are times when you must go to the tag level to apply or to override a style set in your style sheet. **CSS class selector rules**—named sets of formatting instructions—allow you to define a specific-purpose style in the style sheet that can be triggered in the document code. Class selectors are preceded by a period (.), known as a **flag**, that identifies the rule as a class rule. Following the flag is the selector name. Class rules can be applied inline to any element using `class="classname"`. When the browser sees `class="classname"` in an opening tag, it uses the formatting instructions specified in the style sheet for that class. When you specify a class, you do not type the flag. Once you have defined a class in the style sheet, you can change the formatting instructions for the class in the style sheet, and the instructions cascade down to any element using that class. You have identified a few areas of your Web page that still need formatting but that cannot be formatted using type selector rules. You will apply class selector rules to these elements.

STEPS

1. **Return to your code, click just after } that ends the unordered list rule, press [Enter] twice, then type the following code, pressing [Enter] after each line:**

```
.second_bul    {
    list-style-image: url(../images/pm_bul2.png);
}
```

   You created a class selector rule that defines a class called second_bul. You can apply the rule to your second-level unordered lists to change the graphic bullet to pm_bul2.png, which is a square bullet.

2. **Locate the opening `<ul>` tag above the line of code that begins `<li>`join us poolside, click inside the `<ul>` tag just after ul, press [Spacebar], then type `class="second_bul"`**

   As shown in Figure E-13, you have applied the second_bul class to the second-level list under "Family Fun."

3. **Apply the second_bul class to the opening tags of the second-level unordered lists that start above the following list items: "Looking for someone," "Resort counselors are on hand," "Every afternoon from 1 - 3 p.m.," "Skilled skateboarders," "Your evening begins," and "Join your fellow guests," then save your work and view it in your browser**

   Each of the second-level unordered list items starts with a square bullet, as shown in Figure E-14. You notice that the navigation bar near the top of the page remains uncentered.

4. **Return to your code, click in the embedded style sheet just after the closing } following the .second_bul class selector rule, press [Enter] twice, then type the following code, pressing [Enter] after each line:**

```
.nav1    {
    text-align: center;
}
```

5. **Locate the navigation bar code, click after `<p` in the paragraph tag just after the `<p`, press [Spacebar], type `class="nav1"`, then save your work and view your page in your browser**

   The navigation bar moves to the horizontal center of the page, as shown in Figure E-15.

FIGURE E-13: Unordered list tag with applied second_bul class

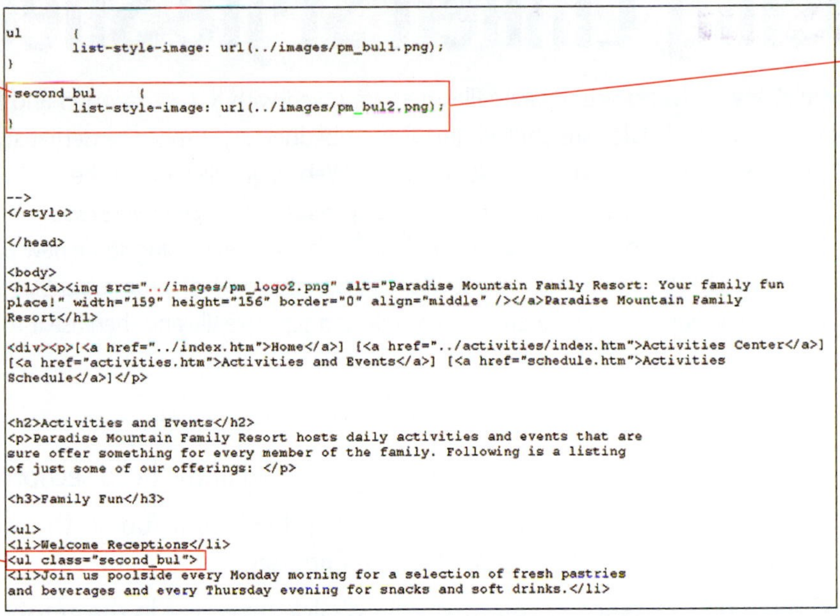

Flag

```
ul        {
          list-style-image: url(../images/pm_bul1.png);
}

.second_bul    {
          list-style-image: url(../images/pm_bul2.png);
}



-->
</style>

</head>

<body>
<h1><a><img src="../images/pm_logo2.png" alt="Paradise Mountain Family fun
place!" width="159" height="156" border="0" align="middle" /></a>Paradise Mountain Family
Resort</h1>

<div><p>[<a href="../index.htm">Home</a>] [<a href="../activities/index.htm">Activities Center</a>]
[<a href="activities.htm">Activities and Events</a>] [<a href="schedule.htm">Activities
Schedule</a>]</p></div>

<h2>Activities and Events</h2>
<p>Paradise Mountain Family Resort hosts daily activities and events that are
sure offer something for every member of the family. Following is a listing
of just some of our offerings: </p>

<h3>Family Fun</h3>

<ul>
<li>Welcome Receptions</li>
<ul class="second_bul">
<li>Join us poolside every Monday morning for a selection of fresh pastries
and beverages and every Thursday evening for snacks and soft drinks.</li>
```

Defined second_bul class

Applied class

FIGURE E-14: Activities page with square second-level bullets

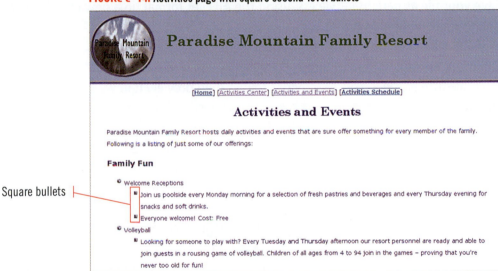

Square bullets

FIGURE E-15: Activities page with centered navigation bar

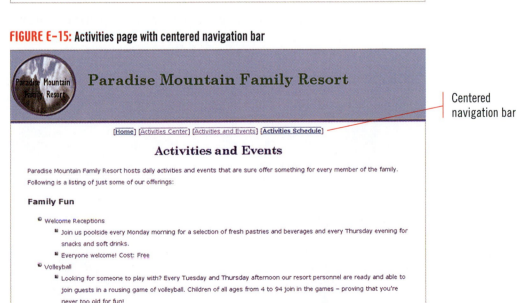

Centered navigation bar

Using Linked Style Sheets

External style sheets are separate files that are saved with a .css extension and linked to documents to which their defined styles are applied. Just like embedded style sheets, external style sheets use type and class selectors. To link an external style sheet to a Web page, click inside the head section and type `<link href="folder/stylesheetname.css" rel="stylesheet" type="text/css" />` substituting the name of your style sheet file for `stylesheetname`. You are developing some new pages to which you want to apply style sheet formatting. You also want to update some of your current pages with style sheet formatting. You decide to save your embedded style as a separate file and then use it to format the other pages in your site.

STEPS

QUICK TIP

To open a second instance of Notepad, choose All Programs/ Accessories/Notepad from the Windows Start Menu.

QUICK TIP

Use the All Files format to ensure that your file is not saved as paradise_style.css.txt. Also, if you did not complete Unit D, copy the media folder to your paradise site folder.

1. **Return to your code, locate the opening style tag in the head section of your document**

2. **Click and drag through the embedded style sheet from "body" through the } following the .nav1 style class, then copy it to the Clipboard**

3. **Open a new instance of your text editor, click anywhere in the empty document, then paste the code you copied from the Clipboard into the new document**

4. **Save your file as paradise_style.css, using the All Files format, in a new root-level folder that you create called css**

   The folder should be at the same level as the spa, activities, images, and media folders, as shown in Figure E-16.

5. **Open the file htm_E-2.txt from the place where you store your Data Files, save it as schedule.htm in the Paradise\activities folder, then preview it in your browser**

   The file contains some placeholder text, the resort logo, some bullet items, and little else. It has not been formatted. You need to insert a link to the external style sheet.

6. **Return to your schedule.htm page code, click in the head section before </head>, type `<link href="../css/paradise_style.css" rel="stylesheet" type="text/css" />`, then press [Enter] twice to insert a link to the external style sheet**

   Your code should resemble Figure E-17.

7. **Locate the navigation bar near the top of the page, click inside the paragraph tag just after <p>, press [Spacebar], then type `class="nav1"`**

8. **Replace Your Name after "Page modified by" at the bottom of the code with your own name, save the file, print the code, then view the page in your browser**

   The file appears formatted with your site styles, as shown in Figure E-18. Because there were no second-level lists, you did not need to apply that class.

9. **Close your browser and text editor**

FIGURE E-16: Paradise site structure with css folder

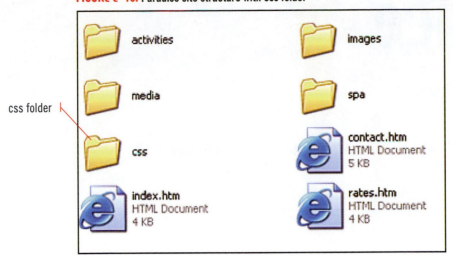

css folder

FIGURE E-17: Linked style applied to head section of document

Linked stylesheet reference typed in head section

```
<!DOCTYPE html PUBLIC "-//W3C//DTD XHTML 1.0 Transitional//EN"
"http://www.w3.org/TR/xhtml1/DTD/xhtml1-transitional.dtd">
<html>
<head>

<title>Paradise Mountain Family Resort Weekly Activities List</title>

<meta name="description" content="Paradise Mountain Family Resort weekly activities
schedule for more information contact the activities center at: 1.970.555.7890" />

<meta http-equiv="Content-Type" content="text/html; charset=iso-8859-1" />

<link href="../css/paradise_style.css" rel="stylesheet" type="text/css" />

</head>

<body>
<h1><a href="../index.htm"><img src="../images/pm_logo2.png" alt="Paradise Mountain
```

FIGURE E-18: Document formatted by linked style sheet

HTML

Practice

▼ CONCEPTS REVIEW

Name the function of each section of code indicated in Figure E-19.

```
1  <!DOCTYPE html PUBLIC "-//W3C//DTD XHTML 1.0 Transitional//EN"
   "http://www.w3.org/TR/xhtml1/DTD/xhtml1-transitional.dtd">
   <html>
   <head>

   <title>Paradise Mountain Family Resort Weekly Activities List</title>

   <meta name="description" content="Paradise Mountain Family Resort weekly activities
    schedule for more information contact the activities center at: 1.970.555.7890" />

2  <meta http-equiv="Content-Type" content="text/html; charset=iso-8859-1" />

3  <style>

4  <!--

5  body    {
               font-family: Verdana, Arial, Helvetica, sans-serif;

        }

6  div      {
               margin-left: 40px;
               margin-right: 40px;
        }

7  .second {
               list-style-image: url(../images/pm_bul2.png);
        }

   -->
   </style>
8  <link href="activities_style.css" rel="stylesheet" type="text/css" />
   </head>
```

9

Match each statement with the term it describes.

10. A feature of CSS
11. A style that formats an individual HTML tag
12. A style sheet that can control the style of many Web pages
13. The file extension of an external style sheet
14. The location of an embedded style sheet

a. Inline
b. CSS
c. External
d. Header
e. Cascade

Select the best answer from the list of choices.

15. **Which of the following should be the first line of code in an XHTML document?**
    a. Document type definition
    b. Embedded style sheet
    c. Link to the external style sheet
    d. Inline style definition

16. **Which type of DTD should be used in an HTML document that is free of formatting attributes?**
    a. XHTML Transitional
    b. XHTML Strict
    c. XHTML Frameset
    d. XHTML Styles

17. **Which one of the following is used before a class selector?**
    a. {
    b. :
    c. ;
    d. .

18. **Where should a link to an external style sheet be placed?**
    a. Inside a comment
    b. Inside the DTD
    c. Inside the body
    d. Inside the head

19. **Where should embedded styles be placed?**
    a. Inside the head
    b. Inside the DTD
    c. Inside the body
    d. Inside `<div>...</div>` tags

20. **Which of the following is used to hide embedded styles from browsers that do not support CSS ?**
    a. `<!--...-->`
    b. `/*...*/`
    c. `<style>...</style>`
    d. `<head>...</head>`

▼ SKILLS REVIEW

1. **Explore CSS formatting.**
    a. Consider how CSS styles can be used to format the pages of the spa site. What styles are appropriate for the spa site?
    b. Which styles should be included in embedded style sheets?
    c. Which styles should be added to an external style sheet?
    d. How can classes be used to format the spa pages?
    e. How can styles be used to format the site's links?

2. **Control text formatting.**
    a. In your text editor, open the file **htm_E-3.txt** from the drive and folder where your Data Files are stored, then save it as **salon.htm** to the paradise/spa directory where you save your site files. If you are asked whether you want to replace the file, click Yes.
    b. Open the **salon.htm** file in your browser to view the unformatted page.
    c. Using your text editor, add the XHTML transitional doctype description at the top of the page above the opening `<html>` tag.
    d. Add a meta tag after the `</title>` tag with a description of the content as "Aphrodite's Salon full-service hair and nail salon."

    e. Add a meta character-set tag under the previous meta tag to let the browser know the page is written in HTML. (*Hint*: Use the code `<meta http-equiv="Content-Type" content="text/html; charset=iso-8859-1" />`.)

    f. Add opening and closing style tags above the basefont tag in the page head.

    g. Add opening and closing comment tags inside the styles tags to hide style code from browsers that do not support CSS.

    h. Add an embedded style rule after the opening comment tag that defines the body page font as Franklin Gothic Book, Arial, Helvetica, sans-serif. (*Hint*: Use the body selector with the declaration `{font-family: Franklin Gothic Book, Arial, Helvetica, sans-serif;}`.)

    i. Delete the basefont style tag in the head. (Because the basefont tag has been deprecated by the W3C in favor of CSS, you replaced this style with the embedded style sheet of your page in the previous step.)

3. Set background colors and images.

    a. Add an embedded style rule for the page body that inserts a background image using the path `../images/bkg_pillar_green1.gif`. (*Hint*: Use the body selector with the declaration `{background-image: url(../images/bkg_pillar_green1.gif);}`.) If you did not complete Unit D, copy the two files in the images folder from the folder where your Data Files are stored and paste them in the paradise/images directory. If necessary, create an images folder in the paradise folder.

    b. Add an embedded style rule for the body that sets the left margin of the page to 150 pixels. (*Hint*: Use the margin-left declaration followed by a colon, with a semicolon after the rule.)

    c. Add an embedded style rule for the body that sets the top margin of the page to 5 pixels.

    d. Add an embedded style rule for the body that sets the right margin of the page to 0 pixels.

    e. Delete the image and left margin information in the `<body>` tag of the page. (*Hint*: The `<body>` tag should not have any attributes.)

    f. Save your work, then open the file in your browser to view the new formatting.

4. Set link properties.

    a. Add an embedded style that formats the unclicked links on the page to bold, a color of #000099, and no decoration. (*Hint*: Add a style of `a:link {font-weight: bold; color: #000099; text-decoration: none;}`.)

    b. Add an embedded style that formats the visited links on the page with a color of #666699 and no decoration.

    c. Add an embedded style that formats the active links on the page to bold, italics, a color of #9933CC, and no decoration.

    d. Add an embedded style that formats the links to bold, italics, a color of #00FF99, and no decoration when the mouse hovers over the link.

    e. Save your work and view the page in your browser.

5. Apply margins.

    a. Add opening and closing `<div>` tags to enclose the main content of the page from below the top navigation bar to just above the `</body>` tag.

    b. Add a style declaration for the `<div>` tag to add 40 pixels of white space above the main page content. (*Hint*: Add `div {margin-top: 40px;}` to the embedded style sheet.)

    c. Save your work, then view the file in your browser.

    d. Verify that additional white space has been added between the top navigation bar and the remainder of the page.

6. Apply text alignment and format lists.

    a. Add an embedded style to format the text in address tags as bold. (*Hint*: Add the style `address{font-weight: bold;}` to your embedded style sheet.)

    b. Add an embedded style to set the color of level-three headings to #336633. (*Hint*: Add the style `h3 {color: #336633;}` to your embedded style sheet.)

    c. Add an embedded style to set the font-size of level-three headings to 20 pixels. (*Hint*: Add `font-size: 20px;` to the h3 style entered in the previous step.)

    d. Save your work, then reload the page in your browser.

    e. Verify the changes to the address text and the level-three headings.

7. Use CSS class rules.

    a. Create a class named circle in the embedded style sheet to format bullets in an unordered list to the open circle style. (*Hint*: Add the code `.circle{list-style-type: circle;}` to your embedded style sheet.)

   b. Place the code `class="circle"` in the `<ul>` tags of the page to apply the circle class to both of the unordered lists in the page.

   c. Replace Your Name between the address tags with your name.

   d. Save your work, reload the file in your browser, then verify the changes to the bullets in the page's lists.

8. Use linked style sheets.

   a. Copy the entire embedded style sheet from your salon.htm page. Do not copy the opening and closing `<style>` tags or the comment tags.

   b. Create an external style sheet by pasting the embedded style sheet into a new empty file, then save it as **salon_style.css** in your paradise/css directory. You should not have the opening or closing `<style>` or comment tags in the external style sheet.

   c. Delete the entire embedded style sheet from your salon.htm file, save the **salon.htm** file, then view the unformatted page in your browser.

   d. Place the link `<link href="../css/salon_style.css" rel="stylesheet" type="text/css" />` to the external style sheet salon_style.css in the salon.htm file's head, before the `</head>` tag.

   e. Resave the **salon.htm** file, then reload the file in your browser.

   f. Verify the page is formatted with the styles in the external style sheet, then print the page in the browser.

   g. Transfer the files to your remote directory.

▼ INDEPENDENT CHALLENGE 1

As you continue developing the Web site for your resort rental business, Star Vacations, you want to use the external and embedded style sheets to format your pages.

   a. In your text editor, open the file **htm_E-4.txt** from the drive and folder where your Data Files are stored, then save it as **features.htm** in the vacations folder where you save your site files. If you are asked whether you want to replace the file, click Yes.

   b. Add a DTD and appropriate meta tags to the page.

   c. Add an embedded style sheet to replace the basefont style information in the header. Don't forget to delete the basefont tag. (*Hint*: Place the following in the embedded style sheet: `body{font-family: Arial, sans serif; color: #000066;}`.)

   d. Add a class named square to the embedded style sheet. that formats the bullets in an unordered list as a square shape (*Hint*: Place the following in the embedded style sheet:
     `.square{list-style-type: square;}`.)

   e. Add `class="square"` to the `<ul>` tag on your page to apply the style to your unordered list.

   f. In your text editor, open a new file, then save it as **star_style.css** in your Vacations folder.

   g. Using Figure E-20 as a guide, add the following styles to your star_style.css external style sheet:

     • Set the body background color to #CCFFCC.

     • Add a top margin of 5 pixels to the body.

     • Format the links as bold, underlined, and a color of #006699.

     • Format the links to a color of #009933 and underlined when the mouse hovers over it.

     • Format level-one headings to 40 pixels with a color of #000099.

   h. Add a link in the features.htm file to the external style sheet.

FIGURE E-20

```
body {
        background-color: #CCFFCC;
        margin-top: 5px;
}
a:link {
        font-weight: bold;
        color: #006699;
        text-decoration: underline;
}
a:hover {
        color: #009933;
        text-decoration: underline;
}
h1      {
        color: #000099;
        font-size: 40px;
}
```

▼ INDEPENDENT CHALLENGE 1 (CONTINUED)

i. Using the search engine of your choice, find a new international resort. Add a link to the resort in the unordered list of the features page.

j. Replace Your Name between the address tags with your name, save your work, display the **features.htm** file in the browser to check your styles, then transfer your completed pages to your remote directory.

Advanced Challenge Exercises

- Find a color that you would like to use as a background when the mouse hovers over the link.
- Add a style to your external sheet that changes the link background to your color when the mouse hovers over the link. (*Hint*: Add `background:#FFFFFF;` to the a:hover style, replacing `#FFFFFF` with the code for your chosen color.)
- Save your external style sheet, and check the link background color.
- Save your files and transfer them to the remote site.

▼ INDEPENDENT CHALLENGE 2

You want to use style sheets to format the water-conservation Web site you are developing for your employer, Metro Water. You decide to put many of the styles for your pages in an external style sheet to ensure uniform formatting throughout your Web site. You will check the external styles by applying them to a page in your Web site.

a. Create an external style sheet, then save it as **metro_style.css** in the water folder where you save your site files.

b. Add rules to format the body of a Web page with the following styles:
- Background color of #CCFFCC
- Top margin of 10 pixels
- Font-family of Verdana, Arial, Helvetica, sans serif
- Font color of #333333

c. Add a style rule to format the links as underlined, a color of #0066FF, and a hover effect of bold.

d. Add a class rule named "small" to change the numbers of the ordered list to lower case alpha characters (*Hint*: Set the list-style-type to `lower-alpha`.)

e. Add a style rule to the `<div>` tag that sets the left margin to 25 pixels.

f. Save the external style sheet.

g. In your text editor, open the **htm_E-5.txt** file from the drive and folder where your Data Files are stored, then save it as **inside.htm** in the water folder where you save your site files. If you are asked whether you want to replace the file, click Yes.

h. Delete the page's basefont style information in the head section.

i. Add `<div>` tags to apply the style defined in Step e to the General Tips section of the page. (*Hint*: There are comments in the page to help you place the opening and closing `<div>` tags in the correct location.)

j. Add `class="small"` to the `<ol>` tag on the page.

k. Place a link to the metro_styles.css style sheet in the page head.

l. Replace Your Name between the address tags with your name, save your work, then display the **inside.htm** file in your browser to make sure the styles have been applied to the page. Your page should match Figure E-21.

m. Save your work and transfer the files to the remote site.

FIGURE E-21

[Home] [Conserving Inside] [Conserving Outside] [Super Saver] [Resources] [Landscaping and Irrigation]

Conservation Tips

Conserving Water Indoors

Are you using more water than y...
he or she would imagine. Cutting...
surprised at how much money th...

If you have questions about wat...
customer surveys, the most comm...

a. How can I tell how much wa...
b. What can I do to conserve w...
c. Is my water usage within re...
d. What's the average daily wa...
e. What if I have a well, doesn...

If you have ever asked yourself a...
links below to find your answers.

[General Tips]

You and your water usage

If you want to know how much w...
month is listed there.

Water District Household Averag...

person per day. However, if you are at the high end of the scale or if you are using more water than average, chances are that you can substantially reduce your water usage. Every drop helps . . . *You CAN make a difference!*

General Tips

- Never pour water down the drain when there may be another use for it such as watering a plant or garden, or for cleaning around your home.
- Verify that your home is leak free. Many homes have hidden water leaks. Read your water meter before and after a two-hour period when no water is being used. If the meter does not read exactly the same, there is a leak.
- Repair dripping faucets by replacing washers. If your faucet is dripping at a rate of one drop per second, you can expect to waste 2,700 gallons per year. This adds to the cost of water and sewer utilities and adds to your water bill.
- Retrofit all household faucets by installing aerators with flow restrictors to slow the flow of water.
- Evaporative coolers require a seasonal maintenance check-up. For more water efficient cooling, check your evaporative coolers annually. Insulate your water pipes. You'll get hot water faster and avoid wasting water while it heats up.
- Install water softening systems only when necessary. Save water and salt by running the minimum amount of regenerations necessary to maintain water softness. Turn softeners off while on vacation.

In the Kitchen

- Operate automatic dishwashers and clothes washers only when they are fully loaded. Set the water level for the size of load you are using.
- When washing dishes by hand, fill one sink or basin with soapy water. Quickly rinse under a slow-moving stream from the faucet.
- Store drinking water in the refrigerator. Don't let the tap run while you are waiting for cool water to flow.
- Do not use running water to thaw meat or other frozen foods. Defrost food overnight in the refrigerator or use the defrost setting on your microwave.
- Kitchen sink disposals require lots of water to operate properly. Start a compost pile as an alternate method of disposing of food waste, instead of using a garbage disposal. Garbage disposals also can add 50 percent to

▼ INDEPENDENT CHALLENGE 2 (CONTINUED)

Advanced Challenge Exercises

- Add an embedded style section to the inside.htm page under the link to the external style sheet, just above the `</head>` tag.
- Add a style to the embedded style sheet that uses the class `small` to change the numbers of the ordered list to lower roman numerals. Add the class name to the ordered list.
- Add an inline style to the `<body>` tag of the page to set the background color to #FFFF99.
- Save your changes to the inside.htm page, and display the file in the browser to check your styles.
- Write a paragraph describing your observations of the precedence of external, embedded, and inline styles.
- Transfer your completed pages to your remote directory.

▼ INDEPENDENT CHALLENGE 3

Style sheets are used to preserve a consistent look for the pages of a Web site. You want to use style sheets, but you are concerned about accessibility and browser support.

a. Go to the Student Online Companion for this text, locate the link for this unit, then go to the W3C Web Accessibility page and review the information for CSS techniques. Write one or two paragraphs answering the following questions:
- How can the use of style sheets make your site more user-friendly?
- What are the issues of accessibility when using style sheets?
- What methods are included in CSS2 that allow content to be generated from style sheets?
- Add your name and today's date to the top of your paper.
- Print the paper.

b. Use the search engine of your choice to research the two versions of CSS: CSS1 and CSS2. Investigate the browser support for CSS1 and CSS2, and then write one or two paragraphs answering the following questions:
- When were the CSS1 and CSS2 versions introduced?
- Which browsers fully support CSS1 and CSS2?
- Which browsers partially support CSS1 and CSS2?
- Add your name and today's date to the top of your paper, then print it.

▼ INDEPENDENT CHALLENGE 4

Now that you've studied style sheets to define styles for Web pages, you are ready to add style sheets to the pages on your Web site.

a. Determine how the different types of style sheets can be used in your Web site. You need to add at least one embedded and one external style sheet to your site.

b. Add at least one style that formats the entire page body.

c. Add at least one style that formats a class.

d. Add at least one style that formats the `<div>` tag.

e. Place links to your external style sheet in the appropriate pages of your site.

f. Transfer your external style sheet and your edited files to the remote location.

HTML

Work progresses on your Bits and PCs Web site and you decide to use an external style sheet to format your pages. In your text editor, open the **htm_E-6.txt** file from the drive and folder where your Data Files are stored, then save it as **index.htm** in the bitspcs folder where you save your site files. Create an external style sheet, then save it as **bit_style.css** in the bitspcs folder where you save your site files. Your external style sheet should format your index page as shown in Figure E-22. Use classes to center the navigation bar and to format the contact information at the bottom of the page. Replace info in the e-mail link label at the bottom of the page with your name. (*Hint*: Both the level-one and level-three headings are formatted with the color #3333FF and the links, including the visited ones, are formatted with the color #006699. Level-one headings are 30 pixels in size.)

FIGURE E-22

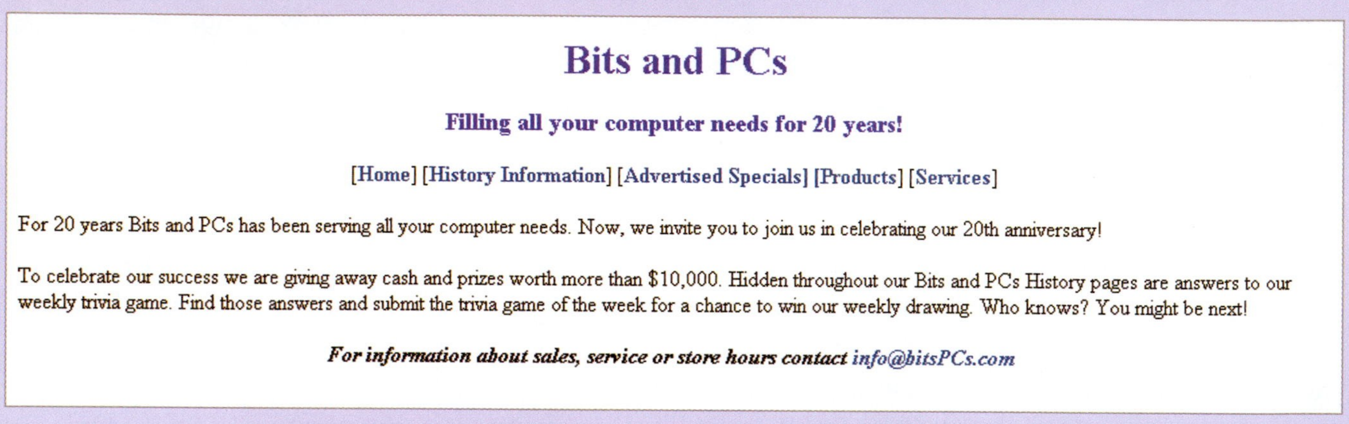

Bits and PCs

Filling all your computer needs for 20 years!

[Home] [History Information] [Advertised Specials] [Products] [Services]

For 20 years Bits and PCs has been serving all your computer needs. Now, we invite you to join us in celebrating our 20th anniversary!

To celebrate our success we are giving away cash and prizes worth more than $10,000. Hidden throughout our Bits and PCs History pages are answers to our weekly trivia game. Find those answers and submit the trivia game of the week for a chance to win our weekly drawing. Who knows? You might be next!

For information about sales, service or store hours contact info@bitsPCs.com

Working with Tables

OBJECTIVES

Plan a table
Create a simple table
Span and align columns and rows
Format table content
Format borders
Modify table backgrounds
Change table dimensions
Position page elements

Although paragraphs are a useful way to present most Web page information, certain types of content require other formats. HTML includes extensive support for one of the most common alternate layouts: the **table**, which allows you to present information in a grid of columns and rows, creating a compact list of items and their related details. Tables are also often used as a method for laying out Web pages. Once you plan and create a table, you can align columns and rows, adjust cells so they span multiple columns or rows, and format cell data, borders, and backgrounds. You can also easily change the table size and its position on the page.  Your current project at Paradise Mountain is to add an activities and events calendar with a listing of activity days and times. Formatting the activity information using a table allows Web page users to easily find information about activities that interest them.

Planning a Table

A table is a useful way to summarize many types of information, including the differences among a list of items or the results of a database search. You can also use tables to tailor Web page design by controlling element positioning. As shown in Figure F-1, table data is organized into rows and columns; a **row** is a single horizontal line of data, and a **column** is a single vertical line of data. The intersection of a row and a column is a single unit of table data called a **cell**. Many aspects of tables are customizable. Figure F-1 also shows several customizations, including table heading formatting, spans, cell alignment, background color, and a caption. Figure F-2 shows the code for the sample table. Table F-1 summarizes the HTML tags used to create a table. As you prepare to create the table for the Paradise Mountain activities page, you plan your table layout.

DETAILS

Some of the many attributes for controlling a table's appearance include:

- **Structure and border**

  You can customize a table to include exactly the number of columns and rows that your data requires. You also can modify a table's structure so that one or more cells span multiple rows or columns. By default, each cell is slightly separated from the cells that surround it. To make the boundaries between cells clearer, you can add cell borders to a table. HTML allows you to customize border color and thickness.

- **Alignment**

  Just as with standard Web page elements or paragraphs of text, you can align cell contents along the cell's right or left edges, or center it between the two edges. Additionally, you can set the vertical alignment flush with the top or bottom cell border, or centered between the two borders. The default alignment for a table cell is horizontally left aligned and vertically centered.

- **Background**

  By default, a Web page table is transparent, showing the same background image or color as the Web page. However, you can apply a custom background color to the entire table, specific rows, or individual cells.

- **Dimensions**

  In addition to customizing the number of rows and columns in the table structure, you can specify the sizes of table elements, as well as the spacing between them. You can set the entire table to a fixed width or height, or you can specify table dimensions as a percentage of the window size. You also can set the amount of blank space around the contents of each cell, as well as the amount of space between cells.

- **Positioning**

  Because tables are so flexible and customizable, Web designers have found many uses for them. Tables are commonly used to position page elements and control page layout. While the W3C recommends CSS over tables as a method of controlling element positioning, some complicated designs are easier to achieve when tables are used.

TABLE F-1: HTML table tags

tag(s)	function
`<table>...</table>`	Defines start and end of table contents
`<tr>...</tr>`	Marks contents of each table row
`<th>...</th>`	Marks contents of a table heading cell and applies table heading format
`<td>...</td>`	Marks contents of a table data cell
`<caption>...</caption>`	When coded within a table, formats text to appear as a table caption

FIGURE F-1: Table components with customizable features

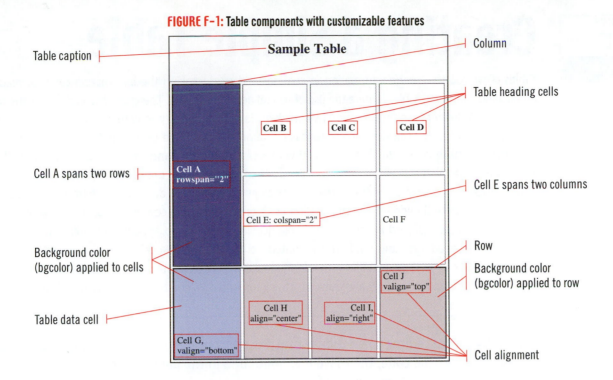

FIGURE F-2: Sample table code

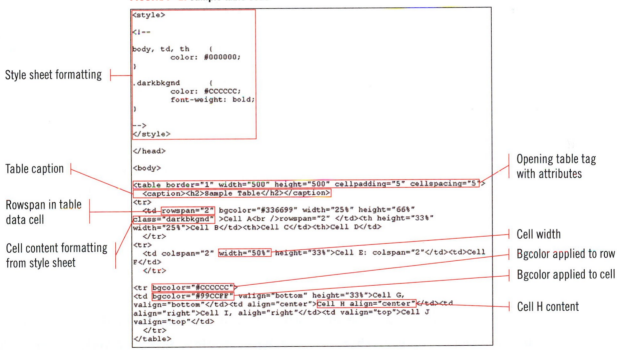

Design Matters

Formatting cell contents

When working with tables it is best to avoid the use of `<font>...</font>` tags for formatting large areas of page content. Because browsers treat each table cell as a separate window, cell content does not inherit properties set using standard HTML formatting, such as the `<font>...</font>` tag outside of the table. (**Standard HTML** is HTML without the benefit of style sheets and XHMTL or DHMTL enhancements.) A better method is to use CSS formatting to declare the font attributes for all table content. You can use the basefont tag to specify a formatting style for the page in order to code for **backward compatibility**—the ability to ensure that your page is displayed as expected in older browsers. In most browsers, CSS formatting overrides standard HTML formatting.

Creating a Simple Table

Tables allow you to arrange information in columns and rows, making the information easier to read and understand. However, tables require the use of several nested elements. Therefore, the code to create even a simple table is longer than most other HTML markup. Tables begin and end with `<table>`...`</table>`—the parent tag for all tables. Table content is contained within table cells. The two types of table cells are **table heading cells**, which are marked with `<th>`...`</th>`, and **table data cells**—marked with `<td>`...`</td>`. All table cells must be contained within a **table row**—designated by the opening and closing table row tags, `<tr>`...`</tr>`. The default alignment for table data cell content is left-aligned and aligned to the vertical middle. The default alignment for table heading content is horizontally aligned in the center and vertically aligned in the middle. Table heading content also appears as boldfaced type, making column or row headings stand out from the contents of the regular data cells. The Activities Center director has given you some text files with information about daily youth-centered activities. You added head and document formatting codes and think that the information will be best displayed in table format.

STEPS

1. **Start your text editor, open the file htm_F-1.txt from the place where you store your Data Files, inspect the code, then save it as youth.htm in the paradise/activities folder in the place where you store your site files**

   The file contains the youth activity information that you received, along with a transitional doctype declaration, the meta character set tag, a link to your style sheet, link tags, and the image logo tag that was added earlier. As shown in Figure F-3, the file also contains several comment tags.

2. **Click after the comment tag that reads `<!-- Start table and row 1 here -->`, press [Enter], type `<table border="1">`, then press [Enter]**

   Your code starts the table and sets a one-pixel border. You'll learn more about borders in another lesson.

3. **Type `<tr>`, click before the comment that reads `<!-- End row 1 here -->`, then type `</tr>`**

   Your code starts and ends the first row. You want to make the first row a heading row.

4. **Click below `<tr>` and before the word Day, type `<th>`, click after Day, type `</th>`, then type opening and closing table heading tags before and after the following items: Time, Activity, Location, Cost, and Notes**

   You have formatted the cells in the first table row as table heading cells.

5. **Click after each of the next Start row comments, press [Enter], press [Delete], then type `<tr>`**

6. **Click before each of the End row comments, type `</tr>`, then press [Enter]**

7. **Type `<td>` before and `</td>` after each of the words or phrases listed in Table F-2**

8. **Click before `<!-- End table here -->`, type `</table>`, save your work, start your Web browser, then preview the file youth.htm in your browser**

   As shown in Figure F-4, the data for the Sunday and Monday events appears in a table of six columns and three rows. The rest of the week's activities need to be added to the table.

9. **Open another text editor window, open the file htm_F-2.txt from the place where you store your Data Files, click before `<tr>` under the comment at the top of the page, then select and copy all of the code and text to the end of the document**

10. **Return to the youth.htm file, click in the blank line above `</table>`, paste the code, then save your work**

    Your table now lists all of the youth activity events.

FIGURE F-3: Text file with XHTML elements and comment tags

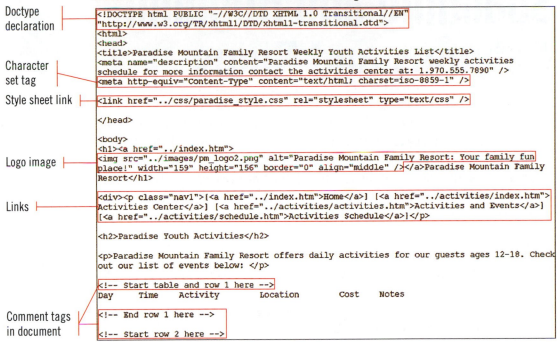

Doctype declaration

```
<!DOCTYPE html PUBLIC "-//W3C//DTD XHTML 1.0 Transitional//EN"
"http://www.w3.org/TR/xhtml1/DTD/xhtml1-transitional.dtd">
<html>
<head>
<title>Paradise Mountain Family Resort Weekly Youth Activities List</title>
<meta name="description" content="Paradise Mountain Family Resort weekly activities
schedule for more information contact the activities center at: 1.970.555.7890" />
```

Character set tag
```
<meta http-equiv="Content-Type" content="text/html; charset=iso-8859-1" />
```

Style sheet link
```
<link href="../css/paradise_style.css" rel="stylesheet" type="text/css" />

</head>

<body>
<h1><a href="../index.htm">
```

Logo image
```
<img src="../images/pm_logo2.png" alt="Paradise Mountain Family Resort: Your family fun
place!" width="159" height="156" border="0" align="middle" /></a>Paradise Mountain Family
Resort</h1>
```

Links
```
<div><p class="nav1">[<a href="../index.htm">Home</a>] [<a href="../activities/index.htm">
Activities Center</a>] [<a href="../activities/activities.htm">Activities and Events</a>]
[<a href="../activities/schedule.htm">Activities Schedule</a>]</p>

<h2>Paradise Youth Activities</h2>

<p>Paradise Mountain Family Resort offers daily activities for our guests ages 12-18. Check
out our list of events below: </p>
```

Comment tags in document
```
<!-- Start table and row 1 here -->
Day      Time     Activity       Location       Cost    Notes

<!-- End row 1 here -->

<!-- Start row 2 here -->
```

FIGURE F-4: Youth activities table code output

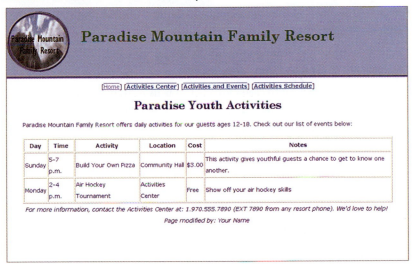

TABLE F-2: Opening and closing points for table cells

row	cell 1	cell 2	cell 3	cell 4	cell 5	cell 6
2	`<td>Sunday</td>`	`<td>5-7 p.m.</td>`	`<td>Build Your Own Pizza</td>`	`<td>Community Hall</td>`	`<td>$3.00</td>`	`<td>This... another</td>`
3	`<td>Monday</td>`	`<td>2-4 p.m.</td>`	`<td>Air Hockey Tournament</td>`	`<td>Activities Center</td>`	`<td>Free</td>`	`<td>Show... skills</td>`

Clues to Use

Using comments in tables

A useful tool in creating tables is the **comment tag**, which you can use to create statements such as (`<!-- Comment information goes here. -->`). You can insert such tags in your code to make notations and to make it easier to find specific content when you want to edit it later. Browsers do not display code or text that is contained within comment tags. Comment tags can contain one or more lines as well as other tags as long as the comment starts with `<!--`, and ends with `-->`.

Spanning and Aligning Columns and Rows

A basic table contains cells of data arranged in columns and rows. However, sometimes the contents of a cell apply to more than one row or column. You can mark a single cell to **span**—cover or become part of—multiple rows or columns by using attributes in the `<th>` or `<td>` tags. When used with a numeric value, the **rowspan** attribute causes a cell to span multiple rows. Likewise, the **colspan** attribute with a numeric value causes the cell to span multiple columns. The Notes column at the end of the youth activities table contains more information than the rest of the table cells. You think the content would look better positioned in a separate row that spans the width of the table below the other information for each day's event.

STEPS

1. **With your youth.htm page code open, drag to select `<th>Notes</th>` in row 1, then press [Delete]**

   You removed the Notes table heading because you are going to reposition the information from that column in a row located under the details for each item.

2. **Click just after `<td>$3.00</td>` in row 2, press [Enter], type `</tr>`, press [Enter] twice, then type `<tr>`**

   You ended the row after the cost column and started a new row, which contains the information formerly in the Notes column.

   QUICK TIP

   The process of spanning table rows is very similar to spanning columns. Instead of using the colspan attribute in a `<th>` or `<td>` tag, you use rowspan.

3. **Click after td in the opening table data tag that starts the next line of code, press [Spacebar], then type `colspan="5"`**

   You caused the content of the cell in the new row to span the width of your table. You did not have to code a second end table row tag because the second row used the existing `</tr>` tag.

4. **Repeat Steps 2 and 3 in each of the remaining rows, then save your work**

   Your code should resemble that shown in Figure F-5, which shows the code for the Monday and Tuesday events.

5. **Click the browser program button on the taskbar, then reload youth.htm**

   The information from the notes column is now formatted in a separate single-cell row that spans the width of the table. You think the dollar amounts in the fifth column would look better aligned to the right.

6. **Click the text editor program button on the taskbar to return to the youth.htm document code**

7. **Locate the opening table data tag for the row 2 cell that contains the content $3.00, click after td in the tag, press [Spacebar], then type `align="right"`**

8. **Repeat Step 7 to align the text for all the other cells in the Cost column, then save your work and reload the youth.htm page in the browser**

   As shown in Figure F-6, the text in the column containing the cost information is aligned to the right, enabling the decimal points in the monetary amounts to line up, but the table requires additional formatting.

```
<tr>
<td>Monday</td> <td>2-4 p.m.</td>        <td>Air Hockey Tournament</td>   <td>Activities
Center</td>        <td>Free</td>
</tr>

<tr>

<td colspan="5">Show off your air hockey skills</td>

</tr><!-- End row 3 here -->

<!-- Insert copied table rows and data below this comment -->

<tr>
<td>Tuesday</td>          <td>10 a.m. - noon</td> <td>Skateboard Instruction and
Demonstration</td>        <td>Skate Park</td>       <td>Free</td>
</tr>

<tr>

<td colspan="5">
<td>Pick up tips and tricks from some of the region's best skateboarders, then practice
what you've learned. All are welcome to watch, but helmets and permission slips are
required for guests wishing to take an active part in this event. Safety equipment is
available for rent at a nominal fee. Contact the Activities Center for more
information.</td></tr>
```

New closing and opening row tags split row

Colspan attribute extends cell to width of several cells

FIGURE F-6: Table containing Notes information in spanned rows

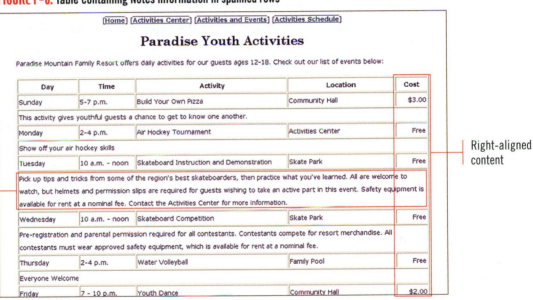

Notes column information moved from last column to cell spanning five columns

Right-aligned content

Clues to Use

Aligning tables and table content

By default, all table contents are vertically centered. Table data contents are horizontally left-aligned and table heading cells are horizontally centered. You can customize the horizontal alignment of a table and its contents using an attribute common to many Web page elements—the align attribute. When set in the <tr>, <th>, and <td> tags, the align attribute determines the alignment of row or cell contents, overriding the defaults. Possible values for align are left, center, and right. When the align attribute is applied to the opening <table> tag, it affects the horizontal alignment of the entire table on the page, but does not affect the alignment of the content within the table cells. You can also control the vertical alignment of table content using the valign attribute. When applied to the <tr>, <th>, or <td> tags, the valign attribute controls the vertical placement of content within the cell. Possible vertical alignment options are top, middle and bottom. Note, however, that valign is not a supported attribute of the <table> tag.

HTML

Formatting Table Content

You can use table attributes to control the amount of space around cell content. The **cellpadding** attribute allows you to control the amount of space between the cell wall and its content, and **cellspacing** allows you to control the amount of space between table cells. You specify both attributes in the opening table tag, not in the `<tr>`, `<td>`, or `<th>` tags. By default, table cells take on the basefont or style sheet formatting specified for the rest of the page. When no formatting attributes are specified in the head section through CSS or the basefont tag, tables use the default browser formatting style. Tables do not take on formatting attributes specified outside of the table in the body section of a document through font or character-formatting tags.  The content of your table data cells seems too close to the cell borders. In addition, the double-spaced format looks out of place in the table, so you decide to add table and style sheet formatting to make the table text more readable.

STEPS

1. **Click the** text editor program button **on the taskbar to return to the** youth.htm **page code**

2. **Click just after border="1" in the opening table tag, press [Spacebar], type** `cellpadding="5" cellspacing="5"`, **then save your work**

   The cellpadding attribute adds five pixels of space between the inner cell walls and the content for each table data and table heading cell. The cellspacing attribute adds five pixels of space between each of the table cells.

3. **Click the** browser program button **on the taskbar, then reload the** youth.htm **page**

   As shown in Figure F-7, the inner cell borders have expanded to five pixels in width, and additional space appears between the cell walls and the cell content.

4. **Use your file management system to find your paradise_style.css style sheet in your paradise\css folder in the place where you save your site files, right-click your style sheet file name or icon, point to** Open With **on the shortcut menu, then click your text editor name**

   > **TROUBLE**
   > If you do not have a style sheet, copy the CSS folder and contents from the Unit F folder in the place where you store your Data Files.

   Your style sheet opens in a separate instance of your text editor program, allowing you to keep your youth.htm page open. (If you did not complete the Unit E lessons, you may copy the css folder, which contains a modified version of the style sheet, from the Unit_F Data Files to your paradise folder in the place where you save your site files.)

5. **Click just after } at the end of the body style rule, press [Enter] twice, then type the following code, pressing [Enter] after each line:**

   ```
   td, th {
        line-height: 1em;
        color: #000033;
   }
   ```

6. **Save your style sheet, then reload your** youth.htm **page in your browser**

   > **TROUBLE**
   > If your line spacing remains unchanged, make sure that you did not type a space between the line-height number (1) and "em".

   The double line spacing has been removed from the text within the cells, as shown in Figure F-8, making it appear more compact, and the text color has been changed to a darker blue.

Expanded space between cells (cellspacing)

Additional space within cells (cellpadding)

Paradise Youth Activities

Paradise Mountain Family Resort offers daily activities for our guests ages 12-18. Check out our list of events below:

Day	Time	Activity	Location	Cost
Sunday	5-7 p.m.	Build your own Pizza	Community Hall	$3.00
This activity gives youthful guests a chance to get to know one another.				
Monday	2-4 p.m.	Air hockey tournament	Activities Center	Free
Show off your air hockey skills				
Tuesday	10 a.m. - noon	Skateboard Instruction and Demonstration	Skate Park	Free
Pick up tips and tricks from some of the region's best skateboarders, then practice what you've learned. All are welcome to watch, but helmets and permission slips are required for guests wishing to take an active part in this event. Safety equipment is available for rent at a nominal fee. Contact the Activities Center for more information.				
Wednesday	10 a.m. - noon	Skateboard Competition	Skate Park	Free
Pre-registration and parental permission required for all contestants. Contestants compete for resort merchandise. All contestants must wear approved safety equipment, which is available for rent at a nominal fee.				
Thursday	2-4 p.m.	Water Volleyball	Family Pool	Free

FIGURE F-8: Line formatting applied to table

Line formatting changes display of text

Paradise Mountain Family Resort offers daily activities for our guests ages 12-18. Check out our list of events below:

Day	Time	Activity	Location	Cost
Sunday	5-7 p.m.	Build your own Pizza	Community Hall	$3.00
This activity gives youthful guests a chance to get to know one another.				
Monday	2-4 p.m.	Air hockey tournament	Activities Center	Free
Show off your air hockey skills				
Tuesday	10 a.m. - noon	Skateboard Instruction and Demonstration	Skate Park	Free
Pick up tips and tricks from some of the region's best skateboarders, then practice what you've learned. All are welcome to watch, but helmets and permission slips are required for guests wishing to take an active part in this event. Safety equipment is available for rent at a nominal fee. Contact the Activities Center for more information.				
Wednesday	10 a.m. - noon	Skateboard Competition	Skate Park	Free
Pre-registration and parental permission required for all contestants. Contestants compete for resort merchandise. All contestants must wear approved safety equipment, which is available for rent at a nominal fee.				
Thursday	2-4 p.m.	Water Volleyball	Family Pool	Free
Everyone Welcome				
Friday	7 - 10 p.m.	Youth Dance	Community Hall	$2.00
Enjoy a selection of snacks and sodas as you dance, mix and mingle with new friends.				
Saturday	1 - 4 p.m.	Kayaking Adventure	Meet in front of Resort lodge	$10.00
Ride in the van to Paradise Lake, then kayak out to Paradise Island where you can spend your time exploring the island swimming in the cove or kayaking around the island. Transportation, snacks and drinks provided.				

For more information, contact the Activities Center at: 1.970.555.7890 (EXT 7890 from any resort phone). We'd love to help!

Page modified by: Your Name

Clues to Use

Using CSS with tables

Prior to CSS, the only method of formatting table content was to set HTML formatting tags inside each cell. However, CSS formatting allows you to set td and th style rules to specify attributes for table cells without applying those formatting commands to each cell individually. This ability to apply style sheet formatting to table cells gives you more flexibility than ever in planning your page design.

Formatting Borders

Just as you can control the arrangement of cells in a table, you can also alter the properties of the borders between cells. By assigning a value in pixels to the **border attribute** in the `<table>` tag, you can change the thickness of the table's outside border. As you have already seen, when the border attribute is present with a value of 1 in the opening `<table>` tag, cell borders appear as lines one pixel wide. However, if the border is set equal to zero, or if the attribute is not present, cells do not display any borders. Setting a value greater than "1" causes the border to appear with a thicker line. In addition to the border attribute, the opening table tag accepts other attributes for controlling the appearance of table borders. You can set the **bordercolor** attribute to control the color of the table border. You can also set the **bordercolorlight** and **bordercolordark** attributes to apply a highlighting effect to your table borders. Table F-3 summarizes border attributes. You want to customize the look of your table by formatting the table borders.

STEPS

QUICK TIP

Not all browsers can display colored table borders. Test your design to make sure that your colored borders work in the browser used by most of your site visitors, or make sure that your design is not compromised if your border color fails to appear.

1. **Click the youth.htm text editor program button on the taskbar to open that instance of your text editor, click after cellspacing="5" in the opening table tag, press [Spacebar], then type** `bordercolor="#99CCFF"` **and save your file**
   You formatted your table borders with a light blue color.

2. **Click the browser program button on your taskbar, then reload your youth.htm file**
   The table is displayed with a light blue border surrounding the table and all of the cells. You would like to test the page with a two-color border.

3. **Click the youth.htm text editor program button on the taskbar, then click between bordercolor and the equal sign in the bordercolor attribute**

4. **Type** `light` **so that the attribute reads bordercolorlight="#99CCFF"**
   Bordercolorlight causes the browser to display the specified color along the top and left borders of the table and all of the table cells.

QUICK TIP

Remember to type the pound sign (#) before the color number.

5. **Click after the closing quotation mark in the bordercolorlight attribute, press [Spacebar], then type** `bordercolordark="#000033"`
   The bordercolordark attribute causes the bottom and right edges of the table and cell borders to display the specified color. You would like to make your table borders thicker and reduce the space between cells.

6. **Click just after the 1 in table border="1", press [Backspace], then type** `2`
   You increased the size of the table borders by 1 pixel.

7. **Click just after the 5 and before the closing quotation mark in the cellspacing value, press [Backspace], type** `2`, **then save your work**
   Your code should resemble that shown in Figure F-9.

8. **Click the browser program button on the taskbar, then reload the youth.htm file in your browser**
   As shown in Figure F-10, there is less space between table cells and the table and cell borders are highlighted with a lighter color on the top and left edges and shadowed with a darker color on the bottom and right edges.

FIGURE F-9: Code for opening table tag

Opening table tag with border attributes

```
<p>Paradise Mountain Family Resort offers daily activities for our guests
ages 12-18. Check out our list of events below: </p>

<!-- Start the table and row 1 here -->

<table border="2" cellpadding="5" cellspacing="2" bordercolorlight="#99CCFF"
bordercolordark="#000033">
  <tr>
  <th>Day</th>  <th>Time</th>    <th>Activity</th>        <th>Location</th>
```

FIGURE F-10: Youth Activities table with border formatting

Tighter cell spacing

Light borders

Dark borders

Paradise Youth Activities

Paradise Mountain Family Resort offers daily activities for our guests ages 12-18. Check out our list of events below:

Day	Time	Activity	Location	Cost
Sunday	5-7 p.m.	Build your own Pizza	Community Hall	$3.00
This activity gives youthful guests a chance to get to know one another.				
Monday	2-4 p.m.	Air hockey tournament	Activities Center	Free
Show off your air hockey skills				
Tuesday	10 a.m. - noon	Skateboard Instruction and Demonstration	Skate Park	Free
Pick up tips and tricks from some of the region's best skateboarders, then practice what you've learned. All are welcome to watch, but helmets and permission slips are required for guests wishing to take an active part in this event. Safety equipment is available for rent at a nominal fee. Contact the Activities Center for more information.				
Wednesday	10 a.m. - noon	Skateboard Competition	Skate Park	Free
Pre-registration and parental permission required for all contestants. Contestants compete for resort merchandise. All contestants must wear approved safety equipment, which is available for rent at a nominal fee.				
Thursday	2-4 p.m.	Water Volleyball	Family Pool	Free
Everyone Welcome				
Friday	7 - 10 p.m.	Youth Dance	Community Hall	$2.00
Enjoy a selection of snacks and sodas as you dance, mix and mingle with new friends.				
Saturday	1 - 4 p.m.	Kayaking Adventure	Meet in front of Resort lodge	$10.00
Ride in the van to Paradise Lake, then kayak out to Paradise Island where you can spend your time exploring the island swimming in the cove or kayaking around the island. Transportation, snacks and drinks provided.				

For more information, contact the Activities Center at: 1.970.555.7890 (EXT 7890 from any resort phone). We'd love to help!

Page modified by: Your Name

TABLE F-3: Table and cell border attributes

tag	attribute	description	example
`<table>`	border	Adds borders around the table and around each cell—numeric value determines border thickness	`<table border="5">`
	bordercolor	Specifies the table border color	`<table border="2" bordercolor="#000066">`
	bordercolorlight	Specifies the color to appear on the top and left edges of table and cell borders	`<table border="2" bordercolorlight="#99CCFF">`
	bordercolordark	Specifies the color to appear on the bottom and right edges of table and cell borders	`<table border="2" bordercolorlight="#99CCFF" bordercolordark="#000033">`

Modifying Table Backgrounds

By default, table cells are transparent; the background color or image for the rest of the Web page appears as the table background. However, you can use background and bgcolor attributes in the opening `<table>`, `<tr>`, `<th>`, or `<td>` tags to assign a background image or color to a table or any part of it. You can also apply these attributes as style rules to the table, tr, th, or td selectors. As with other Web page elements, it is important to use table background color wisely and sparingly to enhance your page content, rather than overwhelm it. 🎨 You want to add color to the heading and notes rows in the youth activities table to add aesthetic value and to make it easier to read.

STEPS

1. **Click the paradise_style.css instance of the text editor on the taskbar**

2. **Click after } of the td, th style rule, press [Enter] twice, then type the following code, pressing [Enter] after each line:**

```
th      {
        background-color: #6699CC;
        color: #336633;
        }
```

The code near the top of your style sheet appears, as shown in Figure F-11. You set a new rule to override the style set in your td, th style rule. According to the rules of CSS proximity, the rule closest to the tag—the rule furthest down on the style sheet—takes precedence over (overrides) any other rules because it is read last. Your new rule gives all table heading cells a blue background and uses the same green color you used in your page heading. You think the notes rows should stand out so that they are easier to read.

3. **Locate the nav1 class at the bottom of your style sheet, click after the } at the end of the style, press [Enter] twice, then type the following code, pressing [Enter] after each line:**

```
.notesrow     {
        background-color: #CCCCFF;
        font-weight: 500;
        }
```

You set a style rule to define the formatting of the notes rows of your table. The background color for each specified row will be a lighter shade of blue than the background of the heading row. Your font will be heavier. The bottom of your style sheet should resemble the code shown in Figure F-12.

4. **Save your work, return to your youth.htm code, then locate the table data cell with the content that begins This activity gives...**

5. **Click just after colspan="5", press [Spacebar], then type class="notesrow"**

6. **Repeat Step 5 for the remaining rows to which colspan="5" has been applied**

7. **Save your work, click the browjser program button on the taskbar, then reload your youth.htm page**

As shown in Figure F-13, the header row background is a steel blue color and the notes rows are light blue.

QUICK TIP
To locate code quickly, press [Ctrl][Home] to place the insertion point at the top of the document, click Edit on the menu bar, then click Find. Type the text you are looking for in the Find what text box, then click Find Next. The text editor highlights the first instance of the text you typed. To find the next instance, click Find Next again.

Clues to Use

Adding a background image to a table

In addition to the bgcolor attribute, the most recent versions of most browser applications support the background attribute for the `<table>`, `<th>`, and `<td>` tags. You can specify the background attribute for the table in the body tag or you can use CSS to set your background image as follows:

`background-image: url(../images/filename.gif)`. You cannot apply a background to a table row. Because table background properties are not fully supported by all browsers, be sure to test your pages for readability in multiple browsers both with and without table background colors and images.

FIGURE F-11: Style sheet with new th and td style rules

```
body        {
            font-family: Verdana, Arial, Helvetica, sans-serif;
            font-size: 14px;
            color: #333366;
            background-color: #FFFFFF;
            line-height: 2em;
            background-image: url(../images/pm_bkgnd2.gif);
            margin-left: 0px;
            margin-top: 5px;
            margin-right: 0px;

}

td, th   {
            line-height: 1em;
            color: #000033;

}

th       {
            background-color: #6699CC;
            color: #336633;

}
```

Style rule for table data and table heading cells

New table heading style rule overrides background and text colors

FIGURE F-12: New class style rule for notes row

```
.second_bul     {
        list-style-image: url(../images/pm_bul2.png);

}

.nav1   {
        text-align: center;

}

.notesrow       {
        background-color: #CCCCFF;
        font-weight: 500;

}
```

New class rule

FIGURE F-13: Youth Activities table with style sheet formatting applied to heading and rows

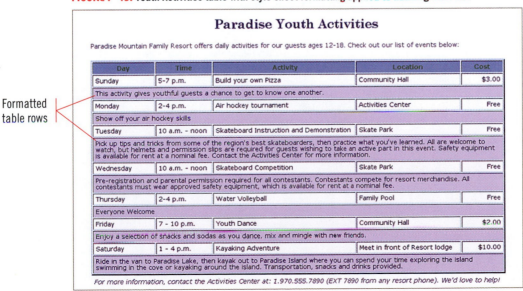

Formatted table rows

Paradise Youth Activities

Paradise Mountain Family Resort offers daily activities for our guests ages 12-18. Check out our list of events below:

Day	Time	Activity	Location	Cost
Sunday	5-7 p.m.	Build your own Pizza	Community Hall	$3.00
This activity gives youthful guests a chance to get to know one another.				
Monday	2-4 p.m.	Air hockey tournament	Activities Center	Free
Show off your air hockey skills				
Tuesday	10 a.m. - noon	Skateboard Instruction and Demonstration	Skate Park	Free
Pick up tips and tricks from some of the region's best skateboarders, then practice what you've learned. All are welcome to watch, but helmets and permission slips are required for guests wishing to take an active part in this event. Safety equipment is available for rent at a nominal fee. Contact the Activities Center for more information.				
Wednesday	10 a.m. - noon	Skateboard Competition	Skate Park	Free
Pre-registration and parental permission required for all contestants. Contestants compete for resort merchandise. All contestants must wear approved safety equipment, which is available for rent at a nominal fee.				
Thursday	2-4 p.m.	Water Volleyball	Family Pool	Free
Everyone Welcome				
Friday	7 - 10 p.m.	Youth Dance	Community Hall	$2.00
Enjoy a selection of snacks and sodas as you dance, mix and mingle with new friends.				
Saturday	1 - 4 p.m.	Kayaking Adventure	Meet in front of Resort lodge	$10.00
Ride in the van to Paradise Lake, then kayak out to Paradise Island where you can spend your time exploring the Island swimming in the cove or kayaking around the island. Transportation, snacks and drinks provided.				

For more information, contact the Activities Center at: 1.970.555.7890 (EXT 7890 from any resort phone). We'd love to help!

Changing Table Dimensions

As with other page elements, you can customize table dimensions using the height and width attributes in the <table>, <th>, and <td> tags. Because all the cells in a row are displayed at the same height and all the cells in a column are displayed at the same width, you only need to set either dimension once for each row or column. Table measurements are flexible: You can specify a table width as a percentage, then set a fixed pixel width for one or more columns. This allows any columns in which no specific sizes have been set to expand or contract with the size of the browser window for a more effective design. You can also add the **nowrap attribute** to a table cell to prevent its contents from wrapping to the next line. Dimension values applied to the <table> tag are in relation to the browser window. Values for the <th> and <td> tags are based on the size of the table. You noticed that some page elements, including your page heading, wrap to a second line at lower resolutions or when the window is made smaller. You want to use table attributes to control these problems.

STEPS

1. **With your youth.htm page open in your browser, click the Restore Down button 🗗 in the upper-right corner of the browser, then, if necessary, drag the right browser border to the left until the page heading wraps to a second line**

   As shown in Figure F-14, the page heading wraps to a second line when the window size is reduced.

2. **Click the youth.htm instance of the text editor, click before <h1> under the opening body tag, type `<table border="0" cellpadding="0" cellspacing="0" width="800">`, then press [Enter]**

3. **Type `<tr><td nowrap>`, click after </h1>, type `</td></tr></table>`, then save your work**

   You used table width settings to prevent your page heading from wrapping. You would like to apply similar settings to one of the columns in your Youth Activities table.

4. **Locate the opening heading tag for the Time column in the youth activities table, click just after th, press [Spacebar], then type `nowrap width="125"`**

5. **Replace Your Name in the Modified by paragraph at the bottom of the page with your own name, update the date, save your work, then print your page code**

6. **Click the browser program button on the taskbar, reload the page, then drag the right browser border to the right and to the left**

   As Figure F-15 shows, the page heading no longer wraps, and the content of each cell in the Time column is displayed on a single line. Because all cells in a column conform to the widest cell, there is no need to set the width properties on the other cells in the column.

FIGURE F-14: Page heading and cell contents wrap in resized window

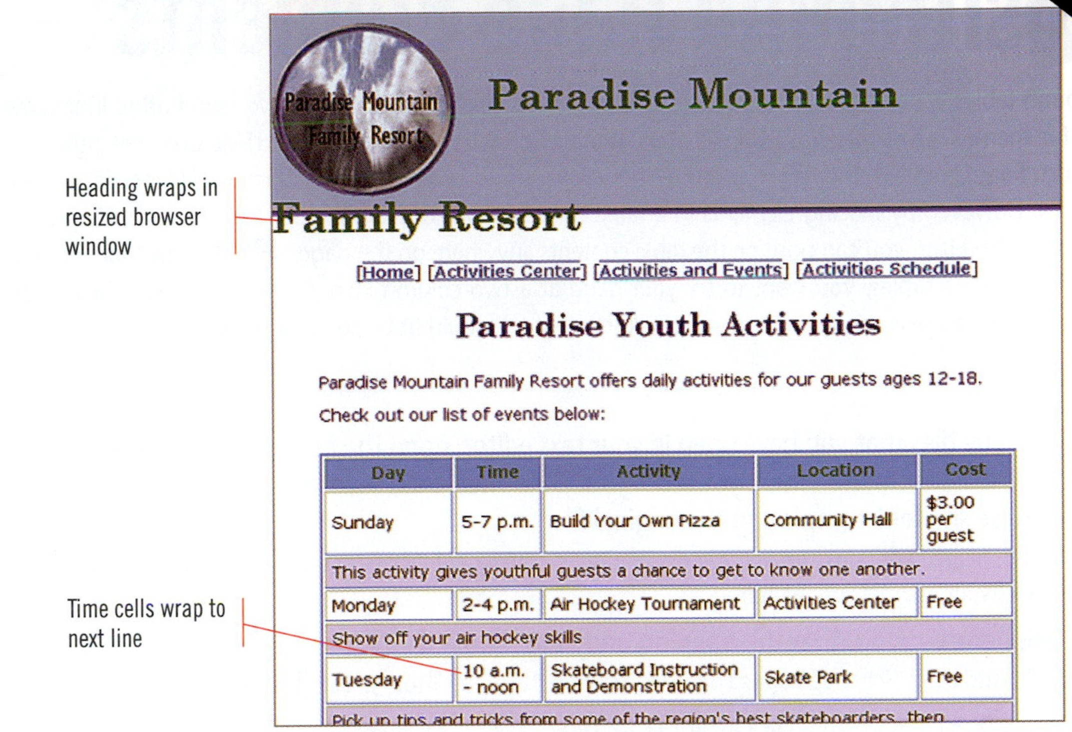

Heading wraps in resized browser window

Time cells wrap to next line

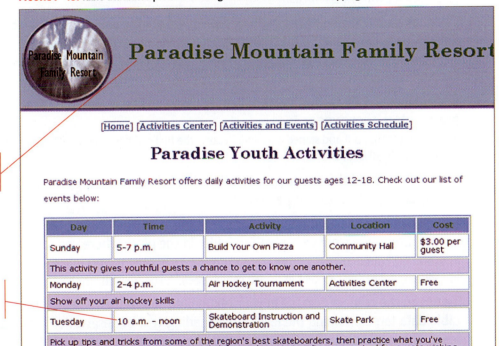

FIGURE F-15: Table attributes prevent heading and cell content from wrapping

Heading does not wrap in resized window

Time cell contents remain on one line

Using nested and stacked tables

You can use **nested tables**—tables that are fully contained within the cell of another table—to produce more complex page designs. You set width and height percentage values for a nested table in relation to the size of the parent cell. To gain even more control over your page layout, you can stack tables. **Stacked tables** are those in which one table ends before another begins. Stacked table sizes are not dependent upon one another, meaning that you can stack a page heading table of one width on top of a navigation table that is set at a different width. When table alignment values are also set, you can have more control over the placement of your page elements.

tioning Page Elements

es were originally developed to display data in a grid, designers have found other innovative
. One of the most popular uses of tables is to create layouts that HTML does not otherwise
example, basic HTML codes do not allow you to position elements in specific locations in the
wever, by placing elements in a table that does not display any borders and by adding blank
d widths, you can position the table contents anywhere on the page. 🎨 Now that you have
e using tables, you want to try your hand at a two-column layout. You have noticed that your
ntact page is very long, and you think the content would fit better in two columns.

QUICK TIP

Although most recent versions of popular browsers support new methods for placing elements, many Web page designers still prefer to use tables because they are supported by older browsers.

1. **Close any files that you have open in your text editor, open the htm_F-3.txt file in your text editor from the place where you store your Data Files, then save it as contact.htm in your paradise site folder, replacing the original file**

   The file, which contains the doctype declaration, the meta characters tag, and a link to your style sheet, replaces your original contact.htm.

2. **Click before `<h1>` under the opening body tag, type `<table border="0" cellpadding="0" cellspacing="0" width="800">`, then press [Enter]**

3. **Type `<tr><td nowrap>`, click after `</h1>`, type `</td></tr></table>`, then save your work**

   You used the table data cell settings that you used in the previous lesson to prevent the heading from wrapping when the window is resized.

4. **Click before `<h3>Reservations</h3>`, type `<table width="90%" align="center">`, press [Enter], type `<tr>`, press [Enter], then type `<td width="50%">`**

   You started creating a table that will appear at 90% of the window size, then you specified that the first cell will be 50% of that table width. The table will be centered on the page.

5. **Click before `<h3>Paradise Garden Day Spa and Fitness Center</h3>`, type `</td>`, press [Enter], then type `<td>`**

   You ended the first cell and started a second. Because the first cell has reserved 50% of the width, there is no need to specify 50% for the second cell.

6. **Click after `</p>` of the paragraph with the id "info", type `</td>`, press [Enter], type `</tr>`, press [Enter], then type `</table>`**

7. **Save your page, click the browser program button on the taskbar, then open your contact.htm page from your paradise folder in the place where you save your site files**

   As shown in Figure F-16, the content now appears in two columns, but the columns do not align at the top. In addition, some of the content in the left column seems to be crowding the content in the right column.

8. **Return to the contact.htm file in your text editor, locate the table row tag above the table data tag containing the level-three heading text of Reservations, click just after tr inside the `<tr>` tag, press [Spacebar], then type `valign="top"`**

   Because you set the vertical alignment in the row, you do not have to set it in either of the table data cells.

9. **Click just after align="center" in the opening table tag of the same table, press [Spacebar], type `cellpadding="10"`, update the "Page modified by" information, save your work, then reload it in the browser and print the Web page**

   As shown in Figure F-17, the cellpadding applied to the opening table tag affects both cells, and the content in the left cell no longer crowds the content in the right.

10. **Close all files and programs, then transfer your files to your remote directory**

FIGURE F-16: Web page with borderless table creates two columns

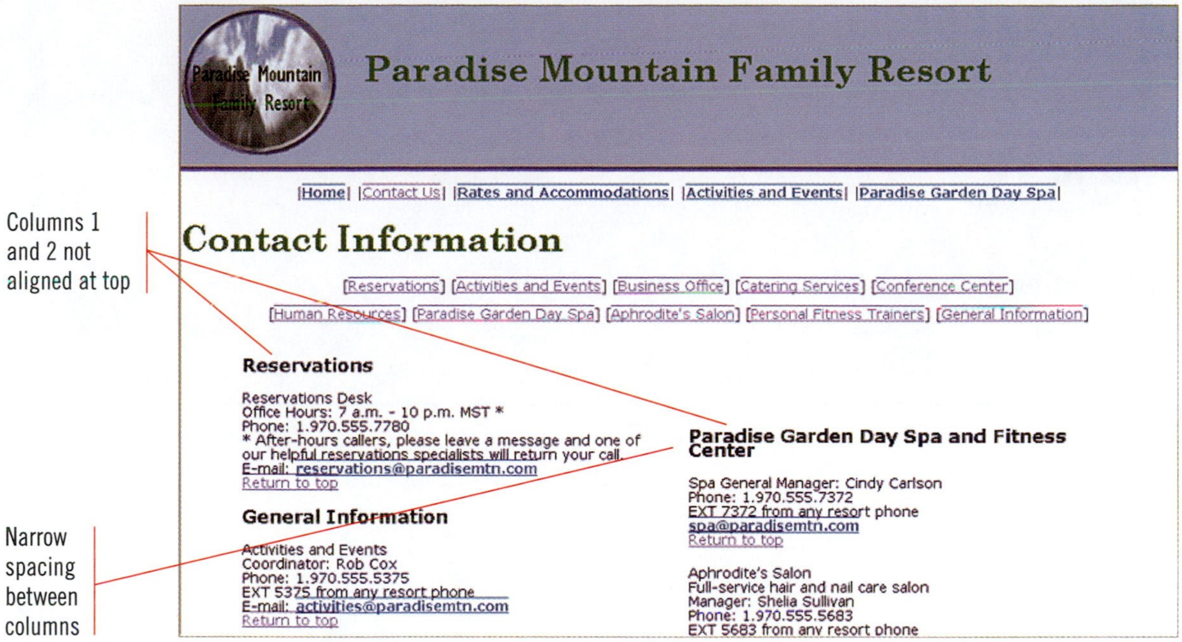

Columns 1 and 2 not aligned at top

Narrow spacing between columns

FIGURE F-17: Table content aligned and padded

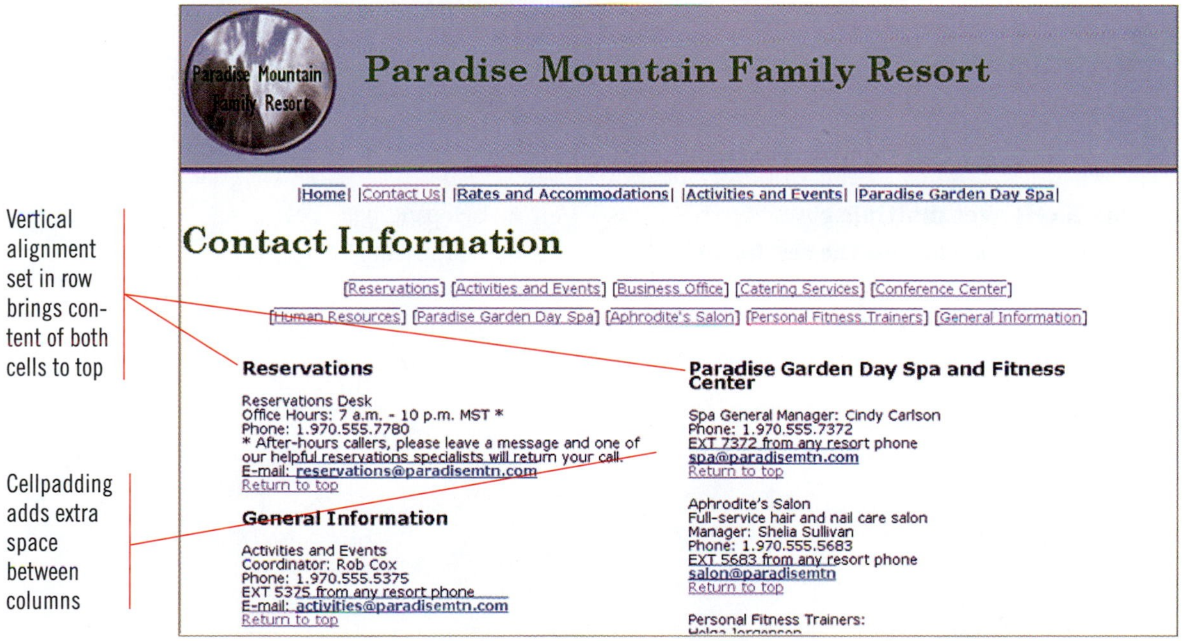

Vertical alignment set in row brings content of both cells to top

Cellpadding adds extra space between columns

Practice

▼ CONCEPTS REVIEW

Name the function of each section of code indicated in Figure F-18.

FIGURE F-18

```
1    <table border="1" width="70%" cellspacing="2" cellpadding="2" align="center">    9
2    <tr>
3    <th>Hand Care</th>
     </tr>
                                                                                       8
     <tr>
4    <td>Deluxe spa manicure (with paraffin treatment)</td><td>$40.00</td>
     </tr>
                                                                                       7
     <tr>
     <td>Deluxe spa manicure (with glycolic treatment)</td><td>$40.00</td>
     </tr>

     <tr>
5    <td>French manicure</td><td>$30.00</td>
     </tr>

     <tr>
6    <th>Foot Care</th>
     </tr>

     </table>
```

Match each statement with the term it describes.

10. Attribute to span a cell over multiple rows
11. Space between the cell content and the cell border
12. Space between table cells
13. Descriptive information about a table
14. Attribute to resize a table

a. Cell padding
b. Cell spacing
c. Rowspan
d. Width
e. Caption

Select the best answer from the list of choices.

15. **Which one of the following tag sets marks the contents of a header cell?**
    a. `<table>...</table>`
    b. `<th>...</th>`
    c. `<tr>...</tr>`
    d. `<td>...</td>`

16. **Which one of the following inserts a comment into an HTML file?**
    a. `<!--comment -->`
    b. `<comment>`
    c. `<comment />`
    d. `<*comment*>`

17. **Which one of the following attributes creates a cell that spans multiple columns?**
    a. Rowspan
    b. Colspan
    c. Cellpadding
    d. Cellspacing

18. **Which of the following changes the background color of a table element to red?**
    a. background-color: #333366;
    b. color: #333366;
    c. bkcolor: #333366;
    d. tablecolor: #333366;

19. **Which one of the following tag sets creates a table row?**
    a. `<table>…</table>`
    b. `<th>…</th>`
    c. `<tr>…</tr>`
    d. `<td>…</td>`

20. **Which one of the following tag sets marks a cell containing table data?**
    a. `<table>...</table>`
    b. `<th>...</th>`
    c. `<tr>...</tr>`
    d. `<td>...</td>`

▼ SKILLS REVIEW

1. **Plan a table.**
   a. Consider how tables can be used to present the information on the pages of the spa site. What pages should use tables?
   b. How would you structure each table?
   c. Are there any table cells that should span over rows or columns?
   d. How can borders and backgrounds be used to clearly present the table information?
   e. How wide should each table be displayed with respect to the browser window?

2. **Create a simple table.**
   a. In your text editor, open the file **htm_F-4.txt** from the drive and folder where your Data Files are stored, then save it as **hands.htm** to the paradise/spa directory where you save your site files. If you are asked whether you want to replace the file, click Yes.
   b. Copy the **bkg_spa.gif** and **spa_logo.gif** files from the drive and folder where your Data Files are stored, then paste the files to the paradise/images directory. If you are asked whether you want to replace the file, click Yes.
   c. Locate the comment in your **hands.htm** file indicating where the table begins, add the opening `<table>` tag, then delete the comment.
   d. Locate the comment in your file indicating where the table ends and add the closing `</table>` tag, then delete the comment.

e. Using Figure F-19 as a guide, create a table structure using the hand care and foot care data. Delete any <br /> tags in the table data area, as well as the hyphens before the prices.

f. Save your work and view the **hands.htm** page in your browser.

FIGURE F-19

```
<table border="1">

<tr>
<th>Hand Care</th>
</tr>

<tr>
<td>Deluxe spa manicure (with paraffin treatment)</td><td>$40.00</td>
</tr>

<tr>
<td>Deluxe spa manicure (with glycolic treatment)</td><td>$40.00</td>
</tr>

<tr>
<td>French manicure</td><td>$30.00</td>
</tr>

<tr>
<th>Foot Care</th>
</tr>

<tr>
<td>Peppermint pedicure with foot & leg mask</td><td>$55.00</td>
</tr>

<tr>
<td>Deluxe spa pedicure (paraffin treatment)</td> <td>$60.00</td>
</tr>

<tr>
<td>Soothing foot bath with manicure</td><td>$45.00</td>
</tr>

</table>
```

3. **Span and align columns and rows.**

   a. Span the heading Hand Care over two columns by adding `colspan="2"` to the first <th> tag.

   b. Span the heading Foot Care over two columns by adding `colspan="2"` to the second <th> tag.

   c. View the table changes in your browser.

   d. Save your work.

4. **Format table content.**

   a. Add one pixel between the cells in the table by adding a cellspacing attribute to the opening table tag. (*Hint*: The opening table tag should now be: `<table border="1" cellspacing="1" >`)

   b. Add four pixels between the cells' content and its borders by adding a cellpadding attribute to the opening table tag. (*Hint*: The opening table tag should now be: `<table border="1" cellspacing="1" cellpadding="4">`)

   c. Using your text editor, create an external style sheet named **hands_style.css** and save it in your paradise/css directory. (A link to this style sheet is already in the head section of your hands.htm file.) In your hands_style.css file, add a style to change the font color of the table text to #009900. (*Hint*: Add the following style: `td, th {color: #009900;}`)

   d. Save your work.

   e. Reload the **hands.htm** file in your browser to view the changes to the table.

5. **Format borders.**

   a. In your hands.htm file, change the table border to the color #999999 by adding a bordercolor attribute to the opening table tag. (Hint: Add `bordercolor="#999999"` to the opening table tag.)

   b. Add the color #006633 to the cell borders and the bottom-right edges of the table. (*Hint*: In the opening table tag, change `bordercolor="#999999"` to `bordercolordark="#006633".`)

   c. Add the color #006633 to the top and left borders of the table. (*Hint*: In the opening table tag, add `bordercolorlight="#006633"` after bordercolordark="#006633".)

   d. Increase the table border to five pixels by changing border="1" to `border="5"` in the opening table tag.

   e. Save your work.

   f. View the changes to the table in your browser.

6. **Modify table backgrounds.**

   a. In your hands_style.css style sheet, add a style of `th {background-color: #CCFFCC;}` to format the table headings with a light green color.

   b. Bold the table data by adding a style to the **hands_style.css** file of `td {font-weight: bold;}`.

    c. Save your work.

    d. Open the **hands.htm** file in your browser to verify the changes to the table.

7. Change table dimensions.

    a. In your hands.htm file, change the width of your table to 600 pixels by adding `width="600"` to the end of the attribute list in the opening table tag.

    b. Locate the first appearance of `<td>$40.00 </td>` in the table section and add a width attribute of 140 pixels by adding `width="140"` inside the opening td tag.

    c. Align the contents of one of the prices by placing `align="right"` in its opening `<td>` tag.

    d. View the right-aligned price in your browser, then delete the align="right" code from the `<td>` tag.

    e. Save your work.

    f. Verify the changes to the table dimensions by viewing the **hands.htm** page in the browser.

8. Position page elements.

    a. In your hands.htm file, change the width of your table to be displayed at 80% of the window size by changing the width attribute in the opening table tag to `width="80%"`.

    b. Display the second column of the table at 30% of the total table size by changing the width="140" in the opening td tag of the second row in the table to `width="30%"`.

    c. Center the table in the browser window by adding `align="center"` to the opening table tag.

    d. Save the changes to your **hands.htm** file.

    e. Verify the table changes by viewing the **hands.htm** page in your browser.

    f. Add your name to the hands.htm and hands_style.css pages using comments at the end of the files, then save and print the pages. (*Hint*: Add `<!-- Your Name -->` to each page. In the hands.htm file, place the comment before the `</body>` tag.)

    g. Transfer the files to your remote directory.

▼ INDEPENDENT CHALLENGE 1

As you continue developing the Web site for your resort rental business, Star Vacations, you want to organize your featured resorts using a table.

    a. In your text editor, open the file **htm_F-5.txt** from the drive and folder where your Data Files are stored, then save it as **features.htm** in the vacations folder where you save your site files. If you are asked whether you want to replace the file, click Yes.

    b. Locate the comment tags indicating the place where a table will be used to organize the resort information. Enclose the resort data with opening and closing table tags, then delete the comments.

    c. Add a border of one pixel to the table.

    d. Add opening and closing `<tr>`, `<td>`, and `<th>` tags to structure the resort data, as shown in Figure F-20.

    e. Add five pixels of spacing between cells.

    f. Add 10 pixels of space between the cells' content and border.

    g. Display the table at 60% of the browser window.

    h. Center the table in the browser window.

    i. Add your name to the address tag at the bottom of the page.

    j. Save your work, display the **features.htm** file in your browser to check your table, then print the file in your browser.

    k. Close all files, then transfer your completed features.htm page to your remote directory.

FIGURE F-20

Resort	Location	Link
Canyon Ranch	Lenox, MA	Canyon Ranch
Arizona Biltmore	Phoenix, Arizona	Arizona Biltmore
Ojai Valley Inn and Spa	Ojai, Calfornia	Ojai Valley Inn and Spa
Banff Park Lodge	Alberta, Canada	Banff Park Lodge
Tomahawk Resort	Ontario, Canada	Tomahawk Resort

HTML

▼ INDEPENDENT CHALLENGE 1 (CONTINUED)

Advanced Challenge Exercises

- Add a caption of Featured Resorts to the table in your **features.htm** file.
- Save your work and display the **features.htm** file in the browser to check your caption.
- In a separate text editor window, open the file **htm_F-6.txt** from the drive and folder where your Data Files are stored, then save it as **star_style.css** in the vacations folder where you save your site files. If you are asked whether you want to replace the file, click Yes. (The star_style.css is an external style sheet for your features.htm page.)
- Add a style to the **star_style.css** file that formats table captions with Lucida Calligraphy or a serif font.
- Save your **star_style.css** file and display the **features.htm** file in your browser to check the formatting of your table caption. (You do not have to add the link to the style sheet because it was in the data file.) If you do not have the Lucida Calligraphy font on your computer, the caption will be displayed in a substituted serif font.
- Close all files, then transfer your completed pages to your remote directory.

▼ INDEPENDENT CHALLENGE 2

You will use tables along with an external style sheet to organize the water-conservation Web site you are developing for your employer, Metro Water. You decide to start by using a table to organize the links in the navigation bar.

a. In your text editor, open the **htm_F-7.txt** file from the drive and folder where your Data Files are stored, then save it as **resources.htm** in the water folder where you save your site files. If you are asked whether you want to replace the file, click Yes.

b. Replace the Add table here comment with a table structure of one row and six columns where each column is displayed as a table heading. (*Hint*: Type the code for one column, copy it, then paste it five times.)

c. Add a border of one pixel to the table.

d. Add two pixels of space between the cells' content and the border.

e. Add three pixels of space between the table's cells.

f. Add an attribute to display the table at 70% of the browser window.

g. Place each of the six links from the top navigation bar into a table heading cell, then delete the entire top navigation bar.

h. Save your file, then view the navigation table in your browser.

i. Create an external style sheet, then save it as **navstyle.css** in the water folder where you save your site files. Add styles to format the links, as shown in Figure F-21.

j. Add a link in the resources.htm file to the navstyle.css style sheet. (*Hint*: Place the following before the `</head>` tag:

`<link href="navstyle.css" rel="stylesheet" type="text/css" />`)

FIGURE F-21

```
a:link {
        color:#0066FF;
        text-decoration:underline;
}
a:hover {
        font-weight:bold;
        color:#CC66CC;
        text-decoration:underline;
}
```

k. Refresh the **resources.htm** file in your browser and verify that the styles in the navstyle.css file have been applied to the table links.

l. Add your name as a comment to the bottom of the page, save your work, print the resources.htm and navstyle.css files, then transfer the files to the remote site.

▼ INDEPENDENT CHALLENGE 2 (CONTINUED)

Advanced Challenge Exercises

- Use the search engine of your choice to research the frame attribute for the `<table>` tag.
- Use the frame attribute in the table on your resources.htm file to place borders only on the left and right sides of the cells.
- Save the **resources.htm** file, print it, then view the table in your browser, verifying the change in the cell borders.
- Close all files, then transfer your completed pages to your remote directory.

▼ INDEPENDENT CHALLENGE 3

Tables are used to organize data and to lay out information on a Web site. You want to add tables to your Web site, but first you need to research how you can make them accessible for all users.

Go to the Online Companion for this book, locate the links for this unit, then click the link for the W3C Web Accessibility page and review the information for tables. Write one or two paragraphs answering the following questions about tables that are used to organize data:

    a. How can captions be used to increase accessibility?

    b. If a caption is not appropriate, how can you use attributes to describe the purpose of the table?

    c. What attribute is especially important for tables with cells that span multiple columns or rows?

    d. How should row and column headers be identified?

    e. Add your name and today's date to the top of your paper, then print it.

Use your favorite search engine to research authoring techniques to ensure HTML tables are easily adaptable for international audiences. Summarize your findings in a paragraph, add your name to the paper, then print the document.

▼ INDEPENDENT CHALLENGE 4

Now that you've used tables to organize data, you are ready to add tables to the pages on your Web site.

    a. Determine how tables can be used in your Web site to clearly present the pages' information. Lay out your tables on paper to determine which table properties can best present your site's information. Not all of your Web pages require tables.

    b. Create tables on pages where they clearly communicate information to a user.

    c. Add row and column spanning where appropriate.

    d. Format the table borders and backgrounds to clearly display the information.

    e. Position and align the contents of your tables appropriately.

    f. Save your work, then print the pages with tables in your browser.

    g. Close all files, then transfer your edited files to the remote location.

▼ VISUAL WORKSHOP

Work progresses on your Bits and PCs Web site, and you decide to use a table to advertise specials on hard drives. In your text editor, open the **htm_F-8.txt** file from the drive and folder where your Data Files are stored, then save it as **specials.htm** in the bitspcs folder where you save your site files. If you are asked whether you want to replace the file, click Yes. Replace the comment in the Data File with a table advertising the hard drive specials shown in Figure F-22. Your table should be displayed at a width of 70% of the browser window with a 5-pixel border. There should be two pixels between cells and four pixels around the cell content. Add your name to the bottom of the page before the e-mail link. Save your work, then print the **specials.htm** page in your browser. (*Hint*: Under the opening table tag, use a caption tag to display the text "Hard Drive Specials.".)

FIGURE F-22

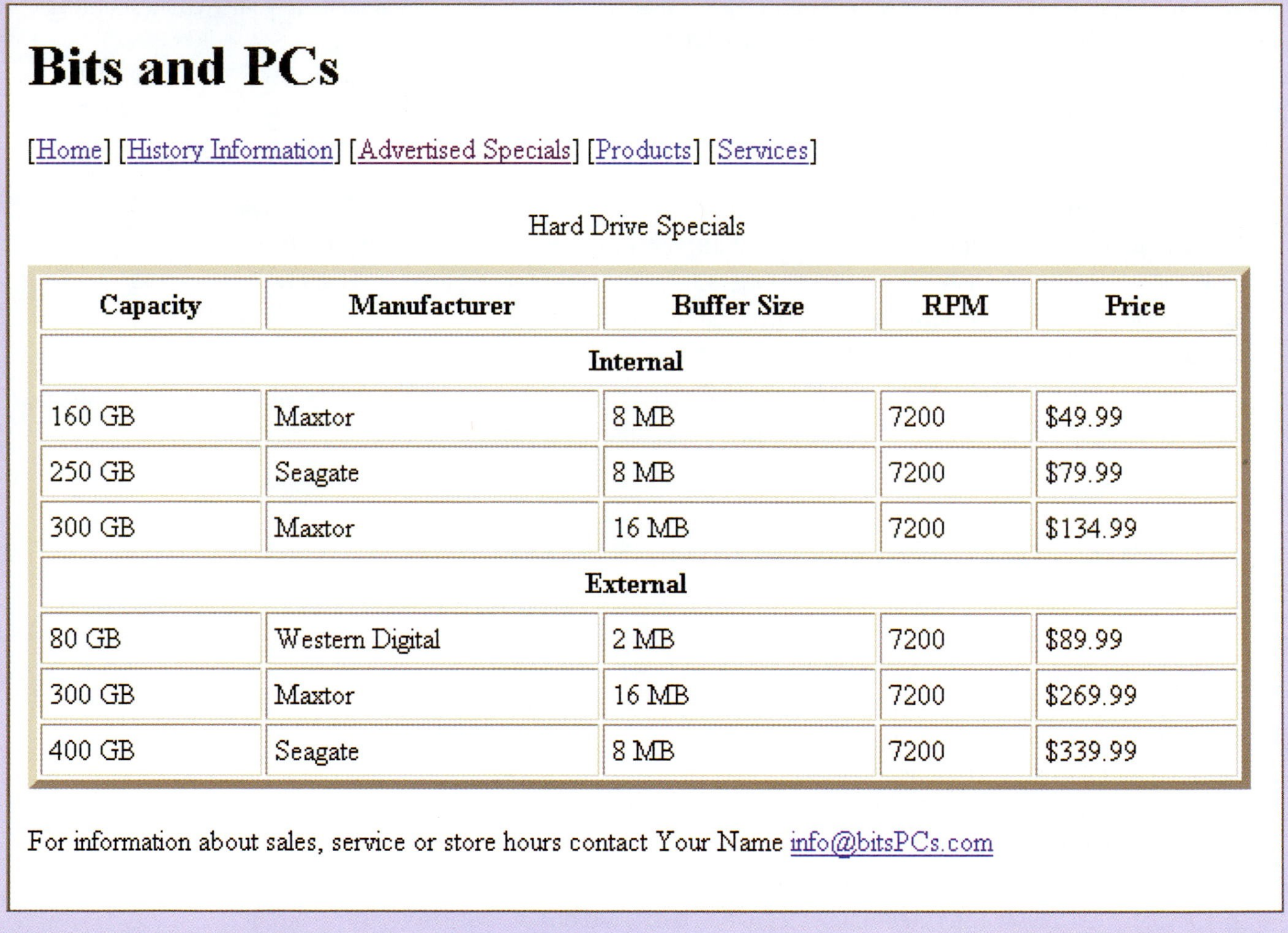

Bits and PCs

[Home] [History Information] [Advertised Specials] [Products] [Services]

Hard Drive Specials

Capacity	Manufacturer	Buffer Size	RPM	Price
Internal				
160 GB	Maxtor	8 MB	7200	$49.99
250 GB	Seagate	8 MB	7200	$79.99
300 GB	Maxtor	16 MB	7200	$134.99
External				
80 GB	Western Digital	2 MB	7200	$89.99
300 GB	Maxtor	16 MB	7200	$269.99
400 GB	Seagate	8 MB	7200	$339.99

For information about sales, service or store hours contact Your Name info@bitsPCs.com

Using Forms to Control Input

OBJECTIVES

In addition to letting you create informational pages for users, HTML also includes methods of making your pages interactive. The main HTML element that makes interactivity possible is a form. A **form** is a set of Web page elements with which you interact to submit a request or provide information. Forms are used for submitting credit card and shipping information for online purchases, completing surveys, and for requesting information. The management team at Paradise Mountain Family Resort wants to use a Web-based survey to find out how resort guests rate the services and activities provided by the resort. You and your Web development team are working to create a Web page form that allows guests to participate in the survey.

Planning a Form

Including a form on your Web site is a simple and straightforward way to allow site visitors to send you feedback or other information. If you are using the Web to sell products or services, forms are vital. As shown in Figure G-1, Web forms can allow users to enter information in several different ways, including predefined choices from which users can select as well as text entry areas. Most forms include several **form fields**—also called **form elements**—such as text boxes or pull-down menus that allow user input. Each field or group of fields is usually next to a **label**—text that explains what information is required in the adjacent field. Before you design your form, you must determine its purpose and the type of information you want to collect. Making those decisions first helps you decide what type of form fields to include. Choosing the right form elements can help ensure that the data you receive meets your needs. You met with Paradise Mountain Family Resort's marketing director to determine what type of information they need to collect. Now it is up to you to review the different types of HTML form fields and to select the most appropriate field for each type of information the director needs.

DETAILS

The types of form fields are:

- **Single-line text box**

    A single-line text box is ideal for requesting limited user input, such as a first or last name, or street address. HTML allows you to specify the size of a single-line text box, as well as the maximum character length of user input you want to allow.

- **Check boxes and radio buttons**

    Check boxes and radio buttons simplify Web forms by allowing users to select from a list of options. Users can select multiple check boxes, which are ideal for a set of options from which a user might choose none, one, or several—as when choosing pizza toppings. On the other hand, radio buttons limit user input to one choice from a set. Radio buttons are the best choice for a mutually exclusive set of choices, such as T-shirt size (S, M, L, or XL). Because it is difficult to account for all possible choices, it is often a good idea to provide a choice for "none" or "other."

- **Pull-down menus and scroll boxes**

    Pull-down menus and scroll boxes both serve a similar function to radio buttons and check boxes: they allow users to make one or more selections from among multiple items. When your list of choices is lengthy, pull-down menus and scroll boxes conserve Web page space. A pull-down menu shows one choice by default, and displays the remaining choices after a user clicks the down arrow. By contrast, a scroll box shows a specified number of choices. Users view hidden options by scrolling through the list.

- **Multiline text areas**

    Multiline text areas—often called comment boxes and check boxes—are designed to allow less-structured input by the user. Text areas allow users to make additional comments or ask questions. You can specify the dimensions of this area on the page.

- **Push buttons**

    HTML includes code to create two kinds of predefined buttons that users can click to execute common form-related tasks. You can configure one of these buttons to submit the information entered by users to the appropriate processing system. The other button allows users to clear information they have entered and start over without reloading the form.

Single-line text boxes

Pull-down menu

Check boxes

Radio buttons

Textarea comment box

Push buttons

Dealing with privacy issues

Surveys consistently show that many Web users are concerned that their personal information is not adequately secure when they interact on the Web. The topic of security is important when considering whether your Web site will include forms, which are often designed to collect information that people want to keep as private as possible. A Web designer is not often in a position to decide a company's policy on use of personal information collected from Web users. You can, however, make site users feel more secure by clearly communicating your organization's policy regarding use of the information you request. Nearly all Web sites that request information allow users to select options within the form that keep their information off e-mail and printed material mailing lists. Sometimes organizations want to collect additional information if users are willing to provide it. Be sure your Web page makes it clear that such fields are optional; that way, you avoid losing the business of potential customers who refuse to answer such questions.

Creating a Text Field

The text and fields that compose a Web page form are always surrounded by the `<form>...</form>` tag. Most form fields use the `<input />` tag with attributes that specify the kind of form field and any special characteristics. The required attribute for input elements is **type**. Input tags are self-closed using the cancel mark (/) at the end of the tag. To create a **text field**—also known as a single-line text box—you set the input type attribute value to "text". Text fields are useful for collecting information such as the user's name. Because most form-processing scripts use the name assigned to each form field for matching collected data with processing instructions and output display, another recommended attribute for all forms and form elements is **name.** Table G-1 explains the syntax and attributes for the `<form>...</form>` and `<input />` tags. You want to include text fields to collect guests' names. You will use tables to arrange the form elements.

STEPS

QUICK TIP
The nonbreaking spaces in the form hold table cells open until you add form elements.

1. **Start your text editor program, open the file htm_G-1.txt from the place where you store your Data Files, save it using the All Files type as survey.htm in your paradise folder in the place where you save your site files, then inspect the code**
   As shown in Figure G-2, the page is set up in a table-based format and contains several comment tags, with prompts regarding the placement of your form elements. First, the form needs opening and closing form tags.

2. **Locate and select the comment `<!-- Begin Form Here -->`, press [Delete], then type**
   `<form name="survey" action="" method="post">`
   The form name value in the opening form tag identifies the form for processing purposes. To accomplish their designated purpose, forms use methods—such as post and get—and actions. **Post** is used to send information to a server, and **get** is used to retrieve information. The form **action** identifies the script or page used to process the form. Because this form will send survey information to the Marketing Department, you specified the post method. You will specify the form action later.

3. **Scroll to the bottom of the document, select the comment `<!-- End Form Here -->`, press [Delete], then type `</form>`**
   All of the form field elements must be coded between the opening and closing form tags. Notice that the opening and closing form tags surround the form table. Tables make it easy to align form fields.

4. **In the page code, locate and select the comment `<!--Label 1 -->`, press [Delete], type `First name:`, press [Spacebar], move to the next line, drag to select the comment `<!-- Input First name text field -->`, press [Delete], then type `<input type="text" name="fname" size="20" />`**
   You set the first form prompt label, "First Name", and its matching form field.

QUICK TIP
Be sure to type the letter "l" (for last name) and not the number "1" in the name value.

5. **Locate and select the Label 2 comment tag, press [Delete], type `Last name:`, move to the next line, select `<!-- Last name text field -->`, press [Delete], type `<input type="text" name="lname" size="20" />`, then save your work**
   You have created first and last name input elements for your form.

6. **Move to the bottom of the page, locate and select the comment tag `<!-- input, e-mail -->`, press [Delete], then type `<input type="text" name="email" size="100" />`**
   The text box for the e-mail address is considerably longer than the others. Your design team has created the rest of the form labels for you, but you need to insert the form fields.

7. **Save your work, start your Web browser, then open the file survey.htm in your browser**
   The text entry boxes and labels in which users can supply their first name, last name, and e-mail address appear on the Web page, as shown in Figure G-3.

8. **Click in the First name text box, type your first name, press [Tab], type your last name in the Last name text box, press [Tab], then type your e-mail address**
   Your text boxes accept input, but the form requires additional form elements.

FIGURE G-2: Commented page code for survey form

```
<p>Dear Valued Guest, </p>
<p>Thank you for taking the time to fill out our guest satisfaction survey. Your answers
help us improve our services at Paradise Mountain Family Resort and are strictly
confidential. None of your personal information will be shared with other organizations.
<br />
 <hr />
<br /></p>
</td>
</tr>
<tr valign="top">
<td>

<!-- Begin Form Here -->
<table border="0" width="90%" id="frm_table" cellpadding="4" align="center">
  <tr valign="top">
    <td align="right" width="25%" nowrap><!-- Label 1 --> </td>
    <td width="25%"><!-- Input First name text field --> </td>
    <td align="right" width="25%" nowrap><!-- Label 2 --> </td>
    <td width="25%"><!-- Last name text field --> </td>
  </tr>
  <tr valign="top">
    <td align="center" colspan="4">Tell us about your visit<br />
    <hr />
    </td>
  </tr>
  <tr valign="top">
    <td colspan="3">At what time of year was your last visit to Paradise Mountain Family
Resort? </td>
    <td>Season: <!-- Dropdown season --></td>
    </td>
  </tr>

  <tr valign="top">
    <td colspan="3">During your last visit, how many people were in your party?  
```

Comments guide element placement

Nonbreaking spaces hold cells open

FIGURE G-3: Web page displaying labeled text boxes

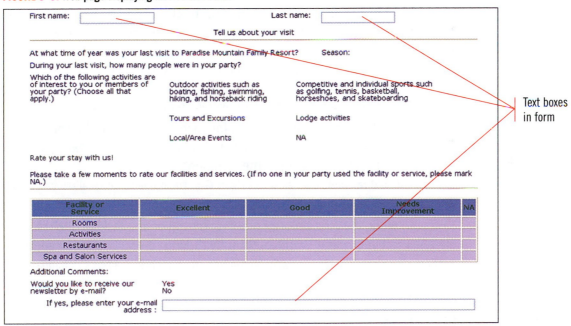

First name: Last name:

Tell us about your visit

At what time of year was your last visit to Paradise Mountain Family Resort?   Season:

During your last visit, how many people were in your party?

Which of the following activities are of interest to you or members of your party? (Choose all that apply.)

Outdoor activities such as boating, fishing, swimming, hiking, and horseback riding

Competitive and individual sports such as golfing, tennis, basketball, horseshoes, and skateboarding

Tours and Excursions   Lodge activities

Local/Area Events   NA

Rate your stay with us!

Please take a few moments to rate our facilities and services. (If no one in your party used the facility or service, please mark NA.)

Facility or Service	Excellent	Good	Needs Improvement	NA
Rooms				
Activities				
Restaurants				
Spa and Salon Services				

Additional Comments:

Would you like to receive our newsletter by e-mail?   Yes   No

If yes, please enter your e-mail address :

Text boxes in form

TABLE G-1: Common form field tags

tag(s)	attribute	description	example
`<form>...</form>`		Defines the form boundaries	`<form method="post">...</form>`
`<input />`	type	Specifies the type of form field to create	`<input type="text" />`
	name	Assigns a form or element name; used by scripts to reference and process forms	`<form name="survey">...</form>` `<input type="text" name="value" />`
	size	Specifies the display length (width) of the form field	`<input type="text" size="20" />`
	maxlength	Sets the largest number of characters allowed in the current form field; extra typing is ignored after this number is reached	`<input type="text" maxlength="40" />`

Adding Radio Buttons

Text boxes allow form users to enter unique bits of information. However, you can reduce the potential for user input error by providing a list of choices. This eliminates the possibility that a user will enter a selection that the form processor doesn't understand or that is not useful. HTML includes several formats for controlling user input; each format is appropriate for different situations and types of information. To create a set of options that a user can see all at once, and from which a user can make only one selection, you create radio buttons. **Radio buttons** are small white circles appearing next to explanatory text. When a user clicks a circle, it fills with black to indicate it is selected. Selecting one button in a group deselects any previously selected button. You create radio buttons using the `<input />` tag, with the type attribute set to "radio." All radio buttons in a set share the same name; however, each button uses a different value. The value of the selected button is returned by the form processor as the user's response to the question. The values you specify vary depending upon how the information will be used. You want to add radio buttons to enable survey users to choose one of several options for some questions. You will configure some button groups with numeric values so they can be processed as numbers in a spreadsheet or database.

STEPS

1. **Click the text editor program button on your taskbar, then in your text editor, locate the comment that begins `<!-- Use the comments below`**

2. **Click just after the comment `<!-- Radio button - name, rooms; value, 3 -->`, before the nonbreaking space ` `, press [Enter], press [Tab], then type `<input type="radio" name="room" value="3" />`**

   You created the first button in the first group of buttons, which you've named "room." Buttons in the same group share a common name, defining a set from which users can make only one selection. You assigned a value of 3 to your first button. The rest of the buttons in the chart need to be configured.

3. **Repeat Step 2 to create radio buttons for each of the rest of the cells in the Rooms row, then create radio buttons for each cell in the Activities, Restaurants, and Spa services rows, using the values shown in the comments**

   Your code should resemble that shown in Figure G-4. The numeric values allow you to process the collected data as numbers in a spreadsheet or database to numerically rank each resort feature.

TROUBLE
If you are able to select more than one radio button in the same row, check your source code to ensure that all the buttons in the same row have the same name.

4. **Save your work, click the browser program button on the taskbar and reload the survey.htm file, then test your ratings radio buttons by clicking several buttons in each group.**

   As shown in Figure G-5, when a radio button in a group is clicked, a black dot appears in the center. When another button is clicked, the first selection is removed. When a user submits the form, the returned value for each field is the value of the selected radio button.

5. **Return to your code, click after the comment `<!-- Radio Button - name, newsletter; value, Yes -->`, press [Enter], press [Spacebar] four times, type `<input type="radio" name="newsletter" value="Yes" checked="checked" />`, then press [Spacebar]**

   The checked attribute signifies that the radio button should appear as selected when the page opens.

6. **Click after the comment `<!-- Radio Button - name, newsletter; value, No -->`, press [Enter], press [Spacebar] four times, type `<input type="radio" name="newsletter" value="No" />`, press [Spacebar], then save your page and view it in the browser**

   The Yes and No values you set for the newsletter radio button group allow you to sort your results by respondents who wish to receive your newsletter. As shown in Figure G-6, the Yes value for the newsletter radio button group is prechecked.

FIGURE G-4: Web page code containing tags for radio button list

Comment tag

Input type radio tag

Cancel mark (closing slash)

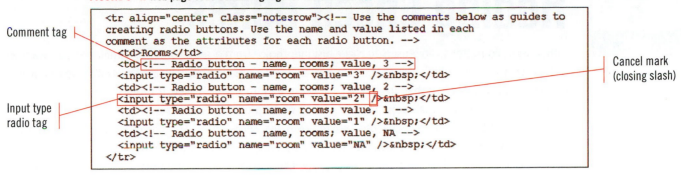

```
<tr align="center" class="notesrow"><!-- Use the comments below as guides to
creating radio buttons. Use the name and value listed in each
comment as the attributes for each radio button. -->
    <td>Rooms</td>
    <td><!-- Radio button - name, rooms; value, 3 -->
    <input type="radio" name="room" value="3" /> </td>
    <td><!-- Radio button - name, rooms; value, 2 -->
<input type="radio" name="room" value="2" /> </td>
    <td><!-- Radio button - name, rooms; value, 1 -->
    <input type="radio" name="room" value="1" /> </td>
    <td><!-- Radio button - name, rooms; value, NA -->
    <input type="radio" name="room" value="NA" /> </td>
</tr>
```

FIGURE G-5: Web page displaying radio button list

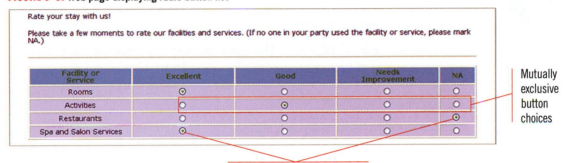

Mutually exclusive button choices

One button selected in each group

FIGURE G-6: Survey page with prechecked radio button

Prechecked radio button

Clues to Use

Using the checked attribute

By default, all the fields in a set of radio buttons appear empty. This means that none of the buttons is selected unless the user clicks one of them. You can include the checked attribute in the `<input />` tag for one of the radio buttons in a set, causing it to appear as selected when the Web page opens. The checked attribute can simplify the form for your users by saving them a click. It is most useful for the least expensive or most commonly selected items in a list. In general, you use the checked attribute in a list that requires a selection by the user; you avoid using it in a list that doesn't require a user to make a selection. Do not use the checked attribute for radio button groups that require users to add personal information such as age or gender.

HTML

Adding Check Boxes

Although radio buttons allow users to make a single choice from a set of options, sometimes you want to allow users to make multiple selections from a list. For situations like this, HTML offers **check boxes**, which display an array of choices that are all visible at once, and from which users may select any, all, or none. A check box appears as a small box next to its label. When a user clicks an empty check box, a check mark appears in the box; clicking a checked box removes the check mark. You create check boxes using the `<input />` tag, with the type attribute set to "checkbox." Unlike radio buttons, each check box should have a unique name. Also unlike radio buttons, you can use the checked attribute for multiple check boxes in the same section of your form to display the box with an initially checked state. If you don't specify a value attribute, the default value returned for a checked box is "On". Unchecked boxes return a value of "Off". Since the values On and Off are not very intuitive, it is a good idea to assign each check box a specific value. Paradise Mountain Family Resort offers a wide variety of activities for their guests. The Marketing Department wants to find out which activities generate the most interest. Because you want guests to be able to choose more than one option, you add the activities to the form as check box fields.

STEPS

1. **In your text editor, click after the comment tag that reads** `<!-- Checkbox name, outdoorActivities-->`**, press [Enter], press [Tab], type** `<input type="checkbox" name="outdoorActivities" value="Yes" />`**, press [Spacebar], press [Enter], then press [Tab]**

   You entered the code to create the first check box. The text following the code becomes the form label. When checked and submitted, the form returns a value of "outdoorActivities Yes". This makes it easy to sort by respondents who enjoy outdoor activities.

2. **Click after** `<!-- Checkbox name, competitiveActivities-->`**, press [Enter], press [Tab], type** `<input type="checkbox" name="competitiveActivities" value="Yes" />`**, press [Spacebar], press [Enter], then press [Tab]**

3. **Click after the comments for tours, lodge_activities, events and NA, then repeat Step 2 to create checkboxes for each of the following labels: Tours and Excursions, Lodge activities, Local/Area Events, and NA, setting each value as Yes**

   You included the "NA" option for respondents who are not interested in activities. Compare your code to that shown in Figure G-7.

4. **Save your page, then click the browser program button on the taskbar and reload the survey.htm page**

   As shown in Figure G-8, two columns of check boxes present selection options for survey users.

Design Matters

Labeling radio buttons and check boxes

The text that you enter as a label next to a radio button or a check box is just like plain text elsewhere on your Web page. Even though form fields would be meaningless to users without labels, HTML has no rules about how to label the fields. Therefore, you are free to put a label to the left or right of a field, or even above or below it. The most important guideline is to make sure it is obvious to a user which label and which field go together. From a design standpoint, it is also important to make the fields easy for users to find. By placing the check box form field in front of the label and using tables to align your content, you make it easier for the user to match form fields with their respective labels.

FIGURE G-7: Source code for survey check boxes

Comment tag with checkbox name

Checkbox with "Yes" value

```
<input type="checkbox" name="outdoorActivities" value="Yes" />
Outdoor activities such as boating,
fishing, swimming, hiking, and horseback riding </td>
<td>
<!-- Checkbox name, competitiveActivities -->
<input type="checkbox" name="competitiveActivities" value="Yes" />
Competitive and individual sports such as
golfing, tennis, basketball, horseshoes, and skateboarding</td>
</tr>

<!-- Activities Table Row 2 -->
<tr valign="top">
<td><!-- Checkbox name, tours-->
<input type="checkbox" name="tours" value="Yes" />
Tours and Excursions
</td>
<td><!-- Checkbox name, lodge_activities-->
<input type="checkbox" name="lodge_activities" value="Yes" />
Lodge activities
</td>
</tr>

<!-- Activities Table Row 3 -->
<tr>
<td><!-- Checkbox name, events-->
<input type="checkbox" name="events" value="Yes" />
Local/Area Events
</td>
<td><!-- Checkbox name, NA -->
<input type="checkbox" name="NA" value="Yes" />NA
</td>
</tr>
```

FIGURE G-8: Web page survey with check boxes

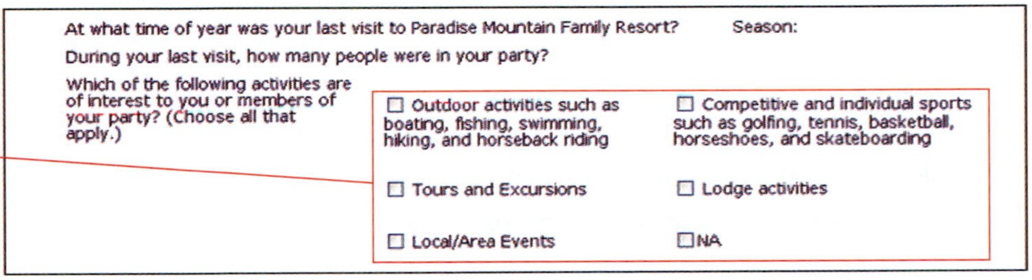

Checkbox list

At what time of year was your last visit to Paradise Mountain Family Resort?   Season:

During your last visit, how many people were in your party?

Which of the following activities are of interest to you or members of your party? (Choose all that apply.)

☐ Outdoor activities such as boating, fishing, swimming, hiking, and horseback riding

☐ Competitive and individual sports such as golfing, tennis, basketball, horseshoes, and skateboarding

☐ Tours and Excursions

☐ Lodge activities

☐ Local/Area Events

☐ NA

Creating a Pull-Down Menu

Radio buttons and check boxes lay out a group of related options so that they all are visible on the Web page. Sometimes, however, you want to save space on your Web page. You may have such an extensive set of choices that it would be impractical to include all of them in the Web page's layout. For this type of situation, HTML allows you to format your options with a more efficient form field called a pull-down menu. A **pull-down menu**—also known as a **select option box** or **drop-down list**—appears on the page like a single-line text field. However, it also contains a down-arrow button that the user clicks to open a menu of choices. In most cases, when the user clicks a choice, the list closes and the user's selection appears in the field. The pull-down menu is popular on Web page forms because it uses space efficiently and because most users are familiar with it from common operating systems and software. To create a pull-down menu, you use the `<select>...</select>` tag set to surround a list of choices. Each choice is marked with the `<option>...</option>` tag set. Table G-2 explains the common attributes used with these tags. You have identified three areas of your form that would make effective use of pull-down menus.

STEPS

1. **In your text editor, locate and select the comment tag `<!-- Dropdown season -->`, in the third row of your form layout table, press [Delete], press [Enter], press [Tab], type `<select name="season">`, press [Enter], press [Tab], then type `</select> <br /> <br />`**

   You typed the opening and closings tags for your drop-down list and placed two line breaks after it. The line breaks add a little extra space and prevent your form from appearing too crowded.

2. **Click just before `</select>`, then type the following code, pressing [Enter] and [Tab] after each line:**

   ```
   <option value="Spring">Spring</option>
   <option value="Summer">Summer</option>
   <option value="Fall">Fall</option>
   <option value="Winter">Winter</option>
   ```

   Your code resembles that shown in Figure G-9. By adding a value to and closing each option, you ensure that your code works with a form-processing script.

3. **Locate and drag to select the comment tag that reads `<!-- dropdown num_guests -->`, press [Enter], press [Tab], type `<select name="num_guests">`, then press [Enter]**

4. **Press [Tab], then type `</select> <br /> <br />`**

5. **Click after `<select name="num_guests">`, press [Enter], press [Tab] twice, then type the following code, pressing [Enter] and [Tab] twice after the first and second lines**

   ```
   <option value="1">   1   </option>
   <option value="2 - 3">2 - 3 </option>
   <option value="4 or more">4 or more</option>
   ```

   Because the first option contains a single character, you insert nonbreaking spaces around it so it is easier for users to see.

6. **Save your work, then reload the survey.htm page in your browser**

   Figure G-10 shows your form with an active pull-down menu. Unlike form element names, which are used by program code to identify form objects, option values are text strings and can contain spaces.

FIGURE G-9: Code for pull-down menu

Opening select tag

Opening option list tag

Closing select tag

```
<tr valign="top">
    <td colspan="3">At what time of year was your last visit to Paradise
Mountain Family Resort? </td>
    <td>Season: 
    <select name="season">
    <option value="Spring">Spring</option>
    <option value="Summer">Summer</option>
    <option value="Fall">Fall</option>
    <option value="Winter">Winter</option>
    </select> <br /> <br />
    </td>
</tr>
```

Closing option list tag

FIGURE G-10: Web page with active pull-down menus

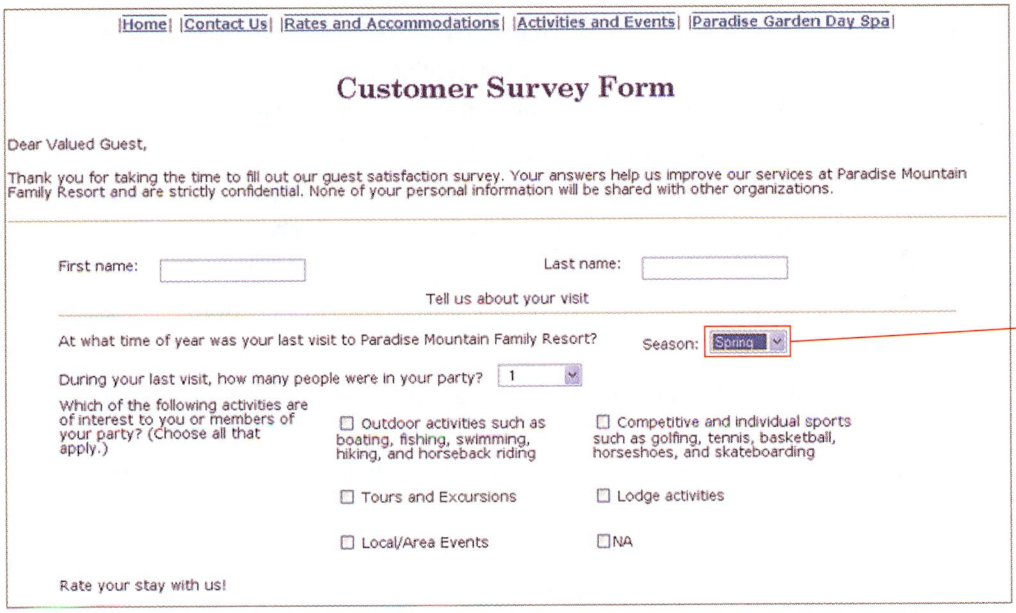

|Home| |Contact Us| |Rates and Accommodations| |Activities and Events| |Paradise Garden Day Spa|

Customer Survey Form

Dear Valued Guest,

Thank you for taking the time to fill out our guest satisfaction survey. Your answers help us improve our services at Paradise Mountain Family Resort and are strictly confidential. None of your personal information will be shared with other organizations.

First name: [   ]   Last name: [   ]

Tell us about your visit

At what time of year was your last visit to Paradise Mountain Family Resort?   Season: [Spring ▾]

During your last visit, how many people were in your party? [1 ▾]

Which of the following activities are of interest to you or members of your party? (Choose all that apply.)

☐ Outdoor activities such as boating, fishing, swimming, hiking, and horseback riding   ☐ Competitive and individual sports such as golfing, tennis, basketball, horseshoes, and skateboarding

☐ Tours and Excursions   ☐ Lodge activities

☐ Local/Area Events   ☐NA

Rate your stay with us!

Active pull-down menu

TABLE G-2: Pull-down menu tags and attributes

tag(s)	function	attribute	description
<select>...</select>	Creates a list field of options in which some choices are hidden	name	Creates a field name used to reference a field for form processing
		size	Sets the number of items that appear on screen; if omitted, choices appear as a pull-down menu; if set to 2 or more, list appears as a scroll box
		multiple	Sets the number of options user may select from the list; if omitted, user may select only one list item
<option>...</option>	Surrounds each item in a selection list; must occur between <select> and </select> tags	value	Specifies the text to be submitted to form-processing system
		selected	Specifies the option to appear in the field text box when the Web page opens in the browser

Adding a Comment Box

An effective method of ensuring that your site visitors have ample opportunity to express all of their concerns when filling out a form is to add an additional form element called a **multiline text area**, also known as a **comment box**. Comment boxes are designed to allow less-structured user input by accommodating multiple lines of user comments. To add a comment box to a page, use the `<textarea>...</textarea>` tag set. You configure the text area tag using the cols attribute for columns and the rows attributes for rows. You decide to allow users to add additional information using a comment box.

STEPS

1. **In your text editor, locate the comment tag that reads** `<!-- Insert textarea here -->`, **drag to select the comment tag and the nonbreaking space,** , **that follows it, press [Delete], then press [Enter]**

2. **Type** `<textarea name="comments" rows="4" cols="40">`, **then press [Enter]**
   Because text area elements display content, including spaces and tabs that you type between the opening and closing tags, you decide not to space or tab after returning to the next line.

3. **Type** `</textarea>`, **then save your page**
   Your code should resemble the code shown in Figure G-11. Although you can add prompting text such as, "Type your comments here" to the content area of a comment box, you decide not to do so because if a site visitor chooses not to add a comment of his or her own, the placeholder text will be returned as the form field value.

4. **Locate the code for the opening table data tag and Additional Comments label that reads:** `<td colspan="2">Additional Comments: </td>`

5. **Click just after colspan="2" inside the opening table data tag, press [Spacebar], then type** `align="right"`
   Aligning the label content to the right brings it next to the comment box letting users know that the label belongs to the box.

6. **Locate the "Page modified by" paragraph at the bottom of the page, replace Your Name with your own name, update the date text to show the current date, then save the page**

7. **Click the browser program button on the taskbar, then reload the survey.htm page**
   As shown in Figure G-12, the comment box appears on the page and is ready for user input.

FIGURE G-11: Code for text area comment box

Textarea code not indented or spaced

```
<tr valign="top">
    <td colspan="2">Additional Comments: </td>
    <td colspan="2">
<textarea name="comments" rows="4" cols="40">
</textarea></td>
    </tr>
```

FIGURE G-12: Web page with comment box

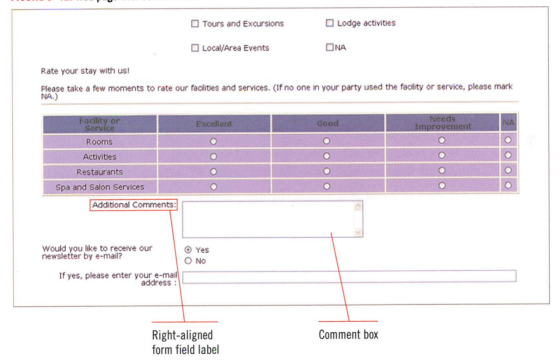

Right-aligned
form field label

Comment box

Adding a Push Button

Once users finish filling out a form, they need to submit their information to your organization for processing. To allow users to execute such tasks, HTML forms include **push buttons**, which are labeled objects that a user can click to perform a task. You create a push button using the `<input />` tag, and you specify its function using the type attribute. The most common push button types are reset, submit, and button. A **reset button** clears all the input in a form, allowing a user to start over. The **submit button** performs one of the most common form activities—submitting information for processing. Input elements of the button type use an Onclick event associated with a script in order to perform a function. For input elements with the attributes submit, reset, or button, you can use the value attribute to change the text on the button face. You want to add submit and reset buttons to your form to make it easy for your site visitors to use.

STEPS

1. In your text editor, select the comment `<!-- Insert Submit button here -->` as well as the nonbreaking space, ` `, that follows it near the bottom of the document, then press [Delete]

2. Type `<input type="submit" value="Complete Survey" name="submit" />`

3. Select the comment that reads: `<!-- Insert Reset button here -->` as well as the nonbreaking space that follows it, then press [Delete]

4. Type `<input type="reset" value="Start Over" name="reset" />`, press [Spacebar], then save your file

   This portion of your HTML document should resemble the code shown in Figure G-13.

5. Click the browser program button on the taskbar, reload the page, then click the Complete Survey button

   The browser reloads the page as shown in Figure G-14 and clears the information you entered in the form. If you have access to a server with form-processing capabilities, you can configure your form to submit information by adding the name of your processing script as the value of the form action. Check with your instructor or server administrator to find out if your server has form-processing capabilities.

6. Close your browser and your text editor, then transfer your updated files to your remote directory

Clues to Use

Using a graphic as a push button

The value attribute allows you to customize the text on a push button to fit its specific function on your Web pages. You can further customize a button to fit your page's overall theme by specifying a graphic to use as a button. To use a graphic as a push button, set the `<input />` tag type attribute to "image," then specify the path and name of the graphic file with the src attribute. Like other images in your Web pages, you should specify alternate text for a graphical button by using the alt attribute.

FIGURE G-13: Web page code containing tags for push buttons

```
<tr valign="top">
  <td> </td>
  <td colspan="2" align="right">
  <input type="submit" value="Complete Survey" name="submit" /> </td>
  <td><input type="reset" value="Start Over" name="reset" /></td>
  </tr>
```

Submit button code

Reset button code

FIGURE G-14: Web page displaying push buttons

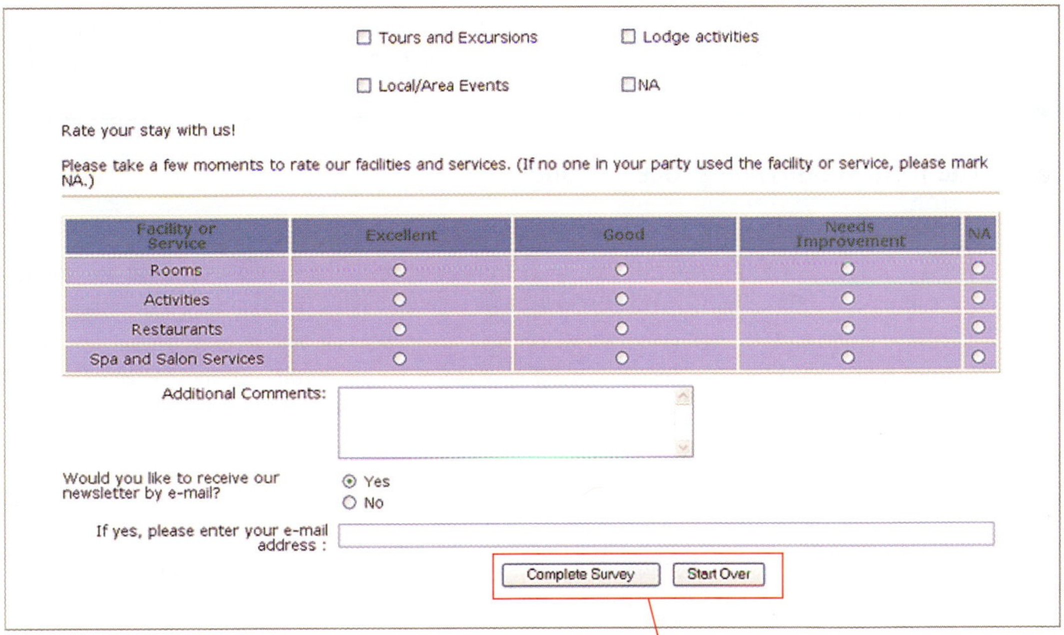

Push buttons

Clues to Use

Using input buttons

Submit and Reset input buttons have built-in **event actions** that allow them to function without additional scripting: When clicked, the Submit button automatically sends form data to the processing file specified in the opening form tag's action attribute. The Reset button automatically clears the form without reloading the page. However, you may want your button to perform an additional action before submitting the form, such as calculating information or sending a response. In these cases, you can use button or image type input elements. Although they look very similar to Submit and Reset elements, button (type="button") and image (type="image") elements require the addition of an onClick event with a reference to an associated file, function, or processing script, as in the following example: `<input type="button" name="submit" value="Send Information" onClick="verify();" />`, where verify() is the name of a function, which is a scripted action.

Connecting a Form's Back End

Like tags to format other Web page elements such as text and graphics, the tags for creating a form only generate the Web page that users see in their browsers; that page is known as the **front end**. Once a user clicks the Submit button, however, the information entered requires processing that is not performed by the page's HTML code. When the code specifies an action in the opening form tag, clicking the submit button automatically instructs the browser to send the entered data to your Web server for processing. The programs that reside on an organization's computer system and that are responsible for processing the submitted data make up the **back end**. Figure G-15 shows the different parts of the front end and the back end and how data moves between them. Generally, Web page designers are responsible for creating the front end, and other people in an organization, such as the Web site administrator, handle the back-end tasks. However, it is important that the front-end designer work with the people responsible for the back end to ensure that the parts of the Web site that both of you create work together as expected. Table G-3 describes form attributes and values for submitting information from the server. You are meeting the Paradise Mountain Family Resort site administrator to begin coordinating your work on the submission process for the visitor survey. You can get more information on connecting to the form's back end by visiting the Student Online Companion for this text.

DETAILS

The form-submission process includes:

- ### Browser packaging

  When a user clicks the submit button, the browser refers to the `<form>` tag attributes for details on how to submit the information. These attributes, which are described in Table G-3, allow you to specify where the information entered in a form is sent, how the browser sends it, and in what format. Your IT Department has not yet finalized the submission requirements, but will provide you with these settings in time to test the system before the site survey page goes online.

- ### Form handler

  The border between a Web site's front end and back end is the communication between the Web server—where the HTML document is stored—and the programs that process the information collected in a form. This communication is facilitated through a form handler, and sometimes takes place using a standardized protocol known as **CGI (Common Gateway Interface)**. CGI is not a scripting language. It is instead an interface between the Web client and the processing script. Most CGI scripts are written in PERL, C++, or JavaScript. They are often compiled as executable programs with .exe or .dll extensions. Other types of form handlers are ASP (Active Server Page), JSP (Java Server Page), and PHP (Hypertext PreProcessor) scripting, which are all used extensively for making connections to database servers.

> **QUICK TIP**
>
> If you don't have access to a form handler, you can test your form using the mailto action of the opening form tag with a valid e-mail address as the action.

- ### Form processing and confirmation

  The final step in submitting form contents is the processing by the appropriate software. Because forms have many uses, they require different types of processing—for example, searching for information in a database, adding information to a database, or transforming in some way the data that was submitted. In any case, form submission and processing generally require an acknowledgement to the user, which confirms that the information was submitted, and which may also contain the results of the submission. For the Paradise Mountain guest survey form, your department is using a simple form handler. However, at such a time when the resort begins to accept online payment for reservations, you have made arrangements to work with a **shopping cart service**, which can bill the user's credit card for the amount of the reservation and inform the resort when the payment has cleared. The interface for one of the most popular shopping cart services, PayPal, is shown in Figure G-16. PayPal provides processing services for both businesses and individuals.

FIGURE G-15: Web page front end and back end

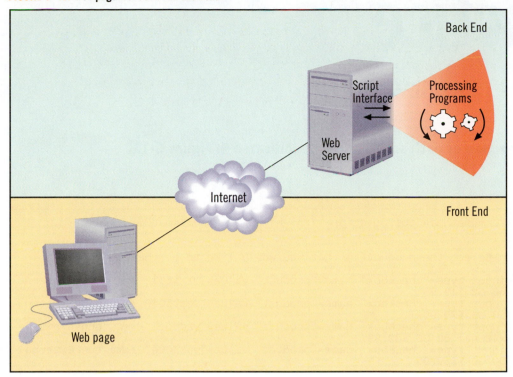

FIGURE G-16: PayPal services Web page

TABLE G-3: `<form>` tag attributes for submitting information

attribute	description	example
method	Indicates how the data entered by the user is submitted to the server; acceptable values are "get"—for calling information from the server—and "post"—for sending information to the server	`method="post"`
enctype	Specifies how the browser formats the user responses on the form before submitting them to the server	`enctype="text/plain"`
action	Indicates the path and name of the processing program that the server must run when the form is submitted	`action= "/cgi-bin/execmacro/input"`

Practice

▼ CONCEPTS REVIEW

Name the function of each section of code indicated in Figure G-17.

FIGURE G-17

```
<form method="post" action="/cgi-bin/execmacro/input">

<p>Select the product(s) that you would like to purchase:
<br />
<input type="checkbox" name="product" value="max160i" /> Maxtor Internal
160 GB $49.99
<input type="checkbox" name="product" value="sea250i" />Seagate Internal
250 GB $79.99
<input type="checkbox" name="product" value="wed80e" />Western Digital
External 80 GB $89.99
<input type="checkbox" name="product" value="max300e" />Maxtor External
300 GB $269.99
</p>

<br />Credit card Information:
<br />Type:
<select name="payment">
<option value="visa">Visa</option>
<option value="mc">MasterCard</option>
<option value="amx">American Express</option>
</select>

<br /> Number:
<input name="num" type="text" size="25" />
<br />Expiration date:
<input name="exp" type="text" size="4" />

<p>
Choose a Shipping Method:

<input type="radio" name="ship"  value="yes" />Ground
<input type="radio" name="ship" value="no" />Air
</p>

<p><input type="submit" value="Order" name="submit" />
<input type="reset" value="Start Over" name="reset" /></p>

</form>
```

1 2 3 4 5 6 7 8 9

Match each statement with the term it describes.

10. Form element that allows multiple user selections
11. Form element that limits user input to one choice
12. Multiline text area
13. Descriptive text that accompanies a form field
14. Required attribute for all input fields

a. Label
b. Type
c. Radio button
d. Comment box
e. Check box

Select the best answer from the list of choices.

15. **Which attribute can you use to display an item as selected in a radio button list?**
    - **a.** Type
    - **b.** Checked
    - **c.** Length
    - **d.** Order

16. **Which of the following attributes determines the number of items that appear by default in a pull-down menu?**
    - **a.** Value
    - **b.** Multiple
    - **c.** Name
    - **d.** Size

17. **Which tag(s) mark a choice in a pull-down menu?**
    - **a.** <form>...</form>
    - **b.** <input />
    - **c.** <select>...</select>
    - **d.** <option>...</option>

18. **Which attribute allows you to customize the text on a push button?**
    - **a.** Text
    - **b.** Type
    - **c.** Name
    - **d.** Value

19. **The Web page that users see in their browsers is called the Web site's:**
    - **a.** Form
    - **b.** Front end
    - **c.** Back end
    - **d.** Script

20. **The interface between the Web client and the processing script is called:**
    - **a.** Browser packaging
    - **b.** CGI
    - **c.** Scripting
    - **d.** Order processing and confirmation

▼ SKILLS REVIEW

1. **Plan a form.**
   - **a.** Consider how a form could be used to sell spa products over the Web. What type of data would you collect on a product order form?
   - **b.** Which form fields would you use on the form?
   - **c.** How would you structure the form?
   - **d.** Which types of push buttons would you place on your form?
   - **e.** How would you connect your form's back end to a Web server?

2. **Create a text field.**
   - **a.** In your text editor, open the file **htm_G-2.txt** from the drive and folder where your Data Files are stored, then save it as **spaproducts.htm** to the paradise/spa directory where you save your site files.
   - **b.** Locate the comment in the file indicating where the first set of text fields begins and place an input tag of `<input type="text" name="name" size="25" />` next to the Name: label to add a field for the customer's name.
   - **c.** In the following line next to the Address: label, place an input tag of `<input type="text" name="address" size="25" />` to add a field for the customer's address.

d. In the following line next to the City: label, place an input tag of `<input type="text" name="city" size="15" />` to add a field for the customer's city.

e. In the following line next to the State: label, place a similar text input tag assigning the name of state and a size of 2.

f. In the following line next to the Zip Code: label, place a similar text input tag assigning the name of zip and a size of 5.

g. In the following line next to the E-mail Address: label, place a similar input tag assigning the name of email and a size of 25.

h. Locate the comment in the file indicating where the second set of text fields begins, and place an input tag of `<input type="text" name="num" size="25" />` next to the Number: label to add a field for the credit card number.

i. In the following line next to the Expiration Date: label, place an input tag of: `<input type="text" name="exp" size="4" />` to add a field for the expiration date.

j. Save your file and view the form in your browser to check your work.

3. Add radio buttons.

a. Locate the comment in the file indicating where the radio buttons begin, and beneath the comment place an input tag of `<input type="radio" name="ship" value="ground" />Ground` to add a radio button choice for Ground shipping.

b. In the next line, place an input tag of `<input type="radio" name="ship" value="air" />Air` to add a radio button choice for Air shipping.

c. Save your work.

d. View the form in your browser to check your work.

4. Add check boxes.

a. Locate the comment in the file indicating where the check boxes begin, and beneath the comment place an input tag of `<input type="checkbox" name="product" value="soap" />Shea Butter Soap $12` to add a check box choice for Shea Butter Soap. Add two nonbreaking spaces by entering `  ` after the price.

b. In the next line, place an input tag of `<input type="checkbox" name="product" value="handcream" />Hand Cream $25` to add a check box choice for Hand Cream. Add two nonbreaking spaces after the price.

c. In the next line, place a similar input tag using a value of salts and a label of Bath Salts $9 to add a check box choice for Bath Salts with two nonbreaking spaces following the choice.

d. In the next line, place a similar input tag using a value of **bodycream** and a label of Body Cream $30 to add a check box choice for Body Cream.

e. Save your work

f. View the form in your browser to check your work.

5. Create a pull-down menu.

a. Locate the comment in the file indicating where the pull-down menu begins, and beneath the comment place the tag `<select name="payment">` to begin the list of choices.

b. In the next line, place an option tag of `<option value="visa">Visa</option>` to add a choice for Visa.

c. In the next line, place an option tag of `<option value="mc">MasterCard</option>` to add a choice for MasterCard.

d. In the next line, place a similar option tag for an American Express choice, using an option value of amx.

e. In the next line, place the tag `</select>` to end the list of choices.

f. Save your work.

g. View the form in your browser to check your work.

6. Add a comment box.

a. Locate the comment in the file indicating where the comment box begins, and place an opening `<textarea>` tag to start a multiline text area for customer product suggestions.

b. Add the attribute `name="newproducts"` to the opening textarea tag to give a name to the comments your customers provide in the box.

    c. Add the attribute `rows="5" cols="45"` to the opening textarea tag to create a box of five rows and 45 columns.

    d. Add the closing `</textarea>` tag to end the multiline comment area.

    e. Save your work.

    f. View the form in your browser to check your work.

7. Add a push button.

    a. Locate the comment in the file indicating where the push buttons begin, and place an `<input />` tag to start a button that can be used to submit your customer form data.

    b. Add the attribute `type="submit"` to the input tag to define the button as a submit button.

    c. Add the attribute `value="Order"` to the input tag to place the label Order on the button.

    d. Add the attribute `name="submit"` to the input tag to assign a name of submit to the button.

    e. Add an `<input />` tag to start a button that can be used to reset the form in the event that a customer would like to clear the form data.

    f. Add the attribute `type="reset"` to the input tag to define the button as a reset button.

    g. Add the attribute `value="Start Over"` to the input tag to place the label Start Over on the button.

    h. Add the attribute `name="reset"` to the input tag to assign a name of reset to the button.

    i. Delete any unnecessary blank lines in your file, then save your work.

    j. View the form in your browser to check the buttons.

8. Connect a form's back end.

    a. Locate the opening form tag in your file. What is the value of the method attribute?

    b. How will the order data entered by your customers be submitted to the server?

    c. What is the value of the action attribute in your form tag?

    d. What does this action value describe about the process the server uses to work with the form data?

    e. Delete all the comments, add a comment with your name, then print the code.

    f. Transfer the **spaproducts.htm** file to your remote directory.

▼ INDEPENDENT CHALLENGE 1

As you continue developing the Web site for your resort rental business, Star Vacations, you decide that forms can help to measure the interest of your customers in new markets. You decide to use a form to gather input about interest in Australian rentals.

    a. In your text editor, open the file **htm_G-3.txt** from the drive and folder where your Data Files are stored, then save it as **survey.htm** to the vacations folder where you save your site files.

    b. Locate the form area where the text fields are placed to collect contact information. Add an input tag to create a text field for the Zip Code label using a name of zip and a size of 5.

    c. Add the input tag to create the text field for the E-mail Address label using a name of email and a size of 25.

    d. Locate the form area where the Yes radio button is placed to collect responses from customers who are interested in Australia rentals. Under the Yes radio button option, add an input tag to create a radio button option for the No label using a name of rental and a value of no.

    e. Locate the form area where the check boxes are placed to collect locations of interest in Australia. Under the Melbourne choice, add the input tag to create a check box choice for the Perth label using a name of location and a value of perth.

    f. Under the Perth choice, add the input tag to create a check box choice for the Hayman Island label using a name of location and a value of hayman.

    g. Locate the form area where customers are asked about other locations of interest in Australia. Add a multiline text area under the comment "What other locations would you like to visit in Australia?" Assign the text area a name of newlocations, and provide space for five rows and 35 columns.

    h. Locate the form area where the pull-down menu is placed to collect length of rentals in Australia. Under the Two Weeks choice, add the option tags to create a choice for the Three Weeks label using a value of "three".

HTML

▼ INDEPENDENT CHALLENGE 1 (CONTINUED)

i. Under the Three Weeks choice, add the option tags to create a choice for the One Month label using a value of "month".

j. Locate the form area where the comment tag indicates a submit button should be placed, and add a submit button with a name of "submit" and the value Submit on the button.

k. Locate the form area where the comment tag indicates a reset button should be placed, and add a reset button with a name of "reset" and the value Start Over on the button.

l. Delete the comments from your file, add a comment line with your name, save and print the file, then display the **survey.htm** file in your browser to check your form.

m. Transfer your **survey.htm** page to your remote directory.

Advanced Challenge Exercises

- Add a size attribute with a value of two to the opening select tag to display two choices in the pull-down menu. (*Hint*: Add `size = "2"` inside the `<select>` tag.)
- Save your work and display the form in your browser to check your pull-down menu.
- Add a comment to your file describing the change in the pull-down menu.
- Transfer your form to your remote directory.

▼ INDEPENDENT CHALLENGE 2

Metro Water publishes monthly newsletters on a variety of topics related to water conservation. You will create a subscription form for Metro Water's customers to sign up for the monthly newsletters.

a. In your text editor, open the **htm_G-4.txt** file from the drive and folder where your Data Files are stored, then save it as **newsletter.htm** in the water folder where you save your site files.

b. Using the Begin form here comment, add an opening form tag with a method of "post" and an action of `/cgi-bin/execmacro/input`.

c. Locate the comment in your file indicating the area for check boxes, then use the table to the right to add check boxes with four newsletter choices. Place each choice on its own line. (*Hint*: Use a line break after each option.)

Check box labels and attributes

Label	Name	Value
Inside Conservation	newsletter	inside
Outside Conservation	newsletter	outside
Landscaping	newsletter	landscaping
Resources	newsletter	resources

d. Locate the comment in your file indicating the area for a comment box and add a multiline text area with five rows and 70 columns for customer input about future newsletters. Assign a name of "newtopics" to the text area.

e. Locate the comment in your file indicating the area for radio buttons, then use the table on the right to add radio buttons that will grant permission for future e-mail contact with your customers.

Radio button labels and attributes

Label	Name	Value
Yes	lecture	yes
No	lecture	no

f. Locate the comment in your file indicating the area for the submit and reset buttons, then use the table on the right to add buttons that will submit or reset the form data. Add the closing `</form>` tag.

Name	Value
submit	Submit
reset	Start Over

g. Delete the comments in the form, add a comment containing your name, save your file, then view the form in your browser.

h. Save your work, print the file, then transfer your **newsletter.htm** file to the remote site.

Advanced Challenge Exercises

- Locate the check box area and the Inside Conservation item. Add a checked attribute with a value of "checked" to the input tag of the Inside Conservation choice in the check box area to display the form with this option selected.
- Save your work and display the form in the browser comparing the check boxes to Figure G-18.
- Add a checked attribute with a value of "checked" to the No choice in the radio button area to display the form with this option selected.
- Save your work and display the form in the browser comparing the radio buttons to Figure G-19.
- Transfer your form to your remote directory.

Select the newsletter(s) that you would like to receive:
☑ Inside Conservation
☐ Outside Conservation
☐ Landscaping
☐ Resources

May we inform you by e-mail of local water conservation lectures?
○ Yes ◉ No

▼ INDEPENDENT CHALLENGE 3

Forms are used to interact with Web site users. You want to add forms to your Web site, but first you need to research how you can make them accessible for all users.

Go to the Student Online Companion for this book, and go to the Unit G link for the W3C Web Accessibility page and review the information for forms. Write one or two paragraphs answering the following questions about forms:

a. How can initial text in the text area tag be used to increase form accessibility?

b. How can push buttons be coded to increase their accessibility?

c. How can forms be designed to allow keyboard access between form elements?

d. Add your name and today's date to the top of your paper, then print the document.

▼ INDEPENDENT CHALLENGE 4

Now that you've used forms to collect user data, you are ready to add forms to your Web site.

a. Determine how forms can be used in your Web site to gather user information

b. Lay out your forms on paper to determine which form elements are necessary to collect user information.

c. Create the forms using your text editor.

d. Add submit and reset buttons.

e. Format your forms appropriately.

f. Add appropriate accessibility features to your forms.

g. Transfer your edited forms to the remote location.

HTML

You have created user groups for your Bits and PCs customers. You will use a form to sign up members for the four groups that you have created. Use Figure G-20 as a guide to create the form in your text editor for the user group membership. Use descriptive names for your form data. Save your form as **usergroups.htm** in the bitspcs folder where you save your site files.

FIGURE G-20

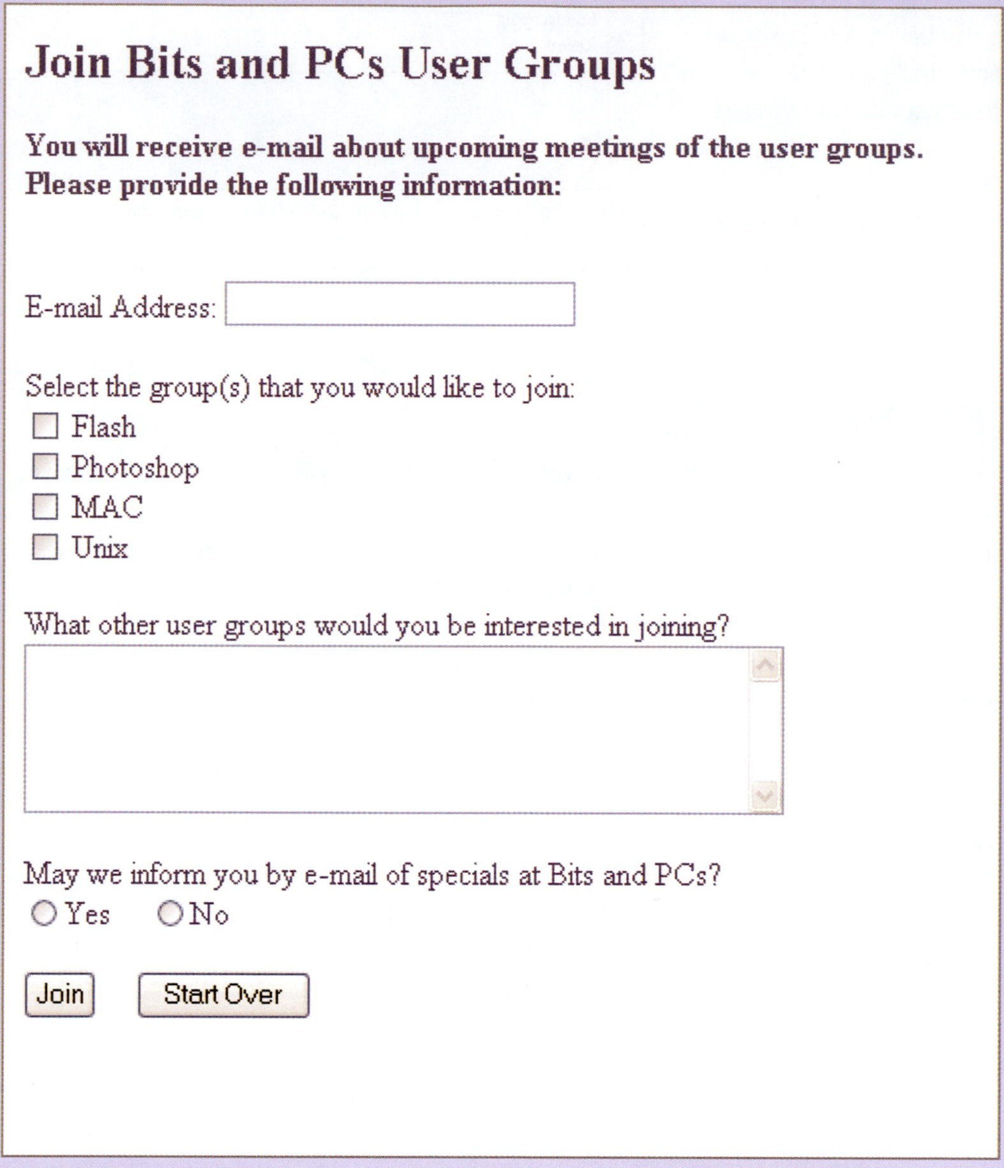

Join Bits and PCs User Groups

You will receive e-mail about upcoming meetings of the user groups. Please provide the following information:

E-mail Address: [   ]

Select the group(s) that you would like to join:
☐ Flash
☐ Photoshop
☐ MAC
☐ Unix

What other user groups would you be interested in joining?

May we inform you by e-mail of specials at Bits and PCs?
○ Yes   ○ No

[Join] [Start Over]

Controlling Page Layout with Frames and Tables

OBJECTIVES

Understand layout tools
Create a navigation bar
Create a frameset
Target links
Format frame borders
Use nested frames
Create a structuring table
Create a template

HTML was originally designed for identifying the content of Web page elements, rather than specifying how the elements should appear in a browser. This meant that early versions of HTML provided no methods of implementing layout and readability features you usually see in print media. However, later versions of HTML allowed more readable and useful Web page layouts through the use of tables, which you learned about in Unit F, and frames. **Frames** allow you to divide the browser into multiple scrollable windows, each of which contains a separate HTML document. Tables let you create single-page, grid-based layouts that resemble frames layouts; they are easy to construct but can be difficult to maintain. Although frames can produce more flexible pages, they can be difficult to use and might not be viewable in all browsers.  You are investigating the possibility of converting Paradise Mountain's site to a new design and are considering the use of frames to standardize your navigation.

Understanding Layout Tools

To successfully convey information, a visual layout must divide it into discrete sections. Although you can divide a page using such HTML elements as headings and line breaks, such a format is **linear**, meaning it limits you to stacking page elements above and below each other, and provides few options for horizontal placement. Frames and tables both let you design more effective HTML layouts by allowing you to place elements anywhere on the screen, and by providing additional means of indicating divisions between them. In a frames page, such as the one shown in Figure H-1, the page is divided into windows that users can scroll individually. Each window contains a separate HTML document. A page organized with a table, like the page shown in Figure H-2, includes the entire page contents in one HTML file. Each option is appropriate for creating different effects. As you prepare to enhance the layout of the Paradise Mountain pages, you review the principal advantages of laying out a Web site using frames and tables.

DETAILS

Some advantages of using frames or tables include:

- **Grid positioning**

    Print media designers frequently use a **grid**, a set of columns and rows, to position and group page elements. Using a grid gives a design a sense of balance, consistency, and organization. You can easily add a grid to a Web page by creating columns and rows with the HTML table tags. Frames can also create a grid structure, as each frame can serve as a separate column or row. The ability to create a layout grid is the underlying feature of tables and frames that makes them both especially valuable for page layout.

- **Unified appearance**

    As you incorporate more pages into a Web site, it becomes important to ensure that users can easily navigate the site. After following a trail of links away from the home page, a user may wish to explore another area of the site. Rather than requiring users to return to the main page, well-designed sites usually include a **site navigation bar**—a set of links to the home page and main sections of the site—that appears on every page. In the most user-friendly sites, the navigation bar and other page elements, appear in the same location on each page, giving all the site's pages a unified appearance. This predictable layout reassures users that they won't get lost, and encourages them to explore the site. You can easily achieve a unified site appearance by implementing a frames-based layout or by creating a table. You can also unify your site by creating a **template**, a Web page coded with the site's page structure and primary elements, and then using the template as the starting point for each new Web page.

- **White space control**

    Tables and frames offer effective methods of controlling white space in page borders and between page elements. This ability to control white space allows designers to create pages that are aesthetically pleasing and easy to read.

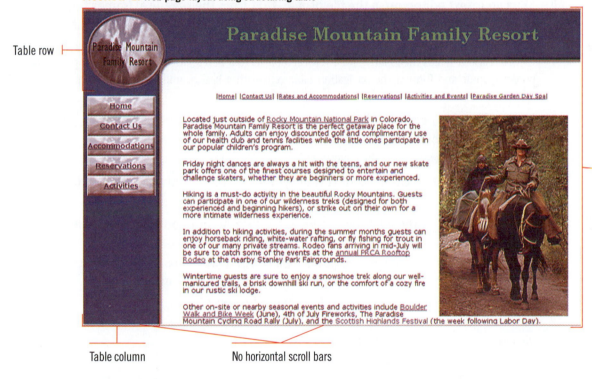

FIGURE H-1: Web page layout using frames

Right frame contains page content

Left frame contains navigation bar

Scroll bars allow frames to move independently

FIGURE H-2: Web page layout using structuring table

Table row

Table-based layout emulates frames site

Table column

No horizontal scroll bars

Design Matters

Exploring style sheet positioning

Although both frames and tables are powerful Web page layout tools, they were created for simpler tasks, and neither offers an exhaustive set of design options. However, Cascading Style Sheets (CSS), as you learned in Unit E, are specifically designed for Web page formatting. CSS formatting is more intuitive and effective than earlier page design methods. CSS formatting not only allows you to control multiple page elements from an external file and apply defined attributes to multiple instances of the same element; it also allows you to control page layout by specifying settings for horizontal and vertical positions. Most browsers support CSS layout, but some older browsers do not. This means that users of older browsers might not see your content in the layout you planned. On the other hand, pages that use CSS layout formatting are more effectively displayed on alternate output devices such as personal digital assistants (PDAs)—making it the layout method of choice for site designers who strive to meet federal accessibility mandates. Nevertheless, frames and tables continue to be effective Web page layout tools—especially for smaller sites.

UNIT H
HTML

Creating a Navigation Bar

Although you can add a simple navigation bar to any page layout, creating a grid layout provides more choices for the bar's formatting and its location on the page. You can position the bar's paragraphs or graphics at the bottom of the screen in a linear layout, but positioning the bar in the same place on each page could require adding imprecise spacing elements, such as line breaks. By contrast, when using frames or tables you can specify the exact dimensions of each component, allowing you to place it in a consistent page location. Additionally, in a grid layout you can create a vertical navigation bar, running along the left or right edge of the browser window, and include other page elements alongside it. You begin your redesign by creating a navigation bar that you can incorporate into the page layout for the Paradise Mountain site.

STEPS

1. **Using your computer's file system, locate and copy the folder named frames and all of its contents from the UnitH\Lessons folder in your Data File location, then paste it into your paradise site folder in the place where you save your site files**
   The folder contains all the Data Files you need for this unit.

2. **Start your text editor, open the file htm_H-1.txt from the paradise\frames folder in your site files location, inspect the code, then save it in the same folder as navbar.htm**
   Your new file uses a linked style sheet that one of your team members created for formatting your site documents. It also contains the link text for a vertical toolbar. Your new style sheet formats your page with a left-border graphic and formats the navigation table cells with a background button image to give them the appearance of standard buttons.

QUICK TIP

You can apply a background button to a table cell without the aid of style sheets by using the background attribute of the table cell.

3. **Locate the table heading cell of the row with the attribute `id="vnavRow1"`, click before Home, type `<a href="main.htm">`, click after Home, then type `</a>`**
   You created the first link in the site navigation bar.

4. **Click before Contact Us in the next row, type `<a href="contact.htm">`, click after Us in the same row, then type `</a>`**

5. **Link the content of the next three rows as follows: Accommodations: rates.htm, Reservations: reserve.htm, Activities: activities/index.htm**
   Because you know your background image will tile if the cell content is too large, you decided to shorten the Activities and Events text. Your code appears similar to that shown in Figure H-3.

6. **Save your work, then preview your file in your browser**
   Figure H-4 shows the finished page. Using the same background graphic for all the table buttons keeps your Web page download time to a minimum.

```
<table width="136" border="0" cellpadding="0" cellspacing="0" align="left" id="vnav">
<tr align="center" id="vnavRow1">
<th width="135" height="40" class="nav2">
<a href="main.htm">Home</a>
</th>
</tr>

<tr id="vnavRow2" align="center">
<th width="135" height="40" class="nav2">
<a href="contact.htm">Contact Us</a>
</th>
</tr>

<tr id="vnavRow3" align="center">
<th width="135" height="40" class="nav2">
<a href="rates.htm">Accommodations</a>
</th>
</tr>

<tr id="vnavRow4" align="center">
<th width="135" height="40" class="nav2">
<a href="reserve.htm">Reservations</a>
</th>
</tr>

<tr id="vnavRow5" align="center">
<th width="135" height="40" class="nav2">
<a href="activities/index.htm">Activities</a>
</th>
</tr>
</table>
```

Table heading cell formatted with CSS as navigation buttons

```
.nav2     {
          background-image: url(../images/btn_pm1_blank.png);
          color: #000033;
          font-weight: 1000;

}
```

FIGURE H-4: Navigation page displayed in browser

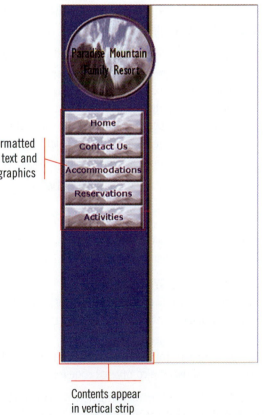

Table cells formatted as links with text and background graphics

Contents appear in vertical strip

Creating a Frameset

In a frames-based layout, the browser is divided into sections called **windows**. Each window—also called a **frame**—displays the contents of a separate HTML document. You create these individual documents with the same tags you use for standard Web pages. The document that controls the layout and organization of your frames is called a **frameset**. The total number of documents required to create a frames-based layout is equal to the number of frames plus one for the frameset. Because there must be at least two windows in a frameset, the minimum number of documents required is three. Figure H-5 shows the relationship between HTML files in a frames page. Table H-1 describes the tags and attributes required to create a frameset. You have divided the contents of your new design into two separate HTML documents, similar to the layout design shown in Figure H-5. Each document will appear in a frame on the Paradise Mountain home page. You begin to lay out the page by creating a frameset.

STEPS

1. **In your browser, open the file main.htm from the paradise\frames folder in the place where you save your site files**

   This is the Paradise Mountain home page that will appear in the right frame of the frameset when users first open the Paradise Mountain frameset. Notice that the page background and heading elements have been stripped from the document. For the content of the left frame, you decide to use the navigation bar you created earlier.

2. **In your text editor, open the file htm_H-2.txt from your paradise\frames folder, and save it as frameset.htm in the same folder**

   The file contains the frameset DTD. You begin by entering the basic tags for your frameset document.

3. **Click in the line below the DTD, type `<html>`, press [Enter] twice, type `<head>`, press [Enter], type `<title>Paradise Mountain online</title>`, press [Enter], type `</head>`, then press [Enter] twice**

   > **QUICK TIP**
   > To create a frameset composed of rows instead of columns, use the rows attribute in place of cols.

4. **Type `<frameset cols="180,*" frameborder="0">`, then press [Enter] twice**

   The opening `<frameset>` tag marks the beginning of the frameset. In a frameset document, this tag replaces the standard HTML `<body>` tag. You use the cols attribute to indicate the width, in pixels, of each column. You specified the width of the first column—the navigation bar—as 180 pixels, and used an asterisk (*) for the width of the second column, indicating that it should occupy the remaining width of the browser window. You set the frameborder attribute equal to zero to remove the default border that appears between frames.

   > **QUICK TIP**
   > To divide a frame, you can enter a `<frameset>. . . </frameset>` tag in place of a `<frame>` tag, then nest `<frame>` tags within this set to specify the sources of the set's frame documents.

5. **Type `<frame src="navbar.htm" name="nav"/>`, press [Enter], type `<frame src="main.htm" name="main"/>`, press [Enter] twice, type `</frameset>`, then press [Enter] twice**

   Each frame requires a `<frame>` tag that specifies the name and location of its source file using the src attribute. It is also important to name each frame using the name attribute, so that each frame's hyperlinks work properly. It is good practice to include additional text that will appear in the window of a browser that does not support frames.

6. **Type `<noframes>`, press [Enter], type `This page was designed to be viewed with frames. You can open individual pages using the <a href="navbar.htm"> navigation bar</a>.`, press [Enter], type `</noframes>`, press [Enter] twice, then type `</html>`**

   Your alternate text provides a link to the navigation bar and ensures that users of older browsers can still access the entire site. Figure H-6 shows the completed code for the frameset Web page.

7. **Save your work, click the browser program button on the taskbar, open the file frameset.htm, then scroll the right window down using the vertical scroll bar**

   The browser displays both frames, as shown in Figure H-7. If necessary, resize the browser window. Notice that each frame includes a scrollbar, allowing you to scroll one side of the screen without moving the other side's contents.

FIGURE H-5: Frameset structure

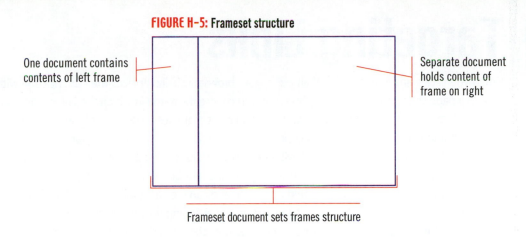

One document contains contents of left frame

Separate document holds content of frame on right

Frameset document sets frames structure

FIGURE H-6: Frameset code

Frameset DTD

Frameset defines frame structure

Content source declared in frame tag

Noframes section provides link for site visitors without frames support

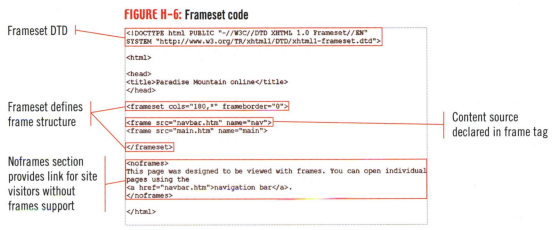

```
<!DOCTYPE html PUBLIC "-//W3C//DTD XHTML 1.0 Frameset//EN"
SYSTEM "http://www.w3.org/TR/xhtml1/DTD/xhtml1-frameset.dtd">

<html>

<head>
<title>Paradise Mountain online</title>
</head>

<frameset cols="180,*" frameborder="0">
<frame src="navbar.htm" name="nav">
<frame src="main.htm" name="main">

</frameset>

<noframes>
This page was designed to be viewed with frames. You can open individual
pages using the
<a href="navbar.htm">navigation bar</a>.
</noframes>

</html>
```

FIGURE H-7: Frameset in browser

Navigation frame

Horizontal scroll bars

Main frame

Vertical scroll bar

TABLE H-1: Frame tags and attributes

tag(s)	description	attributes	function
`<frameset>...</frameset>`	Marks frameset contents and describes their layout	rows	Defines number and sizes of horizontal frames to create
		cols	Defines number and sizes of vertical frames to create
		frameborder	Turns border between frames on or off; set to "0" or "no" to turn borders off
`<frame>`	Specifies a frame's source file and name	src	Defines location and filename for frame contents
		name	Defines frame name for reference by hyperlinks
`<noframes>...</noframes>`	Defines alternate page content for browsers that do not support frames; requires no attributes		

Targeting Links

When you click a link in a standard Web page, your browser usually replaces the current page with the linked one. In a page structured with frames, however, you choose the frame in which the linked page will open. This feature of frames has facilitated a popular frameset layout that fixes a page of links in one frame and displays content in another frame. When users click a link, the content of the navigation frame remains static and the content of the other frame changes. HTML offers two methods for setting the location where a linked page opens. One option is to add the target attribute to a link's <a> tag, and set this attribute equal to the name of the frame in which the linked page should open. You also can create a global setting for all of a page's links by adding the <base /> tag to the page's head section and assigning the tag the appropriate target setting. Table H-2 explains target values with special behaviors. You used the _blank value in Unit B to open a page in a new window. You want the navigation bar to remain visible to users as they explore the Paradise Mountain Web site. You add the <base /> tag to the navbar.htm page's head section and apply the target attribute with a value to make the pages open in the frame on the right side of the frameset.

STEPS

1. **With the file frameset.htm open in your browser, click a link in the vertical navigation bar, then click your browser's Back button**

   When you click a link, the navigation bar is replaced by the link target file and, as shown in Figure H-8, is no longer available in the frameset. By default, a linked page opens in the same frame as the link that opened it.

2. **In your text editor, open the file navbar.htm**

3. **Locate the </title> tag in the head section, click after the closing >, press [Enter] twice, then type <base target="main" />**

   Figure H-9 shows the Web page code containing the <base> tag. When you created the frameset file, you assigned the name "main" to the frame on the right side of the screen. By setting the target attribute in the <base /> tag, you allow users to click any link in the left frame—the navigation bar—to change the contents of the right frame.

4. **Save your work, click the browser program button on the taskbar, then click the Go button next to the browser Address Bar to reload the page**

   Clicking the Go button next to the Address Location box reloads the entire frameset.

5. **Click one of the link buttons in the vertical navigation bar**

   As shown in Figure H-10, the linked page opens in the main content frame, and the navigation bar remains in the left frame, allowing you to continue moving around the site.

6. **Click one of the links in the right (main) window frame**

   The page for the link you clicked opens in the right frame. Because your opening page for the right frame doesn't specify a target value for the links, the linked pages open by default in the same frame, as you intended. You want to make sure that linked pages from other sites (external links) do not appear in your frameset's content window because it could be considered a violation of copyright law.

7. **Open main.htm from your paradise\frames folder in the text editor, then locate the link for the PRCA Rooftop Rodeo, click inside the link just before >, press [Spacebar], then type target="_blank"**

   Because the target URL is not a page that you created, you want it to open in a new window outside of your Web site to make sure you won't violate copyright laws.

8. **Repeat Step 7 for the Boulder Walk and Bike Week, and the Scottish Highlands Festival links, then save your work and test the links in your browser**

   The linked pages open in a new window.

FIGURE H-8: Linked page replaces navigation bar content

Main frame does not change

Linked file opens in navigation frame

FIGURE H-9: Page code with base target

Base target set in head section

```
<!DOCTYPE html PUBLIC "-//W3C//DTD XHTML 1.0 Transitional//EN"
"http://www.w3.org/TR/xhtml1/DTD/xhtml1-transitional.dtd">
<html>

<head>

<title>Paradise Mountain Family Resort: Vertical Site Navigation</title>

<base target="main" />

<meta name="description" content="Paradise Mountain Family Resort
vertical site navigation />
```

FIGURE H-10: Linked file opens in main content frame

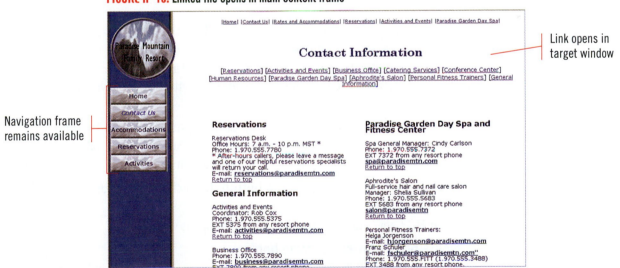

Link opens in target window

Navigation frame remains available

TABLE H-2: Special values for the target attribute

value	link behavior
_blank	Opens in new browser window
_self	Opens in current frame; this is the default setting
_parent	Replaces current frameset; use when you want external links to open with the Back button enabled
_top	Replaces contents of current browser window; use on links to your own frameset to prevent new framesets from opening within existing framesets

HTML

Formatting Frame Borders

Like most other Web page elements, frames support the attributes that change the frames' appearance in a browser. Several of these attributes are similar to those used to format tables. Although narrow borders appear between frames by default, you can use the frameborder attribute in the `<frameset>` tag to remove them or to change their appearance. Once a frameset includes borders, you can use other attributes to control border thickness and color, as well as the width of the margin between a frame's border and its contents. By default, Web page users can move the borders between frames to change the amount of the browser window that each frame occupies. If you want to make sure your layout remains fixed, you can add the noresize attribute to `<frame>` tags to ensure that the frames remain the width or height you specified in the `<frameset>` tag. Table H-3 describes several attributes available for formatting frames. You want to experiment with borders and border formats in your layout.

STEPS

1. In your text editor, open frameset.htm

2. Locate the opening `<frameset>` tag, select the text `frameborder="0"`, press [Delete], then, if necessary, press [Delete] again or press [Backspace] to remove the extra space before the closing >

3. Save your work, click the browser program button on the taskbar, then click the Go button next to the browser's Address Location box to reload frameset.htm

    Clicking the Go button reloads the frameset; however clicking the Reload button while viewing a frameset reloads the pages currently displaying in your browser. As shown in Figure H-11, the frameset appears with a border separating the two windows.

4. Move the mouse pointer over the frame border, then click and drag to the right

    The mouse pointer changes to a double arrow, indicating you can resize the frames. Dragging the border to the right resizes both frames.

5. In your text editor, locate the opening `<frameset>` tag, click before >, press [Spacebar], then type `frameborder="10" border="10" framespacing="10"`

    The border and framespacing attributes change the thickness of borders between frames. Because each attribute is appropriate for different browsers, you use all with the same setting to ensure your frames appear similarly to all users.

QUICK TIP

Use caution in setting the noresize attribute of your frames—this setting could cause some content to become unavailable to some users.

6. Click directly before > in the first `<frame>` tag, press [Spacebar], then type `noresize`

    Figure H-12 shows the completed code for the frameset document. Adding the noresize attribute to a `<frame>` tag prevents users from resizing that frame, as well as adjoining frames, in the browser window.

7. Save your work, click the browser program button, then click the Go button to reload the frameset with its default pages

    As shown in Figure H-13, the border between the two frames appears wider.

8. Move the mouse pointer over the frame border

    Because you added the noresize attribute to the left frame, the mouse pointer does not change to a double arrow and you cannot drag the frame border, which remains in its original location.

FIGURE H-11: Frameset windows separated by border

FIGURE H-11: Frameset windows separated by border

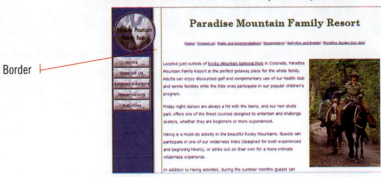

Border

FIGURE H-12: Page code for formatting frame borders

```
<head>
<title>Paradise Mountain online</title>

</head>
<frameset cols="180,*" frameborder="10" border="10" framespacing="10">

<frame src="navbar.htm" name="nav" noresize>
<frame src="main.htm" name="main" >

</frameset>

<noframes>
This page was designed to be viewed with frames. You can open individual
pages using the <a href="navbar.htm">navigation bar</a>
</noframes>

</html>
```

Frame borders
formatted to
work in most
major browers

FIGURE H-13: Frames page with formatted, wider border

Wider frame border

TABLE H-3: Frame formatting attributes

tag	attribute	function	allowable values
`<frameset>`	frameborder	Determines whether or not borders appear	"0" or "no" turns off borders; "1" or another positive number or "yes" enables borders (the default setting)
	border	Specifies the space between frames	A size in pixels
	framespacing	Specifies the space between frames	A size in pixels
	bordercolor	Customizes color of lines separating frames	Hexadecimal color value or corresponding color name
`<frame>`	marginheight	Specifies space between frame contents and top and bottom borders	A size in pixels
	marginwidth	Specifies space between frame contents and left and right borders	A size in pixels
	noresize	Prevents users from changing a frame's dimensions	Requires no value; the presence of noresize enables this option
	scrolling	Controls the appearance of the frame's scrollbars	A "yes" value always includes scrollbars; "no" prevents scrollbars from appearing; when attribute is absent or set to "auto", scrollbars appear as needed

HTML

Using Nested Frames

Thus far you've worked with two-window framesets, but you can also create nested framesets that allow you to divide your browser window into multiple rows or columns or into both rows and columns. In a **nested frameset**, the `<frameset>` tag, with frames and framesets of its own, replaces one of the `<frame>` tags. You can achieve a more sophisticated layout using nested framesets. You decide to use nested framesets to create a page layout with a heading frame, and both a left-border navigation frame and a content frame below the heading.

1. **In your browser, open top.htm from your paradise\frames folder**

   A member of your design team created the top.htm file earlier in the design process. This file uses a top-border graphic and a corner logo graphic with a curved bottom edge.

2. **Open top.htm in your text editor and inspect the code, then close the file without making any changes**

   This file uses a table with CSS formatting to create a horizontal page heading layout that fits in a top frame.

3. **If necessary, open your frameset.htm file in your text editor and save it as frameset2.htm in your paradise\frames folder**

   The file is ready for editing and does not replace your original frameset. You want to create a frameset with three windows. The top frame serves as a page banner with a logo and heading, and spans the width of the navigation and content frames. Because the logo will be in your top frame, you want to replace navbar.htm with a version that does not contain the logo.

4. **Click before `<frameset`, type `<frameset rows="163,*" frameborder="0" border="0" framespacing="0" noresize>`, press [Enter], then type `<frame src="top.htm" name="top" border="0" scrolling="no">`**

5. **Locate the code for the left-border frame, click after navbar, type `2`, save your work, then load frameset2.htm in your browser**

   The file navbar2.htm was created for you by a member of your design team. The combination of the top-border background and the curved logo gives the illusion of a rounded content area. The shadow effect applied to the graphics adds depth to the page appearance; however, all frame borders must be eliminated for the full effect. Also, indenting the nested frame makes your code easier to read.

6. **Return to your frameset2.htm code, click before `<frameset cols="180,*"`, press [Spacebar] twice to indent it, then change the frameborder, border, and framespacing values in the second frameset from 10 to `0`**

7. **Click before the frame tag with the src value navbar2.htm, press [Spacebar] twice, then indent the next two lines of code, ending with the `</frameset>` line**

   The parent `<frameset>` tag you added in Step 4 and 5 needs a closing tag.

8. **Click after `</frameset>`, press [Enter], type `</frameset>`, then save your work**

   You closed the parent frameset. Your code appears similar to that shown in Figure H-14.

9. **Return to your browser, open frameset2.htm from your paradise\frames folder, then click the links to test them**

   As shown in Figure H-15, your new frames-based layout appears in the browser, but the page heading from both top.htm and main.htm are visible.

10. **In your frameset2.htm file, locate the reference to main.htm and change it to main2.htm, then save your work and view it in your browser**

    Your new frameset appears without the double headings. The Home link in the main2.htm page targets frameset2.htm.

```
<frameset rows="163,*" frameborder="0" border="0" framespacing="0"
noresize>

<frame src="top.htm" name="top" border="0" scrolling="no">

    <frameset cols="180,*" frameborder="0" border="0" framespacing="0">

    <frame src="navbar2.htm" name="nav" noresize>
    <frame src="main2.htm" name="main">

    </frameset>

</frameset>
```

Parent
frameset

Nested
frameset

FIGURE H-15: Nested frameset displayed in browser

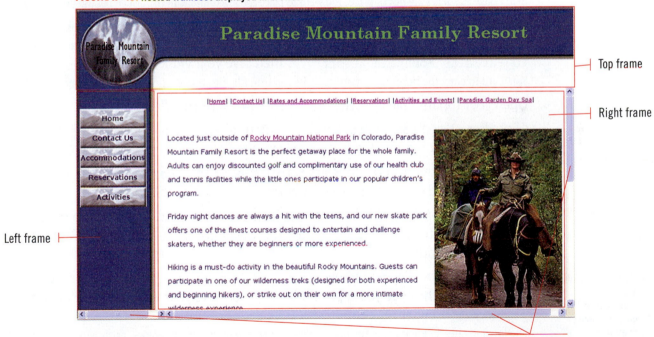

Top frame

Right frame

Left frame

Frameset scrollbars

HTML

Creating a Structuring Table

You can lay out a Web page in a grid using a **structuring table**, which allows you to include all the page elements within one large table. Structuring tables offer positioning benefits similar to frames, yet make your pages accessible to most users whose browsers don't support frames. You decide to try your layout in a structuring table, to compare its appearance with frames. To achieve the same effect using tables, you'll create a heading row, a vertical navigation column, and a content column. Some areas of your frames-based page are already positioned using tables. You will include these sections in your structuring table as nested tables.

STEPS

1. **In your text editor, open the file htm_H-3.txt from your paradise\frames folder in your site file location, then save it as home.htm in the same folder**

   As shown in Figure H-16, the file is a table-based layout page with placeholder text to guide you in the process of nesting tables from your frame source pages in your new document. A class called headrow, which adds a top-border background graphic, was embedded in the document and applied to the first row. The contents of your main2.htm page have already been pasted into the content cell.

2. **Click after width="100%" inside the opening table tag, press [Spacebar], then type cellpadding="0" cellspacing="0" border="1"**

   The design you are working to achieve is dependent upon your ability to precisely position your logo image. Setting the cellpadding and cellspacing to zero helps you achieve the effect you want. Although a borderless structuring table is usually the most effective for layout, you temporarily turn on the borders to help you quickly and easily see if any page elements are out of place. You want to place the logo graphic in the first cell of the heading row.

3. **Drag to select the text in the first cell that reads Logo goes here, press [Delete], type `<img src="images/logo_pm3.png" width="188" height="165" alt="Welcome to Paradise Mountain Resort" />`, then save your work**

   You want to copy the heading content from the top.htm file into the second cell in your home.htm file table.

4. **Open your top.htm file in a separate instance of your text editor**

5. **Click after `<!-- Heading content -->`, drag to select `<br clear="all" />` through the `</h1>`, copy the selected text, then close the file**

6. **In your home.htm file, drag to select `top.htm content goes here`, press [Delete], paste the copied code, then save your work**

TROUBLE
Make sure that you do not copy the closing table data, table row, or table tags for the parent table.

7. **Open your navbar2.htm file in a separate instance of your text editor, locate the table with the attribute `id="vnav"`, drag to select the entire table, as shown in Figure H-17, then copy the code**

TROUBLE
If your page elements don't appear as shown, make note of which elements are out of place by inspecting the grid marks in the browser, then check your code for errors.

8. **In your home.htm file, drag to select `navbar2.htm content goes here`, press [Delete], paste the code you copied in Step 7, then save your work and preview your page in your browser**

   The layout is nearly identical to the one you created with frames. The difference, as shown in Figure H-18, is that you can see the grid work of white borders, which push the logo image slightly to the right.

9. **Return to your home.htm code, locate the opening table tag just below the opening body tag, change the border value from 1 to 0, save your work, then view your page in your browser**

   The border disappears and your page closely resembles your frameset2.htm layout.

FIGURE H-16: Starting code for structuring table

Headrow class adds top border graphic

Placeholder text in table cells

```
</head>

<body>
<table width="100%">
<!-- The heading row starts below this comment -->
<tr valign="top" class="headrow">

<td width="188" height="165">Logo goes here</td>

<td nowrap>top.htm content goes here</td>
</tr>

<tr valign="top">

<td>
<!-- Begin holding table for site navigation -->
<table width="146" cellpadding="5" id="nav_holdTable">
<tr>
<td><!-- Insert site navigation table below -->
navbar2.htm content goes here

</td>
</tr>
<!-- End holding table for site navigation -->
</table>
<!-- End navigation cell -->
</td>

<!-- Content from main2.htm goes in the content cell below. -->
<td>
<p style="text-align: center; font-size: 75%;">|<a href="frameset.htm"
target="_top">Home</a>|  |<a href="contact.htm">Contact Us</a>|  |<a href="rates.htm">Rates
and Accommodations</a>|  |<a href="reserve.htm">Reservations</a>|  |<a
href="activities/index.htm">Activities and Events</a>|  |<a href="../spa/index.htm"
```

FIGURE H-17: Copied code for structuring table

```
<table width="136" border="0" cellpadding="0" cellspacing="0" align="left" id="vnav">

<tr align="center" id="vnavRow1">

<th width="135" height="40" class="nav2">
<a href="main.htm">Home</a>
</th>
</tr>

<tr id="vnavRow2" align="center">
<th width="135" height="40" class="nav2">
<a href="contact.htm">Contact Us</a>
</th>
</tr>

<tr id="vnavRow3" align="center">
<th width="135" height="40" class="nav2" background="images/btn_pm1_blank.png">
<a href="rates.htm">Accommodations</a>
</th>
</tr>

<tr id="vnavRow4" align="center">
<th width="135" height="40" class="nav2" background="images/btn_pm1_blank.png">
<a href="reserve.htm">Reservations</a>
</th>
</tr>

<tr id="vnavRow5" align="center">
<th width="135" height="40" class="nav2" background="images/btn_pm1_blank.png">
<a href="activities/index.htm">Activities</a>
</th>
</tr>
</table>
```

FIGURE H-18: Web page laid out in structuring table

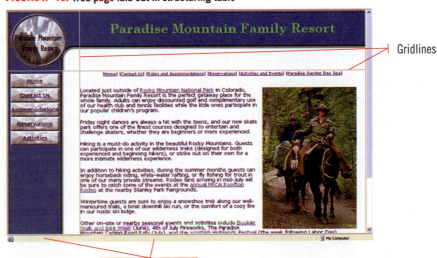

Gridlines

No individual scrollbars

HTML

Creating a Template

Once you finalize your site layout with a structuring table, it is important to implement the layout uniformly on all your Web site's pages. Rather than reentering the code for common elements for every page in your site, however, you can make your design tasks easier by creating a template. A **template** contains the Web page code for the page's structure, along with any text or other elements that appear on every page. You can create a template by removing the page-specific items from your original layout. Then you can use it as a starting point for creating additional pages. It is also good practice to add comments to the code, so that other designers using the template clearly understand where to insert their own page-specific elements. After you presented your layout sample options and explained the advantages and drawbacks of each, your Web design team decided to use your structuring table design for the Paradise Mountain site. You want to create a template from your Web page to make the team's work on the site more efficient, and to ensure that each team member implements the same layout.

STEPS

1. **In your text editor, save a copy of home.htm as template.htm in your paradise folder**
   Because you can use this template for any page in your site, you want to save it in your site root folder.

2. **Click just after `<body>`, press [Enter], type `<!-- Web page structuring table, two rows by two columns -->`, then press [Enter]**

3. **Click after `<tr valign="top" class="headrow">`, press [Enter], then type `<!-- Logo image - Do not change -->`**
   Figure H-19 shows the Web page code containing the first comments, some of which are from your home.htm file.

4. **Click before `<td nowrap><br clear="all" />`, type `<!-- Second column - Page heading goes here   -->`, then press [Enter]**

5. **Click before `<tr align="center" id="vnavRow1">`, type `<!-- Site-standard navigation bar - Do Not Change -->`, then press [Enter]**

6. **Click after `src="` in the image tag for the trail_ride2.jpg image, drag to select the entire source path, press [Delete], type `file.jpg`, click after alt=", select the entire alt statement, press [Delete], then type `Placeholder graphic. Insert your own image and alt statement in this tag.`**

7. **Drag to select the remaining text in the content column, stopping just before `<address style="text-align: center;">`, press [Delete], type `<p>Insert your page text here.</p>`, then press [Enter] twice**

8. **Edit the Day Spa link to remove the ../ so that the spa files are available from the root directory; if necessary, change the href value of both home links to index.htm**

9. **Copy the paradise_style2.css style sheet from the frames\css folder and paste it into the paradise\css folder, then copy the images from the frames\images folder and paste them into the paradise\images folder, clicking No if prompted to replace files**

10. **Edit the "Page modified by" paragraph as necessary with your name and today's date, save your work, preview your template and print it from your browser, then close the file and exit the program**
    Your template appears with site-standard elements and placeholder text, as shown in Figure H-20.

FIGURE H-19: Opening comments in page template code

Comment tags in template

```
<body>
<!-- Web page structuring table, two rows by two columns -->

<table width="100%" cellpadding="0" cellspacing="0" border="0">
<!-- The heading row starts below this comment -->
<tr valign="top" class="headrow">
<!-- Logo image - Do not change -->

<td width="188" height="165"><img src="images/logo_pm3.png" width="188" height="165"
alt="Welcome to Paradise Mountain Resort" /></td>

<td nowrap><br clear="all" />
<br /><br />
<h1 class="heading">Paradise Mountain Family Resort</h1></td>
</tr>

<tr valign="top">

<td>
<!-- Begin holding table for site navigation -->
<table width="146" cellpadding="5" id="nav_holdTable">
<tr>
<td><!-- Insert site navigation table below -->
<table width="136" border="0" cellpadding="0" cellspacing="0" align="left" id="vnav">

<tr align="center" id="vnavRow1">

<th width="135" height="40" class="nav2">
<a href="main.htm">Home</a>
</th>
</tr>

<tr id="vnavRow2" align="center">
<th width="135" height="40" class="nav2">
```

FIGURE H-20: Completed template

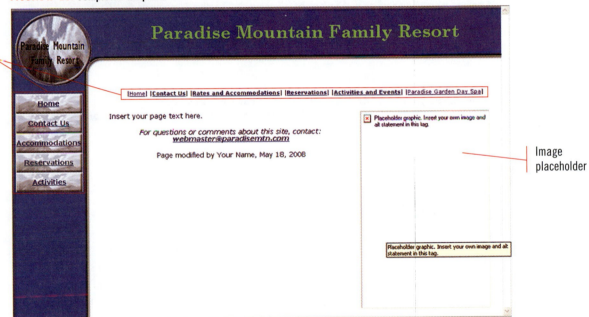

Navigation elements

Image placeholder

Clues to Use

Choosing between frames and tables

Frames offer several features that tables can't match, such as independently scrolling window areas and the ability to maintain site-standard information such as navigation, headings, and footers in easily updated, separate files. However, due to the fragmentation of information on a frames-based site, it is difficult to optimize such sites for search engine listings. Frames-based sites also create some of the problems they were meant to prevent. If, for example, a frame's content page is opened outside of the frameset (as can easily happen when a visitor comes across page content via a search-engine listing), that standardized information you so carefully constructed as part of your frameset is not available. Moreover, framesets are no longer part of the W3C standard. Consequently, most professional Web designers find that the advantages of tables and divisions outweigh the benefits of frames. Because all the page contents of a table or division layout are contained in one HTML file, pages constructed in this manner are easier for users to print, and they provide more accurate data for search engine indexes. Additionally, because a browser's address bar displays the name and location of the table- or division-based pages, they are more accessible to site visitors who want to bookmark them for later use.

HTML

Practice

▼ CONCEPTS REVIEW

Name the function of each section of code indicated in Figure H-21.

FIGURE H-21

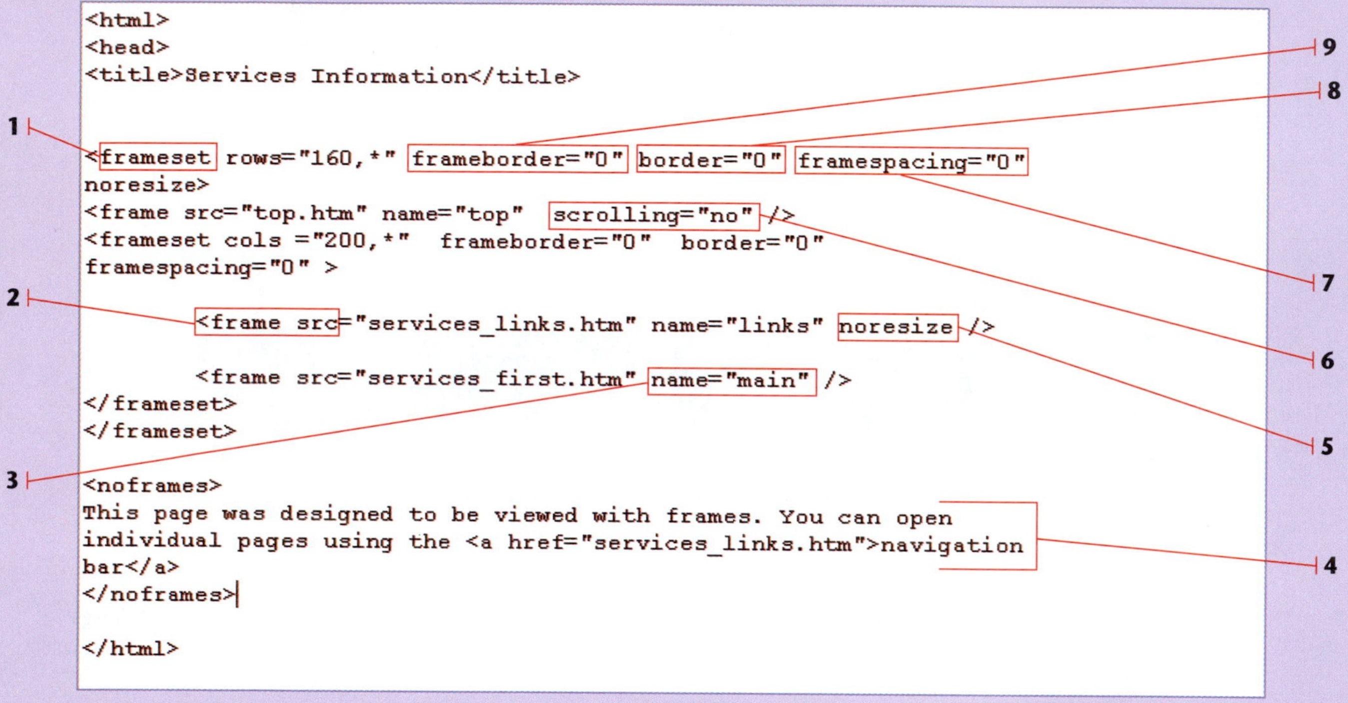

```
<html>
<head>
<title>Services Information</title>


<frameset rows="160,*"  frameborder="0"  border="0"  framespacing="0"
noresize>
<frame src="top.htm" name="top"  scrolling="no" />
<frameset cols ="200,*"  frameborder="0"  border="0"
framespacing="0" >

        <frame src="services_links.htm" name="links"  noresize />

        <frame src="services_first.htm" name="main" />
</frameset>
</frameset>

<noframes>
This page was designed to be viewed with frames. You can open
individual pages using the <a href="services_links.htm">navigation
bar</a>
</noframes>

</html>
```

1
2
3
9
8
7
6
5
4

Match each statement with the term it best describes.

10. Navigation bar
11. Frameset
12. Frame
13. Target
14. Noresize

a. Attribute that prevents the change of a frame's dimensions
b. A set of links to the home page and main sections of a Web site that appears on every page
c. A file specifying the organization of frame files within the browser window
d. A window within a frameset that displays a separate HTML document
e. A method of setting the location where a link page opens

Select the best answer from the list of choices.

15. **In a Web page laid out with frames, each frame displays:**
    a. The contents of a separate Web document.
    b. The contents of a table cell.
    c. The contents of a table.
    d. The same Web document.

16. **Which tag would you use to create a global setting to target a different frame for all of a page's links?**
    a. `<body>`
    b. `<head>`
    c. `<base />`
    d. `<noframes>`

17. How can the pages in a frameset be refreshed?

    a. Click the Refresh or Reload button in the browser.

    b. Click the Go button in the browser.

    c. Hold down [Ctrl] while refreshing the frameset page.

    d. Hold down [Fn] while refreshing the frameset page.

18. Which attribute in the frame tag defines the location for the frame contents?

    a. cols

    b. rows

    c. src

    d. name

19. How many HTML files would you need in order to create a frameset that displays two frames?

    a. One

    b. Two

    c. Three

    d. Four

20. Which tags cannot be used within `<frameset>...</frameset>` tags?

    a. `<frame />`

    b. `<frameset>`

    c. `<body>`

    d. `<noframes>`

▼ SKILLS REVIEW

1. Understand layout tools.

    a. Consider how frames can be used to present the information on the pages of the spa site. How would you lay out the spa pages using frames?

    b. Which spa pages would you lay out using structuring tables?

    c. How would you include the spa logo on your pages if using tables or frames?

    d. What advantages do you see in using frames for the spa site?

    e. What advantages do you see in using structuring tables for the spa site?

2. Create a navigation bar.

    a. Copy the files **wraps.htm**, **packages.htm**, **salon.htm**, and **hands.htm** from the drive and folder where your Data Files are stored to the paradise/spa folder where you save your site files. If you are asked whether you want to replace the files, click Yes.

    b. Copy the file **services_style.css** from the drive and folder where your Data Files are stored to the paradise/css folder where you save your site files.

    c. Copy the **spa_logo.gif** from the drive and folder where your Data Files are stored to the paradise/images folder where you save your site files. If you are asked whether you want to replace the file, click Yes.

    d. In your text editor, open the file **htm_H-4.txt** from the drive and folder where your Data Files are stored, then save it as **services_links.htm** to the paradise/spa directory where you save your site files.

    e. Locate the comment in the file indicating where the navigation bar is placed. Add the link for the massage therapy information by placing `<a href="wraps.htm">` before Massage Therapy and `</a>` after this label in the first table row.

    f. Add the link for the spa packages by placing `<a href="packages.htm">` before Spa Packages and `</a>` after this label in the second table row.

    g. In the third table row, add a link to the salon.htm page for Aphrodite's Salon.

    h. In the fourth table row, add a link to the hands.htm page for Hand and Foot Care.

    i. Delete the comment, save your file, then open the **services_links.htm** file in your browser to view the navigation bar and test its links.

3. Create a frameset.

a. In your text editor, open the file **htm_H-5.txt** from the drive and folder where your Data Files are stored, then save it as **servicesframes.htm** to the paradise/spa directory where you save your site files. Copy the **services_first.htm** file from the drive and folder where your Data Files are stored to your paradise/spa folder.

b. Create a frameset with the configuration shown below in Table H-4 by inserting `<frameset cols="200,*">` under the title information.

TABLE H-4

200 pixels	Remaining browser width

c. Specify your navigation bar, services_links.htm, as the source file with the name of links that will appear in the left frame by inserting `<frame src="services_links.htm" name="links" />` under the `<frameset>` tag.

d. In the servicesframes.htm file, specify a source file of services_first.htm with the name `main` for the right frame by inserting `<frame src="services_first.htm" name="main" />` on the line below the first `<frame />` tag.

e. In the servicesframes.htm file, end the frameset after the second `<frame />` tag using the `</frameset>` tag.

f. Provide alternate page content in the servicesframes.htm file for browsers that do not support frames by adding the following before the closing `</html>` tag: `<noframes> This page was designed to be viewed with frames. You can open individual pages using the <a href="services_links.htm">navigation bar</a> </noframes>`.

g. Save your work, then view the **servicesframes.htm** file in your browser.

4. Target links.

a. If necessary, open the **services_links.htm** file in a separate instance of your text editor.

b. Using a base tag, set a target attribute of `main` for this page so that the contents of the page's links are displayed in the right frame of the servicesframes.htm file. (*Hint*: Under the title information, add `<base target="main" />`.)

c. Save your **services_links.htm** file.

d. Refresh your **servicesframes.htm** file in your browser using the Go button.

e. Check the targets for your links in the left frame to be sure their content can be displayed in the right frame, then close the services_links file.

5. Format frame borders.

a. In the servicesframes.htm file, hide the border of the frames by adding `frameborder="0"` in the opening `<frameset>` tag.

b. To ensure compatibility with the greatest number of browsers, add `border="0"` and `framespacing="0"` to the opening `<frameset>` tag.

c. Prevent users from resizing the left frame by adding `noresize` in the first `<frame />` tag.

d. Save your **servicesframes.htm** file and refresh the page in your browser.

e. Check your work by making sure the left frame cannot be resized and that the borders do not appear.

6. Use nested frames.

a. In your text editor, open the file **htm_H-5.txt** from the drive and folder where your Data Files are stored, then save it as **servicesframes2.htm** to the paradise/spa directory where you save your site files.

b. Create a frameset with the configuration shown in Table H-5 by inserting `<frameset rows="160,*">` under the title information.

TABLE H-5

160 pixels
Remaining browser height

c. Turn off the frame borders and prevent resizing of the frames by adding `frameborder="0" border="0" framespacing="0" noresize` to the `<frameset>` tag.

d. Copy the **top.htm** file from the drive and folder where your Data Files are stored, then save it to your paradise/spa folder. In the serviceframes2.htm file, specify the top.htm page as the source file with the name `top` for the upper frame by inserting `<frame src="top.htm" name="top" />` under the `<frameset>` tag.

e. Prevent scrollbars from being displayed in the upper frame by adding `scrolling="no"` to the `<frame />` tag.

f. Place the frame structure you created in the servicesframes.htm file in the lower frame of the servicesframes2.htm page by copying the code between the title information and the closing `</html>` tag and pasting it above the closing `</html>` tag of the servicesframes2.htm file. Your nested frame configuration is shown in Table H-6.

g. In the servicesframes2.htm file, close the first `<frameset>` tag by adding `</frameset>` after the existing closing `</frameset>` tag.

h. Save your work, then open the **servicesframes2.htm** file in your browser to view the frames. See Figure H-22.

TABLE H-6

top.htm	
services_links.htm	services_first.htm

FIGURE H-22

7. Create a structuring table.

a. In your text editor, open the file **htm_H-6.txt** from the drive and folder where your Data Files are stored, then save it as **servicestable.htm** to the paradise/spa directory where you save your site files.

b. Add the spa logo from the **top.htm** file to the top row of the table by opening top.htm file in your text editor, copying the code between the opening and closing `<body>` tags, then using the comment in the servicestable.htm file as a guide to paste the code in the top row of your table. Close the top.htm file.

c. Add the navigation bar to the left side of your table by opening the **services_links.htm** file in your text editor, copying the code between the opening and closing `<body>` tags, then using the comment in the servicestable.htm file as a guide to paste the code in the first cell of the second row of your table. Close the services_links.htm file.

d. Add the starting text for the table by opening the **services_first.htm** file in your text editor, copying the code between the opening and closing `<body>` tags, then using the comment in the servicestable.htm file as a guide to paste the code in the second cell of the second row of your table. Close the services_first.htm file.

e. Delete any remaining comments from your servicestable.htm file, save your work, then open the **servicestable.htm** page in your browser to check your work.

8. Create a template.

a. In your text editor, save a copy of servicestable.htm as **servicestemplate.htm** to the paradise/spa directory where you save your site files.

b. Provide information about the structure of the table by adding a comment of `<!-- Web page structuring table, two rows with lower row divided into two columns -->` under the opening `<body>` tag.

c. Provide information about the location of the logo image by adding a comment of `<!-- Logo image - Do not change -->` under the first `<tr>` tag in the body of the page.

d. Provide information about the location of the navigation bar by adding a comment of `<!-- Site navigation bar - Do Not Change -->` in the line below the second `<tr>` tag in the body of the page. In the `<td>` tag in the line below this comment, add `width="20%"` to keep the navigation bar sized appropriately when the amount of page text changes in the future.

e. Mark the area where the opening text should be placed by replacing the text in the last `<td>...</td>` tag set with `Insert your page text here`.

f. Add your name to the servicestemplate.htm file using a comment, preview the template in your browser, then save and print the page.

g. Transfer the files to your remote directory.

▼ INDEPENDENT CHALLENGE 1

As you continue developing the Web site for your resort rental business, Star Vacations, you decide to use frames to lay out your rentals page. You decide to place the navigation bar in an upper frame and the linked contents in the lower frame.

a. In your browser, open the file **rentals.htm** from the drive and folder where your Data Files are stored. View the page, then open the source code in your text editor.

b. In a separate instance of your text editor, open the file **htm_H-7.txt** from the drive and folder where your Data Files are stored, then save it as **navbar.htm** to the vacations folder where you save your site files.

c. In your rentals.htm source code, locate the Vacation Rental Listings title and the navigation bar area and paste them between the body tags in your navbar.htm file. (*Hint*: Copy everything from the rentals.htm file between the opening `<body>` tag and "Information coming soon!")

d. Save your **navbar.htm** file.

e. In your text editor, open the file **htm_H-7.txt** again from the drive and folder where your Data Files are stored, then save it as **open_page.htm** to the vacations folder where you save your site files.

f. Locate and copy the five lines above the closing `</body>` tag in your rentals.htm file, paste them between the `<body>` tags in your open_page.htm file, then save the **open_page.htm** file.

g. In your text editor, open the file **htm_H-8.txt** from the drive and folder where your Data Files are stored, then save it as **vacationframes.htm** to the vacations folder where you save your site files.

h. Assign navbar.htm as the source file for the top frame with a name of `links` and an attribute to prevent resizing the frame.

i. Assign open_page.htm as the source file for the bottom frame with a name of `main`.

j. Save the **vacationframes.htm** file.

k. Add a `<base>` tag to your navbar.htm file to set the target for the links to the lower frame and resave the **navbar.htm** file. (*Hint*: The name of the lower frame is `main`.)

l. Copy the files **faq.htm** and **features.htm** from the drive and folder where your Data Files are stored to the vacations folder where you save your site files. If you are asked whether you want to replace the files, click Yes. You will use these files to test the navbar.htm links.

m. Open your **vacationframes.htm** file in your browser and test the Frequently Asked Questions and Featured Resorts links.

n. Add your name to the vacationframes.htm file in a comment, then save your work and print your vacationsframes.htm file from your text editor.

o. Transfer your pages to your remote directory.

Advanced Challenge Exercises

- Refer to Table H-3 in the Format Frame Borders lesson to find the attribute that customizes the border color for a frame.
- Use the appropriate attribute to add a color of #6600FF to the first frame tag in the vacationframes.htm file.
- Save your work and display the **vacationframes.htm** file in your browser to check the border.
- Transfer your vacationframes.htm file to your remote directory.

▼ INDEPENDENT CHALLENGE 2

Metro Water publishes water conservation tips on their Web site. You will use a structuring table to lay out links for a variety of water conservation tips.

a. In your text editor, open the **htm_H-9.txt** file from the drive and folder where your Data Files are stored, then save it as **conservation_links.htm** in the water folder where you save your site files. You will use the code in this file as part of a structuring table on a Web page.

b. In your text editor, open the **htm_H-10.txt** file from the drive and folder where your Data Files are stored, then save it as **tip.htm** in the water folder where you save your site files. You will use the code in this file as part of a structuring table on a Web page.

c. In your text editor, open the **htm_H-11.txt** file from the drive and folder where your Data Files are stored, then save it as **watertable.htm** in the water folder where you save your site files.

▼ INDEPENDENT CHALLENGE 2 (CONTINUED)

d. Using the comment in the watertable.htm file that identifies the location of the structuring table and the code from the files conservation_links.htm and tip.htm, add the table elements to create the rows and columns, as shown in Table H-7.

TABLE H-7

Metro Water Conservation (Format with level-three heading)	
conservation_links.htm width 40%	tip.htm

e. Add the level three formatting, as shown in Table H-7, for the Metro Water Conservation heading. Add the attribute to set the width of the conservation_links.htm cell. Save the **watertable.htm** file and view the file in your browser to check your work.

f. Create a template by adding comments to mark the locations of the page heading, links, and the tip. Save your template as **watertemplate.htm**

g. Add your name to the watertemplate.htm file as a comment and print the page from your text editor.

h. Save your work and transfer your pages to the remote site.

Advanced Challenge Exercises

- Although using tables for page layout is often preferable to using frames, many Web designers do not use tables in this way. Use your favorite search engine to research the challenges associated with using tables for Web page layout.
- Write a paragraph citing four problems associated with page layout using tables. Include the preferred method for Web page layout.
- Add your name and today's date to the top of your paper and print it.

▼ INDEPENDENT CHALLENGE 3

In this unit you used frames to lay out Web pages. You are considering using frames to standardize your site navigation, but first you need to research how you can make them accessible for all users.

Go to the Student Online Companion for this book, locate the link for this unit, then click the link for the W3C Web Accessibility page and review the information on frames. Write one or two paragraphs answering the following questions about frames:

1. How can titles in frames be used to increase their accessibility?
2. What information about frames is important to note in a frameset?
3. What is the best place to add descriptions of the frames in a frameset?
4. Add your name and today's date to the top of your paper, then print it.

▼ INDEPENDENT CHALLENGE 4

Now that you've used frames and structuring tables to lay out Web pages, you are ready to add them to your Web site.

a. Determine how frames and structuring tables can be used in your Web site to standardize navigation.

b. Lay out your Web pages on paper to determine which structure works best.

c. Create the frames and/or structuring tables using your text editor.

d. Create templates for the structures to use for other pages.

e. Format your frames and tables appropriately.

f. Add appropriate accessibility features to your pages.

g. Test and edit your pages, then add your name and the current date. Save and print the pages, then transfer them to the remote location.

▼ VISUAL WORKSHOP

You have created a Web page with links for the services provided by Bits and PCs. You want to use nested frames to lay out the page with a header in the top frame and two columns in the lower frame. The contents of the links in the left frame should appear in the right frame. Use Figure H-23 as a guide to create the page layout in your text editor using the data files: bitshead.htm, first.htm, and bitslinks.htm. Be sure to include a description in the frameset page for browsers that do not display the frames. Add your name as a comment in the frameset page, save your frameset page as **bitsframes.htm** in the bitspcs folder where you save your site files, then print the page.

FIGURE H-23

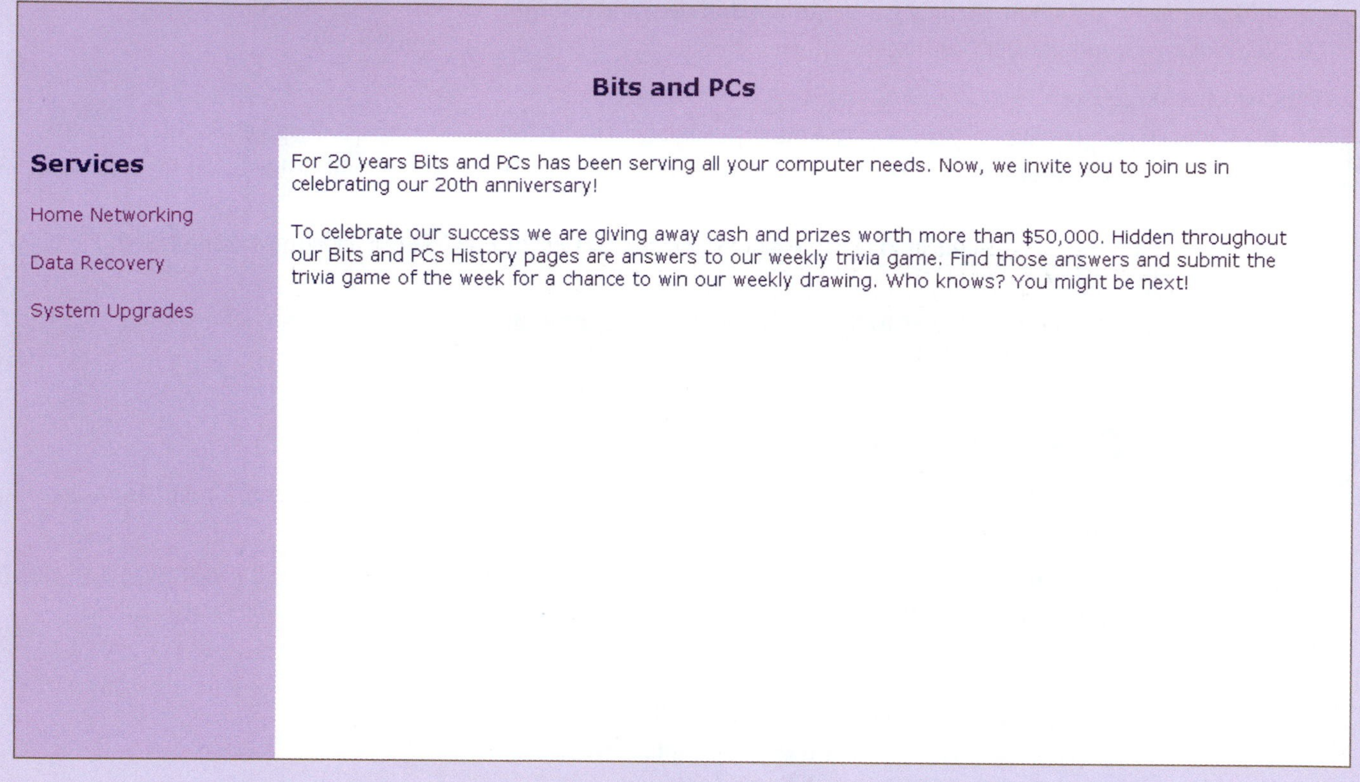

Bits and PCs

Services

Home Networking

Data Recovery

System Upgrades

For 20 years Bits and PCs has been serving all your computer needs. Now, we invite you to join us in celebrating our 20th anniversary!

To celebrate our success we are giving away cash and prizes worth more than $50,000. Hidden throughout our Bits and PCs History pages are answers to our weekly trivia game. Find those answers and submit the trivia game of the week for a chance to win our weekly drawing. Who knows? You might be next!

UNIT
I
HTML

Designing Web Pages

OBJECTIVES

Understand design principles

Examine Web-specific design issues

Explore cross-platform issues

Incorporate images effectively

Create a noframes alternative

Locate Web design resources

Design an accessible Web page

Explore Web writing guidelines

Study usability factors

Understanding how to create a well-designed Web page is the key to attracting users and creating functional Web sites. You don't have to be a graphics design professional to create effective Web pages, but you do need to understand universal design guidelines and the unique design advantages and challenges associated with the Web. You have spent many hours designing and updating the Paradise Mountain Family Resort Web site, and you want to optimize your pages to make them more effective. You have employed a graphics design firm and are utilizing online resources to increase your understanding of and find tips for effective design, usability, and search-engine optimization.

Understanding Design Principles

Web page design incorporates many of the elements used in print design, including graphics, color, typography, and layout. These elements can add visual clues to help readers interpret the function and importance of page elements. However, balance and moderation are essential to good page design. Using too many layout elements makes a page overwhelming and leaves users unclear about its purpose. Attaining a thoughtful balance between plainness and overuse of formatting elements is the key to the effectiveness of any Web page design. Figure I-1 shows an effective layout that incorporates many of the basic design principles. Through your meetings with the design consultants and your Internet research, you put together a list of basic Web design guidelines. Although you have already put some of these principles into practice, it is worth reviewing them to ensure that you are doing all you can to make your site as pleasing and effective as possible.

DETAILS

Some basic design guidelines are:

- ### Use active white space
  The term **white space** refers to any empty part of a page; it may include a color or a background image. **Passive white space** is any large area of unused space that doesn't serve a purpose in your design. Too much passive white space gives a page an unbalanced look. However, the use of **active white space**, empty areas deliberately placed between page elements, gives the site visitor's eyes a place to rest and reinforces the separateness of each element or section. This technique helps the user mentally group the page into sections. Figures I-2 and I-3 demonstrate a before-and-after design layout in which problematic passive white space has been eliminated.

QUICK TIP
Try printing your page on a gray scale printer with the background colors and graphics showing. If there is enough contrast between your background color or image and your text or other elements, your color choices are probably readable by any site visitor.

- ### Choose complementary colors
  You can control color in page and table backgrounds, text, and graphics. You can use colored text to highlight main ideas or to emphasize important points. As with white space, you can also use colors to indicate separate ideas or sections in your layout. However, a word of caution: While you can use color for many purposes, moderation is key. For color differences to have maximum impact, use them sparingly so that each occurrence is not overpowered by others surrounding it. It is best to limit colors to two or three per page, and to be sure that the colors you select complement each other.

- ### Ensure content legibility
  As you plan the rest of your page components, focus also on contrast to make your pages legible. Use images that aren't too bright or too dark. When you deviate from the default black text on a white page, it is important to select font and background colors with enough contrast to make the text stand out from the page background. If you choose to use an image as the page background, you need to ensure that the image provides an appropriate contrast for all page contents.

- ### Use type effectively
  Regardless of the design you choose, it is important that users can read your page text. Consider legibility as you choose each font; select font sizes that aren't illegibly small, and avoid using decorative font families in the body of your document. If you mix fonts, limit yourself to using one font style for headings and another for body text.

- ### Use a style that fits the message
  In addition to testing the design merits of each page element, you need to ensure that all components of your layout reinforce the page's message. For example, the appropriate font family, page colors, and graphics for a business site are quite different from those describing a Mardi Gras festival.

FIGURE I-1: Page layout incorporating design principles

Table-based
layout centered
for balance

Easily accessible
site navigation
and contact
information

Important site
content appears
in first screen

FIGURE I-2: Page with problematic passive white space

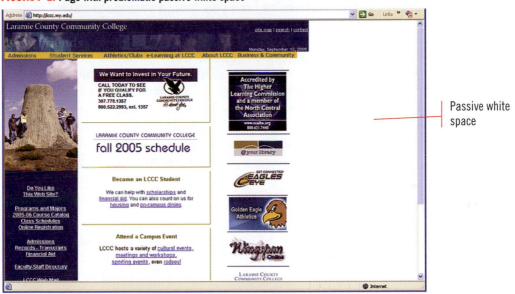

Passive white
space

FIGURE I-3: Passive white space eliminated on redesigned page

Passive white space
eliminated

Examining Web-Specific Design Issues

As you design your pages, it is important to consider Web-specific design issues. Four factors that play an important role in determining how you design your pages are Web users, Web connections, Web browsers, and the Web medium. Although Web pages can resemble traditional media, there are two significant differences. Most printed documents are presented in **portrait orientation**—taller than they are wide. However, Web browsers present information in **landscape orientation**—wider than they are tall. Additionally, Web users interact with Web pages, rather than just look at them. You need to include enough linked material to make your site visitors feel that they are visiting a quality site, but not so much that the user becomes disoriented. Nevertheless, regardless of the constraints it imposes on design, the Web's flexibility also offers designers significant advantages. Through the power of the Web, you can supply up-to-date content at an affordable price. You review the four major factors to consider in creating effective Web sites.

DETAILS

Four factors that determine how you design your pages are:

- ### Web users

  Knowing your users helps you to design a site that is appealing to the audience you are trying to attract. While inexperienced users will always exist, most of today's Web users are fairly knowledgeable about surfing the Web. They know what they are seeking and have little patience for sites with long download times or content that is not readily identifiable. To know who your users are, create a user profile detailing the characteristics of your **target audience**—the users you are trying to attract—then conduct user surveys to determine if these are, in fact, the people who spend the most time on your site. If your users do not match your target-audience profile, you need to work harder at promoting your pages. Attracting the right group of users, however, does you no good if they cannot find information on your site. To help your site visitors find the information they are seeking, use standardized navigation throughout your site and make your site's contents easily identifiable.

- ### Web connections

  You cannot control the speed at which your users connect to the Internet. However, you can make their connection process less painful by working hard to optimize all of your pages. To optimize your pages for quick download, make sure that all graphics are saved in the proper format and that your file sizes are as small as possible, then remove any irrelevant information from your pages.

- ### Web browsers

  The Web browser is the "virtual container" in which your pages appear. Remember that this "container" has a landscape orientation. Therefore, when you plan your page layout, sketch it on a page that you have turned on its side. This practice helps you create pages in which the most important information fits within the first screen of the browser window, an important element of Web design.

QUICK TIP

Web Pages that rely on CSS for special formatting render as plain text HTML documents in older browsers that do not "understand" style sheets. When created with appropriate structuring tags, these documents are viewable in almost any medium.

- ### Web medium

  The Web itself as a medium presents design advantages and challenges. Web pages are not static documents published once, like magazines and newspapers; they are active, changing documents that let you update information on a monthly, weekly, or daily basis. This enables you to keep your content fresh and relevant with current information, so users get the impression that they are always viewing new documents. Because Web users expect to find current content on a site, they quickly become bored with content that never changes. Consequently, you must schedule and budget regular updates to your Web site in order for it to maintain its level of integrity. As shown in Figure I-4, an obvious visual sign of updated content is the changing of page images.

FIGURE I-4: Updated page content

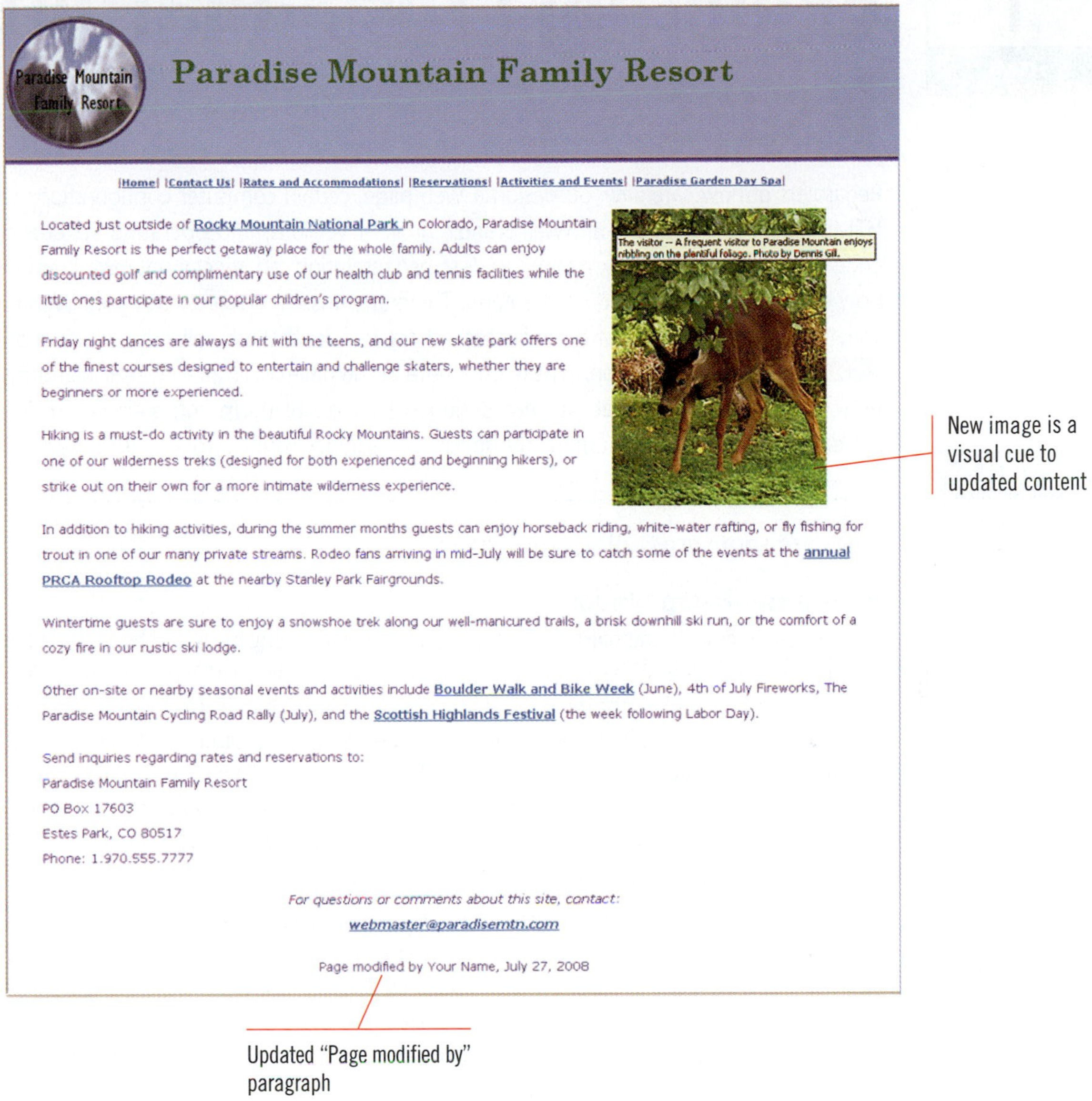

Paradise Mountain Family Resort

|Home| |Contact Us| |Rates and Accommodations| |Reservations| |Activities and Events| |Paradise Garden Day Spa|

Located just outside of Rocky Mountain National Park in Colorado, Paradise Mountain Family Resort is the perfect getaway place for the whole family. Adults can enjoy discounted golf and complimentary use of our health club and tennis facilities while the little ones participate in our popular children's program.

Friday night dances are always a hit with the teens, and our new skate park offers one of the finest courses designed to entertain and challenge skaters, whether they are beginners or more experienced.

Hiking is a must-do activity in the beautiful Rocky Mountains. Guests can participate in one of our wilderness treks (designed for both experienced and beginning hikers), or strike out on their own for a more intimate wilderness experience.

The visitor -- A frequent visitor to Paradise Mountain enjoys nibbling on the plentiful foliage. Photo by Dennis Gill.

New image is a visual cue to updated content

In addition to hiking activities, during the summer months guests can enjoy horseback riding, white-water rafting, or fly fishing for trout in one of our many private streams. Rodeo fans arriving in mid-July will be sure to catch some of the events at the annual PRCA Rooftop Rodeo at the nearby Stanley Park Fairgrounds.

Wintertime guests are sure to enjoy a snowshoe trek along our well-manicured trails, a brisk downhill ski run, or the comfort of a cozy fire in our rustic ski lodge.

Other on-site or nearby seasonal events and activities include Boulder Walk and Bike Week (June), 4th of July Fireworks, The Paradise Mountain Cycling Road Rally (July), and the Scottish Highlands Festival (the week following Labor Day).

Send inquiries regarding rates and reservations to:
Paradise Mountain Family Resort
PO Box 17603
Estes Park, CO 80517
Phone: 1.970.555.7777

For questions or comments about this site, contact:
webmaster@paradisemtn.com

Page modified by Your Name, July 27, 2008

Updated "Page modified by" paragraph

Clues to Use

Understanding Web media

The Web medium is, in fact, a collection of media devices, each of which interprets Web information differently. While users with disabilities can access Web pages using specialized interfaces such as text readers, other users connect to the Web using a variety of devices, such as desktop and laptop computers, Web TV, digital phones, and personal digital assistants (PDAs). To ensure accessibility for all users, use code that is as widely interpretable as possible, including physical formatting tags such as ... instead of <i>...</i>, then add additional formatting through linked style sheets.

Exploring Cross-Platform Issues

Regardless of how carefully you design a Web page, certain computer configurations can render the same HTML differently. Different browser brands, browser versions, and operating systems can interpret source code differently. Additionally, a computer's screen resolution can affect what each user sees on the screen and how each element is aligned on the page. Therefore, it is important to test your Web pages using as many variations as possible of all of these factors—characteristics that are collectively known as a user's **platform**. To give your development team a taste of the differences among user platforms and screen resolutions, you open a page that was not designed for cross-platform compatibility in different browsers and screen resolutions. You also outline the specific appearance issues across platforms and displays.

DETAILS

Here are some cross-platform issues:

- **Browser interpretation**

  Although industry standards for Web document file formatting are issued by independent organizations such as the World Wide Web Consortium (W3C) and the International Organization for Standardization (ISO), it is private companies, not the standardizing organizations, that develop most of today's browsers. Regardless of the published standards, not all browsers comply with these standards. As a result, each browser brand supports different subsets of each version of HTML, XHTML, and XML, and many browsers interpret the features differently. Consequently, it is a good idea to test your files in as wide a variety of different browsers as possible. For a list of downloadable browsers, see the Student Online Companion for this text.

QUICK TIP

If it is likely that your Web page audience uses older equipment, you may want to design pages compatible with the lowest possible resolution of 640 × 480. Consider a flexible option for such a display.

- **Screen resolution**

  You can be assured that a Web page does not appear on your screen exactly as all other readers see it. The reason is that monitor **resolution**—the screen's display dimensions (width by height, in pixels)—varies, depending on a user's monitor and computer hardware. Common resolutions include 800 × 600, 1024 × 768, and 1280 × 1024, with some platforms capable of displaying even larger areas. As the resolution increases, more of the page is visible in the browser window. Designers often create Web pages that consistently appear at different resolutions by using a centered layout table no wider than the lowest common resolution. Another, often better, approach is to create a page with a flexible content area, as shown in Figure I-6. Because most of today's Web site visitors use higher resolutions, pages optimized for low resolutions often include large areas of inactive white space. Better design options are to use a flexible division- or table-based design that allows the content area to expand and contract with the size of the browser window or to center the design on the page so that it remains balanced at all resolution settings.

- **Image display**

  The way your images appear on the Web could be affected by your user's operating system—the core software program that runs the computer's basic operations. Most Web users use an operating system that is IBM PC compatible, such as Windows, DOS, or Linux, or they use an operating system such as OS X, which is designed to run on the Apple Macintosh. Most OS configurations display the majority of Web page elements in the same way. However, there is one exception—images. Among the many properties of a digitized image file are **gamma settings**, which specify the degree of contrast between midlevel gray values. The Macintosh and the PC have different standard gamma settings for their displays; this can cause the same image to appear noticeably different on the two platforms. An image with heavy contrast on a Macintosh may look very dark on a PC, whereas high-contrast Windows images may look flat and washed out on a Macintosh. Web designers generally split the difference, using images with a setting midrange between the Macintosh and PC.

FIGURE I-6: Web page at three different screen resolutions

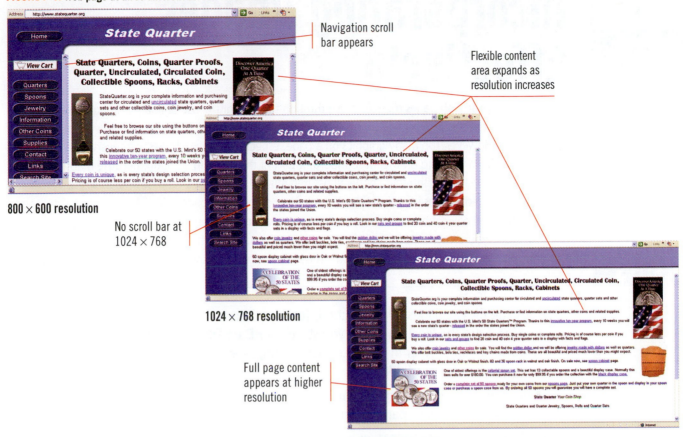

Navigation scroll bar appears

Flexible content area expands as resolution increases

800 × 600 resolution

No scroll bar at 1024 × 768

1024 × 768 resolution

Full page content appears at higher resolution

1280 × 1024 resolution

Design Matters

Designing pages for handheld devices

You can further broaden a page's audience by making the page viewable on handheld devices such as digital phones and **personal digital assistants (PDAs)**. Since PDAs and similar devices support only the most basic HTML tags, documents you prepare for such devices should be stripped clean of most HTML attributes. Moreover, because, as shown in Figure 1-5, the output screens on

such devices are so small (usually from 150 × 140 to 240 × 320), use of tables is not recommended for PDA display. PDA optimized pages should be short with few decorative enhancements. If you are using images to supplant your PDA-ready content, your images must be small, in both dimension and file size, and simple.

FIGURE I-5: Paradise Mountain home page shown in PDA display

Images sized to fit in single screen

Text and links available in scrollable window

Non-PDA supported items such as page backgrounds do not appear

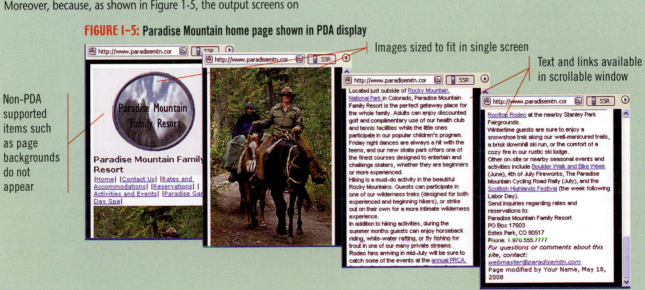

HTML

Incorporating Images Effectively

You can make your Web pages more effective through the thoughtful use of images. Images draw readers' attention and contribute to a page's mood. They can also serve as additional visual clues in locating your site's content. However, too many graphics on a page, especially unrelated ones, can overwhelm users and prevent them from focusing on the most important part of the page. In addition, because many Web users still rely on relatively slow Internet connections, minimizing your page's total download size by including only well-optimized images is vital to ensuring relatively quick downloads. You want to create and test an icon-based navigation bar to help your site visitors find the information they are seeking. As a model of this feature, you create a horizontal navigation bar that appears at the top of the screen. This new bar contains options users need, regardless of which page in the site they open.

STEPS

1. Copy the files activities.gif, contact.gif, food.gif, home.gif, lodging.gif, spa.gif, and deer.jpg from the location where you store your Data Files, then paste them into the paradise\images folder in your site file location, then copy food.htm and paste it into your paradise\frames folder

2. In your text editor, open the file htm_I-1.txt from your Data Files location, then save it as template2.htm in your paradise site folder

QUICK TIP

Be sure not to press [Enter] between the image tag and the line break in your navigation bar code. Doing so could cause the text below some of the icons to drop down a line.

3. Click after <!- HORIZONTAL MENUBAR ICONS ->, press [Enter] twice, then type the following code:

```
<table id="navIcons" width="372" cellpadding="0" cellspacing="0">
<tr align="center">
<td width="62"><a href="index.htm">
<img src="images/home.gif" width="62" height="30" border="0"
alt="Home" /><br />Home</a>
</td></tr></table>
```

You created the table and row structure plus the first cell with a navigation icon of a single-row icon-based navigation bar. Now you want to add cells with images to serve as the rest of your navigation elements.

4. Click before </tr> in the navIcons table, press [Enter], then type <td width="62"> <a href="contact.htm"><img src="images/contact.gif" width="62" height="30" border="0" alt="Contact Us" />
Contact</a></td>

By inserting text below each icon, you enable site visitors to more easily understand your graphic navigation bar.

QUICK TIP

It's a good idea to include an extra line return between each table data tag set; however, depending upon your monitor and text editor settings, your code might wrap in a different place than the code shown in the figure.

5. Enter the remaining lines of code shown in Figure I-7

Figure I-7 shows the completed code that adds the icons to the horizontal toolbar.

6. Save your work, open your browser, then open the file template2.htm

As shown in Figure I-8, the horizontal toolbar appears along the top of the Web page. Each icon is small, minimizing the page's download time. The icons are similar in shape and appearance, which suggests their relatedness without distracting users from other parts of the Web page.

FIGURE I-7: Icon-based navigation bar code

```
<!-- HORIZONTAL MENU BAR ICONS -->

<table id="navIcons" width="372" cellpadding="0" cellspacing="0"><tr align="center">
<td width="62"><a href="index.htm">
<img src="images/home.gif" width="62" height="30" border="0" alt="Home" />
<br />Home</a>
</td>

<td width="62"><a href="contact.htm">
<img src="images/contact.gif" width="62" height="30" border="0" alt="Contact Us" />
<br />Contact</a>
</td>

<td width="62"><a href="rates.htm">
<img src="images/lodging.gif" width="62" height="30" border="0" alt="Rates and
Accommodations" /><br />Lodging</a>
</td>

<td width="62"><a href="food.htm">
<img src="images/food.gif" width="62" height="30" border="0" alt="Resort Dining
Options" /><br />Dining</a>
</td>

<td width="62"><a href="activities/index.htm">
<img src="images/activities.gif" width="62" height="30" border="0" alt="Activities
Center" /><br  />Activities</a>
</td>

<td width="62"><a href="spa/index.htm">
<img src="images/spa.gif" width="62" height="30" border="0" alt="Paradise Garden Day
Spa" /><br />Spa</a>
</td>

</tr></table>
```

FIGURE I-8: Template with icon-based navigation bar

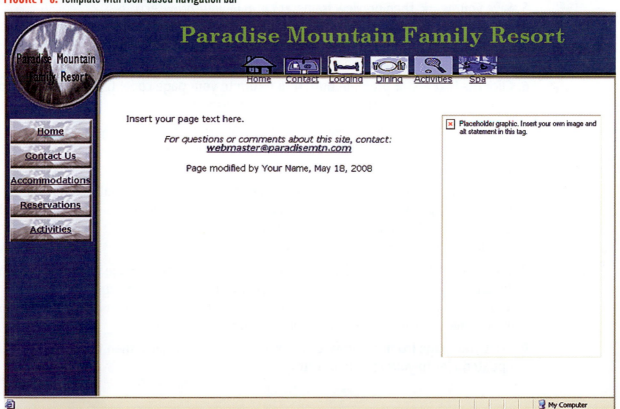

Creating a Noframes Alternative

As you design your Web pages, you can create frames-based pages that work for a variety of users. By following just a few guidelines, you can ensure that your frames-based pages are accessible to users of any platform and browser combination. First, supply a complete set of navigation options in the `<noframes>...</noframes>` section of your frameset, and add the complete content of your frameset's opening main content page to the noframes area. Also make sure that every content page in your site includes text navigation to your main site pages at a convenient location somewhere on the page. Text navigation is usually inserted at the top or bottom of the page. Finally, specify that all links to the frameset include the `target="_top"` attribute value to prevent framesets from opening inside of other frames. You want to optimize your experimental frames-based layout for display in all browsers.

STEPS

TROUBLE

If you did not complete the frames lessons in Unit H, obtain a copy of the necessary files from your instructor.

1. In your text editor, open your main2.htm page from the frames folder in your site file location, click after <body>, drag to select all of the page code between <body> and </body>, copy the code to your clipboard, then close main2.htm

2. Open the file htm_I-2.txt from your Data Files location, then save it as frameset3.htm in your site's paradise\frames folder

3. Click after <noframes>, drag to select the paragraph, including linked text between <noframes> and </noframes>, press [Delete], then paste your copied code

4. Click after <noframes>, press [Enter], then type `<h1 style="text-align:center;">Paradise Mountain Family Resort</h1>`
   You inserted the Page heading at the top of your noframes content.

5. Save your work, then preview frameset3.htm in your browser
   As shown in Figure I-9, your browser supports frames, so your page appears identical to your frameset2.htm page. You want to test your noframes alternative to see how it appears in a browser that does not support frames, so you need to add the noframes content to a test page.

QUICK TIP

Some Web design applications have noframes viewing utilities that you can use to test your framesets to see how they appear in a browser that does not support frames. When you do not have access to such a utility you can build your own test page as you do in these steps.

6. Click the text editor program button to return to your page code, then select and copy all the content from <noframes> to </noframes>

7. Open htm_I-3.txt from the place where you store your Data Files, save it as noframes.htm in your paradise\frames folder, click after the comment near the top of the page, press [Enter] twice, then paste your copied code

8. Click Replace on your text editor's Edit or File menu, in the Find what text box type `noframes>`, press [Tab], type `body>` in the Replace with text box as shown in Figure I-10, click Replace all , then close the Replace dialog box
   Including the > ensures that the comment text will not be replaced.

9. Update the "Page modified by" paragraph at the bottom of the page with your own name (if necessary) and today's date, then save your work and view the page in your browser
   As shown in Figure I-11, the page does not contain all of the formatting used in your frameset, but is an adequate alternative for browsers that do not support frames.

10. Print your page from the browser, close all files and programs, then transfer your updated files to your remote directory

FIGURE I-9: Frameset in browser window

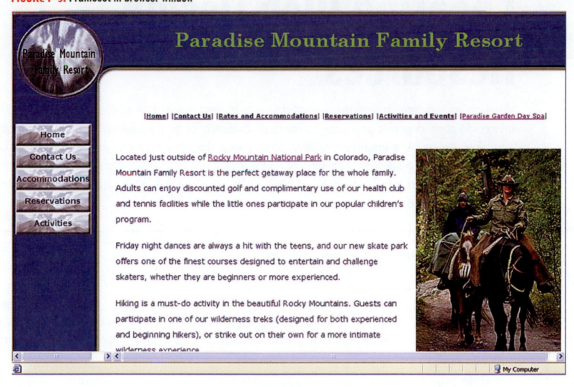

FIGURE I-10: Replace dialog box

FIGURE I-11: No frames test page shown in browser window

Locating Web Design Resources

Although you are familiar with the general design guidelines required by all Web pages, many other guidelines could apply depending on a page's contents, audience, or goal. Additionally, as Web technologies and languages evolve, it is important to stay current with the consensus on how to effectively use them. Fortunately, design guidelines are abundant on the Web itself. You can use a search engine to research relevant design pointers for your Web pages. You review a few main categories of design resources, then describe their uses to the members of your design team.

Some types of Web design resources include:

- **Web design articles**

  The Web contains many sites that focus on HTML and related technologies and regularly add new articles and news. These sites, such as the one shown in Figure I-12, are a great way to keep current on design trends. They also provide advice from experienced designers and can quickly bring you up to date on industry conventions.

- **Style guides**

  Many large organizations—such as corporations and universities—include their Web design guidelines on their Web sites. Although these guides, such as the one shown in Figure I-13, generally contain rules that members of the particular organization must follow when creating Web pages, they can shed light on the reasons some organizations use or avoid specific formatting or elements in their designs. By examining several such guides you also can get a sense of which style rules are in common use on the Web and which are specific to an organization's image or its internal practices.

- **Existing Web sites**

  You can find valuable design ideas on the sites you visit as a Web user. As you read the news, shop, research information, or check e-mail messages on the Web, pay attention to the design of each page that opens. When you find an interesting design, you can check the page code to see how it was created. You also should try to find other Web pages that use the same design; if you are unable to find any, there may be a good reason why other sites haven't implemented the design.

FIGURE I-12: Web design resource featuring regular articles and tutorials

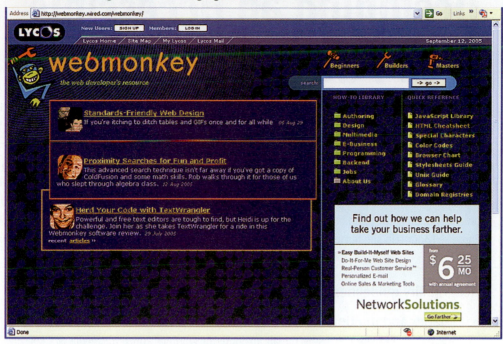

FIGURE I-13: Online Web style guide

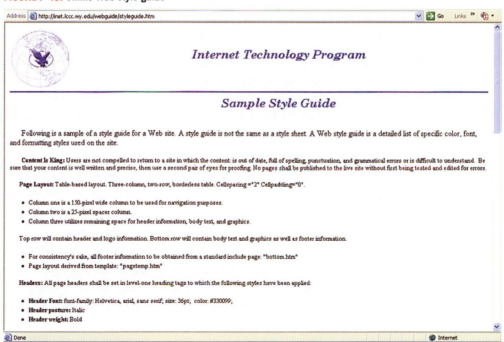

Designing an Accessible Web Page

Careful planning of your Web page design can maximize the page's usability in several ways. Close attention to usability guidelines helps ensure that your pages are accessible for Web users with disabilities, including blindness, color blindness, and cognitive or learning disabilities. Accessibility guidelines stem from three main requirements: The appearance or perception of color should not be necessary for interpreting information; all page elements should make sense when vocalized by a machine rather than viewed on a screen; and content should be clear and logically organized. Verifying that your pages meet these tests ensures their availability not only to people with disabilities but also to Web users with older displays or browsers. You check the Paradise Mountain site template shown in Figure I-14 against a list of the main accessibility guidelines.

DETAILS

Accessibility guidelines tell you to ensure that:

QUICK TIP

To learn more about usability guidelines, search the Web periodically using your favorite search engine. This will help keep you up to date on new technologies as well as federal guidelines, standards, and requirements.

- **Images and multimedia include alternate text**

  Specifying alternate text using the alt attribute for graphics and multimedia is a key means of translating visual or aural information into a format that many devices can interpret. Alternate text can provide a description of a sound file, or explanatory text that is vocalized by a Web interface device for sight-impaired users. You included a description of each icon in the template, using the alt attribute and text.

- **Color differentiation is not required for viewing any part of the page**

  A popular visual design strategy applies color to selected layout elements to indicate a common meaning or similarity. For example, the heading text in your page appears in green to differentiate it from other page text. Because some readers are unable to perceive differences in color—or may be using a monochrome display— you should not rely on color differences as the only formatting distinction between different types of information. Because the text also uses a level-one heading, it remains distinguishable when viewed without color.

- **Headers in data tables are correctly formatted**

  When read aloud by a Web interface for the visually impaired, tables should still be able to convey the information expressed in their visual formats. It is important to format cells in the header row with the `<th>` tag— and equally important not to use this tag for other cells in the table, even if their contents should be formatted as boldface and centered. The cells in your navigation bars do not use table heading formatting.

- **Table contents make sense if read row by row**

  Some older browsers and other Web interfaces have difficulty organizing text that wraps to multiple lines within a table cell. Ideally, cell contents in a data table should cover only a single line. You made sure that your text does not wrap in your navigation tables.

- **Linked text does not rely on its context to indicate its function**

  A widely discouraged element of Web page design, which is slowly disappearing from the Web, is the use of the text "Click here" to create a link. Instead, linked text should always describe the contents of the target page. This style guideline is especially important to visually impaired users who might scan a page using the [Tab] key to move from link to link. All of the links in your navigation bars describe the contents of the Web page they open.

- **Page content is logically organized**

  Ensuring that your pages contain simple, logical information makes them more accessible to people with cognitive disabilities, as well as to anyone who has difficulty reading. Use headings and ordered and unordered lists to clarify the relationships between page elements. Implementing navigation tools such as navigation bars throughout your site explicitly denotes the relationship between different Web pages. The two navigation bars that you incorporated into the Paradise Mountain Family Resort template provide a structural context for all pages in the site. Using the standard default underline format for links makes them instantly recognizable.

FIGURE I-14: Paradise Mountain page template

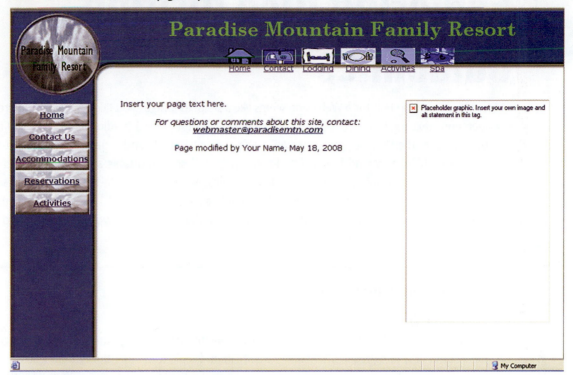

Exploring Web Writing Guidelines

At first glance, writing text for a Web page seems like a snap: as long as you take the layout differences into consideration, text for the Web should be similar to any other visual medium, right? In reality, several unique aspects of the Web require a markedly different writing style and organization. Because text on a screen is more difficult to read than printed text, users are less comfortable and more impatient reading Web pages. Fortunately, just as there are style guidelines available for printed media, many resources on the Web outline and explain effective writing for an online audience. Figure I-15 shows a site with effective content. You researched the writing guidelines for the Web, and tell your design team to use them on all Paradise Mountain pages.

DETAILS

Web writing guidelines include:

- **Keep your writing concise**

  Because it is more difficult to read from a computer monitor than from a printed page, it is best to minimize the amount of reading required to convey information. People read more slowly from a screen than from paper. When comparing printed with online text, a rule of thumb is to keep your sentences short (an average of 15 words), and vary your sentence length. Most importantly, go easy on the modifiers—avoid using several words when a single precise word can do the job.

- **Use short paragraphs with section headings**

  Web users skim most of the text they encounter. As a result, your pages are more useful if they help users find information that is relevant for them. Rather than forcing users to skim—or skip—a long section of text, use plenty of active white space by breaking text up into manageable sections with meaningful headings. This allows users to quickly identify the main points of the page, and then give a closer reading to any section(s) that seem to match their interests.

- **Divide text into page-size stand-alone units**

  Even if you divide information into sections below descriptive headings, you must give attention to the length of text on a single Web page. To allow users to scan and digest the contents of a page, when possible limit the text length to no more than three screens. Instead of displaying a long article on a single page, break it up into sections that can stand on their own, and place each on its own page.

- **Use concise linked text that describes its target**

  In addition to accessibility factors for Web users with disabilities, ensuring that linked text is descriptive yet concise is important in making Web text readable. Because linked text stands out from its surroundings on a page, users are more likely to notice it while scanning. Thus, this text should clearly state a specific point so users can immediately discern where the link will lead. Well-chosen linked text helps reduce the amount of text on your pages, and helps to ensure that all your text communicates its meaning as efficiently as possible.

- **Stop writing when you are finished**

  Don't overwrite about your subject. Rambling sentences and redundant phrases betray the fact that you are padding your content to fill additional space. Your job as a Web content writer is to say what must be said, then stop.

FIGURE I-15: Site with effective Web content

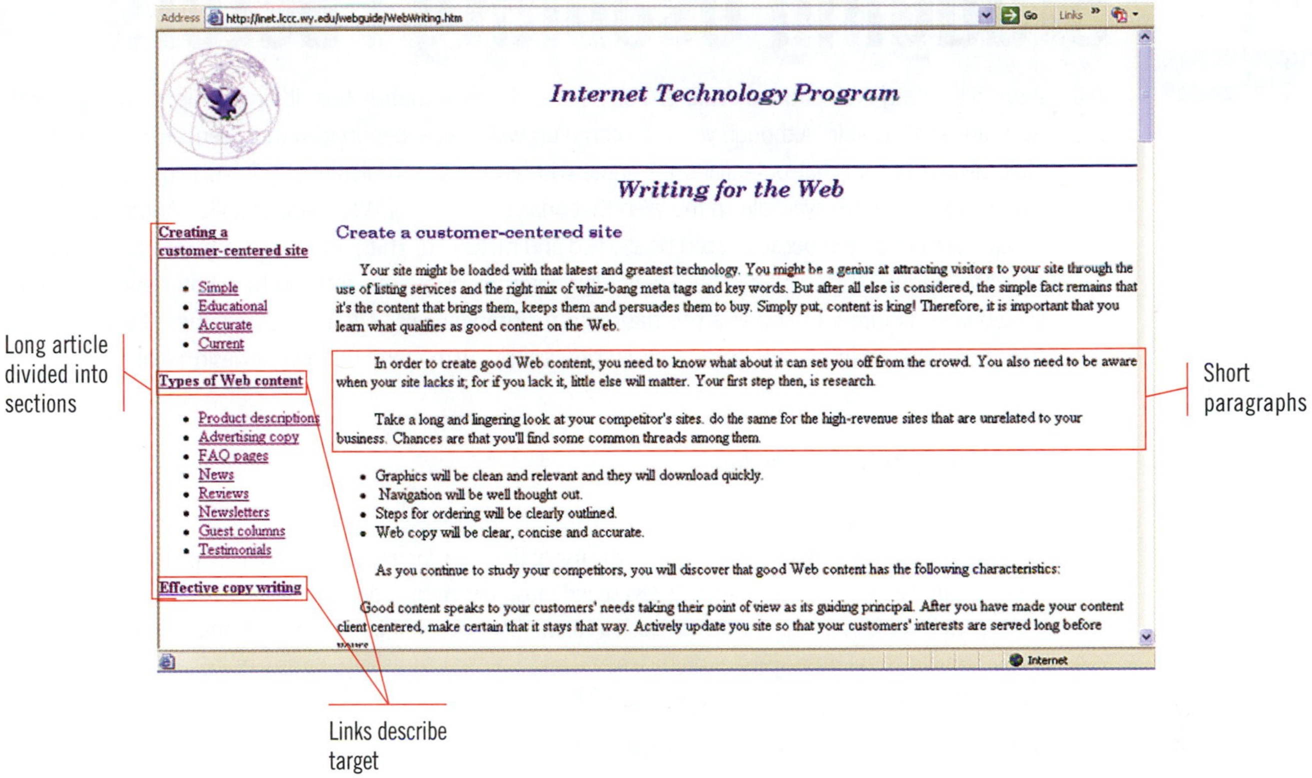

Long article divided into sections

Short paragraphs

Links describe target

Clues to Use

Supplementing your site with guest content

An effective method of enhancing your site's quality and depth is to solicit materials from other contributors. Regularly featured guest columns and articles—especially those written by known experts in your subject area—enhance your site's credibility, generate return site traffic, and save you from the chore of creating all the site content yourself. For example, a pet supplies site could feature regular columns written by a veterinarian; a mountain resort site might feature articles written by local hunting and fishing experts; and an archaeology site could host articles written by noted scholars and historians. Many, but not all, experts are willing to write for free or for a small fee in order to get their work published online. However, when using guest content, it is important that you retain editorial control. You must check all content for accuracy and edit it for clarity, grammar, and punctuation.

Studying Usability Factors

In addition to creating Web pages that are laid out well and convey information, it's important to make sure that your pages are easily usable. Although you may come up with a new design idea that seems more user friendly, you should always ensure that potential users agree with you before implementing it. As with other aspects of design, many resources are available on the Web that analyze aspects of Web page usability. Additionally, usability is a unique area of design because it can be studied and measured. Thus, reviewing some of the available data on what works and what doesn't can be a rewarding investment of time and can help you design more user-friendly Web sites. Figure I-16 shows a site designed for usability. You have gathered some research, and share your notes on important factors in Web site usability with members of your design team.

Web usability guidelines include:

- ### Use a familiar layout

  Web design is becoming more standardized in the use of the most common design elements. Jakob Nielsen, a Web design usability expert, points out that, "Users spend most of their time on *other* sites." This means that Web users usually prefer to use Web page elements—such as menu bars—laid out in a common format with which they are already familiar to increase speed and efficiency. Thus, you should balance creativity in your designs with the interface approach found on the most popular Web sites.

- ### Do not rush to implement the latest technology

  Often, new developments in HTML or other Web technologies promise to simplify the designer's or the user's experience or to allow previously impossible functionality in a Web site. However, implementing new technology can be tricky; if it generates errors for users, you risk your site's reputation as a reliable, usable site—and users may not return. You should take the time to familiarize yourself with the technology and its potential drawbacks before using it, and give yourself time to test your implementation before making it available to users. New technology usually comes with compatibility problems, for disabled users as well as for anyone using an older Web browser. Usually, the best response to a new technology is to wait until the Web design community has established its limits and its most appropriate uses.

- ### Minimize download times

  Given most Web users' emphasis on speed, impatience is common when waiting for a Web page to download. Large Web pages that contain many screens of text, large graphics, or other technologies that require downloading can result in delays. At best, you annoy your audience; at worst, they give up on your page before it finishes loading and go elsewhere. One of the keys to minimizing download time is to avoid animations and large graphics on your Web pages, especially on a site's home page. To ensure a quick download time, try to limit your total home page size to 45 KB or less, then use link titles and text to warn site visitors of slow loading pages.

- ### Keep information up to date

  To persuade users to regularly return to your Web site, you need to give them reason to trust the site and its contents. A crucial element to building this trust, which is specific to the Web, is to regularly update the site's contents and to include text that specifies the date of your last site update. For example, if you located a Web site containing information on a subject of interest, but then discovered that the site was last updated in 1997, you would probably assume that more recent information might be available and that you'd do best to continue your search elsewhere.

- ### Test your design

  One of the best ways of maximizing the usability of your design is also one of the most obvious: test it. While a well-planned test with different types of people can help you exhaustively analyze your Web site, feedback from even a handful of people can identify major stumbling blocks or an aspect that could be dramatically improved by some fine-tuning. Remember, however, to test your pages with members of the target audience. Such users are usually not other designers; they are often people who are less technically adept. Positive reviews from such testers are a good indication that your design is indeed easy to use.

FIGURE I-16: Text-based site designed for usability

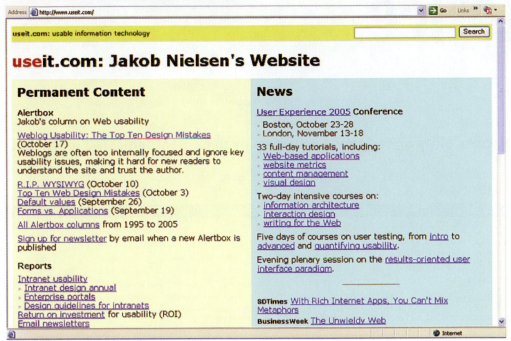

Clues to Use

Estimating page download time

Most Web page files are small, with some being less than 10 KB in file size. However, your total page size is more than just the size of the Web document file. You can estimate your total page download time by adding the file size of your page to the total file size of any support files, including images, multimedia files, external scripts, and external style sheets. Then divide your total page size by the per-second download time based on the most common connection your site visitors are using. A rough estimate of per-second download time is: 3 KB per second over a 28.8 Kbps modem, or a minimum download speed of 6 KB per second over a 56 Kbps modem. Broadband connections can be up to 40 times faster than a 56 Kbps modem, but don't count on the majority of your users having that technology at their disposal.

Practice

▼ CONCEPTS REVIEW

Describe the accessibility or design value of each page element indicated in Figure I-17.

FIGURE I-17

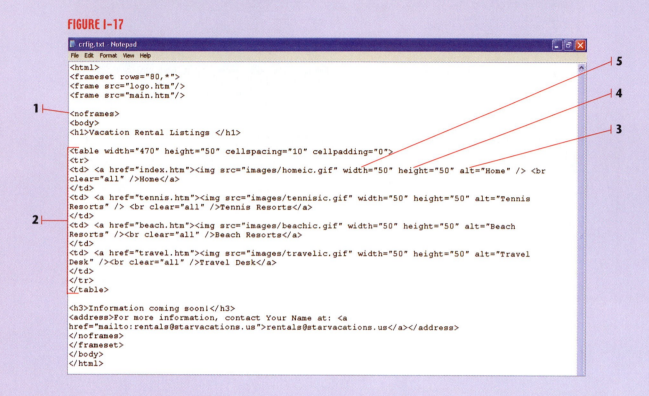

Match each recommendation with the design principle it describes.

6. Use images and text that contrast with the Web page background.
7. Ensure users can easily read text on a Web page.
8. Add unused space to separate page elements.
9. Use sparingly to separate ideas or sections on a page.
10. Ensure the site's colors, fonts, and backgrounds appropriately convey the message.

a. Active white space
b. Style
c. Effective use of typeface
d. Content legibility
e. Complementary colors

Select the best answer from the list of choices.

11. **Web pages are displayed in:**
    - **a.** Normal orientation
    - **b.** Slide orientation
    - **c.** Landscape orientation
    - **d.** Portrait orientation

12. **You can make a Web site's content accessible from every page by using:**
    - **a.** A navigation bar
    - **b.** Forms
    - **c.** White space
    - **d.** Frames

13. **Which one of the following guidelines helps keep the size of your HTML and associated files as small as possible?**
    - **a.** Limit the size and number of graphics.
    - **b.** Ensure the text and background colors are compatible.
    - **c.** Break up long sections of text into short paragraphs.
    - **d.** Add text to a link to describe the target page.

14. **You should schedule and budget regular updates to your Web site in order to:**
    - **a.** Prevent pages from growing too long.
    - **b.** Maintain the integrity of the site.
    - **c.** Minimize the time users wait for pages to download.
    - **d.** Make the site accessible for disabled users.

15. **To give users with disabilities access to your Web pages, you should:**
    - **a.** Limit the use of linked text.
    - **b.** Remove graphics from your pages.
    - **c.** Include alternate text for images and multimedia.
    - **d.** Use HTML code that is as widely interpretable as possible.

16. **Designers generally create Web pages no wider than:**
    - **a.** 640 pixels
    - **b.** 1024 pixels
    - **c.** 800 pixels
    - **d.** 1280 pixels

17. **Most operating systems display Web pages similarly, except for:**
    - **a.** Images
    - **b.** Navigation bars
    - **c.** Link format
    - **d.** Text readability

18. **What is a prudent upper limit on the number of colors on a Web page?**
    - **a.** One
    - **b.** Two or three
    - **c.** One or two
    - **d.** Three or four

19. **Which of the following design strategies is/are recommended in an accessible Web page? (Choose all that apply).**
    - **a.** Headers in data tables must be correctly formatted.
    - **b.** Images include alternate text.
    - **c.** There are fewer than four colors per page.
    - **d.** There are fewer than four links per page.

20. **Which one of the following design strategies is recommended for a PDA page? (Choose all that apply).**
    - **a.** Only the most basic HTML tags are used on a page.
    - **b.** Images must be small in dimension.
    - **c.** Images must be small in file size.
    - **d.** Tables should not be used.

21. **The degree of contrast between midlevel gray values is called:**
    - **a.** Alpha settings
    - **b.** Gamma settings
    - **c.** Color resolution
    - **d.** Midtones

22. **Which design resource focuses on HTML and related technologies?**
    - **a.** Web design articles
    - **b.** Style guides
    - **c.** Existing Web sites
    - **d.** E-commerce sites

23. **Which design resource contains rules for members of an organization?**
    - **a.** Web design articles
    - **b.** Style guides
    - **c.** Existing Web sites
    - **d.** E-commerce sites

24. A usable Web page design should reflect prevalent designs currently in use because:

    a. Users may not return to your site if the new technologies generate errors.

    b. Testing a new design is rarely effective at identifying its weak points.

    c. Users prefer Web page elements in a format that they already understand.

    d. Pages employing old technology do not need to be reviewed for accessibility compliance.

25. The output screen on PDAs is usually:

    a. Between 150 × 140 and 240 × 320   **c.** Between 280 × 240 and 360 × 430

    b. Between 250 × 240 and 340 × 420   **d.** Between 360 × 480 and 480 × 520

▼ INDEPENDENT CHALLENGE 1

As you continue developing the Web site for your resort rental business, Star Vacations, you want to add a horizontal navigation bar to the top of your pages.

    a. In your text editor, open the file **htm_I-4.txt** from the drive and folder where your Data Files are stored, then save it as **rentals.htm** to the vacations folder where you save your site files. If you are asked whether you want to replace the file, click Yes.

    b. Copy the image files **beachic.gif**, **homeic.gif**, **tennisic.gif**, and **travelic.gif** from the drive and folder where your Data Files are stored and save them in the vacations/images folder where you save your site files. Copy the files **beach.htm**, **tennis.htm**, and **travel.htm** from the drive and folder where your Data Files are stored and save them in the vacations folder where you save your site files.

    c. Locate the area where the horizontal navigation bar will be placed and review the first two table cells. Use the table below to add the page links in the third and fourth table cells.

    d. Use the table to the right to add the image tags in the appropriate table cells.

    e. Specify the image sizes for the last two table cells by adding the width and height attributes to the image tags. The images' dimensions are the same as the images in the first two table cells.

Cell	Linked text	Linked page	Linked image	Alternate text
Third	Beach Resorts	beach.htm	images/beachic.gif	Beach Resorts
Fourth	Travel Desk	travel.htm	images/travelic.gif	Travel Desk

    f. Use the table above to add alternate text for the last two images in the navigation bar.

    g. Add your name to the address text at the bottom of the page.

    h. Delete the page comments, save your work, display the **rentals.htm** file in your browser to check your navigation bar, then print the file from your browser.

    i. Close all files, then transfer all of the files to your remote directory.

Advanced Challenge Exercises

    ■ Use the Help menu in your browser to find out how to turn off the display of images. (*Hint*: Search for help to turn off pictures.)

    ■ Turn off the image display in your browser, then refresh your **rentals.htm** page to be sure that the navigation bar is functional without images.

    ■ Turn your image display back on and close your rentals.htm file.

▼ INDEPENDENT CHALLENGE 2

One of the best ways to learn effective Web page design is to critically evaluate a Web page with a less-than-optimal design.

    a. Find at least five Web sites that are poorly designed. As you examine the pages, list the design errors that you notice on each site.

    b. Write a report that includes a paragraph describing the design flaws of each site and explain how you would correct the errors.

▼ INDEPENDENT CHALLENGE 2 (CONTINUED)

c. Find at least five Web sites that lack accessibility features. Add a paragraph to your report describing the accessibility elements that are missing from each site and explain how you would correct the errors.

d. Add your name to the report and print it.

Advanced Challenge Exercises

■ If your Web pages will be viewed from a 256 color (8-bit) computer you need to use browser-safe colors. Use your favorite search engine to research the Web-safe color palette.

■ Arrange a complementary color combination using the Web-safe palette of no more than three colors.

■ Write a report describing how you would use each color on a Web site. Include the hexadecimal and RGB values for each color you selected.

■ Add your name to the report and print it.

▼ INDEPENDENT CHALLENGE 3

Many countries have passed laws regulating the accessibility of Web pages. You want to be sure that your pages incorporate all of the required accessibility features mandated by the countries where your users reside.

a. Go to the Student Online Companion for this book, go to the Unit I link to the W3C Web Accessibility page, and review the information about accessibility policies in countries around the world.

b. Research policies in two different countries where your Web pages might be viewed.

c. Write a paragraph on each country discussing its accessibility guidelines. Include all existing laws that relate to Web accessibility.

d. Add your name and today's date to the top of your paper, then print it.

▼ INDEPENDENT CHALLENGE 4

Now that you've studied design principles, usability, and accessibility, you are ready to apply these features to the pages on your Web site.

a. Determine how white space can be used in your Web site to break the content into sections. Add the appropriate amount of active white space to your pages.

b. Choose complementary colors for your site limiting your choices to two or three per page. Use the colors on your site to separate the sections of the pages.

c. Examine the fonts that are used on your pages to be sure that the text is legible. If your fonts are mixed, check to be sure that a single font is used for headings and another for the body text.

d. Examine your site's images to be sure that they are not too bright or too dark. If you have background images make sure that they provide an appropriate contrast for all of the page elements.

e. Save your work, then print your site pages with changes in your browser.

f. Close all files, then transfer your edited files to the remote location.

▼ VISUAL WORKSHOP

Work progresses on your Bits and PCs Web site, and you decide to add a horizontal navigation bar to the top of your pages. In your text editor, open the **htm_I-5.txt** file from the drive and folder where your Data Files are stored, then save it as **bitsnav.htm** in the bitspcs folder where you save your site files. Copy the image files **help.gif**, **homevw.gif**, **services.gif**, and **specials.gif** from the drive and folder where your Data Files are stored, and save them in the bitspcs/images folder where you save your site files. Copy the file **help.htm** from the drive and folder where your Data Files are stored, and save it in the bitspcs folder where you save your site files. Add the image tags including image size information and appropriate alternate text to the bitsnav.htm file to create the navigation bar shown in Figure I-18. Add your name to the e-mail address at the bottom of the page, then print the page from your browser. (*Hint*: You can find the height and width of an image by viewing its Summary tab in the Properties dialog box.)

FIGURE I-18

Bits and PCs

Filling all your computer needs for 20 years!

For 20 years Bits and PCs has been serving all your computer needs. Now, we invite you to join us in celebrating our 20th anniversary!

To celebrate our success we are giving away cash and prizes worth more than $10,000. Hidden throughout our Bits and PCs History pages are answers to our weekly trivia game. Find those answers and submit the trivia game of the week for a chance to win our weekly drawing. Who knows? You might be next!

For information about sales, service or store hours contact info@bitsPCs.com

Scripting for HTML

OBJECTIVES

Creating pages with HTML and XHTML allows you to present static information in a format that is easily accessible to a wide range of users. However, you can incorporate **scripts**, small programs that run on the viewer's browser, into your Web pages for added functionality and interest. For example, you can use scripts to make your page display different information in response to user input, to automatically update pages with current information, or to display specialized graphics and animations. A well-written script can extend the function of a page beyond the simple presentation of information. It can also make the Web experience more enjoyable for the site visitor.

Understanding Web Scripting

There are two types of Web scripts, **server-side scripts**—separate files that are stored and execute (run) on a remote Web server, and **client-side scripts**—instructions written directly into page code that cause the script to execute on the site visitor's computer. Server-side **scripting**—the process of writing scripts— allows designers and programmers to process secure information and to deliver content, such as database information, that would otherwise not be available to the client. Pages that use server-side scripting are usually saved with .asp, .jsp, or .php extensions. Pages based on server-side scripting may take longer to download and process because processing information must pass back and forth between the client and server. On the other hand, client-side scripting makes it possible to use the processing power of the client computer, thereby cutting download time and saving valuable server resources and bandwidth for applications that must run on the server. Most client-side scripts are written in JavaScript, a scripting language that is cross-platform compliant. For additional information on client- and server-side scripting, visit the Student Online Companion and click the links for this unit. Figure J-1 shows the source code for a Web page containing a script, as well as the Web page generated by that code. You recently attended a design conference and participated in several scripting workshops. You learned that using scripting in Web page development offers several advantages over using HTML alone.

DETAILS

Scripting advantages include:

- **Flexibility**

  You can combine scripting codes in many different ways, opening the door to more variety and creativity in your pages than with HTML alone. For example, you can automatically update the date and time displayed on a page, create rotating banners that display a series of different photos or text content, or allow the end user to customize parts of the page's appearance based on personal preference.

- **Simplification**

  You can script some aspects of your page design to automatically update certain sections of the page, including some navigation elements and contact sections.

- **Immediate response**

  Client-side scripting embedded in your page code eliminates the lag time involved in contacting the remote server, waiting for a response, and downloading new information because client-side scripts can perform their tasks without acquiring extra information from the server.

- **Improved interactivity**

  The quick response time that **local** (client-side) scripting provides allows you to incorporate an impressive amount of user interactivity into your Web pages. Because script processing occurs locally, your script can react almost instantly to any user action.

- **Reduced server load**

  Local execution of scripts is an advantage not just for users, but for Web site administrators as well. The reduced demand on the server, when some of the processing is shifted to local computers, results in more system resources being available for other tasks. This may result in a decrease in download time for people viewing your site's pages and faster processing when a Web page does need to submit a request to the server.

```
<script type="text/javascript" language="JavaScript" >
<!-- HIDE code from older browsers

var name=prompt("For personal service, please type your first name and click OK.","")

        function clearUp() {
                document.info.elements[0].value=""
                document.info.elements[1].value=""
                document.info.elements[2].value=""
                document.info.elements[3].value=""
                document.info.elements[4].value=""
                document.info.elements[5].value=""
}


function submitted() {
        alert("Information submitted!")
}

//-->
</script>
```

Variable inserted in script

User name generated by script incorporated into Web page

Paradise Mountain Family Resort

News from the Mountain
Juanita, welcome to Paradise Mountain's newsletter!

Another Day in Paradise!

Guest Charlcie Gill was the winner of our *Another Day in Paradise* contest. Gill, who lives in Astoria, Oregon, is a self-employed graphic artist/Web design professional. She also works part time for the University of Oregon extension service and serves as a volunteer for several 4-H clubs in her area.

A frequent visitor to Paradise Mountain Family Resort, Gill said she draws inspiration from the beauty and grandeur of the Rocky Mountains. As the winner of our contest, Gill and her family will return to Paradise Mountain for a week in one of our two-bedroom luxury units. While her family plays, Gill will have her choice of one of our full-day spa experiences at our onsite Garden of Eden Day Spa.

Clues to Use

Choosing a scripting language

Several languages are available for writing Web page scripts. The two most common scripting languages for client-side scripting are JavaScript, which was originally developed by Netscape and Sun Microsystems and loosely based on the scripting language called C (the forerunner of C+ and C++), and VBScript, the Microsoft adaptation of its own Visual Basic programming language. Most browsers are compatible with JavaScript. On the other hand, VBScript is not universally compatible, meaning that users of certain browsers or operating systems might be unable to view elements scripted with that language. If you are working on a company intranet site and are certain that all users have the same operating system and browser, VBScript is a fine choice for client-side scripting, but if your pages must be viewable to the general Web population, choose JavaScript to create pages viewable in most major browsers.

Creating a Script

You can add a script to a Web page just as you would add to or edit the Web page's HTML code. To do this, you can use a text editor such as WordPad or Notepad or a good Web page editor—a program that writes Web page code and often adds an autocompletion feature and debugging capabilities. For a browser to recognize a script, the script must be contained within `<script>...</script>` tags. It is also good practice to surround each script with a set of tags that make it invisible to browsers incompatible with scripts. This second set of tags tells incompatible browsers to bypass the script. ▓▓▓▓ While researching scripting fundamentals, you found a sample script that validates a form before submitting it to a server by checking the form to be sure information has been entered in each field. When form fields are empty, the form validation script displays a warning box that reminds the user to complete each field. You decide to try adding this script to your survey form in order to better understand how to insert scripts into HTML code.

1. **Copy the file charlcie.jpg from your Unit J Data Files into your paradise/images folder, start your text editor program, open the file htm_J-1.txt from your Data Files location, then save it as newsletter.htm in your paradise site folder**

   The file contains a newsletter article and, as shown in Figure J-2, some placeholder text and a partial function designed to alert the user that a form has been submitted. You will learn more about functions in a later lesson. The document also includes a short form for requesting the resort's newsletter.

2. **Locate the style sheet link in the head section, select the text [Replace with opening script tags] below it, then press [Delete]**

3. **Type `<script type="text/javascript" language="JavaScript">`, then press [Enter]**

   The beginning of the script is marked with the opening `<script>` tag with attributes specifying the scripting language and type. Specifying both language and type makes your script available to a greater number of browsers. You want to add code to ensure that older browsers are not confused by the scripting commands.

4. **Type `<!-- HIDE code from older browsers`, then press [Enter] twice**

   The tag `<!--` tells an incompatible browser (one that can't process your script) to ignore the code that follows. Compatible browsers process the script. Because all browsers ignore the text in the line with the comment tag, the phrase, "HIDE code from older browsers" makes it easier for programmers to understand the code.

5. **Select the text [Replace with closing script tags], then press [Delete]**

6. **Type `//-->` and press [Enter], then type `</script>`, then press [Enter]**

   Two slashes (//) mark a comment in JavaScript. Two dashes and an end bracket (-->) mark the end of an HTML comment. Used together, these two tags mark the end of the comment and prevent page errors. Figure J-3 shows the Web page source code containing the opening and closing script tags.

7. **Check the lines you added for errors, make changes as necessary, then save your work**

8. **Open the page newsletter.htm in your browser, scroll down to the text fields near the bottom of the page, then fill in sample information**

9. **Click the Send newsletter request! button**

   The browser simulates form submission to a server, then displays the dialog box shown in Figure J-4. This type of feature helps visitors by letting them know their form has been submitted.

10. **Click the OK button to close the dialog box, then return to your text editor**

QUICK TIP

To prevent the Internet Explorer Information bar from appearing and to automatically allow active content to run on your computer, click Tools on menu bar, click Internet Options, select the Advanced tab, then scroll to the Security section near the bottom of the tab and check Allow active content to run in files on My Computer.

Script placeholder text

```
htm_J-1.txt - Notepad
File  Edit  Format  View  Help

<link href="css/paradise_style.css" rel="stylesheet" type="text/css" />

[Replace with opening script tags]
function submitted() {
        alert("Information submitted!")
}
[Replace with closing script tags]

</head>

<body>

<h1><img src="images/pm_logo2.png" alt="Paradise Mountain Family Resort"
align="middle" width="159" height="156" /><font style="font-family:
Century Schoolbook, Times New Roman, Times, serif; color:
#336633;">Paradise Mountain Family Resort</font></h1>

<div id="text">
<h2>News from the Mountain</h2>
```

FIGURE J-3: Source code for Web page dialog box with script elements

Opening script tag

Closing script tag

```
<link href="css/paradise_style.css" rel="stylesheet" type="text/css" />

<script type="text/javascript" language="JavaScript" >
<!-- HIDE code from older browsers

function submitted() {
        alert("Information submitted!")
}

//-->
</script>
```

Opening comment markup hides script from older browsers

Closing comment markup prevents errors

FIGURE J-4: Web page with script-generated dialog box

Dialog box assures users that the form is submitted

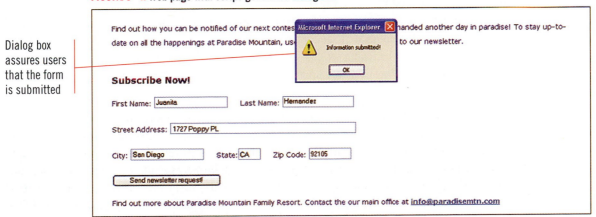

Find out how you can be notified of our next contes [Microsoft Internet Explorer] handed another day in paradise! To stay up-to-date on all the happenings at Paradise Mountain, us [Information submitted! OK] to our newsletter.

Subscribe Now!

First Name: Juanita   Last Name: Hernandez

Street Address: 1727 Poppy PL

City: San Diego   State: CA   Zip Code: 92105

Send newsletter request!

Find out more about Paradise Mountain Family Resort. Contact the our main office at info@paradisemtn.com

Clues to Use

Linking to an external script

In addition to typing script code directly into a Web page, you can add scripts to your pages by using an HTML code that references a separate file containing script code. A script located in an external file that you can link to a Web page is known as a **scriptlet**. Scriptlets make it easier to share code and to reuse scripts on multiple pages by allowing you to use a script without needing to paste its code into each Web page.

Debugging a Script

No matter how carefully you enter scripting code, a script often contains errors, or **bugs**, the first time your browser processes it. In general, a bug causes the script to return unexpected and undesired results. These may include improper formatting, appearance of code in the browser window, or, in the worst case, a browser application **hang** that requires the user to exit the application and restart the browser. It is doubtful that simple errors you make entering the scripts in this book could **hang your browser** (prevent it from working). However, when your results are different than those shown in this text, you can use a process called **debugging** to systematically identify and fix your script's bugs. Two examples of bugs are illustrated in Figure J-5. You review several types of scripting errors that generate undesired results.

DETAILS

Some causes of scripting errors and methods of fixing them include:

- ### Capitalization
  JavaScript is a **case-sensitive** language, meaning that it treats capital and lowercase versions of the same letter as different characters. Thus, depending on the script you are entering, capitalizing or not capitalizing letters can result in errors. Check your work to ensure that you have no capitalization errors in your script.

- ### Spacing
  When entering script code from a printed source, it is easy to add extra spaces or to leave spaces out. Some parts of JavaScript syntax allow for extra spaces, which makes code easier to view and understand. However, incorrect spacing in certain parts of a script can render otherwise perfect code incomprehensible to the browser. The best way to avoid spacing errors is to pay careful attention to spacing when you enter code.

- ### Parentheses ( ), brackets [ ], braces { }, and quotes " "
  JavaScript often uses these four types of symbols to enclose arguments, values, or numbers upon which certain commands are executed. More complex scripts often contain commands nested within other commands. As with HTML coding, the punctuation surrounding each command must be properly opened and closed. In lines or blocks of script where these symbols are concentrated, it can be difficult to check for accuracy. However, to ensure that your script runs properly, you must make sure that each opening symbol is paired with its closing counterpart.

- ### Typographical errors (0 vs. O, 1 vs. I)
  Another common source of coding errors is interchanging characters that appear similar, such as the numeral "0" and the letter "O" or the numeral "1" and the uppercase "i" or lowercase "l". Generally, the context provides clues for determining what character you should be typing. When in doubt, try to analyze what the script is doing in the current line. Once you understand this, it should be obvious which character to type.

- ### Debugging aids
  Many JavaScript-compatible browsers include script-error notification tools and debugging programs. Because these programs can be annoying to Web users who have no plans to correct page script, such features are turned off by default and must be turned on before they can be useful. Check your browser program's Tools or Edit menus to determine the method of activating your browser's script debugger. Figure J-6 shows the Advanced tab of the Internet Explorer, Internet Options window, where debugging is enabled. Figure J-7 shows script error notification windows that describe the types of errors the browser encountered and their locations. Script errors are referenced by their line number in the script. With this information, some investigation of your code, and a bit of thought, you can track down and fix scripting errors.

FIGURE J-5: JavaScript containing common bugs

```
<script type="text/javascript" language="JavaScript" >
<!-- HIDE code from older browsers
function submit() {}

function verify() {
        if (document.info.elements[O].value == "" ||
        document.info.elements[1].value == "" ||
        Document.info.elements[2].value == "" ||
        document.info.elements[3].value == "" ||
        document. info.elements[4].value == "" ||
        document.info.elements[5].value == "" {
                alert("Please complete each field")
        }

                else {
                submit()
        }
}
//-->
</script>
```

Letter "O" instead of numeral zero (0)

Extra space

FIGURE J-6: Internet Options Advanced tab

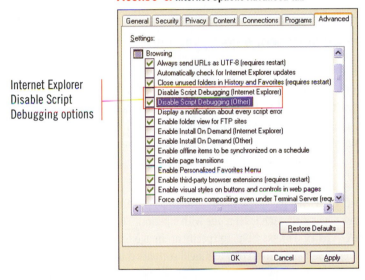

Internet Explorer Disable Script Debugging options

FIGURE J-7: JavaScript Error windows

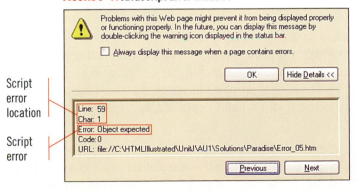

Script error location

Script error

Script error location

Script error

Clues to Use

Commenting a script

While writing a script it can be useful to include comments in ordinary language to explain what the script is doing at particular places. These notes can be helpful for you when editing or debugging your script or for someone else who wants to understand how the script works. To add a comment to a line of the JavaScript code, type // before the line, then type your comment. You also can mark several lines of text in a script as a comment by typing /* at the start of the block and */ at the end. To comment a line of VBScript, use a single quote (').

Understanding Objects

When working with scripts, it is important to understand the Document Object Model (DOM). The **Document Object Model (DOM)** is an object-based collection of programming routines and functions for HTML, DHTML, and XML documents that allows programs and scripts to access and work with the content of a Web page. In the DOM, each element in the window is called an **object**. Each object has a default name and set of descriptive features based on its location and function in the Document Object Model (DOM). These features include **properties**—qualities such as size, location, and type—and **methods**—actions the object can carry out. For example, the *window* object has an associated *alert* method that allows you to create customized dialog boxes. As shown in Figure J-8, the DOM organizes objects in an **object hierarchy**, a tree structure that allows designers to access object properties and methods by describing the object path from the topmost object, *window*, down through the object tree. For example `window.document.form.txtFname.value`, maps the path from the *window* object to the value of a *form* element, in this case a text box named *txtFname*. With a few exceptions, anything found in an HTML or XML document can be accessed, changed, deleted, or added using the Document Object Model. As you research the object hierarchy, you learn different ways to refer to the various elements in a document when writing a script.

DETAILS

To properly reference document objects, you must understand:

- **DOM object hierarchy**

  All objects within the DOM have a position within the DOM hierarchy. The *window* object (the browser itself) has the topmost position within the DOM. The *window* object can contain many objects, such as the *location*, *document*, *history*, and *frames* objects. With the exception of the *window* object, each object in the DOM is contained within a parent object. Some objects, such as *window*, *document*, *tables*, *forms*, and *frames*, contain one or more child objects. Other objects are barren, meaning that they are children but have none of their own.

- **Dot syntax**

  To specify an object on a Web page, you need to detail its position in the hierarchy, beginning on the document level and then separating each level name with a period. This method of referencing objects in the hierarchy is called **dot syntax**. For example, to specify an image on a Web page, begin with document.images. To specify an element such as a button or a text field contained inside a form, you must also specify the *form* object in the object path as follows: `document.form.element` where *element* is one of the objects shown under the form object in Figure J-8.

- **Object numbering**

  Because a document can contain more than one object of each type, each object is automatically assigned a number based on the order in which it appears in the Web page code. In JavaScript, object numbering begins with 0. Consequently, if you write a script that refers to the first image in your HTML code, use the reference, `document.images[0]`. According to the object hierarchy, the second image in your HTML code is `document.images[1]`. Other elements such as forms, hyperlinks, and layers, also are assigned numbers.

QUICK TIP

The quotation marks surrounding information in parentheses indicate to the browser that it is a literal text string, meaning that only the information within the quotation marks, not the quotation marks themselves, is written in the document.

- **Object methods**

  You also use dot syntax to refer to an object's methods. For example, the code `document.write ("Copyright Course Technology, 2008.")` calls on the *write* method of the *document* object. This code causes the information in parentheses to be written in the document. Table J-1 lists the default objects that are part of every browser window, along with their methods.

- **DOM standards**

  DOM standards are set by the World Wide Web Consortium (W3C). However, not all browsers meet current W3C DOM standards. Because standards and programming methods are constantly changing, the only way to ensure that a particular browser supports the objects, properties, and methods you use in your Web applications is to preview your pages in that Web browser.

FIGURE J-8: The Document Object Model

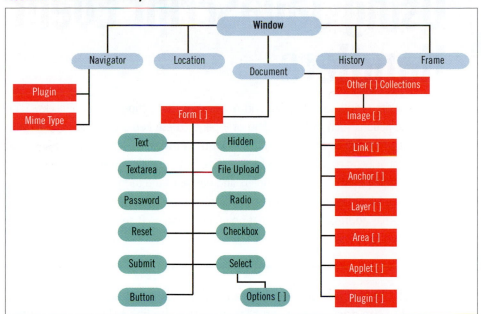

TABLE J-1: Default objects and methods

object name	method name	description
window	*alert(message)*	Displays a dialog box with a message in the window
	close()	Closes the window
	prompt(message, default_text)	Displays a dialog box prompting the user for information
	scroll(x, y)	Scrolls to the x- and y-coordinates in the window
frame	*alert(message)*	Displays a dialog box with a message in the frame
	close()	Closes the frame
	prompt(message, default_text)	Displays a dialog box prompting the user for information
history	*back()*	Returns to the previous page in the history list
	forward()	Goes to the next page in the history list
location	*reload()*	Reloads the current page
document	*write()*	Writes text and HTML tags to the current document
	writeln()	Writes text and HTML tags to add a line break following the new text on the current document
form	*reset()*	Resets the form
	submit()	Submits the form

Clues to Use

Naming an object

When you initially create a page element, it is a good idea to assign it a unique identifier in the form of an ID, using the *id* property, or in the form of a name, using the *name* property. When an object has an identifier, you can refer to it using its ID or name instead of its index number. For example, the code `<form id="newsletter" name="newsletter">` assigns *newsletter* as both the ID and the name of the form. Some scripts call an object by its name; others call an object by its ID. By assigning both a name and ID, you make the object available to both types of scripts. When a parent element has an ID or name, you can use the name or ID to refer to that element as well as to any child elements within it. For example, to refer to the form named *newsletter*, use `document.form.newletter`. To refer to elements within the form, use `document.form.newsletter.elements[0]` (where *elements* refers to the specific child element such as *text*, *radio*, and so on). You can also use names and/or IDs rather than index numbers to refer to child elements.

Using JavaScript Event Handlers

You can write scripts to recognize and respond to user actions, such as clicks. Scripts can also respond to automatic actions such as the loading of a page. These automatic and user actions are known as **events**. Scripts can respond to an event with an **event handler**—a set of instructions executed in response to an event. By specifying event handlers for specific events, you can make your script respond to events when they happen. Table J-2 lists 12 event handlers and describes the triggering action for each one.  You want the Paradise Mountain newsletter page to display a message in the status bar when a user moves the pointer over the e-mail address. You know that pointer positioning is an event, and you can use a script with an event handler to display the message.

STEPS

1. Click the text editor program button to return to your newsletter.htm code, scroll to the end of the document, then click just after the link title that ends with `later."` in the opening `<a>` tag

QUICK TIP

Even though you do not press [Enter], your text editor may wrap the text onto multiple lines. This does not affect the accuracy of your code.

2. Press [Spacebar], then type the following code *without* pressing [Enter]:
   `onMouseOver="window.status='We will reply to your inquiry within 24 hours!'; return true"`
   The *window.status* object refers to the status bar. The first part of your script causes the message "We will reply to your inquiry within 24 hours!" to appear in the status bar when a user positions the mouse pointer over the e-mail link.

QUICK TIP

Be sure you use two apostrophes, rather than a quotation mark, following *onMouseOut= "window.status=.*

3. Press [Spacebar], then type `onMouseOut="window.status=''; return true"`
   The completed script is shown in Figure J-9. The *onMouseOut* event handler instructs the browser to clear the text from the status bar when the mouse pointer is moved off the hypertext link. The text is cleared as indicated by the apostrophes containing no text or spaces between them that follow the second *window.status* object reference.

4. Check the document against Figure J-9 for errors, make changes as necessary, then save your work

5. Reload newsletter.htm in your browser window, then scroll to the bottom of the page
   Notice that the status bar contains information about the loading status of the current Web page.

QUICK TIP

If your message does not appear correctly, check to be sure you have typed the script exactly as shown in Steps 2 and 3.

6. Move the mouse pointer over the link info@paradisemtn.com, but do not click
   The scripted message appears in the status bar, as shown in Figure J-10.

7. Move the mouse pointer off the link
   The message no longer appears in the status bar.

```
<p>Find out more about Paradise Mountain Family Resort. Contact the our main
office at <a href="mailto:info@paradisemtn.com" title="If you do not have a mail program
installed on the system you are currently using, write down this e-mail address and
contact us later." onMouseOver="window.status='We will reply to your inquiry within 24
hours!'; return true" onMouseOut="window.status=''; return true">
info@paradisemtn.com</a></p>
```

Event handlers

FIGURE J-10: Browser displaying status bar message

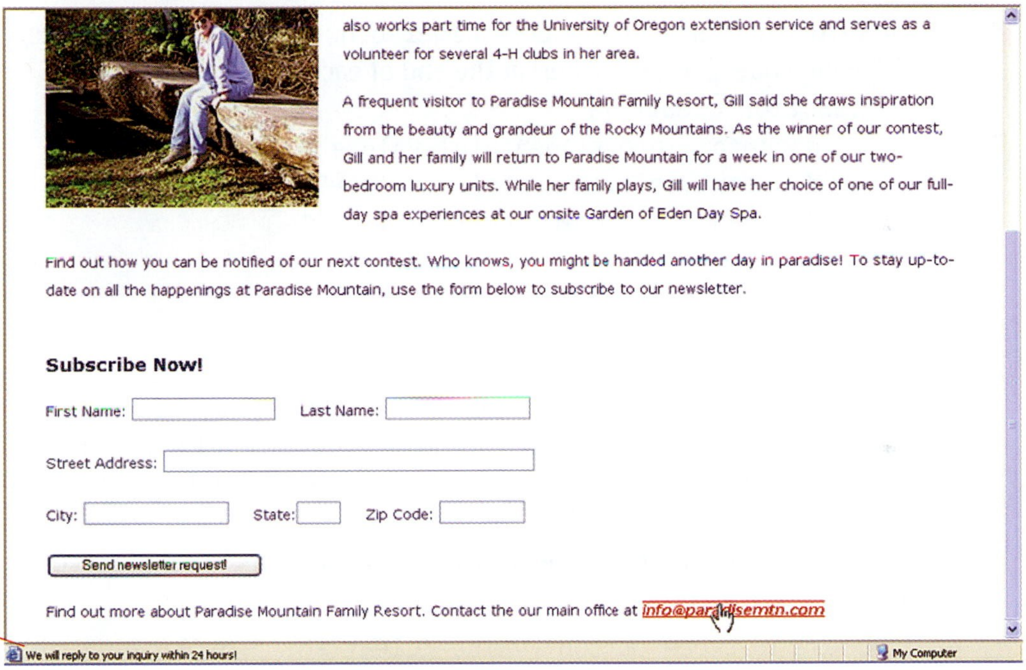

also works part time for the University of Oregon extension service and serves as a volunteer for several 4-H clubs in her area.

A frequent visitor to Paradise Mountain Family Resort, Gill said she draws inspiration from the beauty and grandeur of the Rocky Mountains. As the winner of our contest, Gill and her family will return to Paradise Mountain for a week in one of our two-bedroom luxury units. While her family plays, Gill will have her choice of one of our full-day spa experiences at our onsite Garden of Eden Day Spa.

Find out how you can be notified of our next contest. Who knows, you might be handed another day in paradise! To stay up-to-date on all the happenings at Paradise Mountain, use the form below to subscribe to our newsletter.

Subscribe Now!

First Name: [   ]   Last Name: [   ]

Street Address: [   ]

City: [   ]   State: [   ]   Zip Code: [   ]

[Send newsletter request!]

Find out more about Paradise Mountain Family Resort. Contact the our main office at *info@paradisemtn.com*

Status bar message

We will reply to your inquiry within 24 hours!   My Computer

TABLE J-2: JavaScript event handlers

event handler	triggering action	event handler	triggering action
onAbort	Page loading halted	onLoad	Page or image opens
onBlur	Object not current or highlighted	onMouseOut	Mouse pointer not over link
onChange	Object value changed	onMouseOver	Mouse pointer over link
onClick	Hyperlink or button clicked	onSelect	Text selected
onError	Error executing script	onSubmit	Form submitted
onFocus	Object current or highlighted	onUnload	Different page opened

HTML

Creating a Function

As your scripts become more complex, you can organize named sets of script code in units called functions. A **function** is a named set of instructions that performs a specific task, such as validating form elements or inserting a variable. When you group the lines of your scripts into functions, the code is logically broken down into functional units, which makes it easier to understand and to debug them. You usually define functions in a page's head section, which allows you to quickly find and work with a page's code. It also makes the functions available to all page elements. Additionally, because each function has a name, you can easily refer to it in several different parts of a Web page. This means you do not need to duplicate code each time you want your page to repeat a procedure. ▦▦▦ You want to add a button to the Web page to clear the user's input in the form. You write a function to perform this task.

STEPS

1. **Click the text editor program button to return to your page code, then locate the script you previously typed in the head section**

QUICK TIP
Null is not the same thing as zero.

2. **Click after `<!-- HIDE code from older browsers`, press [Enter] twice, then type the following code, pressing [Enter] at the end of each line:**

```
function clearUp() {
    document.info.elements[0].value=""
    document.info.elements[1].value=""
    document.info.elements[2].value=""
    document.info.elements[3].value=""
    document.info.elements[4].value=""
    document.info.elements[5].value=""
}
```

The code above defines a function that assigns the value **null**, or nothing, to each of the six text fields on the page. This null value is defined with the paired quotation marks that follow each equal sign and that contain nothing between them. Figure J-11 shows the completed function, including the opening and closing braces. The code for a function is always demarcated with braces {}.

3. **Scroll to the end of the document, select the comment `<!-- Insert Clear button here. -->`, then press [Delete]**

4. **Type `<input type="button" value="Clear Form" onClick = "clearUp();">`**
   The button tag includes an event handler to trigger, or **call**, the function *clearUp()* when a user clicks the button. Figure J-12 shows the completed button tag in the document.

5. **Check the document for errors, make changes as necessary, then save your work**

6. **Reload newsletter.htm in your Web browser, fill in the six input fields, then click the Clear Form button**
   The browser clears each of the text input fields. See Figure J-13.

FIGURE J-11: clearUp() function code

```
<script type="text/javascript" language="JavaScript" >
<!-- HIDE code from older browsers

        function clearUp() {
                document.info.elements[0].value=""
                document.info.elements[1].value=""
                document.info.elements[2].value=""
                document.info.elements[3].value=""
                document.info.elements[4].value=""
                document.info.elements[5].value=""
}


function submitted() {
        alert("Information submitted!")
}

//-->
</script>
```

FIGURE J-12: Document code containing clearUp() function reference

```
<form name="info">
First Name: <input type="text" size="20" name="firstname" />    
Last Name: <input type="text" size="20" name="lastname" /><br /><br />
Street Address: <input type="text" size="58" name="address" /><br /><br />
City: <input type="text" size="20" name="city" />    
State:<input type="text" size="3" name="state" />    
Zip Code: <input type="text" size="10" name="zipcode" />
<br /><br />
<input type="button" value="Send newsletter request!" onClick="submitted()" />
<input type="button" value="Clear Form" onClick = "clearUp();">

</form>
```

clearUp()
function
reference

FIGURE J-13: Page with Clear Form button

Guest Charlie Gill was the winner of our *Another Day in Paradise* contest. Gill, who lives in Astoria, Oregon, is a self-employed graphic artist/Web design professional. She also works part time for the University of Oregon extension service and serves as a volunteer for several 4-H clubs in her area.

A frequent visitor to Paradise Mountain Family Resort, Gill said she draws inspiration from the beauty and grandeur of the Rocky Mountains. As the winner of our contest, Gill and her family will return to Paradise Mountain for a week in one of our two-bedroom luxury units. While her family plays, Gill will have her choice of one of our full-day spa experiences at our onsite Garden of Eden Day Spa.

Find out how you can be notified of our next contest. Who knows, you might be handed another day in paradise! To stay up-to-date on all the happenings at Paradise Mountain, use the form below to subscribe to our newsletter.

Subscribe Now!

First Name: [   ]   Last Name: [   ]

Street Address: [   ]

City: [   ]   State: [   ]   Zip Code: [   ]

[Send newsletter request!]   [Clear Form]

Button clears entered
data from form

Assigning a Variable

In scripting, you often instruct your script to utilize specified bits of information known as **values**. For example, the text "We will reply to your inquiry within 24 hours!", which you used earlier in conjunction with an event handler, is a value. Values can also include numeric quantities that scripts can manipulate, as well as user input from form fields. When values are composed of many characters, such as the message text above, or when they change in different situations, such as when the size of the browser window changes, it can be cumbersome to enter them several times in your script. You can make this process easier and more efficient by assigning the value to a **variable**, which serves as a nickname for the object value. When you assign a value to a variable, you enter or look up the value only one time and then you use the variable to refer to the value. Using variables saves you time when writing scripts. Variables provide added flexibility by allowing you to modify the value in only one place and have the modifications reflected instantly throughout the document as indicated by the variable. You want to personalize the site newsletter page by displaying the user's name, so you define a variable that represents the user's name, and use that variable in the scripts.

STEPS

1. **Click the text editor program button to return to your newsletter.htm code, click after `<!-- HIDE code from older browsers`, then press [Enter] twice**

TROUBLE

Pressing [Enter] before the end of the script can cause a scripting error.

2. **Type the following code, pressing [Enter] only after typing the closing parenthesis:**
   ```
   var name=prompt("For personal service, please type your first name and click OK.","")
   ```
   This line of script creates a dialog box that prompts the user to enter his or her first name and assigns the user's input to a variable named *name*. Figure J-14 shows the document source with this line of code inserted. The command *var* tells JavaScript that you are specifying a variable. The word following *var*, in this case, *name*, is the name of the variable you are creating. The value of the new variable follows the name after an equal sign. In this case, the value is the result of user input in a dialog box created by the *prompt* method.

3. **Scroll down to the page's body section, locate and click just after `<h2>News from the Mountain</h2>`, press [Enter] twice, then beginning with the opening script tag, type the code from Figure J-15, exactly as shown**
   The script uses the *write* method of the *document* object to write a line of text near the top of the page. You used the variable *name* to insert the user's name into the page heading. Notice that the code includes level-two heading tags in quotation marks as part of the text string. The tags written into the page code format the content as a level-two heading and apply the formatting specified in the style sheet that is linked to the document.

4. **Scroll down to the beginning of the form section, select the level-three heading, `<h3>Subscribe Now!</h3>`, then press [Delete]**

5. **Type the code shown in Figure J-16, making sure *not* to press [Enter] in the *document.write* line**
   The script places the user's name at a second location in the Web page.

6. **Check the document for errors, make changes as necessary, then save your work**

7. **Click the browser program button to display your newsletter.htm file in the browser, then reload the page**

8. **Type your first name in the prompt dialog box, then click OK**
   The Paradise Mountain home page is now personalized. The name you entered in the prompt dialog box appears in the browser window as shown in Figure J-17.

FIGURE J-14: Script creating a variable

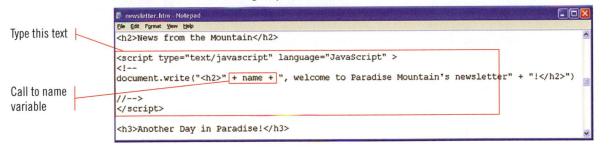

Variable inserted in script

```
<link href="css/paradise_style.css" rel="stylesheet" type="text/css" />

<script type="text/javascript" language="JavaScript" >
<!-- HIDE code from older browsers

var name=prompt("For personal service, please type your first name and
click OK.","")

        function clearUp() {
                document.info.elements[0].value=""
                document.info.elements[1].value=""
```

FIGURE J-15: Level-two heading script with variable

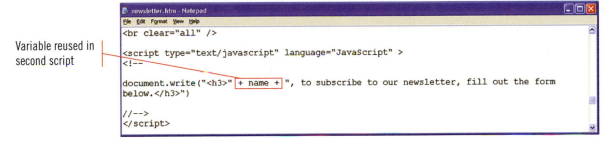

Type this text

Call to name variable

```
newsletter.htm - Notepad
File Edit Format View Help
<h2>News from the Mountain</h2>

<script type="text/javascript" language="JavaScript" >
<!--
document.write("<h2>" + name + ", welcome to Paradise Mountain's newsletter" + "!</h2>")

//-->
</script>

<h3>Another Day in Paradise!</h3>
```

FIGURE J-16: Script reusing a variable

Variable reused in second script

```
newsletter.htm - Notepad
File Edit Format View Help
<br clear="all" />

<script type="text/javascript" language="JavaScript" >
<!--
document.write("<h3>" + name + ", to subscribe to our newsletter, fill out the form
below.</h3>")

//-->
</script>
```

FIGURE J-17: Page with displayed variable information

Page content generated from script

News from the Mountain

Juanita, welcome to Paradise Mountain's newsletter!

Another Day in Paradise!

Guest Charlcie Gill was the winner of our *Another Day in Paradise* contest. Gill, who lives in Astoria, Oregon, is a self-employed graphic artist/Web design professional. She also works part time for the University of Oregon extension service and serves as a volunteer for several 4-H clubs in her area.

A frequent visitor to Paradise Mountain Family Resort, Gill said she draws inspiration from the beauty and grandeur of the Rocky Mountains. As the winner of our contest, Gill and her family will return to Paradise Mountain for a week in one of our two-bedroom luxury units. While her family plays, Gill will have her choice of one of our full-day spa experiences at our onsite Garden of Eden Day Spa.

Find out how you can be notified of our next contest. Who knows, you might be handed another day in paradise! To stay up-to-date on all the happenings at Paradise Mountain, use the form below to subscribe to our newsletter.

Juanita, to subscribe to our newsletter, fill out the form below.

First Name: Juanita   Last Name: Hernandez

Clues to Use

Manipulating variables

In addition to using scripts that display text based on variable values your users enter, your scripts can process values using arithmetic operators, which allow you to manipulate variables mathematically to create new values. For example, you can create a script that reads through your Web page code and counts objects of a specific type, adding 1 to a variable value each time it encounters that object tag. You can also write scripts that use mathematical equations to add, subtract, or multiply values that a user enters.

Creating a Conditional

Sometimes, you want a script to be able to create different results depending on different user actions or on the value of a certain browser attribute. You can set up this situation by creating a **conditional** in your script. A conditional allows your script to choose one of two paths, depending on a condition that you specify. For example, you might want a graphic to be displayed at a smaller size if a user's window is not maximized to keep the graphic fully in view. You could use a conditional to check the dimensions of the user's browser window and then set the graphic dimensions to one of two preset choices. Conditionals allow you to create flexible, interactive scripts with output that can change in different situations. You want to make sure that when visitors submit requests for brochure information, they do not forget to include the zip code. You want your Web page to verify that the user has completed the Zip Code form field before it submits the data to the server. Using a conditional, your page can prompt the user to complete the field if it is left blank.

STEPS

1. **Click the text editor program button to return to your page code, click before //--> in the head section script code, then type the following code, pressing [Enter] at the end of each line:**

```
function verify() {
    if (document.info.elements[5].value == "") {
    alert ("Please complete the Zip Code field.")
    }
    else {
        submitted()
    }
}
```

Figure J-18 shows the code containing the *verify* function. The *if* statement code checks if the value of the Zip Code field is null (contains no information), indicating that the user has left it blank. When the *if* statement returns a value of *true*, the function executes the code that immediately follows it. Here, the *true* result triggers the *alert* command to create a dialog box prompting the user to complete each field. When the *if* statement returns a value of *false*, the function executes the code following the command *else*. In your script, the *else* command runs a function called *submitted()* that informs the user that the information has been submitted.

2. **Scroll to the bottom of the form section, then locate the input button with the *Send newsletter request!* value**

3. **Select the value *submitted()*, after the *onClick* event in the tag, press [Delete], then type verify()**

Your code now reads `onClick="verify()"`.

4. **Check the scripts you added for errors, make changes as necessary, then update the "Page modified by" paragraph with your name and the current date**

5. **Save your work, click the browser program button, then reload newsletter.htm in your Web browser**

6. **Enter your name, scroll down to the form, enter text in all fields except the Zip Code field, then click the Send newsletter request! button**

The script runs and displays the dialog box shown in Figure J-19.

7. **Click the OK button, then fill in each of the fields with sample information and click the Send newsletter request! button**

The script you added verifies that the Zip Code field contains information and then allows the form submit function to execute.

FIGURE J-18: Web document with conditional script

```
<script type="text/javascript" language="JavaScript" >
<!-- HIDE code from older browsers

var name=prompt("For personal service, please type your first name and click OK.","")

        function clearUp() {
                document.info.elements[0].value=""
                document.info.elements[1].value=""
                document.info.elements[2].value=""
                document.info.elements[3].value=""
                document.info.elements[4].value=""
                document.info.elements[5].value=""
}


function submitted() {
        alert("Information submitted!")
}

function verify() {
        if (document.info.elements[5].value == "") {
        alert ("Please complete the Zip Code field.")
        }
        else {
                submitted()
        }
}

//-->
</script>
```

Conditional terms · Condition · false result · true result

FIGURE J-19: Browser showing script-generated alert dialog box

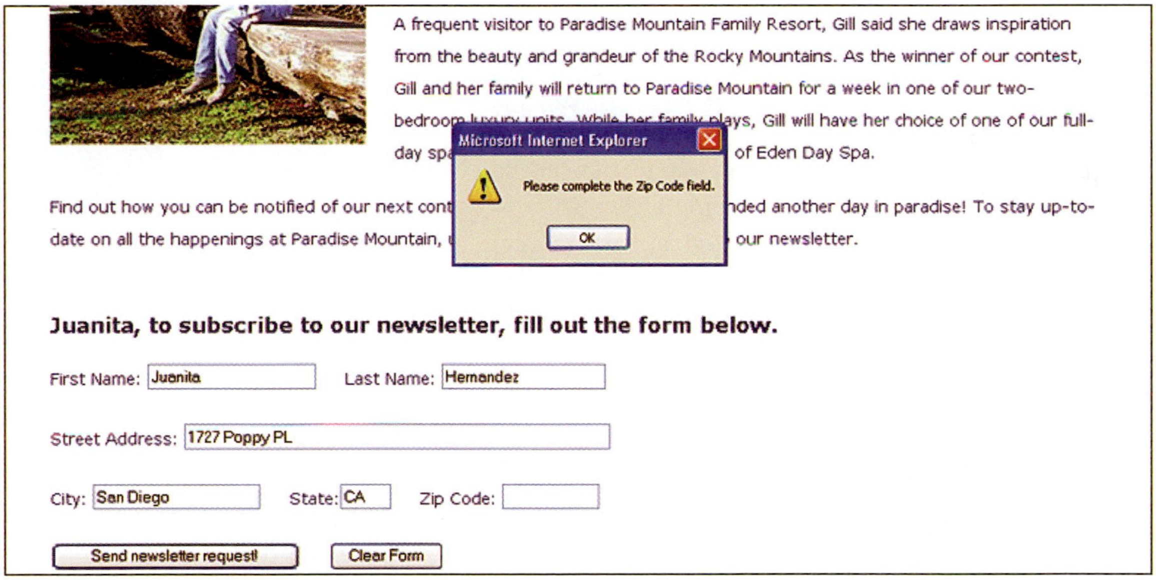

A frequent visitor to Paradise Mountain Family Resort, Gill said she draws inspiration from the beauty and grandeur of the Rocky Mountains. As the winner of our contest, Gill and her family will return to Paradise Mountain for a week in one of our two-bedroom luxury units. While her family plays, Gill will have her choice of one of our full-day spa ... of Eden Day Spa.

Find out how you can be notified of our next cont ... nded another day in paradise! To stay up-to-date on all the happenings at Paradise Mountain, ... our newsletter.

Microsoft Internet Explorer
Please complete the Zip Code field.
OK

Juanita, to subscribe to our newsletter, fill out the form below.

First Name: Juanita   Last Name: Hernandez

Street Address: 1727 Poppy PL

City: San Diego   State: CA   Zip Code:

Send newsletter request!   Clear Form

Clues to Use

Testing multiple conditions

In addition to using a conditional to test a single condition, you can test multiple conditions using logical comparison operators. JavaScript recognizes three logical comparison operators: && ("and"), || ("or"), and ! ("not"). A conditional using the && operator between two or more conditions returns *true* only if all conditions are true. Linking multiple conditions with the || operator, however, returns *true* if any one of the conditions is true. The ! operator returns *true* if its associated condition is not *true*.

Practice

▼ CONCEPTS REVIEW

Name the function of each section of code indicated in Figure J-20.

```
<script type="text/javascript" language="JavaScript">                        ─5
<!-- Hide from Browsers that don't support JavaScript                      ─4


function verify() {
        if (document.info.elements[12].value == "") {
                alert("Please enter the expiration date")               ─3
        } else {
                submitted()
        }
}

var status=prompt("Please let us know if you are a new or returning customer, and click OK","")    ─1

document.write("<h2> As a " + status +  " customer, you will enjoy our latest spa products.</h2>" )

//End of JavaScript hiding -->

</script>    ─2
```

Match each statement with the term it best describes.

6. **Dot syntax**
7. **Event handler**
8. **Debugging**
9. **Method**
10. **Scriptlet**

   a. A JavaScript response to a user's actions
   b. Correcting script errors
   c. A script located in an external file
   d. A hierarchical method of referencing objects in JavaScript
   e. An action carried out by an object

Select the best answer from the list of choices.

11. **Which HTML tag set marks the beginning and end of a script?**
    a. <js>...</js>
    b. <javascript>...</javascript>
    c. <script>...</script>
    d. <language>...</language>

12. **Which of the following scripting languages can be used in an HTML document? Choose all that are correct.**
    a. JScript
    b. JavaScript
    c. ActionScript
    d. VBScript

13. **Which of the following mistakes might result in a JavaScript error? (Choose all that apply.)**
    a. Substituting an uppercase for a lowercase letter
    b. Inserting extra spaces
    c. Omitting a closing brace
    d. Omitting the comment that hides JavaScript from nonsupporting browsers

14. **Which of the following references the second element in a form called** `info`**?**
    a. `info[2]`
    b. `document.info.elements[1]`
    c. `document.info.elements[2]`
    d. `info.elements[2]`

15. **What tag instructs nonsupporting browsers to ignore JavaScript code?**
    a. `<!--    -->`
    b. `<* --    --*>`
    c. `<//    //>`
    d. `</*    /*>`

16. **Which comparison operator returns true only if the values before and after it are both** `true`**?**
    a. `&&`
    b. `||`
    c. `!`
    d. `==`

17. **A set of code that performs a specific task is called a(n):**
    a. Object
    b. Function
    c. Hierarchy
    d. Variable

18. **Which of the following serves as a nickname for an object's value in a script?**
    a. `&&`
    b. Scriptlet
    c. Variable
    d. Function

▼ SKILLS REVIEW

1. **Create a script.**
    a. In your text editor, open the file **htm_J-2.txt** from the drive and folder where your Data Files are stored, then save it as **spascript.htm** to the paradise/spa directory where you save your site files.
    b. Locate the comment in the file indicating where the opening script tags should be placed, and add the opening tag for JavaScript.
    c. Add beginning and ending comments to hide JavaScript code from nonsupporting browsers. Use the file comments to place them in the proper locations.
    d. Add the closing JavaScript tag. Use the file comment to place it in the correct location.
    e. Save your file.

HTML

2. Use JavaScript event handlers

a. Locate the text marking the placement of an event handler at the end of the link at the bottom of the page. Replace the text with an event handler that places a message in the status bar informing users that questions will be answered within 24 hours. Use Figure J-21 as a guide.

b. Use Figure J-21 as a guide to add the appropriate event handler to clear the status bar when a user moves the mouse pointer out of the link area.

c. Review your script for errors. Add your name and the current date to the "Page modified by" paragraph at the bottom of the page, then save your file.

d. Open the **spascript.htm** file in your browser and check your work by moving the mouse pointer over and away from the link at the bottom of the page.

e. Debug your script as necessary, then save your file.

FIGURE J-21

```
<p>For questions or comments about this site, contact:
<br />
<a href="mailto:webmaster@paradisemtn.com" onMouseOver="window.status='Questions will be answered
within 24 hours';return true" onMouseOut="window.status='';return
true">webmaster@paradisemtn.com</a> </p>
```

3. Create a function.

a. Locate the comment in the file indicating where the submitted function is to be placed.

b. Use Figure J-22 as a guide to add a function that informs users that their information has been submitted when they click the Order button.

c. Review your script for errors, then save your file.

d. Open the **spascript.htm** file in your browser and check your work by entering data in the form and clicking the Order button.

e. Debug your script as necessary, then save your file.

FIGURE J-22

```
function submitted() {
        alert("Information submitted!")
}
```

4. Assign a variable.

a. Locate the comment in the file indicating where the variable definition and user message is to be placed. Use Figure J-23 as a guide to define a variable named *status* that keeps track of whether a user is a new or returning customer.

b. Use Figure J-23 as a guide to write a message to customers indicating they will enjoy the spa products.

c. Review your script for errors, then save your file.

d. Open the **spascript.htm** file in your browser and check your work by entering "new" or "returning" in response to the prompt and clicking the OK button.

e. Debug your script as necessary, then save your file.

FIGURE J-23

```
var status=prompt("Please let us know if you are a new or returning customer, and click OK","")

document.write("<h2> As a " + status +  " customer, you will enjoy our latest spa products.</h2>" )
```

▼ SKILLS REVIEW (CONTINUED)

5. Create a conditional.

   a. Locate the comment in the file indicating where the *verify* function is to be placed.

   b. Use Figure J-24 as a guide to add a function that verifies that a date has been entered into the credit card expiration date field before the form data is submitted.

   c. Locate the input tag near the bottom of the form that contains the button named Submit. Change the function that is referenced from *submitted* to *verify*. (*Hint*: The tag should end with `onClick="verify()"`)

   d. Review your script for errors, then save your file.

   e. Reload the **spascript.htm** file in your browser and check your work by submitting an order with a blank expiration date.

   f. Debug your script as necessary, then save your file.

FIGURE J-24

```
function verify() {
        if (document.info.elements[12].value == "") {
                alert("Please enter the expiration date")
        }       else {
                submitted()
        }
}
```

▼ INDEPENDENT CHALLENGE 1

As you continue developing the Web site for your resort rental business, Star Vacations, you decide to add JavaScript to your Australia survey form. You decide to add a function that informs your users that their information has been submitted when they click the Submit button.

   a. In your text editor, open the file **htm_J-3.txt** from the drive and folder where your Data Files are stored, then save it as **survey.htm** to the vacations folder where you save your site files. If you are asked whether you want to replace the file, click Yes.

   b. Locate the JavaScript in the head section of the file. Correct the error in the <script> tag.

   c. Use the guidelines listed in the unit to identify and correct the additional JavaScript errors in the head section.

   d. Preview and edit the page until the Information submitted message is displayed when the Submit button is clicked.

   e. Add a comment line to the script in the head section with your name, then save and print the file from your text editor.

   f. Transfer your **survey.htm** page to your remote directory.

Advanced Challenge Exercises

   ■ Use the search engine of your choice to research JavaScript debuggers for three Web browsers.

   ■ Write one or two paragraphs comparing the features of the products.

   ■ Add your name and today's date to the top of your paper, then print the document.

▼ INDEPENDENT CHALLENGE 2

Metro Water publishes monthly newsletters on a variety of topics related to water conservation. You want to use JavaScript in the subscription form to display information about the newsletters in the status bar when a user moves the mouse pointer over the selections. You also want to notify users that their information has been submitted when they click the Submit button.

a. In your text editor, open the **htm_J-4.txt** file from the drive and folder where your Data Files are stored, then save it as **newsletter.htm** in the water folder where you save your site files. If you are asked whether you want to replace the file, click Yes.

b. Add opening and closing JavaScript tags to the head section of the file.

c. Add comment lines to hide JavaScript code from nonsupporting browsers.

d. Add a function named *submitted* that displays the message "Information submitted!" when a user clicks the Submit button.

e. Locate the <input /> tag for the button named Submit at the bottom of the form. Add an *onClick* event handler that calls the submitted function you created in the previous step.

f. Save your file, then open your **newsletter.htm** file in your browser and submit a form to check your work. Debug your script as necessary.

g. Add an event handler that displays the message "Each newsletter will arrive in a separate e-mail" in the status bar when a user moves the mouse pointer over the newsletter selections. (*Hint*: Add the event handler to the <p> tag that appears before the check boxes in the form.)

h. Add an event handler to remove the message when a user moves the mouse pointer away from the newsletter choices.

i. Save your file, then refresh your newsletter.htm file in your browser and move the mouse pointer over the newsletter selections to check your work. Debug your script as necessary.

j. Add a comment line with your name in the head section, then save and print the file from your text editor.

k. Transfer your **newsletter.htm** page to your remote directory.

Advanced Challenge Exercises

■ In your text editor, assign the name of *info* to your form.

■ Under the E-mail Address field on your form, add an additional field for users to reenter their e-mail addresses.

■ Add a JavaScript function named *verify* that compares the two e-mail addresses, displays the message "Please reenter your email address" if they are different, and calls the *submitted* function if they are the same. Be sure to clear both e-mail fields if they are not the same. (*Hint*: You need to compare document.info.elements[0].value with document.info.elements[1].value.) Change the function that is called when the Submit button is clicked from *submitted* to *verify*.

■ Save your file and refresh the form in the browser. Check your work by entering two different e-mail addresses and clicking the Submit button.

■ Transfer your **newsletter.htm** page to your remote directory.

▼ INDEPENDENT CHALLENGE 3

JavaScript can be used to validate forms and provide user feedback. You want to add JavaScript to your Web site, but first you need to research how you can make the scripted pages accessible for all users.

Go to the Student Online Companion for this book, and go to the Unit J link to the W3C Web Accessibility page and review the information for JavaScript. Write one or two paragraphs answering the following questions about forms:

How is the noscript element used to increase accessibility when JavaScript is used on a Web page?

- **a.** Research methods for increasing accessibility when adding JavaScript to a Web page.
- **b.** How can event handlers be used to maximize accessibility?
- **c.** Add your name and today's date to the top of your paper, then print the document.

▼ INDEPENDENT CHALLENGE 4

Now that you've used JavaScript to validate forms, you are ready to add these features to the forms on your Web site.

- **a.** Determine how JavaScript can be used on the forms in your Web site to validate input data.
- **b.** Determine which functions would be useful on your forms.
- **c.** Create the functions for your forms using your text editor.
- **d.** Add the necessary event handlers to call your functions.
- **e.** Transfer your edited forms to the remote location.

▼ VISUAL WORKSHOP

You want to add JavaScript to the Bits and PCs user group form to make sure users enter their e-mail addresses when completing the form. In your text editor, open the **htm_J-5.txt** file from the drive and folder where your Data Files are stored, then save it as **usergroups.htm** in the bitspcs folder where you save your site files. If you are asked whether you want to replace the file, click Yes. Add two JavaScript functions, submitted and verify, to the head section. The submitted function should display the message "Information Submitted!" The verify function should check the contents of the e-mail form field for data and display the error message shown in Figure J-25 if it is empty, or call the submitted function if it contains data. Be sure to add an event handler to call the verify function. Add your name as a comment in the head section of the file, save your work, then print the file from your text editor. Transfer the **usergroups.htm** page to your remote directory.

FIGURE J-25

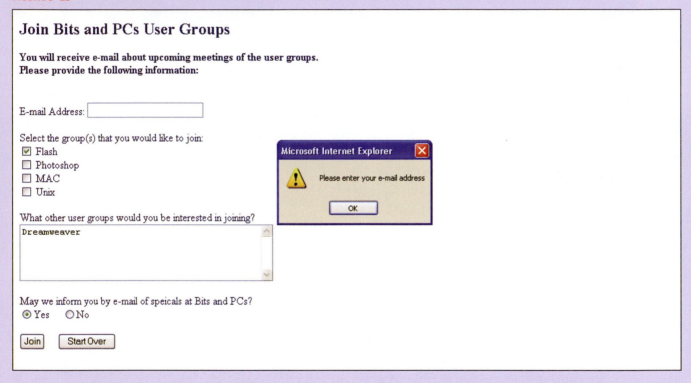

Working with Dynamic HTML (DHTML)

OBJECTIVES

Define Dynamic HTML
Tour DHTML pages
Understand the DHTML Document Object Model
Plan DHTML pages
Research code architecture
Show and hide elements
Change font size dynamically
Change font color dynamically
Keep up with DHTML changes

You have learned how to create well-structured Web pages that use effective style combinations and allow basic user input. By combining Web page design elements and scripting, collectively known as Dynamic HTML (or DHTML), you can increase the interactivity in your pages. DHTML enlivens your Web pages as text and graphics change color, grow, shrink, and move on and off the page in response to user actions.  You are studying Dynamic HTML and want to create a set of pages to help your design team at Paradise Mountain Family Resort better understand this technology and how it works.

Defining Dynamic HTML

During the early 1990s, Web pages were simple documents that users downloaded and viewed on their computers. The interactivity of each Web page was limited to hyperlinks, which accessed other Web pages, opened new e-mail messages, or ran scripts on the server. Web pages with this type of limited interactivity use what is known as **static HTML**. Today, however, many Web pages respond to and even interact with the user by changing appearance based on user actions. Such pages use **Dynamic HTML (DHTML)**, which allows quick responses to user actions without needing to access the server. DHTML is a combination of HTML, style sheets, and scripts that allow documents to be animated or to change based on user interaction.  You are preparing to update the Paradise Mountain Web site, and decide to research DHTML to determine how you can use it to improve the site. Through your research, you learned about several broad categories of DHTML design.

Some DHTML design categories include:

- ### Dynamic style

  When you create a page using standard HTML coding, you specify a style for each text element. Except for hyperlinks that change color depending on their status, these styles remain the same regardless of user actions. However, when you create a page using DHTML, you can incorporate styles—including font size, typeface, and color—that change in response to user actions, such as pointing to a heading. This feature, known as **dynamic style**, allows your pages to emphasize an area only when a user shows interest in it, meaning you can avoid cluttering the page with large text or bright colors.

- ### Dynamic content

  A DHTML Web page can display content based on a user's activities without taking the time to request, download, and display a new Web page. DHTML utilities can hide or display blocks of text or other elements in the current page. Called **dynamic content**, this aspect of DHTML allows you to create simple, well-organized, and visually appealing pages that can instantly display extra information depending upon the user's interests.

- ### Data awareness

  Standard HTML tools allow your Web pages to download chunks of information, such as database contents, from a Web server as a user requests them. With DHTML, this process is instantaneous for the user; for example, a DHTML Web page could be designed to download a complete database, but then display only the information the user wants to view. A Web page equipped to work with data in this way is said to be **data aware**, which means the user can work with information from a Web server without adding to Internet traffic by repeatedly requesting additional pieces of information. Also, data awareness can allow the user to manipulate and change the information directly in the browser window.

- ### Positioning

  As with other formatting options, static HTML leaves many of the choices regarding the positioning of elements in a Web page to the browser's discretion. In addition to displaying pages unpredictably depending on the browser, HTML limits Web page design and does not allow more flexible layouts, such as those in magazines. DHTML provides more control by allowing Web page designers to use division layers to precisely position all page elements. Using this positioning feature, which is unavailable in standard HTML, designers can use window coordinates to position elements on the page. Through what is called "layer-based positioning," you can place an element in relation to other page objects or place it absolutely using window coordinates. You can even position some elements to overlap or occupy the same space as others. The Web page in Figure K-1, which is from an online tutorial on DHTML, uses DHTML to position text in combinations not possible with static HTML.

FIGURE K-1: Web page formatted with DHTML positioning and text effects

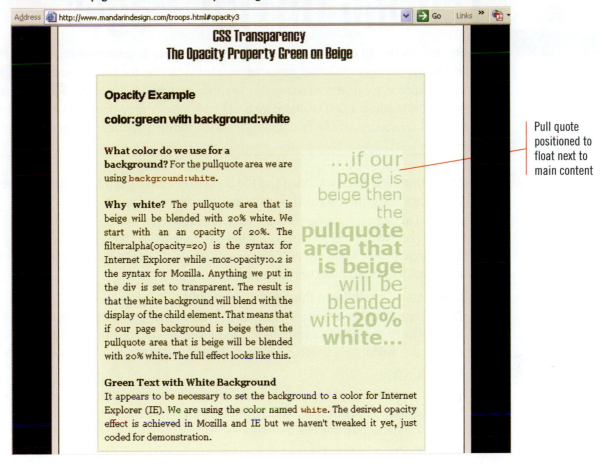

Pull quote positioned to float next to main content

HTML

Touring DHTML Pages

Viewing and interacting with DHTML Web pages is the best way to get acquainted with DHTML. Examining the design and behavior of DHTML pages can also help you plan the features you want to include in your own pages, such as element positioning, dynamic style, and dynamic content. A friend at a neighboring farm is building a DHTML-based Web site and invites you to download his prototype pages. You want to preview them as you begin collecting ideas for updating the Paradise Mountain Web site.

STEPS

1. **Start your Web browser, open the file berryHome.htm from the location where you store your Data Files, then scroll down the page to view its layout**

   As shown in Figure K-2, the page contains several groups of text positioned on the page; each group uses the element positioning features of DHTML so they each consistently appear in the same place on the page. The designer created the sidebar on the right using DHTML style specifications to position the text, specify its width, and set a background color for the text block.

2. **If necessary, scroll down the page, then point to Blue Ray**

   The text color changes from black to purple and the size increases, demonstrating the effects of dynamic style. Dynamic style provides visual cues to users, such as indicating that they can click a link to display related information, and provides more visual interest than the standard blue underline indicating a link.

3. **Click Blue Ray**

   Without reloading the page, a paragraph of detailed information appears below the heading, as shown in Figure K-3. This is an example of dynamic content because your actions changed the page content. Dynamic content lets you display only information the user requests, which streamlines their online experience.

4. **Watch the text in the status bar**

   A message continuously scrolls across the status bar. This feature, created by a script and activated by the page *onLoad* event, is another example of dynamic content.

5. **Below the "Learn more about Jim's!" heading, point to an image or a corresponding text link**

   As the pointer moves over the linked text or image, the image changes from monochromatic to full color. When you move the pointer away from the link, the image returns to its original appearance. Using dynamic content in this way provides navigation cues to the Web page user. These cues are especially useful when you use images as navigation devices. Rather than simply changing a graphic's display properties, the position of the pointer over the link triggers a script that changes the source of the image in the image tag. The pointer movement signals that the image should toggle between two different source files.

6. **Click the Farm Products link to open the file berryTypes.htm, then click the table headings to sort the table data**

   This page contains a data table, shown in Figure K-4, that summarizes information about blueberry bushes. Unlike standard HTML tables, however, this table is generated from an external file as the Web page opens. Linking a Web page to an external data file is known as **data binding**. If you add or change records in the external file, they appear in the Web page the next time it opens—you do not have to change the Web page source code. Data binding is related to **data awareness**, which allows a Web page to load all the records from a database but display only some of them. A user can then access a record instantly without needing to download more information to the browser. You will learn more about data binding in Units L and M.

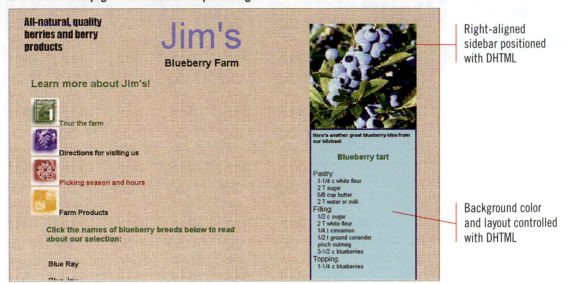

Right-aligned sidebar positioned with DHTML

Background color and layout controlled with DHTML

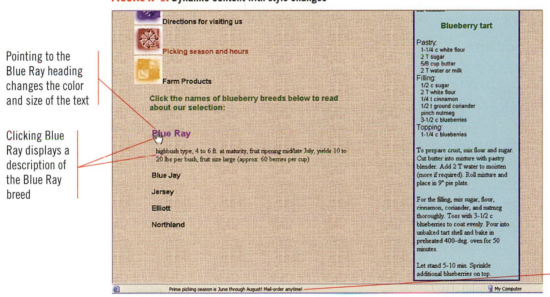

Pointing to the Blue Ray heading changes the color and size of the text

Clicking Blue Ray displays a description of the Blue Ray breed

When this page is open, messages scroll across the status bar

Table bound to an external data source

When you change data in the external source, the same data is updated the next time the Web page opens

Click a column heading to sort the data

Bush	Type	Height	Fruit maturity	Yield per bush	Berry size	Berries per cup
Blue Ray	high	4-6 ft.	mid/late July	10-20 lb	large	60
Blue Jay	high	5-7 ft.	late July	7-10 lb	small/ medium	110
Jersey	high	5-7 ft.	late July	7-10 lb.	small/ medium	110
Elliott	high	5-7 ft.	late Aug./early Sept.	10-20 lb	small/ medium	75
Northland	medium	3-4 ft.	early July	15-20	small	135

HTML

Understanding the DHTML Document Object Model

As you learned in Unit J, developers of early scripting languages created an **object hierarchy** that allows Web page developers to describe and work with the Web page elements in a browser window. This hierarchy, officially called the Document Object Model (DOM), categorizes and groups Web page elements, or objects, into a treelike structure. For example, in the Microsoft DOM, the *window* object is the top-level object, and it contains the *document* object, which contains the objects in the Web page, such as images and links. Netscape Navigator and Internet Explorer have increased the range and versatility of DHTML by including in their browser code their own extended DOM versions, known as DHTML Document Object Models. Although each DOM version references some objects differently, most browsers, including recent versions of Netscape, contain code that recognizes most of the Internet Explorer DHTML DOM. Figure K-5 shows the basic structure of the IE DOM, which makes most browser window elements available to scripts. To take full advantage of DHTML's capabilities on the Paradise Mountain Web site, you review the top level of object classes in the Microsoft DHTML Object Model.

DETAILS

The top level of object classes in the Microsoft DHTML Object Model are:

- **Location**

  The *location* object contains the URL of the current page.

- **Frames**

  The *frames* object contains a separate window object for each frame in the current browser window. When the window is not divided into frames, this object is empty and the entire contents of the document are part of the *document* object. The Microsoft DOM also contains a frames collection within the *document* object to reference its `<iframe>` tag.

- **History**

  The *history* object allows access to the browser's list of previously visited URLs.

- **Navigator**

  The *navigator* object provides information about the browser.

- **Event**

  The *event* object allows interaction with the event currently being processed by the browser, such as mouse movement, clicks, or keystrokes.

- **Screen**

  The *screen* object provides information about the user's screen setup and display properties.

- **Document**

  The *document* object represents the current Web page in the browser window. A *document* object contains many elements, which are listed in Figure K-5. These elements, including links, anchors, and images, help to give each Web page its defining characteristics.

QUICK TIP

You don't need to know the meaning of each element of the *document* object right now. You will learn about some of these elements as you learn more about DHTML.

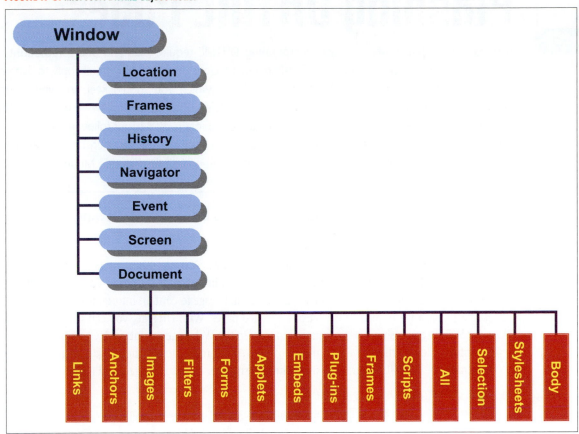

Designing for cross-browser support

Until recently, it was common practice to use a browser-detection script, sometimes called a browser sniffer, to check for a user's browser type and version, and then write a different set of code to generate page content according to the browser type and version. However, browser detection can be difficult to manage. Current browser-detection scripts cannot account for all future browsers and versions. The best approach to coding for cross-browser compatibility is to include a current Document Type Declaration (DTD), which ensures that your design works in browsers that support current standards.

Planning DHTML Pages

Like static Web pages, those pages incorporating DHTML require planning and forethought. Standard HTML design rules, such as careful proofreading and judicious use of headings, still apply to dynamic pages. However, DHTML has its own advantages and pitfalls, which you should keep in mind as you design dynamic pages. In addition to being aware of browser differences, use the following guidelines when working with DHTML.  To ensure that your Paradise Mountain Web pages follow good design principles, you decide to make a list of recommendations based on your DHTML research for designing pages with DHTML. You plan to follow these recommendations as you update the Paradise Mountain Web site.

DETAILS

Recommendations for designing DHTML pages include the following:

- **Organize for dynamic content**

  DHTML allows you to position page elements and show new content in response to user actions. This means that you can fit more content in a dynamic page than in a static HTML page. For example, the hierarchical, or cascading, menu shown in Figure K-6 allows a single page to contain information that would otherwise be formatted as a list of links and a set of associated pages. With DHTML, you can insert cascading menus in your Web pages to simplify navigation and to keep the Web page uncluttered. Cascading menus also organize information so that the user can see how one choice relates to another. Organizing your Web site to take advantage of DHTML features can make the site easier for users to navigate and for you to manage.

- **Use dynamic features purposefully**

  In moderation, Dynamic HTML features can make your pages engaging and easy to use. However, a little goes a long way. Just as in static pages, the best dynamic Web pages are focused and free of distracting elements. The content and message of your Web pages, rather than newly available features, should dictate which dynamic tools you use.

- **Take advantage of design resources**

  Because browser developers are eager to show off their browser's features, they provide links on their corporate Web sites to well-designed pages, including those that support their proprietary features. Reviewing these pages can give you ideas for planning successful dynamic Web pages and introduce you to new features. The W3C Web site (www.w3.org) also provides extensive CSS design resources and tips. However, as you plan your pages, make sure that you do not include proprietary DHTML features for pages that must be accessible to most members of the general public. Figure K-7 shows an effective example of a layer-based menu from one of the online W3C tutorials.

FIGURE K-6: Web page containing a hierarchical DHTML menu

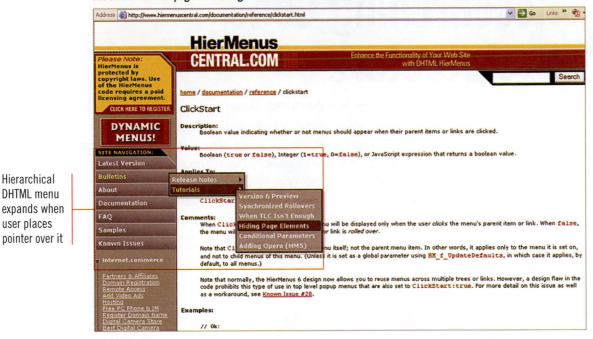

Hierarchical DHTML menu expands when user places pointer over it

FIGURE K-7: Web page using layer-based navigation menu

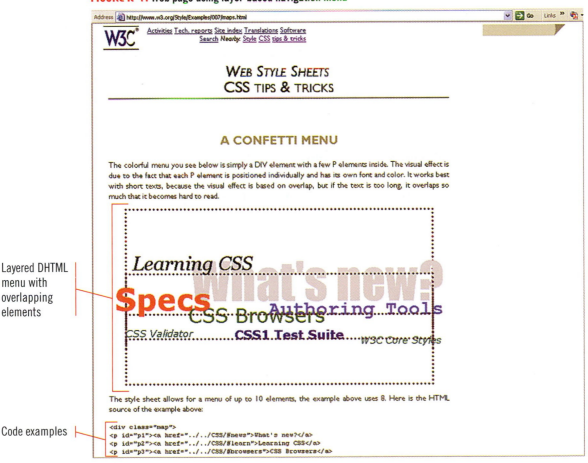

Layered DHTML menu with overlapping elements

Code examples

Researching Code Architecture

After you outline your Web page and identify the DHTML features you want to use, the next step is to write the code that makes these features work. In many cases, it can be difficult to determine how to use scripts and style sheets to create a particular feature. At this point, research on the Web is indispensable to creating a successful DHTML page. For example, you can examine the source code of a Web page that uses a feature appropriate for a page you are designing. You also can find well-documented sample code, code that you are allowed to modify and use for your own purposes, on Web sites.  You want to review successful and attractive DHTML Web pages, so you decide to search for samples on the Web and learn by example. Then you can apply some of the techniques you find to your Web pages for Paradise Mountain.

STEPS

1. **Open a search engine of your choice**

2. **In the Search text box, type Dynamic HTML programming, then click the Find button (or its equivalent)**

   The browser lists links to sites related to DHTML programming.

3. **Review the links you found, then follow one to a site that seems likely to contain tutorials or sample code**

   Articles and sample scripts for DHTML applications might be helpful in creating your own pages. If you cannot find a site with DHTML information and CSS resources, go to the Student Online Companion for this unit.

4. **Scan the site's opening page for links to script libraries or articles about DHTML features, then follow the appropriate links**

QUICK TIP

If necessary, create a folder for scripts in the place where you save your site files.

5. **Locate sample code or a relevant article for an interesting DHTML feature, then download the page or copy the script to a scripts folder**

   A sample online tutorial page with code is shown in Figure K-8.

6. **Save the script or page as DHTML_Download.htm**

7. **As shown in Figure K-9, add comment tags before the script that include your name, a description of the script, and the URL of the site from which you downloaded the page**

   The downloaded file can be a helpful reference when you plan your own DHTML applications.

FIGURE K-8: Web tutorial with downloadable source code for DHTML script

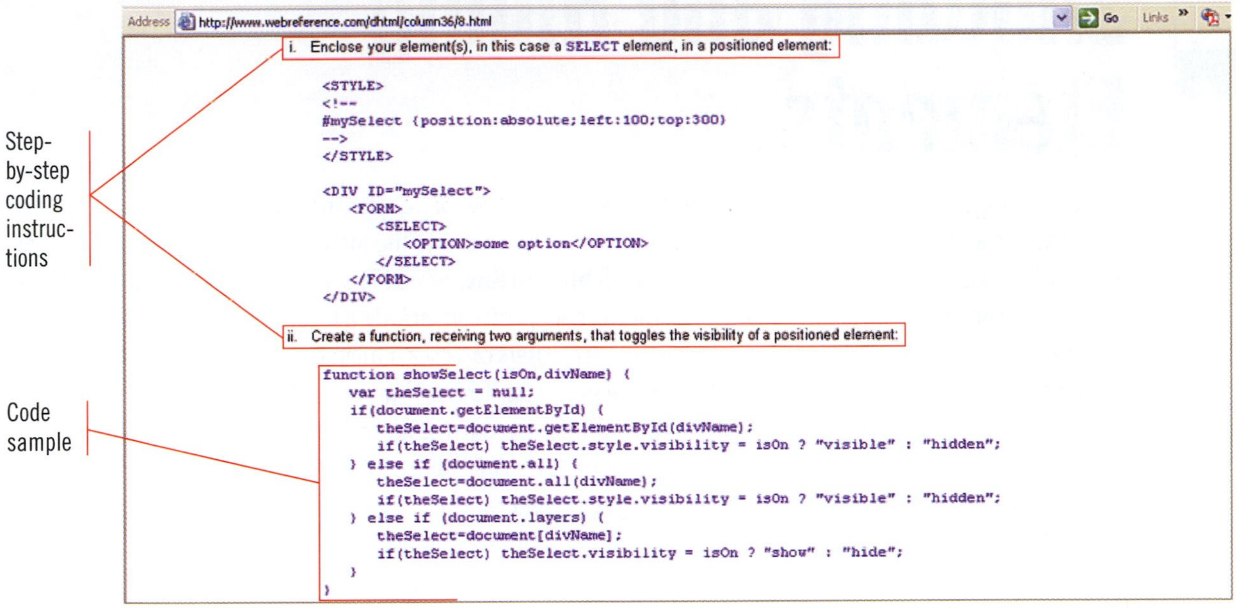

Address http://www.webreference.com/dhtml/column36/8.html   Go   Links »

Step-by-step coding instructions

i. Enclose your element(s), in this case a SELECT element, in a positioned element:

```
<STYLE>
<!--
#mySelect {position:absolute;left:100;top:300}
-->
</STYLE>

<DIV ID="mySelect">
    <FORM>
        <SELECT>
            <OPTION>some option</OPTION>
        </SELECT>
    </FORM>
</DIV>
```

ii. Create a function, receiving two arguments, that toggles the visibility of a positioned element:

Code sample

```
function showSelect(isOn,divName) {
    var theSelect = null;
    if(document.getElementById) {
        theSelect=document.getElementById(divName);
        if(theSelect) theSelect.style.visibility = isOn ? "visible" : "hidden";
    } else if (document.all) {
        theSelect=document.all(divName);
        if(theSelect) theSelect.style.visibility = isOn ? "visible" : "hidden";
    } else if (document.layers) {
        theSelect=document[divName];
        if(theSelect) theSelect.visibility = isOn ? "show" : "hide";
    }
}
```

FIGURE K-9: Downloaded script with student comments

```
<STYLE type="text/css">
<!--
#dv{position:absolute;visibility:hidden;top:0px;left:0px}
-->
</STYLE>
<SCRIPT LANGUAGE="JavaScript" TYPE="text/javascript">
<!--
curPage=8;
//-->
</SCRIPT>
```

Student comments inserted into downloaded script

```
<!-- Isabella Martinez, Nov 11, 2008: This is the script I downloaded from
the DHTML Lab site at:
http://www.webreference.com/dhtml/column36/8.html. The script enables the
designer to show and hide elements based on user interaction. Scroll to the
bottom of the page to actually see the scripted code. The script works with
CSS positioning. The style above sets the visibility to hidden for some
elements. The script below causes the menu choices to show on mouse over.
-->

<SCRIPT LANGUAGE="JavaScript1.2" TYPE="text/javascript">
<!--
function showSelect(isOn,divName) {
    var theSelect = null;
    if(document.getElementById) {
        theSelect=document.getElementById(divName);
        if(theSelect) theSelect.style.visibility = isOn ? "visible" :
"hidden";
    } else if (document.all) {
        theSelect=document.all(divName);
        if(theSelect) theSelect.style.visibility = isOn ? "visible" :
"hidden";
    } else if (document.layers) {
```

Clues to Use

Practicing good code-borrowing etiquette

You can save time and frustration by modifying existing code you download from the Web instead of creating it from scratch. However, to comply with copyright law and be considerate to other designers, you should follow a few simple guidelines. First, be aware that some DHTML code is copyrighted, and you cannot use it without permission from its author, which could involve paying a fee. Some pages and sites, like the one shown in Figure K-8, offer code free for reuse.

In this situation, it is still considered courteous to credit the source of the code in your Web page, usually with the creator's name and the source URL. If you find code you would like to use and are unsure whether you can, it is best to contact the creator for permission. If you don't have permission to use someone else's code, you can still use its basic framework to help you plan the creation of your page and then augment the features with your own coding.

HTML

Showing and Hiding Elements

By working together with embedded scripts, CSS can specify how page elements should be displayed in different situations and in response to user actions. This allows you to create the interactive features that are the hallmark of DHTML. One such feature is the **expandable outline**, which lets you hide and show information based upon user actions. For example, on your home page, you can include a table of contents that is designed as an expandable outline (also called a **collapsible list**). Users can click a main topic to show related subtopics. Then they can click the main topic again to hide the subtopics. To create an expandable outline, you use a combination of style sheets and scripts. You want to use DHTML to create an expandable outline on the DHTML FAQ page you are designing for Paradise Mountain's IT Department that hides the paragraphs containing the answers and displays each answer only when the user clicks its corresponding question. You start with a file to which some content and style information, as well as some scripting, has already been added.

STEPS

1. **Open the file htm_K-1.txt in your text editor from the place where you store your Data Files, then save it as DHTML_FAQ.htm in your paradise directory in the place where you save your site files**

   In addition to content and style information, the file contains a script to hide the answer paragraph.

QUICK TIP

"El" stands for element. Be sure to type "El" or "el" using the letter "l" and not the number "1" or the capital letter I.

2. **Select the code comment /* Add expand function here */, press [Delete], then type the following code, pressing [Enter] at the end of each line:**

```
function expand(el) {
    theEl=eval(el + "answer");
    if (theEl.style.display == "none") {
        theEl.style.display="block";
        theEl.expanded=true;
    }
    else {
        theEl.style.display="none";
        theEl.expanded=false;
    }
}
```

   Figure K-10 shows the new code.

3. **Scroll down to the `<div>` tag for the first question, "What is Dynamic HTML?", select the comment `<!--replace with opening <a> tag-->`, then press [Delete]**

4. **Type `<a href="#" onClick="expand('one'); return false";>`, then move to the end of the line and replace the text `<!-- replace with closing </a> tag-->` with `</a>`**

   Because you use an `<a>` tag with # as a dummy `href`, the pointer becomes a hand when it moves over the question, indicating to the user that clicking the text triggers an action. The remaining code uses the *onClick* event handler to call the expand function and specifies the variable `'one'` for the function to process. The *onClick* event calls the *expand(el)* function that you entered earlier.

5. **Repeat Steps 3 and 4 for the remaining five list items, substituting `'two'` for `'one'` in item two, and so forth**

   Figure K-11 shows a portion of the completed code for the expanding FAQ list.

6. **Use Figures K-10 and K-11 to check the document for errors, make changes as necessary, then save your work**

7. **Open DHTML_FAQ.htm in your browser, then click the first question**

   As Figure K-12 shows, the text for the first question is displayed.

FIGURE K-10: DHTML_FAQ.htm page with added script

```
<script type="text/javascript" language="JavaScript">
<!--

function init(){
            tempColl=document.all.tags("div");
            for (i=0; i<tempColl.length; i++) {
                    if (tempColl(i).className == "answer") {
                            tempColl(i).style.display="none";
                            tempColl(i).expanded=false;
                    }
            }
}

function expand(el) {
        theEl=eval(el + "answer");
        if (theEl.style.display == "none") {
                theEl.style.display="block";
                theEl.expanded=true;
        }
        else {
                theEl.style.display="none";
                theEl.expanded=false;
        }
}

with (document) {
        write("<style type='text/css'>");
        write(".question {position: relative; left: 40px}");
```

Expand function inserted in page code

Expands element to display block if event is true (The *onClick* event is defined in a later script)

Collapses element on second click

FIGURE K-11: <a>...</a> tags added to question items

```
<h3>Click any of the popular questions about DHTML below to see its answer.</h3>

<div id="oneQuestion" class="question"><p><a href="#" onClick="expand('one'); return
false";>What is Dynamic
HTML?</a></p></div>

<div id="oneanswer" class="answer"><p>Dynamic HTML (DHTML) describes a set of new
technologies for designing Web pages that allow new and more precise formatting features,
along with faster access for users.</p></div>

<div id="twoQuestion" class="question"><p><a href="#" onClick="expand('two'); return
false";>Is DHTML a new language?</a></p></div>

<div id="twoanswer" class="answer"><p>DHTML is not a new language. DHTML is simply a
snazzy name for a set of new features that recent Web browsers are equipped to interpret
and use. DHTML features work only within the context of a standard HTML
document.</p></div>

<div id="threeQuestion" class="question"><p><a href="#" onClick="expand('three'); return
false";>How does DHTML
work?</a></p></div>

<div id="threeanswer" class="answer"><p>DHTML uses two new pieces in concert with HTML.
The first is scripts that run on the user's browser, written in a scripting language such
as JavaScript or VBScript. The other is Cascading Style Sheets, a new method of specifying
```

Anchor tag with *onClick* event

Closing anchor tag

Class attribute applied to divisions

FIGURE K-12: Expanding FAQ list

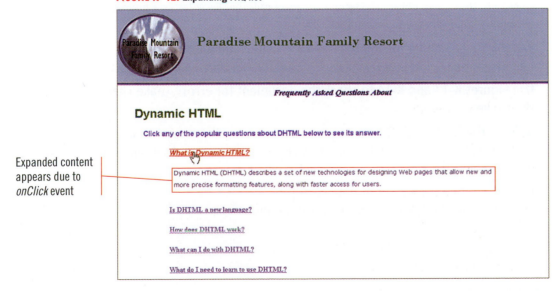

Expanded content appears due to *onClick* event

HTML

Changing Font Size Dynamically

In the last lesson, you used a script to modify the style of an element in response to a user action. Using this general formula, you can add dynamic formatting to most style aspects of any object on your Web pages. A popular application of this method is to change the appearance of text or to swap one graphic for another when a user points to an image. This effect is commonly referred to as a **rollover**. Adding rollover effects to graphics or text is straightforward in newer browsers. However, some older browsers require a considerable amount of extra scripting to dynamically change text. You want to change the text size of the FAQ questions when the user moves the mouse pointer over them. Because the feature is not crucial to the overall layout of your Web page, you decide to focus on creating the feature for newer browsers only.

STEPS

1. **Click your text editor program button to return to the source code for your DHTML_FAQ.htm page**

2. **Scroll to the ending comment `//-->` and `</script>` tag in the document's head section, select the text `/* replace with text size functions */`, press [Delete], then type the following functions, pressing [Enter] at the end of each line**
   ```
   function changeText(whichQuestion) {
      whichQuestion.style.fontSize="18pt";
   }
   function changeTextBack(whichQuestion) {
      whichQuestion.style.fontSize="12pt";
   }
   ```
   Figure K-13 shows the functions entered into the Web page source code. The first function, *changeText*, changes the font size of the object from which it was called to 18-point type. The second function, *changeTextBack*, returns the font size of the calling object to 12-point type.

3. **Scroll to the opening `<a>` tag for the first question item "What is Dynamic HTML?", click after the semicolon following the `return false";` statement, then press [Spacebar]**

4. **Type the following code, pressing [Spacebar] but not [Enter] between each event argument**
   `onMouseOver="changeText(this);" onMouseOut="changeTextBack(this);"`
   This code adds two new arguments to the heading. The first uses the *onMouseOver* event handler to call the *changeText* function you created earlier. The "`this`" is scripting shorthand to tell the function to make changes to the current object. The second argument calls the *changeTextBack* function for the current object in response to the pointer moving off the text.

5. **Repeat Steps 3 and 4 for the remaining five question items**
   Figure K-14 shows source code containing the inline code for dynamically changing text size.

6. **Use Figures K-13 and K-14 to check the document for errors, make changes as necessary, then save your work**

7. **Refresh the DHTML_FAQ.htm page in your browser, then point to a topic item**
   As shown in Figure K-15, the text size increases when you move the mouse pointer over the text. The text color changes to red due to settings in your linked style sheet.

8. **Move the pointer away from the first topic**
   The text for the first topic returns to its original formatting.

FIGURE K-13: Page containing ChangeText and ChangeTextBack functions

changeText
function

change
TextBack
function

```
window.onload=init;


function changeText(whichQuestion) {

        whichQuestion.style.fontSize="18pt";
}
function changeTextBack(whichQuestion) {

        whichQuestion.style.fontSize="12pt";
}
//-->
</script>
```

FIGURE K-14: Page containing code to change the text size

Code to
initiate
changeText
and
ChangeText-
Back
functions

```
<h3>Click any of the popular questions about DHTML below to see its answer.</h3>

<div id="oneQuestion" class="question"><p><a href="#" onClick="expand('one'); return
false"; onMouseOver="changeText(this);" onMouseOut="changeTextBack(this);">What is Dynamic
HTML?</a></p></div>

<div id="oneanswer" class="answer"><p>Dynamic HTML (DHTML) describes a set of new
technologies for designing Web pages that allow new and more precise formatting features,
along with faster access for users.</p></div>

<div id="twoQuestion" class="question"><p><a href="#" onClick="expand('two'); return
false"; onMouseOver="changeText(this);" onMouseOut="changeTextBack(this);">Is DHTML a new
language?</a></p></div>

<div id="twoanswer" class="answer"><p>DHTML is not a new language. DHTML is simply a
snazzy name for a set of new features that recent Web browsers are equipped to interpret
and use. DHTML features work only within the context of a standard HTML
document.</p></div>

<div id="threeQuestion" class="question"><p><a href="#" onClick="expand('three'); return
false"; onMouseOver="changeText(this);" onMouseOut="changeTextBack(this);">How does DHTML
work?</a></p></div>
```

FIGURE K-15: Changed text formatting in Internet Explorer

Text size
increases
and other
formatting
changes
appear on
mouseOver

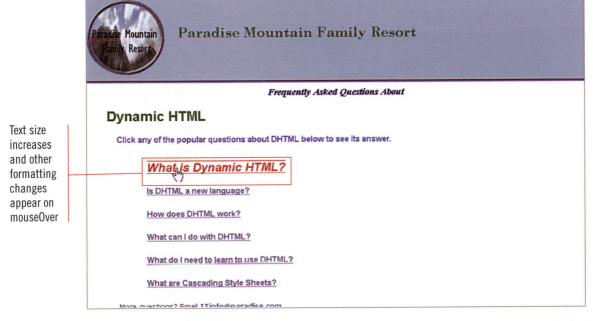

Changing Font Color Dynamically

Just as you can script a page to change text size in response to a user action, you can easily change or modify such scripts to change several other properties that control how text is displayed.  In addition to the increase in text size, you want the heading font color to change when the user points to it to increase the impact of this effect. You can modify the scripts you already created to alter font color and text size when users point to the text.

STEPS

1. Click your text editor program button to return to the source code for your DHTML_FAQ.htm page

2. Scroll to the *changeText* function in the page header, click after the text `whichQuestion.style.fontSize="18pt";`, then press [Enter]

3. Type `whichQuestion.style.color="#CC3366";`

4. Click after `whichQuestion.style.fontSize="12pt";` in the *changeTextBack* function, then press [Enter]

5. Type `whichQuestion.style.color="#000066";`

   Figure K-16 shows the completed changes in the Web page source code containing the color style. The *changeText* function increases the size of the text and changes the color for the selected object. The *changeTextBack* function returns the text to its original size and color.

6. Check the document for errors, make changes as necessary, click after `</a>` in the itemRest division near the bottom of the page, press [Enter], add a "Page modified by" paragraph with your name and the current date then save your work

QUICK TIP

If you clicked other elements on the page, other DHTML effects such as questions showing under or overlines might be present.

7. Save your work, click the browser program button on the taskbar to return to your browser, reload DHTML_FAQ.htm, then point to the What is Dynamic HTML? heading

   As shown in Figure K-17, the text changes size and color, making it stand out from the other questions on the page. If you are using an older generation browser, your text may not change.

8. Move the mouse pointer away from the first heading

   The text returns to its original size and color.

9. Close your browser

10. Print your file, then close your text editor and transfer your page to your remote directory

```
window.onload=init;


function changeText(whichQuestion) {

        whichQuestion.style.fontSize="18pt";
        whichQuestion.style.color="#CC3366";
}
function changeTextBack(whichQuestion) {

        whichQuestion.style.fontSize="12pt";
        whichQuestion.style.color="#000066";
}
//-->
</script>

<style type="text/css">
```

Code to change text color

FIGURE K-17: Color change in browser

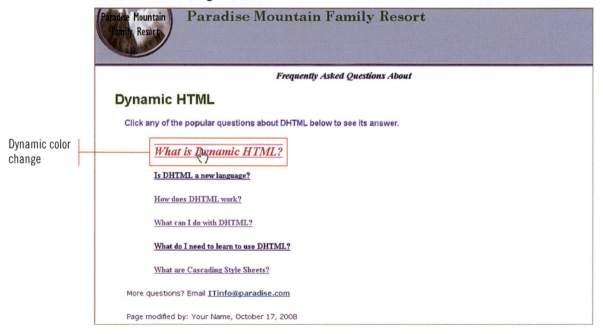

Dynamic color change

HTML

Keeping Up with DHTML Changes

Web and software designers have already developed many ideas and methods for implementing DHTML. As with any developing technology, this body of knowledge continues to grow, and in the process, provides new uses and innovations for DHTML programming. In addition, as browser developers update and expand the capabilities of their products, they introduce possibilities for new DHTML applications. You should therefore stay current with the latest developments in DHTML so that you can adapt your Web pages and keep them up to date. Predictably, the Web is a rich source of information on DHTML. You decide to research the future of DHTML and its updated features.

STEPS

1. **Open a search engine and use the keywords DHTML news or DHTML updates to search for Web pages about the most recent information about DHTML**

   The search engine returns descriptions and links to pages about DHTML. If you have trouble finding links about DHTML, go to the Student Online Companion and visit some of the linked sites.

2. **Follow a link on the search results page to a site containing DHTML information**

3. **Scroll through and scan the opening page for tips on working with DHTML and for news about recent and upcoming developments**

   Figure K-18 shows a Web page offering tips and articles on using DHTML.

4. **Follow links to explanations of new DHTML features or to news about upcoming additions or changes, read one of these articles, then print the article and write your name on it**

5. **Close your Web browser**

FIGURE K-18: Web page containing DHTML tips

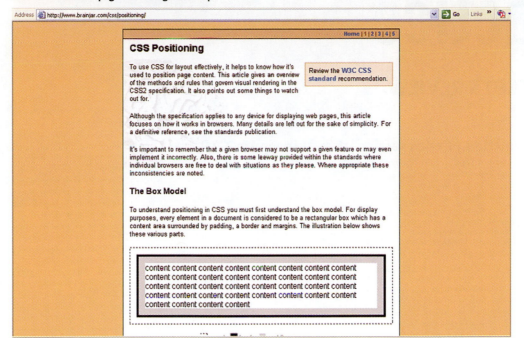

HTML

Practice

▼ CONCEPTS REVIEW

Name the function of each section of code in Figure K-19.

FIGURE K-19

```
<script type="text/javascript" language="JavaScript">
<!--
function expand(el) {
        theEl=eval(el + "answer");
        if (theEl.style.display == "none") {
                theEl.style.display="block";
                theEl.expanded=true;
        }
        else {
                theEl.style.display="none";
                theEl.expanded=false;
        }
}
with (document) {
        write("<style type='text/css'>");
        write(".question {position: relative; left: 40px}");
        write(".answer {display: none; position: relative; left: 50px; width: 90%}");
        write("</style>");
}
window.onload=init;
//-->
</script>
</head>
<body>
<h2>Frequently asked Questions about Dynamic HTML </h2>
<div id="oneQuestion" class="question"><a href="#" onClick="expand('one'); return false"
onMouseOver="changeText(this)" onMouseOut="changeTextBack(this)"><P>What is Dynamic HTML?
</P></a></div>
```

1
2
3
5
4

Match each statement with the term it describes.

6. **Dynamic style**
7. **Proprietary features**
8. **This**
9. **Positioning**
10. **Dynamic HTML**

a. Notation indicating that a function should use the current object
b. Collection of Web page technologies allowing responses to user actions
c. Unique elements and attributes that are written for a specific browser
d. Ability to specify locations of Web page elements
e. Font or color changes in response to user actions

Select the best answer from the list of choices.

11. **Which of the following are features of DHTML? (Choose all that apply.)**
    a. Dynamic style
    b. Dynamic content
    c. Positioning
    d. Data awareness

12. **Positioning allows Web page designers to:**
    a. Create interactive page formatting.
    b. Create predictable layouts.
    c. Download Web page data.
    d. Create interactive page content.

13. **A collapsible list is a good example of:**
    a. Dynamic style.
    b. Dynamic content.
    c. Data awareness.
    d. Absolute positioning.

14. **DHTML uses a hierarchy called:**
    a. W3C.
    b. JavaScript.
    c. CSS.
    d. DOM.

15. **Linking a Web page to an external data file is called:**
    a. Positioning.
    b. Data binding.
    c. Data history.
    d. DOM.

16. **Which object provides browser information in the DOM?**
    a. *Frames*
    b. *Navigator*
    c. *Document*
    d. *Screen*

17. **Which object represents the current Web page in the DOM?**
    a. *Frames*
    b. *Navigator*
    c. *Document*
    d. *Screen*

18. **Which of the following organizes information so that a user can see how one choice relates to another?**
    a. Data binding
    b. Data awareness
    c. Positioning
    d. Cascading menus

▼ SKILLS REVIEW

1. **Show and hide page elements.**
   a. In your text editor, open the file **htm_K-2.txt** from the drive and folder where your Data Files are stored, then save it as **packages.htm** to the paradise/spa directory where you save your site files. If you are asked whether you want to replace the file, click Yes.
   b. Locate the *init* and *expand* functions at the top of the page and review the script code.
   c. Locate the comment at the top of the body section indicating where an *onClick* event handler is to be placed. Place the following *onClick* event in the opening <a> tag after `href="#"`: `onClick="expand('one'); return false"`. This displays the package details when the Rocky Mountain Express name is clicked. Delete the comment.
   d. Add the same *onClick* event to the remaining four opening <a> tags, changing `'one'` to 'two', 'three', 'four', or 'five' respectively.
   e. Check your script for errors, make changes as necessary, then save **packages.htm**.
   f. Open **packages.htm** in your browser to check your work.

2. **Change font size dynamically.**
   a. Locate the *changeText* and *changeTextBack* functions at the top of the page and review the script code.
   b. Edit the code in the *changeText* function to change the font size to 16 pt when the mouse moves over the names of the packages. (*Hint*: The first line of the function should be `whichQuestion.style.fontSize="16pt";`.)
   c. Locate the first opening <a> tag with the *onClick* event. Add an *onMouseOver* event and an *onMouseOut* event to the tag to call the *changeText* and *changeTextBack* functions. (*Hint*: The opening <a> tag should now be `<a href="#" onClick="expand('one'); return false" onMouseOver="changeText(this)" onMouseOut="changeTextBack(this)">`.)
   d. Add the same *onMouseOver* and *onMouseOut* events to the remaining four opening <a> tags.

▼ SKILLS REVIEW (CONTINUED)

   e. Check your script for errors, make changes as necessary, then save the file.

   f. Open **packages.htm** in your browser to check your work.

3. Change font color dynamically.

   a. Edit the code in the *changeText* function to change the font color to #0066FF when the mouse moves over the names of the packages. (*Hint*: The second line of the function should be `whichQuestion.style.color="#0066FF";`.)

   b. Check your script for errors, make changes as necessary, then save the file.

   c. Open **packages.htm** in your browser to check your work.

   d. Add your name to the bottom of the page before the date.

   e. Print the page from your text editor.

▼ INDEPENDENT CHALLENGE 1

As you continue developing the Web site for your resort rental business, Star Vacations, you decide to use DHTML to add a dynamic style to each question in a collapsible list for the Frequently Asked Questions page.

   a. In your text editor, open the **htm_K-3.txt** file from the drive and folder where your Data Files are stored. Add your name as the contact person for information at the bottom of the page, then save the page as **faq.htm** in the vacations folder where you save your site files. If you are asked whether you want to replace the file, click Yes.

   b. Open the **faq.htm** file in your browser to view the collapsible list, then return to your text editor and print the page.

   c. Using the printed page, label each page element indicating which parts of the page are part of the collapsible list and which remain on the Web page at all times.

   d. Review the *init*, *expand*, *changeText*, and *changeTextBack* functions in the head section of the page.

   e. In your text editor, edit the *changeText* function to change the size of the question text to 15 pt when the user moves the mouse pointer over the question.

   f. Edit the *changeText* function to change the color of the question text to #0066CC when the user moves the mouse pointer over the question.

   g. Review the opening `<a>` tag for the question with an `id="oneQuestion."` Copy the *onMouseOver* and *onMouseOut* event handlers from this opening `<a>` tag and paste them in the opening `<a>` tags of the five remaining questions.

   h. Save your work, open the page in your browser, move the mouse pointer over the questions to view the font changes, then print the page from your browser.

   i. Transfer the faq.htm file to your remote directory.

Advanced Challenge Exercises

- Write a paragraph describing in your own words the purpose of the *init* function in the page's header. Use the search engine of your choice to research the code you do not understand.
- In your paper explain how and where the function is called in the page.
- Add your name to the page, then print it.

▼ INDEPENDENT CHALLENGE 2

Your employer Metro Water has asked you to make their Web site more interactive for the users who access water conservation information. You decide to add dynamic font features to the page that supplies water conservation tips for the Metro Water customers.

   a. In your text editor, open the **htm_K-4.txt** file from the drive and folder where your Data Files are stored. Add your name to the bottom of the page, then save the page as **outside.htm** in the water folder where you save your site files. If you are asked whether you want to replace the file, click Yes.

   b. Review the *changeText* and *changeTextBack* functions in the head section of the page, then edit the *changeText* function to change the font size of each tip to 14 pt when the user moves the mouse pointer over the question.

c. Edit the *changeText* function to change the font color of each tip to #3399FF when the user moves the mouse pointer over the tip.

d. Add the necessary event handlers to the opening <a> tags using the *changeText* and *changeTextBack* functions to dynamically change the font of the tips when the user moves the mouse pointer over and away from the tip.

e. Save your work, open the page in your browser, then move the mouse pointer over the questions and then away from the questions to view the font changes. Print the page from your text editor.

f. Transfer the outside.htm file to your remote directory.

Advanced Challenge Exercises

- In the *changeText* function, *whichQuestion* is a parameter that is used in the function. Use the search engine of your choice to research how functions use parameters in JavaScript.

- Use the results of your research to write a paragraph about how the *changeText* function uses the *whichQuestion* parameter. In your paper, include the value of *whichQuestion* when the *changeText* function is called by an event handler in an opening <a> tag.

- Add your name to the page, then print it.

▼ INDEPENDENT CHALLENGE 3

DHTML is used to add formatting and interactivity to Web sites. You want to add DHTML features to your Web site, but first you need to research how you can make the interactive pages accessible for all users.

Go to the Student Online Companion for this book, then go to the Unit K link to the W3C Web Accessibility page and review the information for DHTML accessibility issues. Write one or two paragraphs answering the following questions about DHTML scripts:

a. How can you make DHTML scripts accessible?

b. What are some of the issues involving DHTML scripts and their accessibility?

c. Which DHTML features should be avoided to maximize the accessibility of your pages?

d. Add your name and today's date to the top of your paper, then print the document.

▼ INDEPENDENT CHALLENGE 4

Now that you've seen how DHTML can enhance Web sites, you are ready to use some of these features on your Web site.

a. Determine how the DHTML features from this unit can be used to enhance the pages in your Web site.

b. Identify the pages that would benefit from DHTML scripts, then print the pages and mark the elements that you would like to make interactive to users' actions.

c. Add the DHTML features to your pages to dynamically format the font on at least two pages.

d. If you have a frequently asked questions page, add a collapsible list to make it easier to read the page.

e. Add your name to the pages, print the pages, then transfer the edited pages to your remote site.

▼ VISUAL WORKSHOP

Work progresses on your Bits and PCs Web site, and you decide to add dynamic style to the questions on your Frequently Asked Questions page. In your text editor, open the **htm_K-5.txt** file from the drive and folder where your Data Files are stored, then save it as **questions.htm** in the bitspcs folder where you save your site files. Add the necessary functions and event handlers to your file to change the font as shown in Figure K-20 when the mouse pointer is moved over the questions. The Frequently Asked Questions heading might look different if you do not have the Lucida Calligraphy font installed on your computer. (*Hint*: The font size changes to 16 pt, and the font color changes to #0066FF.) Add your name to the bottom of the page in the e-mail link, then save the file. Open the file in your browser to check your work, then print the questions.htm page in your text editor.

FIGURE K-20

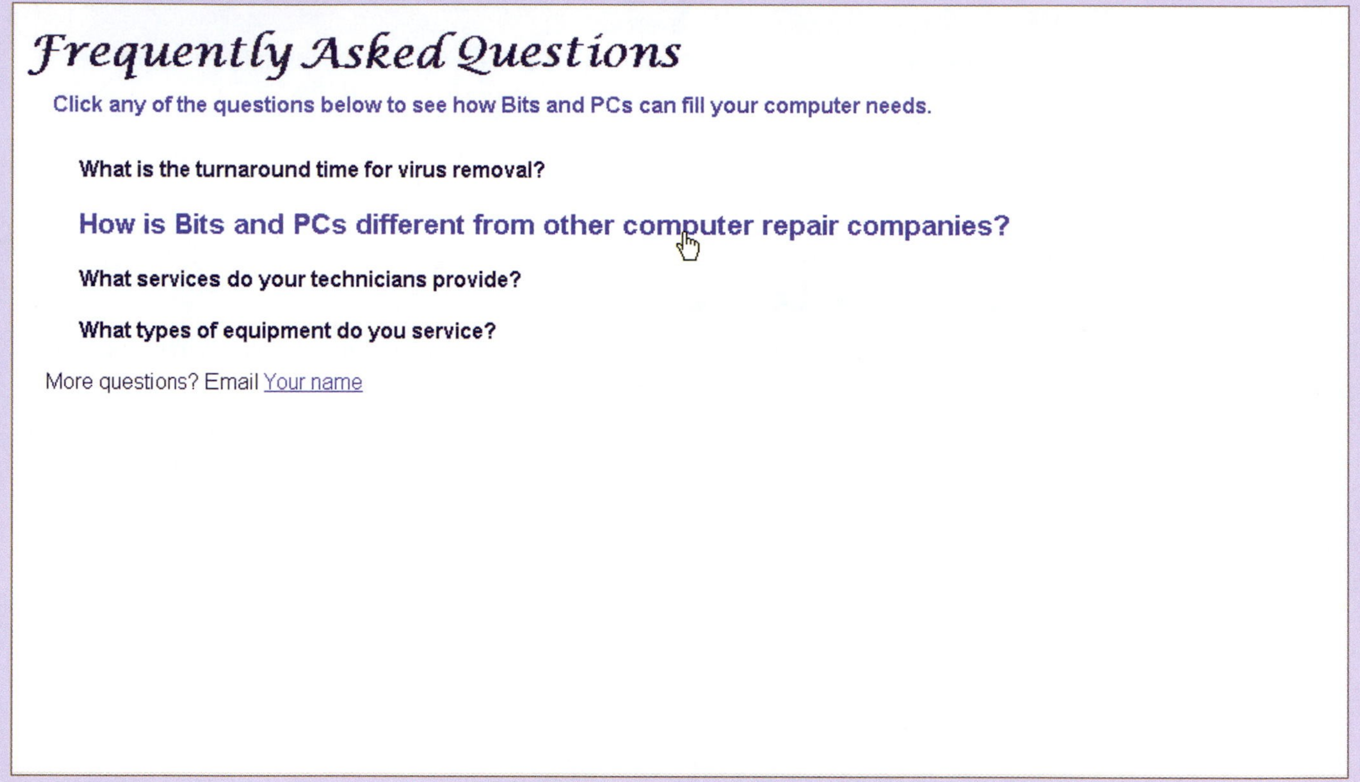

Frequently Asked Questions

Click any of the questions below to see how Bits and PCs can fill your computer needs.

What is the turnaround time for virus removal?

How is Bits and PCs different from other computer repair companies?

What services do your technicians provide?

What types of equipment do you service?

More questions? Email <u>Your name</u>

UNIT
L
HTML

Controlling Content Dynamically

OBJECTIVES

Understand dynamic content
Insert content dynamically
Delete content dynamically
Modify content dynamically
Incorporate an advanced content function
Replace graphics dynamically
Bind data
Manipulate bound data dynamically

Just as dynamic HTML (DHTML) allows you to create pages in which styles change instantly based on user actions, it also provides tools that allow users to modify a page's content. You can use this feature, known as **dynamic content**, to generate all or part of the page when it is opened or to alter the page's contents in response to user events. Many resort guests enjoy participating in overnight, weekend, and weeklong backcountry adventures, but some come unprepared. The resort management has asked you to develop a set of pages for its new Nomad Outfitters Ltd shop, which specializes in camping and backpacking equipment. You want to use dynamic content to make the Web pages more enticing.

Understanding Dynamic Content

Dynamic HTML includes many tools for altering a Web page's appearance in response to user actions. Using scripts to change text attributes such as color and font size affects only the style of elements, leaving the elements themselves, such as text or images, unchanged. Dynamic content tools, however, allow your Web page elements to change based on user input. Dynamic content can create an effect similar to an expanding outline where content that is already part of the page hides or becomes visible in response to user actions. However, true dynamic content is more than showing or hiding content—it involves reordering and replacing page elements. As you learn about dynamic content, you identify several of its main uses and consider ways you can use it on the Nomad Outfitters pages.

DETAILS

Dynamic content can be triggered through:

- **Pointing**

  Dynamic content allows you to change an element in response to a user's mouse pointer movements. You have already learned about the formatting changes you can create using dynamic style. Now, using dynamic content, you can make your page's text and graphic contents available to user changes. Figure L-1 shows a Web page displaying an alternate graphic in response to user pointing.

- **Run-time activities**

  Dynamic content tools can create portions of your Web pages for you at **run time**, the period when a browser first interprets and displays the Web page and runs scripts. A simple example is a script that displays the text "Good Morning!" or "Good Evening!" based on the time of day according to the user's computer clock. You also can program a page to generate a table of contents (TOC) for the page at run time, which allows you to change a page's structure and contents without also revising the TOC each time you make a change to the rest of the page content.

- **Data binding**

  In addition to standard tools for working with Web page text, dynamic content includes special features for easily creating and working with table data. You can use dynamic content tools to associate an external database or text file with a Web page by using data binding, which was introduced in Unit K. Recall that data binding allows the user's browser to generate a Web page table from an external data file at run time. By adding some lines of script, you also can allow users to sort the table on your Web page. Figure L-2 shows a dynamically generated table in a Web page that has been sorted by the Web page user.

FIGURE L-1: Dynamic content responding to user pointing

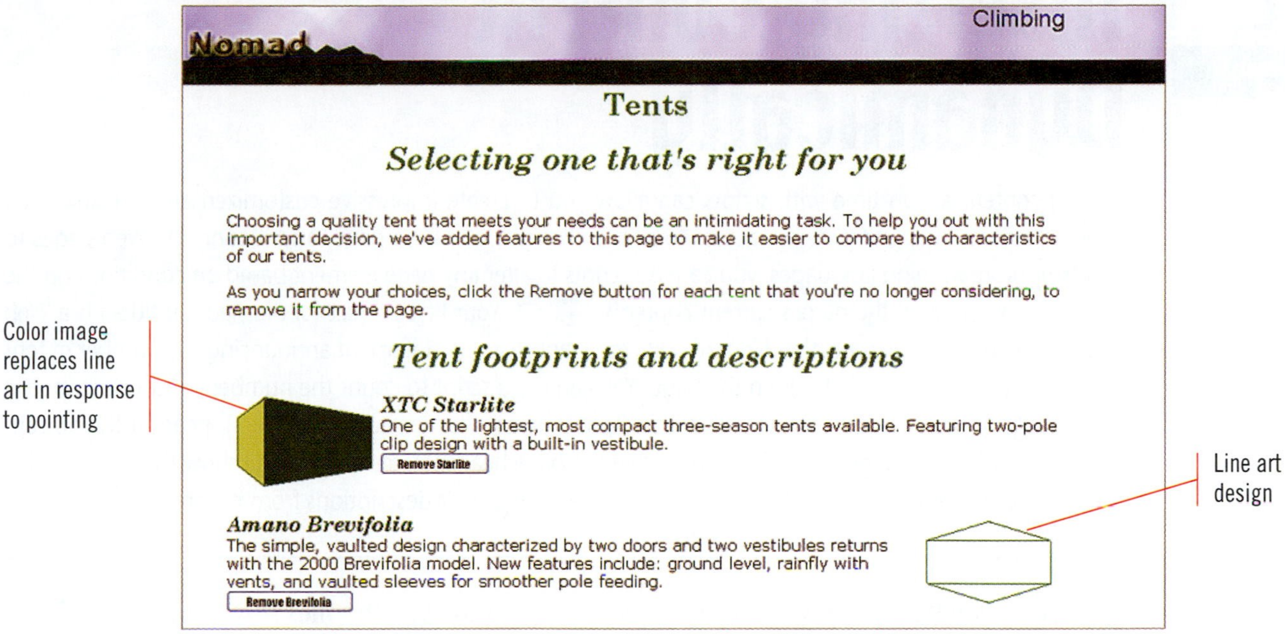

Color image replaces line art in response to pointing

Line art design

FIGURE L-2: Table sorted by user

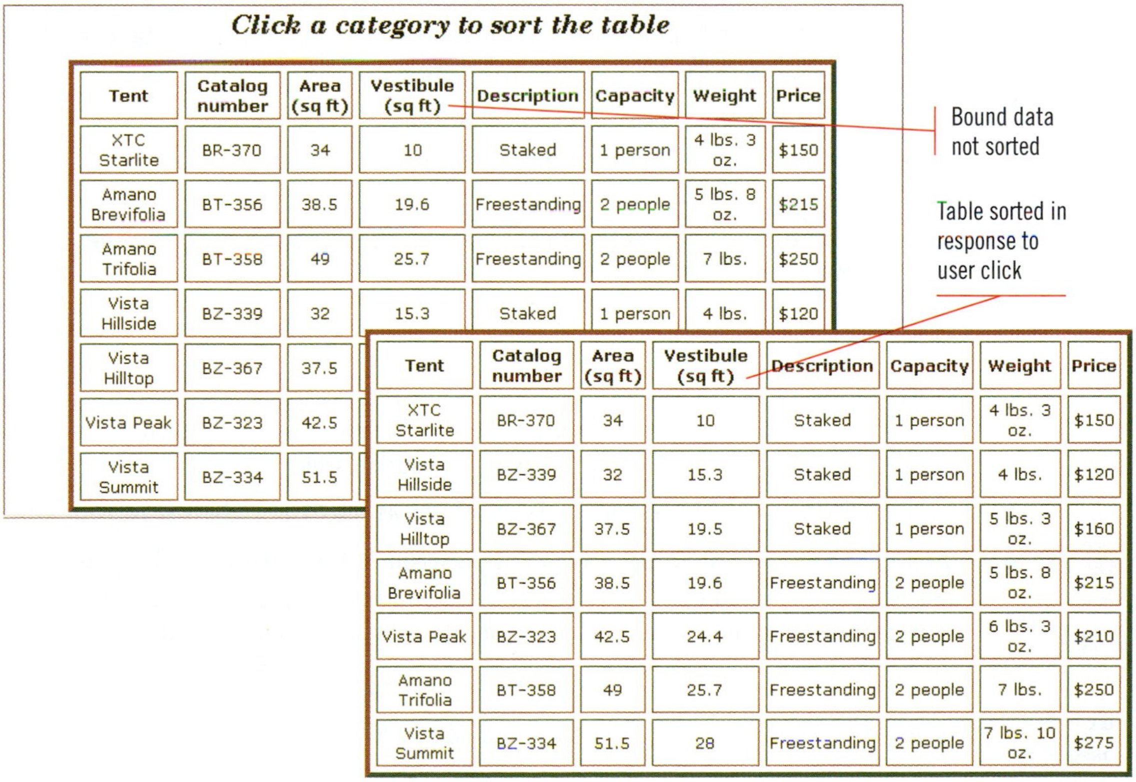

Bound data not sorted

Table sorted in response to user click

Click a category to sort the table

Tent	Catalog number	Area (sq ft)	Vestibule (sq ft)	Description	Capacity	Weight	Price
XTC Starlite	BR-370	34	10	Staked	1 person	4 lbs. 3 oz.	$150
Amano Brevifolia	BT-356	38.5	19.6	Freestanding	2 people	5 lbs. 8 oz.	$215
Amano Trifolia	BT-358	49	25.7	Freestanding	2 people	7 lbs.	$250
Vista Hillside	BZ-339	32	15.3	Staked	1 person	4 lbs.	$120
Vista Hilltop	BZ-367	37.5					
Vista Peak	BZ-323	42.5					
Vista Summit	BZ-334	51.5					

Tent	Catalog number	Area (sq ft)	Vestibule (sq ft)	Description	Capacity	Weight	Price
XTC Starlite	BR-370	34	10	Staked	1 person	4 lbs. 3 oz.	$150
Vista Hillside	BZ-339	32	15.3	Staked	1 person	4 lbs.	$120
Vista Hilltop	BZ-367	37.5	19.5	Staked	1 person	5 lbs. 3 oz.	$160
Amano Brevifolia	BT-356	38.5	19.6	Freestanding	2 people	5 lbs. 8 oz.	$215
Vista Peak	BZ-323	42.5	24.4	Freestanding	2 people	6 lbs. 3 oz.	$210
Amano Trifolia	BT-358	49	25.7	Freestanding	2 people	7 lbs.	$250
Vista Summit	BZ-334	51.5	28	Freestanding	2 people	7 lbs. 10 oz.	$275

Inserting Content Dynamically

Adding content at run time with scripts can allow you to create impressive customized and versatile Web pages. Because the DOM provides access to all the elements of a Web page, and it connects Web pages to scripts or programming languages, you can use scripts to alter any page element based on conditions on the user's computer or on the page's current contents. Your first project for Nomad Outfitters is a Web page that compares the tents that Nomad sells. You want to add a statement announcing the number of tent models that users can read about on the page. You can use a script to count the number of tent descriptions on the page and then insert this value dynamically in the page header statement that appears at the bottom of the page when the page loads. This means that the page header statement will still show the correct value even after the sales department adds to or removes tents and their descriptions from its tent selection.

STEPS

1. **Before you begin, use your computer's file system to copy the files shown in Table L-1 from your Unit L Data Files folder, then paste them into a folder called nomad that you create in your paradise folder in the place where you save your site files**

2. **In your text editor, open the file htm_L-1.txt from your Data Files folder, then save it as tents.htm in your paradise\nomad folder**

   The page is designed to show each tent's floor plan, or footprint, along with the tent's description. You have already included a function in the page header that counts the number of tent-description headings in the page and assigns the number to the variable *totalTents*.

3. **Use your text editor's Find function to locate the comment `<!-- Replace with tent count code -->`, select the comment, then press [Delete]**

QUICK TIP

Be sure to include a space after the word "describes" and a space before the word "tent".

4. **Type the following code, pressing [Enter] at the end of each line:**
   ```
   <script type="text/javascript" language="JavaScript">
   <!--
   countHeaders()
   document.write("<h3 style='text-align: center;'>This page describes ")
   document.write(totalTents)
   document.write(" tent models.</h3>")
   //-->
   </script>
   ```
   Figure L-3 shows the Web page code containing the script. The code formats the text "This page describes" and "tent models." as centered, level-three headings. Between these two bits of text, the script uses the *document.write* method to insert the value counted by the *countHeaders* function, which is assigned to the variable *totalTents*.

5. **Check your document for errors, make changes as necessary, then save your work**

TROUBLE

Although the script works in IE and newer Netscape browsers, your header-counting script may not work in all browsers. If your count does not appear correctly, try using a different browser.

6. **Open tents.htm in your Web browser, then scroll to the bottom of the page**

   As shown in Figure L-4, the level-three heading text you scripted appears near the bottom of the page. The statement includes the number of tents counted by the *countHeaders* function and inserted with a script.

FIGURE L-3: Code for countHeaders script

```
<!-- Insert button code for tent7 -->

<br /><br /><br clear="all" />

</div>

<script type="text/javascript" language="JavaScript">
<!--

countHeaders()
document.write("<h3 style='text-align: center;'>This page describes ")
document.write(totalTents)
document.write(" tent models.</h3>")

//-->
</script>

<h2 align="center">Nomad Ltd has a tent that's right for you!</h2>
```

Scripted text writes header count

Opening and closing script and comment tags

FIGURE L-4: Web page with dynamic tent count

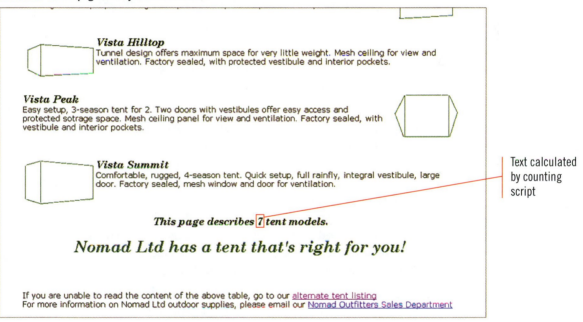

Text calculated by counting script

Vista Hilltop
Tunnel design offers maximum space for very little weight. Mesh ceiling for view and ventilation. Factory sealed, with protected vestibule and interior pockets.

Vista Peak
Easy setup, 3-season tent for 2. Two doors with vestibules offer easy access and protected sotrage space. Mesh ceiling panel for view and ventilation. Factory sealed, with vestibule and interior pockets.

Vista Summit
Comfortable, rugged, 4-season tent. Quick setup, full rainfly, integral vestibule, large door. Factory sealed, mesh window and door for ventilation.

This page describes 7 tent models.

Nomad Ltd has a tent that's right for you!

If you are unable to read the content of the above table, go to our alternate tent listing
For more information on Nomad Ltd outdoor supplies, please email our Nomad Outfitters Sales Department

TABLE L-1: Nomad files

alt_tent.htm	bkg_nomad.gif	brevcolor.gif
brevifolia.gif	hillside.gif	hillsidecolor.gif
hilltop.gif	hilltopcolor.gif	nomad.css
nomad.jpg	peak.gif	peakcolor.gif
starcolor.gif	starlite.gif	summit.glf
summitcolor.gif	tents.txt	tricolor.gif
trifolia.gif		

Deleting Content Dynamically

Besides adding Web page elements dynamically at run time, you can script your Web page to allow users to tailor it to suit their needs. For example, some scripts allow users to move items around or to delete elements from a Web page. This latter feature is especially useful in a content-laden page in which the user might want to pare down the content to pertinent elements or sections. Because users of the tent comparison page will be trying to select a tent based on their needs, you think it would be helpful to allow them to remove information they are not interested in from the page content.

1. **Click your text editor program button to return to your tents.htm source code**

2. **Scroll up the page to view the body text describing the first tent, the XTC Starlite, select the comment** `<!-- Insert button code for tent1 -->`**, then press [Delete]**

3. **Type the following code, pressing [Enter] at the end of each line:**
```
<script type="text/javascript" language="JavaScript">
<!--
//-->
</script>
```
   You entered the opening and closing script tags for the code that will write the button; now you need to enter the button code using the *document.write* method.

4. **Click after** `<!--`**, press [Enter], then, without pressing [Enter] at the end of each line, type**
   `document.write("<button class='button' onClick=tent1.outerHTML=''>Remove Starlite</button>")`
   Be careful not to add a space between the single quotes following outerHTML=. The `<button>` tag set creates a button with a customized function. The text between the tags is the label that appears on the button. Previously a class definition called `.button` was inserted in the page's embedded style sheet that sets the button face text in an 8-point, sans serif font. You use the *onClick* event handler to change the *outerHTML* property of the object named *tent1*, which includes the description and graphic for the first tent. An element's *outerHTML* property includes the element contents and the tags surrounding it, so changing the property to a null value removes the element and its surrounding tags from the Web page.

5. **Repeat Steps 3 and 4 for the remaining six tent descriptions, substituting the button object names and tent names as listed in Table L-2**
   Figure L-5 shows the Web page code containing the button code for the first two tent descriptions.

6. **Check the document for errors, make changes as necessary, then save your work**

7. **Click the browser program button on the taskbar, reload tents.htm in your browser, then scroll down the page until the Amano Brevifolia description appears in the document window**
   The Remove Brevifolia button is visible beneath the tent's descriptive text.

8. **Click the Remove Brevifolia button**
   As Figure L-6 shows, the Web browser removes the tent's description and graphic. Now you want to update the counter so that it reflects the changes users make to the Web page by updating the number of tent descriptions displayed.

FIGURE L-5: Web page containing code for delete buttons

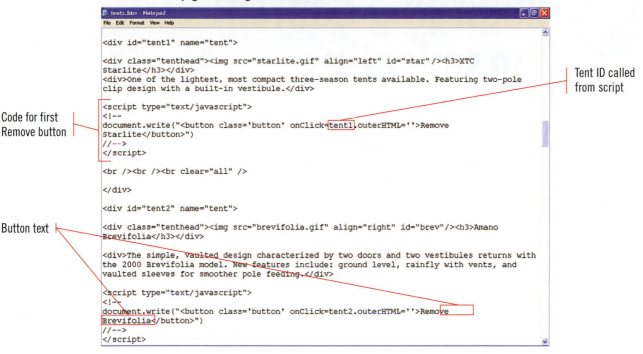

Tent ID called from script

Code for first Remove button

Button text

FIGURE L-6: Page with deleted image and description

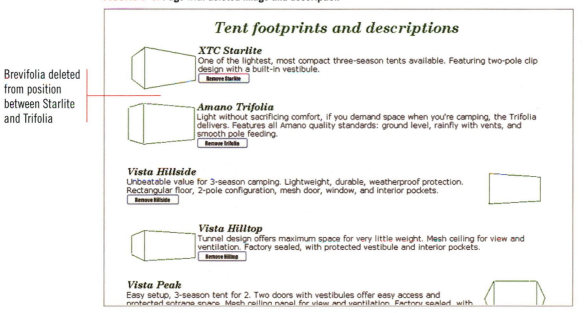

Brevifolia deleted from position between Starlite and Trifolia

TABLE L-2: Tent description IDs and button text

description number	substitute for *tent1*	substitute for Starlite
2	tent2	Brevifolia
3	tent3	Trifolia
4	tent4	Hillside
5	tent5	Hilltop
6	tent6	Peak
7	tent7	Summit

Modifying Content Dynamically

Dynamic content involves more than adding or deleting static Web page content. It lets you create pages that change content in response to various events. For example, you can add interactivity by modifying page content in response to user actions.  Because your page allows users to remove descriptions for tents that don't fit their needs, you want to ensure that the statement showing the number of tents available displays the correct number after user deletions.

1. **Click the text editor program button to return to your tents.htm page code, then, starting from the top, scroll down the page until the function *reCount* appears in the document window**

   The function *reCount* appears between JavaScript comment tags /* */. You previously added the function, then commented it out until you were ready to use it. The function subtracts 1 from the total count of tent descriptions on the page and then uses the *innerHTML* property to update the number that appears in the statement at the bottom of the page. The *innerHTML* property replaces an element but leaves its enclosing HTML tags intact. You use *innerHTML* because you want to replace only the number, which is within HTML tags, and not any of the surrounding text or HTML tags.

2. **Select** `/* Remove these comments to make this function work`, **press [Delete], move to the end of the function, select** `*/`, **then press [Delete]**

3. **Using your text editor's Find utility, type the term tent1 to locate the opening tag for the tent1 script, click after** `onClick=tent1.outerHTML=''`, **then type** `,reCount()` **(including the comma)**

   You added a reference to the *reCount* function in the *onClick* event of the code for the first dynamic button. Your code should resemble that shown in Figure L-7. Now you will add the code to the rest of the buttons. The reference triggers the function code *reCount* when a button is clicked to remove a tent description from the page.

4. **Copy the text** `,reCount()` **and paste it after the onClick command in each button script for the remaining six buttons**

5. **Scroll down to the countHeaders function, click after** `This page describes ")`, **press [Enter], then type** `document.write("<span id='textnum'>")`

   You typed the code that writes an opening span tag with an *id* value of *textnum*.

6. **Click after** `document.write(totalTents)`, **press [Enter], and then type**
   `document.write("</span>")`

   Figure L-8 shows the completed code containing the span tags. By inserting the span tags with an *id* value, you create an inline object named *textnum* that you can manipulate with scripts. Your *reCount* function changes *textnum*'s *innerHTML* property each time the user clicks one of the delete buttons. This use of dynamic content keeps the contents of the Web page statement current with page changes produced by user actions.

7. **Check your document for errors, make changes as necessary, save your work, then click the browser program button on the taskbar and reload tents.htm in the browser window**

8. **Scroll to the bottom of the page, then click the Remove Summit button**

   As before, the tent description total is displayed in the statement. When you click the button, the browser removes the description for the Vista Summit tent, updates the total, as shown in Figure L-9.

9. **Click the Remove Hilltop button**

   The browser removes the Vista Hilltop description, and again changes the tent total to reflect the current number of descriptions on the page.

FIGURE L-7: Code with reCount function

```
tents.htm - Notepad
File Edit Format View Help
<div id="tent1" name="tent">

<div class="tenthead"><img src="starlite.gif" align="left" id="star" /><h3>XTC
Starlite</h3></div>
<div>One of the lightest, most compact three-season tents available. Featuring two-pole
clip design with a built-in vestibule.</div>

<script type="text/javascript">
<!--
document.write("<button class='button' onClick=tent1.outerHTML='',reCount()>Remove
Starlite</button>")
//-->
</script>
```

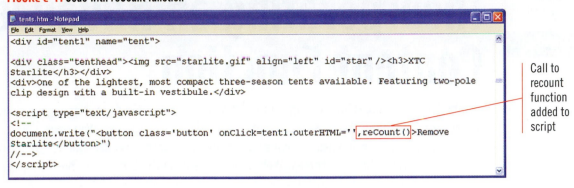

Call to recount function added to script

FIGURE L-8: Code containing span tags

```
<script type="text/javascript" language="JavaScript">
<!--

countHeaders()
document.write("<h3 style='text-align: center;'>This page describes ")
document.write("<span id='textnum'>")
document.write(totalTents)
document.write("</span>")
document.write(" tent models.</h3>")

//-->
</script>
```

JavaScript for opening and closing <span>. . . </span> tags

FIGURE L-9: Web page with updated total

Total updated due to tent deletion

HTML

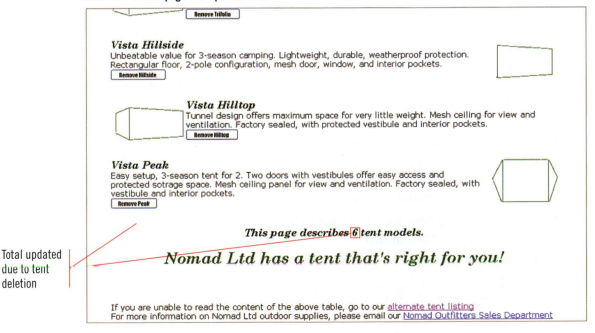

Incorporating an Advanced Content Function

Combining different DHTML tools in your scripts allows you to present or change your page content using a variety of interesting effects. By incorporating special features into your Web page, you can enhance your site visitors' experience and help generate repeat visits to your site. During your research you found a script that cycles through different Web page elements in the same spot, presenting information like a slide show with each new segment of text appearing for a short interval. You decide to use this feature on the tent page you are developing to display some additional information about Nomad Outfitters products.

STEPS

1. **Click the text editor program button on the taskbar to return to your page code, then, starting from the top of the document, scroll down the page until you find the code that reads:**
   ```
   <!-- Replace with text cycle script -->
   <pre>

   </pre>
   ```
   The placeholder text provides a space for your cycle function, which you are ready to place into your Web page. The <pre> and </pre> tags read typed line breaks and so prevent your content from moving up into the banner section before you put the new code in place.

2. **Select the placeholder text including the <pre>...</pre> tags, press [Delete], then type the following code, pressing [Enter] after each line:**
   ```
   <script type="text/javascript" language="JavaScript">
   <!--
   function addCycle() {
   }
   //-->
   </script>
   ```
   The code starts a function called *addCycle*. Now you need to add the content that the function will cycle through on the Web page.

3. **Click before } in your *addCycle* function, press [Tab], type** `cycle(txt1, "Hiking,Bicycling,Camping,Kayaking,Climbing,Find all your gear at,Nomad Outfitters", 30)`, **then press [Enter]**
   This line defines the display parameters for the text you want to cycle as follows: *txt1* indicates the name of the object whose value will be cycled; the text in quotes separated by commas specifies the different words and phrases that should cycle; and the number 30 tells how long one word or phrase should display before cycling to the next word or phrase. The event cycles 1 second for every 10 increments specified in the script, so the text cycles at a regular 3-second interval as specified by 30 in the script. Now you need to type the code that makes your function load and run on the page.

4. **Click after } following your *addCycle* function, press [Enter] twice, type** `window.onload = new Function("addCycle()")`, **then press [Enter]**
   Figure L-10 shows the Web page source code containing the completed script. The script writes the function, then triggers the function cycle, which begins after the page loads.

5. **Check your document for errors, make changes as necessary, save your work, then reload the page in your Web browser**
   The cycling text appears in the upper-right corner of the page, as shown in Figure L-11.

FIGURE L-10: Page source containing script to call cycle function

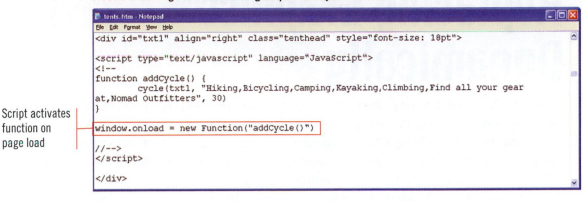

Script activates function on page load

```
<div id="txt1" align="right" class="tenthead" style="font-size: 18pt">

<script type="text/javascript" language="JavaScript">
<!--
function addCycle() {
        cycle(txt1, "Hiking,Bicycling,Camping,Kayaking,Climbing,Find all your gear
at,Nomad Outfitters", 30)
}

window.onload = new Function("addCycle()")

//-->
</script>

</div>
```

FIGURE L-11: Web page displaying cycling text

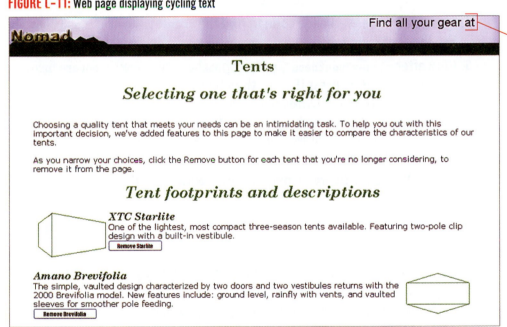

Text content changes every few seconds

Find all your gear at

Nomad

Tents

Selecting one that's right for you

Choosing a quality tent that meets your needs can be an intimidating task. To help you out with this important decision, we've added features to this page to make it easier to compare the characteristics of our tents.

As you narrow your choices, click the Remove button for each tent that you're no longer considering, to remove it from the page.

Tent footprints and descriptions

XTC Starlite
One of the lightest, most compact three-season tents available. Featuring two-pole clip design with a built-in vestibule.

Remove Starlite

Amano Brevifolia
The simple, vaulted design characterized by two doors and two vestibules returns with the 2000 Brevifolia model. New features include: ground level, rainfly with vents, and vaulted sleeves for smoother pole feeding.

Remove Brevifolia

Replacing Graphics Dynamically

Thus far you have used dynamic content tools to modify a Web page's text, but you can also use these features for making dynamic changes to other page elements, including graphics. For example, you can use dynamic content features to change the graphic that appears on the page by using the *onMouseOver* event handler. You could even gradually change a graphic's size to create the effect of animation.  You want to use color to highlight the element to which the user is currently pointing. However, rather than using dynamic style, you created colored versions of each of the tent footprint graphics. The colored version of a text footprint graphic appears in response to mouse movement over each graphic or its associated text.

1. **Click the** text editor program button **to return to your tents.htm source code, then scroll through the page code to find** `<div class="tenthead"><img src="starlite.gif" align="left" id="star">`**, which is located directly below** `<div id="tent1" name="tent">`

2. **Click after** `class="tenthead"`**, then press** [Spacebar]

3. **Type** `onMouseOver="star.src='starcolor.gif'"`**, press** [Enter]**, then type** `onMouseOut="star.src='starlite.gif'"`

> **QUICK TIP**
> Make sure to type an apostrophe (') followed by a quotation mark (") after the source names, not three apostrophes.

4. **Scroll down the Web page code to find the** `<div class="tenthead">` **tag below the opening tent2 division tag**

5. **Click after** `class="tenthead"`**, press** [Spacebar]**, type** `onMouseOver="brev.src='brevcolor.gif'"`**, press** [Enter]**, then type** `onMouseOut="brev.src='brevifolia.gif'"`
   Figure L-12 shows the completed code for the first two tent items. Notice that the image tag for each tent has a unique ID attribute, such as `id="star"`. The *onMouseOver* event swaps a color graphic of the tent floor plan for the original image source. The *onMouseOut* event replaces the color image with the original black-and-white graphic.

6. **Repeat Step 5 for the remaining five list items, using the IDs and graphic files listed in Table L-3**

7. **Check your document for errors, make changes as necessary, then save your work**

8. **Click the** browser program button **on the taskbar, then reload** tents.htm **in your browser**

9. **Scroll down to the list of tent descriptions, then move your mouse pointer over the heading or graphic for the Amano Brevifolia**
   As shown in Figure L-13, when you move the mouse pointer over the black-and-white outline or its associated heading, the image is replaced with a color graphic. Even though you are simply swapping one graphic for another, this action creates the illusion of modifying the original graphic, much like changing text color using style sheets.

10. **Move the mouse pointer away from the second list item**
    The graphic changes back to the line art version.

FIGURE L-12: Event handlers for the first and second list items

Event handlers for Starlite inserted in <div> tag

ID attribute

Image source

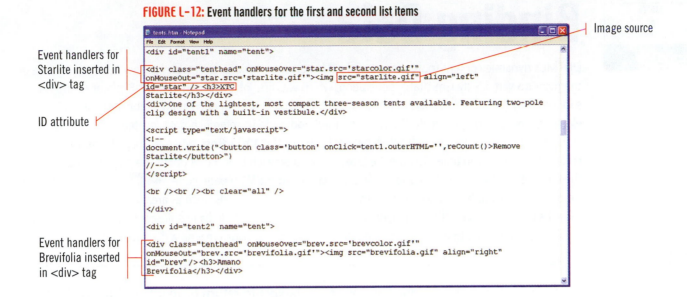

Event handlers for Brevifolia inserted in <div> tag

FIGURE L-13: Web page showing substituted graphic

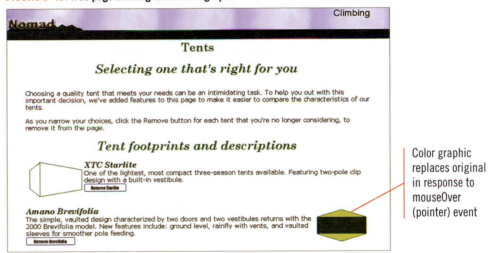

Color graphic replaces original in response to mouseOver (pointer) event

TABLE L-3: List item src and graphic filenames

list item	src	color graphic name (*onMouseOver*)	black-and-white graphic name (*onMouseOut*)
1	star	starcolor.gif	starlite.gif
2	brev	brevcolor.gif	brevifolia.gif
3	tri	tricolor.gif	trifolia.gif
4	hillside	hillsidecolor.gif	hillside.gif
5	hilltop	hilltopcolor.gif	hilltop.gif
6	peak	peakcolor.gif	peak.gif
7	summit	summitcolor.gif	summit.gif

Binding Data

DHTML's dynamic content tools offer specialized features for working with tables in your Web pages. One of the most powerful is dynamic table generation, which was first introduced in Internet Explorer 4, and is now supported by Netscape browsers as well as later versions of IE. Instead of creating a table using a tag for each element, you can simply create the headers, then add code to reference data located in an external file. Linking an external database with a Web page is known as **data binding**. When the page loads, the browser creates the table at run time. Because the table is re-created each time a user opens the page, you can change the contents of the external data source without changing the Web page code. Because it is helpful for tent shoppers to be able to compare the details of different models, such as area and weight, you decide to add a tent data table to the Web page. Nomad Outfitters has provided a text file containing the appropriate information. You want to write code to bind the file to your Web page creating a dynamic table.

STEPS

1. Click the **text editor program button** on the taskbar to return to your tents.htm source code

2. **Scroll to near the end of the code until the `<object>` tags and list of tent descriptions appear in the document window**

   Figure L-14 shows the code including the `<object>...</object>` tags. These tags were entered for you earlier, to set up the external file containing the data for your table as a Web page object. The classid attribute calls the routine for dynamic table generation to format the linked data. The nested `<param>` elements within the object tags denote parameters for the object. The *DataURL* parameter identifies the name of the external file, tents.txt, to be bound. The *true* value for the UseHeader attribute specifies that the data in the external file includes a row of information identifying the contents of each column.

3. **Select the partial comment `<!-- Begin Table Comment: Replace with opening table tag`, then press [Delete]**

   The comment you selected does not contain the ending comment marks (`-->`). To prevent the partial table from appearing as an error while you worked on your page, you placed the entire set of code within a single comment. As shown in Figure L-14, the comment ends at the insertion point for the closing table tag.

4. **Type `<table width="90%" border="4" cellpadding="2" cellspacing="5" id="elemtbl" datasrc="#tentlist" bordercolorlight="#996633" bordercolordark="#006600" align="center">`**

   The table tag causes the code that follows to be formatted as rows in a table. The datasrc attribute refers to the object element with the id *tentlist*. The number sign (#) indicates that the source is an object in the same Web page. The other attributes you typed into the opening table tag format the table with colors that match the rest of your page.

5. **Scroll down to the bottom of the table content area and select the partial comment `End Table Comment: Replace with closing table tag -->`, press [Delete], then type `</table>`**

   The rows within the table tags contain row header display information and links to the columns in the external source. The datafld attribute in each `<div>...</div>` tag names the column header in the external file that marks the column to be associated with the tag.

6. **Check your document for errors, make changes as necessary, then save your work**

7. **Click your browser program button on the taskbar and reload tents.htm, then scroll to the bottom of the page**

   The tent comparison information from the bound data file appears in a table, as shown in Figure L-15. Nomad Outfitters can add, remove, or edit lines from the external file, and the Web page table automatically reflects the most current information each time the Web page is loaded.

TROUBLE

If you are using a Netscape browser and the table does not load, select Options from the Tools menu, click the Advanced button, then click the Download button in the Advanced window to download the browser updates. You can also switch to the Netscape Internet Explorer rendering engine by choosing the Internet Explorer option from the Tools/Options/Site Controls window.

FIGURE L-14: Object and comment tags in Web page source

Code to format bound data

```
<object id="tentlist" classid="clsid:333C7BC4-460F-11D0-BC04-0080C7055A83">
        <param name="DataURL" value="tents.txt">
        <param name="UseHeader" value="true">
</object>

<!-- Begin Table Comment: Replace with opening table tag

<caption><h3>Tent Descriptions<br />Click a category to sort the table</caption>
<thead>
<tr>
<td><strong><div id="tent">Tent</div></strong></td>
<td><strong><div id="catno">Catalog number</div></strong></td>
<td><strong><div id="area">Area (sq ft)</div></strong></td>
<td><strong><div id="vest">Vestibule (sq ft)</div></strong></td>
<td><strong><div id="desc">Description</div></strong></td>
<td><strong><div id="cap">Capacity</div></strong></td>
<td><strong><div id="weight">Weight</div></strong></td>
<td><strong><div id="price">Price</div></strong></td>
</tr>
</thead>
<tbody>
<tr>
<td><div datafld="tent"></div></td>
<td><div datafld="catno"></div></td>
<td><div datafld="area"></div></td>
<td><div datafld="vest"></div></td>
<td><div datafld="desc"></div></td>
<td><div datafld="cap"></div></td>
<td><div datafld="weight"></div></td>
<td><div datafld="price"></div></td>
</tr>
</tbody>
End Table Comment: Replace with closing table tag -->
```

Comment tag surrounds table structure

FIGURE L-15: Tent comparison table

Vista Summit
Comfortable, rugged, 4-season tent. Quick setup, full rainfly, integral vestibule, large door. Factory sealed, mesh window and door for ventilation.

[Remove Summit]

This page describes 7 tent models.

Nomad Ltd has a tent that's right for you!

Tent Descriptions
Click a category to sort the table

Browser-generated table based on external data source

Tent	Catalog number	Area (sq ft)	Vestibule (sq ft)	Description	Capacity	Weight	Price
XTC Starlite	BR-370	34	10	Staked	1 person	4 lbs. 3 oz.	$150
Amano Brevifolia	BT-356	38.5	19.6	Freestanding	2 people	5 lbs. 8 oz.	$215
Amano Trifolia	BT-358	49	25.7	Freestanding	2 people	7 lbs.	$250
Vista Hillside	BZ-339	32	15.3	Staked	1 person	4 lbs.	$120
Vista Hilltop	BZ-367	37.5	19.5	Staked	1 person	5 lbs. 3 oz.	$160
Vista Peak	BZ-323	42.5	24.4	Freestanding	2 people	6 lbs. 3 oz.	$210
Vista Summit	BZ-334	51.5	28	Freestanding	2 people	7 lbs. 10 oz.	$275

If you are unable to read the content of the above table, go to our alternate tent listing
For more information on Nomad Ltd outdoor supplies, please email our Nomad Outfitters Sales Department

HTML

Manipulating Bound Data Dynamically

In addition to dynamic table creation, Microsoft Internet Explorer introduced other cutting-edge tools for working with tables in Web pages. Perhaps one of the most useful is dynamic sorting, which enables users to sort the data in a table by clicking the relevant column heading. To allow users to compare tent statistics based on the most important categories, you add a script that sorts the tent information on a given column when a user clicks that column heading.

STEPS

1. **Click your text editor program button on the taskbar to return to your page code, then locate the function tentClick() near the bottom of the page**

   The function, with separate scripts for each column, has already been entered for you. However, it was disabled with JavaScript comment tags (/* */). Each script sorts the table by the contents of that column using the *tentlist.Sort=* command, and then regenerates the table to show the sort, with the function, *tentlist.Reset()*. Accompanying each script is a line of code triggering the script in response to the *onClick* event for the given column header. You want to remove the comment tags and enter a final script to sort the table by price.

2. **Locate the line of code that reads /*function tentClick() {, select the opening JavaScript comment marker, /*, then press [Delete]**

3. **Move to the bottom of the script and select the closing JavaScript comment tag, */, as well as the comment /*Replace with price script*/ that follows, then press [Delete]**

4. **Press [Enter], then type the following script, pressing [Enter] at the end of each line:**
   ```
   function priceClick() {
       tentlist.Sort="price";
       tentlist.Reset();
   }

   price.onclick=priceClick;
   ```
   Figure L-16 shows the section of your script with the completed price-sorting function. Notice that below the closing script tag, a link was inserted to display information for users whose browsers do not support data binding.

5. **Check the script you entered for errors, click before the final </div> tag, add a Page modified by paragraph with your name and today's date, then save your work**

6. **Click your browser program button on the taskbar to open your browser, reload your page, scroll to the bottom of the page and inspect the table, then print the page**

   The tent comparison table is displayed in its default order. Notice that the Vestibule (sq ft) column is not displayed in any particular order.

7. **Click the Vestibule (sq ft) column heading, scroll down to see the regenerated table, then compare your screen with your printout**

   The table regenerates to show the records in ascending order by vestibule area, as shown in Figure L-17.

8. **Click the Price column heading, then scroll down to see the regenerated table and print the page again**

   The table displays the records in order by price, using the script you entered.

9. **Close the Web browser and text editor, then transfer your new files to your remote directory on the server**

FIGURE L-16: Web page code containing price-sorting script

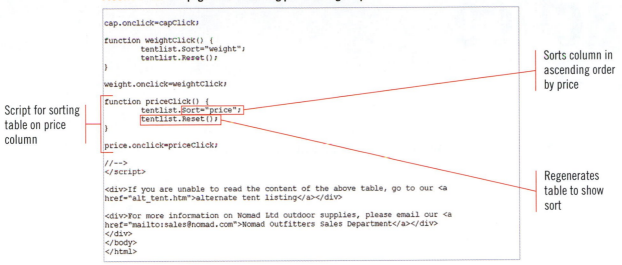

```
cap.onclick=capClick;

function weightClick() {
        tentlist.Sort="weight";
        tentlist.Reset();
}

weight.onclick=weightClick;

function priceClick() {
        tentlist.Sort="price";
        tentlist.Reset();
}

price.onclick=priceClick;

//-->
</script>

<div>If you are unable to read the content of the above table, go to our <a
href="alt_tent.htm">alternate tent listing</a></div>

<div>For more information on Nomad Ltd outdoor supplies, please email our <a
href="mailto:sales@nomad.com">Nomad Outfitters Sales Department</a></div>
</div>
</body>
</html>
```

Sorts column in ascending order by price

Script for sorting table on price column

Regenerates table to show sort

FIGURE L-17: Table with unsorted and sorted data

Tent	Catalog number	Area (sq ft)	Vestibule (sq ft)	Description	Capacity	Weight	Price
XTC Starlite	BR-370	34	10	Staked	1 person	4 lbs. 3 oz.	$150
Amano Brevifolia	BT-356	38.5	19.6	Freestanding	2 people	5 lbs. 8 oz.	$215
Amano Trifolia	BT-358	49	25.7	Freestanding	2 people	7 lbs.	$250
Vista Hillside	BZ-339	32	15.3	Staked	1 person	4 lbs.	$120
Vista Hilltop	BZ-367	37.5	19.5	Staked	1 person	5 lbs. 3 oz.	$160
Vista Peak	BZ-323	42.5	24.4	Freestanding	2 people	6 lbs. 3 oz.	$210
Vista Summit	BZ-334	51.5	28	Freestanding	2 people	7 lbs. 10 oz.	$275

Table sorted in response to click on column head

Tent	Catalog number	Area (sq ft)	Vestibule (sq ft)	Description	Capacity	Weight	Price
XTC Starlite	BR-370	34	10	Staked	1 person	4 lbs. 3 oz.	$150
Vista Hillside	BZ-339	32	15.3	Staked	1 person	4 lbs.	$120
Vista Hilltop	BZ-367	37.5	19.5	Staked	1 person	5 lbs. 3 oz.	$160
Amano Brevifolia	BT-356	38.5	19.6	Freestanding	2 people	5 lbs. 8 oz.	$215
Vista Peak	BZ-323	42.5	24.4	Freestanding	2 people	6 lbs. 3 oz.	$210
Amano Trifolia	BT-358	49	25.7	Freestanding	2 people	7 lbs.	$250
Vista Summit	BZ-334	51.5	28	Freestanding	2 people	7 lbs. 10 oz.	$275

Clues to Use

Suppressing errors

When creating cross-browser code, you may want to add features to your pages that generate error messages in some browsers. To allow your information to get out to everyone who wants to view it without alarming viewers, you can include a script that keeps error messages from appearing in incompatible browsers. By setting the value of the object *window.onerror* to null, you prevent error windows from opening when scripts have problems completing. Take care not to add error suppression until you have completed and debugged your page because error suppression removes an important debugging aid.

HTML

Practice

▼ CONCEPTS REVIEW

Name the function of each section of code indicated in Figure L-18.

```
1 ┤
    <body onload="scrollit('Gift certificates are available for all of
    the spa packages.');">

    <div
2 ┤ onMouseOver="logo.src='spa_logo2.gif'"
    onMouseOut="logo.src='spa_logo.gif'">
3 ┤
    <img id="logo" src="spa_logo.gif" width="420" height="100" />
    </div>

    <script type="text/javascript" language="JavaScript">
    <!--

    document.write("<button onClick=pack1.outerHTML='',reCount()>Remove
    Rocky Mountain Express Package</button>")

    function priceClick() {
4 ┤        packlist.Sort="price";
           packlist.Reset();
    }
5 ┤
    price.onclick=priceClick;

    //-->
    </script>

    </body>
    </html>
```

Match each statement with the term it describes.

6. **DHTML features that make immediate modifications to a page's actual content**
7. **Period when a browser first interprets and displays a Web page**
8. **Associating an external database with a Web page**
9. **HTML property for replacing an element and the HTML tags enclosing it**
10. **HTML property for replacing an element but leaving its enclosing HTML tags**

a. Data binding
b. *InnerHTML*
c. Run time
d. *OuterHTML*
e. Dynamic content

Select the best answer from the list of choices.

11. Linking an external database with a Web page is:

    a. Data binding.

    b. *OuterHTML.*

    c. *InnerHTML.*

    d. Event handling.

12. When linking an external database, the name of the data file is provided in the:

    a. *DataURL* parameter.

    b. `<div>` tag.

    c. `<span>` tag.

    d. *InnerHTML.*

13. Which HTML tag set do you use to list the properties for a dynamically generated table?

    a. `<tbl>...</tbl>`

    b. `<table>...</table>`

    c. `<thead>...</thead>`

    d. `<object>...</object>`

14. Error windows may be prevented from opening when your scripts have trouble running by adding what value to the object *window.onerror*?

    a. Noerror

    b. Void

    c. Null

    d. None

15. Dynamic content can be triggered through which of the following? (Choose all that apply.)

    a. Pointing

    b. Run time

    c. Data binding

    d. Tools menu

▼ SKILLS REVIEW

1. Insert content dynamically.

    a. In your text editor, open the file **htm_L-2.txt** from the drive and folder where your Data Files are stored, then save it as **packages.htm** to the paradise/spa directory where you save your site files. If you are asked whether you want to replace the file, click Yes.

    b. Copy the **spa_logo.gif** and **spa_logo2.gif** files from the drive and folder where your Data Files are stored to the paradise/spa directory where you save your site files.

FIGURE L-19

```
<script type="text/javascript" language="JavaScript">
<!--

countHeaders()
document.write("<h3> We are sure that you will enjoy one of our   ")
document.write("<span id='textnum'>")
        document.write(totalPacks)
        document.write("</span>")
document.write(" spa packages.</h3>")

//-->
</script>
```

    c. Locate the *countHeaders* function at the top of the page and review the script code.

    d. Locate the comment on the page indicating where to insert the package count code.

    e. Use Figure L-19 as a guide to enter the code that writes the number of spa packages calculated by the *countHeaders* function. Delete the comment.

    f. Check your script for errors, make changes as necessary, then save **packages.htm**.

    g. Open **packages.htm** in your browser to check your work.

2. Delete content dynamically.

    a. Locate the area where a button will be placed that removes the Rocky Mountain Express package.

    b. Enter the code: `document.write("<button onClick=pack1.outerHTML=''>Remove Rocky Mountain Express Package</button>")` between the opening `<script>` and closing `</script>` tags to add the button that removes the Rocky Mountain Express package.

    c. Check your code for errors, make changes as necessary, then save **packages.htm**.

    d. Delete the comment line for the button in the script.

    e. Reload **packages.htm** in your browser and check your work by clicking the button to delete the Rocky Mountain package.

3. Modify content dynamically.

    a. Locate the *reCount* function at the top of the page and review the script code.

    b. In the code for the button that removes the Rocky Mountain package, add a call to the *reCount* function in the button tag. (*Hint*: The tag should be `<button onClick=pack1.outerHTML='',reCount()>`. Be careful not to add a space between the quotes and the comma before the function name.)

    c. Check your script for errors, make changes as necessary, then save **packages.htm**.

    d. Reload **packages.htm** in your browser to check your work.

4. Incorporate an advanced content function.

    a. Locate the *scrollit* function at the top of the page and review the script code.

    b. Locate the `<body>` tag and place the code `onload="scrollit('Gift certificates are available for all of the spa packages.');"` inside the tag to call the *scrollit* function to create scrolling text in the status bar.

    c. Check your script for errors, make changes as necessary, then save **packages.htm**.

    d. Reload **packages.htm** in your browser to check your work.

5. Replace graphics dynamically.

    a. Locate the `<img />` tag that displays the spa logo. Above the `<img />` tag, add the following code to change the image when a user moves the mouse over the logo: `<div onMouseOver="logo.src='spa_logo2.gif'" onMouseOut="logo.src='spa_logo.gif'">`

    b. Add a closing `</div>` tag after the `<img />` tag.

    c. Check your code for errors, make changes as necessary, then save **packages.htm**.

    d. Reload **packages.htm** in your browser, and move the mouse over the spa logo to check your work.

6. Bind data.

    a. In your text editor, open the file **htm_L-3.txt** from the drive and folder where your Data Files are stored, then save it as **packages.txt** to the paradise/spa directory where you save your site files. Review the data in the file, then close the file.

    b. Locate the opening `<object>` tag near the bottom of the packages.htm file, and review the attributes and values between the opening `<object>` tag and closing `</object>` tag.

    c. Locate the opening `<table>` tag under the closing `</object>` tag. Add a datasrc attribute with a value of *packlist* to the opening `<table>` tag. (*Hint*: The table tag will be `<table border="1" datasrc="#packlist">`.)

    d. Check your code for errors, make changes as necessary, then save **packages.htm**.

    e. Reload **packages.htm** in your browser and check your table to be sure it contains the data from the packages.txt file.

7. Manipulate bound data dynamically.

    a. Locate the *priceClick* function at the bottom of the file before the closing `</body>` tag. Review the function between the `<script>` tags.

    b. Before the closing `</script>` tag, add the code to call the function *priceClick*. (*Hint*: `price.onclick=priceClick;`.)

    c. Check your code for errors, make changes as necessary, then save **packages.htm**.

    d. Reload **packages.htm** in your browser and check your work by clicking on the price column to sort the data in increasing order by price.

    e. Add your name as a comment in the script area at the bottom of the packages.htm page, then save and print the page.

    f. Transfer the **packages.htm** and **packages.txt** files to your remote directory.

▼ INDEPENDENT CHALLENGE 1

As you continue developing the Web site for your resort rental business, Star Vacations, you decide to change the frequently asked questions page so that it allows users to delete questions to suit their needs. This allows users to print only the questions and answers that apply to their situations.

a. In your text editor, open the file **htm_L-4.txt** from the drive and folder where your Data Files are stored, then save it as **faq.htm** to the vacations folder where you save your site files. If you are asked whether you want to replace the file, click Yes.

b. Locate the area where the first question "How can I list a property?" is answered. Review the button that removes this question and answer.

c. Locate the area where the second question "How do I find the perfect vacation property?" is answered. Review the button that removes this question and answer.

d. Use the examples from the first two buttons to write the button code for questions three through seven.

e. Check your code for errors, add your name to the bottom of the page as the contact person for information, then save **faq.htm**.

f. Open **faq.htm** in your browser and check your work by clicking the buttons to remove the questions. Print the page with all of the questions displayed in your browser.

g. Transfer the **faq.htm** file to your remote directory.

Advanced Challenge Exercises

- Add a ScreenTip to the button that removes question 2 to let users know the button removes the question and the answer.
- Save your work and reload the **faq.htm** page in the browser to check your ScreenTip.
- Transfer your **faq.htm** page to your remote directory.

▼ INDEPENDENT CHALLENGE 2

Metro Water has an e-mail subscription form for its customers to sign up for monthly newsletters. You will add a feature to the form that counts the newsletters offered to your customers.

a. In your text editor, open the **htm_L-5.txt** file from the drive and folder where your Data Files are stored, then save it as **newsletter.htm** in the water folder where you save your site files. If you are asked whether you want to replace the file, click Yes.

b. Locate the script comment that points out where the *countNewsletters* function should be placed. Use Figure L-20 as a guide to enter the *countNewsletters* function to total the number of newsletters on the form. Delete the comment.

FIGURE L-20

```
function countNewsletters() {
    for (var i = 0; i < document.all.length; i++){
        var hit = document.all[i].name;
        if ("new" == hit){
                totalNews++;
                }
        }
}
```

HTML

▼ INDEPENDENT CHALLENGE 2 (CONTINUED)

c. Locate the script comment that points out where the *countNewsletters* function should be called. Use Figure L-21 as a guide to enter the *countNewsletters* function call and the code that will display the results on the form. Delete the comment.

d. Check your code for errors, add your name as a comment in the script that calls the function, then save **newsletter.htm**.

e. Open **newsletter.htm** in your browser and check your work.

f. Print the page from your text editor, then transfer the **newsletter.htm** file to your remote directory.

FIGURE L-21

```
countNewsletters()
document.write("<h4> All ")
document.write("<span id='textnum'>")
        document.write(totalNews)
        document.write("</span>")
document.write(" Metro Water newsletters are distributed
on the first day of each month.</h4>")
```

Advanced Challenge Exercises

- The *alert* function can be used to debug scripts by tracking the value of variables at different points in a script.
- Add two *alert* statements to the script that calls the *countNewsletters* function. The *alert* functions should display the value of the *totalNews* variable before and after the *countNewsletters* function is called.
- Save your work, then reload the **newsletter.htm** file in your browser to check the totals.
- Transfer the **newsletter.htm** file to your remote directory.

▼ INDEPENDENT CHALLENGE 3

You can find and analyze Web pages that employ dynamic features to get ideas for incorporating DHTML. You will search for new dynamic features to add to Web sites.

a. Use the search engine of your choice to locate two Web pages that incorporate dynamic content in ways that are different than those presented in this unit.

b. Print a copy of each page and mark up the areas where the content changes dynamically.

c. In a separate paper briefly describe how the content changes on each page and what triggers the changes.

d. Add the pages' URLs and your name to the paper, then print the paper.

Now that you have used dynamic content to add new features to Web pages, you are ready to add these features to your Web site.

a. Determine how the DHTML features from this unit can be used to enhance the pages in your Web site.

b. Identify the pages that would benefit from user interactivity, then add the appropriate scripts to the pages.

c. Identify the pages that would provide a better user experience with content inserted or deleted dynamically, then add the scripts to the pages.

d. Identify the pages that should bind data from an external file, then add the scripts to create the table using the data. Add sorting capability to the appropriate column headings.

e. Add your name to the pages, print them, then transfer them to your remote directory.

▼ VISUAL WORKSHOP

You have created a text file with data about hard drives that you will offer your Bits and PCs customers. You want to use data binding to create a Web Page table from this external text file that can be sorted by the Bits and PCs customers. In your text editor, open the external data file **hdlist.txt** from the drive and folder where your Data Files are stored and review the contents. Save the **hdlist.txt** file in the bitspcs folder where you save your site files. In your text editor, open the htm_L-6.txt file from the drive and folder where your Data Files are stored, then save it as **specials.htm** in the bitspcs folder where you save your site files. If you are asked whether you want to replace the file, click Yes.

Use Figure L-22 as a guide to create a table on the specials.htm page that displays the data from the text file hdlist.txt in the table columns. Be sure the table is sortable by price and capacity when the column headers are clicked, using the scripts on the page. Add your name as a comment in the script in the specials.htm file, print the file from your text editor, then save and close specials.htm.

FIGURE L-22

Bits and PCs

[Home] [History Information] [Advertised Specials] [Products] [Services]

Hard Drive Specials

Capacity(GB)	Buffer Size(M)	RPM	Price
160	8	7200	$110.99
250	8	7200	$130.99
300	16	7200	$145.99
100	8	7200	$100.99
450	16	7200	$150.00
255	8	7200	$120.99

For information about sales, service or store hours contact info@bitsPCs.com

Positioning with DHTML

OBJECTIVES

Understand DHTML positioning

Position an element absolutely

Position an element relatively

Size an element manually

Stack screen elements

Add a scroll bar

Create a sidebar

Use dynamic positioning

One of DHTML's greatest contributions to Web page design is its ability to precisely position elements on a page. Like other DHTML components, DHTML positioning and sizing features open doors to many possibilities for Web page enhancements. For example, you can change the sizes of elements by percentage based on screen width, or you can set the widths of columns of information as fixed pixels. You can also position elements using top and left page coordinates, or you can position elements in relation to other elements on the screen. Other DHTML features, such as scroll bars and sidebars, complement positioning to help create effective page layouts.  You have been working on pages for Nomad Outfitters, the company that leads the trekking and outback adventures for Paradise Mountain. Now you want to enrich the Web page design for the Nomad Outfitters pages. You will use positioning and other DHTML layout features to create a sophisticated, attractive style.

Understanding DHTML Positioning

Although document layout tools for traditional media, such as posters and magazines, allow precise placement of page elements, HTML lacks such tools for Web page design. However, DHTML allows precise positioning of page elements through an extension of cascading style sheets called **Cascading Style Sheets Positioning (CSSP)**. CSSP allows you to position elements either absolutely, at fixed coordinates on a user's screen, or relatively, based on the position of other screen elements. Although some advanced page layout is possible with basic HTML, CSSP makes the task much easier to code and offers features not possible with HTML alone. To specify positioning using CSSP, you use the position attribute, which is a style sheet property.  As you research CSSP, you learn about several features, including columns, overlapping, and scripted effects, that you would like to include in your Web pages.

Using CSSP you can control:

- **Columns**

  Many Web page designers have created advanced layout features using basic HTML formatting. For example, standard HTML pages can use tables to display text in columns rather than in a single block. However, adding these features in HTML can be difficult and limiting because the tags were not originally designed to provide advanced formatting and their content does not always read the way it should for users of accessibility devices such as text readers. CSSP makes this type of formatting much simpler by allowing you to easily specify each element's width and location on a Web page. CSSP also places elements more predictably when users view pages in different screen resolutions. You plan to use the CSSP float feature to add a sidebar similar to the one shown in Figure M-1 to the Nomad Outfitters tents page.

- **Overlap**

  A design feature not found in HTML but available in CSSP is the ability to overlap screen elements, which allows you to add captions over graphics. You can also create complex layouts such as those that superimpose words in different colors or that overlap parts of images. The Web page in Figure M-1 uses CSSP to overlap page elements. You want to use the overlap feature to create a distinctive design effect in your Web pages for Nomad Outfitters. You plan to place the general category name for each Web page in large, light-colored text behind and above the page headings.

- **Scripted features**

  As with other DHTML tools, combining CSSP with scripts allows you to create many new display features for your Web pages. For example, by changing a graphic's dimensions slightly at regular intervals, you can animate it with DHTML. You also can use scripting to allow users to drag elements to new positions on the Web page as shown in Figure M-2. You plan to add some draggable elements to your tents page to help users visualize the placement of sleeping bags in various tent designs.

FIGURE M-1: Nomad Outfitters page with overlapping and floating DHTML elements

Layered, overlapping elements

Floating sidebar

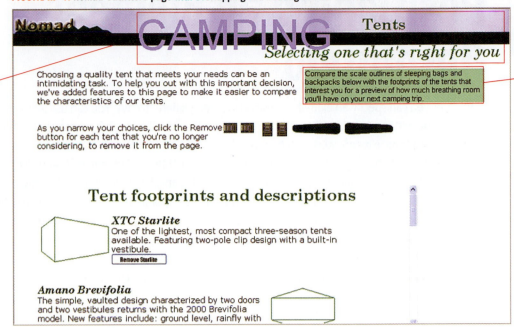

Dynamic positioning allows users to drag page elements to other positions

FIGURE M-2: Page with draggable elements

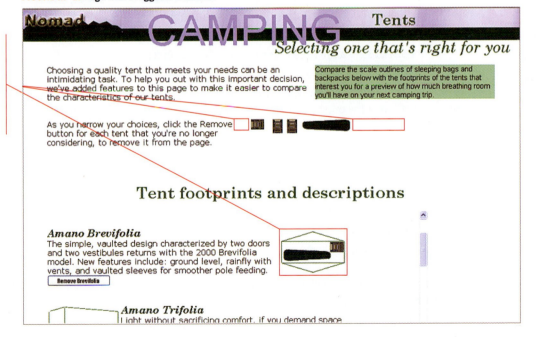

HTML

Positioning an Element Absolutely

With CSSP, you can specify an element's position in several different ways. You can use **absolute positioning** to specify the left and top coordinates of an element relative to the top-left corner of its parent element. For example, a `<span>` element nested within a `<div>` would be positioned relative to the `<div>` element, its parent. In this case, the `<span>` element is known as a child of the `<div>` element. Any element not enclosed by another element is a child of the browser window and is absolutely positioned with respect to the top-left corner of the window. You can specify left and top values in points (pt), pixels (px), inches (in), millimeters (mm), or centimeters (cm). If you don't specify units, the browser defaults to pixels The number of pixels visible on a user's screen varies depending on its resolution. However, even when using pixels, it is a good idea to specify units in order to make your code clearer when debugging it and when others read it. As you develop the Nomad Outfitters tents page, you want to reposition the elements located at the top of the page to decrease the amount of blank space in your original design. You decide to use absolute positioning of the elements to create a more compact layout, and override two default styles to further enhance the page.

STEPS

1. **In your text editor, open the file htm_M-1.txt from the place where you store your Data Files, then save it as tents2.htm in your paradise\nomad folder**

    If you did not complete the lessons in Unit L, create a folder called nomad inside your paradise site folder, then copy the Unit L data files to your nomad folder.

2. **Locate the embedded style sheet in the document's head section, click after the closing } following the *noital* style in your document's embedded style sheet, press [Enter], then type the following code, pressing [Enter] after each line:**

    ```
    #logo {
        position: absolute; top: 0px; left: 0px;
    }
    ```

    The *position: absolute* property tells the browser to set a position based on the top-left corner of the browser window, regardless of the other elements on the page. Figure M-3 shows the document source containing the absolute position code. By applying absolute positioning to the page logo, you remove it from the normal flow of content and allow the page headers to move up and fill in the empty area at the top of the page.

3. **Locate the image tag for the nomad.jpg graphic, drag to select `align="left"` in the image tag, then press [Delete]**

4. **Click before `<img src="nomad.jpg" />`, type `<div id="logo">`, then click after the image tag and type `</div>`**

    As shown in Figure M-4, the logo image is now defined as layer content that can be relatively or absolutely positioned. By placing the position information in the `<div>...</div>` element rather than in the image tag, you make it possible for both older and newer browsers to render your layout, which is often referred to as **cross-browser support**.

5. **Compare your code with that shown in Figures M-3 and M-4 to check your document for errors, make any necessary changes, then save your work**

6. **Open tents2.htm in your Web browser**

    As Figure M-5 shows, the Nomad logo appears absolutely positioned in the upper-left corner of the window and has no effect on the alignment or flow of the page elements. The heading text overlaps the dark part of the top border background image.

FIGURE M-3: Page source with absolute positioning code

```
<link href="nomad.css" rel="stylesheet" type="text/css" />

<style>
<!--
.tenthead {
        font-family: arial, sans-serif;
        font-size: 14pt;
}
.button {
        font-family: impact, arial, sans serif;
        font-size: 8pt;
}
.norm   {
        font-weight: normal;
}
.noital {
        font-style: normal;
}
#logo   {
        position: absolute; top: 0px; left: 0px;
}
-->
</style>
```

Class style removes boldfacing when applied to element → `.norm { font-weight: normal; }`

Class style to remove italics → `.noital { font-style: normal; }`

ID style with absolute position code → `#logo { position: absolute; top: 0px; left: 0px; }`

FIGURE M-4: Applied class and id designations

```
<body>

<div id="logo"><img src="nomad.jpg" /></div>

<div class="content">

<h1>Tents</h1>
```

Applied logo id → `<div id="logo">`

FIGURE M-5: Absolute logo positioning causes page content overlap

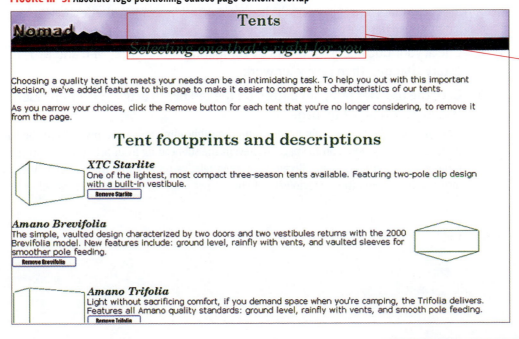

Content moves up on page

HTML

Positioning an Element Relatively

In addition to placing elements at fixed screen coordinates, CSSP allows you to simply offset elements from their default positions in the page flow. This format, called **relative positioning**, is useful when you want your document to always display an element before or after other elements, but at a specified horizontal or vertical offset. You want to indent the page headings but leave them in the general page flow. You use relative positioning to specify the new placement for the headings.

1. **Click the text editor program button on the taskbar to return to your source code, click after the closing } following the** `#logo` **style, press [Enter], then type the following code, pressing [Enter] after each line:**

```
#head {
    position: relative; left: 250px; top: 20px;
}
```

Figure M-6 shows the document code for relative positioning. The *left* property moves the text 250 pixels from the left in relation to its parent element, which could be the browser window or another element, such as a division or a table cell. The top property moves the content down 20 pixels. Unlike absolute positioning, relative positioning leaves an element in the document flow. As a relatively positioned element moves into position, the elements that follow do not move up to fill its former location in the browser window. You want to use relative positioning in your document because you want to indent the headings without allowing the text that follows to overlap the headings and logo graphic.

2. **Scroll to the body section of the document to locate the level-one page heading Tents, click before** `<h1>`, **type** `<div id="head">`, **then press [Enter]**

3. **Click after** `<br />` **in the line below the level-two heading "Selecting the one that's right for you", then type** `</div>`

   As shown in Figure M-7, you enclosed the level-one and level-two headings near the top of the body section in a single division, which you referenced as *id="head"* in order to apply the relative positioning properties you specified in the style section of the document. You used relative positioning because you want the headings, which are centered based on the heading styles set in your linked style sheet, to be indented from the left relative to the content division.

4. **Check your document for errors by comparing it to Figures M-6 and M-7, make any necessary changes, then save your work**

5. **Click the browser program button on the taskbar to activate your browser window, then reload your tents2.htm page**

   As Figure M-8 shows, the main heading and the subheading move 250 pixels from the left of their former location and drop down on the page to prevent the subheading from being written in the dark edge of the top-border background image. Because you used relative positioning, the text after the headings does not move up into the positions previously held by the headings but continues to flow below them.

FIGURE M-6: Page style with absolute and relative position code

```
<style>
<!--
.tenthead {
        font-family: arial, sans-serif;
        font-size: 14pt;
}
.button {
        font-family: impact, arial, sans serif;
        font-size: 8pt;
}
.norm    {
        font-weight: normal;
}
.noital {
        font-style: normal;
}
#logo    {
        position: absolute; top: 0px; left: 0px;
}
#head    {
        position: relative; left: 250px; top: 20px;
}

-->
</style>
```

Absolute position code

Relative position code

FIGURE M-7: Head id applied to page heading sections as a division

Head and logo ids
set in page code

```
<div id="logo"><img src="nomad.jpg" /></div>

<div class="content">

<div id="head">
<h1>Tents</h1>
<h2 class="norm">Selecting one that's right for you</h2>
<br /></div>
```

FIGURE M-8: Page with positioned head element

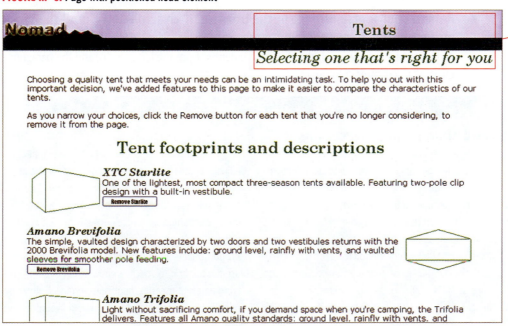

Positioned
head
element

HTML

Sizing an Element Manually

In addition to specifying an element's position on the page, DHTML style properties also allow you to specify an element's dimensions using the height and width properties. You can specify the two dimensions separately by using the same units available for the positioning properties. Additionally, you can size the element relative to its parent by using percentages. If you choose not to specify the height or the width, the browser sizes the element automatically. You want to reformat the descriptive text for each tent model so that it displays indented and in a narrower column. Because you are changing style information for several screen elements, you add properties to the page's embedded style sheet.

STEPS

1. Click the text editor program button on the taskbar to return to your tents2.htm source code

2. Click after the closing } following the #head style in the embedded style sheet in the head section of your document, then press [Enter]

3. Type the following code, pressing [Enter] after each line:

```
.tentbody {
     position: relative; left: 12%; top: 20px; width: 80%;
}
```

Figure M-9 shows the document code including the new tentbody style. The style uses relative positioning with percentages for the left and width attributes in order to accommodate a greater range of browsers and resolutions. By sizing by percentages rather than in fixed pixels, you allow the content area to expand or contract depending upon the size of the browser window and minimize the potential for passive white space.

4. Locate the division tag for the first tent description that reads `<div id="tent1" name="tent">`, click after "tent", press [Spacebar], then type `class="tentbody"`
By applying the *tentbody* class, you set the display properties for the *tent1* division.

5. Repeat Step 4 to apply the *tentbody* class to divisions *tent2, tent3, tent4, tent5, tent6,* and *tent7*
Your completed code should resemble that shown in Figure M-10, which shows the class applied to the *tent6* and *tent7* divisions.

6. Use Figures M-9 and M-10 to check your document for errors, make any necessary changes, then save your work

7. Reload your tents2.htm file in the browser, then scroll down until the tent descriptions appear in the document window
As Figure M-11 shows, each description is indented from the left margin, and the paragraph width is reduced, creating a narrower column.

Design Matters

Positioning and sizing using percentages

Although standard measurement units, such as pixels and points, are most familiar to Web page designers, the ability to use a percentage as a positioning and sizing unit offers advantages for some screen elements. Because elements in the document window appear larger or smaller based on screen resolution, elements aligned or sized in fixed units can appear at different positions, depending on the user's resolution settings. While a column of 150 px may fit perfectly in an 800 × 600 display, that same column may be surrounded by passive white space at 1024 × 768, reducing the effectiveness of your layout. On the other hand, if you size an element that is a child of the document window at 35%, that element automatically adjusts to changes in resolution or window size and maintains the same size relative to the document window. This relative size relationship is not exclusive to the window object as the parent element, but can be set for an element that is a child of any other element, such as a division within the window. In addition to using proportional sizing and positioning with text elements, you can also use the method to specify image sizes. For some applications, specifying an exact measurement is important, but percentage sizing and positioning are important tools in your Web page design toolbox.

FIGURE M-9: Code for .tentbody class

Code for .tentbody class sets relative position and narrows content area to 80% of parent element

```
<style>
<!--
.tenthead {
        font-family: arial, sans-serif;
        font-size: 14pt;
}
.button {
        font-family: impact, arial, sans serif;
        font-size: 8pt;
}
.norm   {
        font-weight: normal;
}
.noital {
        font-style: normal;
}
#logo   {
        position: absolute; top: 0px; left: 0px;
}
#head   {
        position: relative; left: 250px; top: 20px;
}
.tentbody {
        position: relative; left: 12%; top: 20px; width: 80%;
}
-->
</style>
```

FIGURE M-10: Web document code with applied .tentbody class

Opening and closing division tags with .tentbody class apply style to entire division

Next tent division with applied .tentbody class

```
<div id="tent6" name="tent" class="tentbody">

<div class="tenthead" onMouseOver="peak.src='peakcolor.gif'"
onMouseOut="peak.src='peak.gif'"><img src="peak.gif" align="right" id="peak"><h3>Vista
Peak</h3></div>

<div>Easy setup, 3-season tent for 2. Two doors with vestibules offer easy access and
protected sotrage space. Mesh ceiling panel for view and ventilation. Factory sealed, with
 vestibule and interior pockets.</div>

<script type="text/javascript" language="JavaScript">
<!--

document.write("<button class='button' onClick=tent6.outerHTML='',reCount()>Remove
Peak</button>")

//-->
</script>


<br /><br /><br clear="all" />

</div>

<div id="tent7" name="tent" class="tentbody">

<div class="tenthead" onMouseOver="summit.src='summitcolor.gif'"
```

FIGURE M-11: Page displaying adjusted width and position

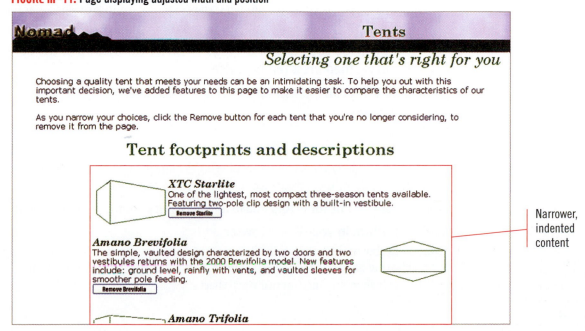

Narrower, indented content

Stacking Screen Elements

Because an absolutely positioned element can appear anywhere on a Web page, including the space occupied by other elements, browsers do not format pages containing these elements as they format standard HTML pages. Instead, each absolutely positioned element is handled as a separate **layer**, which is a transparent, virtual page that can overlap other page elements. To create a layer you use a `<div>` with an *id* property. Web page layers are like sheets of clear acetate with writing or images on them. When the sheets are superimposed as layers in the browser window, all the content of all sheets is available; but some elements may block out others, depending on their order in the stack. To control the order in which each layer stacks on the page, you can specify the element's z-index property. Each layer's **z-index** property determines its position in the stack: higher numbers are located closer to the top of the stack, and elements on these layers will block out elements or superimpose themselves over elements in the same position on lower layers of the stack. The default z-index value for all absolutely positioned elements is 0 (zero). When no other z-index values are specified, you can use a negative z-index value to place an element behind existing content. An element positioned using relative positioning remains on the same layer as the rest of the standard page elements and is not affected by the z-index order. You want to label each of the new Nomad Outfitters pages based on its content category. You want to place the category name at the top of the page so that it appears behind the headings. For the tents page, you decide to add the word "camping" to the heading background in large, light-colored type.

STEPS

1. **Click the text editor program button on the taskbar to return to your page code, locate the `.tentbody` style in the embedded style sheet, click after }, press [Enter] then type the following code, pressing [Enter] after each line:**

```
#backtext   {
            position: absolute; left: 250px; top: 12px;
            font-size: 64pt; font-family: arial; color: #9999FF;
            z-index: -1;
}
```

The new backtext style sets a z-index value of -1 for the backtext element. The first element positioned in a Web page receives a z-index value of 0. Subsequently placed elements receive higher z-index values, resulting in later elements appearing on top of older elements by default. Because you want to make sure the word "CAMPING" appears behind the headings, you assigned it a z-index value lower than 0, the default z-index value.

2. **Scroll down the page code to find the logo division near the top of the body section, click after `</div>`, then press [Enter] twice**

TROUBLE

Z-index positioning may not work in all browsers. Be sure not to use this feature to add content that is critical information to the end user.

3. **Type the following code, pressing [Enter] after each line:**

```
<div id="backtext">
CAMPING
</div>
```

The *id*="*backtext*" property you set for the division displays the properties you defined for *backtext* in the style sheet. Figure M-12 shows the *backtext* division typed into the page code.

4. **Check your document for errors, make any necessary changes, then save your work**

TROUBLE

Depending upon your monitor settings, the "CAMPING" text might appear to the left of your page heading.

5. **Reload tents2.htm in your Web browser**

As Figure M-13 shows, the text "CAMPING" appears behind the headings in a large and light-colored font. This stacked layout allows you to add extra information to the Web page without disrupting the flow of the page. It also adds an interesting, unusual visual effect.

FIGURE M-12: Backtext id applied to CAMPING division

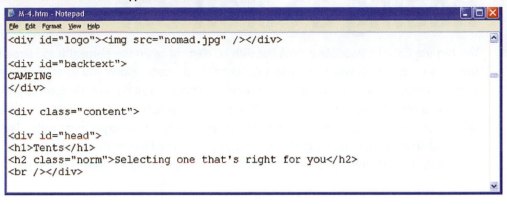

FIGURE M-13: Page with stacked text elements

Stacked page elements

Adding a Scroll Bar

You can use CSSP to associate a scroll bar with an element when the element is too large to fit its defined size. This effect, which you create using the overflow property, allows you to create the equivalent of an independent frame anywhere within your browser window. Most current-day browsers accommodate the overflow property, but some handle it differently, so be sure to check your files in a variety of browsers. To make the tent page layout more concise, you decide to experiment with a layout that formats the list of tent outlines and descriptions in a box with a scroll bar so that users can scroll through the list from top to bottom in the page more quickly and still easily view the tent descriptions.

STEPS

1. Click the **text editor program button** on the taskbar to return to your tents2.htm source code, locate the backtext style in your embedded style sheet, click after **}**, then press **[Enter]**

2. Type the following code, pressing **[Enter]** after each line:

```
#list {
        height: 300px; width: 85%;
        overflow: scroll;
}
```

The code you typed defines the properties that create a display box for an element with the *id* list. You used a fixed pixel height to define your display area, but because you have no way of knowing what resolution and browser settings your site visitors will use, you set the width as a percentage of the page. This prevents the browser from presenting the page with a disproportionate amount of passive white space. Also, because the list of tent descriptions is much longer than 300 pixels, the height specification creates a display area smaller than the object size. The *scroll* value that has been set for the *overflow* property instructs the browser to display scroll bars to allow site visitors to scroll through the entire list. In browsers that do not handle the overflow in the same manner, horizontal scroll bars might also appear.

3. Locate the level-two heading "Tent footprints and descriptions" just above the **tent1** division, click just above the tent1 division, click before **<h2>**, type **<div id="list">**, then press **[Enter]**

QUICK TIP

The *tent7* division contains three line breaks and ends just above the opening script tag for the *countHeaders()* function.

4. Scroll to the end of the list of tent descriptions, locate the closing division tag that follows the button script for tent7, click after **</div>**, then press **[Enter]** twice

5. Type **</div>**

Figure M-14 shows the placement of the opening and closing tag for the list division within the page code. Because some browsers have trouble displaying the relatively positioned elements within the scrolling window, you decide to remove the relative positioning from the *tentbody* class in your embedded style sheet.

6. Locate the **.tentbody** style in your embedded style sheet

QUICK TIP

Do not select the *width: 80%* property.

7. Drag to select **position: relative; left: 12%; top: 20px;** and the space after it, then press **[Delete]**

As shown in Figure M-15, the *tentbody* style class no longer contains any positioning information. In addition, your list style has been added to your embedded style sheet.

8. Check your document for errors, make any necessary changes, then save your page as **tents3.htm**

In saving the tents2.htm file with a new name, you allow your client to decide which version of the page is most pleasing.

TROUBLE

Your page might appear somewhat differently depending upon your browser type and settings. For example, in some browsers a horizontal scroll bar might appear along the bottom of the display area as well.

9. Open **tents3.htm** in your Web browser, then use the scroll bar to view the list of tent footprints and descriptions

As Figure M-16 shows, the list of tent descriptions appears in a condensed area of the page, and a vertical scroll bar on the right edge allows site visitors to scroll the length of the description listing.

Opening list division tag inserted below Tent footprints heading

```
<div id="list">
<h2 class="noital">Tent footprints and descriptions</h2>

<div id="tent1" name="tent" class="tentbody">

<div class="ten   document.write("<button class='button' onClick=tent7.outerHTML='',reCount()>Remove
                   Summit</button>")

                   //-->
                   </script>


                   <br /><br /><br clear="all" />

                   </div>
                   </div>
                   <script type="text/javascript" language="JavaScript">
                   <!--

                   countHeaders()
                   document.write("<h3 style='text-align: center;'>This page describes ")
                   document.write("<span id='textnum'>")
                   document.write(totalTents)
```

Closing list division tag inserted between tent7 button division and countHeaders() function

Adjusted .tentbody style

New #list style with percentage width and overflow set to scroll

```
.tentbody {
        width: 80%;
}
#backtext       {
        position: absolute; left: 250px; top: 12px;
        font-size: 64pt; font-family: arial; color: #9999FF;
        z-index: -1;
}
#list {
        height: 300px; width: 85%;
        overflow: scroll;
}


-->
</style>
```

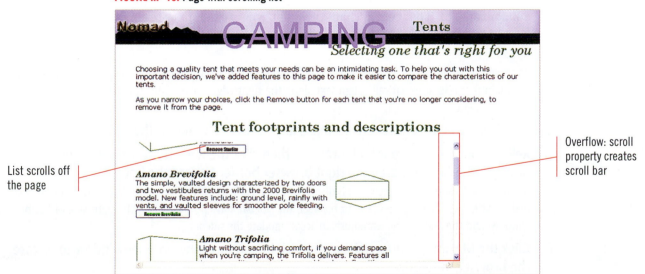

List scrolls off the page

Overflow: scroll property creates scroll bar

HTML

Creating a Sidebar

Using CSSP's placement and sizing properties, you can create and position text blocks independently of each other. You can use the float property to remove an element from the main text flow and display it to the side of the flow in a box called a **sidebar**. The left and right values allow you to specify whether the element is positioned on the right or left side of the main document flow. The float feature allows you to create many text effects, including sidebars, that are difficult to create with HTML alone. You want to add scale outlines of backpacks and sleeping bags to the tents page to give users a better feel for the relative sizes of the tents. To make this area stand out from the page's main text, you decide to enclose it in a sidebar.

STEPS

1. **Click the text editor program button on the taskbar to return to the tents3.htm code**

2. **Locate the *#list* style in your embedded style sheet, click after },press [Enter], then type the following code, pressing [Enter] after each line:**
   ```
   .expl {
       width: 375px;
   }
   ```
   You set a class with a *width* property that you later apply to a section of text to prevent it from expanding too far into the right section of your page.

3. **Press [Enter], then type the following code, pressing [Enter] after each line:**
   ```
   #sidebar {
       width: 40%; float: right;
       font-family: arial; font-size: 11pt; background: #99CC99;
   }
   ```
   The *float* property removes the section from the document flow, and the *right* value specifies that it floats to the right of the flow. The *width* property controls the horizontal space the element occupies. By setting the width as a percentage rather than in fixed pixels, you allow the sidebar to adjust to the size of the page. Some browsers also support a defined *height* property. However, when the *height* property is not set, the browser automatically adjusts the height of a sidebar to fit its contents. By not assigning the *height* property, you create cross-browser compatible code to ensure a uniform appearance.

4. **Locate the division with the id of *head*, click after `</div>` then press [Enter] twice**

5. **Type the following code:**
   ```
   <div style="text-align: left;" id="sidebar">
   Compare the scale outlines of sleeping bags and backpacks below with the
   footprints of the tents that interest you for a preview of how much
   breathing room you'll have on your next camping trip.
   </div>
   ```
   As shown in Figure M-17, you added code and content to create a sidebar. Sidebars that float to the right of the main text also automatically align text along the right edge, so you used an inline style to override the text alignment.

6. **Check your document for errors, make any necessary changes, then save your work**

7. **Reload your page in your Web browser, then click the Restore Down button on the browser window and drag the right browser border toward the left**
   As Figure M-18 shows, your new text is displayed in a rectangle with a colored background to the right of the main text flow. When you resize your browser, the sidebar stays positioned on the right side of the browser window, and the text on the left adjusts to accommodate the sidebar.

8. **Click the Maximize button in the upper-right corner of the browser window to restore the browser to full size**

FIGURE M-17: Page source with code and content for sidebar

Inline style overrides default right text alignment of sidebar id class

```
<div class="content">

<div id="head">
<h1>Tents</h1>
<h2 class="norm">Selecting one that's right for you</h2>
<br /></div>

<div style="text-align: left;" id="sidebar">Compare the scale outlines of sleeping bags
and backpacks below with the footprints of the tents that interest you for a preview of
how much breathing room you'll have on your next camping trip.</div>

<div>Choosing a quality tent that meets your needs can be an intimidating task. To help
you out with this important decision, we've added features to this page to make it easier
```

Sidebar layer identified with id property

Sidebar division layer with content

FIGURE M-18: Floating sidebar adjusts in comparison to document window

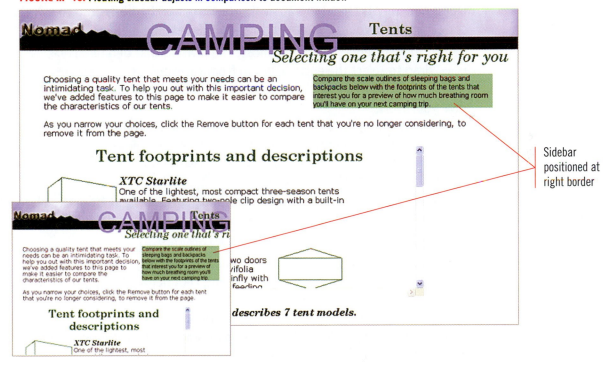

Sidebar positioned at right border

Using Dynamic Positioning

By creating scripts to interact with position and layer information, DHTML allows you to add many special effects and advanced features to your Web pages. One special effect possible with DHTML is **dynamic positioning**. Also known as **dragging**, dynamic positioning combines scripting with style sheet positioning to adjust the position of a selected element based on the coordinates of the mouse pointer, and then assigns the element to its final position once the user releases the mouse button. This drag feature allows users to rearrange elements into an order that is more useful to them than the page's default organization or to interact with Web page models and games. You want to give your site visitors the ability to drag scale outlines of sleeping bags and backpacks over the tent outlines so they can more easily see how much each tent holds.

STEPS

1. Copy the files bag1.gif, bag2.gif, pack1.gif, and pack2.gif in the place where you store your Data Files into your paradise\nomad folder in the place where you save your site files

2. Click the text editor program button to return to your tents3.htm code, locate the *#sidebar* style in your embedded style sheet, click after }, then press [Enter]

3. Type the code shown in Figure M-19, pressing [Enter] after each line, then save your work
   You created the id descriptions as well as a class description, *drag*, in the embedded style section. The *drag* class specifies a z-index of 10 for a draggable element, which ensures that all draggable icons remain on top. You want to position the elements on the page.

4. Open htm_M-2.txt in a separate instance of your text editor, drag to select all of the code, copy it to your clipboard, then close the text file

5. Return to your tents3.htm code, locate the division that begins <div>Choosing a quality tent, drag to select the entire division from <div>Choosing a quality tent, through to remove it from the page.</div>
, press [Delete], then paste your copied code and save your work
   As shown in Figure M-20, the new code contains the original division text as well as divisions containing *id*s and image codes for the icons that you want to insert below your side bar. Each of the icon elements contains a reference to the *drag* class that you specified in the embedded style sheet. Now you need to add the script that allows your icons to be moved.

QUICK TIP
You also can format text elements to be draggable, using ... tags as containers.

6. In a separate instance of your text editor, open htm_M-3.txt from the place where you store your Data Files, copy all the code, then close the text file
   The script handles dragging of absolutely positioned elements.

7. Return to your tents3.htm code, then locate the closing comment tags (//-->) of the script in the head section of your document, click before //-->, paste the copied code, press [Enter], then save your work
   The code associates each image with the *drag* class that you defined in the embedded style sheet with the division layers containing each icon. The script you inserted earlier in the code identifies draggable images through the *canDrag* property.

8. Move to the bottom of the document, click after Department</a>, then type
   ```
   <br /><br />
   <div style="text-align: center;">Page modified by: Your Name, Today's month
   and year</div>
   ```

9. Reload tents3.htm in your Web browser, then drag some of the backpack and sleeping bag outlines onto a tent footprint, print the page, then close all files and transfer your nomad folder to your paradise directory on the server
   In Figure M-21, notice that users can drag icons to new positions, causing the icons to appear on top of the tent outlines.

FIGURE M-19: Page code with positioning styles

Styles defining starting positions for icon elements

.drag class with z-index of 10 positions icon elements on top of other page elements

```
.expl {
        width: 375px;
}
#pack1 {
        position: absolute; left: 505px;
}
#pack2 {
        position: absolute; left: 535px;
}
#pack3 {
        position: absolute; left: 425px;
}
#pack4 {
        position: absolute; left: 460px;
}
#bag1 {
        position: absolute; left: 565px;
}
#bag2 {
        position: absolute; left: 670px;
}
.drag {
        z-index: 10;
}
-->
</style>
```

FIGURE M-20: Document code containing draggable image layers

Original text

New icon code

Applied drag class and canDrag propery set properties for element

Applied expl class sets division width

Original text

```
<div>Choosing a quality tent that meets your needs can be an intimidating task. To help you
out with this important decision, we've added features to this page to make it easier to
compare the characteristics of our tents.</div>
<br /><br />

<div id="pack1" class="drag" canDrag>
<img src="pack2.gif" />
</div>

<div id="pack2" class="drag" canDrag>
<img src="pack2.gif" />
</div>

<div id="pack3" class="drag" canDrag>
<img src="pack1.gif" />
</div>

<div id="pack4" class="drag" canDrag>
<img src="pack1.gif" />
</div>

<div id="bag1" class="drag" canDrag>
<img src="bag1.gif" />
</div>

<div id="bag2" class="drag" canDrag>
<img src="bag2.gif" />
</div>

<div class="expl">As you narrow your choices, click the Remove button for each tent that
you're no longer considering, to remove it from the page.</div><br />

<br /><br /><br />
```

FIGURE M-21: Page with dragged images

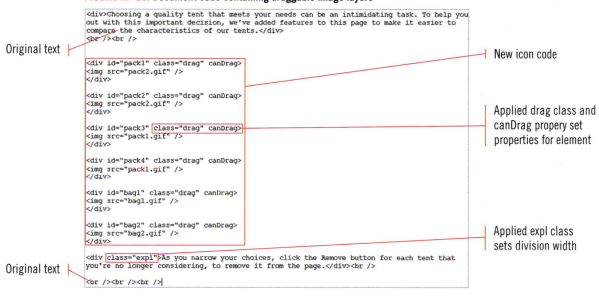

Draggable icons

Icons moved to new position

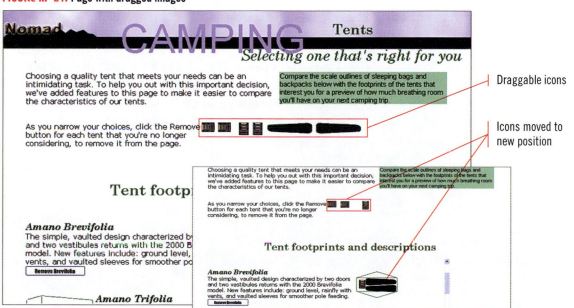

Practice

▼ CONCEPTS REVIEW

Name the function of each section of code indicated in Figure M-22.

FIGURE M-22

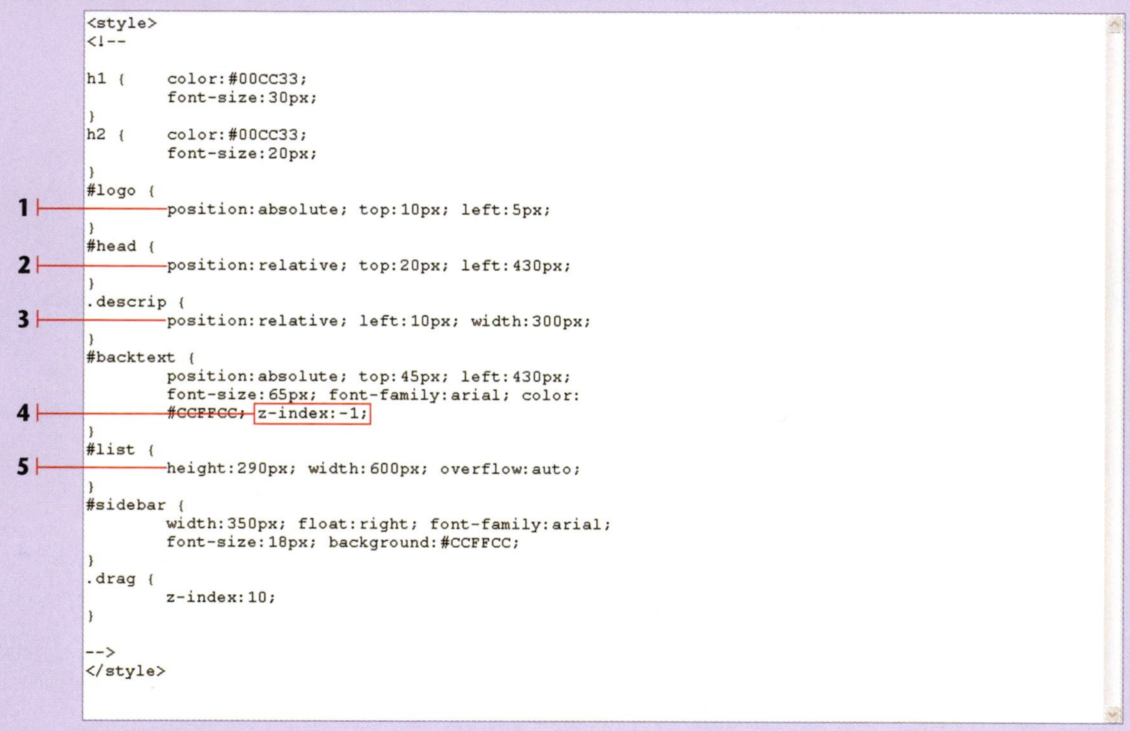

```
<style>
<!--

h1 {      color:#00CC33;
          font-size:30px;
}
h2 {      color:#00CC33;
          font-size:20px;
}
#logo {
1         position:absolute; top:10px; left:5px;
}
#head {
2         position:relative; top:20px; left:430px;
}
.descrip {
3         position:relative; left:10px; width:300px;
}
#backtext {
          position:absolute; top:45px; left:430px;
          font-size:65px; font-family:arial; color:
4         #CCFFCC; z-index:-1;
}
#list {
5         height:290px; width:600px; overflow:auto;
}
#sidebar {
          width:350px; float:right; font-family:arial;
          font-size:18px; background:#CCFFCC;
}
.drag {
          z-index:10;
}

-->
</style>
```

Match each statement with the term it best describes.

6. Absolute positioning
7. Relative positioning
8. Float
9. Height and width
10. Top and left

a. Properties for specifying element dimensions
b. Places an element at fixed left and top coordinates on a page
c. Properties for specifying location
d. Property used to create sidebar
e. Places an element offset from its default position within a page's flow

Select the best answer from the list of choices.

11. **Which CSS-P property allows you to control the amount of an element that is visible?**
    a. Columns
    b. Clip region
    c. Overlap
    d. Sidebar

12. **DHTML allows precise positioning of page elements through an extension of Cascading Style Sheets called**
    a. Absolute positioning.
    b. Cascading Style Sheets–Positioning.
    c. The *Position* style property.
    d. Tables.

13. **The browser places absolutely positioned text (Choose all that apply.)**
    a. At the top-left corner of the browser window.
    b. At the specified coordinates relative to the top-left corner of the parent element.
    c. Behind the main page elements in z-index.
    d. On a separate Web page layer.

14. **As you add new layers to a Web page, the elements on the most recent layers receive**
    a. The same z-index value as earlier layers.
    b. Smaller z-index values than earlier layers.
    c. Larger z-index values than earlier layers.
    d. Negative z-index values.

15. **Which property allows you to add scroll bars to specific elements?**
    a. Scroll bar
    b. Float
    c. Layer
    d. Overflow

16. **Which value should the overflow property be assigned to display a scroll bar for an element?**
    a. Scroll
    b. Absolute
    c. Relative
    d. Float

17. **Which feature allows users to rearrange elements on a Web page?**
    a. Move
    b. Drag
    c. Position
    d. Float

▼ SKILLS REVIEW

1. **Position an element absolutely.**
   a. In your text editor, open the file **htm_M-4.txt** from the drive and folder where your Data Files are stored, then save it as **packages.htm** to the paradise/spa directory where you save your site files. If you are asked whether you want to replace the file, click Yes. Copy the **spa_logo.gif** file from the drive and folder where your Data Files are stored, then paste it in the paradise/images directory in the place where you store your site files. If you are asked whether you want to replace the file, click Yes.
   b. Add a style for an `id` named `logo` below the h2 style in the embedded style sheet. Format the logo `id` with an absolute position of 10 pixels from the top and five pixels from the left of the browser window. (*Hint*: Add `#logo {position: absolute; top: 10px; left: 5px;}` to the embedded style sheet.)
   c. Locate the opening `<div>` tag directly above the `<img />` tag at the beginning of the page body. Add `id="logo"` to the opening `<div>` tag.

    d. Check your file for errors, make any necessary changes, then save your file.

    e. Open **packages.htm** in your browser to view the logo's position. (You will adjust the position of the page heading, now positioned under the logo, shortly.)

2. Position an element relatively.

    a. In the embedded style sheet, below the logo style, add a style for an `id` named head. Format the `head` id with a relative position of 20 pixels from the top and 430 pixels to the left of its parent. (*Hint*: Add `#head {position: relative; top: 20px; left: 430px;}` to the embedded style sheet.)

    b. Locate the opening `<div>` tag directly above the level-one heading of Spa Packages. Add `id="head"` to the opening `<div>` tag.

    c. Check your file for errors, make any necessary changes, then save your file.

    d. Refresh **packages.htm** in your browser to view the position of the page heading.

3. Size an element manually.

    a. In the embedded style sheet, below the `head` style, add a style for a class named descrip. Format the `descrip` class with a width of 300 pixels. (*Hint*: Add `.descrip {width: 300px;}` to the embedded style sheet.)

    b. Locate the opening `<div>` tags directly below the level-three headings of the package names: Rocky Mountain Express, Easy Does It, Eden Paradise, Beautiful Dreamer, and Heavenly Bliss. Add `class="descrip"` to the opening `<div>` tags for these five package descriptions.

    c. Check your file for errors, make any necessary changes, then save your file.

    d. Refresh **packages.htm** in your browser to view the package descriptions displayed in narrow columns.

4. Stack screen elements.

    a. In the embedded style sheet, below the `descrip` class, add a style for an `id` named backtext. Format the `backtext` id with an absolute position of 45 pixels from the top and 430 pixels from the left of the browser window. Add properties to specify the font size as 65 pixels, the font family as arial, the font color as #CCFFCC and a z-index of -1. (*Hint*: Add `#backtext { position: absolute; top: 45px; left: 430px; font-size: 65px; font-family: arial; color: #CCFFCC; z-index: -1;}` to the embedded style sheet.)

    b. Locate the opening `<div>` tag near the beginning of the page body, directly above the text "The Perfect Gift," and add `id="backtext"` to the tag.

    c. Check your file for errors, make any necessary changes, then save your file.

    d. Refresh **packages.htm** in your browser to view the background text behind the Spa Packages heading.

5. Add a scroll bar.

    a. In the embedded style sheet, below the `backtext` id, add a style for an `id` named list. Format the `list` id with a height of 290 pixels, a width of 500 pixels, and an `overflow` property of scroll. (*Hint*: Add `#list {height: 290px; width: 500px; overflow: scroll;}` to the embedded style sheet.)

    b. Locate the opening `<div>` tag near the beginning of the page body directly above the level-three heading for Rocky Mountain Express. Add `id="list"` to the opening `<div>` tag.

    c. Check your file for errors, make any necessary changes, then save your file.

    d. Refresh **packages.htm** in your browser to view the scroll bar for the spa packages.

6. Create a sidebar.

    a. In the embedded style sheet, below the `list` id, add a style for an `id` named sidebar. Format the `sidebar` id with a width of 450 pixels, a `float` property of right, a font family of arial, a font size of 18 pixels, and a background of #CCFFCC. (*Hint*: Add `#sidebar {width: 450px; float: right; font-family: arial; font-size: 18px; background: #CCFFCC;}` to the embedded style sheet.)

    b. Locate the opening `<div>` tag for the text "Compare the spa packages on the left and consider giving one as a gift." near the beginning of the page body. Add `id="sidebar"` to the opening `<div>` tag.

    c. Check your file for errors, make any necessary changes, then save your file.

    d. Refresh **packages.htm** in your browser to view the sidebar.

    e. In your text editor, add your name to the comment above the closing `</body>` tag, print the code, then close the packages.htm file.

▼ SKILLS REVIEW (CONTINUED)

7. Use dynamic positioning.

    a. In your text editor, open the file **htm_M-5.txt** from the drive and folder where your Data Files are stored, then save it as **packages2.htm** to the paradise/spa directory where you save your site files.

    b. In the embedded style sheet, below the `sidebar` id, add a style for a class named `drag`. Format the `drag` class with a z-index of 10. (*Hint*: Add `.drag {z-index: 10;}` to the embedded style sheet.)

    c. Locate the opening `<div>` tag with `class="pkg1"` and add `class="drag"`. Also add `class="drag"` to the next four `<div>` tags with the classes pkg2, pkg3, pkg4, and pkg5.

    d. In the same five opening `<div>` tags, add `canDrag` to mark the text for dragging.

    e. Examine the functions `movePointer`, `checkDrag`, `butPress`, and `checkIt` in the page's head section.

    f. Check your file for errors, make any necessary changes, then save your file.

    g. Open **packages2.htm** in your browser and drag the services on the left into the green area to create a custom package.

    h. In your text editor, add your name to the comment above the closing `</body>` tag and print the packages2.htm code.

▼ INDEPENDENT CHALLENGE 1

As you continue developing the Web site for your resort rental business, Star Vacations, you decide that DHTML positioning will help you lay out the Island Seas Resort page. You will also use DHTML features including a sidebar and a scroll bar to improve the page layout.

    a. In your text editor, open the file **htm_M-6.txt** from the drive and folder where your Data Files are stored, then save it as **island_seas.htm** to the vacations folder where you save your site files. If you are asked whether you want to replace the file, click Yes. Copy the **resort.jpg** file from the drive and folder where your Data Files are stored, then paste it in the vacations/images directory. If you are asked whether you want to replace the file, click Yes.

    b. Locate the embedded style sheet and review the styles for the ids and classes.

    c. Locate the `<img />` tag for the resort.jpg image. Using one of the defined styles from the embedded style sheet, add the *id* or class attribute and value to the `<img />` tag to float the image to the right of the main text flow and assign it a fixed height of 250 pixels.

    d. Locate the opening `<p>` tag above a comment that marks a sidebar content paragraph. Using one of the defined styles from the embedded style sheet, add the *id* or class attribute and value to the `<p>` tag to create a sidebar of text to the left of the main text flow with a fixed height of 200 pixels and a fixed width of 350 pixels. Delete the comment that marks the sidebar text.

    e. Locate the opening `<h3>` tag for the "Property Amenities" text. Using one of the defined styles from the embedded style sheet, add the *id* or class attribute and value to the `<h3>` tag to absolutely position the text 325 pixels from the top and 10 pixels from the left of the browser window.

    f. Locate the opening `<ol>` tag for the ordered list. Using one of the defined styles from the embedded style sheet, add the *id* or class attribute and value to the `<ol>` tag to create a scrollbar of the list items with a height of 145 pixels and a width of 600 pixels.

    g. Locate the opening `<div>` tag below the text "An Island Paradise." Using one of the defined styles from the embedded style sheet, add the *id* or class attribute and value to the `<div>` tag to relatively position the text in the section 40 pixels to the left with a fixed width of 700 pixels. Delete the comment that marks the section text.

▼ INDEPENDENT CHALLENGE 1 (CONTINUED)

h. Check your file for errors by comparing it to Figure M-23

i. Add your name at the bottom of the page in the *mailto*: link, then save the file.

j. Display the file in your browser, and check the position of the page elements and the scroll bar.

k. Print the file from your browser.

l. Transfer the **resort.jpg** file and **island_seas.htm** page to your remote directory.

Advanced Challenge Exercises

■ Internet Explorer does not allow position controls in <body> tags. Use your favorite search engine to research how you can use DHTML to position the entire body of a Web page.

■ Summarize your findings in a paragraph with code examples.

■ Add your name and today's date to the paper, then print it.

FIGURE M-23

```
<img id="image" src="images/resort.jpg" />

<p id="sidebar"><br /><br /><br />
Nestled serenely in a peaceful cove with a sparkling white-sand beach and surrounded by lush
tropical gardens, the Island Seas Resort is so beautiful, the moment you arrive you'll know
<strong><em>you've DISCOVERED PARADISE!</em></strong></p>

<h3 id="head"> Property Amenities </h3>

<ol id="scroll">
<li>Rollaway Bed - $15/Night </li>
<li>Cribs - $10/Night</li>
<li>Convenience Store - On Site</li>
<li>Business Services Available</li>
<li>Fitness Facility</li>
<li>Hourly Shuttle Service from 8:15 a.m. until 5:00 p.m.</li>
<li>Security - 24-Hour</li>
<li>Pool Deck</li>
<li>Gift Shop</li>
<li>White-Sand, Ocean-Front Beach</li>
<li>Children's Pool</li>
<li>Concierge</li>
<li>Restaurant</li>
<li>Babysitting Service</li>
<li>Outdoor Pool</li>
<li>Washer/Dryer</li>
<li>Hot Tub/Whirlpool</li>
</ol>

<h3>An Island Paradise</h3>

<div class="descrip">
<p >Relax and enjoy the unspoiled beauty of pristine white sands at one of the Caribbean's newest
luxury resorts. Situated on its own private beach, the Island Seas Resort is truly a traveler's
dream.</p>

<p>Stroll down the beach to Zonk's Conch Hut to sample one of the island's favorite delicacies.
```

▼ INDEPENDENT CHALLENGE 2

As you continue your work on Metro Water's site, you decide to use DHTML features on the water conservation tips page. You want to use relative and absolute positioning for headings on the page, narrow the width of the tips section, and add background text to the page heading.

a. In your text editor, open the file **htm_M-7.txt** from the drive and folder where your Data Files are stored, then save it as **inside.htm** to the water folder where you save your site files. If you are asked whether you want to replace the file, click Yes.

b. Add an *id* named *head* to the embedded style sheet that sets the font size to 40 pixels and absolutely positions an element 40 pixels from the top and 400 pixels from the left of the browser window's upper-left corner. Locate the opening <h2> tag for the "Conservation Tips" text, and add the head *id* to the tag to fix the position of the page heading.

c. Add a class named *head2* to the embedded style sheet that relatively positions an element 20 pixels from the top and 430 pixels from the left of its default location in the page. Locate the opening <h3> tags for the "Conserving Water Indoors" and "You and your water usage:" text and add the *head2* class to the tags to set the position of the section headings.

d. Add an *id* named *descrip* to the embedded style sheet that relatively positions an element 80 pixels from the left of its default location in the page and fixes its width to 700 pixels. Locate the opening <div> tag above the "General Tips" text and add the *descrip* id to the tag to indent and narrow the width of the tips section.

e. Add an *id* named `backtext` to the embedded style sheet that defines an element's style in the following way:

- Absolute position of 30 pixels from the top and 400 pixels from the left of the browser window's upper-left corner
- Font size of 60 pixels
- Font family of Arial
- Color of #CCFFFF
- Z-index of negative one.

▼ INDEPENDENT CHALLENGE 2 (CONTINUED)

f. Locate the opening `<div>` tag above the "Metro Water" text and add the *backtext id* to the tag to place the Metro Water text behind the page heading.

g. Add your name at the bottom of the page in the *mailto:* link then save the file.

h. Display the file in your browser, checking the position of the page elements and the background text.

i. Print the file from your browser.

j. Transfer the **inside.htm** page to your remote directory.

Advanced Challenge Exercises

■ Change the z-index of the *backtext id* from negative one to three.

■ Save your work. Reload the page in the browser to view the Metro Water text in front of the Conservation Tips heading as seen in Figure M-24. The Metro Water text is in front of the Conservation Tips heading because its z-index is now greater than the z-index for the Conservation Tips heading, which is positioned using the *head id*. (The default z-index value for all absolutely positioned elements is zero.)

FIGURE M-24

■ Using the *head id* that is assigned to the Conservation Tips heading, add a z-index to position it in front of the Metro Water text. (*Hint*: The table below gives an example of a z-index that will work. It also summarizes the relationships between the text, *id*s, and z-indexes.)

FIGURE M-25

Conservation Tips

■ Save your work and reload the page in the browser and compare your page heading to the one shown in Figure M-25.

■ Transfer the **inside.htm** page to your remote directory.

Text	id	z-index
Conservation Tips	head	4
Metro Water	backtext	3

▼ INDEPENDENT CHALLENGE 3

Now that you have learned about positioning using DHTML, you want to add these features to your Web site. You are curious about additional positioning features in CSSP that were not presented in this unit.

Go to the Student Online Companion for this book, and go to the W3C link for this unit, review the information about CSS2 guidelines. Find two new positioning features in CSS2 and write a paragraph about each feature. Be sure to address the following questions for each feature:

a. What does the feature allow you to do on a Web page?

b. What syntax is used to implement the feature?

c. Which browsers support each feature? (*Hint*: You may need to check the Web sites of the browsers for this information.)

d. Add your name and today's date to the top of your paper, then print the document.

▼ INDEPENDENT CHALLENGE 4

Now that you've used DHTML to position Web page elements, you are ready to add these features to your Web site.

a. Determine how DHTML can be used in your Web site to position page elements.

b. Lay out your pages on paper to determine which DHTML features are necessary to position the page elements.

c. Add the DHTML features to your pages. Your pages should include absolute and relative positioning, sidebars, and scrollbars.

d. Test the pages in your browser, and adjust the positioning of elements as necessary.

e. Add your name to the edited pages, print them, then transfer your edited pages to the remote location.

HTML

▼ VISUAL WORKSHOP

Work progresses on your Bits and PCs Web site, and you decide to use DHTML positioning to lay out your services page. In your text editor, open the **htm_M-8.txt** file from the drive and folder where your Data Files are stored, then save it as **services.htm** in the bitspcs folder where you save your site files. If you are asked whether you want to replace the file, click Yes. Create the layout for the services.htm page using Figure M-26 as a guide. Review the *id*s assigned in the page tags and then complete the *id* style definitions for *head, backtext, list,* and *sidebar* in the embedded style sheet. Add your name to the bottom of the page in the e-mail link, save the file, then print the services.htm file in your browser. (*Hint*: The Bits and PCs heading is 70 pixels down and 400 pixels to the right from the top-left corner of the browser window. The Services text is placed five pixels above and 20 pixels to the left of the Bits and PCs heading. The display area for the scroll bar text is 330 pixels high and 300 pixels wide. The sidebar is 600 pixels wide.)

FIGURE M-26

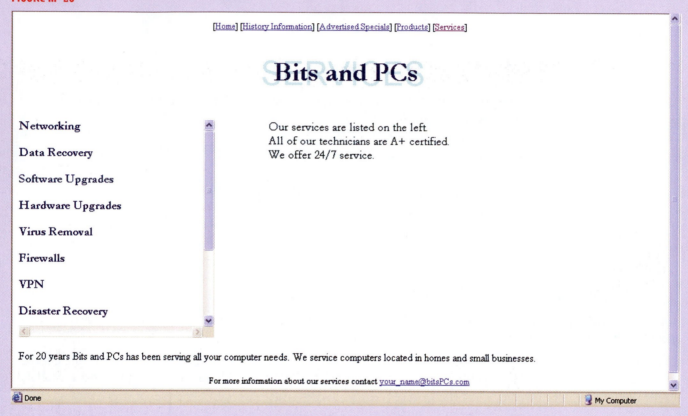

Implementing Dynamic Effects

OBJECTIVES

Understand advanced effects

Filter content

Scale content

Animate element position

Create 3D animation

Apply element transitions

Create a slide show

Create transitions between pages

Using tools such as CSS, dynamic style, dynamic content, and element positioning, you can create interactive Web pages with print-quality formatting and layout. By combining these tools and writing scripts to work with them, you can create and add interesting effects. As you have already learned, browser developers continually add **browser-native**, or proprietary, features that allow you to enhance your pages with dynamic effects using little or no additional scripting. As certain effects become popular, other developers add code to their browsers to allow those effects to appear in their programs as well.  The management at Paradise Mountain Family Resort has asked you to create a Web-based presentation highlighting some of the resort's special features and opportunities. In addition to incorporating CSS formatting and positioning to make the page attractive and easy to read, you plan to add dynamic effects to hold your site visitors' interest.

Understanding Advanced Effects

In addition to the many effects that basic DHTML tools offer, you can create sophisticated visual features through a combination of proprietary effects and simple scripts. Although overuse of any dynamic effect can visually overwhelm users and slow the performance of their computers, the limited and precise use of these advanced features can help you highlight the most important aspects of each page and create entertaining presentations. Introduced as proprietary features in Internet Explorer, many dynamic effects are supported by current browsers. Nevertheless, as you implement these effects, it is a good idea to test your presentation in multiple browsers to ensure that you do not lose essential information in unsupported features. As you organize your presentation, you note advanced features that you can use for dynamic effects.

DETAILS

You can apply dynamic features through:

- **Filtered effects**

  In addition to basic color and size formatting for text and graphics, Internet Explorer offers predefined element formats that affect appearance in complex ways. These formats, known as filters, allow you to create many effects, such as a shadow or glow, as shown in Figures N-1 and N-2.

- **Scripted animation**

  Another way to affect element appearance is by combining a script with CSS position or size information to create the effect of movement or animation. By slowly changing an element's placement or size with a script, you can create the effect of movement without requiring special software or extensive system resources. By using an animation script with off-screen starting coordinates and a timer, you can create **presentation effects** in which elements appear on the screen gradually and in a specified order.

- **Resizing**

  To help ensure your page layouts remain attractive at different screen resolutions and browser window sizes, you can also include simple scripts to resize elements to fit the size of each user's browser window. This aspect of dynamic design helps keep page elements proportional to the window size as well as to each other.

- **Transition effects**

  You can effectively draw attention to a particular page element by scripting its appearance when the page opens. Internet Explorer offers predefined effects called **transitions**, which cause elements to appear gradually and in specific patterns when the page opens or exits. You can apply these effects to selected elements or to the entire page, as shown in Figure N-2.

Shadow filter adds 3D effect

Glow filter

Applied Circle out transition creates slide show effect

Filtering Content

As you have already learned, DHTML includes several tools that let you change the basic appearance of text and graphics by varying the size, color, and other characteristics of selected elements. In addition, many browsers support an extended set of properties, known as filters. **Filters** allow you to modify element appearance in complex ways. Table N-1 lists and describes the filters that are supported by some of today's most popular browsers.  You have already created a presentation page for Paradise Mountain, but you want to call attention to headings in this page without adding more colored text. You decide to try filtering the headings instead.

STEPS

1. Before beginning the lessons in this unit, copy the files earth.gif, logo_pm4.jpg, mountains2.jpg, and roomsPic.jpg from your Data Files location to the paradise\images folder, then copy presentation.css from your Data Files location to your paradise\css folder

2. Start your text editor program, open htm_N-1.txt from the place where you store your Data Files, then save it as presentation.htm in your paradise root folder
   The file contains a set of embedded styles and a link to your external style sheet.

3. Select the text [replace with misshead filter code] in the embedded style sheet, then press [Delete]

4. Type `height: 14pt;`, press [Enter], press [Tab], then type `filter: glow(color: #CC9900);`
   To apply a filter using a `<div>...</div>` or `<span>...</span>` tag, the text must be absolutely positioned or have a defined height or width. To meet this requirement without affecting your layout, you set the font height of your new style to 14 points, which is the same height as your heading text.

5. Select the text [replace with second filter code] in the `#ownit` style definition, then press [Delete]

6. Type `filter: glow(color: #CC9900 strength: 3);`
   Because the font size in the second heading is smaller than in the first, you decide to lower the intensity of the glow by assigning a strength value. This keeps the glow effect proportional to the text dimensions. Figure N-3 shows the completed code for the glow filters in the embedded style sheet. The default glow strength is approximately 5.

7. Locate the level-two heading Our mission, then click before `<h2>`
   You want to apply the filter to the text within the level-two heading tags. To make sure that the filter effects are compatible with most browsers, you want to apply the effect by nesting the heading tags within an identified division layer. Then you can call the filter from the opening `<div>` tag.

8. Type `<div id="misshead">`, click after `</h2>`, then type `</div>`
   You created a division layer that applies the misshead id style to the level-two heading text. The id for the ownit layer has already been set.

9. Check your document for errors, make changes as necessary, then save your work

10. Open presentation.htm in your Web browser
    As shown in Figure N-4, the filtered text appears with a halo of color around each letter.

FIGURE N-3: Code to apply glow filter

Glow filters added to element styles

```
#misshead {
        height: 14pt;
        filter: glow(color: #CC9900);
}
#main   {
        position: absolute; left: 60px;
        width: 275px;
}
#earth  {
        float: right; position: relative; top: -20px;
}
.norm   {
        font-weight: normal;
}
#head1  {
        font-style: italic;
        color: #993366;
}
#head2  {
        font-style: italic;
        color: #669933;
}
#head3  {
        font-style: italic;
        color: #6699CC;
}
#head4  {
        font-style: italic;
        color: #9900CC;
}
#ownit  {
        height: 12pt;
        filter: glow(color: #CC9900 strength: 3);
}
```

FIGURE N-4: Glowing text appears in Web page

Glow effect at default strength

Glow effect with strength set to 3

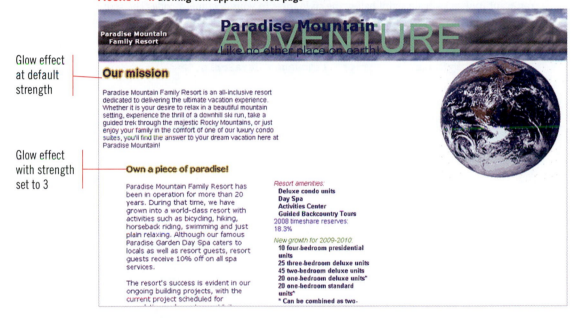

TABLE N-1: Internet Explorer filter effects

filter effect	description	filter effect	description
Alpha	Sets a transparency level	Grayscale	Drops color information from the image
Blur	Creates the impression of moving at high speed	Invert	Reverses the hue, saturation, and brightness values
Chroma	Makes a specified color transparent	Light	Projects light sources onto an object
Drop Shadow	Creates an offset solid silhouette	Mask	Creates a transparent mask from an object
FlipH	Creates a horizontal mirror image	Shadow	Creates a solid silhouette of the object
FlipV	Creates a vertical mirror image	Wave	Creates a sine wave distortion along the x- and y-axes
Glow	Adds radiance around the outside edges of the object	XRay	Shows only the edges of the object

Scaling Content

One drawback of using basic DHTML positioning is that a layout often relies on a particular window size. For example, an indented image may fit well in a layout in a maximized browser window. However, at lower resolutions or in an unmaximized browser window, the element may appear closer to the right edge of the window, thus changing the original layout design. Using basic scripts to complement CSS-P, however, you can automatically adjust the position of your Web page elements based on the browser window size. Because some browsers do not recognize changes in style properties (including element dimensions) after the page has loaded, this automatic adjustment feature does not work in all browsers. Therefore, your page elements must be visible no matter what settings or browsers your site visitors are using.  You laid out your page in a maximized browser window set at a resolution of 1024 × 768 pixels. However, you want the layout to remain as consistent as possible in smaller windows and at lower resolutions.

STEPS

1. **Click the text editor program button on the taskbar to return to your presentation.htm source code**

2. **Locate the embedded style sheet in the head section of your document, click after `</style>`, then press [Enter] twice**

   You want to insert a scale script below the style sheet in your document code. The script scales the image so that it is unlikely to distort the layout of the text when the window is resized.

3. **Type the following script, pressing [Enter] at the end of each line:**

```
<script type="text/javascript" language="JavaScript">
<!--
function change() {
    if (document.body.clientWidth < 800) {
        earth.style.width="25%";
    }
    else {
        earth.style.width="35%";
    }
 }

    window.onresize=change
    window.onload=change
//-->
</script>
```

   Instead of trying to adjust every screen element to fit in a smaller window, you focused on the image on the right edge of the window. Your script adjusts the image to a size that fits into a maximized browser window set at an 800 × 600 resolution. When the window is resized, the image adjusts by percentage so that it leaves more space for the text on the left. Figure N-5 shows the script inserted into a Web document.

4. **Check your document for errors, make changes as necessary, then save your work**

5. **Reload presentation.htm in your Web browser, then make sure your browser window is maximized**

6. **If your display mode is 1024 × 768 or greater, click the Restore Down button in the upper-right corner of the browser window to decrease the size of the document window, then, if necessary, drag the right border inward until your image changes size**

   If your display resolution is set to 800 × 600, note that the earth graphic fits in the window without requiring you to scroll right. Figure N-6 shows the presentation Web page in a reduced window. The scale script you inserted reduced the size of the background graphic to fit better in a limited display area.

QUICK TIP

If you are using a display resolution greater than 800 × 600, you may need to drag the right edge of the browser window to the left a few inches to see the elements rescale.

```
</style>

<script type="text/javascript" language="JavaScript">
<!--
function change() {
        if (document.body.clientWidth < 800) {
                earth.style.width="25%";
        }
        else {
                earth.style.width="35%";
        }
}

        window.onresize=change
        window.onload=change

//-->
</script>

</head>
```

Sets image to 25% of screen if window is less than 800 pixels

Initiates change on page resize or load

FIGURE N-6: Web page displayed in full- and reduced-size windows at 1024 × 768 resolution

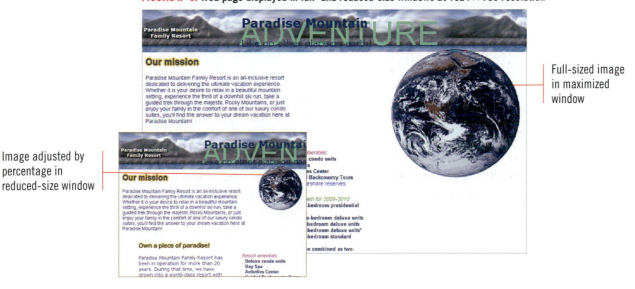

Full-sized image in maximized window

Image adjusted by percentage in reduced-size window

Clues to Use

Scaling by percent

Specifying element dimensions in percentages, rather than pixels or points, has many applications in DHTML design. Usually, you can simply specify the height, width, or font size as percentages. Because these measurements reflect a percentage of the parent element dimension, a percentage-sized element automatically resizes when the window size changes. To make sure the element remains proportionally scaled when specifying element dimensions, be sure to specify only height or width, but not both. Sometimes, screen elements need to change position depending on the screen size or when an element such as a graphic would look distorted if it became too big or too small. In these cases, you need a scaling script to resize your pages.

Animating Element Position

By creating simple scripts to interact with position and layer information, you can add impressive features to your Web pages without requiring extensive system resources on a user's computer. To create basic animation, for example, you can script an element's position coordinates to increase or decrease slowly when the user first opens the page, until the element reaches its final, absolute coordinates. This type of animation is called **position animation**.  You decide to animate the Paradise Mountain logo to move into place when a user first opens the page.

1. Click the text editor program button on the taskbar to return to your presentation.htm source code, then locate *function change()* within the `<script>` tag in the head section of your document

2. Click after `window.onload=change`, press [Enter] twice, then type the following code, pressing [Enter] after each line:

```
function slide() {
  if (800 >= document.all.logo.style.pixelLeft) {
   document.all.logo.style.pixelLeft ++;
   setTimeout('slide()',20);
   }
  else {
   document.all.logo.style.pixelLeft="800";
   }
}
```

The function *slide()* starts with the logo graphic on the left side of the page and then incrementally increases its left coordinate until it reaches the final position of 800. The *setTimeout* values control the amount of time required to fulfill the function. The greater the number, the longer it takes to complete the action. Because you want the logo to travel behind, not in front of, the background heading text, you will change its z-index.

3. Locate the #logo style in the embedded style sheet in the head section of your document, click after `left:0px;`, press [Enter], press [Tab], then type `z-index: -2;`

   The negative z-index ensures that your animation slides behind the other page elements, including the background text (*bgword*) that has a z-index of -1. Now you need to set an event that triggers the action.

4. Click after `<body` in the opening `<body>` tag, press [Spacebar], then type `onload="slide()";`

   The *onload* event handler triggers the slide script every time the browser loads the body section. Figure N-7 shows the code for the event handler to call the *slide()* function.

5. Check your document for errors, make any necessary changes, then save your work

6. Reload presentation.htm in your Web browser

   As Figure N-8 shows, the graphic slides into position from the left edge of the window after you open the page.

FIGURE N-7: Page code with code to create and call slide() function

Slide script advances element if 800 is greater or equal to element position

Slide timer

body onload event triggers slide() function

```
          window.onresize=change
          window.onload=change

function slide() {
          if (800 >= document.all.logo.style.pixelLeft) {
                    document.all.logo.style.pixelLeft ++;
                    setTimeout('slide()',20);
          }
          else {
                    document.all.logo.style.pixelLeft="800";
          }
}

//-->
</script>

</head>

<body onload="slide()";>
```

FIGURE N-8: Paradise Mountain Family Resort logo sliding into position

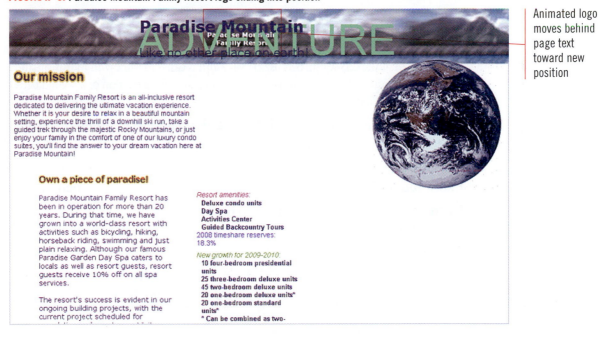

Animated logo moves behind page text toward new position

Creating 3D Animation

As you have already learned, you can easily create simple animation on your Web pages with a script that slowly adjusts an element's top or left attribute over a period of time. DHTML animation creates the effect of movement using only one image and a small script running on the user's browser. By using the width and height properties to incorporate changes in element size, you also can create the illusion of 3D movement. Although too much animation on a page can distract users from the rest of your page content, a short animation, or animation of a small element, can make a page interesting and distinctive. You decide that instead of having the Paradise Mountain logo graphic move into position sideways, you want to use a 3D animation effect to animate the earth graphic so that it appears to approach the user.

STEPS

1. **Open the Data File htm_N-2.txt in your text editor, then save it as presentation2.htm in your paradise root folder**

   The file contains scripting comments to help direct you as you complete your work. Note that the slide animation function has been deleted from the script section of the document.

QUICK TIP
Although it is not required, it is good practice to use a semicolon to mark the end of a line of code in JavaScript.

2. **Locate and select the comment /*replace with 3D animation script*/ in the script area of the document's head section, press [Delete], then type the following script, pressing [Enter] at the end of each line:**

   ```
   function grow() {
    if (earthpic.width<250) {
     x=window.setTimeout('grow()', 100);
     earthpic.width=earthpic.width + 10;
    }
   }

   window.onload=grow;
   ```

   Figure N-9 shows the Web page code containing the script. The script uses the graphic's HTML width property, rather than the CSS width, because HTML width is easier to work with in this situation. Your new script increases the width value by 10 pixels at a time and pauses for a fraction of a second between each increase, which creates the illusion of animation.

QUICK TIP
To prevent animated images with pixilated borders, start with an image that is actually the size of the full-grown image.

3. **Scroll down to the <img /> tag for the earth graphic, click inside the image tag just after id="earthpic", press [Spacebar], then type width="0"**

   By starting with a width of zero (0), the image can grow from nothing until it reaches its full size.

4. **Check your document for errors, make any necessary changes, then save your work**

5. **Open presentation2.htm in your Web browser**

   Figure N-10 shows the page as it is loading. As the page loads, the earth graphic appears and slowly grows as it seems to move toward you.

FIGURE N-9: Web document containing grow script

```
                    window.onload=change

function grow() {
                    if (earthpic.width<250) {
                            x=window.setTimeout('grow()', 100);
                            earthpic.width=earthpic.width + 10;
                    }
        }

                    window.onload=grow;


/*replace with transition function*/

//-->
</script>


</head>
```

Condition statement script checks image width and increases size until Timeout

Script runs on page load

FIGURE N-10: 3D animation of earth graphic

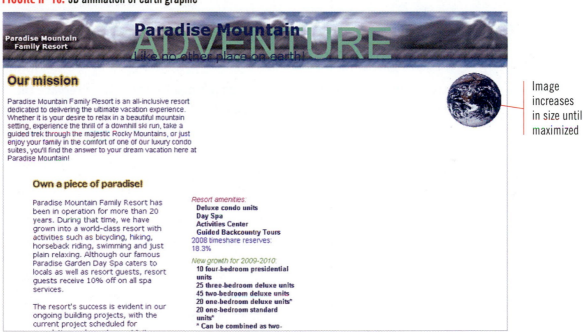

Image increases in size until maximized

Clues to Use

Animated GIF and Flash files

Another popular way to create animation in Web pages is to create animated GIF or Flash files. A GIF is a graphic file in a specific format. Although most GIFs are static, showing only one image, the GIF format also supports animation. To create an animated GIF, you use special software to combine two or more static graphics and to specify the delay between the appearance of each frame. Some of the most popular and widespread uses of GIF animation are in banner advertisements, such as an advertising motto and company logo, and in small, attention-focusing icons. In both of these uses, the statically positioned element alternates between two different frames of information. Animated GIFs are fairly easy to construct using image-editing software such as Adobe ImageReady. You can also download animated GIFs from Web sites for free or for a small fee. For more advanced, movie-quality movement effects, you can use Flash animation, which is generated using Macromedia Flash or other programs such as Adobe ImageReady. DHTML animation is often less expensive to create and often takes less computer memory to download because it uses a single image and the client's processing power to animate. However, animated GIF and Flash files are not limited to specific browsers and are thus accessible by a wider Web audience.

Applying Element Transitions

In addition to hiding and showing an element, or applying filters when an element is displayed, you can affect the way an element becomes visible or hidden by using filter effects known as **transitions**. For example, one popular transition effect is to make an element appear or dissolve gradually in a checkerboard pattern. Transition effects are not available in all browsers; however, Internet Explorer and other browsers that do support transitions use two main transition filters: **blend**, which creates effects that simply fade in or fade out, and **reveal**, which allows the more complex filtering effects. These effects, which can be applied to text as well as graphics, can keep a user's interest and distinguish your pages from others on the Web. You decide to use the blend transition on the Paradise Mountain presentation pages when each page opens.

STEPS

1. Click the **text editor program button** on your taskbar to return to your presentation2.htm page code

2. Click after `left: 0px;` in the #logo style of the page's embedded style sheet, press **[Enter]**, press **[Tab]**, then type the following code, pressing **[Enter]** after each line:

```
visibility: hidden;
filter: blendTrans(duration: 7);
```

   The blend transition can switch from hidden to visible or vice versa. You specified that you want the graphic to start out hidden and then become visible using the *blendTrans* filter. The duration variable details the length of time in seconds of the transition from beginning to end. Next, you need to write the function that activates the transition.

3. Scroll down to the script area in the page's head section, then replace the comment `/*replace with transition function*/` with the following script, pressing **[Enter]** at the end of each line:

```
function doTrans() {
    logo.filters.blendTrans.Apply();
    logo.style.visibility="visible";
    logo.filters.blendTrans.Play();
}
```

   Unlike standard filters, transition filters require scripts to define what happens when they run. The first line of the *doTrans()* function calls the transition's *Apply* method to create the final state defined in the next line, which is "*visible*". Finally, the Play method starts the transition filter itself to create the smooth change from hidden to visible. Figure N-11 shows the Web document code containing the function.

4. Locate, then drag to select the comment `/*replace with function call*/` in the script section at the bottom of the page body section, then type `doTrans()`

   This script, shown in Figure N-12, calls the *doTrans()* function when the page finishes loading in the browser window.

5. Check your document for errors and make any necessary changes, then save your work

6. Refresh **presentation2.htm** in your Web browser

   As Figure N-13 shows, the Paradise Mountain logo slowly fades into view as the page opens.

QUICK TIP

Current versions of Internet Explorer and Netscape browsers support transitions. If the logo does not appear gradually, you might be using a browser that does not support transitions or you may need to adjust your browser settings.

```
                        earthpic.width=earthpic.width + 10;
                }
        }

        window.onload=grow;


function doTrans() {
        logo.filters.blendTrans.Apply();
        logo.style.visibility="visible";
        logo.filters.blendTrans.Play();
}


//-->
</script>

</head>

<body>
```

Transition function

```
</div>

<script type="text/javascript" language="JavaScript">
<!--
doTrans()
//-->
</script>

</body>
</html>
```

Script at bottom of page causes function to run after page loads

Fade-in transition effect on presentation logo

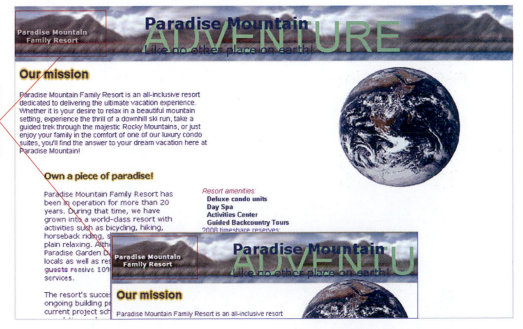

IMPLEMENTING DYNAMIC EFFECTS HTML N-13

HTML

Creating a Slide Show

Presentation software, such as Microsoft PowerPoint, allows you to move through a related set of pages, or **slides**, by clicking the mouse button. You can add this effect to Web pages with scripting. Although standard HTML hyperlinks can create a similar effect, DHTML features enable your users to advance by clicking anywhere on the page, rather than scrolling to locate and click a hyperlink. Also, by eliminating navigation-specific elements, you can keep your pages focused on the presentation topic and create a more unified design. An advantage of DHTML slide shows is that they do not require users to download additional software to view the presentation. You have a second page for your Web presentation and want to script the first page to open the second in response to a mouse click, thus allowing users of most browsers to click anywhere on the Web page and advance to the next page.

STEPS

1. **Copy presentationRooms.htm from the Unit N Data Files, then paste it into your paradise folder in the place where you save your site files**

   The file is the second page of your online presentation.

2. **Click the text editor program button on your taskbar to return to your presentation2.htm page code**

3. **Click after `<body` in the opening `<body>` tag, press [Spacebar], then type**
   `onclick="window.location.href='presentationRooms.htm'";`

   This event handler changes the window's hypertext reference (href) value, or page address, to presentationRooms.htm, the second page of your presentation.

4. **Locate the level-two heading `<h2 class="norm">Like no other place on earth!</h2>`, click after `</div>` that follows it, then press [Enter] twice**

5. **Type the following code, pressing [Enter] at the end of each line:**

   ```
   <div id="instr">
   Click anywhere to advance to next slide.
   </div>
   ```

   This text tells users how to navigate through the presentation. Figure N-14 shows the Web page code containing the event handler and the instruction text. Your starting file already contains an embedded style for formatting the instructions.

   QUICK TIP

   You can direct your final presentation page to return to the home page on your Web site.

6. **Check your document for errors, make any necessary changes, then save your work**

7. **Reload presentation2.htm in your Web browser, then click anywhere on the page**

   The second presentation page opens, as shown in Figure N-15. By adding the event handler to all presentation pages except for the last one, you can enable users to easily page through the presentation online.

FIGURE N-14: Web page code containing event handler and instruction text

onClick event
handler

Instruction
text

```
<body onClick="window.location.href='presentationRooms.htm'">

<div id="logo">
<img src="images/logo_pm4.jpg" />
</div>

<div id="bgword">
ADVENTURE
</div>

<div id="heading">
<h1>Paradise Mountain</h1>
<h2 class="norm">Like no other place on earth!</h2>
</div>

<div id="instr">
Click anywhere to advance to next slide.
</div>


<div id="earth">
<img src="images/earth.gif" id="earthpic" width="0" />
```

FIGURE N-15: Second presentation page

Creating Transitions Between Pages

In addition to creating transition effects for specific elements on a Web page, you can apply transitions when opening or closing a page. In this situation, transitions can grab and hold a viewer's attention, and can help your page to stand out among those a user has recently seen. Each Web page can trigger transitions upon opening and exiting, independent of the preceding or following page. As a final touch, you decide you want Internet Explorer users to see a closing transition with each page in the Web presentation. You decide to start by adding a closing transition that appears when the first page closes.

1. Open the file presentationRooms.htm from your paradise site folder in your text editor, then locate the comment `<!-- Replace with meta tag -->` above the linked style sheet tag in the page's head section

2. Select the comment, press [Delete], then type the following code, without pressing [Enter]: `<meta http-equiv="Page-Enter" content="RevealTrans(Duration: 5,Transition: 19)"; />`

   Figure N-16 shows the Web page code containing the `<meta />` tag. Creating an interpage transition requires no scripting. Instead, you insert an HTML meta tag in the page's head section, calling the transition and defining its properties. You can set the *http-equiv* property, which tells when the transition takes effect, to *"Page-Enter"* or *"Page-Exit"*. You use the content property to specify the transition filter name and parameters, just as you do with the style property for element transitions. In the meta tag, you used the reveal transition's "Strips right down" pattern, indicated by the Transition number 19. Table N-2 lists other reveal transitions and their number codes.

3. Check your document for errors, make any necessary changes, then save your work

4. Click the browser program button on the taskbar, then reload the presentationRooms.htm page

   The page reloads and the transition effect appears.

5. Click your browser's Back button to return to your presentations2.htm page, then click anywhere on the page

   The second presentation page opens using the Strips right down transition, as shown in Figure N-17.

6. Click the text editor program button to return to your code, then experiment with other transition patterns listed in Table N-2, viewing each transition in your browser

7. Close your Web browser program, then print your presentationRooms.htm page code and close your text editor program

8. Upload your new and updated files to your remote directory on the server

```
<!DOCTYPE html PUBliC "-//W3C//DTD XHTML 1.0 Transitional//EN"
"http://www.w3.org/TR/xhtml1/DTD/xhtml1-transitional.dtd">

<html xmlns="http://www.w3.org/1999/xhtml">

<head>
<title>Paradise Mountain: A Rocky Mountain High</title>

<meta name="keywords" content="Paradise Mountain Family Resort, vacation rentals, time
shares, condo suites, hiking, biking, swimming, Estes Park, Colorado" />

<meta name="description" content="Paradise Mountain Family Resort offers the ultimate in
vacation experiences. Come spend a week in paradise and find out for yourself." />

<meta http-equiv="Content-Type" content="text/html; charset=iso-8859-1" />

<meta http-equiv="Page-Enter" content="RevealTrans(Duration: 5,Transition: 19)"; />

<link href="css/presentation.css" rel="stylesheet" type="text/css" />
```

Meta tag with page transition filter

FIGURE N-17: Web page opening with "Strips right down" reveal transition

Second page revealed as transition moves across window

First page

TABLE N-2: Reveal transition effects

reveal transition name	value	reveal transition name	value	reveal transition name	value
Box in	0	Vertical blinds	8	Split horizontal out	16
Box out	1	Horizontal blinds	9	Strips left down	17
Circle in	2	Checkerboard across	10	Strips left up	18
Circle out	3	Checkerboard down	11	Strips right down	19
Wipe up	4	Random dissolve	12	Strips right up	20
Wipe down	5	Split vertical in	13	Random bars horizontal	21
Wipe right	6	Split vertical out	14	Random bars vertical	22
Wipe left	7	Split horizontal in	15	Random	23

Practice

Name the function of each section of code indicated in Figure N-18.

FIGURE N-18

```
<style>
<!--
#logo {
1       position:absolute; left:200; top:10px; visibility:hidden;
        filter:revealTrans(Transition=2, Duration=5);
}

#texthead {
2       width:375px; height:14px; filter:glow(color=#33CCCC);
}
-->
</style>
3  <meta http-equiv="page-exit" content="RevealTrans
   (duration=5,transition=3)"/>

<script type="text/javascript" language="JavaScript">
<!--
function change() {
        if (document.body.clientWidth < 640) {
                bgword.style.fontSize="16pt";
        }
4       else {
                bgword.style.fontSize="22pt";
        }
}
5  window.onresize=change;
   window.onload=change;
6  //-->
   </script>
   </head>
7
   <body onClick="window.location.href='page2.htm'">
```

Match each statement with the term it best describes.

8. Filter
9. Position animation
10. 3D animation
11. Transition
12. Scaling

a. Gradually changes an element's size using the width and height properties
b. Gradually changes an element's appearance as it becomes visible or hidden
c. Gradually moves an element on a Web page
d. Adjusts the size of Web page elements based on the browser window size
e. Modifies the appearance of an element in complex ways

Select the best answer from the list of choices.

13. **Which event handler responds to the user clicking the Web page?**
    a. onLoad
    b. onMouseUp
    c. onClick
    d. onFocus

14. **Which of the following are filters? (Choose all that apply.)**
    a. Shadow
    b. Animation
    c. Blur
    d. Alpha

15. **Which event handler responds to the body section of a page loading in the browser?**
    a. onLoad
    b. onMouseUp
    c. onClick
    d. onFocus

16. **Which HTML tag is used to add a transition from one page to another?**
    a. <head>
    b. <a>
    c. <meta />
    d. <script>

17. **What is the advantage of using DHTML for animation rather than other animation methods on Web pages? (Choose all that apply.)**
    a. DHTML doesn't use scripts.
    b. DHTML doesn't require special software.
    c. DHTML uses few system resources.
    d. DHTML uses animated GIFs.

18. **Which filter adds radiance around the outside edge of the object?**
    a. Drop Shadow
    b. Alpha
    c. Wave
    d. Glow

▼ SKILLS REVIEW

1. **Filter content.**
    a. In your text editor, open the file **htm_N-3.txt** from the drive and folder where your Data Files are stored, then save it as **packages.htm** to the paradise/spa directory where you save your site files. If you are asked whether you want to replace the file, click Yes. Copy the **spa_logo.gif** and **pedi.jpg** files from the drive and folder where your Data Files are stored, then paste them in your paradise/images directory. If you are asked whether you want to replace the files, click Yes. Copy the **rmpkg.htm** file from the drive and folder where your Data Files are stored, then paste it in the paradise/spa directory.
    b. In your packages.htm file, add a style for an id named `texthead` below the <h2> style in the embedded style sheet. Define the texthead id style as a width of 375 pixels, a height of 14 pixels, and a light blue filter glow effect. (*Hint*: Add `#texthead {width:375px; height:14px; filter:glow(color=#99FFFF);}` to the embedded style sheet.)

   c. Locate the comment in the page body indicating where the glow effect id will be placed. Add `id="texthead"` to the opening `<div>` tag to add a light blue glow to the Spa Packages heading, then delete the comment.

   d. Check your file for errors, make any necessary changes, then save your file.

   e. Open **packages.htm** in your browser to view the filter effect.

2. Scale content.

   a. In your text editor, locate the logo id in the embedded style sheet and review its style definition.

   b. Locate the *change* function in the script section below the embedded style sheet and review the function commands. Below the *change* function, add the commands to call it when the page is loaded into the browser and when the browser window is resized. (*Hint*: Add `window.onresize=change; window.onload=change;`.)

   c. Locate the `<img />` tag for the spa_logo.gif image. Add an id of `logo` to the end of the `<img />` tag.

   d. Check your file for errors, make any necessary changes, then save your file.

   e. Refresh **packages.htm** in your browser, and click the Restore Window button to decrease the size of the document window. Check to be sure the logo resizes appropriately. If necessary, drag the right edge of the window to the left to decrease the screen width.

   f. Maximize the browser window.

3. Animate element position.

   a. In your text editor, locate the style description for the logo id in the embedded style sheet and review the position information.

   b. Locate the *slide* function in the script section and review the script code.

   c. Locate the opening `<body>` tag, and insert the code to call the *slide* function when the page is loaded so the logo moves into place from the top. (*Hint*: Add `onLoad=slide()` to the tag.)

   d. Check your file for errors, make any necessary changes, then save your file.

   e. Refresh **packages.htm** in your browser to view the logo position animation.

4. Create 3D animation.

   a. In your text editor, locate the style description for the res id in the embedded style sheet and review the position information.

   b. Locate the *grow* function in the script section and review the script code. Locate the `<img />` tag for the pedi.jpg image and add an id of `res` to the opening `<div>` tag above it.

   c. Locate the opening `<body>` tag, and replace the code that called the *slide* function with the code that calls the *grow* function to animate the pedicure image when the page is loaded. (*Hint*: Replace `onLoad=slide()` with `onLoad=grow()` in the opening `<body>` tag.)

   d. Check your file for errors, make any necessary changes, then save your file.

   e. Refresh **packages.htm** in your browser to view the pedicure image animation.

5. Apply transition elements.

   a. In your text editor, locate the style description for the logo id in the embedded style sheet and add style information that uses the revealTrans filter to transform the logo from hidden to visible. (*Hint*: Add `visibility: hidden; filter: revealTrans(transition=12, duration=5);` to the end of the logo id style definition.)

   b. Locate the script section at the bottom of the page, and insert the code to call the *doTrans* function. (*Hint*: Add `doTrans()` between the script comment tags.)

   c. Check your file for errors, make any necessary changes, then save your file.

   d. Refresh **packages.htm** in your browser to view the logo transition effect.

6. Create a slide show.

   a. In your text editor, locate the style description in the embedded style sheet for the instr id and review the definition.

b. Locate the opening `<body>` tag, and add the code that calls the *onClick* event handler to open the page rmpkg.htm when the page is clicked. (*Hint*: Add `onClick="window.location.href='rmpkg.htm'"` to the opening `<body>` tag.)

c. Use the comment at the bottom of the page to locate the area where a message will be added informing users that clicking the page opens the next page in the slide show. In this location, add a message of "Click anywhere to advance to the next slide." using the instr id in a `<div>` tag to format the message text. Delete the comment.

d. Check your file for errors, make any necessary changes, then save your file.

e. Refresh **packages.htm** in your browser, and click the page to advance to the **rmpkg.htm** file. Use your browser's Back button to return to the **packages.htm** file.

7. **Create transitions between pages.**

a. In your text editor, below the closing `</style>` tag, add a Circle Out transition for the page's exit using the value 5 for the duration. (*Hint*: Add `<meta http-equiv="page-exit" content="RevealTrans(duration=5, transition=3)"/>`.)

b. Check your file for errors, make any necessary changes, then save your file.

c. Refresh **packages.htm** in your browser and check the transition effect by clicking the page to advance to the **rmpkg.htm** file. Use your browser's Back button to return to the **packages.htm** file.

d. In your text editor, add your name to the comment above the closing `</body>` tag and print the page.

e. Transfer the **packages.htm** and **rmpkg.htm** files to your remote directory.

▼ INDEPENDENT CHALLENGE 1

As you continue developing the Web site for your resort rental business, Star Vacations, you decide to use advanced DHTML features to engage visitors to the Island Sea Resort page.

a. In your text editor, open the file **htm_N-4.txt** from the drive and folder where your Data Files are stored, then save it as **island_seas.htm** to the vacations folder where you save your site files. If you are asked whether you want to replace the file, click Yes.

b. Copy the files **resort.jpg**, and **bkg_vaca.gif** from the drive and folder where your Data Files are stored, then paste them in the vacations/images folder where you save your site files. If you are asked whether you want to replace the files, click Yes. Copy the **adventures.htm** file from the drive and folder where your Data Files are stored, then paste it in the vacations folder where you save your site files.

c. Locate the embedded style sheet in your island_seas.htm file and review the defined styles.

d. Locate the `<img />` tag for the resort.jpg image and review the tag attributes and values. Using Figure N-19 as a guide, add a script with the function named *grow* below the closing `</style>` tag to increase the resort.jpg image size when the page is loaded into the browser. Add the event handler in the opening `<body>` tag to call the *grow* function.

FIGURE N-19

```
<script type="text/javascript" language="JavaScript">
<!--

function grow() {
        if (resort.width<200) {
                x=window.setTimeout('grow()', 100);
                resort.width=resort.width + 10;
        }
}

//-->
</script>
```

e. In the embedded style sheet add an id named `texthead` with a style definition that adds a drop shadow filter effect with the color #99CCCC, a width of 375 pixels, and a height of 14 pixels. Add the `texthead` id to the opening `<div>` tag for the Property Amenities heading to add a drop shadow effect to the text.

▼ INDEPENDENT CHALLENGE 1 (CONTINUED)

f. Add an event handler to the `<body>` tag to advance to the adventures.htm file when the page is clicked. Below the closing `</ol>` tag, add the text "Click anywhere to advance to a slide with information about tours." to let the users know they can click the page to get tour information.

g. Add a Box Out closing page transition to the page. (*Hint*: Use a reveal transition of 1 and duration of 5.)

h. Add your name to the e-mail link at the bottom of the page, then save the file.

i. Open the file in your browser to check your work. Click the page to check the transition effect and the slideshow. Use your browser's Back button to return to the **island_seas.htm** page.

j. Print the island_seas.htm code from your text editor.

k. Transfer the **island_seas.htm** and **adventures.htm** pages to your remote directory.

Advanced Challenge Exercises

- The *grow* function is a recursive function. Use your favorite search engine to research recursion in functions.
- Summarize your results in a short paper.
- Apply your research findings to include answers to the following questions in your paper:
  - Which statement in the *grow* function contains the recursive call?
  - What stops the *grow* function?
  - What is the value of *resort.width* and the end of the grow function?
- Add your name and today's date to the paper, then print it.

▼ INDEPENDENT CHALLENGE 2

As you continue your work on Metro Water's site, you decide to use advanced DHTML features to create a slide show about water conservation for your customers.

a. In your text editor, open the file **htm_N-5.txt** from the drive and folder where your Data Files are stored, then save it as **inside.htm** to the water folder where you save your site files. If you are asked whether you want to replace the file, click Yes.

b. Copy the file **mw.gif** from the drive and folder where your Data Files are stored, then paste it in the water/images folder where you save your site files. If you are asked whether you want to replace the file, click Yes. Copy the files **tips1.htm**, **tips2.htm**, **tips3.htm**, and **tips4.htm** from the drive and folder where your Data Files are stored, then paste them in the water folder where you save your site files.

c. In the inside.htm page, locate the `<img />` tag for the mw.gif image, and review the attributes and values. Add a function named *grow* to the script section of the inside.htm page to increase the width of the mw.gif image by 10 pixels every 100 milliseconds until it is 65 pixels wide. Add an event handler in the opening `<body>` tag to call the *grow* function when the page is loaded into the browser.

d. Add an event handler to advance to the tips1.htm page when the page is clicked.

e. Between the opening and closing `<h3>` tags above the contact information, add the text "Click anywhere on this page to view tips for reducing water usage." to let the users know they can click the page to get conservation tips.

f. Add a closing page transition of Split Vertical Out with duration of 5 to the page. (*Hint*: The transition value is 14.)

g. Add the event handlers, page transition code, and instructions for users to advance through the slides in your presentation in the following sequence: tips1.htm, tips2.htm, tips3.htm, and tips4.htm. Clicking the tips4.htm page should return the user to the inside.htm page.

h. Add your name to the bottom of all five pages in the e-mail links, then save the files.

i. Open the **inside.htm** file in your browser, and check the slide show by clicking each page.

j. Print all five pages from your text editor.

k. Transfer the pages to your remote directory.

▼ INDEPENDENT CHALLENGE 2 (CONTINUED)

Advanced Challenge Exercises

- Add a button labeled Next to the bottom of each page that users can click to move to the next slide in the presentation. Be sure to remove the old instructions and event handlers in the pages.
- Add a button labeled Previous to the bottom of each of the tips pages that users can click to move to the previous slide in the presentation. The inside.htm page does not have a Previous button as it is the opening page of the presentation.
- Save your work, then reload the **inside.htm** page in your browser, and check the buttons on each page of the presentation.
- Print all five pages from your text editor.
- Transfer the pages to your remote directory.

▼ INDEPENDENT CHALLENGE 3

Now that you have learned about advanced DHTML effects, you want to add these features to your Web site. You are curious about additional filters and transitions that were not presented in this unit.

Use your favorite search engine to find two new filters and two new transitions. Write a paragraph describing each filter and transition. Be sure to address the following questions for each one:

- **a.** What effect does the filter or transition have on the elements of the Web page?
- **b.** What syntax is used to implement the filter or transition?
- **c.** Which browsers support each filter or transition? (*Hint*: You may need to check the Web sites of the browsers for this information.)
- **d.** Add your name and today's date to the top of your paper, then print the document.

▼ INDEPENDENT CHALLENGE 4

Now that you've used DHTML to add effects to the elements of a Web page, you are ready to add these features to your Web site.

- **a.** Determine how DHTML can be used on your Web site to attract attention to specific page elements.
- **b.** Lay out your pages on paper to determine which elements would benefit from DHTML effects.
- **c.** Add the DHTML code for the effects to your pages. Your pages should include the following:
  - A filter for a heading
  - A transition element
  - An image that scales appropriately when the browser is resized
  - Position animation
  - 3D animation
- **d.** Test the pages in your browser and adjust the DHTML effects as necessary.
- **e.** Add your name as a comment to the edited pages and print the pages.
- **f.** Transfer your edited pages to the remote location.

▼ VISUAL WORKSHOP

Work progresses on your Bits and PCs Web site, and you decide to use filtering and position animation to call attention to the company name. In your text editor, open the **htm_N-6.txt** file from the drive and folder where your Data Files are stored, then save it as **services.htm** in the bitspcs folder where you save your site files. If you are asked whether you want to replace the file, click Yes. Using Figure N-20 as a guide, use the `texthead` id to add a glow filter with the color #9999CC to the Bits and PCs heading. Use the `head` id to add an animation function named *slide* that moves the Bits and PCs heading slowly from its position on the left side of the page to a final position of 390 pixels from the left. Add the event handler that calls the *slide* function when the body section of the page is loaded in the browser. Add your name to the bottom of the page in the e-mail link, save the file, then print the services.htm file from your browser.

FIGURE N-20

UNIT
O
HTML

Structuring Data with XML

OBJECTIVES

Understand Extensible Markup Language (XML)
Define XML elements and structure
Enter XML data
Bind XML data to HTML
Format XML data with HTML
Modify an XML document
Alter XML data view with HTML

In the earliest days of the Web, HTML was a way of structuring information for multiple platforms and browsers. As Web technologies advanced, the combination of HTML and CSS offered a highly effective method of controlling Web page formatting. However, in today's data-rich Web environment with its many new applications, neither HTML nor CSS answer the critical need for a standard but expandable means to define, structure, and deliver data on the Web. Extensible Markup Language (XML) is designed to ensure a universal data structure that can be read by any XML-compliant browser yet still allow Web designers the freedom to create custom **data definitions**—the characteristics, types, and relationships of the data you collect and process—for an endless variety of applications (for example, a book or movie database). The Paradise Mountain Activities Center has asked you to create an "Available Movie Titles" page to list movies in DVD format that the center has on hand for resort guests to check out. The page will display available movie titles data that you store in an XML file and format using custom data definitions.

Understanding Extensible Markup Language (XML)

XML (Extensible Markup Language) is a text-based syntax especially designed to describe, deliver, and exchange structured data. XML documents use the file extension .xml and, like HTML files, can be created using a simple text editor. XML is not meant as a replacement for HTML but rather as a means to extend its descriptive and structural power. XML uses a syntax that is similar to HTML. However, HTML is fairly forgiving when it comes to displaying documents that are not well formed, but XML is not. XML adheres to a strict set of formatting rules that guarantee that a document is well formed. A well-formed document requires that data be uniformly structured in tag sets so it can be read correctly by any XML-compliant browser or editing program.  You are new to using XML, so you decide to research the language before starting to create the available DVD titles list. You decide to carefully review the XML syntax rules for a well-formed document.

Well-formed XML documents adhere to the following rules:

- ### All elements must have start and end tags

  An element consists of the start tag and its corresponding end tag along with the content between the two parts of the tag set. Unlike early HTML coding techniques that allowed you to mark up a document without using some closing tags such as `</p>`, XML requires that both opening and closing tags be present. For example, the first list item in Figure O-1 shows the correct way to code XML with both the start and end tags necessary to create a well-formed XML document. The corresponding line in Figure O-2 lacks the required closing `</li>` tag, and thus violates the first rule of XML syntax.

- ### All elements must be nested correctly

  Although current coding standards tell us that when writing HTML you *should* close last the tag set that you opened first, when writing XML, you *must* do so. Although incorrectly nested HTML elements usually appear correctly in the browser, XML elements that are not correctly nested prevent the page from displaying correctly or, in some cases, prevent it from displaying at all. The second list item in Figure O-1 shows an emphasis tag set `<em>...</em>`, correctly nested inside the list item tag set `<li>...</li>`. The corresponding line in Figure O-2 breaks this rule by placing the closing `</em>` tag after the end list item tag `</li>`. Although the document produced from this code would appear properly in the browser when saved as an HTML document, it is not well formed and, because of the inherent stricter rule enforcement, cannot be displayed as an XML document.

- ### All attribute values must be enclosed in quotation marks

  HTML accepts some values, such as the `image src` value, without quote marks and requires that only certain attribute values, such as URLs and strings, be in quotes. However, in XML, all attribute values must appear in quotes. The third list item in Figure O-1 illustrates the proper way to code by quoting the style attribute value `"font-size: 1.5em;"`. The same line in Figure O-2 shows the style attribute value without quotes and thus is incorrectly marked up for XML.

- ### All empty elements must be self-identifying by ending with />

  An empty element is one that does not have a closing tag such as `<br />`, `<hr />`, and `<img />`. The line break tag at the end of the first line of the fourth list item in Figure O-1 demonstrates the proper way to identify and close an empty element in XML by ending it with `/>`. This forward slash at the end of the tag indicates that the element is not broken (missing its closing tag) but simply empty or open. The same tag in Figure O-2 does not contain the necessary ending slash and, therefore, prevents the XML document from being well formed.

FIGURE O-1: Document correctly marked up for XML

Required opening and closing tags →

Emphasis tag opened last and closed first →

Attribute value enclosed in quotes →

Empty element identified by closing forward slash →

```
<body>

<div style="text-align: center;"><h2>XML Rules and Standards</h2>
<h3>Formatting your XML document</h3></div>

<ol>

<li>All elements must have start and end tags</li>

<li>All elements must be <em>properly nested</em></li>

<li><span style="font-size: 1.5em;">All</span> attribute values must be
enclosed in quotation marks</li>

<li>All empty elements must be self-identifying (self-closing) <br />
    In other words, if you open it, close it!</li>

</ol>

</body>
```

FIGURE O-2: Document incorrectly marked up for XML

Required closing tag is missing →

Emphasis tag should be closed before list item tag →

Attribute value should be in quotes →

Empty element missing closing forward slash →

```
<body>

<div style="text-align: center;"><h2>XML Rules and Standards</h2>
<h3>Formatting your XML document</h3></div>

<ol>

<li>All elements must have start and end tags

<li>All elements must be <em>properly nested</li></em>

<li><span style=font-size: 1.5em;>All</span> attribute values must be
enclosed in quotation marks</li>

<li>All empty elements must be self-identifying (self-closing) <br>
    In other words, if you open it, close it!</li>

</ol>

</body>
```

Clues to Use

Benefits of XML

With XML, it is possible to identify data in meaningful ways. In much the same way that a database lets you identify and organize data with unique fieldnames and records, XML allows you to define custom vocabularies, or element sets, for specific types of data such as books, movies, auto parts, legal cases, and medical information. These custom vocabularies act like the fieldnames in a conventional database to clearly identify and segment data. This new level of semantics improves the ability of search engines to rapidly find relevant information. **Intelligent Web applications**, which seek out choice bits of information on the Web to match the preferences of individual users, can produce more accurate results based on clearly labeled XML data. Additionally, XML offers the means to exchange and process data from otherwise incompatible information repositories on the Internet. XML and DHTML also enable a significant portion of the processing load to be shifted from Web servers to Web browsers (clients). Consequently, applications that require high-level compatibility and performance, such as those in e-commerce, greatly benefit from the use of XML.

HTML

Defining XML Elements and Structure

XML documents are composed of three parts: the prolog, the body and the epilog. The **prolog** contains, in the following order, an XML declaration, comments, a document type declaration, and other comments. Although parts of the prolog are considered optional, the prolog should always include an XML declaration, which is always the first line of code in an XML document. Unlike HTML, XML is not confined to a restricted library of tag sets. XML gives you the freedom to define a limitless set of custom elements known collectively as a **vocabulary** to fit any application or situation. These custom tags are contained within the **body** of an XML document. As shown in Figure O-3, elements within the body section of the document are organized in a treelike hierarchical structure, with child elements fully nested within parent elements. By nesting the child elements within the parent element, you automatically establish a parent-child, or hierarchical, structure similar to the one illustrated in Figure O-4. The optional XML document **epilog** contains any final comments and/or processing instructions. After completing your basic research on XML, you decide to define the XML elements and structure necessary to store the data in the available movies list.

STEPS

1. **Open your text editor, then type** `<?xml version='1.0' encoding='UTF-8' ?>`
   You have typed the prolog, which contains the XML declaration, a processing instruction for the browser or other XML-compliant program reading the document. This processing instruction begins with the opening delimiter `<?` and ends with the closing delimiter `?>`. The instruction included between the delimiters, `xml version='1.0' encoding='UTF-8'`, indicates that the document should be read as an XML file and that it supports a multilingual ASCII character set that is compatible with file systems, parsers, and other software as defined by the International Organization of Standards (ISO).

2. **Press [Enter] twice, then type the following elements with the indentations shown:**
```
<DVDlist>
    <movie>
        <DVDtitle></DVDtitle>
        <actor1></actor1>
        <actor2></actor2>
        <genre></genre>
        <rating></rating>
    </movie>
</DVDlist>
```
   You created the **master**, or **root element**, `DVDlist`, which serves as the parent element for all other elements in the file. Then you created a parent element, `movie`, that contains the child elements `DVDtitle`, `actor1`, `actor2`, `genre`, and `rating`. In doing so, you added the first set of elements to your XML document. Elements in an XML document are ranked from the outermost set to the innermost elements. The rank of an element determines how much of the tree it controls. Figure O-4 is a graphic representation of the XML structure tree for the document that you will create to store your data information.

3. **To create two more instances of the movie elements, select, then copy from `<movie>` to `</movie>` as shown in Figure O-5**

4. **Click after `</movie>`, then press [Enter] twice**

5. **Paste a second movie record**
   A second instance of the movie elements appears in your document.

6. **Press [Enter] twice, then paste another instance of the movie elements**
   Your document should now look like the one shown in Figure O-3.

7. **Using the All Files format, save the file as movies.xml in your paradise\activities folder in the place where you save your site files**
   You are now ready to enter the data into your XML document

FIGURE O-3: Elements and structure of the movie list XML document

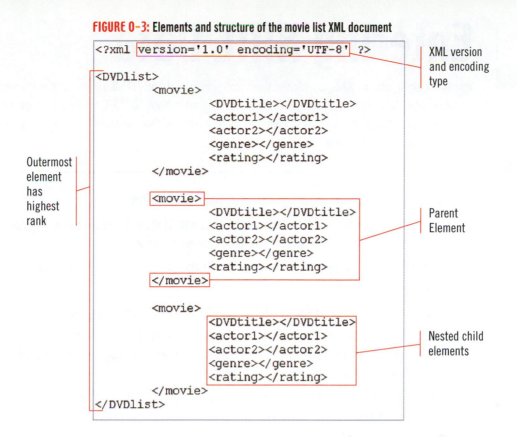

```
<?xml version='1.0' encoding='UTF-8' ?>

<DVDlist>
        <movie>
                <DVDtitle></DVDtitle>
                <actor1></actor1>
                <actor2></actor2>
                <genre></genre>
                <rating></rating>
        </movie>

        <movie>
                <DVDtitle></DVDtitle>
                <actor1></actor1>
                <actor2></actor2>
                <genre></genre>
                <rating></rating>
        </movie>

        <movie>
                <DVDtitle></DVDtitle>
                <actor1></actor1>
                <actor2></actor2>
                <genre></genre>
                <rating></rating>
        </movie>
</DVDlist>
```

XML version and encoding type

Outermost element has highest rank

Parent Element

Nested child elements

FIGURE O-4: Treelike hierarchical structure of an XML document

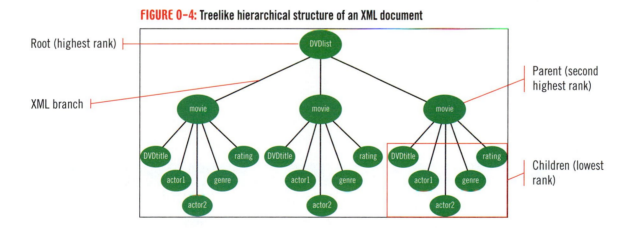

Root (highest rank)

XML branch

Parent (second highest rank)

Children (lowest rank)

FIGURE O-5: Highlighted movie elements to copy

```
<?xml version='1.0' encoding='UTF-8' ?>

<DVDlist>
        <movie>
                <DVDtitle></DVDtitle>
                <actor1></actor1>
                <actor2></actor2>
                <genre></genre>
                <rating></rating>
        </movie>
</DVDlist>
```

Highlighted movie elements to copy

Entering XML Data

You enter data into an XML document the same way you do an HTML page—either manually with an editor or automatically with a sophisticated HTML development tool. You want to enter data about three DVD movies in the XML file to test your knowledge of how this new technology works. You decide to use a text editor to enter the data.

1. Make sure that movies.xml is open in your text editor
2. Click between `<DVDtitle>` and `</DVDtitle>` in the first `<DVDtitle>`...`</DVDtitle>` tag set, as shown in Figure O-6, then type `Chicken Little`
3. Click between `<actor1>` and `</actor1>` in the first `<actor1>`...`</actor1>` tag set, then type `Zach Braff`
4. Click after `<actor2>` in the next tag set, then type `Gary Marshall`
5. Click after `<genre>` in the `<genre>`...`</genre>` tag set, type Animated Children's Comedy, then click after `<rating>` in the `<rating>`...`</rating>` tag set and type PG
   Your code should match the contents of Figure O-7.
6. Type the data indicated in Table O-1 in the appropriate tag sets for the next two instances of the movie elements
   Your document should look like the one shown in Figure O-8.
7. Save the file, then close it

TABLE O-1: Content for movies.xml

DVDtitle	actor1	actor2	genre	rating
Flightplan	Jodie Foster	Peter Sarsgaard	Thriller	PG 13
Just Friends	Ryan Reynolds	Amy Smart	Romantic Comedy	PG 13

Clues to Use

Understanding Document Type Definition (DTD) and XML schemas

As you have already learned, a Document Type Definition (DTD) is the formal specification of the rules for a Web document that specifies which elements are allowed and in what combinations. However, you can create a custom DTD for your XML documents to ensure that any XML document using the DTD is **valid** (complies with the formal specification). For example, a DTD could be set up to ensure that all XML files dealing with drug prescriptions include certain data elements such as the prescribing doctor's name, expiration date, and refill information. Although a DTD can be called from an XML file, it uses a different syntax from XML. An **XML schema** combines the concepts of a DTD, relational databases, and object-oriented designs to create a richer and more powerful way to formally define the elements and structure of an XML document. In addition, XML schemas use the same syntax as XML, so they can appear in the same document. However, support for XML schemas is limited. To learn more about DTDs and XML schemas, visit the Student Online Companion and click one of the XML schema links.

FIGURE O-6: Insertion point position

```
<?xml version='1.0' encoding='UTF-8' ?>

<DVDlist>
        <movie>
                <DVDtitle></DVDtitle>
                <actor1></actor1>
                <actor2></actor2>
                <genre></genre>
                <rating></rating>
        </movie>

        <movie>
                <DVDtitle></DVDtitle>
                <actor1></actor1>
                <actor2></actor2>
                <genre></genre>
                <rating></rating>
        </movie>

        <movie>
                <DVDtitle></DVDtitle>
                <actor1></actor1>
                <actor2></actor2>
                <genre></genre>
                <rating></rating>
        </movie>

</DVDlist>
```

Correct insertion point position

FIGURE O-7: XML document with first data record

```
<?xml version='1.0' encoding='UTF-8' ?>

<DVDlist>
        <movie>
                <DVDtitle>Chicken Little</DVDtitle>
                <actor1>Zach Braff</actor1>
                <actor2>Gary Marshall</actor2>
                <genre>Animated Children's Comedy</genre>
                <rating>PG</rating>
        </movie>

        <movie>
                <DVDtitle></DVDtitle>
                <actor1></actor1>
                <actor2></actor2>
                <genre></genre>
                <rating></rating>
        </movie>
```

Data record

FIGURE O-8: XML document with all data entered

```
<?xml version='1.0' encoding='UTF-8' ?>

<DVDlist>
        <movie>
                <DVDtitle>Chicken Little</DVDtitle>
                <actor1>Zach Braff</actor1>
                <actor2>Gary Marshall</actor2>
                <genre>Animated Children's Comedy</genre>
                <rating>PG</rating>
        </movie>

        <movie>
                <DVDtitle>Flightplan</DVDtitle>
                <actor1>Jodie Foster</actor1>
                <actor2>Peter Sarsgaard</actor2>
                <genre>Thriller</genre>
                <rating>PG 13</rating>
        </movie>

        <movie>
                <DVDtitle>Just Friends</DVDtitle>
                <actor1>Ryan Reynolds</actor1>
                <actor2>Amy Smart</actor2>
                <genre>Romantic Comedy</genre>
                <rating>PG 13</rating>
        </movie>
</DVDlist>
```

Data record 1

Data record 2

Data record 3

HTML

Binding XML Data to HTML

XML-compliant browsers such as Internet Explorer and newer Netscape browsers, support XML by including an XML parser and an embedded XML source object. An **XML parser** dissects and interprets XML elements, whereas the **XML source object** enables binding of the XML data to the HTML document using the DHTML Object Model. Thus, the parser and XML source object cooperate to allow the display, or **rendering**, of XML data in HTML. You want to display the data in the movies.xml file in an HTML document that will become part of Paradise Mountain's Web site. Before you can format the data, you must first create the HTML document and bind the XML data to it.

STEPS

1. **In your text editor, open htm_O-1.txt from the Unit O folder from the place where you store your Data Files, then save it as movies.htm in the paradise\activities folder in the place where you save your site files**

   The text file contains a transitional DTD as well as an xmlns namespace definition link in the opening HTML tag, a link to the Paradise Mountain style sheet, the opening body tag and the standard heading information, including the logo image, for the Paradise Mountain site. An **XML namespace definition (xmlns)** qualifies elements and attribute names used in XML documents by associating them with namespace references. Setting the xmlns in the opening tag tells the parser that the document can accept namespace definitions. For more information on xmlns, visit the Student Online Companion and click on the links to XML Namespace.

2. **Click after** `Paradise Mountain Family Resort</h1>`**, press [Enter] twice, then type** `<h2>Available Movies</h2>`

   The text editor screen now should look like the one shown in Figure O-9. You are ready to bind the XML data you created in the last lesson.

3. **Press [Enter] twice, then type** `<xml id="movies" src="movies.xml" />`

   The `xml` tag uses the `src` attribute to bind the movies.xml data file to your HTML document.

4. **Press [Enter], type** `</body>`**, press [Enter], then type** `</html>`

   With the closing HTML tags entered, your screen should now match Figure O-10.

5. **Save the file**

   You have created an HTML document that binds the XML data entered in the previous lesson. The next step is to construct a table to format and display the bound data in your HTML document.

FIGURE O-9: Beginning HTML markup

```
<!DOCTYPE html PUBliC "-//W3C//DTD XHTML 1.0 Transitional//EN"
"http://www.w3.org/TR/xhtml1/DTD/xhtml1-transitional.dtd">

<html xmlns="http://www.w3.org/1999/xhtml">
<head>

<link href="../css/paradise_style.css" rel="stylesheet" type="text/css" />
<title>Available Movies List</title>

</head>

<body>
<h1><a href="../index.htm">
<img src="../images/pm_logo2.png" alt="Paradise Mountain Family Resort:
Your family fun place!" width="159" height="156" border="0" align="middle"
/></a>Paradise Mountain Family Resort</h1>

<h2>Available Movies</h2>
```

Transitional DTD

Linked style sheet

Opening body tag and site heading information

Page heading

FIGURE O-10: HTML document with data-binding code

```
<!DOCTYPE html PUBliC "-//W3C//DTD XHTML 1.0 Transitional//EN"
"http://www.w3.org/TR/xhtml1/DTD/xhtml1-transitional.dtd">

<html xmlns="http://www.w3.org/1999/xhtml">
<head>

<link href="../css/paradise_style.css" rel="stylesheet" type="text/css" />
<title>Available Movies List</title>

</head>

<body>
<h1><a href="../index.htm">
<img src="../images/pm_logo2.png" alt="Paradise Mountain Family Resort: Your family fun
place!" width="159" height="156" border="0" align="middle" /></a>Paradise Mountain Family
Resort</h1>

<h2>Available Movies</h2>

<xml id="movies" src="movies.xml" />

</body>
</html>
```

Data-binding code

Clues to Use

Understanding XML Parsers

After an XML document is created, it must be analyzed by an XML parser to ensure that the code is properly formatted. Some XML parsers come packaged with XML editing software. Others are part of the browser software used to display XML documents. For example, both Microsoft Internet Explorer and newer Netscape browsers are equipped with their own parsers. XML parsers interpret the document's code and verify that it satisfies all the requirements of a well-formed XML document. XML parsers are strict in their adherence to XML standards. If an element is missing a closing tag or if both the opening and closing tags do not agree in case, the parser reports the error and rejects the document. Although designers who are used to working with XML's more forgiving cousin, HTML, might find this strictness excessive, it is this strict adherence to XML coding standards that enables any XML-compliant browser to open and display any well-formed, valid XML document.

Formatting XML Data with HTML

Once the data in an XML document has been bound to an HTML page, you can use all of the available formatting capabilities in HTML and CSS to control its presentation in a browser. Because XML data often consists of a list or database, the table feature in HTML is an ideal vehicle for displaying it. In addition to conventional table attributes, the `datafld` attribute enables Web page designers to control the binding of XML data to their documents.  You decide to use a table to format and display your movie list data in the XML file.

STEPS

1. **Make sure the file movies.htm is open in your text editor**

2. **Click after `<xml id="movies" src="movies.xml" />`, then press [Enter] twice**
   You want to use a table to display the data from the movies.xml file.

3. **Type the following code, pressing [Enter] after each line:**
   ```
   <table datasrc="#movies" border="1" cellpadding="5"
   align="center">
     <thead>
       <th>DVD Title</th>
       <th>Actor 1</th>
       <th>Actor 2</th>
       <th>Genre</th>
       <th>Rating</th>
     </thead>
   ```
   You typed the opening table tag and the code to create the table headings DVD Title, Actor 1, Actor 2, Genre, and Rating across the top row.

4. **Press [Enter], then type the following code, pressing [Enter] after each line:**
   ```
   <tr>
       <td><span datafld="DVDtitle"></span></td>
       <td><span datafld="actor1"></span></td>
       <td><span datafld="actor2"></span></td>
       <td><span datafld="genre"></span></td>
       <td><span datafld="rating"></span></td>
   </tr>
   </table>
   ```
   The code you typed creates the table cells in which the XML data will appear. The datafld attributes in the code specify the element from the XML document to be bound to each column. The code creates as many rows as necessary to display all the data (records) in your XML file. Your code should appear similar to that shown in Figure O-11.

5. **Check your work to make sure your typing was completely accurate**

6. **Save your work, then open movies.htm in your browser**
   As shown in Figure O-12, the bound XML data appears in a formatted table. The table picks up some of its formatting from the linked style sheet.

> **QUICK TIP**
> You can use all the power and flexibility of DHTML to manipulate XML data once it appears in an HTML document.

```
<img src="../images/pm_logo2.png" alt="Paradise Mountain Family fun
place!" width="159" height="156" border="0" align="middle" /></a>Paradise Mountain Family
Resort</h1>

<h2>Available Movies</h2>

<xml id="movies" src="movies.xml" />

<table datasrc="#movies" border="1" cellpadding="5" align="center">
     <thead>
          <th>DVD Title</th>
          <th>Actor 1</th>
          <th>Actor 2</th>
          <th>Genre</th>
          <th>Rating</th>
     </thead>

     <tr>
          <td><span datafld="DVDtitle"></span></td>
          <td><span datafld="actor1"></span></td>
          <td><span datafld="actor2"></span></td>
          <td><span datafld="genre"></span></td>
          <td><span datafld="rating"></span></td>
     </tr>
   </table>

</body>
</html>
```

Data headings formatted with table heading tags

Span tag holds datafld attribute and value to bind and display data

FIGURE O-12: Web page with bound XML data

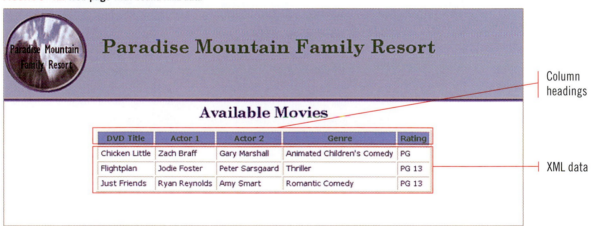

Column headings

XML data

Multiple views of data

Once data is configured for display in your browser, you can present it in many different ways. You can build several different views of the same data depending on the audience. For example, in the case of your movie database, the average user might just want to see the title, actors, and general plot of films, whereas some devoted fans will want to view all the particulars like the date the movie was released, who directed it, and so forth. Because XML only describes data, not its appearance, you are free to use HTML/CSS to create unique views of the data for different classes of users. In addition, with use of DHTML, the view of XML data can be manipulated easily by the end user to suit his or her needs and tastes.

HTML

Modifying an XML Document

You can change an XML document easily using your text editor. Simply open the file and use the edit features to modify the elements and structure of the file.  You want to add a new element to your XML movies file in order to add a short description of each movie.

QUICK TIP
If the movies.xml file does not appear in the file list in the Open dialog box, choose All Files in the Files of type list.

1. **Open the file movies.xml in your text editor**

2. **Click after the first rating element in the location shown in Figure O-13, press [Enter], press [Tab] twice, then type `<description> </description>`**

3. **Repeat Step 2 to create description child elements for the next two movie elements**

4. **In a separate instance of your text editor, open htm_O-2.txt from your Data Files, locate the text under the heading Description 1 that begins, "When an acorn falls to the ground," drag to select the entire description, then copy it to your clipboard**

5. **Click the movies.xml instance of your text editor program button to return to your movies.xml code**

6. **Click between `<description>` and `</description>` in the first movie element, then paste the copied text**

   XML reads tabs and extra spaces coded between the opening and closing tags of each element, so make sure not to press [Enter] or [Tab] to align the pasted description content with the rest of the movie elements.

7. **Repeat Steps 4 and 5 to copy and paste Description 2 and Description 3 into the appropriate movie elements, then close htm_O-2.txt without saving changes**

   The XML document should now contain the text shown in Figure O-14.

8. **Save movies.xml, then close the file**

FIGURE O-13: Correct position for insertion point

```
<?xml version='1.0' encoding='UTF-8' ?>

<DVDlist>
        <movie>
                <DVDtitle>Chicken Little</DVDtitle>
                <actor1>Zach Braff</actor1>
                <actor2>Gary Marshall</actor2>
                <genre>Animated Children's Comedy</genre>
                <rating>PG</rating>                           ─────── First rating
        </movie>                                                       element

        <movie>
                <DVDtitle>Flightplan</DVDtitle>
                <actor1>Jodie Foster</actor1>
                <actor2>Peter Sarsgaard</actor2>
                <genre>Thriller</genre>
                <rating>PG 13</rating>
        </movie>

        <movie>
                <DVDtitle>Just Friends</DVDtitle>
                <actor1>Ryan Reynolds</actor1>
                <actor2>Amy Smart</actor2>
                <genre>Romantic Comedy</genre>
                <rating>PG 13</rating>
        </movie>
</DVDlist>
```

FIGURE O-14: XML document with new description elements

```
<?xml version='1.0' encoding='UTF-8' ?>

<DVDlist>
        <movie>
                <DVDtitle>Chicken Little</DVDtitle>
                <actor1>Zach Braff</actor1>
                <actor2>Gary Marshall</actor2>
                <genre>Animated Children's Comedy</genre>
                <rating>PG</rating>
                <description>When an acorn falls to the ground, a young chicken (Braff)
thinks the sky is falling and causes widespread panic by spreading the inaccurate news.
After his reputation is ruined, the chicken is clobbered by a real piece of the sky as it
falls to Earth.</description>
        </movie>

        <movie>
                <DVDtitle>Flightplan</DVDtitle>
                <actor1>Jodie Foster</actor1>
                <actor2>Peter Sarsgaard</actor2>
                <genre>Thriller</genre>
                <rating>PG 13</rating>
                <description>After the unexpected death of her husband, an airplane
designer, Kyle Pratt (Foster) takes her daughter on board a luxury aircraft to fly from
Berlin to New York. In the middle of the nonstop flight, Julia seemingly disappears without
a trace. Kyle begins to panic when the crew, including the captain and the air marshal
(Sarsgaard), claim the girl never boarded the plane at takeoff.</description>
        </movie>

        <movie>
                <DVDtitle>Just Friends</DVDtitle>
                <actor1>Ryan Reynolds</actor1>
                <actor2>Amy Smart</actor2>
                <genre>Romantic Comedy</genre>
                <rating>PG 13</rating>
                <description>Years after graduating from high school, a man (Reynolds)
reconnects with the girl (Smart) who told him that she just wanted to be friends. This time
he is determined to win her over.</description>
        </movie>
</DVDlist>
```

Description
elements left
"untabbed"
to avoid
extra spacing
in data

HTML

Altering XML Data View with HTML

When you add elements to an XML document, you must make corresponding changes to the HTML document you are using to view the data; otherwise, the new data does not appear. Fortunately, it is easy to bring the HTML document into alignment with the new XML elements. Simply insert the code necessary to display the new elements in the format you want. ████ You decide to display the movie descriptions in the same table with the rest of your movie list data.

1. **Open the file movies.htm in your text editor**

2. **Click after <th>Rating</th>, press [Enter], then press [Tab] twice**

3. **Type `<th>Description</th>`**
   You typed the code to add the heading "Description" to your display table.

4. **Click after `<td><span datafld="rating"></span></td>` in the second table row, then press [Enter]**

5. **Press [Tab] twice, then type `<td><span datafld="description"></span></td>`**

6. **Click before `</body>` at the bottom of your page code, then add a center-aligned Page modified by paragraph with your name and today's date, then press [Enter] twice**
   You added the code to display the description fields from your XML document and added a "Page modified by" paragraph. Your code should resemble that shown in Figure O-15.

7. **Save your work, click the browser program button on your taskbar to display your movies.htm page, then click the Refresh button to reload the page and view your changes**
   The HTML document appears with a new column heading and corresponding data, as shown in Figure O-16.

8. **Print the movies.htm page, then close your browser and text editor**

9. **Transfer your new pages to your remote directory on the server, test your remote files in your browser, then close your FTP program**

FIGURE O-15: Updated code for movies.htm file

```
<img src="../images/pm_logo2.png" alt="Paradise Mountain Family fun
place!" width="159" height="156" border="0" align="middle" /></a>Paradise Mountain Family
Resort</h1>

<h2>Available Movies</h2>

<xml id="movies" src="movies.xml" />

<table datasrc= "#movies" border="1" cellpadding="5" align="center">
    <thead>
      <th>DVD Title</th>
      <th>Actor 1</th>
      <th>Actor 2</th>
      <th>Genre</th>
      <th>Rating</th>
      <th>Description</th>
    </thead>

    <tr>
      <td><span datafld="DVDtitle"></span></td>
      <td><span datafld="actor1"></span></td>
      <td><span datafld="actor2"></span></td>
      <td><span datafld="genre"></span></td>
      <td><span datafld="rating"></span></td>
      <td><span datafld="description"></span></td>
    </tr>
  </table>

<p style="text-align: center;">Page modified by: Your Name, November 28, 2008</p>

</body>
</html>
```

Description heading

Description content cell

FIGURE O-16: Six-column table with new description heading and data

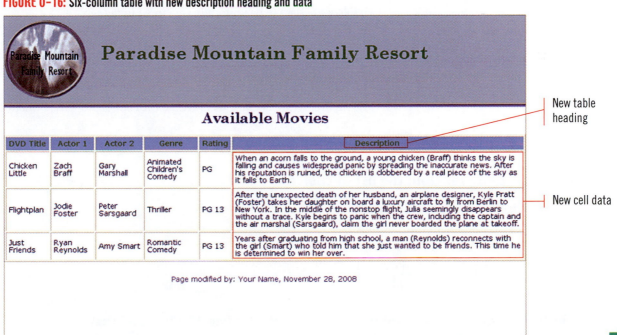

New table heading

New cell data

HTML

Practice

▼ CONCEPTS REVIEW

Name the function of each section of code indicated in Figure O-17.

```
1    <?xml version='1.0' encoding='UTF-8' ?>

2    <packages>
3          <package>
              <name>Rocky Mountain Express</name>
              <price>$100</price>
              <description>Body massage, herbal wrap, and tanning</description>
              <time>1 Hour</time>
          </package>                                                              5

          <package>
              <name>Easy Does It</name>
              <price>$119</price>
4             <description>Facial, herbal wrap, and body scrub</description>
              <time>2 Hours</time>
          </package>
     </packages>
```

Match each statement with the term it best describes.

6. **Valid document**	**a.** The formal specification of rules for an XML document
7. **Parser**	**b.** Requires data to be uniformly structured in tag sets
8. **Well-formed document**	**c.** Uses XML syntax to formally define the elements and structure of an XML document
9. **Schema**	
10. **DTD**	**d.** Text-based syntax designed to describe, deliver, and exchange structured data
11. **XML**	**e.** Follows the rules of a DTD or XML schema
	f. Analyzes XML documents to ensure the code is properly formatted

Select the best answer from the list of choices.

12. The XML declaration should be placed:

    a. As a child element in an XML document.

    b. As the last line of an XML document.

    c. Inside the prolog of an XML document.

    d. Inside the root element of an XML document.

13. Which of the following are syntax rules for an XML document? (Choose all that apply.)

    a. All elements must be nested properly.

    b. All attribute values must be enclosed in quotes.

    c. All elements must be terminated.

    d. All empty elements must be terminated with >.

14. **Choose all of the true statements.**
    a. Child XML elements must be indented from their parents to be properly processed.
    b. XML organizes data in a hierarchical structure.
    c. XML is case sensitive.
    d. XML elements must contain child elements.

15. **Which of the following can be used to display formatted XML data in a browser? (Choose all that apply.)**
    a. Parser
    b. CSS
    c. DTD
    d. Data binding

16. **Which of the following are true statements about the document element or root element? (Choose all that apply.)**
    a. It is the first element in an XML file.
    b. All of the other elements in the document are nested within it.
    c. It must be named `<root>`.
    d. There is only one element of this type in an XML document.

▼ SKILLS REVIEW

1. **Define XML elements and structure.**
    a. Open your text editor, then enter the processing instruction for an XML document. (*Hint*: Enter `<?xml version='1.0' encoding='UTF-8' ?>`.)
    b. Enter a root element of packages for the XML file. (*Hint*: Enter opening `<packages>` and closing `</packages>` tags.)
    c. Add an element named package between opening and closing root element tags. (*Hint*: Enter opening `<package>` and closing `</package>` tags.)
    d. Between the opening `<package>` and closing `</package>` tags, add opening and closing tags for the elements name, price, and description. Use Figure O-18 as a guide.

FIGURE O-18

```
<?xml version='1.0' encoding='UTF-8' ?>
<packages>
        <package>
            <name></name>
            <price></price>
            <description></description>
        </package>

</packages>
```

HTML

▼ SKILLS REVIEW (CONTINUED)

e. Add four more package elements with the children elements of name, price, and description. Use Figure O-19 as a guide.

f. Check your file for errors, make any necessary changes, then save your file as **packages.xml** in the paradise/spa directory in the location where you save your site files.

FIGURE O-19

```
<?xml version='1.0' encoding='UTF-8' ?>
<packages>
        <package>
           <name></name>
           <price></price>
           <description></description>
        </package>

        <package>
           <name></name>
           <price></price>
           <description></description>
        </package>

        <package>
           <name></name>
           <price></price>
           <description></description>
        </package>

        <package>
           <name></name>
           <price></price>
           <description></description>
        </package>

        <package>
           <name></name>
           <price></price>
           <description></description>
        </package>
</packages>
```

2. Enter XML data.

   a. Using Figure O-20 as a guide, enter the data for the packages.xml file.

   b. Check your file for errors, make any necessary changes, then save your file.

FIGURE O-20

```
<?xml version='1.0' encoding='UTF-8' ?>
<packages>
        <package>
           <name>Rocky Mountain Express</name>
           <price>$100</price>
           <description>Body massage, herbal wrap, and tanning</description>
        </package>

        <package>
           <name>Easy Does It</name>
           <price>$119</price>
           <description>Facial, herbal wrap, and body scrub</description>
        </package>

        <package>
           <name>Beautiful Dreamer</name>
           <price>$175</price>
           <description>Body massage, herbal wrap, body scrub, and body mask</description>
        </package>

        <package>
           <name>Eden Paradise</name>
           <price>$165</price>
           <description>Facial, herbal wrap, body massage, manicure, and pedicure</description>
        </package>

        <package>
           <name>Heavenly Bliss</name>
           <price>$215</price>
           <description>Facial, herbal wrap, body massage, body scrub, manicure, and pedicure
           </description>
        </package>
</packages>
```

3. Bind XML data to HTML.

   a. In your text editor, open the file **htm_O-3.txt** from the drive and folder where your Data Files are stored, then save it as **packages.htm** to the paradise/spa directory where you save your site files. If you are asked whether you want to replace the file, click Yes.

   b. Directly below the opening `<body>` tag, enter the `<xml />` tag with the necessary attributes and values to bind the file packages.xml with an id of packages to the html file. (*Hint*: Add `<xml id="packages" src="packages.xml" />`.)

   c. Check your file for errors, make any necessary changes, then save your file.

4. Format XML data with HTML.

   a. In the packages.htm file, locate the opening `<table>` tag and enter a datasrc attribute with a value of #packages to identify the XML file as a data source for the table. (*Hint*: Add `datasrc="#packages"`.)

   b. Locate the first set of `<td> ...</td>` tags in the table, and between them enter `<span datafld="name"></span>` to bind the name element from the XML file to the first table column.

   c. Locate the second set of `<td> ...</td>` tags in the table, and between them enter `<span datafld="price"></span>` to bind the price element from the XML file to the second table column.

   d. Locate the third set of `<td> ...</td>` tags in the table, and between them enter `<span datafld="description"></span>` to bind the description element from the XML file to the third table column.

   e. Check your file for errors, make any necessary changes, then save your file.

   f. Open the **packages.htm** file in your browser.

   g. If you receive an error message, review the HTML and XML files in your text editor, correct the errors, then open the file again in your browser.

   h. Review the XML data in the table.

▼ SKILLS REVIEW (CONTINUED)

5. Modify an XML document.

a. Return to the **packages.xml** file in your text editor and insert a new element named "time" as a child in each package element below the description elements. (*Hint*: Insert `<time></time>` after each closing `</description>` tag.)

b. Add the following data between the `<time>...</time>` element tags: `1 Hour` for the first package, `2 Hours` for the second package, `2 Hours` for the third package, `3 Hours` for the fourth package, and `4 Hours` for the fifth package.

c. Check your file for errors and make any necessary changes.

d. Add your name as a comment below the processing instruction. (*Hint*: XML comments have the same syntax as HTML comments.)

e. Save your file, then print the packages.xml file from your text editor.

6. Alter XML data view with HTML.

a. In your packages.htm file, use your text editor to add a fourth column heading labeled Length of Time to the table. (*Hint*: Add `<th>Length of Time</th>` above the closing `</thead>` tag.)

b. Bind the time element from the XML file to the new column by entering `<td><span dataflld="time"></span></td>` above the table's closing `</tr>` tag.

c. Check your file for errors, make any necessary changes, then save your file.

d. Refresh **packages.htm** in your browser and check the expanded table.

e. In your text editor, add your name to the comment above the closing `</body>` tag and print the packages.htm page.

f. Close all open files, then transfer the **packages.htm** and **packages.xml** files to your remote directory.

▼ INDEPENDENT CHALLENGE 1

As you continue developing the Web site for your resort rental business, Star Vacations, you decide to use XML to organize your tour data.

a. In your text editor, open the file **htm_O-4.txt** from the drive and folder where your Data Files are stored, then save it as **tours.xml** to the vacations folder where you save your site files.

b. At the top of the file, enter the processing instruction for an XML document.

c. Add a new element named price as a child in each tour element below the elements named rtime.

d. Add the following data between the `<price>...</price>` element tags: `$180` for the first tour, `$110` for the second tour, `$80` for the third tour, and `$150` for the fourth tour.

e. Add your name to the comment at the top of the file, then save your file.

f. In your text editor, open the file **htm_O-5.txt** from the drive and folder where your Data Files are stored, then save it as **tours.htm** to the vacations folder where you save your site files.

g. Directly below the opening `<body>` tag, add the `<xml />` tag with the necessary attributes and values to bind the file tours.xml with an id of `tours` to the HTML file.

h. Use the `tours` id to identify the data source for the table.

i. Using your XML file and the table column headings as a guide, add the correct element names as the datafld values to bind the data from the XML file to the table columns.

j. Add your name to the comment at the top of the file, then save your file.

▼ INDEPENDENT CHALLENGE 1 (CONTINUED)

k. Open the **tours.htm** file in your browser and compare your table to Figure O-21.

l. Print the tours.xml and tours.htm files from your text editor.

m. Transfer both pages to your remote directory.

Tours

Name	Departing Time	Returning Time	Price
Kayak Trip	7:00 AM	1:00 PM	$180
Snorkel Trip	9:00 AM	12:30 PM	$110
Island Bus Tour	10:00 AM	12:00 PM	$80
Lucayan National Park Tour	8:00 AM	2:00 PM	$150

Advanced Challenge Exercises

- CSS is another method for displaying XML data in a browser and does not require an HTML page. Use your favorite search engine to research how you can use a style sheet to display XML data in a browser. Investigate how CSS can be used to display XML data as block elements. (*Hint*: Use search terms: XML, display, block elements, CSS).
- In your text editor create a style sheet named **tours.css** to display the tours.xml data. Display the data as block elements in bold with a font size of 18 pt.
- Add your name as a comment at the top of the style sheet, then save the file.
- Add the appropriate link to the tours.css file in your tours.xml file, then save the file.
- Open the **tours.xml** file in your browser and check your work.
- Print the tours.xml and tours.css files from your text editor.

▼ INDEPENDENT CHALLENGE 2

Your employer Metro Water has decided to post their water conservation courses on their Web site. You decide to use XML to structure the course data and HTML to present the course information in a table.

a. In your text editor, open the file **htm_O-6.txt** from the drive and folder where your Data Files are stored, then save it as **courses.xml** to the water folder where you save your site files.

b. At the top of the file, enter the processing instruction for an XML document and a comment with your name.

c. Add a root element named courses.

d. Add element tags named title, dates, day, and time to structure the data inside the opening <class> and closing </class> tags, then save the file.

e. In your text editor, open the file **htm_O-7.txt** from the drive and folder where your Data Files are stored, then save it as **courses.htm** to the water folder where you save your site files.

f. Bind the courses.xml file to the HTML file using an id of courses.

g. Use the courses id to identify the data source for the table.

▼ INDEPENDENT CHALLENGE 2 (CONTINUED)

h. Add the necessary table elements to display the XML data as shown in Figure O-22.

i. Add your name to the comment at the top of the file, then save your file.

j. Open the **courses.htm** file in your browser and check your work.

k. Print the courses.xml and courses.htm files from your text editor.

l. Transfer both pages to your remote directory.

Courses

Class	Session	Day	Time
Conserving Water Inside the Home	January 4 - January 25	Tuesdays	10:00 AM - 12:00 PM
Conserving Water Outdoors	January 5 - January 26	Wednesdays	10:30 AM - 12:30 PM
Conserving Well Water	January 6 - January 27	Thursdays	2:00 PM - 4:00 PM
Household Appliances and Water Consumption	January 7 - January 28	Fridays	1:00 PM - 3:00 PM

Advanced Challenge Exercises

- If you have many records in an XML file you may want to use paging to display the records in groups rather than in one big table. Use your favorite search engine to research how the number of records displayed in a table can be restricted using the datapagesize attribute. Investigate how the methods *previousPage* and *nextPage* can be used to navigate through groups of records in a table.

- In your courses.htm file, add an attribute and value to your opening `<table>` tag to set the maximum number of rows displayed per page to two.

- In your courses.htm file, add a button labeled Next Page that will appear below the table in the browser. This button allows users to move to the next set of data in the XML file.

- In your courses.htm file, add a button labeled Previous Page that will appear to the left of the Next Page button in the browser. This button allows users to move to the previous set of XML data.

- Save your work, then reload the **courses.htm** page in your browser to check your buttons. Compare your table and buttons to Figure O-23.

- Print the courses.htm file from your text editor.

- Transfer the **courses.htm** file to your remote directory.

Courses

Class	Session	Day	Time
Conserving Water Inside the Home	January 4 - January 25	Tuesdays	10:00 AM - 12:00 PM
Conserving Water Outdoors	January 5 - January 26	Wednesdays	10:30 AM - 12:30 PM

[Previous Page] [Next Page]

▼ INDEPENDENT CHALLENGE 3

You know that XML files can be checked with XML parsers, and you want to find out more about these tools.

Use your favorite search engine to research XML parsers. Write a paper answering the following questions:

    a. What are the two types of XML parsers?

    b. How do the two types of parsers differ?

    c. Find a free parser on the Web and provide its URL and note its type.

    d. Add your name and today's date to the top of your paper and print the document.

▼ INDEPENDENT CHALLENGE 4

Now that you've used XML to organize and present data, you are ready to add XML to your Web site.

    a. Determine how XML can be used on your Web site to organize data.

    b. Lay out your pages on paper to determine which pages contain data that can be structured using XML.

    c. Create the XML pages structuring your data.

    d. Create HTML pages to bind the XML data and display it using a table inside a browser.

    e. Open the HTML pages in your browser and make any necessary adjustments.

    f. Add your name as a comment to the XML and HTML pages and print the pages.

    g. Transfer your new pages to the remote location.

▼ VISUAL WORKSHOP

Work progresses on your Bits and PCs Web site, and you have organized your storage inventory in an XML file. In your text editor, open the **htm_O-8.txt** file from the drive and folder where your Data Files are stored, then save it as **inventory.xml** in the bitspcs folder where you save your site files. Create an HTML file that binds the XML data from the inventory.xml file and present it as shown in Figure O-24. (*Hint*: You do not want to display the number of each item in your table. Use the color #663366 for the text and #9999CC for the table heading background.) Add your name to the e-mail link at the bottom of the page, save the file as **inventory.htm** in the bitspcs folder where you save your site files, then open the file in your browser to check your work. Print the inventory.htm file in your text editor then transfer the **inventory.xml** and **inventory.htm** files to your remote location.

FIGURE O-24

Storage Specials

Item	Storage Capacity	Price
Internal Hard Drive	160 GB	$49.99
Internal Hard Drive	250 GB	$79.99
External Hard Drive	300 GB	$269.99
External Hard Drive	80 GB	$89.99
USB Flash Drive	512 MB	$49.99
USB Flash Drive	1 GB	$89.98

For information about sales, service, or store hours contact info@bitsPCs.com

Appendix

Appendix

HTML

OBJECTIVES

Put a document on the Web
Use other FTP client programs
Increase Web site traffic
HTML tag reference
HTML browser-safe colors
HTML color names
Cascading Style Sheet reference
HTML special characters
Formatting with HTML 4.0 attributes

When you create HTML documents for use in a business setting, it is important not only to know how to construct Web pages, but also how to transfer documents and take advantage of resources on the Web. These resources include a variety of search engines and Web sites devoted to helping your business have a Web presence. You also should be aware of the variety of options available for increasing traffic to your Web site. This appendix provides useful HTML code and publishing references for you to use as you create and publish your Web pages.

Putting a Document on the Web

Crucial factors in making your site successful are availability and accessibility. Accessible Web sites are stored on a Web server (a computer that makes files available over the World Wide Web) with adequate bandwidth—data-transfer capacity—so that Web traffic can flow smoothly and quickly. It is also important that the company you choose as your hosting service provides reliable support and backup services so your site is always available. Your school or Internet service provider (ISP)—the company that provides your Internet access—may have a Web server available for your use. Free Web space is also available on many Web sites. However, free sites usually require you to display advertising banners and pop-up windows, both a source of annoyance to visitors, on your pages in exchange for the free service. Figure AP-1 shows a Web page on one such site.

DETAILS

Ensure that your site is ready for users by doing the following:

- **Establish your URL**

  When you place your Web site on a free or inexpensive Web server, the resulting URL is usually a subdirectory on the Web server's domain—for example, www.course.com/users/~torxdesign/. Such a URL is not easy for potential users to remember or to type. The alternative is to register your own domain name, such as www.thomson.com. Domain name registration involves payment of a yearly fee, in addition to paying a Web space provider to store your pages and domain name. In either case, the logistics of setting up your Web site location can take time, so begin making arrangements for a Web server well in advance of your target publishing date.

- **Submit your URL to search engines**

  Submitting your URL for inclusion in search engine databases facilitates potential users locating your site. Each search engine has different site indexing policies. You can access a list of submission instructions by clicking on the About or Businesses link, which is usually near the bottom of a search engine's home page. Figure AP-2 shows the About Google page with a link leading to instructions for submitting a URL. An alternative to submitting your own site URL is to use a search engine submission service. For a nominal fee, these service providers submit your site to a wide variety of search engines. You should be aware, however, that most of these companies use submission "robots"—special software programs that automatically submit your site to a variety of search engines on a rotating basis. Some search engines give less weight to this type of submission.

- **Test your Web pages**

  Extensively test your files using a variety of browsers, operating systems, and display conditions to weed out any errors and design problems before you publish.

- **Ensure Web server compatibility**

  Every hosting service has a list of recommended default file names. Check with your chosen hosting service for a list of recommended file names, then review your filenames to be sure they are named accordingly.

- **Verify hyperlinks**

  Confirm that the hyperlinks in your documents point to the correct filenames. As some operating systems and scripts are case sensitive, it is best practice to use all lowercase in assigning filenames. It is particularly important that all of your files be saved with lowercase extensions. Another common problem with hyperlinks is drive letters that appear in file paths. As you check your links, be sure that no drive-letter paths, such as c:\\ appear in your links. Also, be sure that hyperlinks between pages in your Web site use relative pathnames.

- **Learn the publishing procedure**

  Every Web server uses a unique system for adding new Web sites. Make sure you understand the procedure outlined by your Web space provider, and make sure you have the necessary software.

FIGURE AP-1: Pop-up windows and banners located on a free Web site

FIGURE AP-2: About Google information page

Instructions for submitting site to Google

Using Other FTP Client Programs

Unless you are using a Web development software program that comes with its own file transfer application, you need to establish a method of transferring your files to a Web server. This is usually accomplished through the use of an FTP client program. Before using any FTP client, make sure that you have a valid user ID, password, and directory path as assigned by your instructor or server administrator. If you do not have this information, make sure you get it before attempting to transfer files.

DETAILS

Two common FTP client programs are WS_FTP, which comes in both Home and Pro versions for Windows clients, and Fetch FTP for Apple Macintosh users:

- **WS_FTP by Ipswitch**

  Ipswitch's WS_FTP_Home and Pro programs are high-powered FTP clients that are easy to use and make transfers lightning fast. Figure AP-3 shows the WS_FTP interface with its daily startup tip. While the program walks the user through the install process, WS_FTP Home also supplies its own Getting Started Tutorial. When you start WS_FTP_Home for the first time, you are presented with a Welcome page that supplies a link to the tutorial. If you choose not to view the Getting Started tutorial, simply click the Next button at the bottom of the screen to continue with the setup. (You can always come back to the tutorial at a later time.) (To go directly to the tutorial, go to the Student Online Companion for this book.)

- **Fetch FTP by Fetch Softworks**

  Fetch is an FTP client program by Fetch Softworks. Fetch is designed for use with the Apple Macintosh operating system. It supports FTP and SFTP. As with other FTP clients, Fetch can be used to transfer files from your local computer to another computer on the Internet for document-sharing and Web publishing purposes. Using Fetch, you can also rename, move, delete, and change the permissions of files on a Web server. As shown in Figure AP-4, Fetch uses the graphical user interface common to programs that run on Macintosh operating systems. To view a step-by-step tutorial on using Fetch, go to the Student Online Companion for this book. If you are a student or employee at a public or accredited private school, college, university, or academy or a volunteer at a nonprofit agency, you may qualify for a fee-exempt license. Students and parents in some home-school situations might also be eligible to receive free downloads. Fetch 5.0 supports Mac OS X 10.2.4 or later. If your operating system is older than that, you can download Fetch 4.0, a previous version of Fetch that may still be available for purchase on the Fetch Softworks Web site.

FIGURE AP-3: WS_FTP Home startup screen with Tip

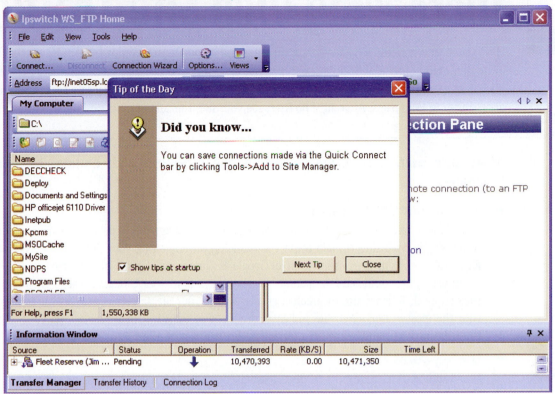

FIGURE AP-4: Fetch GUI windows

Increasing Web Site Traffic

Have you ever wondered why a Web site can be found by one search engine but not by another? How does a site get listed in an index? Some search engines conduct periodic—and laborious—searches of Web sites, and other search engines depend on site submissions to their indices. The key to a successful Web site is its accessibility to Web users. After all, if no users see your site, the caliber of its design is irrelevant.

Make sure users can access your Web pages using search engines by using these guidelines:

- ### Submit your URL to search engines

  One of the simplest steps in getting your site listed by search engines is to provide them with your URL. Most search engine Web sites contain contact information for requesting your site to be added to their index. Figure AP-5 shows the submission form for Google. Because search engine databases have size limits and must continually purge outdated information, you should resubmit your URL on a regular basis to prevent your site's removal. To maximize the number of users sent to your site, target your requests to the search engines with the most visitors. Web site audience measurement statistics are available from comScore Networks, through the comScore Media Metrix service, as shown in Figure AP-6.

- ### Use keywords

  When adding a Web page to its database, a search engine's goal is to locate terms in the page that identify the page's key concepts or focus. It adds these terms, known as **keywords**, to the index for its database. When a user conducts a search, the search engine uses these keywords to determine which URLs it provides as search results. For this reason, it is important that you optimize your page for search-engine submission by using relevant wording throughout your Web page. Because many search engines compare information listed in both the page title—the number-one comparison factor—and the meta tags with the information contained within the text of your Web site, it is important that your title and meta tags contain information your target audience is seeking and that matches your page content. Figure AP-7 shows the source code for a page that has been optimized for search-engine selection.

- ### Plan ahead

  Some search engines can take as long as three months from the time you submit your URL until the time your site is included in their index. In the intervening period, your business may have minimal Web site traffic, which can be a serious problem. If your business plan relies heavily on Web traffic, you may need to schedule the rollout of your Web site prior to the official opening of your business so that it appears in search engine databases.

- ### Make your page a high priority

  Although a search may yield hundreds of sites, most people generally look at only the first few entries in search results. You can give your page a higher priority by skillfully implementing the `<title>` and `<meta />` tags in your Web site. Some search engines look only at the text marked by these tags when indexing, or give extra weight to this text when evaluating your page's relevance to particular topics. The `<meta />` tag includes attributes that allow you to suggest to the search engines the most appropriate keywords, as well as the most appropriate description, for your Web page. Figure AP-7 shows the code for a Web page using `<meta />` tags.

FIGURE AP-5: URL submission form on the Google search engine Web site

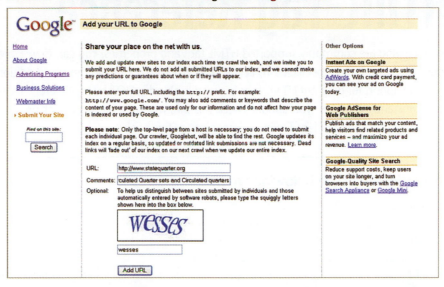

FIGURE AP-6: comScore Media Metrix: the Internet audience measurement service

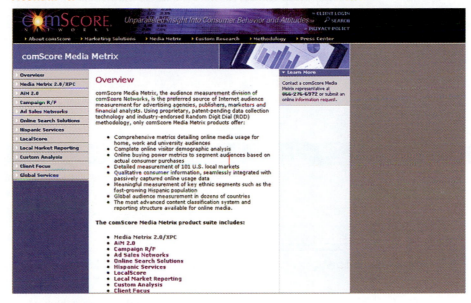

FIGURE AP-7: Web page incorporating optimized `<meta />` title and content tags

Meta tag

Keywords

Description

Title

```
<html>

<head>
<meta name="keywords" content="souvenir, michigan, florida, texas, iowa, wisconsin, california,
oregon,state quarter, commemorative, quarter, uncirculated quarters, 50 states, coin, circulated,
coins, spoon, state spoon, coin shop, collecting, us, U.S., Mint, US Mint, hobby, twenty, five,
cents, twenty-five, numismatics, numismatists, numismatic, money, business,
dealers, dollar, massachusetts, connecticut, conneticut, new york,new jersey, vermont, delaware,
deleware, limited, edition, cent, liberty, in god we trust, dollar, gold, golden, rare, unc, au, ms,
proof, coins, state coins, U.S., Mint, eagle, .25, professional, penny, Sacagawea, nickel, dime,
United, states, p&amp;d, p, d, coin, shops, 1999, 2000, 2001, 2002, 2003, 2004, 2005, 2006, 2007,
2008,  release, Gold, silver, treasure, currency, dealer, new, 1999-2008, redesign, design, state,
uncirculated, circulated" />

<meta name="Description" content="State Quarters and State Quarter products. Coin Jewelry, State
Quarter spoons and spoon display cases Uncirculated Quarter sets and Circulated quarters" />

<meta http-equiv="Content-Type" content="text/html; charset=windows-1252" />
<meta http-equiv="Content-Language" content="en-us" />

<title>State Quarters - Quarter Spoons - Quarter Jewelry - Rolls - Uncirculated state
quarters</title>

</head>

<body background="_themes/quarters/blue-blue_bkgrnd.gif" bgcolor="#FFFFFF" text="#000099"
link="#3366CC" vlink="#666666" alink="#990000">

<table border="0" cellpadding="0" cellspacing="0" width="100%"><tr><td>

<font style="font-family: Arial Narrow, Arial, sans-serif;">

<p style="text-align:center; font-size: 30pt;"><strong>
<img src="_derived/index.htm_cmp_quarters110_bnr.gif" width="600" height="60" border="0"
alt="www.StateQuarter.Org" /></strong><br />
</p>

<br />
```

HTML Tag Reference

The following are commonly supported HTML tags and properties. You can view more detailed information about the latest HTML specifications at the W3C Worldwide Consortium site. Additional information about browser support for different HTML tags is available at Index DOT HTML Reference. Because the World Wide Web constantly changes, you should check this information against current browser versions. (To access these sites, go to the Student Online Companion for this book.)

STEPS

Properties are of the following types:

- *Character*   A single text character
- *Color*   A recognized color name or color value
- *CGI script*   The name of a CGI script on the Web server
- *Document*   The filename or URL of the file
- *List*   List of items separated by commas, usually enclosed in double quotation marks
- *Mime-type*   A MIME data type, such as "text/css", "audio/wav", or "video/x-msvideo"
- *Options*   Limited to a specific set of values (values are shown below the property)
- *Text*   Any legal text string
- *URL*   The URL for a Web page or file
- *Value*   A number, usually an integer

TABLE AP-1: HTML tags

tags and properties		description
`<!-- -->`		Used for comments in documenting the features of your HTML code, often divided into <!-- and -->, which could be separated by several lines
`<a>...</a>`		Marks the beginning and end of a hypertext link
	`href="url"`	Indicates the target, filename, or URL to which the hypertext points
	`name="Text"`	Specifies a name for the enclosed text, allowing it to be a target of a hyperlink
	`rel="Text"`	Specifies the relationship between the current page and the link specified by the href property
	`rev="Text"`	Specifies a reverse relationship between the current page and the link specified by the href property
	`target="Text" (_blank, _top, _self, _parent)`	Specifies the default target window or frame for the hyperlink. Choices: _blank, _top, _self, _parent or the name of the window desired
	`title="Text"`	Provides a title for the document whose address is given by the href property
`<abbr>...</abbr>`		Indicates an abbreviated form (e.g., WWW, HTTP, URI, Mass., etc.)
`<acronym>...</acronym>`		Indicates an acronym (e.g., WAC, radar, etc.)
`<address>...</address>`		The <address> tag is used for information such as addresses, authorship, and so forth; the text is usually italicized and in some browsers it is indented
`<applet>...</applet>`		Supported by all Java-enabled browsers, allows designers to embed a Java applet in an HTML document; it has been deprecated in favor of the OBJECT element

tags and properties		description
`<area>`		Defines the type and coordinates of a hotspot within an image map
	`cords="Value"`	The coordinates of the hotspot; coordinates depend on the shape of the hotspot: *value 2...*
	`Rectangle`	coords=x_left, y_upper, x_right, y_lower
	`Circle`	coords=x_center, y_center, radius
	`Polygon`	coords=x1, y1, x2, y2, x3, y3, ...
	`href="URL"`	Indicates the target, filename, or URL to which the hotspot points
	`shape="Option"` `(rect | circle | poly)`	The shape of the hotspot
	`target="Text"`	Specifies the default target window or frame for the hotspot
`<b>...</b>`		Displays the enclosed text in boldface; use the <strong> tag for greater accessibility
`<base />`		Allows you to specify the URL for the HTML document; it is used by some browsers to interpret relative hyperlinks
	`href="URL"`	Specifies the URL from which all relative hyperlinks should be based
	`target="Text"`	Specifies the default target window or frame for every hyperlink in the document
`<basefont />`		Sets the base font size (using the size attribute). Font size changes achieved with font are relative to the base font size set by basefont. If basefont is not used, the default base font size is 3. Basefont is deprecated in favor of Cascading Style Sheets.
`<bdo>...</bdo>`		Allows authors to turn off the bidirectional algorithm for selected fragments of text
`<bgsound />`		Used to play a background sound clip when the page is first opened; the embed tag is preferred and leaves the user more control.
	`loop="Value"`	Specifies the number of times the sound clip should be played; loop can either be a digit or infinite
	`src="Document"`	The sound file used for the sound clip
`<big>...</big>`		Increases the size of the enclosed text; the exact appearance of the text depends on the browser and the default font size
`<blockquote>... </blockquote>`		Used to set off long quotes or citations, usually by indenting the enclosed text on both sides; some browsers italicize the text as well
`<body>...</body>`		Encloses all text, images, and other elements that the user sees on the Web page
	`Alink="Color"`	Color of activated hypertext links, which are links the user is currently clicking, but has not yet released
	`background="File"`	The graphic image file used for the Web page background
	`bgcolor="Color"`	The color of the Web page background
	`bgproperties="Fixed"`	Keeps the background image fixed so that it does not scroll with the Web page
	`leftmargin="Value"`	Indents the left margin of the page by the number of pixels specified in value
	`link="Color"`	Color of all unvisited links
	`text="Color"`	Color of all text in the document

tags and properties		description
	topmargin="Value"	Indents the top margin of the page by the number of pixels specified in value
	vlink="Color"	Color of previously visited links
 		Forces a line break in the text
	clear="Option"	Causes the next line to start at the spot where the specified margin is clear (left | right | all | none)
<button>...</button>		Buttons created with the button element function just like buttons created with the input element, but they offer richer rendering possibilities; the button element may have content
<caption>...</caption>		Encloses the table caption
	align="Option"	Specifies the alignment of the caption with respect to the table (left | right | center | top | bottom)
<center>...</center>		Horizontally centers the enclosed text or image; the center tag is deprecated in favor of Cascading Style Sheets
<cite>...</cite>		Used for citations and usually appears in italics
<code>...</code>		Used for text taken from the code for a computer program, and usually appears in a fixed width font
<col />		Allows authors to group together attribute specifications for table columns
<colgroup>...</colgroup>		Creates an explicit column group
<dd>...</dd>		Formats text to be used as relative definitions in a <dl> list
<del>		Used to markup sections of the document that have been deleted with respect to a different version of a document
<dir>...</dir>		Encloses an unordered list of <li> items, formatted in narrow columns; deprecated in favor of <ul>
	text="Option"	Specifies the type of bullet used for displaying each <li> item in the <dir> list: (circle | disc | square)
<dfn>...</dfn>		Used for the defining instance of a term, that is, the first time the term is used; the enclosed text is usually italicized
<div>...</div>		Used to set the text alignment of blocks of text or images
<dl>...</dl>		Encloses a definition list in which the <dd> definition term is left-aligned, and the <dt> relative definition is indented
<dt>		Used to format the definition term in a <dl> list
...		Used to emphasize text; the enclosed text usually appears in italics
<fieldset>...</fieldset>		Allows authors to group thematically related controls and labels
<font>...</font>		Used to control the appearance of the text it encloses; the font tag is deprecated in favor of Cascading Style Sheets

tags and properties	description
`color="Color"`	The color of the enclosed text style attributes can be applied as: style="color: color;"
`face="List"`	The font face of the text; multiple font faces can be specified, separated by commas; the browser tries to render the text in the order specified by the list
`size="Value"`	Size of the font on a seven-point scale (1 is smallest, 7 is largest); it can be absolute or relative. Specifying size=5 sets the font size to size 5 on the scale; specifying size=+5 sets the font size 5 points larger than default tag
`<form>...</form>`	Marks the beginning and end of a Web page form
`action="URL"`	Specifies the URL to which the contents of the form are to be sent
`Enctype="Text"`	Specifies the encoding type used to submit the data to the server
`Method="Option"`	Specifies the method of accessing the URL indicated in the action attribute (post | get)
`target="Text"`	The frame or window that displays the form's results
`<frame>...</frame>`	Defines a single frame within a set of frames
`bordercolor="Color"`	Specifies the color of the frame border
`Frameborder="Option"`	Specifies whether the frame border is visible (yes | no)
`framespacing="Value"`	Specifies the amount of space between frames, in pixels
`marginheight="Value"`	Specifies the amount of space above and below the frame object and the frame borders
`Marginwidth="Value"`	Specifies the amount of space to the left and right of the frame object, in pixels
`name="Text"`	Label assigned to the frame
`Noresize`	Prevents users from resizing the frame
`scrolling="Option"`	Specifies whether scroll bars are visible (yes | no | auto); auto (the default) displays scroll bars only as needed
`src="Document"`	Specifies the document or URL of the object to be displayed in the frame
`<frameset>...</frameset>`	Marks the beginning and the end of a set of frames
`border="Value"`	The size of the borders, in pixels
`bordercolor="Value"`	The color of the frame borders
`cols="List"`	The size of each column in a set of frames; columns can be specified either in pixels, as a percentage of the display area, or with an asterisk (*), indicating that any remaining space be allotted to that column (for example, cols="40,25%,*")
`rows="List"`	The size of each row in a set of frames; rows can be specified either in pixels, as a percentage of the display area, or with an asterisk (*), indicating that any remaining space be allotted to that column (for example, rows="40,25%,*")

`<h1>...</h1>`
`<h2>...</h2>`
`<h3>...</h3>`
`<h4>...</h4>`
`<h5>...</h5>`
`<h6>...</h6>`
	The six levels of text headings ranging from the largest (<h1>) to the smallest (<h6>); text headings appear in a bold face font

tags and properties		description
`<head>...</head>`		The head element contains information about the current document, such as its title, keywords that may be useful to search engines, and other data that is not considered document content
`<hr />`		Creates a horizontal line
	`align="Option"`	The alignment of the heading (left | right | center)
	`color="Color"`	Specifies a color for the line
	`Noshade`	Removes 3D shading from the line
	`size="Value"`	The size (height) of the line in pixels
	`width="Value"`	The width (length) of the line either in pixels or as a percentage of the display area
`<head>...</head>`		Encloses code that provides information about the document
`<html>...</html>`		Indicates the beginning and end of the HTML document
`<i>...</i>`		Italicizes the enclosed text; WAI recommends the use of ... instead of <i>...</i>
`<iframe>...</iframe>`		Allows authors to insert a frame within a block of text. Inserting an inline frame within a section of text is much like inserting an object via the object element: they both allow you to insert an HTML document in the middle of another; they may both be aligned with surrounding text, etc.
`<img />`		Used to insert an inline image into the document
	`align=Option`	Specifies the alignment of the image; specifying left or right aligns the image with the left or right page margin; the other alignment options align the image with surrounding text (left | right | top | texttop | middle | absmiddle | baseline | bottom | absbottom)
	`alt="Text"`	Text to appear if the image cannot be displayed by the browser
	`border="Value"`	The size of the border around the image, in pixels
	`controls`	Display VCR-like controls under moving images; used in conjunction with the dynsrc property
	`dynsrc="Document"`	Specifies the file of a video, AVI clip, or VRML worlds displayed inside the page
	`height="Value"`	The height of the image in pixels
	`hspace="Value"`	Controls the amount of space to the left and right of the image, in pixels
	`Ismap`	Identifies the graphic as an image map; for use with server-side image maps
	`loop="Value"`	Specifies the number of times a moving image should be played; the value must be either a digit or infinite
	`lowsrc="File"`	A low-resolution version of the graphic that the browser should initially display before loading the high-resolution version
	`src="File"`	The source file of the inline image

tags and properties	description
`start="Item"`	Tells the browser when to start displaying a moving image file
`(fileopen | mouseover)`	The file is open; mouseover directs the browser to start when the mouse moves over the image
`usemap="#map_name"`	Identifies the graphic as an image map and specifies the name of the image map definition to use with the graphic; for use with client-side image maps
`vspace="Value"`	The amount of space above and below the image, in pixels
`width="Value"`	The width of the image in pixels
`<input>...</input>`	Creates an input object for use in a Web page form
`align="Option"` `(left | right | top | texttop | middle | absmiddle | baseline | bottom | absbottom)`	Specifies the alignment of an input image; similar to the align attribute with the `<img />` tag
`checked`	Specifies that an input check box or input option button is selected
`loop="Value"`	Specifies the number of times a moving input image should be played; the value must be either a digit or infinite
`lowsrc="file"`	A low-resolution version of the input image that the browser should initially display before loading the high resolution version
`maxlength="Value"`	Specifies the maximum number of characters inserted into an input text box
`name="Text"`	The label given to the input object
`size="Value"`	The visible size, in characters, of an input text box
`src="Document"`	The source file of the graphic used for an input image object
`start="Option"` `(fileopen | mouseover)`	Tells the browser when to start displaying a moving image file; similar to the start property for the `<img>` tag
`type="Option"` `(checkbox | hidden | image | password | radio | reset | submit | text | textarea)`	Specifies the type of input object • checkbox creates a check box • hidden creates a hidden object • image creates an image object • password creates a text box that hides the text as the user enters it • radio creates an option button • reset creates a button that resets the form's fields when pressed • submit creates a button that submits the form when pressed • text creates a text box • textarea creates a text box with multiple line entry fields
`value="Value"`	Specifies the information that is initially displayed in the input object
`vspace="Value"`	The amount of space above and below the image, in pixels
`width="Value"`	The width of the input image, in pixels
`<ins>...</ins>`	Used to mark up sections of the document that have been inserted with respect to a different version of a document
`<label>...</label>`	May be used to attach information to controls

tags and properties		description
`<legend>...</legend>`		Allows authors to assign a caption to a FIELDSET; the legend improves accessibility when the FIELDSET is rendered nonvisually
`<kbd>...</kbd>`		Used to make text look as if it came from a typewriter or keyboard; text is displayed with a fixed-width font
`<li>...</li>`		Identifies list items in a <dir>, <menu>, <ol>, or <ul> list
`<link />`		Specifies the relationship between the document and other objects
	`href="URL"`	The URL of the <link> tag links the user to the specified document
	`id="Text"`	The file, URL, or text that acts as a hypertext link to another document
	`rel="URL"`	Directs the browser to link forward to the next page in the document
	`rev="URL"`	Directs the browser to go back to the previous link in the document
	`title="Text"`	The title of the document named in the link
`<map>...</map>`		Specifies information about a client-side image map (it must enclose <area> tags)
	`name="Text"`	The name of the image map
`<menu>...</menu>`		Encloses an unordered list of items, similar to a <ul> or <dir> list
`<meta />`		Used to insert information about the document that is not defined by other HTML tags and properties; it can include special instructions for the Web server to perform
	`content="Text"`	Contains information associated with the name or http-equiv attributes
	`http-equiv="Text"`	Directs the browser to request the server to perform different HTTP operations
	`name="Text"`	The type of information specified in the content attribute
`<nobr>...</nobr>`		Prevents line breaks for the enclosed text
`<noframes>...</noframes>`		Enclosing body tags to be used by browsers that do not support frames
`<noscript>...</noscript>`		The noscript element allows authors to provide alternate content when a script is not executed
`<object>...</object>`		The object element allows authors to control whether data should be rendered externally or by some program, specified by the author, that renders the data within the user agent
`<ol>...</ol>`		Encloses an ordered list of <li> items; typically, ordered lists are rendered as numbered lists
	`start="Value"`	The value of the starting number in the ordered list

tags and properties		description
	type="Option" (A | a | I | i | 1)	Specifies how ordered items are to be marked. A = upper case letters. a = lowercase letters. I = uppercase Roman numerals. i = lowercase Roman numerals. 1 = Digits. The default is 1.
`<optgroup>...</optgroup>`		The optgroup element allows authors to group choices logically
`<option>...</option>`		Used for each item in a selection list; this tag must be placed within <select> tags
	selected	The default or selected option in the selection list
	value="Value"	The value returned to the server when the user selects this option
`<p>...</p>`		Defines the beginning and ending of a paragraph of text
	align="Option" (left | center | right)	The alignment of the text in the paragraph
`<pre>...</pre>`		Retains the preformatted appearance of the text in the HTML file, including any line breaks or spaces; text is usually displayed in a fixed-width font
`<q>...</q>`		User agents should render quotation marks in a language-sensitive manner (see the lang attribute); many languages adopt different quotation styles for outer and inner (nested) quotations, which should be respected by user agents
`<samp>...</samp>`		Displays text in a fixed-width font
`<script>...</script>`		The script element places a script within a document. This element may appear any number of times in the head or body of an HTML document. The script may be defined within the contents of the script element or in an external file.
	src="URL"	This attribute specifies the location of an external script
	type="Text"	This attribute specifies the scripting language of the element's contents and overrides the default scripting language
	language="Text"	Deprecated. This attribute specifies the scripting language of the contents of this element. Its value is an identifier for the language, but since these identifiers are not standard, this attribute has been deprecated in favor of type.
	defer	When set, this boolean attribute informs the browser that the script is not going to generate any document content so the browser can continue parsing and rendering
`<select>...</select>`		Encloses a set of <option> tags for use in creating selection lists
	multiple	Allows the user to select multiple options from the selection list
	name="Text"	The name assigned to the selection list
	size="Value"	The number of visible items in the selection list
`<small>...</small>`		Decreases the size of the enclosed text; the exact appearance of the text depends on the browser and the default font size
`<span>...</span>`		Defines content to be inline but imposes no other presentational idioms on the content; thus, authors may use span in conjunction with style sheets
`<strike>...</strike>`		<strike> and <s> are deprecated; render strike-through style text
`<strong>...</strong>`		Used to strongly emphasize the enclosed text, usually in a bold font

tags and properties		description
`<style>...</style>`		Contains information that identifies the style sheet in use
`<sub>...</sub>`		Displays the enclosed text as a subscript
`<sup>...</sup>`		Displays the enclosed text as a superscript
`<table>...</table>`		The HTML table model allows authors to arrange data—text, preformatted text, images, links, forms, form fields, other tables, etc.—into rows and columns of cells
	`summary="Text"`	This attribute provides a summary of the table's purpose and structure for user agents rendering to nonvisual media such as speech and Braille
	`align="Text" (left|center|right)`	Deprecated. This attribute specifies the position of the table with respect to the document. Permitted values: left: The table is to the left of the document center: The table is to the center of the document right: The table is to the right of the document
	`width="Value"`	This attribute specifies the desired width of the entire table and is intended for visual user agents. When the value is a percentage value, the value is relative to the user agent's available horizontal space. In the absence of any width specification, table width is determined by the user agent.
	`id, class`	document-wide identifiers
	`Lang`	language information
	`Dir`	text direction
	`Title`	element title
	`Style`	inline style information
	`bgcolor="Value" or Text`	table background color
	`frame, rules, border`	borders and rules
	`cellpadding="Value"`	cell margins
	`cellspacing="Value"`	cell margins
`<tbody>...</tbody>`		Contains the body content of a table and should be nested within the <table> tags and after the table header and table footer elements
`<td>...</td>`		Cell data is contained within the <td> tags nested within <tr> tags and the <tbody> and <table> tags
	`scope="Scope-name"`	This attribute specifies the set of data cells for which the current header cell provides header information
	`abbr="Text"`	This attribute should be used to provide an abbreviated form of the cell's content
	`axis="cdata"`	This attribute may be used to place a cell into conceptual categories that can be considered to form axes in an n-dimensional space
	`headers="idrefs"`	The list of header cells that provide header information for the current data cell

tags and properties		description
	rowspan="Number"	This attribute specifies the number of rows spanned by the current cell. The default value of this attribute is one ("1"). The value zero ("0") means that the cell spans all rows from the current row to the last row of the table section (thead, tbody, or tfoot) in which the cell is defined.
	colspan="Number"	This attribute specifies the number of columns spanned by the current cell. The default value of this attribute is one ("1"). The value zero ("0") means that the cell spans all columns from the current column to the last column of the column group (COLGROUP) in which the cell is defined.
	Nowrap	Deprecated. When present, this Boolean attribute tells visual user agents to disable automatic text wrapping for this cell. Style sheets should be used instead of this attribute to achieve wrapping effects. Note: If used carelessly, this attribute may result in excessively wide cells.
	width="Length"	Deprecated; this attribute supplies user agents with a recommended cell width
	height="Length"	Deprecated; this attribute supplies user agents with a recommended cell height
<textarea>...</textarea>		Creates a text box
	cols="Value"	The height of the text box in characters
	name="Text"	The name assigned to the text box
	rows="Value"	The width of the text box in characters
	wrap="Option" (off | virtual | physical)	Specifies how text should be wrapped within the text box. off turns off text wrapping. virtual wraps the text, but sends the text to the server as a single line. physical wraps the text and sends the text to the server as it appears in the text box.
<tfoot>...</tfoot>		TFOOT must appear before TBODY within a TABLE definition so that user agents can render the foot before receiving all of the (potentially numerous) rows of data
<th>...</th>		Defines a cell that contains header information
<thead>...</thead>		Defines a table header grouping that contains replicating table heading information. Must contain at least one table row grouping.
<title>...</title>		Used to specify the text that appears in the Web browser's title bar
<tr>...</tr>		Acts as a container for a row of table cells (<td> or <th>)
<tt>...</tt>		Displays text in a fixed width, teletype style font
<u>...</u>		Underlines the enclosed text, should be avoided because it confuses users with hypertext, which is typically underlined
<ul>...</ul>		Encloses an unordered list of <li> items; typically, unordered lists are rendered as bulleted lists
	Type="Option" (circle | disk | square)	Specifies the type of bullet used for displaying each <li> element in the <ul> list
<var>...</var>		Used for text that represents a variable, and usually appears in italics

HTML

HTML Browser-Safe Colors

The following list of 216 hexadecimal color values is supported by all Web browsers. To view these colors, you must have a video card and monitor capable of displaying up to 256 colors. These colors were designed to be displayed the same in all browsers when rendered using their hexadecimal triplet code.

TABLE AP-2: Browser-safe colors

Color Code	RGB Values	Color Sample	Color Code	RGB Values	Color Sample
#FFFFFF	255,255,255		#FF00CC	255,000,204	
#FFFFCC	255,255,204		#FF0099	255,000,153	
#FFFF99	255,255,153		#FF0066	255,000,102	
#FFFF66	255,255,102		#FF0033	255,000,051	
#FFFF33	255,255,51		#FF0000	255,000,000	
#FFFF00	255,255,000		#CCFFFF	204,255,255	
#FFCCFF	255,204,255		#CCFFCC	204,255,204	
#FFCCCC	255,204,204		#CCFF99	204,255,153	
FFCC99	255,204,153		#CCFF66	204,255,102	
#FFCC66	255,204,102		#CCFF33	204,255,051	
#FFCC33	255,204,051		#CCFF00	204,255,000	
#FFCC00	255,204,000		#CCCCFF	204,204,255	
#FF99FF	255,153,255		#CCCCCC	204,204,204	
#FF99CC	255,153,204		#CCCC99	204,204,153	
#FFCC99	255,153,153		#CCCC66	204,204,102	
#FF9966	255,153,102		#CCCC33	204,204,051	
#FF9933	255,153,051		#CCCC00	204,204,000	
#FF9900	255,153,000		#CC99FF	204,153,255	
#FF66FF	255,102,255		#CC99CC	204,153,204	
#FF66CC	255,102,204		#CC9999	204,153,153	
#FF6699	255,102,153		#CC9966	204,153,102	
#FF6666	255,102,102		#CC9933	204,153,051	
#FF6633	255,102,051		#CC9900	204,153,000	
#FF6600	255,102,000		#CC66FF	204,102,255	
#FF33FF	255,051,255		#CC66CC	204,102,204	
#FF33CC	255,051,204		#CC6699	204,102,153	
#FF3399	255,051,153		#CC6666	204,102,102	
#FF3366	255,051,102		#CC6633	204,102,051	
#FF3333	255,051,051		#CC6600	204,102,000	
#FF3300	255,051,000		#CC33FF	204,051,255	
#FF00FF	255,000,255		#CC33CC	204,051,204	

Color Code	RGB Values	Color Sample	Color Code	RGB Values	Color Sample
#CC3399	204,051,153		#993300	153,051,000	
#CC3366	204,051,102		#9900FF	153,000,255	
#CC3333	204,051,051		#9900CC	153,000,204	
#CC3300	204,051,000		#990066	153,000,102	
#CC00FF	204,000,255		#990033	153,000,051	
#CC00CC	204,000,204		#990000	153,000,000	
#CC0099	204,000,153		#66FFFF	102,255,255	
#CC0066	204,000,102		#66FFCC	102,255,204	
#CC0033	204,000,051		#66FF99	102,255,153	
#CC0000	204,000,000		#66FF66	102,255,102	
#99FFFF	153,255,255		#66FF33	102,255,051	
#99FFCC	153,255,204		#66FF00	102,255,000	
#99FF99	153,255,153		#66CCFF	102,204,255	
#99FF66	153,255,102		#66CCCC	102,204,204	
#99FF33	153,255,051		#66CC99	102,204,153	
#99FF00	153,255,000		#66CC66	102,204,102	
#99CCFF	153,204,255		#66CC33	102,204,051	
#99CCCC	153,204,204		#66CC00	102,204,000	
#99CC99	153,204,153		#6699FF	102,253,255	
#99CC66	153,204,102		#6699CC	102,253,204	
#99CC33	153,204,051		#669999	102,253,153	
#99CC00	153,204,000		#669966	102,253,102	
#9999FF	153,153,255		#669933	102,253,051	
#9999CC	153,153,204		#669900	102,253,000	
#999999	153,153,153		#6666FF	102,102,255	
#999966	153,153,102		#6666CC	102,102,204	
#999933	153,153,051		#666699	102,102,153	
#999900	153,153,000		#666666	102,102,102	
#9966FF	153,102,255		#666633	102,102,051	
#9966CC	153,102,204		#666600	102,102,000	
#996699	153,102,153		#6633FF	102,051,255	
#996666	153,102,102		#6633CC	102,051,204	
#996633	153,102,051		#663399	102,051,153	
#996600	153,102,000		#663366	102,051,102	
#9933FF	153,051,255		#663333	102,051,051	
#9933CC	153,051,204		#663300	102,051,000	
#993399	153,051,153		#6600FF	102,000,255	
#993366	153,051,102		#6600CC	102,000,204	

Color Code	RGB Values	Color Sample	Color Code	RGB Values	Color Sample
#993333	153,051,153		#660099	102,000,153	
#660066	102,000,102		#333300	051,051,000	
#660033	102,000,051		#3300FF	051,000,255	
#660000	102,000,000		#3300CC	051,000,204	
#33FFFF	051,255,255		#330099	051,000,153	
#33FFCC	051,255,204		#330066	051,000,102	
#33FF99	051,255,153		#330033	051,000,051	
#33FF66	051,255,102		#330000	051,000,000	
#33FF33	051,255,051		#00FFFFFF	000,255,255	
#33FF00	051,255,000		#00FFCC	000,255,204	
#33CCFF	051,204,255		#00FF99	000,255,153	
#33CCCC	051,204,204		#00FF66	000,255,102	
#33CC99	051,204,153		#00FF33	000,255,051	
#33CC66	051,204,102		#00FF00	000,255,000	
#33CC33	051,204,051		#00CCFF	000,204,255	
#33CC00	051,204,000		#00CCCC	000,204,204	
#3399FF	051,153,255		#00CC99	000,204,153	
#3399CC	051,153,204		#00CC66	000,204,102	
#339999	051,153,153		#00CC33	000,204,051	
#339966	051,153,102		#00CC00	000,204,000	
#339933	051,153,051		#0099FF	000,153,255	
#339900	051,153,000		#0099CC	000,153,204	
#3366FF	051,102,255		#009999	000,153,153	
#3366CC	051,102,204		#009966	000,153,102	
#336699	051,102,153		#009933	000,153,051	
#336666	051,102,102		#009900	000,153,000	
#336633	051,102,051		#0066FF	000,102,255	
#336600	051,102,000		#0066CC	000,102,204	
#3333FF	051,051,255		#006699	000,102,153	
#3333CC	051,051,204		#006666	000,102,102	
#333399	051,051,153		#006633	000,102,051	
#333366	051,051,102		#006600	000,102,000	

Color Code	RGB Values	Color Sample	Color Code	RGB Values	Color Sample
#333333	051,051,051		#0033FF	000,051,255	
#0033CC	000,051,204		#0000CC	000,000,204	
#003399	000,051,153		#000099	000,000,153	
#003366	000,051,102		#000066	000,000,102	
#003333	000,051,051		#000033	000,000,051	
#003300	000,051,000		#000000	000,000,000	
#0000FF	000,000,255				

HTML Color Names

The following is a list of extended color names and their corresponding hexadecimal triplets supported by most Web browsers. To view these colors, you must have a video card and monitor capable of displaying up to 256 colors. As with other aspects of Web page design, you should test these color names on a variety of browsers before committing to their use. Different browsers may render these colors differently or not at all.

TABLE AP-3: HTML extended color names

color name	value	RGB	preview	color name	value	RGB	preview
aliceblue	#F0F8FE	240,248,254,		darkpurple	#871F78	135,031,120,	
antiquewhite	#FAEBD7	250,235,215,		darksalmon	#E9967A	233,150,122,	
aqua	#00FFFF	000,255,255,		darkslateblue	#6B238E	107,035,142,	
aquamarine	#70DB93	112,219,147,		darkslategray	#2F4F4F	047,079,079,	
azure	#F0FFFF	240,255,255,		darktan	#97694F	151,105,079,	
beige	#F5F5DC	245,245,220,		darkturquoise	#7093DB	112,147,219,	
black	#000000	000,000,000,		darkviolet	#9400D3	094,000,211,	
blue	#0000FF	000,000,255,		darkwood	#855E42	133,094,066,	
blueviolet	#9F5F9F	159,095,159,		dimgray	#545454	084,084,084,	
brass	#B5A642	181,166,066,		dustyrose	#856363	133,099,099,	
brightgold	#D9D919	217,217,025,		feldspar	#D19275	209,174,117,	
bronze	#8C7853	140,120,083,		firebrick	#8E2323	142,035,035,	
brown	#A52A2A	165,042,042,		forestgreen	#238E23	035,142,035,	
cadetblue	#5F9F9F	095,159,159,		gold	#CD7F32	205,127,050,	
chocolate	#D2691E	210,105,030,		goldenrod	#DBDB70	219,219,112,	
coolcopper	#D98719	217,135,025,		gray	#C0C0C0	192,192,192	
copper	#B87333	184,115,051,		green	#00FF00	000,255,000,	
coral	#FF7F50	255,127,080,		greencopper	#527F76	082,127,118,	
crimson	#DC143C	220,020,060,		greenyellow	#93DB70	147,219,112,	
cyan	#00FFFF	000,255,255,		hotpink	#FF69B4	255,105,B4	
darkblue	#00008B	000,000,139,		huntergreen	#215E21	033,094,033	
darkbrown	#5C4033	092,064,051,		indianred	#4E2F2F	078,047,047,	
darkcyan	#008B8B	000,139,139,		indigo	#4B0082	075,000,130,	
darkgoldenrod	#B8860B	184,134,011,		ivory	#FFFFF0	255,255,240,	
darkgray	#A9A9A9	169,169,169,		khaki	#9F9F5F	159,159,095,	
darkgreen	#006400	000,100,000,		lavender	#E6E6FA	230,230,205	
darkkhaki	#BDB76B	189,183,107,		lightblue	#C0D9D9	192,217,217,	
darkmagenta	#8B008B	139,000,139,		lightcoral	#F08080	240,128,128,	
darkolivegreen	#4F4F2F	079,079,047,		lightcyan	#E0FFFF	224,255,255,	
darkorange	#FF8C00	255,140,000,		lightgray	#A8A8A8	068,068,068,	
darkorchid	#9932CD	102,050,205,		lightgreen	#90EE90	144,238,144,	

color name	value	RGB	preview	color name	value	RGB	preview
lightpink	#FFB6C1	255,182,193,		pink	#BC8F8F	188,143,143,	
lightsteelblue	#8FBDBD	143,189,189,		plum	#EAADEA	234,173,234,	
lightwood	#E9C2A6	233,194,166,		powderblue	#B0E0E6	176,224,230,	
lime	#00FF00	000,255,000,		purple	#800080	128,000,128,	
limegreen	#32CD32	050,205,050,		quartz	#D9D9F3	217,217,F3	
magenta	#FF00FF	255,000,255,		red	#FF0000	255,000,000,	
mandarinorange	#E47833	228,120,051,		richblue	#5959AB	089,089,171,	
maroon	#8E236B	142,035,107,		royalblue	#4169E1	065,105,225,	
medium aquamarine	#32CD99	050,205,102,		saddlebrown	#8B4513	139,069,13	
mediumblue	#3232CD	050,050,205,		salmon	#6F4242	111,066,066,	
medium forestgreen	#6B8E23	107,142,035,		sandybrown	#F4A460	244,164,096	
medium goldenrod	#EAEAAE	234,234,174,		scarlet	#8C1717	140,023,023	
mediumorchid	#9370DB	147,112,219,		seagreen	#238E68	035,142,68	
mediumseagreen	#426F42	066,111,066,		sienna	#8E6B23	142,107,035,	
mediumslateblue	#7F00FF	127,000,255,		silver	#E6E8FA	230,232,250	
medium springgreen	#7FFF00	127,255,000,		skyblue	#3299CC	050,102,204,	
medium turquoise	#70DBDB	112,219,219,		slateblue	#007FFF	000,127,255,	
mediumvioletred	#DB7093	219,112,147,		snow	#FFFAFA	255,250,250,	
mediumwood	#A68064	166,128,100,		spicypink	#FF1CAE	255,028,174,	
midnightblue	#2F2F4F	047,047,079,		springgreen	#00FF7F	000,255,127,	
mintcream	#F5FFFA	245,255,250,		steelblue	#236B8E	035,107,142,	
mistyrose	#FFE4E1	255,228,225,		summersky	#38B0DE	056,176,222	
navyblue	#23238E	035,035,142,		tan	#DB9370	219,147,112,	
neonblue	#4D4DFF	077,077,255,		teal	#008080	000,128,128,	
neonpink	#FF6EC7	255,110,199,		thistle	#D8BFD8	216,191,216,	
newmidnightblue	#00009C	000,000,156,		tomato	#FF6347	255,099,071,	
newtan	#EBC79E	235,199,158,		turquoise	#ADEAEA	173,234,234,	
oldgold	#CFB53B	207,181,059,		verydarkbrown	#5C4033	092,064,051,	
olive	#808000	128,128,000,		verydarkgray	#CDCDCD	205,205,205,	
orange	#FF7F00	255,127,000,		violet	#4F2F4F	079,047,079,	
orangered	#FF2400	255,036,000,		violetred	#CC3299	204,050,102,	
orchid	#DB70DB	219,112,219,		wheat	#D8D8BF	216,216,191,	
palegoldenrod	#EEE8AA	238,232,170,		white	#FFFFFF	255,255,255,	
palegreen	#8FBC8F	143,188,143,		yellow	#FFFF00	255,255,000,	
paleturquoise	#AFEEEE	175,238,238,		yellowgreen	#99CC32	102,204,050,	

Cascading Style Sheet Reference

The following are CSS1 fourth-generation browser supported styles. CSS formatting can be applied inline as part of the style attribute (`<tag style="text-align: center;">`), or embedded within the head section in the `<style>...</style>` tag. In actual use in styles, semicolons should appear at the end of each style value.

TABLE AP-4: CSS1 fourth-generation browser supported styles

property	explanation/syntax	example
Font properties		
font-style	*normal*	`{font-style: italic;}`
	oblique (similar to italic, but created manually rather than using italic typeface)	
	italic	
font-variant	*normal* (default)	`{font-variant: small-caps;}`
	small-caps	
font-weight	*extra-light*	`{font-weight: extra-bold;}`
	demi-light	
	light	
	medium	
	bold	
	demi-bold	
	extra-bold	
font-size	A number with a unit abbreviation	`{font-size: 16pt;}`
	• Points (*pt*)	
	• Pixels (*px*)	
	• Inches (*in*)	
	• Centimeters (*cm*)	
	• Percentage of default point size (%)	
	• Multiple of width of *m* character in current font family (*em*)	
line-height	Sets distance between baselines of two adjacent elements; specify multiplication factor for font size as a value (such as 1.2), percentage (120%), or measurement (1.2em)	`{line-height: 1.2;}`
font-family	Any combination of the following, in order of preference: • Specific typeface name (*times new roman*) • General type family (*times*) • Font type (*sans-serif*)	`{font-family: "times new roman", times, garamond, serif;}`

property	explanation/syntax	example
font	Shorthand for setting all six font-related attributes at once; no commas, except between font-family settings; order: font-style, font-variant, font-weight, font-size, line-height, font-family	`{font: italic small-caps extra-bold 16pt 0.75in "times new roman", times, garamond, serif;}`
text-decoration	• *none*	`{text-decoration: italic;}`
	• *underline*	
	• *italic*	
	• *line-through*	
Color and background properties		
color	Hexadecimal or keyword color equivalent for element color	`{color: #99cc66;}`
background-color	Hexadecimal or keyword color equivalent for background color	`{background-color: #000066;}`
background-image	• *none*	`{background-image: url(me.jpg);}`
	• *url(url)*	
background-repeat	Specifies if and how background image is repeated	`{background-repeat: repeat-x;}`
	• *repeat* (tiles over entire background)	
	• *repeat-x* (repeats in single band horizontally)	
	• *repeat-y* (repeats in single band vertically)	
	• *no-repeat* (single image only)	
background-attachment	• *scroll* (image scrolls with foreground)	
	• *fixed* (image remains fixed as foreground scrolls)	`{background-attachment: fixed;}`
background-position	Specifies initial position of background image; coordinates (in percent) match point at those coordinates on image with those coordinates on background	`{background-position: 100% 100%;}`
background	Shorthand for setting all five background attributes at once; no commas; order: background-color, background-image, background-repeat, background-attachment, background-position	`{background: #000066 url(me.jpg) repeat-x fixed 100% 100%;}`
Text properties		
word-spacing	Specifies additional width to insert between words (default=normal); may be negative	`{word-spacing: 0.4em;}`
letter-spacing	Specifies additional width to insert between words (default=normal); may be negative	`{letter-spacing: 0.1em;}`
text-decoration	• *underline* • *overline* • *line-through* • *none* (default)	`{text-decoration: underline;}`

property	explanation/syntax	example
vertical-align	• *baseline* • *sub* • *super* • *top* • *text-top* • *middle* • *bottom* • *text-bottom* • Percentage value; positive and negative numbers possible; specifies percentage of the element's line-height property in relation to the parent baseline	`{vertical-align: super;}`
text-transform	• *capitalize* capitalizes first character of each word • *uppercase* capitalizes all letters • *lowercase* makes all letters lowercase • *none*	`{text-transform: capitalize;}`
text-align	• *left* • *right* • *center* • *justify*	`{text-align: center;}`
text-indent	Positive and negative numbers possible, specifies indentation of first line, in an exact measurement, or a percentage of parent element width	`{text-indent: 3em;}`
line-height	Sets distance between baselines of two adjacent elements; specify multiplication factor for font size, as a value (such as 1.2), percentage (120%), or measurement (1.2em)	`{line-height: 1.2;}`
Box properties		
margin-top	Sets element's top margin as measurement or percentage of parent element width	`{margin-top: 2%;}`
margin-right	Sets element's right margin as measurement or percentage of parent element width	`{margin-right: 2em;}`
margin-bottom	sets element's bottom margin as measurement or percentage of parent element width	`{margin-bottom: 2%;}`
margin-left	sets element's left margin as measurement or percentage of parent element width	`{margin-right: 2em;}`
margin	Shorthand property for specifying margin-top, margin-right, margin-bottom, and margin-left properties; order: top, right, bottom, left; if only one value given, applies to all four; if one or two values missing, missing value copied from opposite side	`{margin 2% 2em;}`
padding-top	Sets an element's top padding, as measurement or percentage of parent element width	`{padding-top: 0.3em;}`
padding-right	Sets an element's right padding, as measurement or percentage of parent element width	`{padding-right: 20%;}`

property	explanation/syntax	example
padding-bottom	Sets an element's bottom padding, as measurement or percentage of parent element width	`{padding-bottom: 0.3em;}`
padding-left	Sets an element's left padding, as measurement or percentage of parent element width	`{padding-left: 20%;}`
padding	Shorthand property for specifying padding-top, padding-right, padding-bottom, and padding-left properties; order: top, right, bottom, left; if only one value given, applies to all four; if one or two values missing, missing value copied from opposite side	`{padding: 0.3em 20% 0.2em;}`
border-top-width; **border-right-width;** **border-bottom-width;** **border-left-width;**	• thin • medium • thick • measurement	`{border-top-width: 2pt;}`
border-width	Shorthand property for specifying all four border thicknesses; order: top, right, bottom, left; if only one value given, applies to all four; if one or two values missing, missing value copied from opposite side	`{border-width: 3em;}`
border-style	Can specify between one and four styles, with same organization as border-width above • *none* • *dotted* • *dashed* • *solid* • *double* • *groove* • *ridge* • *inset* • *outset*	`{border-style: groove;}`
border-color	Hexadecimal or keyword color equivalent for element color; can specify between one and four colors, with same organization as border-width above	`{border-color: navy red red;}`
border-top **border-right** **border-bottom** **border-left**	Shorthand properties for setting each border's width, style, and color	`{border-bottom: thick solid red;}`
border	Shorthand property for setting same width, color, and style on all four borders of an element	`{border: thin inset green;}`
width	Element width, as a length or percentage; negative values are allowed (default=auto)	`{width: 200px;}`
height	Element height, as a length or percentage, negative values are allowed (default=auto)	`{height: 50%;}`
float	Moves element to left or right and wraps text on opposite side	`{float: left;}`
clear	Specifies if an element allows floating elements around it, or should be moved clear of them • *none* • *left* • *right* • *both*	`{clear: both;}`

property	explanation/syntax	example
Classification properties		
display	• *block* • *inline* • *list-item* • *none*	`{display: inline;}`
white-space	• *normal* white space collapsed • *pre* formatted like HTML PRE element • nowrap wrapping triggered only by ` ` elements	`{white-space: nowrap;}`
list-style-type	Specifies marker style for list items • *disc* • *circle* • *square* • *decimal* • *lower-roman* • *upper-roman* • *lower-alpha* • *upper-alpha* • *none*	`{list-style-type: lower-alpha;}`
list-style-image	Specifies an image to use as a list item marker	`{list-style-image: url(reddot.jpg);}`
list-style-position	• *inside* less space between marker and item • *outside* more space between marker and item (default)	`{list-style-position: inside;}`
list-style	Shorthand property for setting list-style-type, list-style-image, and list-style-position	`{list-style: lower-alpha url(reddot.jpg) inside;}`

HTML Special Characters

The following table lists a portion of the HTML extended character set, also known as the ISO Latin-1 Character set. Characters in this table can be entered either by code number or code name. For example, to insert the registered trademark symbol ((r)) you use either &reg or &#174.

Although code names can be easier to remember and type than code numbers, not all code names are recognized by all browsers. Some older browsers that support only the HTML 2.0 standard do not recognize the code name "&times," for instance. Code names that may not be recognized by older browsers are marked with an asterisk. If you are planning to use these symbols in your document, you may want to use the code number instead of the code name.

TABLE AP-5: HTML special characters

character	code	code name	description
	&#00; – &#08;		Unused
	&#09;		Tab
	&#10;		Line feed
	&#11; – &#31;		Unused
	&#32;		Space
!	&#33;		Exclamation point
"	&#34;	&quot;	Double quotation mark
#	&#35;		Pound sign
$	&#36;		Dollar sign
%	&#37;		Percent sign
&	&#38;	&amp;	Ampersand
'	&#39;		Apostrophe
(	&#40;		Left parenthesis
)	&#41;		Right parenthesis
*	&#42;		Asterisk
+	&#43;		Plus sign
,	&#44;		Comma
-	&#45;		Hyphen
.	&#46;		Period
/	&#47;		Forward slash
0–9	0 – 9		Numbers 0–9
:	&#58;		Colon
;	&#59;		Semicolon
<	&#60;	&lt;	Less than sign
=	&#61;		Equal sign
>	&#62;	&gt;	Greater than sign
?	&#63;		Question mark
@	&#64;		Commercial at

character	code	code name	description
A–Z	A – Z		Letters A–Z
[	&#91;		Left square bracket
\	&#92;		Back slash
]	&#93;		Right square bracket
^	&#94;		Caret
_	&#95;		Horizontal bar
`	&#96;		Grave accent
a–z	a – z		Letters a–z
{	&#123;		Left curly brace
|	|		Vertical bar
}	&#125;		Right curly brace
~	&#126;		Tilde
	&#127; – 		Unused
,	&#130;		Low single comma quotation mark
ƒ	&#131;		Function sign
„	&#132;		Low double comma quotation mark
…	&#133;		Ellipses
†	&#134;		Dagger
‡	&#135;		Double dagger
ˆ	&#136;		Circumflex accent
‰	&#137;		Per mile sign
Sˇ	&#138;		Capital S with hacek
‹	&#139;		Left single angle quotation mark
Œ	&#140;		Capital OE ligature
	 – 		Unused
'	&#145;		Single beginning quotation mark
'	&#146;		Single ending quotation mark
"	&#147;		Double beginning quotation mark
"	&#148;		Double ending quotation mark
•	&#149;		Middle dot
–	&#150;		En dash
—	&#151;		Em dash
~	&#152;		Tilde

character	code	code name	description
™	&#153;	&trade;	Trademark symbol
sˇ	&#154;		Small s with hacek
›	&#155;		Right single angle quotation mark
œ	&#156;		Small oe ligature
	 – ž		Unused
Ÿ	&#159;		Capital Y with umlaut
			Nonbreaking space
¡	&#161;	&iexcl;	Inverted exclamation point
¢	&#162;	&cent;	Cent symbol
£	&#163;	&pound;	Pound sterling
¤	&#164;	&curren;	General currency symbol
¥	&#165;	&yen;	Yen sign
‖	&#166;	&brvbar;	Broken vertical bar
§	&#167;	&sect;	Section sign
¨	&#168;	&uml;	Umlaut
©	&#169;	&copy;	Copyright symbol
ª	&#170;	&ordf;	Feminine ordinal
«	&#171;	&laquo;	Left angle quotation mark
¬	&#172;	&not;	Not sign
-	&#173;	&shy;	Soft hyphen
®	&#174;	&reg;	Registered trademark
¯	&#175;	&macr;	Macron
°	&#176;	&deg;	Degree sign
±	&#177;	&plusmn;	Plus/minus symbol
2	&#178;	&sup2;	Superscript 2
3	&#179;	&sup3;	Superscript 3
´	&#180;	&acute;	Acute accent
µ	&#181;	&micro;	Micro symbol
¶	&#182;	&para;	Paragraph sign
·	&#183;	&middot;	Middle dot
ç	&#184;	&cedil;	Cedilla
1	&#185;	&sup1;	Superscript 1
º	&#186;	&ordm;	Masculine ordinal
»	&#187;	&raquo;	Right angle quotation mark
¼	&#188;	&frac14;	Fraction one-quarter
½	&#189;	&frac12;	Fraction one-half
¾	&#190;	&frac34;	Fraction three-quarters
¿	&#191;	&iquest;	Inverted question mark

Formatting with HTML 4.0 Attributes

Before styles came into common use, font formatting was applied using a different set of values within the `<font>    </font>` tag. HTML was not originally designed as a formatting language, but Web users started to demand that Web pages have formatting similar to that found in print media. To accommodate this demand, formatting attributes such as face, color, and size were developed. These were not efficient because they had to be applied in multiple locations on a page, and formatting with these tags was necessarily limited. For example, there was no control of line spacing and there were only seven size formats. In spite of the fact that HTML 4.0 attributes have been deprecated by the W3C, there are still millions of Web pages that use them, so it's a good idea to become familiar with them so you can recognize them and edit them if necessary.

attribute	value	function	examples
face	typeface name	Changes font typeface; may list several alternate fonts in order of preference	`<font face="Arial, Helvetica, sans serif">`This text appears in the Arial or Helvetica typeface. If neither Arial or Helvetica are available on the system, the default sans serif font will be displayed`</font>`
color	#hexadecimal color value	Changes text color; color can be specified as any six-digit value with digits from 0 (zero) to 9 and A through F	`<font color="#000066">`This text appears in navy blue.`</font>`
color	color name	Changes text color identified by a standard color name	font color="navy">This text also appears in navy blue`</font>`
size	numeric value from 1 through 7	Changes text size according to its HTML number value: 1, 6 point; 2, 10 point; 3, (default size) 12 point; 4, 14 point; 5, 18 point; 6, 24 point; 7, 36 point	`<font size="7">`This text appears in the largest size available.`</font>`
size	+# (1 to 4) –# (1 or 2)	When paired with a number 1 through 4, changes font size to the numeric equivalent of font default size (3) plus the number specified. When paired with a number 1 or 2, changes the font size to the numeric equivalent of the font default size (3) minus the number specified	`<font size="+1">`This text appears one size larger than the default text—equivalent to a font size 4`</font>` `<font size="+3">`This text is equivalent to a font size 7`</font>`
size	–# (1 or 2)	When paired with a number, reduces font size by the numeric equivalent of the default font size minus the number	`<font size="-1">`This text appears one size smaller than the default text—equivalent to a size 2`</font>`

Project Files List

Unit	File supplied on Data Disk		Location file is used in unit
A	htm_a-1.rtf		Lessons
A	htm_a-2.rtf		Skills Review
B	contact.htm **activities** folder containing index.htm		Lessons
B	hands.htm packages.htm salon.htm services.htm thermacore.htm **spa** folder containing index.htm		Skills Review
B	faq.htm features.htm rentals.htm **listings** folder containing index.htm		Independent Challenge 1
B	outside.htm inside.htm saver.htm **irrigation** folder containing index.htm htm_B-1.txt		Independent Challenge 2
C	htm_C-1.txt htm_C-2.txt htm_C-3.txt		Lessons
	htm_C-4.txt htm_C-5.txt inside.htm		Independent Challenge 1 Independent Challenge 1 (ACE) Independent Challenge 2
	htm_C-6.txt		Visual Workshop

D	htm_D-1.txt
	paradise/images folder containing:
	  clear.gif (used as spacer for
	  bg_samples page)
	  trail_ride1.jpg
	  trail_ride2.jpg
	  pm_logo1.jpg
	  pm_logo2.png
	  pm_bkgnd.gif
	  bed2.jpg
	  frontroom.jpg
	  masterbath.jpg
	  bath2.jpg
	  floorplan2bedroom.gif
	  kitchen.jpg
	  masterbedroom.jpg
		paradise/images/samples folder containing:
		  bkg_samples.htm
		  heather_bkg.htm
		  blu_heather_bkg.htm
		  background.htm
		  pm_bkgnd.htm
		  LB_PlamsThatch3.htm
		  heather_bkg.jpg
		  pm_bkgnd1.jpg
		  blu_heather_bkg.jpg
		  LB_PlamsThatch3.jpg
		
		paradise/media folder containing:
		  paradise.wmv
			Lessons

D	htm_D-2.txt
	htm_D-3.txt
	
	spa folder containing:
	  wraps.htm
	  imagemap.txt
	  hands.htm
		paradise/images folder containing:
		  bkg_spa.gif
		  pedi.jpg
		  spa_logo.gif
		  spa_nav.gif
			Skills Review

Unit	File supplied on Data Disk		Location file is used in unit
	spa/media folder containing: 　spa.wmv		
D	htm_D-4.txt vacations/images folder containing: 　bkg_vaca.gif 　Map.gif 　resort.jpg	vacations folder containing: 　eu.htm 　ak.htm 　hi.htm 　map.txt	Independent Challenge 1
D	vacations_ace/media/folder containing: 　islandseas.wav		Independent Challenge 1 (ACE)
D	htm_D-5.txt water/media folder containing: conserve.wav	water folder containing: 　saver.htm water/images/folder containing: 　mw.gif	Independent Challenge 2
D	water/images folder containing: 　water_bg1.jpg 　water_bg2.jpg 　waterHead2.gif		Independent Challenge 2 (ACE)
D	bitspcs/images folder containing: 　apple.gif 　apple.bg.gif 　woz-jobsbyLuckow.jpg	bitspcs/media folder containing: 　apple.wav	Visual Workshop
E	pm_bkgnd2.gif pm_bul1.png pm_bul2.png htm_E-1.txt htm_E-2.txt		Lessons
E	htm_E-3.txt	images folder containing: 　bkg_pillar_green1.gif 　spa_logo.gif	Skills Review
E	htm_E-4.txt		Independent Challenge 1
E	htm_E-5.txt		Independent Challenge 2
E	htm_E-6.txt		Visual Workshop
F	htm_F-1.txt htm_F-2.txt htm_F-3.txt		Lessons
F	htm_F-4.txt bkg_spa.gif spa_logo.gif		Skills Review
F	htm_F-5.txt htm_F-6.txt		Independent Challenge 1 Independent Challenge 1 (ACE)
F	htm_F-7.txt		Independent Challenge 2
F	htm_F-8.txt		Visual Workshop
G	htm_G-1.txt		Lessons
G	htm_G-2.txt		Skills Review
G	htm_G-3.txt		Independent Challenge 1
G	htm_G-4.txt		Independent Challenge 2

Unit	File supplied on Data Disk	Location file is used in unit
H	**paradise/frames folder containing:** htm_H-1.txt htm_H-2.txt htm_H-3.txt	Lessons
H	wraps.htm packages.htm salon.htm hands.htm services_style.css spa_logo.gif htm_H-4.txt htm_H-5.txt top.htm htm_H-6.txt services_first.htm	Skills Review
H	htm_H-7.txt rentals.htm htm_H-8.txt faq.htm features.htm	Independent Challenge 1
H	htm_H-9.txt htm_H-10.txt htm_H-11.txt	Independent Challenge 2
H	bitshead.htm first.htm bitslink.htm	Visual Workshop
I	htm_I-1.txt htm_I-2.txt htm_I-3.txt activities.gif contact.gif food.gif home.gif lodging.gif spa.gif deer.jpg food.htm	Lessons
I	htm_I-4.txt beachic.gif homeic.gif tennisic.gif travelic.gif beach.htm tennis.htm travel.htm	Independent Challenge 1
I	htm_I-5.txt help.gif homevw.gif services.gif specials.gif help.htm	Visual Workshop
J	htm_J-1.txt charlcie.jpg	Lessons

Unit	File supplied on Data Disk	Location file is used in unit
J	htm_J-2.txt	Skills Review
J	htm_J-3.txt	Independent Challenge 1
J	htm_J-4.txt	Independent Challenge 2
J	htm_J-5.txt	Visual Workshop
K	htm_K-1.txt berryHome.htm berryTypes.htm berries.txt berrybush.jpg construction.htm construction.jpg image1off.jpg image1on.jpg image2off.jpg image2on.jpg image3on.jpg image3off.jpg image4on.jpg image4off.jpg mat.jpg	Lessons
K	htm_K-2.txt	Skills Review
K	htm_K-3.txt	Independent Challenge 1
K	htm_K-4.txt	Independent Challenge 2
K	htm_K-5.txt	Visual Workshop
L	alt_tent.htm bkg_nomad.gif brevcolor.gif brevifolia.gif hillside.gif hillsidecolor.gif hilltop.gif hilltopcolor.gif nomad.css nomad.jpg peak.gif peakcolor.gif starcolor.gif starlite.gif summit.gif summitcolor.gif tents.txt tricolor.gif trifolia.gif htm_L-1.txt	Lessons
L	htm_L-2.txt spa_logo.gif spa_logo2.gif htm_L-3.txt	Skills Review
L	htm_L-4.txt	Independent Challenge 1
L	htm_L-5.txt	Independent Challenge 2

Unit	File supplied on Data Disk	Location file is used in unit
L	hdlist.txt htm_L-6.txt	Visual Workshop
M	htm_M-1.txt htm_M-2.txt htm_M-3.txt bag1.gif bag2.gif pack1.gif pack2.gif	Lessons
M	htm_M-4.txt spa_logo.gif htm_M-5.txt	Skills Review
M	htm_M-6.txt resort.jpg	Independent Challenge 1
M	htm_M-7.txt	Independent Challenge 2
M	htm_M-8.txt	Visual Workshop
N	earth.gif logo_pm4.jpg mountains2.jpg roomsPic.jpg presentation.css htm_N-1.txt htm_N-2.txt presentationRooms.htm	Lessons
N	htm_N-3.txt spa_logo.gif pedi.jpg rmpkg.htm	Skills Review
N	htm_N-4.txt resort.jpg bkg_vaca.gif adventures.htm	Independent Challenge 1
N	htm_N-5.txt mw.gif tips1.htm tips2.htm tips3.htm tips4.htm	Independent Challenge 2
N	htm_N-6.txt	Visual Workshop
O	htm_O-1.txt htm_O-2.txt	Lessons
O	htm_O-3.txt	Skills Review
O	htm_O-4.txt htm_O-5.txt	Independent Challenge 1
O	htm_O-6.txt htm_O-7.txt	Independent Challenge 2
O	htm_O-8.txt	Visual Workshop

Glossary

_blank Frames attribute that opens the link in new browser window; can be used with non-frames pages.

_parent Frames attribute that causes the link to replace the content of the current frameset; use _blank or _parent for links to pages outside of a frameset.

_self Frames attribute that opens the link in current frame; this is the default setting.

_top Frames link attribute that causes the link to replace the contents of current browser window; always use when creating links from a content page back to the main frameset.

Absolute link Link that includes the target page's full Web site location and directory information (for example, <a href="http://www.course.com/sl/default.htm">); most useful to reference a specific page on a different Web site. *See also* Relative link.

Absolute positioning Element positioning specified at fixed screen coordinates by setting the left and top coordinates of an element on the Web page relative to the top-left corner of the window object. *See also* Relative positioning.

Absolute URL Complete URL including the protocol (http://), server name, domain name, path, and filename of the file to open.

Action Form attribute that indicates the path and name of the processing program that the server must run when the form is submitted.

Active link State of a link in the process of being clicked; also, the state of a link as a site visitor clicks the Back button to return to the page after link is clicked. The highlighted link color is red by default in some browsers, purple by default in others.

Active link attributes Attributes that must often be set to make active links readable against a background graphic or color.

Active white space Planned white space that serves a purpose in page design.

Add-on Small program you can download from the Web for free to extend a browser's capabilities; required for viewing some multimedia formats, including Flash animation.

Alert Method associated with the *window object* that allows you to create customized dialog boxes.

Alignment The horizontal placement of text or graphics on the page.

Alignment attribute options Alternative ways of horizontally aligning Web elements, including left, right, center, and, justify.

Alt attribute Also known as an alt statement, an attribute that causes alternative text to display or when the mouse pointer rests over the graphic in the browser if for any reason the image does not appear; used by screen readers to describe graphics or graphic links.

Anchor tag In code, a tag that surrounds information users click to navigate to another location; also called a link tag.

Animated GIF GIF file that combines two or more images into a single file to give the illusion of movement or to display banner images.

Attributes Extra settings available in most HTML tags that allow you to add to or change a tag's default features.

Attribute string Series of attributes applied to the same opening element tag.

Back end Programs that reside on an organization's computer system and that are responsible for processing the data submitted from forms. *See also* Front end.

Background images Pictures that appear behind text or other graphics on a Web page; stored as separate GIF, JPG, or PNG files, usually in the site's images directory.

Backward compatibility The ability to ensure that your page is displayed as expected in older browsers.

Bandwidth Data transfer capacity of a Web user's Internet connection.

Basefont tag <basefont /> HTML tag that sets the font for an entire page. W3C has recently deprecated it in favor of newer formatting methods; however, literally millions of pages on the Web still use this tag to format Web pages.

Baseline The imaginary line on which text or graphics vertically align, not counting the extenders.

bgcolor attribute Attribute that specifies a background color using a color name value or its hexadecimal equivalent, such as #FFFFFF, which represents the color white.

Blend A simple fade-in or fade-out effect.

Block-level Tags Tags that control sections of page content, such as <blockquote> and <address>.

Blockquote tag <blockquote>...</blockquote> The tag set that alters the default white space on either side of the affected text.

Body section Web page section, enclosed in <body>...</body> tags, that contains the page content, such as heading and paragraph elements.

Boldfaced text Text with a heavier (thicker) line stroke than the default text for a typeface; can be applied to text using the ... or ... tags. The latter is recommended because text readers and visual browsers recognize it.

Border Box surrounding a displayed HTML element such as an image. Also an attribute that allows you to set the size of an element's border; when used with frames, specifies the space between frames.

Bordercolor Attribute that allows you to set the border color of a table.

Bordercolordark Attribute that allows you to define the color of the bottom and right edges of a table.

Bordercolorlight Attribute that allows you to define the color of the top and left edges of a table.

Broadband Internet connection technologies that allow faster downloads than traditional dial-up modems.

Brochure sites Web sites that display information similar to that found in a printed brochure; not designed to sell a product, but may contain links to sites where products and services are sold.

Browser *See* Web browser.

Browser-native features Proprietary features that allow you to enhance your pages with dynamic effects using little or no additional scripting.

Browser packaging The appearance of the form and of the page from which it is displayed.

Bugs Scripting errors that cause a script to return unexpected and undesired results—may include improper formatting, appearance of code in the browser window, or could prevent your browser from working. *See also* Hang.

Business e-commerce sites Web sites that contain catalog information and order-processing elements such as shopping carts.

Business sites Web sites that contain an organization's product information, mission statement, and contact information.

Cable modem A broadband connection device that allows for faster data transmission than a dial-up connection.

Call A piece of code that specifies the name and location of an internal or external object that will be pulled into or run from a Web page.

Cascade *See* Cascading Style Sheets (CSS).

Cascading Style Sheets (CSS) Web page formatting method that uses rules you create and apply to your Web pages; cascade refers to the ability to apply multiple styles to the same document. Can be applied at the tag level as inline attributes of almost any HMTL tag, at the page level in an embedded style sheet, or externally from a linked style sheet.

Cascading Style Sheets positioning Styles that allow you to position elements absolutely or relatively.

Case-sensitive Describes a language or system that treats capital and lower-case versions of the same letter as different characters.

Cell In a table, the intersection of a row and a column.

Cellpadding In a table, an attribute that allows you to control the amount of space between the cell wall and its content.

Cellspacing In a table, an attribute that allows you to control the amount of space between table cells.

CGI (Common Gateway Interface) An interface between the Web client and the processing script; most CGI scripts are written in PERL, C++, or JavaScript.

Character kerning The space between letters within a word.

Character set Defined list of characters recognized by hardware and software; most Web documents use the ISO-8859-1 character set.

Check box Input form field that appears as a small box, each of which displays a single choice among an array of choices that are all visible at once and from which users may select any, all, or none; when a user clicks an empty check box, a check mark appears in the box; clicking a checked box removes the check mark.

Child elements Code elements within a parent tag set. *See also* Parent element.

Click event When a site visitor clicks a link or other object on the page.

Client-side script Instructions written directly into page code that causes the scripts to execute (run) on the site visitor's computer.

Clip property Property that allows you to control how much of an element is visible on your Web page by acting as a layer above the element, covering all of it except for a hole you define; supports only rectangular shapes.

Code *See* Source code.

Coded line breaks Line breaks that are forced using the HTML line break tag <br />.

Collapsible list Table of contents created using a combination of CSS and scripting that is designed as an expandable outline in which users can click a main topic to show related subtopics and click again to hide subtopics.

Color depth The number of bits per pixel that can be displayed on a computer screen. The more bits per pixel in an image, the more colors it can display.

Colspan Attribute to cause a cell to span multiple columns. *See also* Rowspan.

Column A single vertical line of data.

Comment box A form area in which site visitors can enter text; designer specifies the maximum number of characters the box can contain. *See also* Multiline text area.

Comment tag A tag such as (<!-- Comment information goes here. -->, used to make notations and to make it easier to find specific content in your source code; not visible in browser windows.

Common screen resolutions 800 × 600, 1024 × 768, and 1280 × 1024

Content-specific links Links from keywords in your Web page content area to quality external resources.

Coords Pixel coordinates that describe the boundaries of the hot spot in an image map, such as coords="94, 205, 0, 205, 0, 42, 132, 137".

Conditional A script that allows you to create different results depending on different user actions or on the value of a certain browser attributes; allows your script to choose one of two paths.

Crop Cut unnecessary elements from graphics to optimize images.

Cross-browser support Coding that makes it possible for both older and newer browsers to render your layout.

CSS *See* Cascading Style Sheets.

CSS class selector rules Named sets of formatting instructions that allow you to define a specific-purpose style in the style sheet and that can be triggered in the document code; the selector name is preceded by a period (.) known as a flag that identifies the rule as a class rule.

CSS declaration Code containing one or more properties and values that describe the CSS style.

CSS selector Code that specifies the element to which a CSS style is applied.

CSS style rule Instructions that describe the formatting of XHTML elements; composed of a selector and a declaration. *See also* CSS style selector and CSS style declaration.

CSSP *See* Cascading Style Sheets positioning.

Data awareness Condition that allows pages to display data from an outside source and that allows users to manipulate and change linked information directly in the browser window.

Data binding Linking a Web page to an external data file which allows a Web page to load all the records from a database but display only some of them or to access a record instantly and manipulate it without downloading more information to the browser. *See also* Data awareness.

Data binding Linking a Web page to an external database or text document to create a data display at run time.

Data definitions The characteristics, type, and relationships of data.

Debugging The process of systematically identifying and fixing your script's bugs.

Declaration In a style rule, one or more properties and values that describe the style; a colon follows each declaration property and a semicolon follows each declaration property value.

Decoration Formatting enhancements used to emphasize text or block elements including bold text, underline, overline, and box frames.

Description Located in the head section of an HTML document, a metatag that provides a description of your Web page content; useful for supplying search engines with a preferred site description to appear under the results page link.

DHTML Dynamic Hypertext Markup Language, a Web technology that enables a Web page to react to user input without sending requests to the Web server.

Dimension Width and height of an HTML/XHTML element as displayed on a page.

Division Block-level elements often used to treat several block-level elements as one unit.

Division tag <div>...</div> Block-level tag that uses attributes to affect changes in sections of text and to control page output.

Document object Represents the current Web page in the browser window and contains all document elements, including links, anchors, and images, to help to give each Web page its defining characteristics.

Document Object Model (DOM) An object-based collection of programming routines and functions for HTML, DHTML, and XML documents that allows programs and scripts to access and work with the content of a Web page.

Document Type Definition (DTD) Also called a doctype declaration, a tag in the first line of source code to tell the browser what type of XHTML the page is written in, so the browser can correctly interpret the code.

Dot-slash notation A combination of dots and forward slashes that serve as path designators from one folder to another up and down the directory tree.

Dot syntax A method of referencing objects in the object hierarchy.

Download time The amount of time it takes for a Web page and its files to transfer from their location on the Web to a user's browser.

Dragging A combination of scripting and style sheet positioning that allows users to adjust the placement of a selected element based on the coordinates of the pointer and then assign the element to its final position once the user releases the mouse button. *See also* Dynamic positioning.

Drop-down list Expanding form field that allows users to select one or more choices out of several options. *See also* Pull-down menu.

Drop-down menu *See* Drop-down list and Pull-down menu.

DSL Digital Service Line, a high bandwidth connection to the Internet often described as broadband.

Dynamic content DHTML-based pages in which styles change instantly based on user actions and can allow users to modify a page's content—can be used to generate all or part of the page in response to events.

Dynamic HTML (DHTML) A combination of HTML, style sheets, and scripts that allows Web documents to interact with the user and to be animated or changed in response to user and browser events without needing to access the server.

Dynamic positioning. A DHTML effect that allows users to drag and position page elements to different locations on the page; accomplished using scripts that allow interaction with position and layer information. *See also* Dragging.

Em The height and width of the lowercase letter "m" of a chosen font family.

E-mail links Code instructions that give users the ability to click a link that automatically opens an e-mail message; they use the mailto protocol with an e-mail address as the href attribute value.

Embed tag <embed /> Tag used to embed sound or video files to display as Web page content. Requires the source (src) attribute, which specifies the path to the media file used on the Web page.

Embedded media Sound or video files that are displayed as part of a Web page to make the files available to site visitors. Can be used for wav, avi, mpg, and mp3 files.

Emphasized text ... Marks text as emphasized; interpreted by browsers as italic. Interpretable by different Web interfaces; use instead of <i>...</i>.

Enctype Form attribute that specifies how a browser formats the user responses on a form before submitting them to the server.

Epilog Final section of an XML document—contains any final comments and/or processing instructions.

Event handler A set of instructions that are executed in response to an event.

Event object Allows interaction with the event currently being processed by the browser, such as mouse movement or the press of a button.

Events Browser or user actions such as *load, unload,* and *click. See also* Event handler.

Expandable outlines DHTML feature that allows you to hide and show information based upon user actions.

Extensible Hypertext Markup Language (XHTML) A revision of HTML that transforms the language into a rigorous system in line with related programming languages used for other applications.

Extensible Markup Language (XML) A sister language to HTML, used to describe, deliver, and exchange structured data from many databases and multiple platforms in a clear format. This language is case-sensitive and all elements in such documents must be closed.

Extension-specific A characteristic of some file transfer programs, which require that files transferred have specific file extensions.

External style sheets Separate files, saved with a .css extension, that are linked to documents to which their defined styles are applied.

External Web files Files that are hosted on another server or Web site than the site currently being accessed.

File type The format in which files are saved—also called file format. Choosing the right format can greatly affect file size and function. Supported Web image formats include JPEG (jpg), GIF (gif), and PNG (png).

File Transfer Protocol (FTP) One of the most common methods of transferring files to a server, usually using an FTP client program. *See also* FTP Client and Secure File Transfer Protocol.

Filtered effects Predefined element formats in Internet Explorer that affect appearance in complex ways.

Filters DHTML Presentation tools that allow you to modify element appearance in complex ways.

Flag The period (.) character that precedes a class selector.

Flash animation A highly compressed multimedia presentation created with proprietary technology from Macromedia Inc. Can be used as a movie file or for as animated navigation elements.

Font A complete set of characters, including letters, numbers and special characters, in a particular size and style of type.

Font stack A list of acceptable fonts included as part of the font-family style or font attribute string for the <font> or <basefont> tag.

Form A set of Web page elements with which users interact to submit a request or provide information.

Formatting A powerful tool for visually organizing the content on your Web pages, making it easier for users to identify valuable content and to navigate your site.

Form element *See* Form field.

Form field A form input area such as a text box, radio button, or pull-down menu that allows user input.

Form handler Program that facilitates communication between the form's front end and back end.

Form label Text entered next to a radio button or a check box that describes the option's function.

Frame A single window in a multiple-window layout that displays the contents of a separate HTML document.

Frameborder Attribute that specifies the border size in a frameset.

Frames Layout method that divides the browser into multiple scrollable windows, each of which contains a separate HTML document.

Frameset Layout control document that specifies the placement and source content of each frame within a frames-based layout; contains one document for each frame and one document (the frameset) as the frames-placement control.

Framespacing Frames attribute that specifies the space between frames.

Frames object Contains a separate window object for each frame in the current browser window.

Freeware Software you can download from the Internet without charge.

Front end The Web page containing the form that users see in their browsers and from which they submit or request information. *See also* Back end.

FTP Client A program that allows users to transfer files to a server without using command-line instructions, such as InternetSoft FTP Commander or Ipswitch WS_FTP.

FTP Commander An FTP client program created by InternetSoft that lets you transfer files between a local computer and a Web server.

Full-page tile A square image that repeats until the entire page background is filled; usually associated with the background attribute or background style.

Function A named set of scripted instructions that is logically broken down into functional units and performs a specific task.

Gamma settings Digitized image file properties that specify the degree of contrast between midlevel gray values; can cause noticeable differences in same image on different platforms.

Get Method.

GIF A proprietary graphic format by CompuServ/Unisys that supports 1-bit transparency and is used for line art and animations; requires a licensing fee in some cases.

Graphical user interface (GUI) A technology that allows users to interact with a computer using icons, folders, pictures, and buttons.

Grid positioning A series of columns and rows used to position and group page elements; gives a design a sense of balance, consistency, and organization.

Hand-coding Creating Web pages by entering the HTML tags yourself, rather than using software to automatically generate code based on a design.

Hang A condition often caused by faulty scripting that prevents your browser from working and requires you to exit the browser application and restart it.

Head *See* Head section.

Head section The portion of a Web page that includes identifying and descriptive information, such as meta tags with the page description and keywords.

Height Attribute that specifies the vertical measurement of an HTML/XHTML element in pixels.

Hexadecimal equivalent Six-digit number used to describe the color of a Web page element, such as #FFFF00, which represents yellow.

Hexadecimal triplet Six-digit number used to describe a color; named because it is comprised of three pairs of numbers; one for the red value, one for the green value, and one for the blue value. *See also* Hexadecimal equivalent.

Hexadecimal A numbering system based on 16 digits (0 – 9 and A – F). *See also* Hexadecimal equivalent.

Hierarchical structure Organization of information into content sections, from general at the top to more specific beneath it; often used for organizing large sites or sites with potential for fast growth.

High-bandwidth High-speed Internet connections such as T1, T3, DS1, OC1, DSL, and cable modems.

History object Allows access to the browser's list of previously visited URLs.

Hot spot A linked area within an image map; defined with a coordinate system that uses the x – y axis of an image. *See also* Image map.

Hover event When the site visitor rests the mouse pointer over a link or other page object.

Href The required attribute for a link tag; stands for hypertext reference.

Href value In a link tag, the file name and path of the link target location.

Hspace Attribute that defines, in pixels, the amount of space between the left and right sides of an image or multimedia element and the surrounding text.

HTML document A text file made up of text and HTML instructions that a browser displays as a Web page.

HTML file *See* HTML document.

Hyperlink *See* Link.

Hyperlinking The ability to jump from one content point to another by clicking hypertext links. *See also* Link.

Hypertext links *See* Link.

Hypertext Markup Language (HTML) The language upon which all Web pages are based.

ID An identifier for any HTML element that can serve as an anchor point for jump links.

Image file extensions The three or four characters that follow the dot (.) in an image file name, such as jpg, jpeg, gif, and png.

Image map Graphic that has different areas linked to different Web files. Each of these mapped areas is a hot spot. *See also* Hot spot.

Import To bring in Web page content from another location, such as a word processing document.

Improved compression The shrinking of audio and video file sizes.

Inline images Graphics that are displayed as content on a page.

Inline style A style applied as an attribute.

innerHTML A property that replaces an element but leaves its enclosing HTML tags intact.

Input element Type of form field that, depending upon its type attribute value, can be a radio button, checkbox, text field, push button, reset button, or submit button.

Intelligent Web applications Applications that seek out choice bits of information on the Web to match the preferences of individual users; can produce more accurate results as a result of clearly labeled XML data.

Internal links Links to pages on the same Web site.

International Organization for Standardization (ISO) International organization that helps set standards for Web documents and networks.

Internet The global network of computers that includes the World Wide Web.

Internet Protocol Address Also called an IP address, a four-part numeric address that makes it possible for Web users to find information stored on a particular server.

IP address *See* Internet Protocol Address.

ISDN Integrated Services Digital Network, a high bandwidth connection to the Internet or other networks.

JavaScript Scripting language developed by Netscape and Sun Microsystems and loosely based on C.

JPEG *See* JPG.

JPG (or JPEG) Photographs and other images with a variable compression that allows tradeoff between better image quality and smaller file size.

Jump links Links that allow users to move from a link to a specific point on that page or on another page. Also called menu links.

Keywords Terms in a Web page that identify the page's key concepts or focus; a search engine uses these to determine ranking when adding a Web page to its database.

Landscape orientation Layout that is wider than tall.

Layer An essentially transparent, virtual page that can overlap other page elements; created using `<div>...</div>` tags with an id property. When superimposed over other layers or page elements, some layer contents may block out others, depending on their order in the stack.

Line spacing In page text, the amount of white space between lines.

Linear A Web site structure in which pages are organized in "book style," with one page leading into the next. Also describes a Web page layout that limits stacking of page elements above and below each other, and provides few options for horizontal placement.

Linear layout A layout method in which elements are stacked above and below each other, providing few options for horizontal placement.

Link A specially-formatted Web page object that the user can click to open a different Web file or to move to a specified location on the current Web page or to a specified location on another Web page.

Link states On a Web page, the four possible ways a link can appear, depending on how they have been used; the four link states are normal, visited, hover, and active.

Link tag *See* Anchor tag.

Link titles ScreenTips (pop-up text balloons) that appear when site visitors rest the mouse pointer over a link in which a link title has been specified; useful as accessibility tools for sight-impaired users.

Linked images Graphics that Web page users click to link to another location; by default, linked images display a one-pixel border in the color of linked text on the page.

Local scripting *See* Client-side scripting.

Location object Contains the URL of the current page.

Logical formatting Formatting tags that indicate an element's specific role and enable the formatting to be heard via text readers as well as seen in visual browsers. *See also* Physical formatting.

Macromedia Flash animation Animation created using the Macromedia Flash program; requires the Flash player program to be installed on the Web page user's computer for viewing.

Magic targets Link targets that begin with an underscore character, usually used in sites that use frames (sites that display parts of the page in several windows simultaneously); useful for opening linked files in a new window from any page.

Margin Added space around an element.

Mark up Add HTML tags to source code so pages can be viewed using a browser.

Markup Tags surrounding page content that tell the browser how to interpret and display Web page information.

Menu links *See* Jump links.

Meta tags Placed in the head section of an HTML document, tags that provide additional information to help search engines identify and describe your page content, such as the description and keywords metatags.

Method Form attribute that indicates how data entered by the user is submitted to the server; acceptable values are "get"—for calling information from the server—and "post"—for sending information to the server.

Methods Actions that objects can carry out.

Middle When set, causes image middle to line up with the vertical middle of text line between baseline and text top.

Multimedia The integration of sound and/or video with Web page text and graphics.

Multiline text area A large form field designed to allow less-structured, paragraph-length user input, allowing users to make additional comments or ask questions. *See also* Comment box.

Name Required attribute for HTML objects such as form fields that are accessed by a script or that submit information; defines the data field to which information is submitted or identifies the object that is accessed by the script.

Navigation bar A set of links arranged in either a horizontal or vertical display. Top-level navigation bars usually contain links to the home page and main section pages of a Web site, and usually appear on every page; can be text- or graphic-based page element with links to other pages.

Navigator object Provides information about the browser.

Nested Frames Framesets placed within framesets; allows for both horizontal and vertical frames within the same window.

Nested list A list that is wholly contained within another list. The opening list tag of a nested list appears before the closing list tag of the parent list.

Nested tables Tables that are fully contained within the cell of another table; often used to produce more complex page designs.

Nested tags In Web page code, tags that are fully contained within another tag.

Net structure Sketch of the relationship of pages within a Web site.

Network A group of interconnected computers that can be used to share files and to communicate with one another. Networks can be local, (LAN), organization-based (Intranet), or worldwide. The largest worldwide network is the Internet.

Non-frames alternative Text or other elements coded into a frameset for display in browsers that do not support frames.

Non-linear content Information that does not need to be read in a particular order, such as on the World Wide Web.

Noresize Frames attribute that prevents frames from being resized in the browser window.

Nowrap attribute Attribute that prevents table cell content from wrapping to the next line.

Null An assigned value representing and empty set or nothing—not zero.

Object Each element in the browser window with its own default name and set of descriptive features based on its location and function in the Document Object Model (DOM).

Object hierarchy A tree structure that allows designers to access object properties and methods by describing the object path from the topmost object, *window*, down through the object tree.

Object tag set <object>...</object> Used for implementing scripts on a Web page. Also used for implementing Java applets and Flash or other multimedia. When used with Flash, embeds a call to the download site for the Flash player making it easy for users to obtain and install the program.

Open tag Tags that do not have corresponding closing elements, such as the line break tag <br />.

Optimize To adjust an object's resolution, dimension, file type, and color depth to create the smallest file size possible for Web delivery.

Ordered list A list in which each item is automatically numbered or lettered. *See also* Unordered list.

outerHTML An element property that includes the element contents and the tags surrounding it; changing the property to a null value removes the element and its surrounding tags from the Web page.

Padding Added space within an element, such as a table cell.

Page-level formatting tags Tags such as ..., ... and <font>...</font> that apply formatting at the page level by applying formatting codes directly to text or other elements within the body section of a document. Most have been deprecated by the W3C in favor of style-sheet formatting.

Page title In the head section of an HTML document, the name of a page, enclosed in the <title>...</title> tags.

Paragraph tag *See* Paragraph tag set.

Paragraph tag set <p> ... </p> Marks paragraph text within the body of an HTML document.

Parent element A tag set in which another tag is nested.

Passive white space White space that serves no purpose and that can be distracting to the site user.

Personal digital assistant (PDA) Handheld device used for scheduling, contacts, and many other purposes, on which Web page information can be displayed.

Personal sites Web sites that can be used to communicate with friends or family, post professional résumés or portfolios, or honor a favorite public figure.

Physical formats Formats that can only be recognized visually; not recognized by text readers and other accessibility devices. *See also* Logical formatting.

Pipe A character (|) often used as a dividing element between adjacent sets of linked text in a text- based horizontal navigation bar.

Pixels Adapted from the term "pixel element," single points of light that make up the display on a computer screen; abbreviated as "px."

Placeholder File containing text explaining that a target page is incomplete; serves as a link target for an unfinished Web page. Also, a set of text elements or simple graphics that represent page content not yet developed.

Platform The unique characteristics of a Web user's computer system, including browser brand, browser version, operating system, and screen resolution.

Portrait orientation Layout that is taller than wide.

Position animation Scripted effect that interacts with position and layer information and relies on the user's system resources to create basic animation.

PNG A Web-compatible graphic format developed by Microsoft; supports 32-bit (gradient) transparency and can be used for line art as well as for photographs.

Post *See* Method.

Posture A characteristic of type that refers to its angle on the page, such as italic.

Presentation effects A combination of animation scripts with starting coordinates, timers, and filters that allow you to specify which elements appear on the screen gradually and in what order.

Prolog First part of an XML document, containing, in the following order, an XML declaration, comments, a document type declaration, and other comments (optional).

Properties Object qualities such as size, location, color, or type.

Proprietary features Unique elements and attributes that are written for specific browsers; generally supported by only one of the major browsers; most useful in single-browser settings, such as intranets where all users run the same browser.

Public support sites Web sites that contain downloadable user manuals, forms, and software drivers. Can also be part of a company intranet that enables users to upload and download company documents and to access shared databases.

Publicly accessible Web site A site that is hosted on an Internet server and does not require log-in permission for file viewing.

Pull-down menu Expanding form field that allows users to select one or more choices out of several options; also known as a select option box or drop-down list, appears on the page as a single-line text field with a down-arrow button the user clicks to open a menu of choices. *See also* Drop-down menu and Scroll box.

Push button A labeled form object that a user clicks to perform a task; created using the <input /> tag. *See also* Submit button and Reset button.

Radio button Input form field of the type "radio" that appears as a small white circle, usually next to explanatory text; allows users to select one of several choices. Fills with black when selected.

Relative link Link that includes only information about the target page's location relative to the current Web page (for example, <a href="justice.htm">); most useful for referencing other pages in a site, without needing to type the entire path to each page. *See also* Absolute link.

Relative positioning Element positioning based on an offset relative to other page elements. *See also* Absolute positioning.

Render To process and display data.

Reset button An input object of the type "reset"; when clicked, erases form information without sending it. *See also* Push button and Reset button.

Resolution A monitor's screen display dimensions (width by height), in pixels; for example, 800 × 600.

Resolution The screen's display dimensions (width by height, in pixels); varies according to a user's monitor and computer hardware.

Reveal A transition that allows more complex filtering effects, which can be applied to text as well as graphics.

Rollover A popular DHTML application that changes the appearance of text or swaps one graphic for another when the user points to the text or image.

Root element In well-formed HTML code, element names contained within the opening and closing html tags.

Root folder Top-level folder for a Web site; contains all Web site files.

Row In a table, a single horizontal line of data.

Rowspan Attribute that causes a cell to span multiple rows *See also* Colspan.

Run time The period when a browser first interprets and displays the Web page and runs scripts.

Sans serif fonts Literally means "without serifs;" fonts in this group do not have decorative tails. *See also* Serif font.

Screen object Provides information about the user's screen setup and display properties.

Script A small program coded into a Web page that runs on a viewer's browser.

Scripting The process of writing scripts.

Scriptlets Reusable script code that can be shared by multiple pages without the need to paste the code into each page.

Scroll box Expanding form field that allows users to select one or more choices out of several options. *See also* Drop-down menu and Pull-down menu.

Scrolling Frames attribute that controls the appearance of the frame's scrollbars; a "yes" value always includes scrollbars, and "no" prevents scrollbars from appearing. When attribute is absent or set to "auto," scrollbars appear only as needed.

Seamless Applied to images, indicating that the end user cannot tell where one repetition of the image ends and the next begins.

Secure File Transfer Protocol A method of transferring files to a server that also includes encryption for addition security.

Select option box *See* Pull-down menu.

Selector In a style declaration, specifies the element to which a style is applied.

Serif fonts Fonts with small "tails" called serifs at the ends of the lines that make up each letter. *See also* Sans serif fonts.

Server *See* Web server.

Server-side script Script that runs on a remote Web server.

Shopping cart service Service provider that provides order processing, billing, and credit card services.

Sidebar A floating text box specified using the float property with positioning coordinates; removes an element from the main text flow and displays it to the side of the flow.

Single-line text box Form input field that allows users to enter a limited number of alphanumeric characters such as first or last name, street address, or e-mail address; designer can specify the size and maximum number of characters permitted.

Site navigation bar *See* Navigation bar.

Site storyboard A sketch of a Web site's organization and structure.

Slides Related set of pages in a presentation.

Source *See* Source code.

Source code The text and HTML code that make up a Web document.

Span In a table, to cover or become part of multiple rows or columns.

Sponsored links Links that site owners have paid search engines to place at the top of their list of found references.

Stacked tables One or more tables in which the code for one table ends before the code for another begins; not dependent upon one another for width, height, or placement.

Stacked tags In Web page code, tags that are closed before the next tag begins or are opened after the previous tag has ended.

State The condition of a link that indicates how it has been or will be used, such as active, visited, or hovered.

Static HTML Web page code that provides limited interactivity based on hyperlinks to open other pages or generate new e-mail messages.

Storyboard *See* Storyboard layout sketch.

Storyboard layout sketch Drawing that shows the desired arrangement of the major elements you want to include in your Web page.

Storyboarding Planning Web page or Web site design by sketching the elements you want to include and how you want them arranged.

Streaming Multimedia Technology A method of transferring data that allows it to be processed in a steady, continuous stream, allowing the browser or plug-in to start displaying the data before the entire file has been transmitted.

Structuring table A grid-based page layout upon which a page template is based.

Style sheets Files composed of one or more CSS rules that dictate the way page content appears; can be embedded within a document's head section to control page formatting, or saved as separate files to control formatting for multiple pages. *See also* Cascading style sheets.

Submit button An input object with the type "submit"; when clicked, submits information for processing. *See also* Push button and Reset button.

Syntax The language rules and structures of a programming language such as XHTML.

T-1 and T-3 connections Dedicated phone line technologies that are actually bundles of copper phone lines; T-1 bundles 24 individual lines, and T-3 bundles 67 lines, each of which supports 64 Kbps of file-transfer capacity.

Table A grid-based layout of columns and rows; used to control page layout or display data.

Table data tag (<td>...</td>) In a table, indicates a table data cell, the most basic data unit in a table.

Table heading tag (<th>...</th>) In a table, identifies table heading content; its content is horizontally centered and bold.

Tag Each HTML instruction in an HTML document.

Tag set A pair of opening and closing HTML tags, such as <style> </style>, that surround a page element.

Target The Web page that opens when a user clicks a link.

Target audience Users you are trying to attract to your site.

Template Document containing the Web page code for a page's structure, along with any text or other elements that appear on every page; used as a basis for designing pages to ensure consistency within a site.

Text attribute Sets the text color for a Web page.

Text box An input element that allows users to input a short line of text. *See also* Single-line text box.

Text image A graphic showing text; best used sparingly to implement formats that HTML cannot reliably create.

Text jumping Common to graphic-heavy pages; text on a page begins to load and then must "jump" out of the way to make room for an image that appears later in the page-load process.

Tile Repeat an image across and down the page to fill the background.

Transition effects Internet Explorer predefined effects that cause elements to appear gradually and in specific patterns when the page opens or exits; can be applied to selected elements or to an entire page.

Transitions Filtered effects, such as dissolve, swipe, and circle-in, that affect the way an element becomes visible or hidden by gradually displaying the object or page; not available in all browsers.

Type Required attribute for input form fields; defines the way a form field appears in a form and the type of data a form field accepts.

Type selectors Also called tag selectors, specifies elements by their names and applies the CSS rule to all tags of the same name.

Typeface A series of fonts such as Times Bold, Times Italic, and Times New Roman, which are different fonts in the same family.

Uniform Resource Locator (URL) A Web site address consisting of the hypertext transfer protocol (http:), the Web server name (usually www), and the domain name, such as course.com.

Unordered list A list in which a bullet character, instead of a number or letter, designates each list item. *See also* Ordered list.

Upload Transfer, such as files to a Web server.

URL *See* Uniform Resource Locator.

User ID A unique identifying number assigned to a server user by a system administrator that, along with a password, grants the server user permission to transfer files to that server.

Values Attribute modifiers that specify or change a tag's behavior or function; in scripting, specified bits of information, such as text or numeric quantities, that scripts can manipulate or display; can also include user input from form fields.

Variable A nickname for the object value that allows you to enter or look up the value only once; saves time because it allows you to modify the value in only one place and have the modifications reflected instantaneously throughout the document as indicated by the variable.

VBScript Microsoft scripting adaptation of the Visual Basic programming language; not compatible with all platforms.

Vlink Visited link.

Vspace An HTML attribute that sets the amount of vertical space in pixels between the surrounding text and the top and bottom of an inline image, media player, or object.

Web browser A software program, installed on a user's computer, that allows users to view Web pages.

Web media A collection of media devices, each of which interprets Web information differently.

Web page A file containing text and HTML markup that is saved with an appropriate extensions such as, .htm, .html, .shtml, .dhtml, .asp, .jsp, etc. Also known as a Web document.

Web server A computer permanently connected to the Internet, usually by means of lines reserved for that purpose, that stores published Web documents for delivery to client computers.

Web site A group of related Web pages published to a Web server.

Webcasting Media programming delivered over the Internet, rather than through air waves.

Weight A characteristic of type appearance, such as boldfaced.

White space Any empty area in a Web page layout.

Word spacing The amount of space between words.

World Wide Web (Web, WWW) Information contained on the vast network of interconnected computers known as the Internet. Information on the Web is divided up into sites and files.

Write access Permission to transfer files to a server or update files in a directory.

XHTML *See* Extensible Hypertext Markup Language.

XHTML Frameset XHTML document that uses frames to partition the browser window into two or more windows.

XHTML Strict XHTML document that contains no layout or formatting markup and that uses only CSS to apply formatting effects.

XHTML Transitional XHTML document that takes advantage of CSS but might contain small markup adjustments, such as bgcolor or text and link attributes in the body tag, to make pages backward compatible.

XML (Extensible Markup Language) A text-based syntax especially designed to describe, deliver, and exchange structured data. XML documents use the file extension .xml and can be created using a simple text editor. *See also* Extensible Markup Language.

XML body Main section of an XML document—contains vocabulary elements.

XML epilog Optional XML document section that contains any final comments and/or processing instructions.

XML namespace definition (xmlns) An object that qualifies elements and attribute names used in XML documents by associating them with namespace references—Setting the xmlns in the opening tag tells the parser that the document can accept namespace definitions.

XML parser Application that dissects and interprets XML elements to ensure that the code is properly formatted; works with the XML source object to allow the display of XML data. *See also* XML source object.

XML prolog Top section of an XML document; contains the XML declaration, comments, a document type declaration, and other comments.

XML schema Combines the concepts of a DTD, relational databases, and object-oriented designs to create a richer and more powerful way to formally define the elements and structure of an XML document; uses same syntax as XML.

XML source object Enables binding of the XML data to the HTML document using the DHTML Object Model; works with XML parser to allow the display of XML data.

XML vocabulary Custom XML elements created to fit any application or situation.

XML-compliant browsers Browsers such as Internet Explorer and Netscape that support XML by including an XML parser and an embedded XML source object.

Z-index Layer property used to determine a layer's position in the stack; higher numbers are located closer to the top of the stack, and elements on these layers will block out elements or superimpose themselves over elements in the same position on lower layers of the stack. Can be 0 (the default) or a negative or positive number.

Index

reusing variables in scripts, J-14–J-15

reveal filters, N-12

rich text format (.rtf) files, A-10

right alignment, CSS formatting, E-12

rollover effects, using, K-14

root element described, E-2

rows, table
    aligning, F-6–F-7
    creating frameset, H-6
    described
    in page layout grids, H-2–H-3
    sizing, F-14–F-15
    tags, F-4

rowspan attribute, F-6–F-7

.rtf files, A-10

rules, CSS class, E-14–E-15

▶ S

saving
    files using keyboard, B-8
    HTML documents in text format, A-6–A-7
    text documents as HTML, A-9

scaling content dynamically, N-6–N-7

screen elements, stacking, M-10–M-11

screen resolution
    PDAs (personal digital assistants), I-7
    and Web page design, I-6

ScreenTips and link titles, B-16

<script> tags, J-4

scripting
    creating conditionals in, J-16–J-17
    creating function, J-12–J-13
    JavaScript event handlers, using, J-10–J-11
    referencing document objects, J-8–J-9
    Web, generally, J-1–J-3

scripts
    assigning variables in, J-14–J-15
    CGI, ASP, JSP, PHP, G-16
    comments, adding, J-7
    creating Web, J-4–J-5
    CSSP, combining with, M-2
    debugging, J-6–J-7
    described, A-4
    linking to external, J-5
    suppressing error messages with, L-17
    using dynamic sorting, L-16–L-17

scroll bars on Web pages, H-3, H-7, M-12–M-13

scroll boxes, using as form element, G-2–G-3

seamless background tiling, D-10

search engines
    described, A-2
    submitting your URL to, AP-2, AP-6

sections on Web pages, A-4–A-5

Secure File Transfer Protocol (SFTP), A-16

Security Alerts, Windows, A-17, A-18

<select> tag, push buttons, G-10–G-11

selection option boxes, G-10

selectors, CSS rules, E-4, E-14–E-15

semicolons (;)
    in CSS rules, E-4
    and JavaScript, N-10
    in style values, C-10

server-side scripts, J-2

servers
    FTP Servers properties, A-18
    posting files to, write access, A-16

showing, hiding DHTML page elements, K-12–K-13

sidebars, creating, M-3, M-14–M-15

site maps, creating, B-2

site navigation bars on Web pages, H-2

site structure charts, creating, B-2–B-3

size
    customizing font, C-12–C-13
    and heading tags, A-12–A-13
    of image files on Web pages, D-2
    specifying image, D-8–D-9

sizing
    and noresize frame attribute, H-10
    page elements with DHTML, M-8–M-9
    scaling content dynamically, N-6–N-7
    table borders, F-10–F-11
    tables, F-14–F-15

slashes (/)
    in dot-slash notation, B-6
    in HTML code, A-8
    in input tags, G-4
    and Web paths, B-6
    and XML elements, O-2–O-3

slide shows, creating, N-14–N-15

sniffers, browser, K-7

software, Web development packages, A-16

sorting
    table data dynamically, K-5, L-16–L-17
    z-index positioning, M-10

sound files, embedding, D-16

source code
    data file, J-5
    described, A-2
    examining on Web, K-10
    printing, A-14–A-15
    viewing in Microsoft browser, C-10
    viewing Web page, A-10
    for Web page, A-5

spaces
    in image code, D-4
    in link tags, B-7
    in table cells, F-8–F-9
    use in W3C coding standards, A-8

spacing, controlling with CSS, E-2

<span> tags, M-4, M-16

spanning and aligning table columns, rows, F-6–F-7

special characters, HTML, AP-31–AP-34

sponsored links, B-9

square brackets ([])
    in JavaScript, J-6
    and jump links, B-12

square bullets, E-15

src attributes, D-4–D-5, D-18

stacked tables, F-15

stacked tags, A-8–A-9

stacking screen elements, M-10–M-11

Standard HTML, F-3

states, and link properties, E-8

static HTML, K-2

storyboard for Paradise Mountain Web page, A-5

storyboarding, planned Web site, A-4, B-2

streaming media, D-16

streaming multimedia technology, D-16

<strong> tag, C-6–C-7

structuring tables, creating, H-14–H-15

style guides, locating, I-12–I-13

style sheets
    cascading. *See* CSS
    modifying, F-8
    using linked, E-16–E-17

<style /> tag, AP-26, E-4

style values and font selection, C-10

submit buttons, G-14

support Web sites, B-2

surveys, Web page, G-7, G-9

syntax
    dot, J-8
    XHTML, E-3